INDIAN AFFAIRS
ANNUAL
2008

INDIAN AFFAIRS ANNUAL 2008

(In 9 Vols.)

Vol. 2

Chronology of Events

(05-05-2007 to 18-06-2007)

Shailendra Sengar

KALPAZ PUBLICATIONS

KALPAZ PUBLICATIONS

DELHI - 110052

Indian Affairs Annual 2008

Rs. 6300 (Set)

ISBN: 81-7835-693-7 (Set)
ISBN: 81-7835-695-3 (Vol. 2)

Published in 2008 in India by
Kalpaz Publications
C-30, Satyawati Nagar,
Delhi-110052
E-mail: kalpaz@hotmail.com
Phone : 9212729499

Laser Type Setting by: Quick Media, Delhi
Printed at : Singhal Print Media, Delhi

INDIAN AFFAIRS ANNUAL 2008

Chronology of Events

(05-05-2007 to 18-06-2007)

739. (5-5-2007) NEW DELHI : The President of India said that I am indeed delighted to participate in the "Businessworld-FICCI-SEDF Corporate Social Responsibility Award" for the year 2006. I congratulate the award winners and greet the industry chiefs, entrepreneurs and distinguished guests. I am happy that Corporate Social Responsibility Award scheme has been instituted by Federation of Indian Chambers of Commerce and Industry (FICCI) in partnership with Businessworld and Social Economic Development Foundation (SEDF) for recognizing excellence in fulfillment of Corporate Social Responsibility by Industrial houses. This is a major contribution of FICCI towards business-government-civil society partnership to enhance the quality of life of the common people. While I was interacting with the group of societal reformers (NGOs) from various parts of the country during the 2007 Republic Day get together at Rashtrapati Bhawan, they expressed that large scale participation of corporate houses in societal missions will further speed up the benefits of development reaching all the sections of society, empowering the people and ensuring continuity of services to the citizens. While I am with you, I would like to share my experience during my address to European Parliament at Strasbourg on 25th April 2007. At the invitation of the President of European Parliament, I delivered a talk on the topic "Dynamics of Unity of Nations". The subject is relevant to industry and business ventures.

740. (5-5-2007) NEW DELHI : There is no specific request from the International Labour organisation to the Government of India to incorporate preventive measures in the occupational safety and health policies. However, the International Labour Standards on Occupational Safety and Health adopted by the International Labour Conference from time to time emphasise the need for preventive measures in the Occupational Safety and Health policies of the member countries of the International Labour Organisation. Such a need is incorporated in the Convention No. 155 of the International Labour Organisation. The Government of India have not ratified this Convention for various reasons, including the fact that the national laws are presently not totally in consonance with the provisions of the above ILO Convention. The Factories Act, 1948 requires that where any worker in a factory contracts any disease specified in Schedule III thereof, the manager or the medical practitioner concerned, shall send details of the same to the Chief Inspector of the Factories of the concerned state to ensure that facilities are provided to protect the safety and health of such workers. These provisions of the Factories Act are applicable to all workers irrespective of their gender. The Schedule III contains 29 diseases, including certain case of poisoning. This was stated by the Minister of State (Independent Charge), Labour & Employment, Shri Oscar Fernandes in a written reply in Lok Sabha today.

741. (5-5-2007) NEW DELHI : Human capital is the most critical resource, which needs to be tapped properly for India to achieve a sustained growth in the manufacturing sector. This was stated by Dr. V. Krishnamurthy, Chairman, National Manufacturing Competitiveness Council (NMCC), while launching the Post Graduate Programme for Executives for Visionary Leadership in Manufacturing (PGPEX-VLM), here today. Dr. Krishnamurthy said that while India had done well by recording impressive growth in the manufacturing sector, the biggest concern today was that of having highly skilled manpower to run the sector. He complemented the stakeholders of PGPEX-VLM and noted that this was the first occasion when the Indian Institute of Technology (IIT) and Indian Institute of Management (IIM) have joined hands to run a post graduate programme. "The programme is expected to generate 300 visionary leaders in the manufacturing field in the next three years", he said. Dr. Krishnamurthy also thanked Confederation of Indian industry (CII), Japanese International Cooperation Agency, Ministry of Human Resources Development and in particular, Prof. Shoji Shiba of Japan who along with IIT/Kanpur, IIT/Madras and IIM/Calcutta helped to develop the programme. The Japanese Ambassador to India, Mr. Yasukuni Enoki, expressed happiness of about Japanese involvement in the development of PGPEX-VLM and hoped that the programme would enable India to regain its dominant position in the world in manufacturing which, he pointed out, the country had enjoyed in the pre-colonial era – in the 16th and 17th centuries. Shri R. Seshasayee, President of CII, in his keynote address, expressed optimism regarding the association of industry and the academic world which has come together to develop the PGPEX-VLM. He highlighted 3 key challenges facing the Indian industry viz., development of quality higher education; enabling the manufacturing industry to attract and retain best talent and to develop a critical mass of intellectual property through R&D initiatives. He hoped that these concerns would be ably met through PGPEX-VLM programme. The programme is of one-year duration and the first session (2007-08) will commence in August 2007. The eligibility for admission is a first class degree in any branch of engineering along with minimum 5 years of experience in manufacturing and related sector. The tuition fee for the programme would be

Rs.5 lakh. The launch programme was also attended by Shri Ravi Mathur, Jt. Secretary, Ministry of HRD; Shri Rajeev Ranjan, NMCC, Prof. Shekhar Chaudhri, Director, IIM/Calcutta; Prof. Sanjay G. Dhande, Director, IIT/Kanpur; and Prof. M.S. Ananth, Director, IIT/Madras.

742. (5-5-2007) NEW DELHI : The number of defaulting establishments (un-exempted sector) as on March 31, 2004, 2005 and 2006 was 51990, 40608 & 76476 respectively. This includes the establishments which have defaulted in remittance of employees' share of contribution. Recovery of dues is effected in accordance with the provisions of the Employees' Provident Funds & Miscellaneous Provisions Act, 1952. This includes prosecution under Section 14 of the Act, filing of complaints under Section 406/409 of IPC, attachment of properties/bank accounts and arrest of defaulters. The amount outstanding from defaulting establishments (including employees' share) was Rs. 1724.19 crore (un-exempted sector) as on March 31, 2006. Complaints under Section 406/409 of Indian Penal Code are filed against the defaulting establishments who deduct employees' share but fail to remit the same to the Employees' Provident Fund Organisation. This was stated by the Minister of State (Independent Charge), Labour & Employment, Shri Oscar Fernandes in a written reply in Lok Sabha today.

743. (5-5-2007) NEW DELHI : The Ministry of Labour & Employment has not prepared nor is likely to prepare any policy for payment of unemployment allowance to the unemployed youth of the country particularly to Scheduled Castes/Scheduled Tribes/Other Backward Classes. However, under the National Rural Employment Guarantee Act 2005, implemented by the Ministry of Rural Development there is a provision for making payment of unemployment allowance; this provision covers, inter-alia, unemployed youth belonging to SC/ST/Other Backward Classes. This was stated by the Minister of State (Independent Charge), Labour & Employment, Shri Oscar Fernandes in a written reply in Lok Sabha today.

744. (5-5-2007) NEW DELHI : As against a projected fishable potential of 3.93 million tonnes, only about 3 million tonnes of marine fish is being exploited currently. As such, no drastic effect of large-scale fishing on our marine ecosystem has been reported. With the aim of attaining sustainability and to minimize possible adverse effect on marine ecosystem the Government has made ample provisions for regulation of fishing in the Marine Fishing Regulation Act of Coastal States/ UTs. As per this, (a) closed season is observed both on east and west coasts, (b) catching of endangered species is banned; (c) destructive fishing methods are prohibited, (d) outside the territorial waters, the Government of India has made letter of permission compulsory for entry into India's Exclusive Economic Zone (EEZ) for fishing, (e) only Indian flag vessels are allowed to fish in the EEZ, (f) only resources specific fishing methods are permitted, (g) the total number of vessels that could be allowed in each resources specific category has been worked out and notified, and (h) an Inter-Ministerial Empowered Committee has been set up to oversee deep sea fishing activities at the Centre. This information was given by Shri Kanti Lal Bhuria, Minister of State for Agriculture in written replies to questions in the Lok Sabha today.

745. (5-5-2007) NEW DELHI : A multi-pronged approach has been adopted under Sarva Shiksha Abhiyan (SSA) for reducing drop-out rates. One set of interventions are towards strengthening of schools and improving the quality of education through improvement in school infrastructure, recruitment of additional teachers, annual school grants, regular training of teachers, regular academic support to teachers etc. In addition, several interventions under SSA also aim at community support, flexible schooling for children who are drop-outs, older children or children in difficult circumstances, and special provisions to promote education of girls, children from disadvantaged sections of society or children with special needs. Drop-out rates have been declining since the launch of Sarva Shiksha Abhiyan. It declined from 34.9% in 2002-03 to 29.0% in 2004-05. This information was given by the Minister of State for Human Resource Development Smt. D. Purandeswari in a written reply in the Rajya Sabha.

746. (5-5-2007) NEW DELHI : Ground Infrastructure for utilization of EDUSAT has been largely created by Indian Space Research Organisation (ISRO), which invested Rs. 89.00 crore in the programme till December 2006. University Grants Commission (UGC), through its body Consortium for Educational Communication (CEC) is utilizing EDUSAT facility for curriculum based education. UGC-CEC uses EDUSAT network for live transmission of their classroom programme which is received by all institutions having Satellite Interactive Terminals (SITs) or Receive Only Terminals (ROTs). The students attending the session can interact and ask questions to the experts through audio-video conferencing or text mode or through telephone. All India Council for Technical Education (AICTE) is sponsoring telecasting of programmes through AICTE-EDUSAT network mostly for curriculum based teaching as also for conducting training programmes and seminars. The Council is also engaged in the development of digital course wares. The infrastructure of EDUSAT is being utilized by Indira Gandhi National Open University (IGNOU) for curriculum based education, teachers' training, professional educational courses and for conducting teleconferencing sessions for software content generation. NCERT is conducting inter-active orientation/training programmes of teachers and teachers' educators. Department of Science & Technology (DST) is utilizing EDUSAT network for group discussion, lectures, demonstrations, video-shows, training and capacity building programmes. This information was given by the Minister of State for Human Resource Development Smt. D. Purandeswari in a written reply in the Rajya Sabha.

747. (5-5-2007) NEW DELHI : The Ministry of Rural Development has sanctioned Rs. 41.93 crore to the State Government of Madhya Pradesh towards part payment of first instalment of funds against the provisional allocation of Rs.251.62 crore made for the Government of Madhya Pradesh under Accelerated Rural Water Supply Programme (Normal) of Rajiv Gandhi National Drinking Water Mission, during the year 2007-08. The balance amount of first instalment will be released after receipt of AG report for 2003-04 covering the amount sanctioned under PM's Programme. Up to 15 per cent of funds released under this sanction may be utilized for Operation & Maintenance and up to 5 per cent of funds may be spent for taking sustainability measures. States have been requested to delegate powers for management of Rural Water Supply Schemes through the Panchayati Raj Institutions (PRIs) as per the Constitution of India. As such Operation and Maintenance of the completed RWS Scheme should be transferred to the PRIs. No expenditure shall be incurred on taking water quality problems form the present release, as there is a separate allocation for the purpose. This release is for execution/ completion of schemes to provide safe drinking water facilities to rural habitations and schools under the Centrally Sponsored ARWSP and according to Priorities set in ARWSP guidelines and through other instructions issued from time to time..

748. (5-5-2007) NEW DELHI : The Ministry of Rural Development has sanctioned Rs. 13.82 crore to the State Government of Kerala towards first instalment of funds against the provisional allocation of Rs.82.93 crore made for the Government of Kerala under Accelerated Rural Water Supply Programme (Normal) of Rajiv Gandhi National Drinking Water Mission, during the year 2007-08. The balance amount of first instalment will be released after receipt of AG report for 2004-05. Up to 15 per cent of funds released under this sanction may be utilized for Operation & Maintenance and up to 5 per cent of funds may be spent for taking sustainability measures. States have been requested to delegate powers for management of Rural Water Supply Schemes through the Panchayati Raj Institutions (PRIs) as per the Constitution of India. As such Operation and Maintenance of the completed RWS Scheme should be transferred to the PRIs. No expenditure shall be incurred on taking water quality problems form the present release, as there is a separate allocation for the purpose. This release is for execution/ completion of schemes to provide safe drinking water facilities to rural habitations and schools under the Centrally Sponsored ARWSP and according to Priorities set in ARWSP guidelines and through other instructions issued from time to time.

749. (5-5-2007) NEW DELHI : The Ministry of Rural Development has released Grants-in-aid amounting to Rs. 1.45 crore as part of first instalment out of the allocation of Rs.8.70 crore to North District of Tripura, as Central assistance for the implementation of the Sampoorna Grameen Rozgar Yojana (SGRY) during the current financial year (2007-08). Grants-in-aid amounting to Rs.1.77 crore as second instalment has been released to the West Tripura District after deducting Rs.2.94 crore on account of excess carry over and Rs.1.57 crore on account of late receipt of proposal from the DRDA under the scheme for the year 2006-07. An amount of Rs.9.55 crore has also been released as 3rd/additional instalment to 3 districts of Tripura, namely North (Rs.2.17 crore), South (Rs.3.44 crore) and

West (Rs.3.93 crore) for the year 2006-07. The release is towards plan expenditure and will be utilized for approved items of works subject to the conditions laid down in the SGRY Guidelines. No deviations from the guidelines is permissible.

750. (5-5-2007) NEW DELHI : The Ministry of Rural Development has released Grants-in-aid amounting to Rs. 47.16 crore as third/additional instalment of Central assistance to 23 districts of Tamil Nadu for the implementation of the Sampoorna Grameen Rozgar Yojana (SGRY) during the financial year (2006-07). Grants amounting to Rs.26.60 crore as part of first instalment has also been released to 19 districts of the State under the scheme for the year 2007-08.

751. (5-5-2007) NEW DELHI : The Ministry of Rural Development has released part payment of first instalment of Central share of funds amounting to Rs. 1.61 crore under the 'Swarnjayanti Gram Swarojgar Yojana' (SGSY) during the year 2007-08 to 17 DRDAs of Punjab.

752. (7-5-2007) BALLIA: Virtually rejecting the CPI's demand for a review of Left support to the UPA Government, the CPI(M) has made it clear that it will continue to support the Congress-led coalition to keep away "communal forces" from power. - PTI

753. (8-5-2007) NEW DELHI : Shri Arjun Singh, Minister for Human Resource Development has said that we should not forget, that 1857 uprising not only promoted unity in India but also recognised a pluralist culture. Shri Singh was today inaugurating National Seminar on '1857-Renaissance of Indian Languages'. He further said that in this seminar scholars of different languages have assembled and they will discuss different aspects of 1857 uprising but we should never forget the role of language is not to divide the society but to unite it. 'The language of 1857 uprising may be Urdu or Hindi, or Bangla or, it may be any other language, it does not matter, but we should see the underlined current which united the freedom fighters. We should understand and absorb that underlined current', he added. The Central Institute of Hindi, Ministry of HRD, Govt. of India in collaboration with the National council for promotion of Urdu is organizing this seminar from the 8th of May till the 10th of May, 2007. In his key note address, Prof., Sabysachi Bhattacharya, Chairman Indian Council of Historical Research explored the link between 1857 uprising and Indian languages, development of Indian culture and as to what was the common people's understanding of the uprising. He said in fact, it became a metaphor for freedom struggle by its sheer scale and expanse. He further concluded that the uprising of 1857 developed deeper unity between Hindus and Muslims. Prof. Bhattacharya concluded that in view of all these facets, this event takes a central point in the history of India during India's struggle for independence. Chairman of National Book Trust, Shri Bipin Chandra, presided over the function. The welcome address was given by the Vice-Chairman, Kendriya Hindi Shikshan Mandal, Prof. Ram Sharan Joshi and Prof. Shambhunath, Director, Central Institute of Hindi presented the theme of the seminar. Prof. Ali Javed, Director National Council for Promotion of Urdu Language (NCPUL) proposed a vote of thanks. The aim of this national seminar is to highlight the role of 1857 in the renaissance of India. The conference also aims at evaluating the effect of the renaissance on the modern developments in the Indian Languages. The purpose is to find out how the northern Indian Languages, especially Urdu, Hindi, Punjabi, Kashmiri, Dogri, Rajasthani etc. were struggling with the problems of self-identity in the process of their modernization and to explore how communicability and interrelationship was being established due to the cultural and linguistic interaction among the different Indian Languages. Prominent scholars like Prof. Kamala Prasad, Prof. Imtiaz Ahmed, Shri, Sudeep Banerjee, Shri. Prabhash Joshi, Prof. Purushottam Aggarwal, Shri. Nadir Ali Khan, Prof. Iqbal Hussain and Prof. Iktedar Alam Khan will participate in the seminar.

754. (8-5-2007) NEW DELHI : A statement giving State and UT-wise drop out rates at secondary (classes I-X) stage in 2004-05 and transition rates of the children from class V in 2003-04 to class VI in 2004-05, is given at Annexure. Drop out rates of Standard XII and information in respect of students taking admission in the first year of college after completing 12th class and their drop out rates are not being maintained. A multi-pronged approach has been adopted under SSA for reducing drop-out rates. One set of interventions are towards strengthening of schools and improving the quality of education through improvement in school infrastructure, recruitment of additional teachers, annual school grants, regular training of teachers, regular academic support to teachers etc. In addition, several interventions under SSA also aim at community support, flexible schooling for children who are drop-outs, older children or children in difficult circumstances, and special provisions to promote education of girls, children from disadvantaged sections of society or children with special needs. This information was given by the Minister of State for Human Resource Development Smt. D. Purandeswari in the written reply in the Lok Sabha today.

755. (8-5-2007) NEW DELHI : The Sixth Pay Commission is mandated to give its recommendations within 18 months from the date of its constitution, that is, 5.10.2006, following which the Government will take further necessary action. The terms of Reference of the Sixth Pay Commission include examination of desirability and the need to sanction any interim relief till the time the recommendations of the Commission are made and accepted by the Government. The Government will take a decision on grant of interim relief to Central Government employees, after a recommendation in this regard is received from the Pay Commission. Shri Pawan Kumar Bansal, Minister of State for Finance gave this information in reply to a question raised by Shri Rudra Narayan Pany in Rajya Sabha today.

756. (8-5-2007) NEW DELHI : Government has decided to import 15 lakh tonnes of pulses such as Urad, Tur, Moong, Masur, Gram and Yellow peas through National Agriculture Federation of India Ltd. (NAFED), Metals and Minerals

Trading Corporation (MMTC), PEC Ltd. and State Trading Corporation (STC). The pulses will be imported at the most competitive prices available in the international market. As on April 25, 2007, 2.87 lakh tonne of pulses have been contracted and 52,039 tonnes have already reached the Indian ports. Edible oils are under the Open General License and they have been imported as there is always an excess demand over domestic supply. No specific decision has been taken by Government to import edible oils in the current financial year. Shri Pawan Kumar Bansal, Minister of State for Finance gave this information in reply to a question raised by Shri Motiur Rahman in Rajya Sabha today.

757. (8-5-2007) NEW DELHI : As Inflation is a manifestation of the demand-supply gap, concerted efforts are required to check inflation. While monetary policy attempts to moderate demand, the supply side is strengthened by the Government through fiscal measures and improvements in the distribution system. As part of its monetary policy, RBI has, from time to time, announced changes in the policy rates as warranted to regulate liquidity. During 2006-07, the repo rate was raised on five occasions (June, July, October, 2006 and January and March 2007) by 25 basis points each time to reach a level of 7.75 per cent. The reverse-repo rate was raised from 5.75 per cent to 6.00 per cent in July 2006; the CRR was raised four times by 25 basis points on each occasion (December 2006, January, February, and March 2007) to reach a level of 6.00 per cent. During 2007-08, the CRR has further been revised upward by 25 basis points each effective April 14, 2007 and April 28, 2007, respectively. The approach towards External Commercial Borrowing is calibrated to take into account the emerging market situation on an ongoing basis. As on date, there has been no comprehensive change in the ECB guidelines announced by the RBI in August, 2005. Shri Pawan Kumar Bansal, Minister of State for Finance gave this information in reply to a question raised by Dr. Murli Manohar Joshi and Shri Ram Jethmalani in Rajya Sabha today.

758. (8-5-2007) NEW DELHI : Public sector banks are free to determine their own rates of interest on domestic term deposits of Various maturity values, whereas interest rates on small savings deposits, including term deposits and PPF are benchmarked to average yield on Government Securities of comparable maturity in the secondary market, as recommended by Expert Committee on Administered Interest Rates under the Chairmanship of Dr. Y.V. Reddy, the then Dy. Governor, Reserve Bank of India. Currently the benchmark yield for Government Securities of shorter maturities (1 year/2 year) are higher by 69 basis points and 61 basis points, respectively, compared to the rates on 1 year/2 years Post Office Time Deposits. However, 3 year Time Deposit rates are on par with G-sec. yields; and in the case of medium and longer maturities of 5 years and above, the small savings rates still enjoy a spread ranging from 2 basis points to 152 basis points. In so far as senior citizens are concerned, their deposits under the 5 year Senior Citizens Savings Scheme enjoy a spread of 152 basis points over G-sec. yield for comparable maturity. As regards EPF deposits, the rate of interest is recommended by the Central Board of Trustees (EPF) and there is no linkage of rate of interest on EPF balance with the interest on investments in PPF/Time Deposit in post offices and public sector banks. Any increase in the small savings interest rates will require a concomitant increase in the on lending rates to the States for whom net collections under small savings schemes constitute a significant portion of revenue. The risk free, assured, regular returns, easy availability and liquidity of small savings schemes as well as the tax benefits enjoyed on PPF, NSC (VIII Issue) and Post Office Savings Accounts continue to contribute to the attractiveness of the small saving schemes. Shri Pawan Kumar Bansal, Minister of State for Finance gave this information in reply to a question raised by Shri Rajkumar Dhoot in Rajya Sabha today.

759. (8-5-2007) NEW DELHI : As per available information the total resources of iron ore in Bailadila deposits have been placed at 1135.31 million tones. At present, National Mineral Development Corporation (NMDC) holds six mining leases for iron ore in Bailadila mines over a total lease area of 5861.76 hectares. In addition to these, one prior approval for grant of mining lease for iron ore over an area of 413.74 hectares in Bailadila R.F. No.13 in favour of NMDC, one prior approval for grant of prospecting licence in favour of Essar Steel Ltd. over an area of 2285 hectares in Bailadila R.F. No. 3 and one prior approval for grant of prospecting licence in favour of Tata Iron & Steel Ltd. over an area of 2500 hectares in Bailadila R.F. No.1 have been conveyed to the State Government. The total production of iron ore in Bailadila area during 2006-07 was of 20.45 million tones and the quantity exported was 2.05 million tones. Above information was given by the Minister of Mines Shri Sis Ram Ola in a written reply in the Lok Sabha today.

760. (8-5-2007) NEW DELHI : All the 17 major Doordarshan Kendras have been fully digitized during the 10th Plan period. As part of modernization process, 48 major All India Radio Stations are proposed to be provided with Hard Disc based system along with server and storage systems. Of these,. 14 are in North Zone, 13 in West Zone, 10 in South Zone, six in North East and five in East Zone. The Government also proposed to modernize small studios and to open new small studios. 30 small studios have been partially digitalized during the 10th Plan period and a new small studio is under implementation at Tirupati as part of continuing schemes. Low end hard disc system are to be provided at 61 AIR stations. Of these, 16 are in North Zone, nine each in North East and East Zones, 15 in West Zone and 12 are located in South Zone. AIR has planned three new studios at Medium Wave (MW) stations, two at FM stations and one new FM transmitter in different parts of the country. Besides, provision of 24 small studios at new FM transmitter sites has also been made. This information was given by Minister of Information & Broadcasting and Parliamentary Affairs, Shri P. R. Dasmunsi in written reply to a question in Lok Sabha today.

761. (8-5-2007) NEW DELHI : Doordarshan has launched two channels in UK, namely, DD-India and DD-News. These were launched on 16.4.4007 by M/s Rayat Television Enterprises Ltd., of M/s Rayat Group Ltd. after entering into an agreement with Prasar Bharati for the distribution of DD-India and DD-News channels in UK for a period of five years. DD-India has seven Hindi and six English news bulletins daily while DD-News has nineteen English and twenty-four Hindi news bulletins daily, respectively. This information was given by Minister of Information & Broadcasting and Parliamentary Affairs, Shri P. R. Dasmunsi in written reply to a question in Lok Sabha today.

762. (8-5-2007) NEW DELHI : If in Delhi the rebellion spread like wild fire, then in other places such as Muzzafarnagar, Saharanpur, Allahabad, Kanpur, Barelli, Banaras, Bihar and Jhansi it irrupted like a volcano. In rural areas, the spread was the fastest and fiercest where the peasantry came out in large numbers against the oppressive revenue system introduced by the Company Lords. Peasants rebellion in India have been traditionally tax rebellion. Gujjars were the worst rebels through out the rebellion. Between the rivers Jamuna and Ganga, away from the GT Road, at Dadri, Sarsawa, Deoband, Bijnour, Moradabad and Rohilkhand, Gujjar turbulence was so intense that it seemed the company's rule has ended. According to one estimate more than a million Gujjars participated in the revolt. A regular system of correspondence existed between the Gujjars living in different parts of the country. The participation of these pastoral and nomadic communities made the rebellion a truly people's revolt. The Rangars and the Rajput communities were out to prove that the Rajput valour is not a thing of the past. The Britishers forgot rather conveniently that the Kisan (peasant and cultivator) of the peace time in India becomes a Jawan (solider) in war time. Jai Jawan, Jai Kisan had been a traditional Indian slogan. An extra ordinary fact stands out in the midst of the story of the great rebellions and that is even the main rebel leaders regarded the Mughal Emperor as their Badshah (King). Even those areas where the rebels established their authority they ruled in the name of the Mughal King. Rao Tula Ram of Rewari established his own government but collected the revenue in the name of the Delhi King. Nana Saheb declared himself a Peshwa at Kanpur but under the Mughal authority. The coins were struck in the name of the Emperor and the orders were issued in the name of the Delhi Badshah. The date on the coins were both in Hijri and Samvat as was the custom in the Mughal Court. Nana Saheb was a brave solider but his daughter Maina who was burnt alive at Bithoor was equally brave. People forgot their differences, communities set aside, their traditional rivalries the whole country faced their enemy as a united community.

763. (8-5-2007) NEW DELHI : No separate year-wise targets have been fixed for the development of market yards and modernization of G&P factories. However, the original target for Development of Market Yards under Technology Mission on Cotton (TMC) (Mini Mission –III) launched in February 2000 was 111. Against this target, 108 Market Yards have been completed by the end of the March 2007 (*i.e.* Xth Plan). The achievement is thus 97.29% of the original target. Similarly, the original target for Modernization of Ginning & Pressing Factories under Mini Mission –IV was 500, against which development of 544 market yards have been completed till the end of the Xth Five Year Plan. Thus achievement under Mini Mission – IV is 107% against the original target. Taking into account the fast pace of the achievements of the target and satisfactory progress of Mini Mission –III & IV the Government of India in June, 2005 thought it prudent to revise and thereby increase the original targets to Development of 250 Market Yards and Modernization of 1000 G& P factories. At the time of revising the target under TMC (MM-III & IV), it was well envisaged that this revised target would spill over to the XIth Plan period. Thus it will not be correct to say that the achievements in comparison to the targets have not been satisfactory. As on today against the revised target, 226 Market Yards have been sanctioned and 907 G& P factories have been sanctioned. The achievement of the revised targets in terms of number of project sanctioned is 90.40% in case of MM-III and 90.70% in case of MM-VI. As modernization of market yard and G& P factories have a long gestation period, it is expected that the project will be completed in the first two years of the XIth Plan period.

764. (8-5-2007) NEW DELHI : According to information received from the State Governments and NCT Delhi, 179 cases were registered against the Students Islamic Movement of India (SIMI) under various provisions of Unlawful Activities (Prevention) Act, Indian Penal Code, Explosive Substances Act, Prevention of Terrorism Act, Arms Act, Essential Services Act, etc. These cases are at different stages of trial in the courts. However, the activities of SIMI are under constant watch of law enforcement agencies. This information was given by the Minister of State for Home, Shri Sriprakash Jaiswal in a written reply to a question in the Lok Sabha today.

765. (8-5-2007) NEW DELHI : The Government proposes to issue multipurpose national identity cards to citizens of the country. However, keeping in view the complexities of the processes and technology, a pilot project is under implementation on an experimental basis in selected sub-districts of 12 states and one union territory. The government proposes to implement the scheme in the entire country after taking into account the experiences gained and lessons learnt from the pilot project. The production and distribution of identity cards will be completed by July, 2007. Rs. 44.36 crore has been sanctioned for the pilot project. This information was given by the Minister of State for Home, Shri Manikrao H. Gavit in a written reply to a question in the Lok Sabha today.

766. (8-5-2007) NEW DELHI : During 2006-07, a total amount of Rs.1065.25 crore was released to various State Governments under the Modernization of State Police Forces (MPF) Scheme. This includes release of an additional amount of Rs.100 crore for purchase of equipment for fighting naxalism against the proposals received from the State Governments of Andhra Pradesh (Rs.15 crore), Bihar

(Rs.15 crore), Chhatisgarh (Rs.24.75 crore), Jharkhand (Rs.15 crore), Maharashtra (Rs.6.75 crore), Orissa (Rs.15 crore) and West Bengal (Rs.8.50 crore). Under the MPF Scheme, the States have been categorized into "A" and "B" Categories with 100% and 75% Central funding respectively. J&K and seven North Eastern States viz., Arunachal Pradesh, Assam, Manipur, Meghalaya, Mizoram, Nagaland and Tripura have been classified as "A" category States in view of problems of insurgency, militancy and terrorism faced by these states. This information was given by the Minister of State for Home, Shri Sriprakash Jaiswal in a written reply to a question in the Lok Sabha today.

767. (8-5-2007) NEW DELHI : The Coir Board, a statutory organization set up under the Coir Industries Act, 1953, implements various schemes for the development of coir industry in coconut producing States for which annual budget allocations are provided by the Ministry of Agro and Rural Industries.

768. (8-5-2007) NEW DELHI : The Ministry of Rural Development has sanctioned Rs. 54.62 crore to the State Government of Jammu & Kashmir towards part payment of first instalment of funds against the provisional allocation of Rs.327.72 crore made for the Government of Jammu & Kashmir under Accelerated Rural Water Supply Programme (Normal) of Rajiv Gandhi National Drinking Water Mission, during the year 2007-08. The balance amount of first instalment will be released after receipt of AG report for 2004-05. Up to 15 per cent of funds released under this sanction may be utilized for Operation & Maintenance and up to 5 per cent of funds may be spent for taking sustainability measures. States have been requested to delegate powers for management of Rural Water Supply Schemes through the Panchayati Raj Institutions (PRIs) as per the Constitution of India. As such Operation and Maintenance of the completed RWS Scheme should be transferred to the PRIs. No expenditure shall be incurred on taking water quality problems form the present release, as there is a separate allocation for the purpose. This release is for execution/completion of schemes to provide safe drinking water facilities to rural habitations and schools under the Centrally Sponsored ARWSP and according to Priorities set in ARWSP guidelines and through other instructions issued from time to time.

769. (8-5-2007) NEW DELHI : The Ministry of Rural Development has released Grants-in-aid amounting to Rs. 24.08 crore as third/additional instalment of Central assistance to 11 districts of Orissa for the implementation of the Sampoorna Grameen Rozgar Yojana (SGRY) during the financial year (2006-07). Grants amounting to Rs.6.55 crore as part of first instalment has also been released to 5 districts of the State under the scheme for the year 2007-08.

770. (8-5-2007) NEW DELHI : Grants-in-aid amounting to Rs. 8.35 crore as third/additional instalment of Central assistance to 2 districts of Jharkhand, viz. Deoghar (Rs. 4.17 crore) and E. Singhbhum (Rs.4.18 crore) has been released by the Ministry of Rural Development for the implementation of the Sampoorna

Grameen Rozgar Yojana (SGRY) during the financial year (2006-07). The release is towards plan expenditure and will be utilized for approved items of works subject to the conditions laid down in the SGRY Guidelines. No deviations from the guidelines is permissible. The expenditure on implementation of the programme with regard to cash component is on 75:25 basis between the Central and the State Government, respectively. The Zila Parishads/DRDAs will release the entire funds allocated to them directly to the respective three tiers of the PRIs in the proportion as given in SGRY Guidelines within 15 days of receipt of funds from the Centre or the State without waiting for matching Share either from the Centre or the State.

771. (8-5-2007) NEW DELHI : Grants-in-aid amounting to Rs.2.10 crore has been released by the Ministry of Rural Development to 3 DRDAs of West Bengal, viz. South 24 Pgns (Rs.123.16 lakh), Nadia (Rs.68.27 lakh) and Murshidabad (Rs.18.77 lakh) towards Restoration of cut on account of late submission under the 'Swarnjayanti Gram Swarojgar Yojana' (SGSY) during the year 2006-07. The amount should be utilized on the Programme as per approved guidelines of SGSY. The funding pattern will be 75:25 by the Centre and the State. The State Government should release its share within one month of the date of release of the Central assistance. Under SGSY, assistance is given to the poor family living below the poverty line for taking up self-employment. It actively promotes group approach by organising the rural poor into Self-Help Groups.

772. (8-5-2007) NEW DELHI : The Ministry of Rural Development has released part payment of first instalment of Central share of funds amounting to Rs. 60.79 crore under the 'Swarnjayanti Gram Swarojgar Yojana' (SGSY) during the year 2007-08 to Gopalganj DRDA of Bihar. The amount should be utilized on the Programme as per approved guidelines of SGSY. The funding pattern will be 75:25 by the Centre and the State. The State Government should release its share within one month of the date of release of the Central assistance. Under SGSY, assistance is given to the poor family living below the poverty line for taking up self-employment. It actively promotes group approach by organising the rural poor into Self-Help Groups.

773. (8-5-2007) NEW DELHI : The Ministry of Labour & Employment has revised the minimum rate of stipend payable to trade apprentices under rule 11 of the Apprenticeship Rules, 1992. In a Gazette notification issued by the Directorate General of Employment and Training, the minimum stipend per month under the new rate shall be Rs. 1090 during the first year of training, Rs. 1240 during the second year, Rs. 1440 during the third year and Rs. 1620 during the fourth year of training. Earlier these rates per month were Rs. 820, Rs. 940, Rs. 1090 and Rs. 1230 during the first, second, third and fourth year of training respectively. The new rates are effective from March 21, 2007. The Apprenticeship rules have been amended in this regard in consultation with the Central Apprenticeship Council.

774. (8-5-2007) NEW DELHI : Under the umbrella scheme of Development of Primitive Tribal Groups, the Ministry of Tribal Affairs, provides funds to the different States which have STs known as Primitive Tribal Groups to provide life and disability insurance cover to the head of each PTG family under a scheme of the Life Insurance Corporation of India known as the Janashree Bima Yojana. This was stated by Shri P.R. Kyndiah, Minister for Tribal Affairs in a reply to a question by Shri Hemlal Murmu in Lok Sabha today. He further stated that the details of funds released and spent by the various State Governments, during last five years under the Janashree Bima Yojana of Life Insurance Corporation of India are as under: Statement showing details of funds released and expenditure reported by the States for Janashree Bima Yojana.

775. (8-5-2007) NEW DELHI : The Ministry of Women and Child Development is implementing a Centrally Sponsored Progrmme for Juvenile Justice under which grant-in-aid is provided to the State Government/UT administrations to meet 50% of their expenditure requirements for construction and maintenance of homes under the Juvenile Justice (Care and Protection of Children) Act, 2000 and upkeep of the children staying in these homes. This was stated by Smt. Renuka Chowdhury, Minister for Women and Child Development in a reply to a question by Shri Badiga Ramakrishna and Shri Mahavir Bhagora in Lok Sabha today.

776. (8-5-2007) NEW DELHI : The Minister for Chemicals and Fertilisers and Steel Shri Ram Vilas Paswan has said, the new policy on Petroleum, Chemicals and Petrochemical Investment Regions will transform India's image in the sector to scale greater heights. He was speaking here today after releasing the policy. Shri Paswan said, apart from helping the overall development of the region, the PCPIRs will help in generating employment. It will give a thrust to industrialization in the regions by way of setting up of downstream units. This in turn, he said, will lead to development of socio-economic infrastructure in the areas in and around the regions. The Minister said, the role of state governments will be in providing the physical infrastructure and utilities linkages under its jurisdiction. While doing so, the state governments should ensure that the rehabilitation policy for the families likely to be displaced should be humane. Shri Paswan said, it will be the government's effort to ensure that the land owner gets his due, while at the same time the process of land transfer, being a complex issue, is between the private developer and the land – owner directly, as far as possible. Later talking to newsmen, Shri Paswan said, the first PCPIR will come up by the year-end. The PCPIRs would be specifically delineated investment regions with and area of around 250 square kilometres for manufacturing facilities for domestic and export led production in petroleum, chemicals and petrochemicals along with associated services and infrastructure. They may include one or more Special Economic Zones, Industrial Parks, Free Trade and Warehousing Zones, Export Oriented Units or Growth Centres duly notified under the relevant central or state legislation policy. Each PCPIR will have a refinery/petrochemical feedstock company as an anchor tenant. The Government of India will ensure the availability of external physical infrastructure including Rail, National Highways, Ports, Airports and Telecommunication facilities in a time bound manner. This infrastructure will be created/upgraded through Public Private Partnerships to the extent possible. The state governments will be responsible for providing infrastructure facilities like power, water, sewerage and health, safety and environmental concerns. The Department of Chemicals and Petrochemicals will be the nodal department of the Government of India. A high-powered committee will be constituted by the centre to scrutinize applications for setting up the PCPIR and then monitor and expedite the implementation. Describing it as a historic occasion the Secretary, Department of Chemicals and Petrochemicals Smt. Satwant Reddy said, the chemical industry in the country has evolved to be an innovative industry. She said, with world class infrastructure in place, the Petroleum, Chemical and Petrochemical Investment Regions will be infrastructure driven and not incentive driven. She said, the scale of the industries and synergy between different units will help the growth of the region. The President of Federation of Indian Chamber of Commerce and Industry Shri Habil Khorakiwala hailed the new policy as path breaking. He said, it will facilitate cluster formation of industries and the policy is like an approach to develop a master plan. He was emphatic that this is happening for the first time in the country. He said, this will also provide great employment opportunity.

777. (8-5-2007) NEW DELHI : The Polavaram project is under Appraisal in Central Water Commission. Issues regarding Irrigation Planning, Hydel Civil Design, Cost aspect, Back water study and Interstate aspects are yet to be finalized. As per Resettlement and Rehabilitation Plan of October 2005 prepared by the Government of Andhra Pradesh, an area of 587.77 ha of Orissa is likely to be submerged. The population likely to be affected is 6316. However, the above figures are to be confirmed by conducting a joint survey by the State Governments. The project is to be executed in accordance with Godavari Water Disputes Tribunal Award and Inter-State Agreement on the project between State Governments of Andhra Pradesh and Orissa. This information was given by the Minister of State for Water Resources, Shri Jai Prakash Narayan Yadav in response to a question by Ms. Pramila Bohidar and Shri B.J.Panda in the Rajya Sabha today.

778. (8-5-2007) NEW DELHI : There is no serious concern for the Lower Assam districts of Barpeta and Nalbari due to Tsatichu landslide dam, as the volume of water in the Tsatichu landslide dam, as the volume of water in the Tsatichu lake is negligible at present. The expert team has visited the landslide dam area on 21st December 2006 upto the point from where a realistic technical assessment of the hazard potential of the slide dam could be done and all the required technical details could be gathered. The team has observed that the landslide dam was stable and there was negligible water in the Tsatichu lake. This information was given by the Minister of State for Water Resources, Shri Jai Prakash Narayan Yadav in response to a question by Smt. Syeda Anwara Taimur in the Rajya Sabha today.

779. (8-5-2007) NEW DELHI : Under the Indus Waters Treaty 1960, waters of the Indus, the Jhelum and the Chenab are available for the unrestricted use of Pakistan except for some specified uses by India. Waters of the Ravi, the Beas and the Satluj are available for the unrestricted use of India, except for some specified uses by Pakistan while these rivers flow in their territory and have not yet finally crossed over into Pakistan. A letter of October, 2002 from the Hon'ble Minister of Irrigation, Government of Gujarat, mentioned the visit of Hon'ble Minister of Water Resources to Gujarat in September, 2002 and requested the Central Government to use its powers to compel the concerned States not to neglect the legitimate claim of Indus Water for Kachch region of Gujarat and to take up the allocation of Eastern River Waters issue with the concerned States at the earliest. The State Government was informed that for getting a share of the waters of the rivers Ravi, Beas and Satluj for the Kutch region of Gujarat, the beneficiary States to whom the waters of these rivers have been allocated, have to agree to help Gujarat by sparing a portion from their allocated waters. It would therefore be appropriate if the State of Gujarat requests the beneficiary States to provide water out of their allocated shares for the Kutch region and only an amicable settlement with the beneficiary States could benefit Gujarat. This information was given by the Minister of State for Water Resources, Shri Jai Prakash Narayan Yadav in response to a question by Shri Jayantilal Barot in the Rajya Sabha today.

780. (8-5-2007) NEW DELHI : Shri Abhishek Singhvi said that the our continuing concern with the events in Gujarat is reflected now in a written communication by a Congress Member of Parliament from Gujarat, our chief whip Shri Madhusudan Mistry who has written in detail to the Home Minister and a copy to the Prime Minister about the widespread apprehension in respect of the engineered killing, liquidation of Mr. Vanzara and the blaming of a particular community for that act. This concern of ours is based on information, facts was shared with you earlier but we have now, to put it on record, written in detail to the authorities and we have said if I may quote from the letter of May 8, 2007, there is a widespread apprehension that the senior DIG, officer may be killed on one pretext or the other and the BJP functionary including Chief Minister may organize things in such a way that the people of Gujarat would believe that a muslim killed DIG Mr. Vanzara. This would in turn engineer riot-like situation throughout the state of Gujarat, polarizing the population both Hindu and Muslim and the BJP team would then go for the elections to try to capture power on that plank and that they have this sinister design and we have a report that the elder brother of the DIG fears about the life and safety of his younger brother namely, Mr. Vanzara. This letter really ought to have been addressed to the state authority, it is really meant for the custodian of law and order, the chief minister. The Home Minister is being requested to take all steps to ensure that such things do not happen and I request you to ensure such measures which nullify any such design of polarizing the society in Gujarat so as to assure peoples' safety and security .But the real point is that this letter should really be addressed to and is meant for the chief minister of Gujarat, the administration of Gujarat which as you and I know are the real custodians of law and order. Unfortunately we know from established track record, from past experience that any such communication to the rightful custodians of law and order is futile. We believe that this is a classic case were the central government is entitled to use all its power, explicit and implicit, to aid, advise, warn, suggest, persuade the state government to ensure that the relevant evidence of all the wrong doings in Gujarat is not physically liquidated. To a question that the BJP has alleged that the Congress may be behind this conspiracy, Shri Singhvi, replying in Hindi said, then I think the matter can be sorted out easily if this matter is handed over to the CBI by the Gujarat government. To a question on the credibility of your report, Shri Singhvi said that this report is based on reliable sources. If it was not credible, if it was not reliable, if it was not well founded, we would not have the next day converted into writing and written to the highest authorities of the country. To a question on the law and order in the state of Gujarat, Shri Singhvi said that the rules of the state jurisdiction, state law and order, federal system and those traditional rules were premised on the basic premise of a state which does not participate in legality. Now the boundary of those rules are breaking down and once the boundaries of those rules are breaking down then all other enabling implied or other powers available in the constitution or else where must be tried to be used. To a question whether Congress Party sees more than encounter, Shri Singhvi said that I have already clarified on earlier occasion that it is completely wrong and misleading and digressive to characterise this as a mere encounter or as a mere law and order and that is precisely what the BJP and the govt. of Gujarat is trying to do. This is repeated, recurrent state complicity, state awareness, state tolerance and state encouragement where the guardians of law themselves have become lawless and it is much more in the aberrational behaviour of an individual police officer which might be described as an encounter death. To a question as to what is the governor doing in Gujarat? Shri Singhvi said I think those like you who raise such questions need to read the constitution again, need to re-educate and re-equate yourself with our constitutional scheme. Unlike, the BJP, which has scant regard to constitutional norms, we do not at the same scant disregard.

781. (8-5-2007) NEW DELHI : As per information furnished by the Ministry of Finance, the amount collected through the Education Cess for the years 2004-05, 2005-06 and 2006-07 (up to February, 2007) is as under: The proceeds of Education Cess utilized exclusively for the Sarva Shiksha Abhiyan (SSA) and Mid-Day Meal Scheme (MDM) of the Government after exhausting the funds provided to these schemes by way of Gross Budgetary Support (GBS) Allocations to States are not being made separately against the Education Cess. Financial assistance to them is released under individual schemes of SSA & MDM related to Elementary Education in accordance with the guidelines of such schemes and against their respective budgetary allocations. This information was given by the Minister of State for Human Resource Development, Shri M.A.A. Fatmi in a written reply in the Lok Sabha today.

782. (8-5-2007) NEW DELHI : Minister for Tourism and Culture Smt. Ambika Soni informed the Rajya Sabha today that the Archaeological Survey of India undertakes the conservation of Taj Mahal strictly in accordance with the archaeological norms. Apart from conservation and preservation of the monument, the Archaeological Survey of India also undertakes development of its gardens and facilities for tourists. A total expenditure of Rs. 2.86 crores was incurred on the above account during the last three years. In a written reply Smt. Soni said, in addition, the Ministry of Tourism has taken up a project at an estimated cost of Rs. 39.34 crores for Agra Revitalisation and Visitor Management for Taj Mahal. The integrated project is expected to be completed within a period of 36 months.

783. (8-5-2007) NEW DELHI : Minister for Tourism and Culture Smt. Ambika Soni informed the Rajya Sabha today that Archaeological Survey of India had undertaken a pilot project for digitizing and cataloguing 10,000 photo archives through the American Institute of Indian Studies. In a written reply she said, there was no objection to this project.

784. (8-5-2007) NEW DELHI : Minister for Tourism and Culture Smt. Ambika Soni informed the Rajya Sabha today that the Government of NCT of Delhi had submitted a proposal for construction of a road link connecting NH-24 with Lala Lajpat Rai Road. The proposed link road is passing through at a distance of 340 metres from the protected limits of Humayun's Tomb. The proposal of the Government of NCT of Delhi was examined by an Expert Advisory Committee constituted by the archaeological Survey of India, and based on the deliberations of the Committee, the Archaeological Survey of India had issued a conditional No Objection Certificate to the proposed link road. As the response of the Government of NCT of Delhi to the conditionalties has not been received, the NOC has been kept under suspension. In a written reply she said, no alternate proposal has so far been received by the Archaeological Survey of India.

785. (8-5-2007) NEW DELHI : The Minister of Tourism and Culture Smt. Ambika Soni informed the Rajya Sabha today that hotels fix their own tariff structure. Due to shortage of hotel accommodation in some metro cities and important tourist destinations, the room tariffs are reported to be high. In a written reply she said, Ministry of Tourism has requested State/ UT Government and other land owning agencies like DDA, Ministry of Civil Aviation, Indian Railways etc. to allocate land for building hotels especially in the budget category. They have been advised to follow investor friendly land policies and single window approach for promoting hotel projects and also for allotting sites on revenue sharing basis, granting extra FSI/ FAR for hotels, permitting extra commercial usage in the hotels etc., so that the Budget Hotels are promoted. Further, in order to increase the number of rooms in the budget category, a scheme for approval of Guesthouses and Incredible India Bed & Breakfast establishments has been introduced.

786. (8-5-2007) NEW DELHI : In a new initiative to propel India's manufacturing growth to a new high, a path breaking Post Graduate Programme for Executives called "Visionary Leadership in Manufacturing" (PGPEX-VLM) was launched here yesterday by Dr. V. Krishnamurthy, Chairman, National Manufacturing Competitiveness Council (NMCC). Dr. Krishnamurthy described this initiative as a milestone in building up human capital, which is India's biggest asset. The Programme will generate "300 visionary leaders in the manufacturing sector in the next three years", he said, while underlining that this was the first time that Indian Institute of Technology (IIT) and Indian Institute of Management (IIM) had joined hands to run a post graduate programme. Dr. Krishnamurthy also indicated that India's manufacturing growth could reach 14% in the coming year and the real challenge would be to sustain this growth so that share of manufacturing in India's GDP could be stepped up from the current 17% to 30%. The programme is of one-year duration and the first session (2007-08) will commence in August 2007. The eligibility for admission is a first class degree in any branch of engineering along with minimum 5 years of experience in manufacturing and related sector. The tuition fee for the programme would be Rs.5 lakh. The programme is one of the major initiatives taken by the NMCC to improve the competitiveness of Indian manufacturing industry in association with the Confederation of Indian Industry (CII), Japanese International Cooperation Agency, the Ministry of Human Resource Development and Prof. Shoji Shiba who has been associated for more than a decade with very successful manufacturing leadership programmes at the Massachusetts Institute of Technology and has helped develop the Visionary Leadership Programme in India along with IIT/Kanpur, IIT/Madras and IIM/Kolkata. The Japanese Ambassador to India, Mr. Yasukuni Enoki, expressed happiness of about Japanese involvement in the development of PGPEX-VLM and hoped that the programme would enable India to regain its dominant position in the world in manufacturing which, he pointed out, the country had enjoyed in the pre-colonial era – in the 16th and 17th centuries. Shri R. Seshasayee, President of CII, in his keynote address, expressed optimism regarding the association of industry and the academic world which has come together to develop the PGPEX-VLM. He highlighted 3 key challenges facing the Indian industry viz., development of quality higher education; enabling the manufacturing industry to attract and retain best talent and to develop a critical mass of intellectual property through R&D initiatives. He hoped that these concerns would be ably met through PGPEX-VLM programme.

787. (8-5-2007) NEW DELHI : The Minister of Rural Development in his opening remarks in the Consultative Committee Meeting of the Ministry, held here yesterday late in the evening, highlighted the achievements of the Ministry under different schemes during the Tenth Plan and outlined the Eleventh Plan projections with focus on budget for the year 2007-08. He informed the members of the Committee that during 2006-07, 90.25 crore man days were generated under the National Rural Employment Guarantee Act (NREGA) and that its coverage will be extended to all the districts by 2009-10. Sampoorna Grameen Rozgar Yojana (SGRY) will be submerged in to NREGA in all the districts during the same period and the annual plan under the scheme will be prepared in line with the NREGA guidelines, he informed. During the Tenth Plan, 15.72 lakh SHGs have been formed and its universalisation by bringing one member from each BPL household within the fold of SHG forms part of the Action Plan under Swarnjayanti Gram Swarozgar Yojna (SGSY). Under Indira Awas Yojna (IAY), during the Eleventh Plan, it is proposed to construct 30 lakh houses every year and under Bharat Nirman the target is to construct 60 lakh houses during 2005-2009. IAY guidelines have been changed to introduce earmarking of funds for minorities and also provision has been made under SGSY from 2006-07 to fix separate targets for the identified minority communities. Under PMGSY (Pradhan Mantri Gram Sadak Yojna), performance targets for 2007-08 are to connect 14,000 habitations and to complete a road length of 55,000 Kms. Under Total Sanitation Campaign (TSC), action plan proposes to provide 100% access to toilets in individual households during the Eleventh Plan, the Minister informed. The three area development programmes, namely IWDP (Integrated Wasteland Development Programme), DPAP (Drought Prone Areas Programme) and DDP (Desert Development Programme) have been merged into one programme, *i.e.* Integrated Watershed Management Programme (IWMP) from the current year which will run on a national programme mode and be implemented by dedicated agencies at the national, state and district levels. Similarly, Computerization of Land Records (CLR), Strengthening of Revenue Administration (SRA) and Updation of Land Records (ULR) have been merged in to one scheme of National Programme for Comprehensive Land Resource Management (NPCLRM) to facilitate the process of computerization, updating, maintenance of land records and validation of titles with a view to providing location-specific information for development planning with major focus on citizen services, the Minister informed the Members of the Committee and he invited their suggestions for further improving the performance of the Rural Development programmes during the Eleventh Plan Period.

788. (8-5-2007) NEW DELHI : In accordance with the provisions of the Act governing the professional bodies, the Government has nominated eight persons on the Council of the Institute of Chartered Accountants of India and five persons on the Council of the Institute of Company Secretaries of India. On the Council of the Institute of Cost and Works Accountants of India (ICWAI) there are four Government nominees. However, when the Council of ICWAI is reconstituted in July, 2007 under the provisions of the Act, as amended, it would be possible to nominate five persons.

789. (8-5-2007) NEW DELHI : The Government approved setting up of Serious Fraud Investigation Office on 9th January 2003. However, it started functioning from 1st October 2003. A Coordination and Monitoring Committee (CMC), co-chaired by Secretary, Ministry of Company Affairs (MCA) and Chairman, SEBI was set up in March, 1999 to settle the policy issues regarding the delinquent companies/promoters and to monitor the progress in regard to action against vanishing companies. 229 companies were originally identified as vanished. With the continuous efforts of CMC, 115 companies have been traced back, as these companies were found to be regular in filing statutory returns, etc., resulting in the number of Vanishing Companies being reduced to 114 as of now. The Serious Fraud Investigation Office has no role to play with regard to the monitoring of action taken against Vanishing Companies. This information was given by Shri Prem Chand Gupta, Minister of Company Affairs in reply to the questions raised by Shri S. Anbalagan in Rajya Sabha today.

790. (8-5-2007) NEW DELHI : Defence Communication Seminar (DEFCOM) 2007 is being conducted at New Delhi, commencing Thursday. The theme for seminar is "Strategies for Future Defence Networks and Relevance of Electromagnetic Interference/ Electromagnetic Compatibility (EMI/EMC) in future Battlefields. The Seminar is being conducted for a period of three days, from 10 May to 12 May 07. The inaugural session will be conducted on 10 May 07. Shri AK Antony, Hon'ble Raksha Mantri is to be the Chief Guest and General JJ Singh, Chief of Army Staff, will be the guest of honour during the inaugural session. The closing session will be chaired by Hon'ble Raksha Rajya Mantri Shri M Pallam Raju on 12 May 07. The Defence Communication Seminar christened as DEFCOM, is an annual event, jointly conducted by Corps of Signals of the Indian Army and the Confederation of Indian Industries (CII). The seminar aims to improve the synergy between the Armed Forces and the Telecom, IT Industry. It is an ideal forum in which the Armed Forces highlight their peculiar communication and IT requirements so that the industry can align their policies and products to be able to provide best possible solutions for the Armed Forces. The communication infrastructure of the Indian Army is undergoing a paradigm shift from Platform Centric to Network Centric Warfare. The erstwhile voice predominant network has been replaced by a state-of-the-art packet switched infrastructure, which can handle voice, video and data simultaneously, also called "Triple Play" in telecom parlance. The communication media consists of optical fibers, digital microwave radios, satellites and tactical wireless equipment. Future battlefields will be cluttered with a plethora of electromagnetic emitters which would include communication equipment, radars, jammers etc. Management of the electromagnetic space to avoid interference amongst these system would be a major challenge. Future wars will be very short and intense with flexibility and mobility of forces being the key. The winner would be the one who can concentrate his forces at the decisive point quicker than the opponent. To achieve this, the communication infrastructure needs to be survivable, robust and secure. Recent experience in Iraq, Afghanistan and Lebanon further underscore this point. Reliance on wireless communication networks would be tremendous and issues related to electromagnetic interference and compatibility would play a paramount role in the success during battle. The Indian Army has set its vision on being Network Enabled by the year 2009 and being 'Network Centric' by the year 2012. Network upgrade is an ongoing process and DEFCOM 2007 aims at gathering views form experts in the Armed Forces, the Industry Defence Research and Development Organisation (DRDO), Ministry of Defence and academia in order to arrive at a consensus on the most appropriate way forward. The seminar will also provide the Indian Industry an insight into network requirements from the Defence Forces perspective. It will also act as a sounding board wherein network planners and managers of the Defence Forces will apprise the Industry of challenges and complexities of interoperability and synchronization of the Defence Networks. DEFCOM INDIA 2007 will provide and ideal platform to the Indian Industry to interact with a wide cross section of Defence Force officers so that a well – coordinated strategy for future Defence Networks may be formulated.

791. (8-5-2007) NEW DELHI : Maj Gen (Mrs.) Shashi Bala of Army's Nursing Services is to be felicitated by the prestigious Florence Nightingale award for nursing services by the President, Dr. APJ Abdul Kalam on Saturday. Maj Gen (Mrs.) Shahi Bala is presently the Additional Director General of Military Nursing Services (MNS) at the Army HQ. She belongs to New Delhi and had her early nursing education in Mumbai. She holds a Masters degree in Nursing. Immediately after joining MNS, she rendered services to the battle casualties of 1971 Indo – Pak War. She has 37 years nursing experience and has been awarded the Vishisht Seva Medal in the past. She is an eminent researcher, academician and author of various aspects of nursing care.

792. (8-5-2007) NEW DELHI : The Minister of State for Communications & Information Technology, Dr. Shakeel Ahmad, informed the Lok Sabha today, in a written reply to a question by Shri S. Ponnuswamy that the Electronics hardware Technology Park (EHTP) Scheme of the Government of India is governed by the Foreign Trade Policy of the Department of Commerce. Upto December 2006, 108 units were operational under the EHTP Scheme. Dr. Ahmad further informed the House that Income tax benefit is available to the developers under the "Special Economic Zones Scheme", promoted by the Department of Commerce and also under the "Industrial Park Scheme", promoted by the Department of Industrial Policy and Promotion under Section 80-1A of the Income Tax Act. Technology Parks can be set up under either of the above schemes.

793. (8-5-2007) NEW DELHI : The Minister of State for Communications & Information Technology, Dr. Shakeel Ahmad, informed the Lok Sabha today, in a written reply to a question by Shri Santosh Gangwar, Smt. Manorama Madhavarj and Shri Braja Kishore Tripathy that Telecom Regulatory Authority of India (TRAI) has released a draft regulation on 23rd April 2007, for putting in place a mechanism called "National Do Not Call Registry (NDNC)" for curbing the unwanted telemarketing calls. This was based on the stakeholders responses to a consultation process for finding a solution to restrict unsolicited commercial communication to subscribers who do not want such calls, internal discussions and international practices. Dr. Ahmad further stated that keeping in mind the concerns of their consumers, mobile service providers have already introduced "Do not Disturb" facility, for the subscribers who do not wish to receive information on product and services of their mobile service provider. Also, TRAI has advised the mobile subscribers through advertisement in leading newspapers to use this facility. TRAI has proposed to implement NDNC through National Informatics Centre (NIC) Department of Information Technology, he added.

794. (8-5-2007) NEW DELHI : The Minister of State for Communications & Information Technology, Dr. Shakeel Ahmad, informed the Lok Sabha today, in a written reply to a question by Shri Mahavir Bhagora that at present there are 133 projects with Centre for Development of Advanced Computing (CDAC). No project completed by or pending with CDAC is under Centrally Sponsored Scheme.

795. (8-5-2007) NEW DELHI : A two-day seminar on modern internal audit concepts, standards, practices and techniques for the professional development of senior civil servants handling internal audit assignments for the Government begins here tomorrow. This is part of an ambitious modernization project launched by the organization of the Controller General of Accounts for development of a multidimensional accounting classification system, for gradually transiting to accrual basis of accounting, and, for development of an advanced system of internal controls. The seminar is being organized by the Institute of Government Accounts and Finance (INGAF) in collaboration with the Indian affiliates of the Institute of Internal Auditors, a global organization, with headquarters in Florida and the Indian Institute of Management, Bangalore. The paradigm shift in public expenditure management has been necessitated by the change in emphasis from outlays to outcomes, introduction of a quarterly exchequer control based expenditure management system, and, the attempt to improve transparency and accountability in governance processes. The seminar has been planned to address the need of recasting the current, essentially regulatory system of internal controls and to respond to the crying requirement of toning up audit functions for effective risk management and performance monitoring. INGAF, the training arm of the Controller General of Accounts, has, over the years, earned recognition as a premier research and training institute in the field of public expenditure management and budgetary reforms not only within the country but also the SAARC, CIS, African and Latin American countries.

796. (8-5-2007) NEW DELHI : The Defence Minister of Italy Mr. Arturo Parisi called on Defence Minister Shri A K Antony at Defence Headquarters in New Delhi today. Both the leaders discussed matters of mutual interest and defence cooperation. Mr. Parisi who arrived here on May 7, 2007, on a four-day state visit has already visited Hindustan Aeronautics Limited and Bharat Electronics Limited establishments at Bangalore. The visiting dignitary will fly back on May 10, 2007.

797. (8-5-2007) NEW DELHI : Government has set up the Sixth Central Pay Commission to go into the question of pay, allowances and other facilities/benefits etc. of Central Government Employees including Armed Forces Personnel. The three services have submitted a joint memorandum to the Sixth Central Pay Commission seeking inter alia, the improved pay scales for the Armed Forces Personnel. The Armed Forces have also sought a better package for Personnel Below Officers' Rank (PBOR) that includes brighter career prospects and enhanced pensionary benefits. This information was given by the Defence Minister Shri AK Antony in a written reply to Smt SG Indira in Rajya Sabha today.

798. (8-5-2007) NEW DELHI : Senior Officers of the Armed Forces are not permitted to negotiate for commercial employment in private sector while in service. Further, Officers of the rank of Colonel and above (and equivalent ranks in Navy and Air Force) are required to obtain permission of the Government before taking commercial employment within two years of the date of retirement. Before granting this permission the competent authorities have to satisfy themselves inter-alia that any official information, knowledge or contacts which the officer might have gained while in service would not be used to give the prospective employer an unfair advantage. Also, appointments with companies/firms which operate in sensitive areas of defence procurements or which have subsidiary firms having contracts with Ministry of Defence as also appointments with foreign government or foreign firms are not allowed. However, defence officers have been seeking voluntary retirement and are resigning for various reasons including (a) supersession for promotion (b) being placed in a permanently low medical category (c) compassionate reasons, such as, looking after ailing parents/children/siblings, to look after ancestral property, attend to litigation etc. (d) failure to acquire minimum technical qualifications prescribed for promotion (e) increase in employment opportunities on the civil side.

799. (8-5-2007) NEW DELHI : It has been decided by the Government to set up an Expert Panel to determine whether there is a need to re-locate and reconfigure the existing Security Forces, keeping in mind the security needs of the State. However, the quantum of troops deployed in the State of Jammu and Kashmir is continuously assessed and reviewed by the Army based on the changing threat perception. This information was given by the Defence Minister Shri AK Antony in a written reply to Shri Ajay Maroo and Shri TS Bajwa in Rajya Sabha today.

800. (8-5-2007) NEW DELHI : Sainik Schools are established on receipt of a specific request from a State Government agreeing to provide funds for the creation and maintenance of basic infrastructure, equipment and facilities besides scholarships for the cadets of the State. Requests for establishment of Sainik Schools have been received from the State Governments of Sikkim, Chhattisgarh and Karnataka. Government of Karnataka has allotted 55.93 acres of land to start the Sainik School at Kudige. It has also conveyed its willingness to fulfil all obligations including the financial commitment of Rs. 25 crore spread over six to seven years for construction of permanent infrastructure of the school and the recurring expenditure of about Rs. 1.3 crore per annum. An inspection of the site selected for establishing the Sainik School has been carried out. A confirmation from Service Hqrs regarding availability of officers for being posted as Principal, Headmaster and Registrar in the school has been received. There are 21 Sainik Schools in the country.

801. (8-5-2007) NEW DELHI : The Government has imported defence items including raw materials for its use during the last three years also. These items are sourced from various countries including Russia, the USA, the UK, France, Israel, Germany, Australia, Italy, Ukraine, etc. Divulging the details relating to these items on the floor of the House would not be in the interests of national security.

802. (8-5-2007) NEW DELHI : The Joint Venture Brahmos was established through Inter-Government Agreement in February, 1998 for design, development, production and marketing of Brahmos supersonic cruise missile with share capital of $250 million, contributed by India and Russia in the ratio of 50.5% and 49.5%, respectively. The share capital was enhanced by $50 million to include the development of aircraft version of the missile. Therefore, the contribution from the Indian side was Rs. 634 crores. DRDO also contributed Rs. 370 crores to realize the required infrastructure, technologies, production facilities and systems for Indian Armed Forces. Performance improvement of the missile system is an on-going process and suitable actions have been initiated. This information was given by the Defence Minister Shri AK Antony in a written reply to Shri Jai Parkash Aggarwal in Rajya Sabha today.

803. (8-5-2007) NEW DELHI : Government is aware that a number of fishermen from Tamil Nadu are being attacked and killed by Sri Lankan Navy during the recent years. There have been incidents of firing on Indian fishing boats in Palk Bay and Gulf of Mannar area and recently slight increase in such incidents has been noticed. To protect the Indian fishermen, surveillance and patrolling are regularly done by the Indian Navy and the Indian Coast Guard in the Indian waters of the Palk Bay and the Gulf of Mannar. Air surveillance is also undertaken. The surveillance mechanisms include coastal patrol, international maritime boundary patrol, air patrol, shallow water patrol and radar surveillance. Further, the Government of India has strongly taken up the issue of firing on Indian fishermen with the Government of Sri Lanka. The need to act with restraint and to treat India's fishermen in a humane manner has been repeatedly emphasized to the Government of Sri Lanka. During the period from 1991 to mid April 2007, 77 fishermen of Tamil Nadu have been killed in such incidents. Government of Tamil

Nadu provides immediate relief to the family of such deceased fishermen according to its norms. In addition, if the deceased belonged to the Fishermen Cooperative Society, his family is also provided financial relief under the Fishermen Accident Group Insurance Scheme operated by the Department of Fisheries through the National Federation of Fishermen Cooperative Ltd. This information was given by the Defence Minister Shri AK Antony in a written reply to Shri C Perumal in Rajya Sabha today.

804. (8-5-2007) NEW DELHI : The General Contract of December, 2000 was signed with Russians for licence manufacture of Su-30 MK-I aircraft by HAL as per the Standard of Preparation (SOP) for direct purchased aircraft contracted by MoD in 1996. Electronic Warfare System was not included in the General Contract because the system was not identified for the aircraft at that time. The Su-30 MK-I aircraft manufactured by HAL under licence is of the same SOP as that of Stage III aircraft supplied directly by Russia. HAL is not ill equipped for setting up repair and overhauling facilities. Su-30 MK-I aircraft were inducted in the Air Force in 2004 and would become due for overhaul from 2010 onwards. The repair and overhaul facilities are planned to be set up by HAL in 2008. This information was given by the Defence Minister Shri AK Antony in a written reply to Shri K. Malaisamy and Shri SPM Syed Khan in Rajya Sabha today.

805. (8-5-2007) NEW DELHI : About *55* different products have been developed by Life Sciences Laboratories of DRDO which are critical for survival of troops in extreme conditions. Some of the products are Air crew protective equipment and clothing; Nuclear, Biological and Chemical (NBC) Protection and Detection Kits; Drugs; Mosquito repellants; Nutritional products, etc. Formal agreements for transfer of technologies have been signed with private companies for various products developed by DRDO. A revenue of Rs. 4.30 crore in the year 2004, Rs. 11.73 crore in 2005 and Rs. 14.62 crore in 2006 have been received for these products. This information was given by the Defence Minister Shri AK Antony in a written reply to Smt Prema Cariappa and Shri Santosh Bagrodia in Rajya Sabha today.

806. (8-5-2007) NEW DELHI : There has been a steady improvement in the settlement of industrial disputes through conciliation officers of the Central Industrial Regulations Machinery (CIRM) also known as the Chief Labour Commissioners' (Central) Organisation. Since 2000-01 the number of settlements arrived at in conciliation proceedings has been going up. The number of settlements was 764 in 2000-01 while it rose to 1506 in 2004-05. Some of the notable achievements on industrial relations front during the recent past have been the long term settlement in cement industry benefiting nearly 1.25 lakh workers and in Hindustan Copper Limited benefiting 6000 workers. The success rate of averting the threatened strikes through mediation by conciliation officers continues to be 97 to 98 per cent. A number of proposed strikes have been averted in banking industry, major port trusts, oil industry, mines, Government of India Security and Currency Press,

Mints etc. However, over the years there is a steady fall in the number of Industrial disputes referred to CIRM. Consequently the number of disputes being seized in conciliation is also showing a decline. There is also decline in the cases of threatened strikes. Similarly the number of awards received for implementation is also on decline. There is also no improvement in the number of awards implemented mainly due to stay orders from the courts and non-availability of sanction under 197 Cr. PC from the employing Ministry. However in the year 2005-06, 80 per cent settlements were fully implemented. The officers of CLC(C) organisation successfully completed Phase I and Phase II of General Verification within record time of 3 years. They verified the membership of 18,168 trade unions affiliated to 13 Central Trade Unions (CTU) with claimed membership of 42 million workers. The final phase of verification *i.e.*, declaration of provisional results and inviting objections from CTU Organisations is yet to be undertaken due to status quo order given by the Kolkata High Court. An All India Conference of Deputy Chief Labour Commissioners (C) and Regional Labour Commissioners (C) is being held in the capital from Thursday (10th May 2007) to critically analyse the performance of the CLC's (C) Organisations during the last one year. The two-day Conference being inaugurated by the Minister of State (Independent Charge), Labour and Employment, Shri Oscar Fernandes will also deliberate on the ways and means for improving settlement of industrial disputes.

807. (8-5-2007) NEW DELHI : State Governments are 'appropriate' Governments for implementation of the Child Labour (Prohibition & Regulation) Act, 1986 in their respective areas. As per the information received from the State Governments, 2229 violations of the recent notification banning employment of children under 14 as domestic help and in hospitality sector were detected. 38818 inspections were carried out by some State Governments from whom reports were received and 211 prosecutions have been filed. The State Governments have been advised for taking appropriate measures for effective implementation of this notification. In this connection, Chief Ministers of all State Governments/UTs have been addressed for creating wide awareness on the issue and for the strict enforcement of the ban. Government of India has also held consultations with the State Governments, NGOs, and other stake holders, at Zonal Conferences held at Bangalore (Southern Zone), Guwahati (North East Zone), Ranchi (Eastern Zone), Amritsar (Northern Zone) and Goa (Western Zone). During the conferences, the action plans of the State Governments were discussed for effective implementation of the Notification and for the rehabilitation of these children. NGOs and other members of civil society also participated in these consultations. The Government is implementing the National Child Labour Project Scheme in 250 districts of 20 States of the country. Under the Scheme, children withdrawn from work are provided education, nutrition, vocational training, stipend and health care etc. and are finally mainstreamed to regular education system. This was stated by the Minister of State (Independent Charge), Labour & Employment, Shri Oscar Fernandes in a written reply in the Rajya Sabha today.

808. (8-5-2007) NEW DELHI : International Labour Organisation (ILO) in its report "Global Employment Trends for Women – 2007" has indicated that in South Asia, 36% of the women are economically active as compared to 82.2% of men. Lower participation of women in the workforce is due to various factors like societal attitudes, low literacy rate, less trained women force etc. Under the National Policy for Empowerment of Women, Government is taking various measures to create an environment for the development of women through positive economic and social policies, to enable them to realize their full potential, greater employment and equal access to education and health. In addition, Government has been running number of Programmes/Schemes with a view to enhance and broaden the employment opportunities including self-employment and development of entrepreneurial skills of women. A number of training institutions have been set up by the Central Government in different parts of the country specifically for the skill training of women which include National and Regional Vocational Training Institutes. This was stated by the Minister of State (Independent Charge), Labour & Employment, Shri Oscar Fernandes in a written reply in the Rajya Sabha today.

809. (8-5-2007) NEW DELHI : The estimated number of women workers engaged in different agricultural operations in rural areas was 2,72,40,738 during 2004-05 survey. This figure was 2,93,08,675 during 1999-2000 survey. Gender-wise information on the contribution of women employed in agriculture sector to national income is not maintained. Persons who operate their own farm or non-farm enterprises or are engaged independently in the profession or trade on own-account or with one or a few partners are deemed to be self-employed in household enterprises. This was stated by the Minister of State (Independent Charge), Labour & Employment, Shri Oscar Fernandes in a written reply in the Rajya Sabha today.

810. (8-5-2007) NEW DELHI : Estimates of employment and unemployment among major religious groups in the country are obtained through quinquennial labour force surveys conducted by National Sample Survey Organization. Last such survey conducted pertains to the year 2004-05.

811. (8-5-2007) NEW DELHI : The total number of educated job seekers including youth, all of whom may not necessarily be unemployed, registered with Employment Exchanges in the country as on 31-12-2005 was around 28 million. The Approach paper to The Eleventh Five Year Plan envisages creation of 70 million new work opportunities. This is for both educated/skilled and unskilled unemployed including youth. In order to tackle the problem of unemployment among both educated and uneducated persons including youth, Government is attempting employment generation in the normal growth process of the economy as well as through special employment generation programmes. The special programmes include Swarnajayanti Gram Swarojgar Yojana, Sampoorna Grameen Rojgar Yojana, Pradhan Mantri Gram Sadak Yojana, Prime Minister's Rojgar

Yojana, Swarna Jayanti Shahari Rozgar Yojana, etc. Besides these, Government is also implementing National Rural Employment Guarantee Scheme in the 313 identified districts of the country, which provides for at least 100 days of guaranteed wage employment in a financial year to every household in the rural areas whose adult members volunteer to do unskilled manual work. This was stated by the Minister of State (Independent Charge), Labour & Employment, Shri Oscar Fernandes in a written reply in Rajya Sabha today.

812. (8-5-2007) NEW DELHI : There has been an increase in the contribution of labour to the Net Domestic Product (NDP). According to the National Account Statistics published by Central Statistical Organisation, the contribution of labour to the Net Domestic Product at Current Prices increased from 33.8% during 1993-94 to 36.5% during 2004-05. The contribution of labour in the economy is measured in terms of compensation paid to employees in the form of wages and salary to Net Domestic Product (NDP) at the current prices. This was stated by the Minister of State (Independent Charge), Labour & Employment, Shri Oscar Fernandes in a written reply in the Rajya Sabha today.

813. (8-5-2007) NEW DELHI : Available reports indicate that infiltration from across the border in Jammu and Kashmir has declined this year as compared to last year. The infiltration for the period (January-March, 2007) was 39, as compared to 59 in the corresponding period of last year. The Centre in tandem with the State Government, have adopted a multi-pronged approach, to contain cross-border infiltration in Jammu and Kashmir, which includes, inter-alia, strengthening of border management and multi-tired and multi-modal deployment along International Border/Line of Control and near the ever changing infiltration routes, construction of border fencing, improved technology, weapons and equipment for security forces, improved intelligence and operational coordination and synergising intelligence flow to check infiltration and pro-active action against the terrorists within the State. The counter infiltration efforts are reviewed periodically at various levels in the State Government (including the two Unified Headquarters headed by the Chief Minister of Jammu and Kashmir) and into the Central Government. This information was given by the Minister of State for Home, Shri Sriprakash Jaiswal in a written reply to a question in the Rajya Sabha today.

814. (8-5-2007) NEW DELHI : The Government has not set up any committee for investigation of cracks on National Highways. Stating this in a written reply in the Lok Sabha today. The Minister of State Shri Muniyappa said that the assessment of cracks and other damages to the National Highways is a continuous process. Based upon such assessments, the repairs/ remedial measures, both immediate and long-term, are taken up within available resources and inter-se priority. The National Highways are maintained in traffic worthy condition within the available resources. However, in case of disruption of traffic movement due to severe damages and breaches on any section of National Highway, traffic is diverted through alternative routes. Necessary actions are taken for immediate repair and permanent remedial measures on such damaged sections of the National Highways within the available funds.

815. (8-5-2007) NEW DELHI : Port facilities to meet the existing demand of passenger movement and cargo movement were available through 56 berthing structure namely 8 mainland-island wharves / jetties, 14 inter-island jetties, 7 vehicle ferry jetties and 27 local ferry jetties prior to the Tsunami that occurred on 26.12.2004. Tsunami caused severe damage to the port infrastructural facilities. Thereafter restoration activities were geared up in a time bound manner to ensure that minimum port facilities to meet the demand are available. At present five Ships are operating between A&N Islands to Mainland ports and 78 vessels are operating between Port Blair and other Islands, which includes passenger, cargo, touring vessels and other utility vessels which are adequate to meet the demand.

816. (8-5-2007) NEW DELHI : Government of Maharashtra has urged Department of Shipping to advise Mumbai Port Trust to jointly work with that Government for land development plan of Eastern Coastal Part of Mumbai City. Department of Shipping has apprised the State Government of the position relating to availability of land with Mumbai Port Trust and its usage. Mumbai Port Trust has received a draft report prepared by the Urban Design Research Institute (UDRI), the agency appointed by Government of Maharashtra in respect of development of Eastern Water Front from the Government of Maharashtra in June, 2005. The draft report prepared by UDRI was based on old data and incorrect assumptions which needed to be updated and revised. The comments on the draft report were forwarded to the Government of Maharashtra on 9.9.2005. Subsequently, the draft report was discussed in the Mumbai Port Trust in a series of meetings in consultation with the concerned organisations including representatives of Government of Maharashtra to take into account the port's business. The updated/revised report is yet to be received from UDRI/Government of Maharashtra.

817. (8-5-2007) NEW DELHI : The Minister of External Affairs, Shri Pranab Mukherjee informed the Lok Sabha today in a reply to a Starred question that a number of decisions have been taken to simplify the Passport Issuance Procedures with effect from 23 December 2006. These guidelines have made the issuance of passports simpler and speedier for the passport applicants. The average time taken for issuing a passport is now 30 days subject to completion of requisite formalities.

818. (8-5-2007) NEW DELHI : China is in illegal occupation of approximately 38,000 square kilometres in the Indian State of Jammu & Kashmir. In addition, under the so-called Sino-Pakistan Boundary Agreement of 1963, Pakistan illegally ceded 5,180 square kilometres of Indian territory in Pakistan Occupied Kashmir to China. China also illegally claims approximately 90,000 square kilometres of Indian territory in the State of Arunachal Pradesh, and about 2000 square kilometres in the Middle Sector. Government have conveyed to the Chinese side that Jammu and Kashmir and Arunachal Pradesh are integral parts of India. India and China are engaged in discussions to arrive at a fair, reasonable and mutually acceptable solution to the boundary question. The ninth and tenth rounds of talks between the Special Representatives of India and China were held in India from 16-18 January 2007 and from April 20-22, 2007 respectively. The two Special Representatives continued their discussions on a framework for the boundary settlement on the basis of the Agreement on Political Parameters and Guiding Principles signed on 11 April 2005. Both sides agreed to hold the next (eleventh) round of talks at a mutually convenient time, which will be decided through diplomatic channels. The above information was given by the Minister of External Affairs, Shri Pranab Mukherjee in a written reply to a question in Lok Sabha today.

819. (8-5-2007) NEW DELHI : The Minister of State in the Ministry of External Affairs, Shri E. Ahamed informed the Lok Sabha today in a written reply to a question that the Government have decided to introduce e-passports, also known as bio-metric passports, initially for diplomats and officials as a pilot project by the end of 2007. Based on the experience gained from this pilot project, it is proposed to start issuance of e-passports in the ordinary category by the end of 2008. A Technical Committee has been constituted to finalise the technical specifications of the e-passports and this matter is under examination. The cost of converting ordinary into bio-metric passports will be worked out on the basis of the technical specifications that are finalised. The Government have been continually taking a number of steps to bring about more transparency in Passport Offices. These include computerisation of all Passport Offices, introduction of on-line registration, tele-enquiry, passport adalats, strengthening of grievance redressal mechanism, etc. The National Institute of Smart Government (NISG), Hyderabad has prepared a comprehensive study on passport issuance system. The implementation of this report will, inter alia, enhance further transparency in the functioning of Passport Offices.

820. (8-5-2007) NEW DELHI : There have been incidents of firing on Indian fishermen by the Sri Lankan Navy in the recent past. During January-April 2007, there have been seven such incidents in which three fishermen have been killed. Government have strongly taken up the matter of incidents of firing on Indian fishermen by the Sri Lankan Navy with the Government of Sri Lanka. The need for the Sri Lankan Navy to act with restraint and for our fishermen to be treated in a humane manner has been repeatedly emphasised to them. In response, the Government of Sri Lanka have denied that their Navy ever enters Indian territorial waters and claimed that their Naval ships were not deployed in areas where the incidents occurred. An immediate cash relief of Rs. 1 Lakh is being paid to the legal heir of the deceased by the Government of Tamil Nadu from the Chief Minister's Public Relief Fund. Apart from this, the family of the deceased fisherman is being paid a sum of Rs. 50,000 under the Fishermen Accident Group Insurance

Scheme, if the deceased is a member of any Fishermen Cooperative Society. The above information was given by the Minister of External Affairs, Shri Pranab Mukherjee in a written reply to a question in Lok Sabha today.

821. (8-5-2007) NEW DELHI : Outlay of Rs.6500 crore has been provided in Budget Estimate of the current fiscal year for construction of rural roads under Pradhan Mantri Gram Sadak Yojana (PMGSY). This sum has been allocated State-wise as per details furnished in Annexure-I. In addition, Rs.4500 crore would be available from a Special Window of National Bank for Agriculture and Rural Development (NABARD) under Rural Infrastructure Development Fund (RIDF). Drawal of funds by the States from this window would be subject to performance under the programme vis-a-vis physical and financial targets fixed for the current year. During the year 2007-08 under Bharat Nirman – the target under New Connectivity is 43989.93 Kms to connect 20071 habitations & Upgradation of 59316.28 Kms. The State-wise details have been given in Annexure-II. This was stated by the Minister of State in the Ministry of Rural Development, Smt. Suryakanta Patil in reply to a question in Rajya Sabha today.

822. (8-5-2007) NEW DELHI : As per the reports received from the Indian High Commission, Nairobi, Kenya, and Kenyan Airways authorities, a Kenyan Airways Flight No. KQ 507 from Douala (Cameroon) to Nairobi (Kenya) crashed on 5th May, 2007, in a mangrove swamp, 10 km south – east of Douala, in Cameroon. The plane which carried 105 passengers including 15 Indians, went down with its nose in the swamp in a marshland making it very difficult to access the site for finding out the survivors. As per information given in the press statement by the Kenyan Airways on 1100 hrs local time, 8.5.07, the recovery is still going on under very difficult circumstances. The Ministry of Overseas Indian Affairs is in constant touch with the Indian High Commission in Nairobi, Kenya, to ascertain the latest position and also the details of the arrangements being made regarding facilitation of travelling and accommodation of near relatives of the deceased from India to the Kenya / Cameroon and also for identification, transportation of the bodies of the victims etc. Indian High Commission has informed that the Kenyan Airways have announced that they would bear the cost of two return tickets per boarded passenger for the next of the kin who wished to travel to Duala. Accommodation would also be provided for reasonable duration by the airways.

823. (8-5-2007) NEW DELHI : The Ministry of Rural Development has sanctioned Rs. 19.48 crore to the State Government of Himachal Pradesh towards part payment of first instalment of funds against the provisional allocation of Rs.116.90 crore made for the Government of Himachal Pradesh under Accelerated Rural Water Supply Programme (Normal) of Rajiv Gandhi National Drinking Water Mission, during the year 2007-08. The balance amount of first instalment will be released after receipt of AG report for 2004-05. An amount of Rs. 9.33 lakh has also been released to the State Government towards part of first instalment of ARWSP-DDP funds against the total allocation of Rs.56.00 lakh for 2007-08. Up to 15 per cent of funds released under this sanction may be utilized for Operation & Maintenance and up to 5 per cent of funds may be spent for taking sustainability measures. States have been requested to delegate powers for management of Rural Water Supply Schemes through the Panchayati Raj Institutions (PRIs) as per the Constitution of India. As such Operation and Maintenance of the completed RWS Scheme should be transferred to the PRIs. No expenditure shall be incurred on taking water quality problems form the present release, as there is a separate allocation for the purpose. This release is for execution/completion of schemes to provide safe drinking water facilities to rural habitations and schools under the Centrally Sponsored ARWSP and according to Priorities set in ARWSP guidelines and through other instructions issued from time to time.

824. (8-5-2007) NEW DELHI : Grants-in-aid amounting to Rs. 1.41 crore as third/additional instalment of Central assistance to 3 districts of Sikkim, viz. East District (Rs. 51.17 lakh), West District (Rs.45.50 lakh) and South District (Rs.43.74 lakh) has been released by the Ministry of Rural Development for the implementation of the Sampoorna Grameen Rozgar Yojana (SGRY) during the financial year (2006-07). Grants-in-aid of Rs.30.31 lakh as part of first instalment, out of the allocation of Rs.1.81 crore to the West District has also been released under the scheme for the year 2007-08. The release is towards plan expenditure and will be utilized for approved items of works subject to the conditions laid down in the SGRY Guidelines. No deviations from the guidelines is permissible. The expenditure on implementation of the programme with regard to cash component is on 75:25 basis between the Central and the State Government, respectively. The Zila Parishads/DRDAs will release the entire funds allocated to them directly to the respective three tiers of the PRIs in the proportion as given in SGRY Guidelines within 15 days of receipt of funds from the Centre or the State without waiting for matching Share either from the Centre or the State.

825. (8-5-2007) NEW DELHI : The target under Pradhan Mantri Gram Sadak Yojana (PMGSY) guidelines is to connect all unconnected habitations having a population of 1000 or more. Under Bharat Nirman (Rural Roads Component), a total of 40,436 habitations with population of 1000 or more are targeted to be connected by all weather road by 2009.

826. (8-5-2007) NEW DELHI : The Ministry of Rural Development has released grants-in-aid amounting to Rs. 22.34 crore to 33 DRDAs (Annexure-I) of Maharashtra towards part payment of first instalment during the year 2007-08 under the 'Swarnjayanti Gram Swarojgar Yojana' (SGSY). Second instalment of Central share of funds amounting to Rs. 22.49 lakh to 2 DRDAs of Maharashtra, viz. Nagpur (Rs.19.64 lakh) and Yavatmal (Rs.2.85 lakh) has also been released towards Restoration of cut on account of State short Release of Central share of funds during the year 2006-07 under the scheme. The amount should be utilized on the Programme as per approved guidelines of SGSY. The funding pattern will be 75:25 by the Centre and the State. The State Government should release its share within one month of the date of release of the Central assistance. Under SGSY, assistance is given to the poor family living below the poverty line for taking up self-employment. It actively promotes group approach by organising the rural poor into Self-Help Groups.

827. (8-5-2007) NEW DELHI : State level communication campaign to enhance awareness about the programme have been undertaken through print, audio visual media and cultural fora for publicizing the programme. State and district level Monitoring and Vigilance Committees have been set up. States have been asked to set up Village level Vigilance and Monitoring Committees for local monitoring. National level Monitors and Area Officers of the Ministry visit various districts to oversee the progress of the implementation of the Act. Comprehensive MIS has been developed which places all vital data in the public domain. Capacity building measures for social audit has also been undertaken. The Ministry is regularly monitoring not only the physical parameters but qualitative indicators as well. This was stated by the Minister of State in the Ministry of Rural Development, Shri Chandra Sekhar Sahu in reply to a question in Rajya Sabha today.

828. (8-5-2007) NEW DELHI : The Government has recently approved a Scheme for providing support for establishing 100,000 broadband, internet enabled, Common Service Centres (CSCs) in rural areas of the country. These Centres would be opened in the ratio of 1 CSC for every 6 Census villages in a State. These Centres would provide a mix of Government and private services in rural areas. This was stated by the Minister of State in the Ministry of Rural Development, Smt. Suryakanta Patil in reply to a question in Rajya Sabha today.

829. (8-5-2007) NEW DELHI : As reported by the States, there are about 2 % habitations not covered with drinking water source within 1.6 km. The major problems encountered by the States for covering these habitations are that population lives in scattered habitations on isolated hilly terrain, the high cost of water supply system network due to inaccessibility of habitations, multi stage pumping, depleting surface streams, lack of ground and surface sources availability near the habitations, difficulty in procurement and transportation of materials, long gestation period, poor recharge of ground water due to hard rock in many places and deterioration of water quality. Under Bharat Nirman, a time bound plan of action for covering such habitations has been formulated. This was stated by the Minister of State in the Ministry of Rural Development, Shri Chandra Sekhar Sahu in reply to a question in Rajya Sabha today.

830. (8-5-2007) NEW DELHI : There has been growing demand for relay and transmission of Punjabi programmes. All regional language programmes are being telecast in the regional channels only and regional language Punjabi satellite channel signal is available throughout the country. This information was given by Minister of Information & Broadcasting and Parliamentary Affairs, Shri P. R. Dasmunsi in written reply to a question in Rajya Sabha today.

831. (8-5-2007) NEW DELHI : The Ministry of Information & Broadcasting has approached Ministry of Finance for lowering the custom tariffs on the import of jumbo rolls. Cameras for shooting, sound equipment and film rolls are part of the imports made by the film industry. To understand the initiatives needed for further growth of the film industry, the Ministry had constituted five Core Groups to look into different aspects including taxation and duties. The reports of these Groups are under examination in the Ministry. As per reports of FICCI – Price Water House Coopers, 2006, the key reasons behind low box office collections are low admission prices, low occupancy level in theatres, low capital/investment level in the number of film prints and ineffective marketing. This information was given by Minister of Information & Broadcasting and Parliamentary Affairs, Shri P. R. Dasmunsi in written reply to a question in Rajya Sabha today.

832. (8-5-2007) NEW DELHI : Union Minister of State for Environment and Forests, Shri Namo Narayan Meena said biotechnology will dominate the 21st century just as information technology dominated the last century. Addressing the 10th meeting of the Consultative Committee of the Ministry of Environment and Forests, last night, he informed the meeting that the stay on Genetic Engineering Approval Committee has been vacated today during judicial hearing. The entire research activities of the country which was at a standstill, will get momentum and Genetic Engineering Approval Committee will be able to work speedily. Shri Meena assured along with treating this field as a priority area with investments, priority will be given to proper risk assessment and appropriate measures to mitigate its adverse impacts. Before the presentation on living modified organisms-LMOs and Genetically Modified Organisms (GMOs), he said in bio-pharma and bio-seeds industries, the turnover has already crossed a billion mark and the growth rate is estimated as 40 per cent. Referring to the approval of transgenic crop Bt cotton and 20 recombinant therapeutic products in India, he said 62 hybrids of cotton have been approved for commercial cultivation across 9 cotton growing states viz; Andhra Pradesh, Gujarat, Haryana, Karnataka, Madhya Pradesh, Punjab, Rajasthan and Tamil Nadu after reviewing the performance and other criteria. The area under cotton cultivation has increased from 72,000 acres in 2002 to 93 lakh acres in 2006. Overall production has gone up to 24.4 million bales in 2005-06 as compared to 15.8 million bales in 2001-02. The productivity has increased from 308 kg. Per hectare to 450 kg. Per hectare during the same period. The Minister of State added the pesticide usage has also come down by 2260 MT during 2005-06. Though there has been overall acceptance of the Bt technology by cotton growing farmers, the issues and concerns raised are being examined by the Regulatory Agencies. He said Bt cotton is the first GM crop in the country, which is making us to pass through learning phase. Sale of illegal/ spurious seeds insect resistant management, compliance of conditions etc. are various issues which will be taken care of by the Ministry. This Ministry is the Nodal Ministry for implementation of Cartagena Protocol on Bio-Safety. This is an International Agreement under Convention of biological diversity. The Ministry is also implementing a World Bank GEF capacity building project on bio-safety which includes strengthening the national capacity for effective legislative frame-work, operational mechanism, establishing bio-safety data base and supporting a network for research in the area of risk assessment and monitoring.

833. (8-5-2007) NEW DELHI : Prime Minister Dr. Manmohan Singh has congratulated Mr. Nicolas Sarkozy on his election as the next President of France. In his message the Prime Minister spoke of the importance of the friendship between India and France and said he looked forward to meeting the President elect.

834. (8-5-2007) NEW DELHI : Justice S. Ratnavel Pandian, former Judge of the Supreme Court of India took over as Chairperson of the National Commission for Backward Classes on 14th August, 2006 has been conferred the status of Union Cabinet Minister in the Table of Precedence for the duration of the term of his office. Justice S. Ratnavel Pandian was born on 13th March, 1929 at Thiruppudaimarudhur village in Thirunelveli District of Tamil Nadu, and had his schooling from Theerthapathi High School, Ambasamudram. He was graduated from Saint Xavier's College at Palayamkottai and thereafter obtained his law degree at Madras Law College in 1954. After practicing as an Advocate for nearly 17 years in the High Court of Madras, he was elevated as Judge of the High Court in February, 1974. Justice Pandian was the acting Chief Justice of the Madras High Court from 18.1.88 to 29.1.88 and from 13.3.88 to 13.12.88. On 14th December, 1988, he was sworn in as Judge of the Supreme Court of India. During his tenure in the Supreme Court, Justice Pandian gave a number of landmark judgements including the judgement in the famous Indira Sawhney case. Justice Pandian retired from the Supreme Court on 12th March, 1994. After retirement from the Supreme Court, Justice Pandian headed from 1994 to 1997 the Fifth Central Pay Commission which gave its final report in April 1997.

835. (8-5-2007) NEW DELHI : Prime Minister, Dr. Manmohan Singh launched the Doordarshan programme 'Gitanjali' on the Hindi rendition of select songs of Gurudev Rabindranath Tagore today. A DVD containing these five songs of Gurudev was released by the Speaker Lok Sabha, Shri Somnath Chatterjee. UPA Chairperson, Smt. Sonia Gandhi released the Publications Division book 'Satyagraha' which is a documentation on Mahatma Gandhi's Satyagraha, on the occasion. The Event was part of celebrations of 146th birth anniversary of Gurudev. The Prime Minister in his address said that the Event captures the undying spirit of our freedom struggle. Through this we pay homage to the memory of Gandhiji and Gurudev Rabindranath Tagore. In his remarks, Shri P. R. Dasmunsi, Minister of Information & Broadcasting and Parliamentary Affairs, said that both Gandhiji and Gurudev inspired millions of Indians for independence. Gurudev expressed different facets of human existence in lyrical songs. His songs like 'Ekla Chalo Re' instilled confidence in the masses. The programme will be available on the prime band of Doordarshan every Sunday, he added. The Minister said that in due course, these songs would be translated and rendered in Marathi, Malayalam, Kannada and Telegu also. During the celebration of 150 years of 1st war of independence, this effort is a true tribute to Gurudev as well as the martyrs of freedom, the Minister said.

836. (8-5-2007) NEW DELHI : The Prime Minister, Dr. Manmohan Singh, switched on the live telecast of Gurudev Rabindranath Tagore's 'Gitanjali' on Doordarshan National Channel on the occasion of 146th birth anniversary of Gurudev, here today. Lok Sabha Speaker, Shri Somnath Chatterjee released the DVD of Tagore's selected songs in Hindi. Smt. Sonia Gandhi released 'Satyagraha', a documentation on Mahatma's Gandhi's Satyagraha, produced by the Publication Division of Ministry of Information and Broadcasting.

837. (8-5-2007) NEW DELHI : The Minister of State for Communications & Information Technology, Dr. Shakeel Ahmad, informed the Rajya Sabha today, in a written reply to a question by Shri B.K. Hariprasad that the roaming charges levied by different operators have to be within the ceiling tariff prescribed by the Telecom Regulatory Authority of India (TRAI). After due consultation process with all the stakeholders, TRAI found justifiable grounds for review of the tariff structure applicable for roaming services that had been fixed five years back. The Minister further stated that the Cellular Operators Association of India had submitted that the customer tariffs are already lowest in the world and consistently coming down and thus, roaming tariffs should also be left to market forces. Based on in-depth analysis of various elements of cost, data on costs, views of stakeholders, the prevailing tariff for calls originated in home networks and other relevant factors, TRAI has prescribed a composite ceiling charge for regional/national roaming effective from 15th February, 2007. The Cellular Operators have already revised roaming tariff accordingly.

838. (8-5-2007) NEW DELHI : The Minister of State for Communications & Information Technology, Dr. Shakeel Ahmad, informed the Rajya Sabha today, in a written reply to a question by Shri V. Hanumantha Rao that the Department of Posts has introduced "Logistics Post" on 10.8.2004 for transmission of large parcels and consignments between identified stations, with minimum charge for 50 Kgs. weight. The Minister further stated that Section 4 of the Indian Post Office Act, 1898 bestows exclusive privilege on the Central Government for handling letters with some exceptions. The Logistics Post is not covered under the said exclusive privilege. Accordingly, there is no proposal to ban private couriers from doing business in this category of service.

839. (8-5-2007) NEW DELHI : The Momins family of Ahmedabad had been earning its livelihood by repairing watches and clocks for generations. However, putting an end to the era of hand wound watches, arrived the electronic ones. The Momins lost their traditional business as they could not keep pace with the fast changing technology. Bereft of customers, they, once the most sought after watch makers by the people, converted the shop into a Pan corner. A few among them migrated to nearby Mumbai to make a living. The family which was considered as a family of technicians was reduced to a family of wage earners, for no fault of their own. They had nothing around to fall back upon, to upgrade their skills. Momins could be no exception, there are thousands of such families forced to live in similar circumstances. For them institutes like Industrial Technical Institutes (ITIs) have come as a hope in despair.

840. (8-5-2007) NEW DELHI : Shri Prem Chand Gupta, Union Minister for Company Affairs laid the foundation stone of "Corporate Bhawan" at Jaipur today. The Ministry of Company Affairs (MCA) is in the process of redefining and restructuring itself. It has taken up an initiative called the 'New Look MCA' as an integral part of this effort. This initiative aims at improving the physical environment of the Ministry's offices by taking up construction of new office complexes and modernization of the existing office complexes. Laying of the foundation stone of "Corporate Bhawan" at Jaipur is an important landmark in this initiative of the Ministry. Smt. Vasundhara Raje, Chief Minister, Rajasthan was also present on the occasion as the Chief Guest. The offices of the Registrar of Companies and Official Liquidator are presently functioning from rented premises in Jaipur, with inherent constraints in providing a modernized work environment. The Corporate Bhawan at Jaipur is proposed to house the office of the Registrar of Companies, the office of Official Liquidator and provide accommodation for a Bench of the National Company Law Tribunal, proposed to be set up in future. As all the related offices will be housed in one building, it would further improve the logistics and efficiency in delivery of services for the State of Rajasthan. The Corporate Bhawan will be a state of the art building conducive to efficient functioning and meaningful partnership with all stakeholders including corporates. The project is envisaged to be completed over a period of 18 months at an estimated cost of Rs. 10.00 crore. The Ministry is already in the process of constructing/ acquiring similar office complexes at other places, Chandigarh and Cuttack being the next in the series for which the land tie-ups and execution agencies have also been finalised. The Ministry of Company Affairs is abuzz with a number of initiatives, and its performance has already been rated very high in various circles. Implementation of the MCA21 e-Governance project has already brought significant credit to the Government. All registration related services are now available on-line in a transparent manner with speed and certainty. More than 18 lakh documents have been filed on-line as on March 31, 2007 with incorporation of over 44,000 companies on-line. It is heartening to note that more than 90%

of the stakeholders are availing of this facility directly, using the portal from the comfort of their offices or homes.

841. (8-5-2007) NEW DELHI : Prof. Saifuddin Soz, the Union Minister of Water Resources launched the redesigned bilingual and dynamic website of Ministry of Water Resources (http://www.mowr.gov.in) here today. He said that the working of the Ministry will be transparent and the dissemination of information will be easier. The redesigning website will be comprehensive and will be updated regularly. As a measure to implement Information Technology Strategic Plan (ITSP), the Ministry of Water Resources has redesigned its website so as to disseminate and access information about the Ministry for the general users, its own employees, citizens, coordinating States and Union Territories and other Ministries and Departments in Government of India. The Ministry has developed a bilingual and dynamic website keeping in view the new concept of E-Governance to provide effective governance. The re-designed website has been incorporated three level links to enhance the content presentation in a manageable unit. Main Links, 2nd Level Links, 3rd Level Links. Bio-graphical sketches have hyperlinks of the Union Minister of Water Resources, Minister of State (WR), Secretary (M/o WR), Head of the organizations under the Ministry both English and Hindi. Photo Gallery of Union Minister and Minister of State, updated contents/material, detailed information of attached and subordinate offices under the Ministry, updated list of Public Information Officers', Asst. Public Information Officers and Appellant Authority under the Right to Information have been incorporated. Integrated search engine facility has been provided to facilitate the common user. Specific emphasis have been given on cyber security to make it secure and hacking free website. The URL of re-designed website of the Ministry is http://www.mowr.gov.in.

842. (8-5-2007) NEW DELHI : Under the Basic Services to the Urban Poor (BSUP) component of the Jawaharlal Nehru National Urban Renewal Mission (JNNURM), during the year 2006-07, the total Central share approved for the 151 projects, which include housing development as well as infrastructure projects, was Rs. 4435.93 crore. Out of this amount the funds released by the Ministry of Finance was Rs. 901.77 crore. The total number of dwelling units covered in these projects was 435564. This was stated by the Minister of State (Independent Charge) for Housing and Urban Poverty Alleviation, Kumari Selja in a reply to a question by Shri Su. Thirunavukkarasar in the Rajya Sabha today. She further stated that under the Integrated Housing & Slum Development Programme (IHSDP) component of the JNNURM, for the cities other than the Mission cities, during the year 2006-07, the total Central share approved for the 194 projects, which include housing development as well as infrastructure projects, was Rs. 1404.57 crore. Out of this amount the funds released by the Ministry of Finance was Rs. 492.61 crore. The total number of dwelling units covered in these projects was 143557. The Central funds released to the States/UTs during 2006-07 under the urban poverty alleviation scheme of Swarna Jayanti Shahari Rozgar Yojana

(SJSRY), implemented by the Ministry of Housing & urban Poverty Alleviation since 1.12.1997, were Rs. 248.68 crore.

843. (8-5-2007) NEW DELHI : During the course of implementation of the Scheme of Swarna Jayanti Shahari Rozgar Yojana (SJSRY), it was observed that there was a need to have a relook at the guidelines of the scheme and certain modifications would be required to enhance the effectiveness of the scheme in tackling the issue of urban poverty. Accordingly, proposals were formulated for the modifications in the Guidelines of Swarna Jayanti Shahari Rozgar Yojana. The major changes proposed were regarding enhancement in project cost ceiling for individual micro-enterprises under Urban Self Employment Programme (USEP) component, increase in average per capita expenditure for skill training, change in funding pattern of the Scheme from 75:25 (Centre : State) to 90:10 for the special category North Eastern and hilly States, removal of educational limit prescribed for the self-employment component, reducing the minimum group Members required to form Development of Women & Children in Urban Areas (DWCUA) Groups from 10 to 5, enhancing the Administrative Expenditure limits, etc. This was stated by the Minister of State (Independent Charge) for Housing and Urban Poverty Alleviation, Kumari Selja in a reply to a question by Smt. N.P. Durga in the Rajya Sabha today. She further stated that as per the prescribed procedure, Expenditure Finance Committee (EFC) appraised these proposals in its Meeting held on 8th August, 2005 and approved the same. However, it was subsequently decided to continue the Scheme of SJSRY, in its present form, during the 10th Plan period and for continuing this scheme into the 11th Plan, an evaluation needs to be done. Evaluation study has since been completed, she added.

844. (8-5-2007) NEW DELHI : Dr. Dasari Narayana Rao, Minister of State for Coal informed the Rajya Sabha in a written reply today that the Neyveli Lignite Corporation (NLC), a major public sector producer of lignite and lignite based power in the country, has plans for development of blocks in open cast mining, underground coal gasification and coal bed methane in Rajasthan and Gujarat. In addition to the existing mining and power generation activities in Tamil Nadu, the company is expanding its operations in Rajasthan. Dr. Rao further said that NLC also takes up exploration activities in lignite blocks in the country to augment lignite production. NLC is also designated as a data centre for lignite resource database. Therefore, keeping in view the future plans of NLC and to ensure that the resources are put to use in a planned and scientific manner, it has been provided that a State Government company or undertaking shall obtain a certificate from NLC to the effect that they have no plan or willingness to undertake mining operation in the concerned lignite block. The present arrangement is under review, the Minister added. Regarding Raneri Lignite block in Bikaner district of Rajasthan, NLC proposes to utilize the deposits from this block for an Underground Coal Gasification project, which was sanctioned on 08.08.2005. "It is expected to be completed within four years form the date of sanction," Dr. Rao said.

845. (8-5-2007) NEW DELHI : The Union Minister for Railways Shri Lalu Prasad inaugurated the First Meeting of the Railway – Industry Coordination Committee here today. Addressing the premium rail customers belonging to the Indian Industry, Shri Lalu Prasad Yadav said that the operating ratio in the Indian Railways is the best in the world and has reached the level of 78 per cent. The Railways have been able to increase their share in the transportation of cement and steel after many decades and a historic landmark has been achieved by earning a cash surplus of Rs. 20000 crores during the year 2006-07. The Minister said that this historic turnaround has been achieved by adopting policies according to the needs of the market and by playing the volume game. He requested the cement and steel customers to take advantage of the plan for development and modernization of loading terminals and sidings for which the Railways were willing to bear 50 per cent of the expenditure and were prepared to give 5 per cent freight discount under the Engine on Load scheme. He informed the industry that the Railways wanted to start a similar plan in the development and modernization of unloading terminals also. He requested that the cement and steal industries enter into long term agreements with the Railways for a period ranging from 5 to 30 years so that those signing such agreements would be supplied rakes on demand even during the busy season. The railways have decided that any decision on the freight discount scheme would be compulsorily taken by the zonal administration within 2 months. To remove complaints regarding claims and refunds etc. it has been decided to organize special camps in all zonal railways in the first week of every quarter. The General Managers will ensure that such claims/refunds do not remain pending for more than 3 months. The Railways hope that the Railway share in the cement and steel transportation will increase to 200 million tonnes each by the year 2011-12. In his concluding remarks, Shri Lalu Prasad said that, with the help of its customers, the railway will be able to increase freight loading from 726 million tonnes in 2006-07 to 1150 million tonnes during the next five years.

846. (8-5-2007) NEW DELHI : The safety of road users including on National Highways is primarily the responsibility of the concerned State Government. However, on the recommendation of Committee on Infrastructure, a Committee was constituted by this Ministry under the Chairmanship of Shri S. Sundar, former Secretary of the then Ministry of Surface Transport to deliberate and make recommendations for setting up an effective and dedicated agency for Road Safety and Traffic Management. The Committee had submitted its report on 20th February, 2007. The main recommendations of the Committee, include creation of National Road Safety and Traffic Management Board through an Act of Parliament. The Board would have advisory as well as regulatory functions. Under regulatory functions, the Board would set standards for the Motor Vehicles and set standards for designing of roads. In its advisory role, the Board would assist Central Government in the matters relating to road safety and traffic management and would promote road safety research, road user behaviour strategies, lay guidelines for establishing medical care and rehabilitation, etc. Enabling provisions have been made for creation of similar bodies at State level. This information was given by the Minister of State for Shipping, Road Transport and Highways, Shri K.H. Muniyappa in a written reply in the Rajya Sabha today.

847. (8-5-2007) NEW DELHI : Government has approved implementation of National Highways Development Project (NHDP) Phase III, V & VI under Public Private Partnership (PPP) on Build, Operate and Transfer (BOT) (Toll) mode. In case, the projects are not viable on BOT (Toll) mode under phase-III, then the projects would be taken up on BOT (Annuity) mode with the approval of the Government. If again, the projects are not viable on BOT (Annuity) mode, then the projects would be taken up on Engineer, Procure and Construct (EPC) mode. Under Government funding, the cost of construction and maintenance thereof is borne by the Government and toll revenue (as per the per km toll rates fixed by the Government) on perpetuity is collected by the Government. Under BOT (Toll) mode, the Concessionaire is required to meet the upfront cost of the construction and the expenditure on annual maintenance for the concession period. Viability gap funding (VGF) limited to 40 % is approved by the Government. The investment on project is recovered through toll revenue, as per the per km toll rates fixed by the Government, collected by the concessionaire and retained by them. Under BOT (Annuity) mode, the Concessionaire is required to meet the upfront cost of the construction and the expenditure on annual maintenance for the concession period. The cost of project is recovered through Annuity payment (semi annually). However, the toll revenue is collected by the Government. BOT (Toll) mode is advantageous to Government as the risk of traffic growth and recovery of revenue lies on the private entrepreneur who raises fund to build and operate the projects and therefore, lower Government funding is required to implement it. This information was given by the Minister of State for Shipping, Road Transport and Highways, Shri K.H. Muniyappa in a written reply in the Rajya Sabha today.

848. (8-5-2007) NEW DELHI : National Highways Authority of India (NHAI) is implementing HIV/ AIDS awareness campaign through Non-Governmental Organisations (NGOs). Accordingly, NHAI is implementing HIV/ AIDS awareness campaign along NH-2 (Delhi-Kolkata), NH-28 (Lucknow-Muzaffarpur), NH-26 and NH-7 (Lalipur to Anantpur-Andhra Pradesh/ Karnataka Border) and on NH-76 & NH-25 (Chittorgarh-Jhansi). Presently, four NGOs have been awarded contracts for implementing HIV/ AIDS awareness campaign along NH-28 (Lucknow-Muzaffarpur). The NHAI has set up one HIV/ AIDS Prevention and Control Unit with experts for assisting NHAI in implementing this programme. Presently, the NHAI's HIV/ AIDS Prevention and Control Programme is being implemented as part of loan commitments to the World Bank and the Asian Development Bank (ADB) along the identified stretches as mentioned above. NH-5 is not covered under this mission. This information was given by the Minister of State for Shipping, Road Transport and Highways, Shri K.H. Muniyappa in a written reply in the Rajya Sabha today.

849. (8-5-2007) NEW DELHI : Any accident including the death or injury to any seafarer of any nationality on board a ship registered in foreign country while the said vessel is on or near the coast of India can be investigated by an officer appointed under section 359 of the Merchant Shipping Act, 1958. During the course of investigation, the vessel or its crew can be detained for the purpose of conducting the investigation. However, if the death is due to any criminal act such as murder, the relevant provisions of the Indian Penal Code/Criminal Penal Code would apply and the Merchant Shipping Act, 1958 does not have any provisions to address such issues. In cases where an Indian seafarer gets injured and dies on a foreign registered ship while the vessel is at high seas, it is the jurisdiction of the respective flag administration to conduct investigation into the cause of such accident or criminal incident. The Government of India, being a substantially interested state, however, has now also started participating as observer in such investigation wherever possible. Further, whenever feasible, the Indian Embassy/ High Commission officials are intimated to investigate the matter in the first port of call in the foreign countries.

850. (8-5-2007) NEW DELHI : The President Dr. A.P.J. Abdul Kalam will give away the National Awards to the eminent individuals and industries in various disciplines in different categories here tomorrow on the occasion of the National Technology Day. Every year May 11 is being celebrated as national Technology Day through out the country by the scientific and industrial organisations, as well as educational institutions. The event is coordinated by the Ministry of Science & Technology in three segments, the first one being a Lecture Session followed by new products release and finally Distribution of national Awards by the Chief Guest, the President of India in the presence of Shri Kapil Sibal, Minister of Science & Technology and Earth Sciences This year's lecture will be delivered by Dr. Jamshed J. Irani, former Managing Director of Tata Iron and Steel Company Limited (TISCO). Mr. Irani is presently the Director of Tata Sons Ltd.

851. (8-5-2007) NEW DELHI : The Minister of Health and Family Welfare in his opening remarks in the Consultative Committee meeting of the Ministry, held here yesterday in the evening, said that he would like to share the experience of his ministry regarding the progress made in the National Mental Health Programme (NMHP) in the country and also bring out the difficulties faced in reaching the unreached, that is the mentally ill who have been away from benefits of modern treatment due to stigma, ignorance and paucity of services. The mentally ill are the most vulnerable members of our society and are most prone to abuse, neglect and despair. Due to the very nature of illness, which in severe cases takes away the insight, these citizens form a voiceless population Underlining the importance of the programme he said that at any given time about 10% of the population suffers from various mental and behavioural disorders. Out of these, approximately 10% suffer from severe mental disorders. And 10% of those suffering from severe mental disorders require long term treatment. Out of those requiring long term treatment, approximately 10% require hospitalization. From this estimate about 10 crore population suffer from some mental ailment at any given time. The burden of neuropsychiatry disorders is estimated to be a whopping 12% of the total disease burden and imposes a heavy burden on the family and society in terms of morbidity, loss of productivity and mortality in terms of suicide in extreme cases. A large number of people with mental problems do not seek help due to ignorance, stigma and lack of availability of services. However, most of these ailments could be treated at an outpatient basis and only a very small proportion requires hospitalization. This has led to acceptance of community-based treatment of mental disorders worldwide. Besides being less expensive community based interventions are more accessible, acceptable, less stigmatizing and less prone to human rights abuse leading to early integration back in the community. Replying to the concern expressed by the members of the committee, the Minister accepted that our county faces an acute shortage of mental health professionals. He said that with a large population in our country on one hand and very few psychiatrists being available on the other hand, less than one psychiatrist is available for every 3 lac population. The psychiatrist / population ratio in rural areas that account for 70% of country's population, could well be under one for every million. To address this huge burden, NMHP was started in 1982 to provide comprehensive community mental health services fully integrated with general health care services and to change from custodial to therapeutic community care. This model was adapted as the district mental health programme (DMHP) and it was implemented The Minister informed the members that till now funds have been given to 129 districts for implementing District Mental Health Programme across 30 States/ UTs, 23 Mental Hospital for modernization and 70 Psychiatry wings in Medical colleges/general hospitals. He further said that there is still a long road ahead and the Government is envisaging modifications in the NMHP to make it more comprehensive by incorporating mental health promotive activities like school & college mental health services, stress management at work place and suicide prevention activities in the district mental health programme. This would require an increase in the total five-year budget of a DMHP in a district to about Rs. 2 crores each from the existing Rs. 1.2 crore. It is envisaged to cover the remaining districts of the country under DMHP. For proper and effective utilisation of funds, a robust monitoring mechanism under NMHP is also being planned. Acute shortage of manpower in the field of mental health could be met by having more training institutes on the lines of NIMHANS. This would require a large investment for creating this infrastructure which would bring fruits in medium and long term period.

852. (8-5-2007) NEW DELHI : There have been reports in the media regarding election to the Office of the President. Various political parties are consulting each other in this regard. The Prime Minister has had some preliminary and exploratory discussions on this matter with some political leaders. News reports mentioning specific names are speculative and premature.

853. (8-5-2007) NEW DELHI : The Minister of State (Independent Charge), Labour & Employment, Shri Oscar Fernandes has urged the officers of the Chief Labour Commissioner's (Central) Organisations to ensure a high level of compliance of labour standards. Inaugurating the Annual Conference of the Dy. Chief Labour Commissioners (C) and the Regional Labour Commissioners (C) here this morning, Shri Fernandes said that the compliance should be ensured not only through prosecution but through persuasion and education of the employers. He said that the labour administration must adapt to the changes in view of the present globalisation scenario to make itself effective and relief oriented. He said, "Now the officers must play a pro-active role as the facilitator, the advisor and the guide to employers, unions and workers so that there is a willing voluntary compliance of provisions of the labour laws by employers and at the same time the workers are made aware of their duties and responsibilities." Shri Fernandes said that there is a need to set high standards of professionalism in order to bring about a marked change in the work culture. He urged the Conference to discuss the term 'Inspector Raj' and the tag attached to it. The Labour Minister said that the CLC's (C) Organisations has a greater responsibility since 93 per cent of the country's workforce is employed in the unorganised sector. He appreciated the efforts of the organisation in undertaking special crash programmes to ensure payment of minimum wages to the workers in this sector. Shri Fernandes said that the cases must be disposed off as early as possible so that workers are able to receive relief well in time. The Minister said that the conference is taking place on the day the country is celebrating the 150 years of its first war of independence and the workers expect something good from this conference. In her key not address, the Secretary, Labour and Employment, Smt. Sudha Pillai said that there is a need for introspection about the role of labour inspectors as it has come to scrutiny and criticism the employers as well as some trade unions said that we need to pose questions to ourselves as to whether inspections are being held honestly. Smt. Pillai said that the purpose of the inspections should be to provide relief to workers and not merely to harass the employer or the establishments. She said that the Ministry treats the CLC(C) Organisations as its eyes & ears as the inputs from it are helping in formulation of policies. She complemented the work of the officers of this Organisations in completing the Phase I and Phase II verification of trade union in a record time. Earlier, the Chief Labour Commissioner (C), Shri S.K. Mukhopadhyay called for increasing the rate of settlement of industrial disputes through conciliation. He said that the success rate of settlement was around 30 per cent. Shri Mukhopadhyay said that during last year 30,000 inspections were conducted, 12,000 prosecutions were launched and 10,000 convictions secured.

854. (8-5-2007) NEW DELHI : The 51st meeting of the Central Wakf Council under the Chairmanship of Mr. A.R. Antulay, Minister for Minority Affairs is to be held here tomorrow. The Council will review its Educational and Development programmes and functioning of its Planning and Advisory, Education and Women Welfare, Wakf Development and Monitoring Committees. It will also approve

Revised Estimates of the Council for the year 2006-07 and Budget Estimates for the current year and its Annual and Audit Reports for the year 2005-06. The meeting will also confirm the minutes of the meeting of the 50th Meeting held on May 24, 2006.

855. (8-5-2007) NEW DELHI : The Ministry of Rural Development has sanctioned Rs. 14.88 crore to the State Government of Uttrakhand towards first instalment of funds against the provisional allocation of Rs.89.30 crore made for the Government of Uttrakhand (Uttrakhand Payjal Sansadhan Vikas Avam Nirman Nigam, Dehradun) under Accelerated Rural Water Supply Programme (Normal) of Rajiv Gandhi National Drinking Water Mission, during the year 2007-08. The balance amount of first instalment will be released after receipt of AG report for 2004-05. Up to 15 per cent of funds released under this sanction may be utilized for Operation & Maintenance and up to 5 per cent of funds may be spent for taking sustainability measures. States have been requested to delegate powers for management of Rural Water Supply Schemes through the Panchayati Raj Institutions (PRIs) as per the Constitution of India. As such Operation and Maintenance of the completed RWS Scheme should be transferred to the PRIs. No expenditure shall be incurred on taking water quality problems form the present release, as there is a separate allocation for the purpose. This release is for execution/completion of schemes to provide safe drinking water facilities to rural habitations and schools under the Centrally Sponsored ARWSP and according to Priorities set in ARWSP guidelines and through other instructions issued from time to time.

856. (8-5-2007) NEW DELHI : The Ministry of Rural Development has sanctioned Rs. 10.02 crore to the State Government of Haryana towards part payment of first instalment of funds against the provisional allocation of Rs.60.13 crore made for the Government of Haryana under Accelerated Rural Water Supply Programme (Normal) of Rajiv Gandhi National Drinking Water Mission, during the year 2007-08. An amount of Rs. 5.55 crore has also been released to the State Government towards part of first instalment of ARWSP-DDP funds against the total allocation of Rs.33.28 crore for 2007-08. Up to 15 per cent of funds released under this sanction may be utilized for Operation & Maintenance and up to 5 per cent of funds may be spent for taking sustainability measures. States have been requested to delegate powers for management of Rural Water Supply Schemes through the Panchayati Raj Institutions (PRIs) as per the Constitution of India. As such Operation and Maintenance of the completed RWS Scheme should be transferred to the PRIs. No expenditure shall be incurred on taking water quality problems form the present release, as there is a separate allocation for the purpose. This release is for execution/completion of schemes to provide safe drinking water facilities to rural habitations and schools under the Centrally Sponsored ARWSP and according to Priorities set in ARWSP guidelines and through other instructions issued from time to time.

857. (8-5-2007) NEW DELHI : Grants-in-aid amounting to Rs. 3.08 crore as third/additional instalment of Central assistance to 3 districts of Meghalaya, viz. East Khasi Hills (Rs. 142.15 lakh), West Khasi Hills (Rs.94.16 lakh) and Ri Bhoi District (Rs.72.05 lakh) has been released by the Ministry of Rural Development for the implementation of the Sampoorna Grameen Rozgar Yojana (SGRY) during the financial year (2006-07). Grants-in-aid of Rs.62.72 lakh as part of first instalment, out of the allocation of Rs.3.76 crore to the West Khasi Hills has also been released under the scheme for the year 2007-08. The release is towards plan expenditure and will be utilized for approved items of works subject to the conditions laid down in the SGRY Guidelines. No deviations from the guidelines is permissible. The expenditure on implementation of the programme with regard to cash component is on 75:25 basis between the Central and the State Government, respectively. The Zila Parishads/DRDAs will release the entire funds allocated to them directly to the respective three tiers of the PRIs in the proportion as given in SGRY Guidelines within 15 days of receipt of funds from the Centre or the State without waiting for matching Share either from the Centre or the State.

858. (8-5-2007) NEW DELHI : Grant-in-aid amounting to Rs.6.54 lakh has been released by the Ministry of Rural Development to the District Rural Development Agency of Daman & Diu towards part payment of first instalment of Central Share for the year 2007-08 under DRDA Administration. The funding pattern under the scheme is 75:25 between Centre and the State. The utilization of funds is to be in accordance with the DRDA administration guidelines and the release of the second instalment during 2007-08 is subject to the fulfillment of all the conditions as per the DRDA Administration guidelines.

859. (8-5-2007) NEW DELHI : Following is the text of the Prime Minister, Dr. Manmohan Singh's Address at the function to commemorate 150th Anniversary of First War of Independence at Parliament today: "One hundred and fifty years ago, in the late afternoon of May 10, 1857, sepoys in Meerut mutinied and attacked the symbols of British imperial power – the telegraph office, the jail, the record room and, the bungalows in which the sahibs lived. As evening fell, a group of about 100 sepoys rode on horseback to Delhi. They arrived at the Lal Qila early in the morning of May 11, and announced to the old Mughal Emperor, Bahadur Shah, that they had revolted against the British. They demanded that he should provide leadership to this rebellion. Thus began the great uprising of 1857 which took the British more than one year to suppress. San-Sattavan, as the people of our sub-continent remember it, was the first significant moment in India's struggle to free herself from British domination. From Delhi to Patna, from the Terai to Jhansi, along the mighty Ganga and the calm water of Jamuna—sepoys and princes, peasants and taluqdars, artisans and intellectuals, came together to fight British rule. A military mutiny quickly transformed itself into a battle for freedom. Both Karl Marx and Benjamin Disraeli, watching the events from London-and from two very different ideological perspectives-conceded that the uprising was nothing short of a "national revolt". The rebels of 1857 fought for freedom from foreign rule. They also fought to protect their **deen** and **dharma.** We must not make the mistake today of interpreting these terms in the narrow sense of the word 'religion'. What the rebels fought to defend was 'a way of life' which they feared the British were destroying. As an alien imposition, British rule threatened cherished notions of an ancient culture and civilisation. The people of India resisted this intervention in their way of life.

860. (8-5-2007) NEW DELHI : Farm commodity prices monitored by the Department of Consumer Affairs have generally remained steady or have shown mixed trend in different centres across the country in the week ending 4.5.2007. Wheat prices remained steady at 13 reporting centres and declined at 4 centres. Wheat prices have shown increase only at Delhi. Government has notified extension of duty free import of wheat till December 31 this year. Sugar prices remained steady across majority of the centres and declined at a number of centres. DGFT has lifted ban on exports of sugar through notification dated January 23, 2007. Gram prices remained steady over the week across most of the centres and declined at Delhi, Jaipur and Shillong. Tur dal prices were also steady across most of the centres. As on 8th May, public sector agencies have contracted import of 4.37 lakh tonne pulses. This comprises contract for 2.58 lakh tonne yellow peas, 1.32 lakh tonne urad, 15000 tonne moong, 30000 tonne tur and 2000 tonne dunpeas. At Delhi, over the week ending 4th May, prices of rice, tur and mustard oil remained steady and prices of tea, sugar, gram and onion declined. Prices of wheat, vanaspati, potato and groundnut oil, however, shown an increase over the week. Price of mustard oil and milk have remained steady for one month; that of atta for six months and that of packed salt for two years.

861. (8-5-2007) NEW DELHI : The President Dr. A.P.J. Abdul Kalam has said that for success in all missions creative leadership is required. Creative leadership should be the means to exercise the vision to change the traditional role from the commander to the coach, manager to mentor, from director to delegator and from one who demands respect to one who facilitates self-respect. For a prosperous and developed India, the important thrust will be on the growth in the number of creative leaders in every laboratory, institution, every industry, every department and finally every organization in the ministry. Dr. Abdul Kalam said this while giving away the National Awards to the eminent individuals and industries in various disciplines in different categories here today to coincide with the celebrations of the National Technology Day. Shri Kapil Sibal, Minister of Science & Technology and Earth Sciences, Dr. Jamshed J. Irani, Director of Tata Sons Ltd., Dr. R. Chidambaram, Principal Scientific Advisor to the Government, Dr. T. Ramasami, Secretary, Department of Science & Technology, eminent scientists and technologists and various other entrepreneurs were present on the occasion. This year's Technology Day lecture was delivered by Dr. Jamshed J. Irani who was also former Managing Director of Tata Iron and Steel Company Limited

(TISCO). Interacting with the audience, which consisted of mostly of scientists and technologists, entrepreneurs, members from academia and the governmental, the President shared the connectivity among economic development, competitiveness, technology and marketing and evolution of a creative leaders.

862. (8-5-2007) NEW DELHI : Government of India have announced the sale (re-issue) of "7.55 percent Government Stock, 2010" under Market Stabilization Scheme for a notified amount of Rs. 6,000 crore (nominal). The Government Stock will be sold through price based auction using multiple price method. The auction will be conducted by the Reserve Bank of India, Mumbai Office, Fort, Mumbai on May 16, 2007 (Wednesday). Up to 5% of the amount notified for the sale of stock is reserved for allotment to eligible individuals and Institutions on non-competitive basis as per the Scheme for Non-Competitive Bidding Facility in the Auction of Government Securities. Bids in the prescribed form obtainable from the Regional Director, Reserve Bank of India, Mumbai Office (Public Debt Office), Fort, Mumbai-400 001 and RBI website www.rbi.org.in should be submitted to that Office on May 16, 2007. The NDS members should submit competitive as well as non-competitive bids in electronic format using Primary Market Operation (PMO) module of NDS. All bids should be submitted by 12.30 P.M. The result of the auction will be announced on May 16, 2007 and payment by successful bidders will be during banking hours on May 17, 2007 (Thursday).

863. (8-5-2007) NEW DELHI : In exercise of the powers conferred by clause (1) of article 222 of the Constitution of India, the President, after consultation with the Chief Justice of India, is pleased to transfer Shri Justice Jagdish Bhalla, Judge of the Allahabad High Court as a Judge of the Chhattisgarh High Court and to direct him to assume charge of his office in the Chhattisgarh High Court on or before 25th May, 2007.

864. (8-5-2007) NEW DELHI : The Union Minister of External Affairs, Shri Pranab Mukherjee today said that India remains committed to scientific research and technical cooperation in the Polar Regions. "Antarctica being a common heritage of mankind and the foremost symbol of peaceful use and cooperation, needs to be protected for posterity", Shri Mukherjee said while addressing the closing session of the XXX Antarctic Treat Consultative Meeting, here. The following are the excerpts from the Address of Shri Pranab Mukherjee, delivered on the occasion: "I am happy to be here to address you at the concluding session of a very successful and historic 30th Antarctic Treaty Consultative Meeting. Historic in the sense that India has hosted this meeting for the first time coinciding with the 25th year of its joining the Treaty. The two-week long deliberations have resulted in some significant outcomes and decisions. These mutually agreed decisions not only strengthen the Antarctic Treaty in providing good governance to the Antarctic continent, but underline the need of cooperative research and environmental protection. The Treaty has certainly grown in stature and strength in last 48 years with newer entrants joining its fold. Adoption of the Madrid

Protocol on Environment Protection in 1991 was a significant landmark for the Antarctic Treaty. It indicated the concern of Treaty Party nations about the fragile Antarctic ecosystems and their significance at global level. The Protocol is a testimony of farsightedness and a global vision of mentors of the Antarctic Treaty. It has gained further importance at a time when we are passing through one of the most critical phase of global environmental scenario, especially after the report of the UN's fourth Intergovernmental Panel on Climate Change. It is becoming increasingly clear that to counter the projected impacts of global warming, we need coordinated effort across the world. The intensive collaborative research work that is being carried out during the ongoing International Polar Year 2007-08, therefore assumes greater importance. I am sure the policy and law makers world over will be benefiting by the research work being carried out by the Polar Scientists in Antarctica, in taking informed decisions and remedial steps against the impacts of global warming. I am happy to note that the Meeting has adopted a comprehensive report of the 10th meeting of the Committee for Environmental Protection, which has included a specific agenda on 'Climate Change' for its deliberations during the next ATCM. This is significant considering the report on Climate Change by the IPCC.

865. (8-5-2007) NEW DELHI : The Union External Affairs Minister, Shri Pranab Mukherjee today said that the Government has constituted two Committees, namely an Expert Group on Haj to recommend ways and means to make further improvements in management of Haj pilgrims from India and another Committee to study measures to look into the reforms of the existing system of management of Haj pilgrimage and prepare an appropriate and viable model for Haj Management. Both the Committees have held several rounds of discussions and their recommendations will help the Government in further improving Haj Management, Shri Mukherjee said. He was delivering the inaugural address at the All India annual Conference for Haj 2007, here. Speaking on the occasion, Shri Mukherjee said, "I take this opportunity to flag an important area of concern that is proving as a bottle-neck to streamlining Haj Management in India. This is the delay in the formation of State Haj Committees by some States in accordance with the provisions of the Haj Committee Act 2002. I would like to urge all those States who have so far not constituted their State Haj Committees to do so expeditiously." The following is the text of the address of Shri Pranab Mukherjee, delivered on the occasion: "At the outset, I express my gratitude for organizing this programme. My colleague, Shri Ahmed was to come but he could not come due to injury to his leg. I am very glad to be with you all this morning to inaugurate the All India Annual Haj Conference. At the outset, I would like to compliment and congratulate the Government of the Kingdom of Saudi Arabia for the arrangements made for the last Haj and for its successful completion. As you know, acceding to our request, they increased our quota by 10,000. I would also like to commend the efforts made by the Haj Committee of India, the Indian Missions in Saudi Arabia, the Airline companies and all other individuals and agencies for their contribution in the smooth and successful organization of Haj pilgrimage and the arrangements made for the last Haj. It is a matter of great pride for us that one of the largest contingent of Haj pilgrims in the world goes from India. I am glad to learn that over 1,50,000 Indian pilgrims performed the Haj last year, which is an all-time record. Indeed, under the UPA Government the pilgrim quota has been considerably increased during the last three years. In this connection, I would like to express my sincere gratitude to the Government of the Kingdom of Saudi Arabia and the Custodian of the Two Holy Mosques for acceding to the request made by the Government of India for enhancement of our quota. For millions of Muslims all over the world, and India is no exception, pilgrimage to the Holy places of Makkah and Medinah is a cherished life-long dream and the Government of India is committed to ensure that the best possible arrangements are put in place for the comfort and well being of Indian pilgrims. The External Affairs Ministry under the guidance of my colleague Shri E. Ahamed has put in dedicated effort in bringing about perceptible improvements in Haj management during the last three years. I congratulate him, his colleagues and senior officers.

866. (8-5-2007) NEW DELHI : Twenty-eight Research Projects have been completed by serving Armed Forces Personnel under Fellowship Scheme at the Institute for Defence Studies and Analyses (IDSA) since September 2000 till date on subjects such as structure of Indian Army, terrorism, counter-terrorism strategy, modernization of Army, security scenario in the Asia Pacific region etc. One Officer from the Air Force is with the IDSA for over four years at present. The officer is doing research in a field important from military point of view, and in which no other suitable researcher is available. The officer has been retained at the Institute's request and with the consent of the Air Force, which does not envisage any operational role for the officer. Eight Armed Forces personnel deputed at IDSA have undertaken 38 foreign travels since September 2000 till date. These visits were made to neighbouring countries, Germany, US, Italy, Canada etc. to participate in Seminars/Conferences of Military importance and relevant to their research subjects. This information was given by the Defence Minister Shri AK Antony in a written reply to Shri Harishchandra Chavan in Lok Sabha. INDUCTION OF AWACS Presently there is no proposal from the Indian Air Force for the induction of Airborne warning and Control System (AWACS). However, government had earlier concluded a contract in March 2004 for procurement of AWACS aircraft. This information was given by the Defence Minister Shri AK Antony in a written reply to Shri Santosh Gangwar and others in Lok Sabha.

867. (8-5-2007) NEW DELHI : Indo-US Naval exercise, code named Malabar, was jointly conducted from April 6 to April 11, 2007 off the Japanese Island of Okinawa and a Tri-lateral exercise with the US Navy and the Japanese Maritime Self-defence Force was also conducted off Tokyo Bay on April 16, 2007. The objective of conducting such joint exercises is to promote mutual cooperation, and gain from the experience of other navies especially in the field of advance technology available with them. It also facilitates inter operability in times of need in situations like disaster management etc. The exercise was dovetailed into the overseas deployment of some Indian naval ships to the North Pacific, which involved visit of five ships to six countries. The total expenditure on this overseas deployment was Rs. 5.81 crore (approximately), including the joint exercise. Further, the expenditure on operation of the foreign naval ships during the exercise was borne by the respective participating countries. An Indo-US Framework for Maritime Security Cooperation has been agreed to between the two governments. The Framework envisages bilateral cooperation in the areas of prevention of/ response to piracy and trafficking in arms and drugs, combating marine pollution, search & rescue operations at sea, enhancement of maritime capabilities through technology cooperation, etc. This information was given by the Defence Minister Shri AK Antony in a written reply to Shri Kishanbhai V Patel and Shri Milind Deora in Lok Sabha.

868. (8-5-2007) NEW DELHI : Representatives of the Indian Air Force had participated in the development trials of the Akash Missile System conducted by DRDO, as observers and provided user's inputs for improvement in the system performance. Some trials at the development stage had not been fully successful. User's trial are likely to commence shortly. No decision has been taken so far by the Government for induction of Akash Missile system in the Army. This information was given by the Defence Minister Shri AK Antony in a written reply to Prof Mahadeorao Shiwankar in Lok Sabha.

869. (8-5-2007) NEW DELHI : The Minister for Steel, Chemicals and Fertilisers Shri Ram Vilas Paswan has asked the public sector National Mineral Development Corporation (NMDC) to increase its production target to 31.6 million tonnes of iron ore. This is 17 percent higher than the previous year's production of 27 million tones. Reviewing the performance of NMDC here today, the Minister said, the company should increase its production in iron ore mines including Kumaraswamy and Donimalai. Shri Paswan said, NMDC should improve the road infrastructure and invest in equipment to increase output. He said, as the economy is growing at 8-9 percent year, the demand for steel is buoyant and NMDC should increase its iron ore production. Congratulating the company for entering into a joint venture with SAIL and RINL for setting up a greenfield steel plant of 2-3 million tonnes, the Minister said the project report should be prepared at the earliest. Secretary Ministry of Steel Shri R.S. Pandey who was present on the occasion said, the government is prepared to talk to the concerned state governments if there are any bottlenecks in any specific mine and also hold tripartite meetings with the steel producers on improving the off take from these mines. Shri Pandey said, the company should target to sell 20 per cent of its output on spot basis. During 2006-07, NMDC increased its iron ore output by 18 per cent to 27 million tonnes. Its net profit increased 25.8 per cent to Rs. 2300 crore during the year against

Rs. 1828 crore in 2005-06. The total turnover rose by 11.9 per cent to Rs. 4150 crore, up from Rs. 3707 crore during 2005-06. Shri Paswan also asked the company to increase its expenditure on corporate social responsibility. During the last financial year NMDC has spent Rs.24.66 crore mostly on education, health, drinking water facilities, approach roads and culverts. He also directed NMDC to prepare a Vision Plan for utilizing over Rs 5000 crore reserves. The Minister took stock of the on-going projects and assured the company of full support from the Ministry of Steel. The Company will celebrate 150th anniversary of 1857 uprising by announcing special programmes.

870. (8-5-2007) NEW DELHI : Environmental clearance to 163 mw hydel power project at the Athirapally Waterfalls in Kerala are under consideration. A sub committee of the Expert Appraisal Committee for River Valley & Hydroelectric Projects visited the proposed sites of Athirapally hydroelectric project during April 2007. The findings of the Committee includes: People living in Athirapally, whose income is mainly tourist dependent are agitated, efforts to assuage their worries have not been adequately addressed by KSEB. There are two tribal settlements – one with 18 families above the FRL and at the upstream side of the dam and the other with 58 families at downstream(about 400 mt from the dam) site of the dam – who somehow developed a strong notion that they would be displaced. During that period of power generation the intense flows spill over the crest of the weir into the stream without providing enough flows in the canals for irrigation. The tail end areas of the canals would be worst affected, particularly during late stages of the Rabi crop season. The present condition of the weir and the head reaches of the canals need repair. The low level sluices in the weir and the canal head reaches have large leakages. The ground water levels in the canal commands have been falling to the dissatisfaction of the people in the command. Drinking water supply is also consequently getting affected. The site visit report of the sub committee is being placed before the meeting of the Expert Appraisal Committee (EAC) scheduled to be held on 16th May, 2007 for its recommendation. After EAC's recommendations are available, Government will take a decision. This information was given by the Minister of State in the Ministry of Environment and Forests, Shri Namo Narain Meena in a written reply to question by Shri K.E.Ismail in the Rajya Sabha today.

871. (8-5-2007) NEW DELHI : The deployment of the troops in Siachen glacier and their continuous human traffic does not have environmental affect on this region. In proportion to the vastness of the Siachen glacier these activities have negligible effect on its melting. Minister of State in the Ministry of Environment and Forests, Shri Namo Narain Meena said in the Rajya Sabha today that the observations made by the Pakistan's Environment Minister are not based on factual data. Though media reports from Pakistan occasionally refer to the environmental benefits of the demilitarisation of the area, no proposal has been received by the Government of India from Government of Pakistan regarding environmental aspects of Siachen Glaciers. As per the information made available by the Geological Survey of India, the total retreat of Siachen Glacier during the last 95 years (1909-2004) is about 500 meters at an average annual rate of 5.3 meter per year only. Shri Meena further informed that the Geological Survey of India has also undertaken studies on recession of several Himalayan glaciers, including Siachen glacier. These studies revealed that the majority of glaciers of Himalayan region are passing through a phase of recession, as has been the case with the glaciers located in other parts of the world. The rate of recession in Himalayan region in different climatic zones is found to be variable in different years. This variable rate of recession can be attributed to the several climatic factors.

872. (8-5-2007) NEW DELHI : The oceanic region adjoining the Indian subcontinent is likely to warm at its surface by about 1.5-2.0 degree Centigrade by the middle of this century and by about 2.3-3.5 degree Centigrade by the end of the century. This indication is derived from modern simulation studies. Replying to a question whether Government is aware that towns and cities along India's Eastern Coast would be devasted with global warming intensifying cyclones and rising sea levels eroding vast stretches of the shore lines by Shri Mahendra Mohan, Minister of State in the Ministry of Environment and Forests, Shri Namo Narain Meena further said the past observations on the mean sea level along the Indian coast show a long-term rising trend of about 1.0 mm/year. The recent data suggests a rising trend of 2.5 mm/year in the sea-level along Indian coastline. The corresponding thermal expansion, related sea-level rise is expected to be between 15 cm and 38 cm by the middle of this century and between 46 cm and 59 cm by the end of the century. According to a study conducted by the Ministry of Environment & Forests on the impacts of climate change on various sectors including coastal zones, in the event of one meter sea-level rise, 5764 Km2 of land in coastal areas of India is projected to lose, displacing approximately 7.1 million people along with 4200 Kms of roads by the end of the 21st century. Further the coastal areas are also vulnerable to projected increase in frequency and intensity of extreme weather events like storm surges and cyclones. In the eastern coast, the vulnerable districts include Jagatsinghpur and Kendrapara in Orissa and Nellore in Andhra Pradesh and Nagapattinam in Tamil Nadu.

873. (8-5-2007) NEW DELHI : Former soldiers have picked up arms again, this time to fight the rising menace of Naxalite violence in Bihar. Raised last year, the Bihar Auxiliary Force recruited 5,000 ex-servicemen in November and December. The "young" force, consisting of veteran soldiers, proved its mettle when they foiled a Maoist raid on a bank under Riga police station in Sitamari district near Nepal border. This was stated by Major General Harwant Krishan, Director-General (Resettlement), DGR, on the sidelines of a training course for retiring soldiers in New Delhi today. The DGR also disclosed that Rajasthan state government has hired about 1,200 ex-servicemen as forest guards. The desert state was stunned two years ago when a Wildlife Institute of India survey confirmed that a poaching mafia had robbed Sariska reserve of its entire tiger population of about 16-18 in numbers. General Krishan said the DGR had helped secure re-employment for about 16,000 ex-servicemen since January this year. In Haryana, the ex-servicemen have been found useful for meter-reading jobs in private agencies contracted by Haryana State Electricity Board and for undertaking "Below Poverty Line" head count in the state. General Krishan said talks are in advanced stage with the Delhi Metro and DTC to institutionalise a framework for recruitment of ex-servicemen. Earlier, General Krishan addressed about 50 soldiers, due for retirement shortly, undergoing a two-day Career Transition Course for Personnel Below Officers Rank (PBORs) at the Rajputana Rifles Regimental Centre, Delhi Cantt. Representatives of five private companies were present on the occasion to brief about employment opportunities and possible campus recruitment. The DGR said companies have been asked to maintain a salary bar to avoid exploitation of ex-servicemen. Due to its high attrition rate, re-employment of ex-servicemen is a priority for the government and the DGR has rendered great utility in their rehabilitation. About 60,000 men of the roughly 12 lakh strong defence forces retire every year, making up about five percent of the workforce.

874. (8-5-2007) NEW DELHI : The Indian Air Force today phased out its Canberra aircraft after fifty years of its glorious service. The phasing out ceremony was held at Air Force Station Agra and was presided over by the Chief of Air Staff, Air Chief Mshl FH Major. The ceremony comprised the fly past by the mighty bombers and concluded with the handing over of 'form 700' to the Chief by Wg Cdr Mathur, the CO of Canberra Squadron. For over fifty years, the Canberra has been a familiar sight the world over, both in war and peace. Designed in 1944 to meet a specification for a jet bomber, the Canberra has had an unrivalled history in the world of military aviation. During its lifetime the Canberra equipped over sixty RAF squadrons plus a number of special flights. It was license built both in Australia and the USA, in the latter as the B-57, some 400 odd were built. It also proved a best seller overseas, being operated by seventeen air forces, and seeing active service with many of them. No. 5 squadron IAF was the first to equip with the Canberra Bomber in May 1957, and by 1959 two more squadrons, No 16 and 35, had become operational on type. The eight PR-57s were operated by 106 SR Squadron, while the T-54s were formed into a jet bomber Operational conversion Unit, namely JBCU. The Canberras were mostly based at Agra. Target-towing version was added to the inventory of the IAF in 1975. Canberra, the only bomber of the Indian Air Force until late seventies, came to India in 1957. An aircraft of British origin, the twin-engine jet bomber has been a proud possession of the Indian Air Force. The high altitude bomber was a force to reckon with in the then prevailing war scenario in the Indian subcontinent. Cruising at four-fifth the speed of sound at 40,000 feet, Canberra was the right weapon carrier then, to carry the war well beyond the frontiers, deep into enemy's territory. Canberra got the first taste of operation on 18th December 1961 when 16 Squadron and

35 squadron were tasked to carry out reconnaissance and bombing of Dabolim airfield. Canberras of No. 35 Squadron were the first jet aircraft of the IAF to bear its arsenal on an enemy. On 18 Dec. 1961 the squadron dropped 60,000 lbs bombs over Dabolim airfield against the Portuguese. It is worth mentioning that the highly accurate bombing damaged only the target with no civilian causalities and the ATC and the aircraft on the dispersal were deliberately not targeted. By the 20th Goa had been reclaimed. The Belgian Congo broke out in political turmoil in 1961 and the UNO was called in for help. When the situation in Katanga (UHHQ) and the capital Leopoldville worsened, India was requested to send strike aircraft on behalf of United Nations. Earmarked for this task was the proud No. 5 squadron. On October 9th 1961, under the command of Wg Cdr A Suares with twelve aircrew and ninety support personnel, six Canberra aircraft took off from Agra for Ndjili airport, Leopoldville over 6000 km away via Jamnagar and Nairobi as the first ever Indian Fighter bomber contingent to take part in UN operations. The Canberras were a major contributor towards the UN aim of establishing peace in Congo. Through the Canberras stood down in the Chinese conflict and did not fly any combat sorties, recce sorties till went through. The Canberras flew 22 Photo Recce missions between 13 Oct. to 11 Nov. 1962 totalling more than fifty hours. Areas of Aksai chin and Eastern sector were covered to monitor enemy encroachment. The Canberras performed magnificently in the conflict. Canberra's mettle was tested for the first time in 1965 Indo-Pak war. Numerous high level bombing missions were successfully flown during the course of the short war. In recognition of their bravery and valour many Canberra crew, were awarded Maha Vir Chakras, Vir Chakras and other gallantry awards. Battle scenario changed dramatically for Canberra bombers after the 1965 war, Entry of radars and high performance fighters with night combat capability meant curtains for the high level sub-sonic bomber. However, air space close to the ground was still a grey area for the radars and the fighters and this was well exploited by the Canberra. Canberras were soon zooming at high speeds across the Gangetic Plains, the lush green fields of Punjab and Haryana, the sandy deserts of Rajasthan, the marshy lands of Saurashtra and the cool waters of the Arabian Sea, honing the new techniques for low level penetration and pull up attacks.

875. (8-5-2007) NEW DELHI : The Annual supplement to the Foreign Trade Policy released in April, 2007 had stated that service tax on exports shall be exempted. Various newspapers have been reporting that differences persist between the Finance and Commerce ministries on this issue. On the issue concerning rebate or refund of service tax paid on various input services used for goods or services exported, it is hereby clarified that there are no differences between the Finance and Commerce Ministries and this decision was taken with the approval of the Commerce Minister, the Finance Minister and the Prime Minister. The taxes paid on inputs or input services used for manufacture of export goods or for providing export services are already being neutralized under rebate, refund and drawback schemes. However modalities for refund/rebate service tax on certain services, which are not input services, but are related to goods or services exported from India, and to neutralize service tax on services received/rendered abroad are being worked out in consultation with the Department of Commerce.

876. (8-5-2007) NEW DELHI : With a view to provide better educational facilities to the children of far flung areas of the country, a Sainik School is being set up at Punglwa in district Peren, near Dimapur in Nagaland. This will be the first Sainik School in Nagaland and third in entire North East. The Defence Minister Shri A.K. Antony will inaugurate the Sainik School at Punglwa tomorrow. The Nagaland Chief Minister Shri Neiphiu Rio and Chairman of Sainik School Society and Minister of State for Defence Shri M M Pallam Raju will also attend the inaugural ceremony. Spread over an area of 300 acres, the school is located in the scenic foothills of Pauna range, about 47 kms from Dimapur. This will be the 21st Sainik School in the country. The school will go a long way in meeting the aspirations of the mostly tribal people and integrating the remote region with the rest of the country. Established under the aegis of Sainik Schools Society, the school has been set up due to the hard work and persistent initiative of Nagaland Chief Minister Shri Neiphiu Rio, who is himself an alumnus of the Sainik School. In an appropriate gesture its foundation stone was laid at the hands of Shri Rio on February 16, 2004. The school building has been constructed by the National Building Construction Corporation (NBCC). The school has received over 14 crore rupees funds from the union ministry for Development of North-Eastern Region (DONER) and Rs. 2 crores grant-in-aid from the state government for infrastructure. The school has a well-equipped computer lab and LCD projector auditorium, while plans are afoot to set up a modern swimming pool, horse-riding club and shooting range. The residential school, only for boys, will be affiliated to the Central Board of Secondary Education (CBSE). It will impart studies through English medium and will provide only Science stream education to senior secondary students. The aim of the school is to prepare boys for entry into the National Defence Academy. The school also aims to bring quality public school education within the reach of the common man.

877. (8-5-2007) NEW DELHI : A section of the media has reported about the midterm review of the Defence Offset Policy at a seminar to be held on 14th of this month. In this connection it is clarified that the offset policy has been designed by Ministry of Defence carefully after studying all aspects between direct and indirect offset. In order to encourage Indian Defence Industry, a well considered decision was taken not to allow indirect offset. There is no rethinking on this subject as reported in a section of the media. The said seminar on May 14, has nothing to do with the review of offset provisions.

878. (8-5-2007) NEW DELHI : The Ministry of Rural Development has released Grants-in-aid to Punjab amounting to Rs. 5.58 crore as third/additional instalment of Central assistance to 6 districts, Rs. 1.56 crore as second instalment to 4 districts and Rs.1.72 crore as first instalment being equal to 60% of total allocation to the

Kapurthala District as central assistance for the implementation of the Sampoorna Grameen Rozgar Yojana (SGRY) during the financial year (2006-07). During the current financial year (2007-08) Rs. 1.72 crore as part of first instalment has been granted by the Ministry to 3 districts of Punjab as central assistance under the scheme.

879. (8-5-2007) NEW DELHI : The Ministry of Rural Development has sanctioned Rs. 31.89 crore to the State Government of West Bengal towards part payment of first instalment of funds against the provisional allocation of Rs.191.37 crore made for the Government of West Bengal under Accelerated Rural Water Supply Programme (Normal) of Rajiv Gandhi National Drinking Water Mission, during the year 2007-08. Up to 15 per cent of funds released under this sanction may be utilized for Operation & Maintenance and up to 5 per cent of funds may be spent for taking sustainability measures. States have been requested to delegate powers for management of Rural Water Supply Schemes through the Panchayati Raj Institutions (PRIs) as per the Constitution of India. As such Operation and Maintenance of the completed RWS Scheme should be transferred to the PRIs. No expenditure shall be incurred on taking water quality problems form the present release, as there is a separate allocation for the purpose. This release is for execution/completion of schemes to provide safe drinking water facilities to rural habitations and schools under the Centrally Sponsored ARWSP and according to Priorities set in ARWSP guidelines and through other instructions issued from time to time.

880. (8-5-2007) NEW DELHI : The Ministry of Rural Development has released Grants-in-aid amounting to Rs. 12.35 crore as third/additional instalment of Central assistance to 5 districts of Chhattisgarh for the implementation of the Sampoorna Grameen Rozgar Yojana (SGRY) during the financial year (2006-07). Grants amounting to Rs.1.88 crore as part of first instalment has also been released to Durg District of the State under the scheme for the year 2007-08.

881. (8-5-2007) NEW DELHI : The Ministry of Rural Development has sanctioned Rs. 1.19 crore of Grants-in-aid to 26 District Rural Development Agencies (DRDAs) of Assam towards part payment of first instalment of Central Share for the year 2007-08 under DRDA Administration.

882. (8-5-2007) NEW DELHI : The Ministry of Rural Development has sanctioned Rs. 67.39 crore to the State Government of Maharashtra (Maharashtra Jeevan Pradhikaran, Mumbai) towards part payment of first instalment of funds against the provisional allocation of Rs.404.40 crore made for the Government of Maharashtra under Accelerated Rural Water Supply Programme (Normal) of Rajiv Gandhi National Drinking Water Mission, during the year 2007-08. Up to 15 per cent of funds released under this sanction may be utilized for Operation & Maintenance and up to 5 per cent of funds may be spent for taking sustainability measures. States have been requested to delegate powers for management of Rural

Water Supply Schemes through the Panchayati Raj Institutions (PRIs) as per the Constitution of India. As such Operation and Maintenance of the completed RWS Scheme should be transferred to the PRIs. No expenditure shall be incurred on taking water quality problems form the present release, as there is a separate allocation for the purpose. This release is for execution/completion of schemes to provide safe drinking water facilities to rural habitations and schools under the Centrally Sponsored ARWSP and according to Priorities set in ARWSP guidelines and through other instructions issued from time to time.

883. (8-5-2007) NEW DELHI : Grant-in-aid amounting to Rs.6.54 lakh has been released by the Ministry of Rural Development to the District Rural Development Agency of Lakshadweep towards part payment of first instalment of Central Share for the year 2007-08 under DRDA Administration. The funding pattern under the scheme is 75:25 between Centre and the State. The utilization of funds is to be in accordance with the DRDA administration guidelines and the release of the second instalment during 2007-08 is subject to the fulfillment of all the conditions as per the DRDA Administration guidelines.

884. (8-5-2007) NEW DELHI : The Ministry of Rural Development has sanctioned Rs. 66.91 crore to the State Government of Uttar Pradesh (Uttar Pradesh Jal Nigam, Lucknow) towards part payment of first instalment of funds against the provisional allocation of Rs.401.51 crore made for the Government of Uttar Pradesh under Accelerated Rural Water Supply Programme (Normal) of Rajiv Gandhi National Drinking Water Mission, during the year 2007-08. Up to 15 per cent of funds released under this sanction may be utilized for Operation & Maintenance and up to 5 per cent of funds may be spent for taking sustainability measures. States have been requested to delegate powers for management of Rural Water Supply Schemes through the Panchayati Raj Institutions (PRIs) as per the Constitution of India. As such Operation and Maintenance of the completed RWS Scheme should be transferred to the PRIs. No expenditure shall be incurred on taking water quality problems form the present release, as there is a separate allocation for the purpose. This release is for execution/completion of schemes to provide safe drinking water facilities to rural habitations and schools under the Centrally Sponsored ARWSP and according to Priorities set in ARWSP guidelines and through other instructions issued from time to time.

885. (8-5-2007) NEW DELHI : The inaugural function of the National Celebration to Commemorate 150th Anniversary of the First War of Independence 1857 saw a colourful cultural extravaganza. About 2000 artists from various parts of the country performed their arts in the backdrop of recreation of the history of freedom struggle. The artists reflected the spirit of unity in diversity. The function held at Red Fort was attended by President, Vice-President, Prime Minister, Speaker of Lok Sabha, Chairperson of UPA, Minister for Human Resource Development, Minister of Youth Affairs & Sports and others. Thousands of youth were also present. These youngsters are a part of the Rally (Yatra) which started from Meerut on 7th May 2007. Volunteers marched down from Victoria Park in Meerut to Red Fort to celebrate the spirit of revolution of 1857. May 11 is the historic day when the soldiers and revolting principalities declared Bahadur Shah Zafar the emperor and established a strong front to take on the mighty British Empire. Although the siege did not remain for long with the Indian patriots and on September 21, 1857 Delhi fell to the British Empire, but it did reflect the passion and communal harmony and love for motherland.

886. (8-5-2007) NEW DELHI : "Technology is a non-linear tool which can effect fundamental changes in economic competitiveness" I am very happy to participate in the National Technology Day Award Function 2007 organized by Ministry of Science and Technology. This day reminds us of our resolve to achieve self reliance in indigenous technologies needed for societal transformation. My greetings to the organizers, scientists, technologists and entrepreneurs and congratulations to the award winners. While I am with you, I would like to talk to you on the topic "technology and innovation power competitiveness".

887. (9-5-2007) NEW DELHI : Congress Spokesperson Smt. Jayanti Natrajan said that yesterday the Election Commission has issued an order directing the BJP to publicly condemn and disown the contents on the venomous CD that was earlier to be distributed by the BJP in Uttar Pradesh. As the entire nation is aware, this CD was released at the Press Conference of senior leaders of the BJP and on the cover of the CD was the election symbol of the BJP as well as the address of its party's office in Lucknow. Senior most BJP leaders Shri Advani and Shri Vajpayee also figured prominently in this CD. This is not the first time that the BJP has distributed such inflammatory CDs and literature. I believe that at its national executive meeting in December, 2006 at Lucknow, the BJP released similar inflammatory CD attempting to spread the worst type of communal poison in the country. Today the BJP has sought to distance itself from the CD by saying that it was not officially distributed but it was a mistake. This does not absolve the BJP from its culpability in flagrantly violating the law of the land, the sentiment of people and of attempting to divide and destroy the secular fabric of our nation. Apart from the election code, the distribution of such inflammatory material, capable of creating enmity and hatred among different communities, is a violation under section-152-A, 153-B and 505 of the Indian Penal Code. Clauses 3 and 3A of sec. 123 and 125 of the Representation of People's Act and also a violation of 16-A of Election symbols order of 1968. The BJP is liable to be punished under all these sections. If there is any credence at all in the stand of the BJP that it had nothing to do officially with CD but the release of the CD was an unauthorized act. It is the beholden duty of the BJP, if it believes in the spirit of the Constitution of India and in communal harmony, to publicly condemn the CD and to that effect obey the specific order of the Election Commission. If the BJP refuses to do so, as has been stated by some spokespersons of the BJP, then the Indian National Congress demands that a CBI enquiry should be ordered. Also, further enquiry under the FIR that was first registered and the guilty should be punished in the most stringent fashion. The Indian National Congress expected from the Election Commission a more stringent punishment at an earlier point of time. There could not have been a more lenient view of such a serious offence and in our view the punishment or rather the request made to the BJP is not in keeping with the ignomity and gravity of the offence committed by the BJP. If the BJP does not follow and obey the instructions and order of the Election Commission to review its order based upon the refusal of the BJP to comply this order and award a stronger and more stringent punishment to a party that is not clearly violating, not just democratic norms but seeking to destroy harmony in society and the secular fabric of our country. To a question on the action taken by the Election Commission against BJP, Smt. Jayanthi said that we believe, in the circumstances, it was a lenient view by the Election Commission. To a question as to what action Congress would like Election Commission to take if BJP refuse to comply, Smt. Natrajan said that certainly, we would call upon the Election Commission to review their order. To a question that the BJP was not allowing the House to function properly, Smt. Natrajan said that unfortunately the BJP has still not come to terms with the fact that they lost the Lok Sabha elections and since then they have not allowed the House to function. Every single problem, every single issue they raise is designed to prevent the House from functioning. On our part we would suggest that all issues be brought to Parliament and discussed in a healthy manner by the representatives of the people and the BJP should function as a constructive Opposition rather than destroying the institution of Parliament. To a question as to what is Congress Parties view on the Sethusamudram project, Smt. Natarajan said that as far as Congress is concerned the Sethusamudram project or any project that has been undertaken by the Central government. It is not some thing that the Indian National Congress alone has taken, it is same thing that the UPA alliance has taken and any view that has to be taken, will be taken jointly by the entire UPA coalition.

888. (10-5-2007) NEW DELHI : To a question on the statement made by Delhi Chief Minister, Smt. Sheila Dikshit, Shri Singhvi, replying in Hindi, said that Smt. Dikshit has made it clear that she did not want to hurt the feelings and sentiments of the people coming to Delhi from UP or Bihar. If at all it has hurt the feelings of some people, she apologized for the same. To a question on the two-party system suggested by the President, Shri Singhvi said that I think any suggestion, any idea coming from the highest office of the land deserves consideration in the sense that it has to be looked at, it has to be examined from all angles and these are ideas which in any democratic system we must investigate, discuss and debate. Debate always enriches us in this respect. Obviously, there cannot be a question of the Congress Party unilaterally giving you any view on this. This is certainly an idea which has all kinds of issues, merit, demerit, plus and minuses. And I am sure in a civil society and in democratic polity it should be discussed. To a question on electing new President, Shri Singhvi said it would be more accurate to say that three names have been floated by the Media as alleged to have been floated by the Congress. To a question about the statement made by the Lok Sabha Deputy Speaker, Shri Singhvi said that I cannot comment on individual views. In a democracy people may have, but certainly we can say that once a decision has been taken by the government of India and by several state governments, that decision is under implementation even as we speak. Any stand or view different from that decision is nothing but an expression of a personal opinion. To a question as to how Congress Party responds to the Deputy Speaker's behaviour, Shri Singhvi said that there is no question of a scene or behaviour, as you put it. A view was expressed which is inconsistent with the view of the government and any such view has to be described as nothing more and nothing less than personal opinion. He has expressed his view which is entirely personal and it is not the stand of the government To a question on difference of opinion in the DMK, Shri Singhvi said that regarding the internal affairs of a party of Tamil Nadu is concerned, we have absolutely nothing to say. These are matters internal to that political party and they do not concern Congress. Secondly, obviously wherever there is violence of an unauthorized, illegal or wrongful kind of any kind by anybody, it is not specific to Tamil Nadu. We obviously do not condone or accept such violence, we only say such violence should be prevented.

889. (11-5-2007) NEW DELHI : Shri Abhishek Singhvi said that the Indian National Congress welcomes the verdict of the people of Uttar Pradesh in the Assembly elections. This verdict is against the misrule and the anti-people policies of the Samajwadi Party government. We are also happy to note that the people of Uttar Pradesh have again rejected a communal party like the BJP. So far as our party, the Congress Party, is concerned we are conscious that the mandate of the people is perhaps to sit in the Opposition and we shall discharge our duty to the best of our ability. To a question that Rahul, Priyanka and Smt. Sonia Gandhi should own responsibility for this defeat in Uttar Pradesh, Shri Singhvi said that the Congress Party functions as a cohesive party. We take full responsibility as an All India National Party for the verdict. You must remember that our figure in Uttar Pradesh, in fact, stood at 16 and we have therefore improved but certainly this is not to say that we are happy with our result. We are certainly disappointed and we shall strive to improve. As far as the persons whose names you are taking are concerned, the one person, who has led from the front, Mr. Rahul Gandhi has made it clear time and again that he is in Uttar Pradesh for a long haul and there are long-term structural reasons from which the Congress is bound to emerge victorious in the near future. We will take these results and analyse these results very carefully and you will see that we will emerge better, stronger, bigger and more victorious than ever. To a question that as you said that you would sit in the Opposition, does that mean you will not support BSP? Shri Singhvi said that the verdict is not for us to form the government or sit in the government, we respect that verdict. As far as the majority party is concerned, there is no question of anybody seeking our support therefore there is no question of our suo-motu extending our support. Let us wait and watch what happens. As of now this question of support is entirely hypothetical. To a question that Congress failed to encash on Mr. Rahul's campaign, Shri Singhvi said that I don't think that there is anything of the sort which you think in terms of encashing or not encashing. Mr. Rahul Gandhi led from the front, he led an energetic and enthusiastic campaign which electrified the electorate. We have improved our position however there is hope for lot more improvement and we are not deterred by the results, we take them as a spur and as an incentive for far better performance in the near future and you shall see that happening. To a question that Priyanka was a better vote catcher than Rahul, Shri Singhvi said that your interpretation, your conclusions are completely misplaced. You are trying to draw conclusions on unrelated events all-together. To a question on Presidential elections, Shri Singhvi said that the process of the Presidential election would have to be gone into by all the leading political players. This is a very important post-election moment and these processes always take place in the informal recesses of the political process. They are not for me and you to share but you will know the result of those procedure at an appropriate time. To a question that Muslims in Uttar Pradesh have not been impressed by the schemes announced for them by the Central government, Shri Singhvi said that I don't agree with the premise of your question all together. We appealed to the electorate of Uttar Pradesh to vote for us and they have voted for us in the manner and the quantum which they wanted to and we accept that verdict. To a question as to who will be your enemy number one in Uttar Pradesh now, Shri Singhvi said that we do not view the political process of enemy No.1 or enemy No.2. However, we do know the emergence of other party as a reason for us to improve our performance. Certainly the Congress in Uttar Pradesh has to reinvent and reassimilate the rainbow of coalition which has been historically our trend and you can take it that we are aware of our strength and weaknesses. You can take it that every possible attempt will be made and you will see the momentum you saw in the last two months will be maintained and this time we will convert it into far better figure for the future.

890. (11-5-2007) NEW DELHI : BJP National Spokesperson and State Incharge of Goa Shri Rajiv Pratap Singh Rudy today said that the misdeeds, corruption and pathetic governance record of the Congress Party in Goa stands fully exposed before the eyes of the people to the extent that even so called loyal soldiers of the party are now in a hurry to desert the sinking ship. While addressing the press, Mr. Rudy charged the Congress Party of now trying to somehow cling onto power by fighting the elections through a camouflage campaign whereby the party was secretly encouraging some of its candidates to contest the election under the banner of other regional parties or as independents. This was being done as the Congress Party is fully aware of the poor image of its government in the state which would be a definite disadvantage for its candidates while seeking votes from the educated and aware citizens of Goa. Further buttressing his point, Mr. Rudy highlighted that the Congress Party is still unable to explain why the brother of Mr. Churchill Allemao, Mr. Joquem Allemao is the party's official candidate while

Mr. Churchill Allemao has himself floated a regional outfit to accommodate proxy candidates of the Congress. The BJP considers this as the "cheat and deceit formula of the Congress" to misguide the Goan people. Despite Mr. Allemao rubbishing the Congress party over the last six months, they did not expel him even while knowing fully well that he had announced the dates for his resignation from the Lok Sabha. All these instances are clearly indicative of the fact that the Congress Party is surreptitiously resurrecting its nominees in a camouflaged manner being fully aware that they have lost own their credibility in Goa. The recent last minute desertions by official Congress candidates is also a clear example of the a "cheat and bluff startegy" clearly highlighted by Atanasio Monserrate "Babush" ditching the party at the very last minute as also the Chief Minister's own son Vishwajit Rane contesting as an independent. The Congress Party is divided and disgruntled house clamouring to retain power by any means, he added. Mr. Rudy said that instead of earlier addressing issues to prevent rampant corruption, runaway inflation, and improve governance, the Congress party's sole objective is retention of power. With this aim in mind, the Congress Party's post election strategy is to fraudulently cobble a coalition of power hungry individuals so that the blatant sale of Goa and its people's interests can continue unabated, he said. However, the people of Goa will never allow this to happen and will give a clear mandate to the BJP to form an efficient, clean and responsive government under the able leadership of the dynamic Mr. Manohar Parrikar, whose last innings as Chief Minister is considered as a golden period in Goa's socio-economic development, he added. Mr. Rudy pointed out that once the final results are out, in contrast to a cohesive stable BJP, the power hungry and desperate Congress party would try to cheat the people's mandate by coming together as a loose federation of unstable and independent members for forming the next government so that the systematic loot and sale of Goa can continue for their own personal benefit. "Goa and its interests are not for sale" he emphasized and added that the people of the state would aggressively oppose it. In the interest of Goa's prosterity, he appealed to the people to fully reject the proxy and camouflaged campaign strategy of the Congress party and give a clear majority to the BJP to form a stable and pro-people government.

891. (12-5-2007) NEW DELHI : Speaking at the Florence Nightingale Awards for Nursing Personnel today, the Health And Family Welfare Minister, Dr. Anbumani Ramados said that under the National Rural Health Mission project, the country requires about 2 lakh nursing personnel to provide comprehensive health care. In order to achieve the requirements of NRHM, State Governments have been advised to enhance the capacity of the ANMs and GNMs by establishing additional nursing training institutions. Welcoming the outstanding personalities of nursing profession from all over the country who have come to receive the award, he said, undoubtedly, it is your hard work, commitment and perseverance that has brought you all to this stage of achievement and helped to bag the prestigious national award. The Minister said that said that way back in 1989, the last National Award function was held. I feel proud to announce that His Excellency Dr. APJ Abdul Kalam have conferred to revive this achievement awards once again and I consider myself fortunate for organizing this ceremony in its own grace and also to name it as "Florence Nightingale Award". His Excellency Dr. A P J Abdul Kalam the President of India, presented the awards To seventeen nursing personnel for their meritorious services. Smt. Panabaka Lakshmi, Minister of State, Shri Naresh Dayal, Secretary Health and Family Welfare were also present at the function.

892. (12-5-2007) NEW DELHI : Nursing Services in India have expanded considerably since Independence. Along with this expansion a diversification in nursing services in the medical care field has also taken place. Great imbalances in the manpower situation can be noticed as far as nursing is concerned. As compared to the developed countries, the nurse's population ratio in India is not adequate. In India there is one nurse to 2250 people while in the developed countries the number of people served by one nurse ranges from 150 to 200. Even developing countries like Indonesia, Kenya, Srilanka and Thailand have a better nurse population ratio. The nurse patient ratio, however, varies form 1:5 to 1:60 or 1:1000 in different Institutions. Nurses have a very vital role to play in the patient care service in a hospital. Their role is, indeed, noble. They provide succour and relief to the patients at all times and particularly in times of need. National Awards for Nurses are given as a mark of highest recognition for the meritorious services of the nurses and nursing profession in the country. Till the year 1989, 31 awards were allocated (18 for Nurses, 10 for Auxiliary Nurse Midwives and 3 for Lady Health Visitors). However, this Award could not be continued and has been revived from this year. One award is earmarked for each State/Union Territory subject to the availability of nursing personnel with meritorious services. Each award carries a Certificate of Merit and Cash award of Rs.50, 000/-. Today, on the occasion of birthday of Florence Nightingale, Hon'ble President of India presented the Awards to 17 Awardees selected by the Central Selection Committee. This day is celebrated all over the world as "International Nurses Day."

893. (12-5-2007) NEW DELHI : The Indian Meteorological Department has alerted the Board of Control for Cricket in India (BCCI) about the possible impact of rains which may affect the Indo-Bangladesh ODI and Test series which is currently going on in the hosting country. This was announced by Shri Kapil Sibal, Minister of Science & Technology and Earth Sciences while briefing the media here today. He informed that a letter has been duly sent to Shri Sharad Pawar, President of BCCI to this effect.

894. (12-5-2007) NEW DELHI : The two-week long XXX Antarctic Treaty Consultative Meeting (ATCM) concluded here yesterday. The meeting was inaugurated by the Minister for Science & Technology and Earth Sciences Shri Kapil Sibal on 30th April 2007 in which Prof. U.R. Rao, an eminent Indian Space Scientist and Former Chairman, Space Commission was elected as the Chairman of the XXX ATCM. The meeting during its two-week long delebrations concluded as follows: The Committee for Environmental Protection (CEP) after reviewing the revised draft Management Plans for two Antarctic Specially Managed Area (ASMA) of Larsemann Hills and Amundsen-Scott South Pole Station, referred them to ATCM, which were finally adopted by ATCM. The CEP, after reviewing, advised the ATCM that the draft Comprehensive Environmental Evaluation (CEE) of the new Indian Research Base at Larsemann Hills adequately meets the requirement, which was subsequently endorsed by ATCM. This clears the way for India to go ahead with development of a detailed plan of the Research Base at the site selected by India. In that direction, India will be finalizing the CEE of the new Base in next few months. This year more than 37000 tourists entered the Antarctic Treaty Area-an increase of about 14% over the last season. The meeting adopted a Resolution for regulation of ship-based tourism in the Antarctic waters. It also decided to address the safety issues in a more cohesive way. The issue of land-based tourism was discussed at length which if not regulated may lead to more than a minor or transitory impact on Antarctica. Some parties have raised concern about this and urged concrete steps need to be taken as limiting possible future development of tourist infrastructure in Antarctica.

895. (12-5-2007) NEW DELHI : Shri Sharad Pawar, Union Minister of Agriculture has said that there is urgent need for policies and programmes that can invigorate productivity in the farm sector. Presiding over the 78th Annual General Body meeting of the ICAR Society here today, Shri Pawar urged upon the agricultural scientists to prove that the 'kisan' is a force to reckon with and be a partner to achieve a higher growth rate in agriculture and food and nutritional security. The Minister opined that there is an urgency to shift from mono-cropping to horticulture and high value added crops. The decline of soil health due to deficiency of micronutrients and falling organic matter needs to be checked, he added. Shri Pawar also called for appropriate technological intervention covering cropping/ farming system models, integrated water and nutrients management and packages, resource conservation technologies, reclamation technologies for acidic and saline /alkaline and participatory management approaches. Pointing out the availability of huge area of waste land in the country, the Minister suggested that wide range of bio-fuel crops could be grown here. Delineating the achievements of the ICAR in areas like development of improved varieties and hybrids, quality seed production, better agricultural education, technical inputs for improving production and export of inland and marine fishery resources, Shri Pawar informed that "ICAR Guidelines for Intellectual Property Management and Technology transfer/commercialisation" has been approved by the Governing Body.

896. (12-5-2007) NEW DELHI : The Prime Minister said that I am happy to participate in the National Awards Function organized by the Ministry of Health and Family Welfare for recognizing the meritorious services of the nursing professionals in the country as a part of the International Nurses Day to rightly remember the great nurse Florence Nightingale. My congratulations to the award winners and greetings to the doctors, nurses, medical professionals and distinguished guests participating in this programme. In a hospital when no doctors, no relatives are around during night time, the nurses provide consolation and relief to the patients. At that time nurses appear to be divine lights to the patients in giving treatment and confidence. As children, we are all nursed by our mothers. I would like to share with you all, few thoughts on the topic "Let my care remove the Pain" As I am in the midst of nursing community, the legend of Florence Nightingale, the mother of nursing profession comes alive in my memory. She volunteered to work for three years in the battlefield taking care of thousands of wounded soldiers travelling from England to Turkey in a ship. She walked four miles every night among sick soldiers with a lamp for light. The grateful soldiers would kiss the shadow of Florence Nightingale as she passed by. She is definitely an example of "giving" for removing the pain of the suffering people. She opened the first nursing school and she wrote the first text book of nursing in 1860. She inspired many women to take to nursing as a respectable career. I particularly like her view on education. She says "education is to teach not to know, but to do". There is a big message for educationists from this statement. Now, I would like to share with you an experience, which I had in Tripura where care, compassion and technology allowed an young boy with a congenital heart disease to blossom.

897. (14-5-2007) NEW DELHI : Six Towns in the country namely Kottayam, Puri, Tirupati, Ujjain, Vrindavan and Thanjavour have been selected in the pilot phase of the Eco-City Programme. The projects undertaken under the pilot phase of the Programme for the respective towns are under various stages of implementation. The Programme which was initiated during the Tenth Five Year Plan is being continued during the first year of the Eleventh Plan. This Eco-City Programme was initiated by the Ministry of Environment and Forests in the Tenth Five Year Plan, which is being implemented by the Central Pollution Control Board (CPCB) through the concerned State Pollution Control Boards and Municipalities. The Programme has been conceptualized to improve the environment and bring in visible results through implementation of identified environmental improvement projects in the selected towns/cities. The specific objectives of the Programme are to identify the environmental problems in the selected towns through participatory approach to designi and prepare details of the prioritized environmental improvement projects; and to create landmarks that show visible environmental improvement. The Plan size including the schemes for implementation during the remaining years of the Eleventh Five Year Plan is not finalized as yet.

898. (14-5-2007) NEW DELHI : The Ministry of Environment and Forest is implementing Centrally Sponsored Integrated Forest Protection Scheme (IFPS). For the State of Madhya Pradesh, during the financial year 2006-2007. A sum of Rs. 79.19 lakhs was revalidated and an amount of Rs. 200 lakhs was released as Second instalment of work programme of 2005-2006 under IFPS. In addition, against the work programme of 2006-2007 a sum of Rs.125.00 lakhs was also released. Under the Centrally Sponsored Development of National Parks & Sanctuaries Scheme, technical and financial assistance is provided to the state governments as and when requests are received in the form of Annual Plan of Operations (APOs) from the states. For the State of Madhya Pradesh, during 2006-07 out of total unspent balance of Rs. 132.451 lakhs of 2005-06, Rs. 123.633 lakh were revalidated against the approved items and Rs. 8.818 lakh were adjusted against the amount released during 2006-07. In addition, Rs.759.46 lakhs has also been released against fresh APO to the various National Parks and Sanctuaries of the state during 2006-07. This information was given by the Minister of State in the Ministry of Environment and Forests, Shri Namo Narain Meena in a written reply to question by Shri Vijay Kumar Khandelwal and Shri Krishna Murari Moghe in the Lok Sabha today.

899. (14-5-2007) NEW DELHI : The State Government of Assam has constituted a Task Force for translocation of Rhinos. Three meetings of the Task force have already been convened for finalizing the re-introduction programme. Necessary action for the recruitment of frontline staff is under process. The estimated cost of the project is Rs. 1,54,04,954.00 against which Rs. 30,77,100.00 has been spent so far. This information was given by the Minister of State in the Ministry of Environment and Forests, Shri Namo Narain Meena in a written reply to question by Shri M.K. Subba in the Lok Sabha today.

900. (14-5-2007) NEW DELHI : The Karnataka Government has submitted 11 towns under National River Conservation Plan (NRCP). These proposals are: Bagalkot, Maddur, Gokak, Baillahongol, Shahbad, Hospet, Gangawati, Kanakpura, Yadgir, Dandeli, Siraguppa. Subsequently, the State Government submitted proposal for Madikeri town in lieu of Gokak. Due to funds constrains, these proposals could not be considered and the State Government of Karnataka had been informed accordingly. In March 2006, the State Government submitted one more proposal namely, Soundatti town, which was rejected as it did not satisfy the criteria stipulated under NRCP. This was communicated to the State Government. This information was given by the Minister of State in the Ministry of Environment and Forests, Shri Namo Narain Meena in a written reply to question by Shri Iqbal Ahmed Saradgi in the Lok Sabha today.

901. (14-5-2007) NEW DELHI : The Associated Chamber of Commerce and Industry (ASSOCHAM) of India came out with a forecast paper on "Aftermath of commonwealth games 2010" and a paper entitled "set up CNG stations in NCR". It also brought out a press statement on "Solid waste management and its disposal" recently. The forecast paper has projected that the Commonwealth event is likely to provide, opportunities in various sectors, possible medical and eco-tourism and highlights the initiatives in construction /upgradation of Games villages, flyovers, roads etc. The ASSOCHAM analysis suggests that a multi-pronged strategy be evolved for more CNG stations and wider distribution of CNG in Delhi and NCR. The paper on "Solid waste management and its disposal" emphasizes the need for a National Waste Policy, highlights Kerala state special purpose vehicle which integrates 60 municipalities to generate power from solid waste and the need to commit resources, involve the community and private entrepreneurs to work with the local government for proper management of solid waste. A set of rules entitled Municipal Solid Waste (Management & Handling) Rules, 2000 has been notified by the Ministry under the Environment (Protection) Act, 1986 to ensure proper collection, transportation and disposal of solid waste generated in the country. This information was given by the Minister of State in the Ministry of Environment and Forests, Shri Namo Narain Meena in a written reply to question by Shri Milind Deora in the Lok Sabha today.

902. (14-5-2007) NEW DELHI : Based on the results of the written part of Civil Services (Main) Examination, 2006 held by the Union Public Service Commission in October-November, 2006 and the interviews for Personality Test held in April-May, 2007, following is the list, in order of merit, of candidates who have been recommended for appointment to the: 'Indian Administrative Service', 'Indian Foreign Service', 'Indian Police Service'; and 'Central Services, Group 'A' and Group 'B'.' A total number of 474 candidates have been recommended for appointment including 214 General (including 13 Physically Challenged candidates), 144 Other Backward Classes (including 03 Physically challenged candidates), 80 Scheduled Castes (including 02 Physically challenged candidates) and 36 Scheduled Tribes candidates. Appointment to the various Services will be made according to the number of vacancies available with due consideration to the provisions contained in Rules 2 and 19 of the Rules of the Examination and subject to the final decision of the Supreme Court/ High Court /C.A.Ts. on the S.L.Ps. /R.As /W.Ps. O.As. pending therein. The number of vacancies reported by the Government for the Indian Administrative Service is 89 (45 General, 24 Other Backward Classes, 13 Scheduled Castes and 07 Scheduled Tribes); for the Indian Foreign Service is 20 (10 General, 05 Other Backward Classes and 05 Scheduled Castes); for the Indian Police Service is 103 (51 General, 28 Other Backward Classes, 16 Scheduled Castes and 08 Scheduled Tribes); for the Central Services Group 'A' is 294 (152 General, 80 Other Backward Classes, 43 Scheduled Castes and 19 Scheduled Tribes) and for Central Services Group 'B' is 27 (15 General, 07 Other Backward Classes, 03 Scheduled Caste and 02 Scheduled Tribe). This includes 18 vacancies for Physically Challenged candidates in the Indian Administrative Service and Central Services Group-"A"& "B". In accordance with Rule 16 (4) & (5) of the Civil Services Examination Rules 2006, the Commission is maintaining a consolidated Reserve List of 116 candidates which includes 58 General, 41 Other Backward Classes and 15 Scheduled Caste and 02 Scheduled Tribes candidate ranking in order of merit below the last recommended candidate under respective category. UPSC has a "Facilitation Counter" near Examination Hall in its campus. Candidates can obtain any information/clarification regarding their examinations / recruitments on the working days between 1000 hours to 1700 hours in person or over telephone Nos. 23385271 / 23381125/23098543. Result will also be available on the U.P.S.C. website *i.e.* http//www.upsc.gov.in. However, marks on the website will be available after 15 days from the date of declaration of result.

903. (14-5-2007) NEW DELHI : The funds under Sarva Shiksha Abhiyan (SSA) are sanctioned by the Government of India based on the Annual Work Plan and Budget of the respective State. The size of funding is decided on the basis of norms laid down in the Framework for Implementation of SSA, the requirements projected in the State plan including the State share provided in the State Government's annual budget. An outlay of Rs. 12198.37 lakh has been approved by the Government of India for implementation of SSA including the National Programme for Education of Girls at Elementary Level and Kasturba Gandhi Balika Vidyalaya schemes in Himachal Pradesh for the year 2007-08. The Gross Enrolment Ratio is 108.90 for primary level and 108.50 for upper primary level. The girls enrolment is 48% of total enrolment. The dropout rate for primary level is 7.74 and for elementary level 15.89. The teacher pupil ratio for primary is 1:21 and for upper primary 1:17. The Government of India has not received any complaint of diversion of funds allocated for the implementation of SSA in Himachal Pradesh. The achievements made by Himachal Pradesh under SSA are annexed. This information was given by the Minister of State for Human Resource Development, Shri M.A.A. Fatmi in a written reply in the Rajya Sabha today.

904. (14-5-2007) NEW DELHI : The samples of poultry and ducks from Matigara, Darjeeling District in West Bengal & Kuttanad in Kerala have tested negative for Avian Influenza (H5 & H7) as per report received from High Animal Security Disease laboratory (HSADL), Bhopal. Unusual mortality in birds had recently been reported from these two places. In Matigara, unusual mortality was reported from Aziz poultry farm, resulting in death of 2500 birds on 5-6th May, 2007. A team headed by Deputy Director (AH) reached the farm on 07.05.07. The dead birds found at site were buried under the supervision of the team following proper procedure. Postmortem revealed Newcastle disease (Ranikhet) with Infectious Bursal Disease (IBD) (Gumboro). Samples were sent to HSADL, Bhopal, which have been tested negative for Avian Influenza (H5&H7). No further unusual mortality has been reported from Matigara. In Kuttanad, reports had been received about the death of about 2000 ducks in five days in some villages on 27.04.07. The Scientists of Avian Disease Diagnostic Laboratory, Thiruvalla along with a team of veterinarians visited the sites and conducted detailed examination and autopsy on the duck carcasses. The samples were collected and sent to HSADL, Bhopal, which have been tested negative for Avian Influenza (H5&H7). No further unusual mortality has been reported from Kuttanad.

905. (14-5-2007) NEW DELHI : In reply to a question whether the Government have provided the 20,000 Maulana Azad Merit-cum-Means Scholarships as announced by the Finance Minister to the Minorities during the last Budget, the

Minority Affairs Minister, Shri A.R. Antulay informed the house today that a scheme for 20,000 scholarships called the merit-cum-means based scholarship to students belonging to minority communities has been formulated and a provision of Rs.54.00 crore has been made for it this year.

906. (14-5-2007) NEW DELHI : A section of media has carried a news report stating that the RSS has urged the Government to table in Parliament the report of the Mukherjee Commission which went into the issue of disappearance of Netaji Subhash Chandra Bose. In this connection, it is clarified that the report of the Mukherjee Commission was tabled in Parliament on 17th May, 2006 along with the action taken report. Its copies were widely distributed to media. The report is also available on the MHA's website, "http://mha.nic.in".

907. (14-5-2007) NEW DELHI : The Union Minority Affairs Minister Sh. A.R. Antulay has given details of grants given by Maulana Azad Education Foundation during the last five years in reply to a question in the Rajya Sabha today.

908. (14-5-2007) NEW DELHI : The Ministry of Rural Development implement and monitor its programmes through the State Governments, District Rural Development Agencies/Zila Parishads and other implementing agencies. The DRDA/Zila Parishads coordinate with the various line departments at the district level in preparing action plan as per the available resources and need of the district and monitors the implementation of rural development programmes through various existing monitoring mechanism stipulated in the programme guidelines. The general problems in the implementation of some schemes are mainly on account of delay in preparation of shelf of projects, shortage of officials at different levels, geographical locations of districts and delay in release of matching share by a few States etc. This was stated by the Minister of State in the Ministry of Rural Development, Smt. Suryakanta Patil in reply to a question in the Lok Sabha.

909. (14-5-2007) NEW DELHI : The Members of Parliament (Lok Sabha) have been nominated as Chairmen or Co-Chairmen of the District Level Vigilance & Monitoring Committees (V&MCs). Members of Parliament from Rajya Sabha have also been associated as Co-chairman of District Level V&MCs. Instructions have been issued to the State Governments and District Administrations that the logistics and infrastructural facilities required for the functioning of the District V&MCs may be provided by the District Administration from the facilities already available at the District Headquarters. This was stated by the Minister of State in the Ministry of Rural Development, Smt. Suryakanta Patil in reply to a question in the Lok Sabha.

910. (14-5-2007) NEW DELHI : In reply to a question whether any decision has been taken so far in the matter of establishment of Fluorosis Mitigation Centre (FMC) in the country, the Minister of State in the Ministry of Rural Development, Shri Chandra Sekhar Sahu informed that it has been decided to set up Regional

Fluorosis Mitigation Centres at Gandhinagar and Hyderabad by way of upgradation of existing Institutions. In this regard, the respective State Governments have been requested to send their detailed proposals for strengthening the identified institutions. This information was given by the Minister in reply to a question in the Lok Sabha.

911. (14-5-2007) NEW DELHI : A ban has also been imposed on grant of emigration clearance to women below the age of 30 years if they are seeking employment as housemaids/domestic workers in any ECR (Emigration Check Required) country. This was stated by Smt. Renuka Chowdhury, Minister for Women and Child Development in a reply to a question by Dr. Prabha Thakur in Rajya Sabha today.

912. (14-5-2007) NEW DELHI : The Ministry of Women and Child Development is implementing a scheme namely, 'An Integrated programme for Street Children' for prevention of destitution and withdrawal of children from a life on the street. The scheme provides shelter, nutrition, health care, sanitation and hygiene, safe drinking water, education and recreational facilities and protection against abuse and exploitation to these children. The number of beneficiaries during last three years is available on website of the Ministry, viz. www.wcd.nic.in.

913. (14-5-2007) NEW DELHI : The Ministry of Women and Child Development is implementing a Centrally Sponsored Progrmme for Juvenile Justice under which grant-in-aid is provided to the State Government/UT administrations to meet 50% of their expenditure requirements for construction and maintenance of homes under the Juvenile Justice (Care and Protection of Children) Act, 2000 and upkeep of the children staying in these homes. This was stated by Smt. Renuka Chowdhury, Minister for Women and Child Development in a reply to a question by Shri Badiga Ramakrishna and Shri Mahavir Bhagora in Lok Sabha today.

914. (14-5-2007) NEW DELHI : The Government has been receiving representations from trade unions for abolition or enhancement of the eligibility limit and calculation ceilings under the Bonus Act, 1965. A proposal regarding amendment to the Payment of Bonus Act, 1965 to enhance eligibility limit of Bonus from Rs. 3,500/- per month to Rs. 7,500/- per month and calculation ceiling from Rs. 2,500/- per month to Rs. 3,500/- per month as per recommendation of the Second National Commission on Labour (NCL) was deliberated in the 41st Session of Indian Labour Conference (ILC) held from 27-28th April, 2007 in New Delhi. After the deliberations, the increase in calculation ceiling from Rs. 2,500/- per month to Rs. 3,500/- per month has been unanimously agreed by all the stakeholders. However, the proposal to increase the eligibility limit from Rs. 3,500/- per month to a suitable level higher than Rs. 7,500/- per month or to Rs. 10,000/- per month as agreed by stake holders other than employers, is under consideration of the Government. Given the procedures/steps involved and related financial implications, it is not possible, at present, to specify a definite timeframe for carrying out the amendment to the Act. The number of persons likely to be covered cannot be estimated as the Payment of Bonus Act, 1965 is applicable to every factory and every other establishment in which twenty or more persons are employed on any day during an accounting year. This was stated by the Minister of State (Independent Charge) for Labour and Employment, Shri Oscar Fernandes in written reply in the Lok Sabha today.

915. (14-5-2007) NEW DELHI : In the Tenth Five Year Plan, total 50 million employment opportunities were projected to be generated. Nearly 20 million employment opportunities were projected to be crated by selective innovative programmes and policy leading to a changed pattern of growth in favour of labour intensive sectors; remaining 30 million were projected to come from the normal buoyancy of growth. As per two most recent quinquennial rounds of National Sample Survey Organisation (NSSO) survey on employment and unemployment, employment opportunities on Current Daily status basis were estimated at 337.20 million in 1999-2000 (55th round) which has gone up to 382.66 million in 2004-05 (61st round). Thus, 45.46 million employment opportunities over a period of 5 years have been generated. This was stated by the Minister of State (Independent Charge) for Labour and Employment, Shri Oscar Fernandes in written reply in the Lok Sabha today.

916. (14-5-2007) NEW DELHI : Vocational training is provided to about 7.42 lakh trainees in 107 trades every year through a network of 5114 Industrial Training Institutes/Centres. Government has taken steps to upgrade 400 Government ITIs into Centres of Excellence with the World Bank assistance. 100 ITIs have been taken up for upgradation through domestic funding and the remaining 1396 Government ITIs are being upgraded in a Public Private Partnership mode at a cost of Rs. 2.50 crore per ITI being provided by the Central Government as interest free loan. About 2.53 lakh apprentices are trained every year in 154 trades under Apprentices Act, 1961 to meet the demand of skilled manpower in the country. There is no proposal under the consideration of the Government to import skilled and trained manpower to work on projects in India nor is there any specific policy in force on hiring foreign labour and workers by the Indian companies. This was stated by the Minister of State (Independent Charge) for Labour and Employment, Shri Oscar Fernandes in written reply in the Lok Sabha today.

917. (14-5-2007) NEW DELHI : Following are the Opening Remarks of the Prime Minister, Dr. Manmohan Singh at the Full Planning Commission meeting, here today: "I have been looking forward to this meeting of the Planning Commission which gives us an opportunity to discuss issues related to agriculture as a prelude to the meeting of the NDC on 29th May. When our Government came to power in May 2004, we emphasized the importance of reversing the prolonged slowdown in agriculture witnessed after 1996 which in turn had led to growing rural-urban imbalances and also to acute rural distress in some areas. When we met last in October 2006 to finalise the Approach Paper to the XI Plan, while we were ambitious in setting a growth rate of 10% for the economy, we were also aware of the areas of concern. There were concerns regarding the levels of poverty, concerns regarding the poor performance of agriculture, concerns regarding the need to generate employment and the persisting regional disparities. In many ways, these problems are inter-related and if we are able to improve the growth rate of agriculture, we would be mitigating the other problems to some extent. At less than 2%, poor agricultural growth is a cause of rural distress. This meeting has been called with a view to focusing on specific strategies to improve the short term and medium term performance of this vital sector which still continues to support almost 2/3rd of our rural population. We have already taken a number of initiatives to deal with the problem. These include actions aimed at dealing with the immediate problem of suicide prone districts. We have also launched the National Horticulture Mission, established the National Rainfed Area Authority, the National Fisheries Development Board, and increased the Plan allocation in agriculture. However, these efforts need to be expanded into a broader based strategy for agricultural revitalization. The Approach to the XI Plan proposed a target of doubling the rate of growth of agriculture from less than 2% between 1996 and 2004 to 4% per annum. This is a key element of the strategy for inclusive growth and we have repeatedly stated that it will not come from following a purely business as usual approach. Recognising this, the NDC, when it approved the Approach Paper last year, also set up a Committee under the chairmanship of the Agriculture Minister Shri Sharad Pawar Ji to present a strategy to achieve this objective. The NDC Committee has worked diligently on this subject, setting up several sub-Committees chaired by different Chief Ministers. The report of the NDC Committee, which has been circulated, draws on a number of other reports of expert groups and presents a broad agenda of the policy changes needed in agriculture. I would like to congratulate Shri Sharad Pawar Ji for his leadership in getting the NDC Committee to complete its work in a relatively short time. We must now use the Committee's recommendations to outline the agricultural strategy we propose to build into the Eleventh Plan. The Planning Commission has been interacting with the Ministry of Agriculture to come up with the main components of this strategy. Some of what needs to be done rests with the Central Government but much of it must be done by the States. We know that there are substantial yield gaps in all States-between yields actually achieved at the farm level, and the yields that are feasible given the agro-climatic constraints and the existing technology.

918. (14-5-2007) NEW DELHI : The Finance Minister of Fiji Sh. Mahendra Chaudhury called on the Tourism & Culture Minister Smt. Ambika Soni here today. During their half-an-hour meeting both the leaders discussed ways to boost tourism and culture ties between the two countries. The visiting Minister said that there is a an increase in tourist traffic from India to Fiji and to boost it further he held a fruitful meeting with Indian tour operators and is hopeful that they will promote tourism in Fiji through package tours. Shri Chaudhury said air connectivity between the two countries is an area where improvement is required. He said his

Government is keen to invite Indian investors in hotel and hospitals sectors and currently negotiating with some big names in India in these two sectors. Smt. Soni stressed the need to promote tourism between the two countries through package tours.

919. (14-5-2007) NEW DELHI : Foreign Direct Investment (FDI) upto 100% on the automatic route is permitted in Floriculture, Horticulture, Development of Seeds, Animal Husbandry, Pisciculture, Aquaculture, Cultivation of vegetables and mushrooms, under controlled conditions and services related to agro and allied sectors. FDI upto 100% with prior Government approval is also permitted in tea plantation subject to divestment of 26% equity in favour of Indian partner / Indian public within a period of five years; and prior approval of the State Government concerned in case of any future land use change. Besides the above, FDI is not allowed in any other agriculture sector/activity. This information was given in the Lok Sabha today by Shri Kanti Lal Bhuria, Minister of State for Agriculture in written reply.

920. (14-5-2007) NEW DELHI : Bio-control agents are emerging as an important component of Integrated Pest Management which is the cardinal Principle of Pest Control. Though they are eco-safe products, can not be a complete alternative to chemical pesticides. To promote biological control as an important component of Integrated Pest Management (IPM), Government of India is implementing a Scheme "Strengthening & Modernization of Pest Management Approach in India" since 1991-92. Under this, 31 Central IPM Centres are functioning with the objectives of pest/disease monitoring, production and release of bio-control agents/ bio-pesticides, conservation of bio-control agents and Human Resource Development in IPM. The use of bio-control agents is promoted through awareness creation among farmers/State extension functionaries by organizing series of Farmers Field Schools. Since 1994-95 to 2005-06, CIPMCs have produced and released 25385 millions of bio-control agents in the farmers' fields covering an area of 77.88 lakh hectares. For promotion of biological control, Government of India is providing Grants-in-aid to States/UTs/NGOs for setting up of production facilities of biological control agents. This information was given in the Lok Sabha today by Shri Kanti Lal Bhuria, Minister of State for Agriculture in written reply.

921. (14-5-2007) NEW DELHI : The Department of Agriculture and Cooperation has launched a Centrally Sponsored Scheme of National Bamboo Mission for implementation across the country during the year 2006-07. Altogether 14 proposals were received in this Department from the States of Arunachal Pradesh, Assam, Chhattisgarh, Meghalaya, Manipur, Mizoram, Nagaland (2 proposals), Orissa, Rajasthan, Sikkim, Tripura, Uttarakhand and West Bengal for promotion of Bamboo during 2006-07. These proposals were duly considered by the National Steering Committee of the Mission it its meetings held on 27th February and 19th March, 2007 and approved the same. The proposals involve various components namely nurseries, area expansion, human resource development, pest and disease management, micro-irrigation, etc. This information was given in the Lok Sabha today by Shri Kanti Lal Bhuria, Minister of State for Agriculture in written reply.

922. (14-5-2007) NEW DELHI : The Government has set up six Agri Export Zones (AEZs) in the country for development of floriculture and promotion of exports. These AEZs are in the States of Tamil Nadu (two AEZs) one in Dharmapuri district and another in Nilgiris district, one AEZ in Maharashtra covering the districts on Pune, Nasik, Kohlapur and Sangli, one AEZ in Karnataka covering the districts of Bangalore Urban, Bangalore Rural, Belgaum, Kolar, Kodagu and Urban, Bangalore Rural, Belgaum, Kolar, Kodagu and Tumkur, one AEZ in Sikkim covering East Sikkim district and one AEZ in Uttarakhand covering the districts of Dehradun, Pant Nagar, Udham Singh Nagar, Nainital and Uttarkashi. In addition, the Government is implementing various schemes for the development of horticultural crops including floriculture. Under the Centrally Sponsored Schemes of (i) Technology Mission for Integrated Development of Horticulture in North Eastern States (TMNE) including Sikkim, Himachal Pradesh, Jammu & Kashmir and Uttarkhand, being implemented since 2001-02 and (ii) National Horticulture Mission, being implemented since 2005-06, assistance is provided to the farmers for cultivation of flowers. Besides, National Horticulture Board is also providing assistance under the Scheme of 'Development of Commercial Horticulture through Production and Post Harvest Management', in which flowers are also covered. This information was given in the Lok Sabha today by Shri Kanti Lal Bhuria, Minister of State for Agriculture in written reply.

923. (14-5-2007) NEW DELHI : The Government is promoting Integrated Nutrient Management (INM), which envisage soil test based balanced and judicious use of chemical fertilizers including secondary and micronutrients in conjunction with organic manures and bio-fertilizers under various schemes. The Government is providing financial assistance for strengthening/setting up of soil testing laboratories @ Rs. 10 lakhs through the Centrally Sponsored Scheme, Balances & Integrated Use of Fertilizers under Macro Management of Agriculture Scheme. The Government is also providing Rs. 50 lakhs for establishment of mechanized comport plants for conversion of biodegradable municipal solid waste into organic manure under the same scheme. There is no state-wise allocation of funds under the scheme, however, State Govts./Uts are implementing the scheme through their annual work plans. In addition, Government is also providing financial assistance @ Rs. 40 lakhs/unit for setting up of Fruits and vegetable waste compost, Rs. 20 lakhs for setting up of bio-fertilizer production units and Rs.1.50 lakhs for setting up of vermiculture hatcheries under Central Sector Scheme, National project of Organic Farming through Project proposals of the States. There is no indication of large scale degradation of soil fertility in the country. However, there are few instances of deterioration of soil fertility/certain nutrient deficiencies in some parts of the country, especially in Indo-Gangetic plains due to inadequate and imbalanced use of chemical fertilizers. This information was given in the Lok Sabha today by Shri Kanti Lal Bhuria, Minister of State for Agriculture in written reply.

924. (14-5-2007) NEW DELHI : In order to produce and supply seeds of brackishwater shrimp or freshwater prawn to farmers, hatcheries have been set up in various maritime States of the country. Besides, two hatcheries have been set up by Marine Products Export Development Authority (MPEDA) as independent societies in Andhra Pradesh and Orissa. There is no proposal for setting up of new hatcheries at present as the hatcheries set up in the private sector so far are able to meet the current demand of seed. The two freshwater prawn hatcheries under construction in Gujarat and Maharashtra with French assistance are to be completed by December, 2008. This information was given in the Lok Sabha today by Shri Taslimuddin, Minister of State for Agriculture in written reply.

925. (14-5-2007) NEW DELHI : Under the Basic Services to the Urban Poor (BSUP) component of the Jawaharlal Nehru National Urban Renewal Mission (JNNURM), during the year 2006-07, the total Central share approved for the 151 projects, which include housing development as well as infrastructure projects, was Rs. 4435.93 crore. Out of this amount the funds released by the Ministry of finance was Rs. 901.77 crore. The total number of dwelling units covered in these projects was 435564. This was stated by the Minister of State (Independent Charge) for Housing and Urban Poverty Alleviation, Kumari Selja in a reply to a question by Shri Su. Thirunavukkarasar in the Rajya Sabha today. She further stated that under the Integrated Housing & Slum Development Programme (IHSDP) component of the JNNURM), for the cities other than the Mission cities, during the year 2006-07, the total Central share approved for the 194 projects, which include housing development as well as infrastructure projects, was Rs. 1404.57 crore. Out of this amount the funds released by the Ministry of Finance was Rs. 492.61 crore. The total number of dwelling units covered in these projects was 143557. The Central funds released to the States/UTs during 2006-07 under the urban poverty alleviation scheme of Swarna Jayanti Shahari Rozgar Yojana (SJSRY), implemented by the Ministry of Housing & urban Poverty Alleviation since 1.12.1997, were Rs. 248.68 crore. The beneficiaries under the Scheme during 2006-07, as reported by the States/UTs through Quarterly Progress Reports (QPRs), are as under: Number of urban poor assisted to set up individual/group micro-enterprises- 56357 Number of urban poor imparted skill training- 73203 Number of Mandays of work generated under wage employment- 26.95 lakh Under the Scheme of 'projects under 10% lumpsum provision for the North Eastern Region including Sikkim', under which projects related to housing (predominantly for the urban poor), slum development and poverty alleviation are executed in the North Eastern States including Sikkim, during 2006-07, Rs. 50 crore were released to various executing agencies for new/ongoing projects. However, as the scheme targets for overall development of the region, the exact number of beneficiaries under the scheme can not be quantified. Under Valmiki Ambedkar Awas Yojana (VAMBAY), during 2006-07, Rs. 10.69 crore were release to the executing agencies for various ongoing projects. Total number of dwelling units and toilets covered under these projects were 21511 and 249 respectively.

926. (14-5-2007) NEW DELHI : During the course of implementation of the Scheme of Swarna Jayanti Shahari Rozgar Yojana (SJSRY), it was observed that there was a need to have a relook at the guidelines of the scheme and certain modifications would be required to enhance the effectiveness of the scheme in tackling the issue of urban poverty. Accordingly, proposals were formulated for the modifications in the Guidelines of Swarna Jayanti Shahari Rozgar Yojana. The major changes proposed were regarding enhancement in project cost ceiling for individual micro-enterprises under Urban Self Employment Programme (USEP) component, increase in average per capita expenditure for skill training, change in funding pattern of the Scheme from 75:25 (Centre : State) to 90:10 for the special category North Eastern and hilly States, removal of educational limit prescribed for the self-employment component, reducing the minimum group Members required to form Development of Women & Children in Urban Areas (DWCUA) Groups from 10 to 5, enhancing the Administrative Expenditure limits, etc. This was stated by the Minister of State (Independent Charge) for Housing and Urban Poverty Alleviation, Kumari Selja in a reply to a question by Smt. N.P. Durga in the Rajya Sabha today. She further stated that as per the prescribed procedure, Expenditure Finance Committee (EFC) appraised these proposals in its Meeting held on 8th August, 2005 and approved the same. However, it was subsequently decided to continue the Scheme of SJSRY, in its present form, during the 10th Plan period and for continuing this scheme into the 11th Plan, an evaluation needs to be done. Evaluation study has since been completed, she added.

927. (14-5-2007) NEW DELHI : The provisions of the Indian Penal Code, 1860, apply to all offences, punishable under the Code, whether committed by way of ragging or otherwise. The Supreme Court of India had constituted a Committee under Dr. R.K. Raghavan to suggest measures to check incidents of ragging and suicide in the educational institutions. The Committee has since submitted its report to the Hon'ble Supreme Court for consideration. This information was given by the Minister of State for Human Resource Development, Smt. D. Prandeswari in a written reply in the Rajya Sabha today.

928. (14-5-2007) NEW DELHI : The funds are not allocated to the State Governments but directly to the following institutions namely to the Central Universities through the University Grants Commission (UGC), Indira Gandhi National Open University (IGNOU), Indian Institutes of Technology (IITs), Indian Institute of Information Technology & Management (IITM), Gwalior; Indian Institute of Information Technology (IIIT), Allahabad; Indian Institute of Information Technology (IIIT), Jabalpur; National Institutes of Technology (NITs); National Institute of Industrial Engineering (NITIE), Mumbai; National Institute of Foundry & Forge Technology (NIFFT), Ranchi; National Institute of Technical Teachers Training and Research (NITTTRs); School of Planning & Architecture (SPA), New Delhi; Indian School of Mines (ISM), Dhanbad; Community Polytechnics;

Sant Longowal Institute of Engineering & Technology (SLIET); Indian Institutes of Management (IIMs) and Indian Institute of Science (IISc), Bangalore. This allocation is intended for benefiting students belonging to the two categories enrolled in these institutions. Ordinarily, the annual provision in the budget is utilized by these institutions. This information was given by the Minister of State for Human Resource Development, Smt. D. Prandeswari in a written reply in the Rajya Sabha today.

929. (14-5-2007) NEW DELHI : According to 2001 Census the literacy rate of scheduled castes was 54.69% as against the national average of 64.84%. Whereas the increase in the overall literacy rate of the country during 1991-2001 was only 12.63%, the increase in the literacy rate of scheduled castes during the same period was 17.28%. The Universalization of Elementary Education and eradication of adult illiteracy form the two-pronged strategy for improving the literacy rate of the country. Sarva Shiksha Abhiyan (SSA) is a comprehensive programme for universalizing quality Elementary Education by 2010. The SSA promotes diverse strategies, specially targeting scheduled caste children. The SSA seeks to develop context specific interventions to tackle the problems of education of scheduled caste children.

930. (14-5-2007) NEW DELHI : The Government has launched a Pilot Scheme for "National Project for Repair, Renovation & Restoration of Water Bodies directly linked to Agriculture" in January 2005. The water bodies having culturable command area of more than 40 hectares and upto 2000 hectares are included under the Scheme in one or two districts each in States: The restoration of 1098 water bodies has been approved in 26 districts of 15 States under the Scheme at a cost of Rs.299.9155 crore to be shared by Centre and State in the ratio of 3:1. As announced in the Budget Speech for 2006-07 of the Hon'ble Finance Minister, it has been decided that the expansion of the Scheme at national level will be with external funding in the XIth Plan. The funding pattern of the Scheme will be 75% as World Bank loan by State Government and 25% as Central subsidy. This information was given by the Minister of State for Water Resources, Shri Jai Prakash Narayan Yadav in response to a question by Shri Anandrao V. Adsul, Shri Ravi Prakash Verma and Shri Adhalrao Patil Shivajirao in the Lok Sabha today.

931. (14-5-2007) NEW DELHI : Irrigation is one of the basic inputs for agriculture. However, the agriculture is dependent on many other factors such as seeds, extension services & marketing, watershed development, credit facilities etc. There has been a gradual increase in the plan outlay for the irrigation sector over the different plan periods. The total expenditure for major & medium irrigation and minor irrigation during the First plan was Rs. 441.86 crore and the outlay for the Tenth Plan for major & medium and minor irrigation was Rs.84734.64 crore. However, the public investment in irrigation sector as percentage of the total plan investment exhibit decline over time. Irrigation being a State subject, irrigation projects are conceived, planned and implemented by the State Governments as per their own priority. The National Common Minimum Programme (NCMP) states that irrigation will receive the highest investment priority and all on-going projects will be completed according to a strict time schedule and that water management in all its aspects, both for irrigation and drinking purposes will receive urgent attention. The Government of India provides central assistance to the State Governments for completion of on-going irrigation projects under the Accelerated Irrigation Benefit Programme (AIBP). The AIBP criteria have been relaxed and procedures simplified to cover more projects under this programme. Further, the draft Approach Paper for XI Plan also envisages to double the rate of growth of irrigated area and to improve water management, rainwater harvesting and watershed development. This information was given by the Minister of State for Water Resources, Shri Jai Prakash Narayan Yadav in response to a question by Shri Balashowry Vallabhaneni in the Lok Sabha today.

932. (14-5-2007) NEW DELHI : Studies carried out by the Central Ground Water Board (CGWB), under the Ministry of Water Resources have indicated the problem of salinity in ground water in various parts of the country. CGWB monitors ground water quality at regional scale through a network of over 15000 observation wells throughout the country. The salinity of water varies from area to area even within a State and hence no State-wise ranking is done. Salinity in ground water is of two types viz. inland salinity, wherein, fresh water floats over saline water and coastal salinity. Inland salinity has been noticed in parts of Andhra Pradesh, NCT of Delhi, Gujarat, Haryana, Kerala, Madhya Pradesh, Orissa, Rajasthan, Tamil Nadu, Uttar Pradesh and West Bengal. While, salinity in coastal aquifers has been noticed in parts of Goa, Gujarat, Karnataka, Kerala, Maharashtra, Tamil Nadu, Andaman & Nicobar Islands, Diu and Pondicherry. 'Water' being a State subject, it is the responsibility of the concerned State Governments to plan, finance and execute schemes to desalinate water. Ministry of Water Resources has not received any proposal for technical assistance in the matter from the States. However, the Ministry of Rural Development (Department of Drinking Water Supply) provides financial and technical assistance to States through a Centrally Sponsored Schemes, namely Accelerated Rural Water Supply Programme (ARWSP), for supply of drinking water as per the stipulated norms. 20% of ARWSP funds is retained at the Centre and released to States on need-basis to tackle water quality problems. To ensure safe drinking water supply to all the urban population of the country, the Ministry of Urban Development have launched two new programmes, viz. Jawaharlal Nehru National Urban Renewal Mission (JNNURM) and Urban Infrastructure Development Scheme for Small and Medium Towns (UIDSSMT), to provide infrastrcture facilities to 5161 urban towns of the country. The project envisages to provide safe drinking water to every citizen of India within a time frame of 7 years. This information was given by the Minister of State for Water Resources, Shri Jai Prakash Narayan Yadav in response to a question by Subrata Bose in the Lok Sabha today.

933. (14-5-2007) NEW DELHI : The Sardar Sarovar Dam was originally scheduled for completion by January, 1998 according to the Revised Implementation Schedule, December, 1989 of Sardar Sarovar Narmada Nigam Limited. Due to the pendency of Writ Petition (Civil) No.319/1994 in the Hon'ble Supreme Court filed by the Namada Bachao Andolan, the work on main dam remained suspended since 1995. The writ petition was disposed off by the Hon'ble Supreme Court in October 2000 and permitted further raising of the dam up to 90.0 m and Narmada Control Authority (NCA) was directed to prepare an action plan for further raising of the dam pari-passu with completion of Resettlement and Rehabilitation (R&R) and environmental safeguard measures. Accordingly, NCA formulated an action plan for further raising of the dam according to which, the dam was scheduled to be completed up to Full Reservoir Level (FRL) of 138.68 m by June 2005. However, owing to slow progress of Resettlement and Rehabilitation of project affected persons, the dam could be raised up to 121.92 m only by the end of December, 2006. The estimated cost of the Sardar Sarovar Project as approved by the Planning Commission at 1986-87 price level was Rs.6406.04 crore. According to the State Government of Gujarat, the estimated cost of the project at 2005-06 price level is Rs. 33822.60 crore. This information was given by the Minister of State for Water Resources, Shri Jai Prakash Narayan Yadav in response to a question by Shri Harin Pathak, Shri Harilal Madhavaji Bhai Patel, Shri Madhusudan Mistry and Shri Mahesh Kanodia in the Lok Sabha today.

934. (14-5-2007) NEW DELHI : Placed below is the provisional Customs & Central Excise Revenue collection for the month of April 2007 along with the comparative data for the corresponding period of the previous year and growth rate over previous year.

935. (14-5-2007) NEW DELHI : In order to produce and supply seeds of brackishwater shrimp or freshwater prawn to farmers, hatcheries have been set up in various maritime States of the country. Besides, two hatcheries have been set up by Marine Products Export Development Authority (MPEDA) as independent societies in Andhra Pradesh and Orissa. There is no proposal for setting up of new hatcheries at present as the hatcheries set up in the private sector so far are able to meet the current demand of seed. The two freshwater prawn hatcheries under construction in Gujarat and Maharashtra with French assistance are to be completed by December, 2008. This information was given in the Lok Sabha today by Shri Taslimuddin, Minister of State for Agriculture in written reply.

936. (14-5-2007) NEW DELHI : The Ministry of Rural Development has released Rs. 75.00 crore as part payment of second instalment of the ADB assisted projects – RRSIP-Batch-II under Pradhan Mantri Gram Sadak Yojana (PMGSY) to Chhattisgarh Rural Road Development Agency (CGRRDA), which is the autonomous agency for receiving funds under the programme. The grant is towards the Plan expenditure and will be subject to the conditions laid down from time to time in the guidelines of the PMGSY and supplementary directions. The

Pradhan Mantri Gram Sadak Yojana aims to provide all-weather basic access to about 1.72 lakh habitations of population of 500 or more (250 or more in Hill States (including North East), desert and tribal areas). PMGSY roads are constructed to high technical standards and backed by 5 year maintenance contracts. The construction cost is fully borne by the Government of India as a Centrally sponsored Scheme, while the State Governments are responsible for providing maintenance funds.

937. (14-5-2007) NEW DELHI : The Ministry of Rural Development has released Rs.65.00 crore as part payment of second instalment for Phase V of Pradhan Mantri Gram Sadak Yojana (PMGSY) to Assam State Road Board (ASRB), Guwahati, which is the autonomous agency for receiving funds under the programme. The grant is towards the Plan expenditure and will be subject to the conditions laid down from time to time in the guidelines of the PMGSY and supplementary directions. The Pradhan Mantri Gram Sadak Yojana aims to provide all-weather basic access to about 1.72 lakh habitations of population of 500 or more (250 or more in Hill States (including North East), desert and tribal areas). PMGSY roads are constructed to high technical standards and backed by 5 year maintenance contracts. The construction cost is fully borne by the Government of India as a Centrally sponsored Scheme, while the State Governments are responsible for providing maintenance funds.

938. (14-5-2007) NEW DELHI : Grant-in-aid amounting to Rs.8.11 lakh has been released by the Ministry of Rural Development to the District Rural Development Agency of Union Territory of Pondicherry towards part payment of first instalment of Central Share for the year 2007-08 under DRDA Administration. The funding pattern under the scheme is 75:25 between Centre and the State. The utilization of funds is to be in accordance with the DRDA administration guidelines and the release of the second instalment during 2007-08 is subject to the fulfillment of all the conditions as per the DRDA Administration guidelines.

939. (14-5-2007) NEW DELHI : The Ministry of Rural Development has released grants-in-aid amounting to Rs. 8.58 crore to 32 DRDAs (Annexure-I) of Rajasthan towards part payment of first instalment during the year 2007-08 under the 'Swarnjayanti Gram Swarojgar Yojana' (SGSY). The amount should be utilized on the Programme as per approved guidelines of SGSY. The funding pattern will be 75:25 by the Centre and the State. The State Government should release its share within one month of the date of release of the Central assistance. Under SGSY, assistance is given to the poor family living below the poverty line for taking up self-employment. It actively promotes group approach by organising the rural poor into Self-Help Groups.

940. (14-5-2007) NEW DELHI : The Ministry of Rural Development has released grants-in-aid amounting to Rs. 5.63 crore to 33 DRDAs (Annexure) of Gujarat towards part payment of first instalment during the year 2007-08 under the

'Swarnjayanti Gram Swarojgar Yojana' (SGSY). The amount should be utilized on the Programme as per approved guidelines of SGSY. The funding pattern will be 75:25 by the Centre and the State. The State Government should release its share within one month of the date of release of the Central assistance. Under SGSY, assistance is given to the poor family living below the poverty line for taking up self-employment. It actively promotes group approach by organising the rural poor into Self-Help Groups.

941. (14-5-2007) NEW DELHI : The following is the text of intervention of Finance Minister Shri P. Chidambaram at the meeting of full Planning Commission held here today: "I welcome the initiative taken to hold a meeting of the full Planning Commission on the subject of food and agriculture. On more than one occasion, the UPA Government has reaffirmed that agriculture must top the agenda of the policy makers and must hold the first charge on our resources. An important lesson that we have learnt in the last three years is that a country with a large population like India has to be self-sufficient or nearly self-sufficient in essential items of food such as cereals, pulses, oil seeds, sugar and milk. Any supply-demand gap in essential food articles has the effect of exacerbating the problems relating to maintenance of price stability. While imports are an answer to the supply-demand gap, practical experience shows that, unlike a small country, a large country has less room to manoeuvre and inevitably has to suffer a higher rate of inflation. The only way forward, in my view, is to increase production and productivity of essential food articles. Further, having regard to the fact that nearly 60 per cent of the population is dependent on agriculture for its livelihood, the goal of "inclusive growth" can be realized only if incomes from agriculture and related activities can be considerably enhanced. It is only higher production and higher productivity that can result in higher incomes to our farmers. I would urge the members of the full Planning Commission to note the following facts. In the period from 1998-99 to 2006-07: The area under food grains has stagnated between 120 million and 125 million hectares. Of this, the area under wheat has stagnated between 25 million and 27.5 million hectares, and the area under paddy has stagnated between 41 million and 45 million hectares. Leaving the outlier years, production of wheat has stagnated between 68 million and 73 million tonnes and the production of rice has stagnated between 85 million and 91 million tonnes. Productivity has also stagnated. In case of wheat it is approximately 2,700 kgs per hectare and in the case of rice it is approximately 1,950 kgs per hectare. I would therefore respectfully urge that we urgently address the issues relating to production and productivity. At an earlier meeting of the full Planning Commission I had urged that we should develop State-specific plans for agriculture. We have found that plan schemes administered by Central Ministries/Departments tend to ignore the special problems and special needs of different States. Furthermore, since many schemes are operationally stand-alone schemes administered by different Ministries/Departments, it is difficult to see how they fit into a coordinated strategy either at the national level or at the State level. The better approach would be to evolve State-specific schemes, aggregate them and then fit them into operational schemes to be administered by different Ministries/Departments. I now turn to the question of improving farm incomes.

942. (14-5-2007) NEW DELHI : All the forest villages in Maharashtra totalling 73 have been converted into revenue villages. About 24 schemes from Maharasthra are pending for clearance under the Forest Conservation Act, 1980 are pending. This information was given by the Minister of State in the Ministry of Environment and Forests, Shri Namo Narain Meena in a written reply to question by Shri Haribhau Rathod in the Lok Sabha today.

943. (14-5-2007) NEW DELHI : Following are the closing remarks of the Prime Minister, Dr. Manmohan Singh at the Full Planning Commission meeting, here today: "I think we have had a fruitful discussion analysing the performance of agriculture and identifying strategies for improving the performance of this vital sector of our economy. As I had said earlier, reversing the prolonged slowdown in agriculture and enhancing its growth rate to 4% per annum is critical to the well-being not just of the large population that is dependent on agriculture but also to ensuring equitable, inclusive growth in all regions of our country. There are a large number of long term issues that have been thrown up and I am sure that the XI Plan would come up with effective strategies to tackle the same. On the input side, there are issues such as improving the management of water resources; raising the quality of inputs such as seeds, fertilizers and pesticides and improving the access to credit both in terms of quantity and in terms of its reach. On the post-harvest side, there are issues such as improving marketing and post harvest management. There are institutional issues such as improving the quality of agricultural research and making it more relevant to the actual needs of different regions; reforming the cooperative system by implementing the Vaidyanathan Committee' s recommendations; designing credible and effective agricultural insurance schemes; and, improving extension services and making them truly responsive to local needs. Further, we have the specific issue of tackling the stagnation in rainfed agriculture. We also have the larger issue of increasing the total investment in agricultural sector-both public and private. The problems in all these areas are well known and long term solutions have been worked and will be implemented in the XI Plan. However, we need strategies that deliver results in the short run as well. This is necessary so that the rural economy too benefits from the acceleration in growth taking place in the rest of the economy and our farmers and rural poor are filled with a sense of hope for their future. Based on our discussions today, I sense that it is possible to identify such strategies which can provide tangible gains in the next 2-3 years. One of the noticeable features of today's discussion is the presence of large yield gaps in many crops. There are gaps in the yields between states and regions. There are gaps between actual yields and the yields that are technologically feasible. By focusing efforts on bridging this yield gap, I am certain that we can achieve substantial results in a short time frame. However, there is no easy solution to this. The gaps in yields may arise from a variety of factors. They could be due to differences in soil and climatic characteristics; they could be due to differences in irrigation and water availability; they could be due to differences in farming practices; they could be due to differences in technologies. Bridging these gaps requires localised, state-specific strategies based on local agro-climatic conditions and constraints. I believe that working together with the States, it should be possible to evolve such viable plans. And the Central Government should be willing to support such plans on a reasonably large scale-on a scale which would make a visible impact on the ground.

944. (14-5-2007) NEW DELHI : There has been a steady rise in the population of older persons in India over the past few decades. The life expectancy, which was around 29 years in 1947, is now closer to 65 years. The same is expected to increase to 71 years by 2026. The number of older persons in the population is expected to increase by more than double from 71 million in 2001 to 173 million in 2026 – an increase in their share to the total population from 6.9 to 12.4 percent. Availability of advanced medical facilities, better quality of life and increased nutrition intake has contributed to this phenomenon of demographic ageing. The trend clearly reveals that ageing has become a major social challenge and there is a need to give more attention to the care and protection for the older persons. Keeping in view of the importance of this demographic ageing, the Government announced the National Policy on Older Persons which, inter-alia visualizes support for financial security, health care and nutrition, shelter, emphasis upon education, training and information needs, provision of appropriate concessions and discounts etc. to senior citizens and special attention to protect and strengthen their legal rights such as to safeguard their life and property. It recognizes persons as 60+ as senior citizens. The Government constituted a National Council for Older Persons (NCOP) under the Chairmanship of Minister for Social Justice and Empowerment to advise and aid the Government on policies and programmes for older persons and also to provide feedback to the Government on the implementation of the National Policy on Older Persons as well as on specific programme initiatives for older persons. The NCOP is the highest body to advice and coordinate with the Government in the formulation and implementation of policy and programmes for the welfare of the aged. The NCOP has been reconstituted in 2005 on completion of the term of the earlier Council. At present, there are 44 members in the Council, consisting of representatives of Central Ministries, State Governments, NGOs and experts in the field of ageing. In recent times, society is witnessing withering of the joint family system, as a result of which a large number of parents are not being looked after by their children. Many older persons, particularly widowed women are now forced to spend their twilight years all alone, having been abandoned by their children. To address these problems being faced by the parents and the elderly, this Ministry formulated a legislation in the name of "Maintenance and Welfare of Parents and Senior Citizens Bill – 2007" which inter-alia contains provisions for providing maintenance to the parents and senior citizens by their families. Providing of better health facilities, care, protection of life and property to the senior citizens are some of the other mail provisions of the Bill. Though the above Bill contains provisions on medical facilities for senior citizens, it also important to ensure that there appropriate Health Insurance Schemes, which offers protection to the senior citizens from the exorbitant medical expenditure are available to the senior citizens. There has been persistent demand from the senior citizens associations for formulating such insurance policies. Taking into consideration of the situation, the National Insurance Company, came up with Varistha Mediclaim policy for the senior citizens last year. The other three public sector insurance companies will also offer similar products to the senior citizens. Meeting of the National Council on Older Persons have been convened on 15th June,2007 to discuss the "Maintenance and Welfare of Parents and Senior Citizens Bill – 2007" and the recent budget announcements namely introduction of new financial product namely "reverse mortgage" for senior citizens and the new health insurance schemes for the older persons to be offered by the public sector insurance companies.

945. (14-5-2007) NEW DELHI : The Prime Minister said that I am indeed delighted to participate in the Inauguration of the CII Education Summit. My greetings to the organizers, education planners, education providers, regulators, accreditation agencies, vocational trainers, representatives of industry and other distinguished guests. The topic selected for CII Education Summit: "Innovating for Excellence" is very important. Since, I am in the midst of experts in education; I would like to discuss on "Mission of Education: Capacity Building."

946. (14-5-2007) NEW DELHI : The Universalisation of Elementary Education and eradication of adult illiteracy form the two-pronged strategy for improving the literacy rate of the country. Sarva Shiksha Abhiyan (SSA) is a comprehensive programme for universalizing quality elementary education by 2010. The National Literacy Mission aims to impart functional literacy to adult illiterates in the 15-35 age-group. According to the Census 2001, the literacy rate of the country is 64.84% and except Bihar, the literacy rate of other States is more than 50%. A statement indicating the State-wise literacy rates is enclosed as Annexure. The Approach Paper to the XI Plan of the Planning Commission has set a target of achieving 85% literacy rate by the end of the Plan period. This information was given by the Minister of State for Human Resource Development Shri M.A.A. Fatmi in a written reply in the Rajya Sabha today.

947. (15-5-2007) NEW DELHI : The Forms for Return of Income are assessment year specific. Vide Notification S.O. No. 762(E) dated 14th May, 2007, the Central Board of Direct Taxes have notified following eight Return Forms for assessment year 2007-08 under a new series:- ITR-1- return of income for Individuals having salary / pension / family pension and interest income and no other income. ITR-2- return of income for Individuals and HUFs having income from any source except from business or profession. ITR-3- return of income for Individuals and HUFs being partners in firms and not having proprietory business or profession. ITR-4- return of income for Individuals and HUFs having proprietory business or profession. ITR-5-combined form for return of income and fringe benefits for Firms/AOP/BOI. ITR-6- combined form for return of income and fringe benefits for Companies. ITR-7- combined form for return of income and fringe benefits for Charitable / religious trusts, political parties and other non-profit organizations. ITR-8- stand alone form for return of fringe benefits for persons who are not liable to file return of income but are liable to file return of fringe benefits All these Forms (except Form ITR-7) have been designed as annexure-less so as to make them amenable for electronic filing. Last year, electronic filing was made compulsory for corporate tax-payers. This year, electronic filing has been made compulsory for firms also which are liable to tax audit under section 44AB. Corporate taxpayers and such firms may either file their return electronically under digital signature or may transmit the data of the return electronically. On successful electronic transmission of data (without digital signature), the Income Tax Department will electronically send the taxpayer a duly filled one-page verification form (Form ITR-V). The taxpayer will have to take a print out of two copies of Form ITR-V, duly verify and sign the two copies, furnish one copy to the Income tax Department and obtain acknowledgement on the other copy for his own record. All other categories of taxpayers (other than charitable trusts, institutions, etc.) will have the option to file the return in a paper form or electronically, as mentioned above, or in a bar-coded return form. These forms alongwith the instructions for guidance to fill these forms are available on the Income Tax Department's website http://www.incometaxindiaefiling.gov.in. These forms are applicable from 14.5.2007. The return for assessment year 2007-08 shall not be accepted in the old forms. However for earlier years, taxpayers should use old forms. The old forms for Assessment year 2006-07 are also available on above mentioned website.

948. (15-5-2007) NEW DELHI : The Vice President of India Shri Bhairon Singh Shekhawat formally launched the 5% Ethanol-Blended Petrol (EBP) programme in New Delhi today. He also inaugurated M/s. Shaheed Matbar Singh Negi Filling Point, a petrol/diesel station located at Rohini allotted to the family of Shaheed Matbar Singh Negi who sacrificed his life while defending the Indian Parliament from terrorists' attack on 13th December, 2001. Shri Murli Deora, Minister of Petroleum and Natural Gas presided over the function which was attended by several dignitaries, including Shri Dinsha Patel, Minister of State for Petroleum and Natural Gas and Shri Sajjan Kumar, Member of Parliament among others. Speaking on the occasion Vice President paid rich tributes to Shaheed Matbar Singh Negi who made supreme sacrifice while defending the Indian Parliament – the symbol of our democracy – from terrorist attack. He was awarded with the Ashok Chakra posthumously for his gallant act. He complemented Ministry of Petroleum & Natural Gas for this gesture in honouring nation's martyrs. In his address Shri Deora said that this petrol station is a token of the nation's homage to a brave martyr. He added that nine petrol pumps have been allotted to the families of the martyrs who laid down their lives defending the Indian Parliament from terrorists' attack on December 13th, 2001. In addition, Petroleum Ministry allotted 303 petrol pumps and 142 LPG distributorships to the families of the martyrs of Operation Vijay "Kargil" so that they can live with honour and dignity. Regarding EBP programme which is part of the UPA Government's commitment to put in place policies that enhance the country's energy security, Vice President Shri Shekhawat stressed the importance of such measures towards energy security. Shri Deora informed that based on its availability, the Government may consider introduction of 10% Ethanol blending in Petrol in future. Today we are blending 5% Ethanol with 95% of Petrol. The total requirement of Ethanol by PSU Oil Marketing Companies is approx. 560 thousand kilolitres per annum in the notified States and Union Territories. Stating that the entire EBP programme is based on Ethanol produced within the country, he clarified that no Ethanol have been imported for EBP Programme. The programme marks a significant step in utilising alternative, renewable and environment-friendly sources of energy like ethanol to supplement hydrocarbon fuels. Shri Deora pointed out that Government issued notifications for implementation of EBP on all-India basis with effect from November 2006, except in Jammu & Kashmir, North-Eastern States, Andaman & Nicobar and Lakshdweep where Ethanol cannot be made available due to logistic reasons. Supply of EBP commenced initially in Uttar Pradesh, Uttaranchal and subsequently in Maharashtra, Delhi, Karnataka, Tamil Nadu, Goa and Andhra Pradesh. Oil companies have also issued a letter of intent for procurement of Ethanol in the States of Bihar and Jharkhand and supplies will commence shortly. This national initiative was first launched on 5th April, 2007 at Hyderabad. Shri Dinsha Patel also louded the bravery of Shaheed Matber Singh Negi in defending the Parliament and emphasised the useful role of ethanol in supplementing fuel availability in the country. The EBP Programme of the Ministry of Petroleum and Natural Gas is primarily based on indigenously produced ethanol from sugarcane molasses, which, besides augmenting fuel availability in the country, would also provide better returns for sugarcane farmers. Further, ethanol is environment-friendly as it enhances combustion of petrol, resulting in lower emission of pollutants.

949. (15-5-2007) NEW DELHI : To a question whether Parliament would be adjourned before schedule date, Congress Spokesperson Shri Singhvi said that I am not privy to the kind of information you are privy to. You know the decision is taken by the appropriate authorities of Parliament and we have absolutely no such intimation which you appear to have. But let me tell you it is not the first time that Parliament has been adjourned or its termination preponed by a day or two. To a question whether Congress Party is supporting preponed adjournment of Parliament, Shri Singhvi said that there is no question of supporting or opposing something which is not available as a proposal or a decision. Secondly, the preponement of a session's end happened not once but umpteen times, it happens almost every other session and if it happens it will be a day or two difference. To a question that BJP has its own candidate for Presidential poll, Shri Singhvi said that I think it is premature to make any final comment on that. If it happens, then so be it. But the decision, first and foremost, both in view of the electorate collage and in view of the ruling coalition has to be taken within the UPA and those supporting the UPA. What the NDA may or may not do is for them to consider. To a question that a Congress Lok Sabha MP has proposed the name of Smt. Gandhi, Shri Singhvi said that there is no question of this decision being taken by any one person, there is no question of a decision being taken by a group of persons, this is a collegiate, collective decision of the highest post in the country, at the highest level of decision making, in the Congress Party, in the UPA and each of the supporting units. It requires great amount of internal discussion, anybody can express its own view which he is entitled to in a democracy but there is no question of that being anything more than a personal view. To a question whether Congress Party would stick to its own nominee or the choice of the Left acceptable, Shri Singhvi said that these are all matters internal to the UPA. To a question about the law and order situation in Tamil Nadu, Shri Singhvi said that let us be very clear that there are two or three aspects to be remembered. Law and order is a state subject and we have no doubt that appropriate steps are being taken and will be taken by the state government which is entirely their jurisdiction. Secondly and most importantly, we do not comment on the internal affairs of a supporting coalition partner. This is a matter for, by and of and within the DMK. Thirdly, let us be very clear, the formal decision has to be and was taken by the Prime Minister as per the appropriate constitutional convention. However, in any coalition you will not have coalition dharma in running a govt. where the absolute view of one party can prevail. Coalition requires the necessary give and take in the spirit of which a certain change in the ministerial fabric. To a question that the situation in Tamil Nadu is similar to Gujarat as law and order is concerned, Shri Singhvi said that if you are trying to equate the degree, the nature and scope of a law and order situation in Tamil Nadu to that of Gujarat, then I can only say that you have got it wrong. To a question that the Prime Minister is weak, Shri Singhvi said that the coalition dharma, coalition spirit, coalition governance, the paradigm the world over is, that you do not consider on unilateralism, you take into account the views of your coalition partners and that is a universal phenomenon. And your saying that Prime Minister is weak is altogether wrong. The Prime Minister is incharge of the decision and the Prime Minister takes it after the widest possible consultations, including consultations with allies who are concerned. To a question on the Taj corridor issue, Shri Singhvi said that is a directly subjudice matter but more than that, at the moment a report has been filed which says specifically that without the statutorily mandated sanction required from the Governor, which is awaited, you cant take a decision.

950. (15-5-2007) NEW DELHI : The Vice President, Shri Bhairon Singh Shekhawat said that terrorism is the single biggest challenge we face as a nation.

We know all too well as to what it means to be the terror's victim. One of the greatest duties that befalls on a society is to take care of the dependants of those who have laid down their lives for the nation. Addressing while launching the ethanol blended petrol and inaugurating the retail outlet allotted to the survivor of late Shri Matbar Singh Negi, a martyr in the terrorist attack on our Parliament, Shri Shekhawat said the oil sector has been in the forefront of discharging this national duty in ample measure serving the nation's cause, retail outlet dealerships are allotted to the widows or next-of-kin of martyrs for their livelihood security. The Ministry of Petroleum and Natural Gas deserves our hearty compliments for this humanistic orientation and compassionate approach. The Vice President said that the supply of ethanol-blended petrol marks the beginning of a new era of green transport fuels. The new eco-friendly fuel is expected to contribute toward a cleaner environment and benefit millions of sugarcane farmers. Since ethanol is obtained from the renewable source of sugarcane molasses available throughout the country, its sustained demand will enlarge the area of sugarcane cultivation and better returns to farmers. In a sense, this fuel-mix has the potential to contribute significantly towards enhancing the strength and resilience of our national economy by ensuring prosperity of our farmers, protection of environment and reduced dependence on import of petroleum products. Shri Shekhawat said that through ethanol blending, we can significantly reduce the net emission of green house gasses so as to counter the alarming threats of global warming. For the country, which imports nearly 70 per cent of its petroleum requirements, ethanol is a renewable source of energy available indigenously for import substitution. Ethanol alternative will also help us overcome the uncertainties and fluctuations of spiraling international oil prices. The country's sustainable development in the long run will depend upon the dynamic partnership between the petro-agro sector in ensuring not only progressive ethanol blending with petrol but also in securing ethanol blending with diesel as well. Union Minister for Petroleum & Natural Gas Shri Muril Deora and the Minister of State for Petroleum and Natural Gas Shri Dinsha Patel also addressed on the occasion.

951. (15-5-2007) NEW DELHI : The Minister of State for Defence Production Rao Inderjit Singh has called for increased interaction between defence enterprises and private industry for the success of the offset policy, as envisaged in the Defence Procurement Policy (DPP), 2006. Presiding over a seminar on the Mid-Term Review of the Offset Policy of the Ministry of Defence here yesterday, he said we can ill-afford to ignore the policy as it is beneficial to the country as well as industry. Urging MoD officials to be more frank and open in their dealings with the private industry, he highlighted the perils of foreign dependence, especially on technology, and urged all the stakeholders to ensure that India finds its rightful place as an exporter of arms in the near future. He assured the industry to give a good push to the offset policy and sought their cooperation. The seminar, organized by the Department of Defence Production, was attended among others by the Secretary (Defence Production) Shri KP Singh, Scientific Adviser to

Defence Minister Shri M. Natrajan, heads of Defence PSUs and representatives of top industry and business chambers. Participating in the seminar, some speakers welcomed the idea of offset banking and encouragement to Small and Medium Enterprises (SMEs). They also opined that the strong IT base of the nation must get a good push for software outsourcing. Representatives of CII and FICCI, while complimenting the government for encouraging SMEs, suggested that a review of the Offset Policy might be attempted after about two years from now.

952. (15-5-2007) NEW DELHI : The President, Dr. A.P.J. Abdul Kalam will take two classes on Nano Technology for students of B. Tech., PG and Phd. at the Indian Institute of Technology (IIT) at Kharagpur on May 17th during his visit to West Bengal. Dr. Kalam will also interact with teachers and students at the National Council of Education function at Jadavpur University in Kolkata during the visit. The President who will reach Kolkata on the night of May 16th will in his other programmes on May 17th also lay the Foundation Stone of the Dr. B.C. Roy Multi-Specialty Research Centre at IIT, Kharagpur and visit the Manovikas Kendra at Kolkata and interact with special children there. In other functions in the West Bengal capital, he will launch the Centenary Endowment Scheme of Calcutta Club Limited, inaugurate the Conference on Development of East and North East India, as well as pay a visit to the National Library. After completing these programmes, Dr. Kalam returns to New Delhi on the night of May 17th.

953. (15-5-2007) NEW DELHI : A delegation of MPs and MLAs from Andhra Pradesh led by TDP Leader, Mr. N. Chandrababu Naidu called on the Prime Minister today to submit a memorandum regarding the Babli Project issue. The Prime Minister urged the delegation not to politicize the issue. He said that river waters are a national resource and all political parties must work together to ensure equitable utilization of this national resource. Stating that the matter was presently before courts, the Prime Minister assured the delegation that the Central Government would ensure that justice is done to both Andhra Pradesh and Maharashtra. He urged the leaders of all political parties not to create tension and instead create an atmosphere in which such contentious issues are resolved amicably to the mutual satisfaction of all sides.

954. (15-5-2007) NEW DELHI : Simplification of procedures for the export of agricultural commodities including reduction in agencies and clearances required are considered by the Government wherever possible keeping in view the domestic regulations and the requirements of the importing countries. As part of this exercise streamlining and simplification of documentation and regulatory clearances for perishable agricultural produce is under way. This was stated by the Minster of State for Commerce & Industry, Shri Jairam Ramesh in a written reply in Lok Sabha today. A Number of clearances are required for export of agricultural commodities. These depend upon the commodity to be exported, the domestic regulations and the requirements of the importing countries. For instance, export of mango to Japan requires Vapour Heat Treatment of the fruit while for export to the United States of America irradiation is essential. For export of groundnuts an export certificate from APEDA is required. Pre shipment inspection is essential for export of meat. These are amongst the other requirements that have to be met for these commodities. As part of its ongoing programme for development of infrastructure to facilitate export of agricultural produce the Agriculture and Processed Food Products Export Development Authority (APEDA) has set up Centres for Perishable Cargo (CPCs) to maintain cold chain at international airports at Delhi, Hyderabad, Chennai, Bangalore, Trivandrum and Mumbai. Provision of such facilities at airports in Cochin, Bagdogra, Kolkata, Goa, Nashik and at Haldia seaport has been taken up.

955. (15-5-2007) NEW DELHI : A consultant firm was engaged to carry out a study to assess the role of MMTC Ltd., STC Ltd. and PEC Ltd. in the liberalized Indian economy and to recommend the business model and the processes these organizations should adopt and the structural changes, if any, required to adopt the recommended business model and processes for their long-term sustainability and growth. The consultant firm has, among others, recommended the merger of these organizations. MMTC Ltd., STC Ltd. and PEC Ltd. have been asked by the Government to consult the employees for their feedback on the recommendations of the consultant firm. There is no decision of the Government as yet on the issue of merger of these organisations. This was stated by the Minister of State for Commerce, Shri Jairam Ramesh, in a written reply in the Lok Sabha today.

956. (15-5-2007) NEW DELHI : The import of Cement is under Open General License (OGL) and anyone can import the requisite quantity provided it conforms to the BIS standards. In order to augment domestic availability of cement, the import duty on cement was brought down to Nil from 12.5% as on 21st January, 2007. The Government in its Budget announcement, has also introduced a dual excise duty structure on cement (excise duty of Rs.600 per metric tonne (PMT) of cement with MRP more than Rs.190 per bag and excise duty of Rs.300 PMT on cement with MRP of Rs.190 or less per bag. In addition to the above, the Ministry of Finance has removed the countervailing duty (equivalent to the excise duty and special additional custom duty of 4% on cement w.e.f. 3rd April, 2007). The importers have to adhere to the Cement (Quality Control) Order, 2003, which provides for mandatory BIS Certification. This was stated by the Minister of State for Commerce, Shri Jairam Ramesh, in a written reply in the Lok Sabha today.

957. (15-5-2007) NEW DELHI : During the Fourteenth SAARC Summit held in New Delhi on 3-4 April, 2007, India announced its decision to allow duty free access to India to the Least Developed Countries (LDCs) of SAARC which are signatories of the Agreement on South Asian Free Trade Area (SAFTA), before the end of this year. These LDC countries are Bangladesh, Bhutan, Maldives and Nepal. Afghanistan, which was inducted as a member of SAARC during the Fourteenth SAARC Summit would also be an LDC and signatory of SAFTA after completing the required formalities. In terms of the phased Trade Liberalization

Programme (TLP) of SAFTA, which has become operational from 1st July 2006, India as a Non-Least Developed Country (NLDC) of SAARC and signatory of SAFTA, had already decided to reduce tariffs to zero percent for SAARC LDCs, except on the items kept in the Sensitive List, by 31.12.2008. With the present decision India would complete SAFTA TLP for LDCs one year in advance. India has already been giving market access to Nepal and Bhutan as per the bilateral Trade agreements signed with these countries. Except Bangladesh the export potential of Maldives and Afghanistan, which has become new member of SAARC is not significant. Further, SAFTA tariff concessions for LDCs would exclude those items kept in the Sensitive List of India under SAFTA. The present decision is therefore not likely to have any serious impact on Indian industry and trade. This was stated by the Minister of State for Commerce, Shri Jairam Ramesh, in a written reply in the Lok Sabha today.

958. (15-5-2007) NEW DELHI : Shri Sanjay K. Raut, a senior Indian Information Service officer of 1985 batch passed away following a massive heart attack yesterday. He was posted as Dy. Director General, Directorate of Field Publicity in Bhubaneshwar. Raut served in various media units of the Ministry of Information & Broadcasting in Orissa and Delhi. He was known as a thorough professional and an able administrator. Raut was also a poet and a short story writer in Oriya language. Minister of Information & Broadcasting and Parliamentary Affairs, Shri P. R. Dasmunsi in his tribute to the late officer has described him as "an outstanding officer dedicated to his work whose passing away is as much a loss for his colleagues as for his near and dear ones."

959. (15-5-2007) NEW DELHI : The United States of America (USA) has allowed the import of Indian mangoes irradiated at 400 Gy dose to mitigate mango stone weevil. The irradiation facility was approved on April 26, 2007 by United States-Animal and Plant Health Inspection Service (US-APHIS). The first consignment of mangoes was dispatched to the United States on April 27, 2007. There was accordingly no export of mangoes to USA in last 3 financial years. Opening up of the US market for Indian mangoes affords greater opportunities for the Indian mango growers.

960. (15-5-2007) NEW DELHI : Registration under section 12A of the Income tax Act, 1961 is a pre-condition for availing exemption of income under sections 11 and 12 of the said Act by a charitable or religious trust or institution. For obtaining such registration, the trust or institution has to make an application in Form no. 10A to the Commissioner of Income-tax within one year from the date of its creation or establishment. Where such application is made after the expiry of one year, the Commissioner may condone such delay, if he is satisfied that the delay was for sufficient reasons. In such case, the exemption under sections 11 and 12 will be available from the date of creation or establishment of the trust or institution. Otherwise, it will be available only from the financial year in which the application for registration is made. Finance Act, 2007 has removed the requirement of filing the application within one year of the creation or establishment of the trust or institution. It has also removed the power vested with the Commissioner for condonation of delay by stipulating that for any application made on or after the 1st day of June, 2007, registration will be granted from the financial year in which the application is made. Therefore, in order to avail of the benefit of condonation of delay for earlier years, any trust or institution which has not filed its application within one year of its creation or establishment may file such application before the 1st day of June, 2007. Applications filed on or after the 1st day of June, 2007 will entitle the applicant to claim exemption of income from the financial year in which the application is made and not for earlier years.

961. (15-5-2007) NEW DELHI : During the course of enquiries carried out by the Income Tax Department, instances of tax evasion by private educational institutions, running various courses, some of which are not recognized by the UGC/AICTE, have come to notice. So far as Service Tax is concerned, proceedings have been initiated against some of the institutes for evasion of service tax on services provided by them in relation to commercial training or coaching. The Indian Institute of Planning and Management (IIPM), New Delhi has not paid income tax in the last two Assessment years, *i.e.* A.Y. 2005-06 and A.Y. 2006-07 as the income was claimed as exempt under section 10(23C) (vi) of the Income-tax Act, 1961. Service tax paid by IIPM, New Delhi and its other associated companies, during last two years, is nil. IIPM has incurred an expenditure of Rs.17,28,27,370/- and Rs.31,62,69,231/- on advertisement for the financial years 2004-05 and 2005-06 respectively. The source of funding of such advertisement is out of various receipts from activities carried out by IIPM as reflected in the Income & Expenditure statements. Shri S.S. Palanimanickam, Minister of State for Finance gave this information in reply to a question raised by Shri Dharam Pal Sabharwal in Rajya Sabha today.

962. (15-5-2007) NEW DELHI : The Securities and Exchange Board of India (SEBI) has informed that compliance with Clause 49 of the listing agreement, containing provisions relating to corporate governance, is mandatory for entities seeking listing for the first time, at the time of seeking in-principle approval for such listing and for existing listed entities having a paid up share capital of Rs. 3 crore and above or net worth of Rs. 25 crore or more at any time in the history of the company. BSE has informed that for the quarter ended March 31, 2007, of the 204 companies in BSE Group A, all companies are compliant with Clause 49 except for 13 companies. NSE has informed that for the quarter ended March 31, 2007, of the 50 companies that comprise the NSE Nifty, all companies are compliant with Clause 49 except for 7 companies. According to SEBI, no listed company that has not complied with the provisions of clause 49 has been fined or their officers imprisoned after 2000. There are 4784 and 1250 companies listed on the BSE and NSE, respectively, as on May 10, 2007. The names of the companies which are listed on BSE and NSE are available on their websites http://bseindia.com and http://nseindia.com respectively. Shri Pawan Kumar Bansal, Minister of State for Finance gave this information in reply to a question raised by Shri Jai Parkash Aggarwal in Rajya Sabha today.

963. (15-5-2007) NEW DELHI : A few cases of misuse of duplicate PAN card have been reported. The number of persons having duplicate PANs is 13.1 lakhs as on 31.3.2007. The information relating to surrender of PANs voluntarily is not maintained separately in the date base. However, the number of duplicate PANs deleted as a result of the de-duplication exercise as on 11.5.2007 is 8,49,293. Several persons were allotted more than one PAN, particularly, during the period between 1996 and 2003.

964. (15-5-2007) NEW DELHI : The refunds are issued and dispatched through post offices within one month from the date of signing by the Assessing Officer. However, refunds pertaining to the jurisdiction of Commissioners of Income Tax, Delhi-IX, XIV, XV and XVI are issued directly by State Bank of India under Refund Banker Scheme. As per the instructions, the refunds are to be issued within four months from the date of receipt of return and dispatched within 30 days from the date of signing. However, in some cases the instructions could not be followed due to reasons attributable to assessees like. (i) Non-quoting or wrong quoting of PAN number by the assessee (ii) Non-furnishing of bank account details by the assessee (iii) Pending de-duplication of PAN. Shri S.S. Palanimanickam, Minister of State for Finance gave this information in reply to a question raised by Shri Rajeev Chandrasekhar in Rajya Sabha today.

965. (15-5-2007) NEW DELHI : Since the inception of Kisan Credit Card (KCC) Scheme in August 1998, 665.63 lakh KCCs have been issued till 31st March, 2007. The credit limit to farmers is fixed on the basis of their credit-worthiness. The entire credit limit is disbursed to them in cash with discretion to purchase inputs of their choice from outlets of their choice; thus, enabling the farmers to take advantage of market conditions. Due to the cash credit nature of loans disbursed through KCC, there is reduction in the quantum of interest paid by the farmer. Further, transaction cost for the farmer for availing of loan from the bank is also reduced. With a view to make KCC more comprehensive in its coverage of credit needs of the farmers through a single window, the scope of the KCC scheme has been extended to cover term loans for agriculture and allied activities and a reasonable component for consumption loan. The banks have also been advised to ensure that the crop loans are routed through KCC only. Shri Pawan Kumar Bansal, Minister of State for Finance gave this information in reply to a question raised by Smt. Sushma Swaraj in Rajya Sabha today.

966. (15-5-2007) NEW DELHI : The proposal to bring all international payment gateways like Visa and Master Card and wire transfer agencies in the category of institutions obliged to report cash transactions and suspicious transactions is under consideration of the Government. If and when such agencies are brought under the Prevention of Money-laundering Act, 2002, they will be required to furnish reports in accordance with the provisions of the Act. During the period from 1.4.2006 to 31.3.2007, the Financial Intelligence Unit, India, has received 21,40,768 Cash Transaction Reports and 817 Suspicious Transaction Reports from reporting entities. Shri S.S. Palanimanickam, Minister of State for Finance gave this information in reply to a question raised by Shri B.K. Hariprasad in Rajya Sabha today.

967. (15-5-2007) NEW DELHI : So far as IRS (IT) is concerned, 49 officers have taken voluntary retirement during 2006-07 and till 1st May, 2007. Requests from 5 officers for voluntary retirement are also under process. So far as IRS (C&CE) is concerned, 38 officers have taken voluntary retirement during 2006-07 and till 1st May, 2007. Requests from 3 officers for voluntary retirement are also under process. The reason behind these retirements is largely personal. Under Govt. of India CCS (Pension) Rules, an officer is entitled to seek voluntary retirement. Shri S.S. Palanimanickam, Minister of State for Finance gave this information in reply to a question raised by Shri Ajay Maroo and Shri Devdas Apte in Rajya Sabha today.

968. (15-5-2007) NEW DELHI : The Government has given approval for induction of certain foreign investors as shareholders in the BSE and NSE, in accordance with its policy on foreign investment in stock exchanges. As required by the BSE (Corporatisation and Demutualisation) Scheme, 2005 and the Regulations framed by SEBI, BSE is required to reduce the equity shareholding by its trading members to 49%. The member brokers do not have any stake in NSE. BSE has informed that depending upon the need and circumstances, it may consider IPO at an appropriate time. NSE has informed that presently no plan for an IPO is under its consideration. Shri Pawan Kumar Bansal, Minister of State for Finance gave this information in reply to a question raised by Shri Gireesh Kumar Sanghi in Rajya Sabha today.

969. (15-5-2007) NEW DELHI : The Bank notes are not devoid of the legal tender characteristics just because they are soiled. Inherently, the banks are obliged to accept them. Reserve Bank of India (RBI) has directed the banks to sort the notes into issuable and non-issuable notes and supply only issuable/clean notes to the public. RBI has also exhorted the public, through media, to insist upon only clean notes from the banks. RBI has been monitoring the implementation of the policy by the banks through regular inspections and incognito visits to the bank branches. In case of any violation of extant guidelines of RBI by a bank, appropriate regulatory action is taken by RBI. Shri Pawan Kumar Bansal, Minister of State for Finance gave this information in reply to a question raised by Smt. Hema Malini in Rajya Sabha today.

970. (15-5-2007) NEW DELHI : The Pharmaceutical Advisory Forum set up by the Ministry of Chemicals and Fertilisers has unanimously recommended that

20 per cent of the MP-LAD and MLA-LAD funds should be earmarked for treatment of poor people for medical treatment. Briefing newsmen after the meeting here today the Minister for Chemicals, Fertilisers and Steel Shri Ram Vilas Paswan said, the funds to be spent on selected illness can be directly paid to the hospitals providing treatment. He said, this will also reduce the burden on public expenditure on health and will be transparent. Health Ministers of States, Industry representatives, Drug Controllers, representatives of consumer bodies and Non Government Organisations, attended the meeting. The meeting, third in the series, also decided to set up a working group on health insurance scheme for BPL families. The working group headed by Joint Secretary in the Department of Chemicals and Petrochemicals will submit its report within two months. The 11 member-working group has among others health secretaries of Andhra Pradesh, Punjab, Rajasthan, Bihar, Mizoram, and Tamil Nadu and representatives of industry associations as its members. The forum also decided to set up a working group on Drug banks. The group will study the Rajasthan model and other models. The Drug bank, proposed to be set up in all the districts is intended to provide medicines free to BPL patients and senior citizens. Several states and members of the forum suggested that the list of Scheduled drugs should be expanded. They also agreed to launch a nationwide campaign to increase consumer awareness on drug prices. The Minister expressed his disappointment over the drug companies not fulfilling their commitment to reduce the price of 886 medicines, which they had voluntarily agreed to. He said a recent survey indicated that only 9 companies have reduced the prices of 295 medicines. The forum urged the drug companies to fulfil their pledge. Earlier delivering the keynote address, Shri Paswan said Special Schemes have been proposed to make drugs accessible to families below poverty line (BPL). These schemes would have to be implemented by various stakeholders including Central Government, State Governments and the Industry. He said, while the endeavours of the Government is that the poorest of poor of Indian citizen gets access to drugs at reasonable prices, it is also being ensured that Indian pharma industry emerges as a global leader. Various policy initiatives through fiscal and non-fiscal measures have been proposed relating to manufacturing and R&D in Pharma Sector. The Minister said, the Government is taking all possible measures to support the growth of Pharmaceutical Industry and on the other hand the Government's objectives continue to be ensuring availability of quality medicines at reasonable prices. Government would also like to ensure that the essential medicines become affordable and access to such medicines is also increased. For this purpose, the National Pharmaceutical Policy, 2006 has come up with several new policy initiatives. We would like to support the industry trade and other stakeholders for implementing these policy measures, he added.

971. (15-5-2007) NEW DELHI : India post is organizing a month long exhibition on postage stamps on wild life and nature. The exhibition at National Philatelic Museum was inaugurated here today by the famous wild life and nature photographer, film maker and a devoted environmentalist Mr. Mike. H. Pandey. On this occasion a special cancellation was released by the Department The

Cancellation is especially designed for this occasion and shows a Banyan tree. The Exhibition shows the amazing variety of flora and fauna of our country. From one of the earliest, post independent stamp issued on Rhinoceros to the latest stamps on Endangered Birds, Himalayan Lakes and scented stamps on Roses, the postage stamps present the Indian naturescape at its most vibrant and exotic. However, this bio diversity is to be protected and conserved. In the exhibition, Mr. Mike H. Pandey has displayed some photographs and posters from his collection. Veteran philatelist, Shri Manohar Lal has also put up a display of about 300 exhibits on stamps and philatelic maxim/post cards. The World Wide Fund for Nature (WWF) has put up a stall and display of various photographs and posters. India Post has issued 113 stamps on the various issues under the theme Nature. These stamps feature animals, flowers and trees, eco systems, birds and various others. These are put on display in this exhibition. Stamps on Himalayan Panda, Kashmir Stag, Snow Leopard, flowers like Rhododendron, orchids, Indian Medicinal Plants, rare animals such as Olive Ridley Turtles, River Dolphin, endangered birds such as the Great Indian Bustard etc., can be seen in this exhibition. The month long exhibition will have a number of interesting events including film shows, paintings and photography exhibition, slide shows and lectures and screening of films on wildlife. The next important occasion is on June 5th, the World Environment Day, when some of the events will be organized. Wildlife and Conservation Experts will also be giving lectures and talks.

972. (15-5-2007) NEW DELHI : Under Production Sharing Contract (PSC) regime, 29 exploration blocks have been awarded so far in KG Basin to various Indian and foreign companies, either alone or in consortium with other companies. As a result of exploration activities, as of now, 21 gas discoveries have been made in these blocks in KG Basin out of which gas inplace reserves in 4 discoveries have been established to the tune of 396 BCM. The development plans of two discoveries have been finalized. Other discoveries are at various stages of appraisal/evaluation by the operators. This information was given by the Minister of Petroleum & Natural Gas Shri Murli Deora in a written reply in the Rajya Sabha today.

973. (15-5-2007) NEW DELHI : The number of proposals received by the Ministry of Information & Broadcasting for producing regional films on social causes such as girl child development etc. during the last three years is 75 of which 67 pertain to CFSI and eight to the FD. Of CFSI proposals, three were found suitable. Two feature films have been made and one is under production. None of the proposals submitted to FD were approved because scheme for production of short fiction films was discontinued from 2002-03. The NFDC has framed byelaws for the regulation of the schemes for the film production and related activities. In CFSI, the proposals received are first vetted by a script Committee which goes into the synopses of making a children's film and then put up to Production Committee for budgetary approval. However, no separate guidelines have been framed for grant of financial assistance to regional films. Films Division does not grant financial assistance for production of any film. It produces films through in-house directors and also assigns films to outside producers on contract basis. Hence, no guidelines have been framed for giving financial assistance. This information was given by Minister of Information & Broadcasting and Parliamentary Affairs, Shri P. R. Dasmunsi in written reply to a question in Lok Sabha today.

974. (15-5-2007) NEW DELHI : There is no definite trend of increase in cases of suicide and fratricide in the Central Police Forces. Courts of Inquiry have been conducted and necessary action taken, wherever required. Eligible dependents of the deceased are appointed as per approved scheme and family pension, gratuity, leave encashment, etc. are also sanctioned to them in such cases. Measures such as Yoga classes, recreation facilities, games, psychiatrist consultation, etc. are provided by the Forces to reduce stress amongst their personnel. This information was given by the Minister of State for Home, Shri Sriprakash Jaiswal in written reply to a question in the Lok Sabha today.

975. (15-5-2007) NEW DELHI : The Government proposes to enact a law to regulate all private detective agencies in the country so as to ensure that they work within the ambit of law and are accountable to a regulatory mechanism. A bill in this regard is likely to be introduced in Parliament shortly. At present, the Government does not have any regulator to regulate the activities of the private detective agencies. Therefore, information about the working of the private detective agencies is not available. This information was given by the Minister of State for Home, Shri Sriprakash Jaiswal in written reply to a question in the Lok Sabha today.

976. (15-5-2007) NEW DELHI : Six members of Indian Army Mountaineering Expedition reached the summit of Mt Everest at 0545h (IST) this morning. The six summiteers are Capt. DJ Singh, Sub Maruti Khandagle, Hav Balwant Singh Negi, Hav Tshering Angchok, Hav Amardev Bhatt and Sep Sachin Patil. The expedition team is being led by Lt. Col IS Thapa of the 4 MARATHA LIGHT Regiment. With this unprecedented feat, the Indian Army has furthered its formidable reputation in the international mountaineering fraternity having summitted Mt Everest four times. Infact in last seven years, Army mountaineers have scaled a 8000 Mtr peak every year to include Mt Everest (8848m) in 2001, 2003 & 2005 and Annapurna – I (8096m) in 2004, which is a remarkable achievement. The Army Everest Expedition team was flagged off by Gen JJ Singh, Chief of the Army Staff on 20 Mar 07. Gen JJ Singh being a mountaineer himself, evinced keen interest in planning and conduct of the expedition at every stage and personally monitored the progress of the team during the expedition. It had left Delhi for Lhasa via Kathmandu on 28 Mar 07 and reached Base Camp at 16,990 ft on 07 Apr. 07. It established Advance Base Camp at 21,190 ft on 16 Apr. 07 and Camp – 1 (23,120 ft) on 18 Apr. 07. Stocking of Summit Camp at a height of 27,220 ft was carried out on 21 Apr. 07, after which the team was forced to return to

Base Camp due to inclement weather conditions. The team recommenced its move upwards from Base Camp on 10 May 07 and reached Summit Camp on Monday 14 May 07. On the night of 14 May 07 the team started from Summit Camp towards the summit. Walking in pitch dark night with the help of headlamps, the team made steady progress and stood on summit of Mt Everest at 29,028 feet – literally on top of the world, at break of the dawn today. The expedition is being conducting and coordinated by Army Adventure Wing of Directorate General of Military Training at Army Headquarters.

977. (15-5-2007) NEW DELHI : The issue of workers' participation in management has been scheduled for discussion in the meeting of the Tripartite Committee being held in New Delhi tomorrow (16/5/07). The meeting will be presided over by the Minister of State (Independent Charge) Labour and Employment, Shri Oscar Fernandes and will be attended by the representatives of employees and employers. The main focus of the discussion will be participation of workers' at the Board level. At the earlier meeting of the Tripartite Committee held in February 2006, there was divergence of views between the employers and the workers. The employees' representatives wanted that Participation of Workers in Management Bill, 1990 should be accepted without any dilution. The employers' Association were agreeable for participation of workers at the shop and plant level but not at the apex level. The Participation of Workers in Management Bill, 1990 was introduced in the Rajya Sabha on May 30, 1990. It provides for specific and meaningful participation of workers in management at shop floor level, establishment level and Board of Management level in industrial establishments. It also provides for formulation of one or more scheme to be framed by the Central Government for giving effect to the provisions of law which will include, among others, the manner of representation of workmen at all the three levels. The Bill proposed to constitute one or more Council at the shop floor level and the Council at the establishment level having equal number of persons to represent the employer and the workers. The Bill also envisages a Board of Management at the apex level where representatives of the workmen as defined under the Industrial Disputes Act shall constitute 13 per cent and persons representing other workers shall constitute 12 per cent of the total strength of such management. The Bill was referred to the Parliamentary Standing Committee of Labour and Welfare, Lok Sabha on 12/7/94 which submitted its report to the Lower House on 18/12/2001. The Parliamentary Standing Committee of Labour and Employment also stated in its meeting held in April, 2005 that the Participation of Workers' in Management Bill, 1990 needs to be pursued. The second National Commission on labour has also recommended that a scheme of workers participation in management should be provided through legislation. The Commission said that it may be initially applicable to establishment employing 300 or more persons. For the smaller establishments, a non statutory scheme may be provided. As stated by the Parliamentary Standing Committee, the Ministry of Labour and Employment has decided to pursue the Bill after consulting social partners with some modifications in view of the new social and economic parameters that have evolved since 1990. Tomorrow's meeting has been called to facilitate one more round of discussion with the stakeholders for arriving at necessary consensus on the issue of participation of workers at the apex level.

978. (15-5-2007) NEW DELHI : As per the Modified Rehabilitation Scheme approved by the Board for Industrial and Financial Reconstruction (BIFR) and Group of Ministers (GOM), it has been decided to close down 12 non functional mills out of the 30 mills to be revived through Joint Venture as there is no production activity in these mills and most of the employees have taken retirement under the Modified Voluntary Retirement Scheme (MVRS). Two of these mills have been closed as per the decision and 10 mills are to be closed further. MVRS has been offered to the remaining employees of these mills also. Government has offered a liberal Modified Voluntary Retirement Scheme (MVRS) to safeguard the interests of workers affected by the closure of unviable mills of NTC. The scheme provided for increasing ex-gratia payment to the workers by 50% to 100% depending upon date of revision of wages. Besides, Department of Public Enterprises (DPE) has formulated a scheme for counseling, re-training and re-deployment of employees of Public Sector and NTC employees are exposed to such programmes. The existing liabilities of closed mills are dealt by NTC for their disposal. This was stated by the Minister of State for Textiles, Shri E.V.K.S. Elangovan in a reply to a question by Shri Sugrib Singh and shri M.P. Veerendrakumar in the Lok Sabha today. It was proposed to revive thirty mills through joint venture. However, as production had completely ceased in12 of these mills and most of the employees have taken MVRS, BIFR and GOM approved to revive the balance 18 mills through joint venture with majority stake to NTC, including development of India International Trade Tower at the land of one of these 18 mills, viz. India United Mill No. 6, Mumbai.

979. (15-5-2007) NEW DELHI : As per the information with Board of Industrial Financial Reconstruction (BIFR), 156 textile units have been declared sick till on 31.10.2006 as below:- This was stated by the Minister of State for Textiles, Shri E.V.K.S. Elangovan in a reply to a question by Shri Ramdas Athawale in the Lok Sabha today. He further stated that the Government has no separate funding scheme for streamlining/ modernization of sick textile mills. However, Government have taken a number of steps for revival of sick industrial units which, inter-alia, include guidelines of the Reserve Bank of India (RBI) to banks, amalgamation of sick units with healthy units, setting up of BIFR under the Sick Industrial Companies (Social Provisions) Act, etc. The RBI has been issuing from time to time elaborate guidelines covering all areas of industrial rehabilitation viz. detection of industrial sickness at incipient stage, identification of sick/weak units, carrying out viability study of the units, then extending relief and concessions to only viable units, coordination among banks and financial institutions and banks themselves, norms for promoters' contribution, extended period for repayment/rescheduling of loans, conversions and waivers of penal rate/compound interest etc. BIFR has been set up with a view to arranging the timely detection of sick and potentially sick companies and for the speedy determination of preventive, ameliorative and remedial measures, which need to be taken in respect of such companies. It appoints operating agencies for preparation of rehabilitation proposals in respect of potentially viable units. It takes decision on rehabilitation on the basis of its findings.

980. (15-5-2007) NEW DELHI : The Ministry of Rural Development has released Grants-in-aid amounting to Rs. 19.48 crore as third/additional instalment of Central assistance to 12 districts of Kerala for the implementation of the Sampoorna Grameen Rozgar Yojana (SGRY) during the financial year (2006-07). The details of the allocation are as under : The release is towards plan expenditure and will be utilized for approved items of works subject to the conditions laid down in the SGRY Guidelines. No deviations from the guidelines is permissible.

981. (15-5-2007) NEW DELHI : The Ministry of Rural Development has released Grants-in-aid amounting to Rs. 40.59 crore as third/additional instalment of Central assistance to 22 districts of Karnataka for the implementation of the Sampoorna Grameen Rozgar Yojana (SGRY) during the financial year (2006-07). Grants amounting to Rs.19.87 crore as part of first instalment has also been released to 16 districts of the State under the scheme for the year 2007-08. The details of the allocation are as under : The release is towards plan expenditure and will be utilized for approved items of works subject to the conditions laid down in the SGRY Guidelines. No deviations from the guidelines is permissible.

982. (15-5-2007) NEW DELHI : The Government is aware that infrastructural constraints are a major impediment to the growth of textiles industry in India. The Government, to neutralize the weakness of fragmentation of various sub-sectors of the textiles and non-availability of quality infrastructure, launched the Scheme for Integrated Textile Parks (SITP) in 2005 to strengthen infrastructural facilities in potential growth areas by merging the then existing schemes, viz., the Apparel Parks for Exports Scheme (APES) and the Textiles Centres Infrastructure Development Scheme (TCIDS). This was stated by the Minister of State for Textiles, Shri E.V.K.S. Elangovan in a reply to a question by Shri K.J.S.P. Reddy in the Lok Sabha today. He further stated that as on March 31, 2006, the total employment in textiles sector was about 88.02 million. He said that textiles activity is mainly concentrated in the decentralised and private sectors. As such, Government does not provide any incentive to textiles workers. However, various welfare and relief schemes are being implemented in the organized and decentralised sub-sectors.

983. (15-5-2007) NEW DELHI : Smt. Renuka Chowdhury, Minister for Women and Child Development visited destitute women at old age homes here today on the occasion of World Family Day. She personally checked all facilities being provided to the inmates and spent more than one hour with them. On the occasion, Mrs. Chowdhury said the Government has number of plans for the welfare of women. Very soon a scheme would be drawn for the rehabilitation of destitute women in collaboration with the State Governments. The Minister also took a medical team with herself for health check ups of the inmates of old age homes. She distributed fruits, tonics and medicines and had a cup of tea with them.

984. (15-5-2007) NEW DELHI : The ban imposed on import of rice by Russia recently with effect from 1/5/2007 is violative of the Protocol signed in February 2007 and the Government of India is taking up the matter with the Russian authorities. This was stated by Shri Jairam Ramesh, Minister of State for Commerce, in a written reply in the Lok Sabha today. The Russian Agency on Veterinary and Phytosanitary Surveillance (ROSSELKHOZNADZOR) issued a notification on 27 April, 2007 imposing a ban on import of rice from India to Russia due to the purported detection of pesticides. The Russian side has started the cause as detection of demethoate, which is not admissible under Russian regulations. Earlier, on 4/12/2006, Russian Agency on Veterinary & Phytosanitary Surveillance (ROSSELKHOZNADZOR) issued a press release announcing a suspension on import of rice from Thailand, Vietnam, Sri Lanka, USA including India due to the purported detection of pesticides. As a result of efforts made by the Government of India to revoke the announced suspension, a delegation from the Federal Service for Veterinary and Phytosanitary Surveillance of the Russian Federation (FSVPSRF) visited India during 19th to 24th February, 2007. At the end of the visit, a protocol was negotiated which has now been signed by both the sides, the Minister added.

985. (15-5-2007) NEW DELHI : The ban imposed on import of rice by Russia recently with effect from 1/5/2007 is violative of the Protocol signed in February 2007 and the Government of India is taking up the matter with the Russian authorities. This was stated by Shri Jairam Ramesh, Minister of State for Commerce, in a written reply in the Lok Sabha today. The Russian Agency on Veterinary and Phytosanitary Surveillance (ROSSELKHOZNADZOR) issued a notification on 27 April, 2007 imposing a ban on import of rice from India to Russia due to the purported detection of pesticides. The Russian side has started the cause as detection of demethoate, which is not admissible under Russian regulations. Earlier, on 4/12/2006, Russian Agency on Veterinary & Phytosanitary Surveillance (ROSSELKHOZNADZOR) issued a press release announcing a suspension on import of rice from Thailand, Vietnam, Sri Lanka, USA including India due to the purported detection of pesticides. As a result of efforts made by the Government of India to revoke the announced suspension, a delegation from the Federal Service for Veterinary and Phytosanitary Surveillance of the Russian Federation (FSVPSRF) visited India during 19th to 24th February, 2007. At the end of the visit, a protocol was negotiated which has now been signed by both the sides, the Minister added.

986. (15-5-2007) NEW DELHI : The Government of India has introduced the Anganwadi Karyakartri Bima Yojana under the LIC's Social Security Scheme, for Anganwadi Workers (AWWs) under the Integrated Child Development Services (ICDS) Scheme. This was stated by Smt. Renuka Chowdhury, Minister for Women and Child Development in a reply to a question by Smt. Minati Sen in the Lok Sabha today. She further stated that the premium under the Scheme is Rs. 280/- per annum per member out of which Rs. 100/- is paid by LIC from Social Security Fund, Rs. 100/- by the Government of India and Rs. 80/- by the Anganwadi Workers / Helper (insured member). The premium of Rs. 80/- payable by these Workers, has since been waived off w.e.f. 1.4.2007 for two years. The total amount accrued so far from the premium of AWWs/AWHs is Rs. 46256720, Rs. 38797600 and Rs. 36770640 during the year 2004-05,2005-06 and 2006-07 respectively.

987. (15-5-2007) NEW DELHI : Duty Free Credit Entitlement (DFCE) Scheme for status holders was started from 1/4/2003. The scheme was limited to Status Holders who had exports of at least Rs.25 crore in 2003-04 and incremental growth of 25%. The scheme was tightened, modified and renamed as Target Plus Scheme in September 2004. Target Plus Scheme was designed with objective to reward incremental growth in exports. Status Holders contribute more than 60% to India's export efforts and to achieve substantial higher exports, fillip to these exporters was granted by Target Plus Scheme. As on 30/4/2007, out of 1923 applications received, 897 claims have been disbursed by grant of duty credits of Rs.4725 crore, 229 applications have been rejected wherein claim amount was Rs.574.63 crore. Applications complete in all respects received till 31/3/2007 have been considered by Zonal Committee and decided. A total of 797 applications, where the claim amount is Rs.3792.10 crore, were found deficient and incomplete. Government has modified Target Plus Scheme for exports during 2005-06 by providing duty credit benefits at 5% of incremental exports, removing petroleum, cereals, ores, sugar and gems & jewellery from purview of the scheme, and by lowering eligibility criteria to Rs.5 crore from Rs.10 crore. After being in operation for exports during 2004-05 and 2005-06, Target Plus Scheme has been abolished for exports from 1/4/2006 onwards. This was indicated by Shri Kamal Nath, Union Minister of Commerce & Industry, in the Lok Sabha today.

988. (15-5-2007) NEW DELHI : The Ministry of Women and child Development has requested all State Governments and Union Territory Administrations to make a demand survey of working women's hostels and to recommend proposals for places on that basis. The number of new hostels set up will depend upon the proposals received as per the assessment of demand. This was stated by Smt. Renuka Chowdhury, Minister for Women and Child Development in a reply to a question by Shri Dushyant Singh in the Lok Sabha today. She further stated that Rs. 15 crore has been provided in the Budget of 2007-08. NCJ/DT

989. (15-5-2007) NEW DELHI : Gen JJ Singh laid the foundation stone for a group housing scheme for army personnel here today. The Army is to construct

648 apartments in Dwarka locality here, for group housing of its personnel. These dwelling units are to come up at two sites. One of the sites measuring about 4 acres is in Sector 22 and the other is about 6.5 acres in Sector 23. The apartments will range from two bedroom small family apartments to penthouses. The buildings will be upto 8 to 10 storeys high. The apartments are being constructed by Army Welfare Housing Organisation (AWHO) on a no profit, no loss basis. In the past, AWHO has completed similar projects in Delhi, NOIDA, Gurgaon and Faridabad besides projects in over twenty other towns

990. (15-5-2007) NEW DELHI : Minister for Tourism and Culture Smt. Ambika Soni informed the Rajya Sabha today that the Archaeological Survey of India has filed a case before the Hon'ble High Court, Patna praying for removal of the unauthorized and illegal constructions within the protected monument of 'Tomb of Sher Shah' in Sasaram. The Superintending Archaeologist, Archaeological Survey of India, Patna Circle has approached the District Authority for revival of inlet and outlet channels and to prevent the immersion of idols, washing of cloth, etc. to ensure flow of clean water.

991. (15-5-2007) NEW DELHI : Minister of Tourism and Culture Smt. Ambika Soni has said that the Government of India, Ministry of Culture has agreed to provide financial assistance of Rs. 9.00 crores to the Gujarat Council of Science City (GCSC) for setting up a Science city at Ahmedabad in Gujarat. Out of Rs. 9.00 crores, the Ministry has so far released Rs. 8.00 crores. In a written reply in the Rajya Sabha today she said, the Ministry of Culture has received request from GCSC for release of balance amount Rs. 1.00 crore for the project. However, due to non-receipt of Annual Audited Statements Accounts of the GCSC for the year 2002-03 onwards and Utilization Certificate for the grants released during year 2005-06, the Ministry is unable to release the balance amount of Rs. 1.00 crore.

992. (15-5-2007) NEW DELHI : The President of India, as advised by the Prime Minister, has accepted the resignation of Shri Dayanidhi Maran, Minister of Communications and Information Technology, from the council of Ministers, with immediate effect. Further, as advised by the Prime Minister, the President of India has directed that the portfolios of the following Ministers shall be changed and allocated as indicated.

993. (15-5-2007) NEW DELHI : Delay in completion of projects results in cost over-run. The other reasons for cost over run are inadequate provision in the original estimates, change in the scope of the project mostly extension of command area, geological surprises, unexpected increase in the cost of land acquisition, Resettlement and Rehabilitation, forest land acquisition, cost escalation of construction material, labour etc. In view of normal gestation period of major projects as 10 to 15 years and that of medium projects as 5 to 8 years, the major projects started during or before 1992 and medium projects started during or before 8th plan which will be continuing as ongoing in 11th plan may be considered as delayed projects. As per the Working Group Report for 11th Plan, Plan-wise break-up of such ongoing projects likely to spill over into 11th Plan are given as under: Among the above 205 projects, 62 major and 49 medium projects are approved projects. As per the information available in Central Water Commission, total original approved cost of these 111 projects was Rs.20,420 crore whereas, the latest estimated cost is Rs.1,16,242 crore. Generally the projects are delayed due to fund constraints, resettlement and rehabilitation issues, land acquisition, forest and environmental clearance, Inter-departmental bottlenecks, contractual problems and changes in the scope of the projects etc. Irrigation is a State subject and planning, execution, funding as well as priority of construction and completion of projects is within the purview of State Government. In order to expedite completion of ongoing irrigation projects, the Central Government launched Accelerated Irrigation Benefit Programme in 1996-97 under which, Central Loan Assistance/Grant amounting to Rs.23231.8659 crore has been provided to the States till date. This information was given by the Minister of State for Water Resources, Shri Jai Prakash Narayan Yadav in response to a question by Shri Ekanath K. Thakur in the Rajya Sabha today.

994. (15-5-2007) NEW DELHI : The average annual water availability in the country is assessed as 1869 billion cubic metre (BCM). Based on the population of 1027 million as per the 2001 census, the per capita available works out to be 1820 cubic metre per year. However, there is considerable temporal and spatial variations in the water availability in the country and due to population growth, the per capita water availability is also declining year after year. There are also instances of over-exploitation of ground water leading to lowering of water table in certain areas. Water being a state subject, several measures for development and management of water resources are undertaken by the respective State Governments which include creation of storages, restoration of water bodies, rain water harvesting, artificial recharge to ground water and adoption of better management practices etc. Government of India provides assistance to the State Governments for completion of on-going irrigation projects under the Accelerated Irrigation Benefit Programme (AIBP). Further, a pilot scheme titled "National Project for Repair, Renovation and Restoration of Water Bodies directly linked to Agriculture" has been approved by Government of India in January 2005. Government of India also provides support under centrally sponsored scheme for Command Area Development and Water Management (CAD&WM) with a view to bridging the gap between irrigation potential created and potential utilized. Government has also constituted an Advisory Council on Artificial Recharge to Ground Water under the Chairmanship of Union Minister of Water Resources with the main objective to popularize the concept of artificial recharge to ground water among all stakeholders. This information was given by the Minister of State for Water Resources, Shri Jai Prakash Narayan Yadav in response to a question by Shri Uday Pratap Singh in the Rajya Sabha today.

995. (15-5-2007) NEW DELHI : The average annual water availability in the country is assessed as 1869 billion cubic metre (BCM). Based on the population of 1027 million as per the 2001 census, the per capita available works out to be 1820 cubic metre per year. However, there is considerable temporal and spatial variations in the water availability in the country and due to population growth, the per capita water availability is also declining year after year. There are also instances of over-exploitation of ground water leading to lowering of water table in certain areas. Water being a state subject, several measures for development and management of water resources are undertaken by the respective State Governments which include creation of storages, restoration of water bodies, rain water harvesting, artificial recharge to ground water and adoption of better management practices etc. Government of India provides assistance to the State Governments for completion of on-going irrigation projects under the Accelerated Irrigation Benefit Programme (AIBP). Further, a pilot scheme titled "National Project for Repair, Renovation and Restoration of Water Bodies directly linked to Agriculture" has been approved by Government of India in January 2005. Government of India also provides support under centrally sponsored scheme for Command Area Development and Water Management (CAD&WM) with a view to bridging the gap between irrigation potential created and potential utilized. Government has also constituted an Advisory Council on Artificial Recharge to Ground Water under the Chairmanship of Union Minister of Water Resources with the main objective to popularize the concept of artificial recharge to ground water among all stakeholders. This information was given by the Minister of State for Water Resources, Shri Jai Prakash Narayan Yadav in response to a question by Shri Uday Pratap Singh in the Rajya Sabha today.

996. (15-5-2007) NEW DELHI : Central Ground Water Authority (CGWA) has been constituted under sub-section 3 of Section 3 of the Environment (Protection) Act, 1986 vide notification dated 14.01.1997 and subsequent amendments for the purpose of regulation and control of ground water development and management in the country. The Central Ground Water Authority has undertaken the following regulatory measures to control the development of ground water: (i) Central Ground Water Authority is regulating withdrawal of ground water by industries/ projects in 1065 Over-exploited, critical and semi-critical areas. List of these areas has been circulated to the State Pollution Control Boards and Ministry of Environment & Forests which refer the new industries/ projects falling in these areas to CGWA for obtaining permission. Pre-conditions in case of permissions are mandatory adoption of rain water harvesting system, monitoring of ground water abstraction as well as monitoring of ground water level and quality etc. by the industry. (ii) CGWA has notified 43 Over-exploited areas in the country for regulation of ground water development and management. For enforcement of the regulatory directions issued under Section 5 of EPA. 1986, concerned Deputy Commissioners/District Magistrates have been authorized to take necessary action in case of violation of directives of CGWA in the notified areas. In these notified areas, installation of new ground water abstraction structures is not permitted without prior specific approval of the Authority. For more effective regulation of ground water development and management, Advisory Committee under the Chairmanship of District Collector/Deputy Commissioners have been constituted. (iii) Directions have been issued Group Housing Societies, Institutes, Hotels, Industries, Farm Houses, etc. in the notified areas of Delhi, Faridabad, Gurgaon and Gaziabad and other areas of NCT Delhi where ground water table is below 8 metres from ground surface, to adopt roof top rain water harvesting system. The last date for adoption of rain water harvesting has been extended upto 30.6.2007. (iv) CGWA have also notified 65 Over-exploited areas in various Sates, for registration of ground water abstraction structures, which showed a very steep decline in ground water levels and required action for regulation. Several measures for development and management of irrigation are undertaken by the respective State Governments which include creation of storages, restoration of water bodies, rain water harvesting, artificial recharge to ground water and adoption of better management practices etc. However, Government of India is providing Central Assistance to the State Governments through various schemes/ programmes, such as Accelerated Irrigation Benefits Programmes (AIBP); Command Area Development and Water Management (CADWM) Programme; National Project for Repair, Renovation and Restoration of Water Bodies directly linked to Agriculture etc. The Government of India also encourages rain water harvesting and recharge to ground water for conservation of water. The Central Ground Water Board (CGWB), under the Ministry of Water Resources, has also circulated Manual/ Guide on Artificial Recharge to Ground Water to the States/Union Territories to enable them to formulate area specific artificail recharge schemes to check the declining trend of ground water levels. Ministry of Water Resources have circulated a revised Model Bill to regulate and control the development and management of ground water to the Sates/ Union Territories in 2005. This information was given by the Minister of State for Water Resources, Shri Jai Prakash Narayan Yadav in response to a question by Shri Dharam Pal Sabharwal in the Rajya Sabha today.

997. (15-5-2007) NEW DELHI : The Government is finalising a new Central Act for regulating fisheries and fishing in the Exclusive Economic Zone (EEZ). Informing this to the Members of parliamentary Consultative Committee here today Shri Sharad Pawar, Union Minister of Agriculture, Consumer Affairs, Food and Public Distribution added that institutional and legal mechanisms are being put in place to regulate deep-sea fishing. Recently an Inter-Ministerial Empowered Committee has been set up to oversee deep-sea fisheries development. The National Fisheries Development Board, set up last year, would address development needs of deep-sea sector as well. Emphasising the importance of deep-sea fisheries, the Minister explained that out of the country's marine fisheries potential at 3.93 million tonnes, about 3 million tonnes comes from the inshore belt where there is very little scope for further augmenting fish production. The major bulk of exploitable surplus of 0.8 million tonnes thus lies in the offshore/deep sea belt. The Minister said that effectively exploiting deep-sea fishery potential is a challenge because deep-sea fishing is highly capital intensive and technology driven. Empowering the indigenous fleet for deep-sea fishing, acquisition of modern technology, human resource development and post harvest support including marketing support are the key elements for developing our deep sea fishing sector, the Minister said. The meeting was also attended by Secretary, Department of Animal Husbandary and Dairying, Ms. Charusheela Sohoni, Secretary, Department of Consumer Affairs, Shri Yashwant Bhave and senior officers of the Ministry. The members who attended the meeting include S/Shri Hansraj Gangaram Ahir, Bhanu Pratap Singh Verma, K. Francis George, M. Appadurai, Kailash Baitha, and Ms. Archana Nayak (Lok Sabha) Thennala G. Balakrishna Pillai, M. Venkaiah Naidu, Shri Sharad Joshi and Pyarelal Khandelwal (Rajya Sabha).

998. (15-5-2007) NEW DELHI : Maharashtra, Gujarat and Andhra Pradesh show the most satisfactory performance under the Jawaharlal Nehru National Urban Renewal Mission. They have secured 57.5 per cent of the total project value with 44, 40 and 30 projects approvals respectively. West Bengal, Tamil Nadu, Karnataka and Madhya Pradesh closely followed these with 17,16,14 and 13 project sanctions respectively. The remaining States can be considered slow moving for the year 2006-07. 205 projects costing Rs.16966 crore for 42 cities in 21 States were sanctioned under the JNNURM during 2006-07. The Government released the first instalment of additional central assistance worth Rs.1353.06 crore upto 31st March 2007. The Secretary, Ministry of Urban Development, Shri M. Ramachandran reviewed the progress under the JNNURM recently. The committed liability of the Government of India for these projects is Rs.8229.46 crore. The Projects, which have been sanctioned so far, include 64 water supply projects, 39 sewerage, 27 drainage and 20-soil waste management. These projects accounted for 78.4 per cent of the total projects sanctioned. They were followed by 39 roads/flyovers, 8 public transport and 6 urban renewal projects. As per appraisal reports, 40 projects worth Rs.1285.07 crore will be completed during the current year 2007-08. Another 63 and 49 projects worth Rs.3488.82 and Rs.6121.91 crores will be completed during the next two years *i.e.* 2008-09 and 2009-2010 respectively as per commitment given by the cities/States. During the last financial year, 5 workshops for the elected representatives of the urban local bodies, 6 workshops for senior municipal functionaries and 7 workshops for second level municipal functionaries were conducted. A national conference and workshop on heritage was organized at Mysore, in Karnataka. Six regional workshops for technical and managerial staff of State/urban local bodies for improving the quality of detailed project reports were held at different cities. Five regional workshops for review of JNNURM activities and its progress as well as for rolling out the credit rating initiative were held in different cities. Peer Experience and Reflective Learning (PEARL) programme was launched in Hyderabad with the objective to create manageable network between JNNURM cities for cross learning and knowledge sharing. Since the launch of Jawaharlal Nehru National Urban Renewal Mission on the 3rd of December 2005, 29 meetings of the Central Sanctioning and Monitoring Committee have been held. In the first meeting, which was held in the current financial year, 5 projects were approved and another 43 projects are under appraisal. Community Participation Fund of Rs.90 crore has also been approved in this meeting. This money will fund community-based projects prepared by the area Sabhas and Community based organizations.

999. (15-5-2007) NEW DELHI : Dr. Dasari Narayana Rao, Minister of State for Coal informed the Chief Minister of Orissa Shri Navin Patnaik that the Ministry of Coal has sanctioned coal linkages and allotted coal blocks to support generation of additional 10,200 MW power in the State. Shri Navin Patnaik met Dr. Dasari Narayana Rao here today to request allocation of additional coal blocks for power projects in view of growing needs of the State for rapid industrialization and economic growth. Giving details Dr. Rao informed the CM that his Ministry has sanctioned long term linkages for new capacity of 3000 megawatt. These include 2000 megawatt power plant to be set up by NLC, 500 megawatt plant of Navbharat Power Pvt. Ltd., 250 MW each of KVK Nilachal Power Pvt. Ltd. and Jindal Photo Ltd. In addition, one coal block has been allotted for Darlipalli thermal plant of NTPC (3200 MW). The Minister further said that 3 coal blocks viz. Meenakshi, Dipside of Meenakshi and Meenakshi-B have been allocated for Orissa Ultra-mega Power Project (4000 MW). Dr. Rao added that his Ministry is already supplying coal or has decided to make coal available to support about 15,000 MW power generation in Orissa. He further informed that a quantity of 22 million metric tonne (MMT) of coal is being supplied to power utilities of OPGENCO & NTPC in the State to support generation of about 5,000 megawatt of power. Of this, 18 MMT coal is being supplied for two thermal power plants of NTPC at Talcher and about 3 MMT to OPGENCO. He assured all assistance to the State for augmenting coal supply for meeting their growing requirements for industrialization and economic development.

1000. (15-5-2007) NEW DELHI : In pursuance of the judgement of the Supreme Court of October 6, 1993 in the Supreme Court Advocates on Record & Anrs. Vs. the Union of India, the judge strength of the High Courts is reviewed every three years. As per the guidelines, the required strength of permanent Judges in a High Court is worked out by dividing the average institution of main cases during the last five years by the national average or the average rate of disposal of main cases per Judge per year in that High Court, whichever is higher. Similarly, the required strength of Additional judges in a High Court is worked out by dividing the number of main cases pending over two years by the national average or the average rate of disposal of main cases per Judge per year in that High Court, whichever is higher. If the disposal per Judge in the concerned High Court is below even that of the national average then instead of increasing the strength, the concerned High Court is required to take steps for improvement in the rate of disposal of vases. If the average disposal of concerned High Court is above the national average then increase in Judge strength is accordingly considered. The strength of Additional Judges is reviewed only if there is an increase in the arrears of the pending cases during the last five years and the disposal per Judge is above the national average.

1001. (15-5-2007) NEW DELHI : More than Rs. 1.75 crore have been paid as unemployment allowance under the Rajiv Gandhi Shramik Kalyan Yojana to insured workers covered under the Employees' State Insurance Scheme (ESIS). The scheme has been introduced by the Employees' State Insurance Corporation working under the aegis of Labour and Employment Ministry. Under it the insured persons facing involuntary unemployment on or after 1st April, 2005 on account of closure of a factory or establishment, retrenchment or permanent invalidity of not less than 50% arising out of non-employment injury, are entitled to claim unemployment allowance up to 50% of their wages for a maximum period of 6 months during the entire service. The only condition is that such insured workers must have contributed to ESI Scheme for five or more years.

1002. (15-5-2007) NEW DELHI : The Central Board of Secondary Education (CBSE) has informed that it has already provided certain relaxation and concession to physically challenged students, namely, exemption to appear in third language in the case of dyslexic, blind students and those suffering from speech/hearing defects; physiotherapy exercises in place of physical and health education courses of the Board in class-X and XII; option of studying one compulsory language as against two language in class-X.

1003. (15-5-2007) NEW DELHI : In order to strengthen basic science research within the university system, a Task Force under the Chairmanship of Prof. M.M. Sharma was constituted by the Central Government. In its Report, the Task Force has inter alia, recommended creation of 1000 positions of Research Scientists at various levels, five fold increase in the number of Ph.Ds from Indian universities within a span of ten years with proper standards, promotion of formal linkage between the Universities and national level institutions including the CSIR laboratories through joint research projects and training, inbuilt component of research in post-graduate programmes pertaining to Science and Technology, upgradation of infrastructural facilities in universities to promote quality scientific research, and, creation of networking centres in Basic Sciences in leading Departments of Universities to promote collaborative research. The recommendations have been accepted by the Government and the Task Force has been converted into an Empowered Committee to implement its recommendations. The University Grants Commission has included the proposals under its plan for allocation of funds. Education Ministers of State Governments have also been apprised of these initiatives at the recent Conference of State Education Ministers in April, 2007 at New Delhi. This information was given by the Minister of State for Human Resource Development Smt. D. Purandeswari in a written reply in the Lok Sabha today.

1004. (15-5-2007) NEW DELHI : According to an estimate based on National Sample Survey Organisation (NSSO) Report No. 409, 50th round (1993-94) only 5.06% youth in labour force in the country are vocationally trained. The Prime Minister in his independence Day (2006) speech had announced to launch a Mission on Vocational Education. Consequent upon the announcement a Task Force has been constituted on 6.12.2006 by the Planning Commission to suggest steps to promote Vocational Education and Training during 11th Plan period and beyond. This information was given by the Minister of State for Human Resource Development Shri M.A.A. Fatmi in a written reply in the Lok Sabha today.

1005. (15-5-2007) NEW DELHI : Shri J. P. Batra, Chairman, Railway Board inaugurated at Vigyan Bhawan today a Seminar on High Speed Corridors on Indian Railways. The Seminar was jointly organized by the Ministry of Railways, Planning Commission and the Asian Institute of Transport Development. The subjects for the different sessions included Economic Growth & Mobility, case for High Speed Passenger Services, Project Financing and Technology Platform etc. In his inaugural remarks, Shri Batra said that the seminar on High Speed Corridors was taking place at a very opportune moment. Out of the four broad classes of products viz. freight, commuter, intercity and High Speed, the Indian Railways were doing well in the first three classes but lacked the fourth product. High Speed Corridors provide the commuter with an alternate mode for travelling punctually, fast, safely and with better comfort than any other mode and Internet has ensured that passengers also carry their office with them. A number of countries viz. Japan, Korea, China, Taiwan, France, Germany, Italy, Netherlands, Russia, Sweden etc. have either joined the bandwagon or are in the process of joining it. Various high speed corridors are already being planned in America. Elaborating on the need for High Speed Corridors in India, Shri Batra said that the need for a cleaner mode of transport for movement of people from one end to the other and also in view of global warming, it is imperative that High Speed trains fare better over all other modes of transport. The concern for affordability of high speed trains in India can be brushed aside by quoting the example of Shinkansen of Japan. Despite high initial cost, the daily average transport density of Tokaido Shinkansen is 2,20,000 passengers and it contributes nearly 500 billion yens per year just from the time saved for its passengers. Another example is the high speed railway in France. The socio-economic profitability combining the money and time saved by the passengers of the South East TGV is estimated to generate a return of 30 per cent on investments. In his concluding remarks, Shri Batra, in his concluding remarks, said that the idea was to scrutinize the feasibility of high speed corridors in India not only as an environmentally clean and viable alternative to meet the ever increasing transport demand but also to explore the possibility of high speed trains playing the vehicle of economic growth in the country. He requested the State Governments to partner with the Indian Railways in this new initiative and help boost the economic growth of their cities. H also asked the Industry to come forward with innovative solutions for making these projects a success.

1006. (15-5-2007) NEW DELHI : The Government is not considering to discontinue Prime Minster's Rozgar Yojana (PMRY). The complaints received from beneficiaries are being looked into and remedial measures are being taken. This was stated by Shri Mahabir Prasad, Minster of Small Scale Industries and Agro & Rural Industries in a written reply in Lok Sabha today. Complaints received from the beneficiaries are referred to the concerned banks for corrective action. Various steps have also been taken by the Central Government which include banks being asked to endorse one copy of the loan sanction letter to the concerned District Industries Centre (DIC) so that the latter can assist the beneficiaries in completing pre-disbursement formalities, instructions to banks to dispose of the applications within the prescribed time frame, provided the loan application is complete in all other respects. Instructions had also been issued making the District Selection Committee responsible for selection and recommendation of projects and beneficiaries, the Minister added.

1007. (15-5-2007) NEW DELHI : The Government has proposed to launch five new Schemes for Agro & Rural Industries. The proposals are only in preliminary stage and only a token budget provision for 2007-08 has been made for each of the five schemes. No targets, however, have been fixed.

1008. (15-5-2007) NEW DELHI : The Ministry of Rural Development has released grants-in-aid amounting to Rs. 16.94 crore to 48 DRDAs (Annexure) of Madhya Pradesh towards part payment of first instalment during the year 2007-08 under the Swarnjayanti Gram Swarojgar Yojana' (SGSY). An amount of Rs. 8.02 has also been released to Chhindwara DRDA of Madhya Pradesh towards Restoration of cut on account of late submission of Central Share of funds under the scheme during the year 2006-07. The amount should be utilized on the Programme as per approved guidelines of SGSY. The funding pattern will be 75:25 by the Centre and the State. The State Government should release its share within one month of the date of release of the Central assistance. Under SGSY, assistance is given to the poor family living below the poverty line for taking up self-employment. It actively promotes group approach by organising the rural poor into Self-Help Groups.

1009. (15-5-2007) NEW DELHI : Grants-in-aid amounting to Rs. 9.05 lakh has been released by the Ministry of Rural Development to the DRDA Hamirpur (Rs.2.71 lakh) and Chamba (Rs.6.34 lakh) of Himachal Pradesh towards Restoration of cut on account of late submission of Central share of funds under the 'Swarnjayanti Gram Swarojgar Yojana' (SGSY) for the year 2006-07. The Ministry of Rural Development has also released grants-in-aid amounting to Rs. 1.38 crore to 11

DRDAs of Himachal Pradesh towards part payment of first instalment of Central Share of funds during the year 2007-08 under the scheme as per details given below: The amount should be utilized on the Programme as per approved guidelines of SGSY. The funding pattern will be 75:25 by the Centre and the State. The State Government should release its share within one month of the date of release of the Central assistance.

1010. (15-5-2007) NEW DELHI : The Ministry of Rural Development has sanctioned Rs. 79.36 lakh of Grants-in-aid to 13 District Rural Development Agencies (DRDAs) of Punjab towards part payment of first instalment of Central Share for the year 2007-08 under DRDA Administration as per details below: The funding pattern under the scheme is 75:25 between Centre and the State. The utilization of funds is to be in accordance with the DRDA administration guidelines and the release of the second instalment during 2007-08 is subject to the fulfillment of all the conditions as per the DRDA Administration guidelines.

1011. (15-5-2007) NEW DELHI : Inter State Coordination Committees have been constituted to periodically review poaching problems along borders, to enable collaborative antipoaching strategy along the sensitive borders in six states having tiger reserves / protected areas. They are Ranthambore Tiger Reserve in Rajasthan, and Palpur Kuno Wildlife Sanctuary in M.P, Bandipur Tiger Reserve in Karnataka, Mudumalai Wildlife Sanctuary/National Park in Tamil Nadu, Wyanad Wildlife Sanctuary in Kerala and Pench Tiger Reserve in Maharashtra and Madhya Pradesh.

1012. (15-5-2007) NEW DELHI : Companies raise capital in the stock market on the basis of valid incorporation under the Companies Act, 1956, compliance with the Rules/Regulations under the Companies Act, 1956 and the SEBI Act, 1992, listing agreements with the Stock Exchange concerned and subject to the Guidelines and Regulation of SEBI as the Capital market regulator. As such, no instances of fake companies have come to notice in the stock market in the last two years. The details of the efforts made by the Government for the protection of small investors in the stock market are as under: The enactment of the SEBI Act, 1992 for setting up of SEBI to protect the interests of investors in securities and to promote the development of, and to regulate the securities market and related matters; Setting up of an Investor Education and Protection Fund (IEPF) by an amendment enacted in 1999, in the Companies Act, 1956, by addition of Section 205(C) in the Act, for promotion of investors' awareness and protection of their interests; Setting up of the Serious Fraud Investigation Office (SFIO) under the Ministry of Company Affairs to investigate cases of corporate fraud and to prosecute such Directors and Officers of the company who may have conducted the affairs of the company in a fraudulent manner detrimental to, *inter alia*, the interest of investors. Implementation of MCA 21, the e-governance programme of the Ministry of Company Affairs, under which disclosures made through documents filed by the companies as required by statute are available for viewing in electronic form, on-line, on round the clock basis to stakeholders on payment of prescribed fees. This initiative is aimed at ensuring enhanced transparency as to the management, governance and financial affairs of companies, thereby enabling protection of the interest of investors/stakeholders. This information was given by Shri Prem Chand Gupta, Minister of Company Affairs in reply to the questions raised by Smt. Sushma Swaraj in Rajya Sabha today.

1013. (15-5-2007) NEW DELHI : The Government initiated the process for comprehensive revision of the Companies Act, 1956 by preparing a concept paper on company law which was placed on the website of the Ministry on August 4, 2004 for information and comments by stakeholders. Thereafter, on December 2, 2004, an Expert Committee headed by Dr. J J Irani was constituted to subject various views/opinions received to merit evaluation and make recommendations to the Government on revision of the Companies Act, 1956. The Committee submitted its report on May 31, 2005. The Irani Committee, while observing that the law should take into account the requirements of different kinds of companies and prescribing the essential requirements of their corporate governance structure, recommended that Small and Private Companies should be provided greater flexibility and freedom of operation while enabling compliance at low cost. To unleash the entrepreneurial talent of the people in the information and technology driven environment, law should recognize One-Person Company (OPC). Such companies should be provided with a simple legal regime through exemptions. Taking into account the recommendations of the Irani Committee as also other inputs received by the Government, a draft Companies Bill is under preparation, in consultation with Ministry of Law, to be introduced in the Parliament once finalized with requisite approvals. This information was given by Shri Prem Chand Gupta, Minister of Company Affairs in reply to the questions raised by Shri Jai Parkash Aggarwal in Rajya Sabha today.

1014. (15-5-2007) NEW DELHI : This Ministry of Company Affairs has chalked out an elaborate plan for investor education and protection under Investor Education & Protection Fund (IEPF) for the year 2007-2008. This includes: (i) Organising seminars/ programmes on investor education through associations registered under IEPF to educate the investors about the Initial Public Offers (IPOs), Capital market instruments and mutual funds; (ii) Conducting 'Training the Trainers' Programme for capacity building of the Non Governmental Organisations/Voluntary Organisations; (iii) Media Campaigns through Electronic and print medium to create investor awareness and spread Financial Literacy amongst potential investors; Investor Education and Protection Fund (IEPF) has been established under Section 205C of the Companies Act, 1956 by way of Companies (Amendment) Act, 1999 for promotion of investors' awareness and protection of the interests of investors. The Ministry has taken the following steps to protect the small investors from being defrauded: (i) MCA-21, an e-governance initiative, has been launched with a view to bring transparency and certainty in the delivery of services to the stakeholders and empower the investors by providing access to the public information about the companies. (ii) A new concept of Director Identification Number has been introduced for existing or intending directors, which would help in establishing the identity of a Director and also help in correlating his participation in other corporate entities. (iii) A website, namely www.watchoutinvestors.com, which is a national registry of economic defaulters and covers information on convictions by various regulatory bodies, has been created to help, free of cost, the investors to protect themselves from unscrupulous promoters, companies and entities. (iv) An "Investor Helpline" www.investorhelpline.in project has also been launched under IEPF through Midas Touch Investors Association to provide a mechanism for redressal of grievances and to create investor awareness, free of cost. This information was given by Shri Prem Chand Gupta, Minister of Company Affairs in reply to the questions raised by Shri V. Hanumantha Rao in Rajya Sabha today.

1015. (15-5-2007) NEW DELHI : The Information & Broadcasting Ministry has permitted 222 private satellite TV channels to uplink from India as on 30.4.2007. Six TV channels uplinked from abroad have also been permitted to downlink in India. In addition to this, 54 foreign TV channels have been provisionally permitted to downlink in India. The proposals of 71 private satellite TV channels for permission to uplink from India are at various stages of scrutiny in accordance with the existing uplinking guidelines. The criteria for grant of permission uplink private satellite TV channels are prescribed under the Guidelines for Uplinking from India which are available on the Ministry's website (http://www.mib.nic.in). All programmes of satellite TV channels transmitted or re-transmitted through cable service are required to adhere to the provisions of the Programme/Advertising Codes prescribed under the Cable Television Networks (Regulation) Act, 1995 and rules framed thereunder. The channels are required to keep a record of programmes downlinked for a period of 90 days and to produce the same before any agency of the Government as and when required, as prescribed under the downlinking guidelines. Government has also sanctioned setting up of Electronic Media Monitoring Centre to monitor contents of satellite TV channels. This information was given by Minister of Information & Broadcasting and Parliamentary Affairs, Shri P. R. Dasmunsi in written reply to a question in Lok Sabha today.

1016. (15-5-2007) NEW DELHI : DAVP has been writing to newspapers refusing to publish PSU Advertisements, as per the clause 18 (f) of the Advertisement Policy. No response has been received as yet from them. The Indian Newspaper Society (INS) has directed all the member newspapers not to publish advertisements of PSUs and Autonomous Bodies at DAVP rates. The recommendations of the Rate Structure Committee regarding print media advertisements rates have been implemented with effect from 01.01.2006. This information was given by Minister of Information & Broadcasting and Parliamentary Affairs, Shri P. R. Dasmunsi in written reply to a question in Lok Sabha today.

1017. (15-5-2007) NEW DELHI : During 2005-06, out of a total 225 Central Public Sector Enterprises (CPSEs), 157 were profit making and 58 were loss making. For 10 CPSEs no information is available. This was stated by Shri Sontosh Mohan Dev, Minister of Heavy Industries and Public Enterprises in a written reply to a question in the Rajya Sabha today. The Minister said that the reasons for losses were manifold and enterprise specific. However, some common problems faced by the sick and loss making CPSEs include obsolete plant and machinery, outdated technology, resource crunch, low capacity utilization, interest burden, stiff competition, weak marketing, surplus manpower etc. The National Common Minimum Programme inter alia stipulates that while every effort will be made to modernise and restructure sick public sector companies and revive sick industries, chronically loss making companies will either be sold-off, or closed, after all workers have got their legitimate dues and compensation. The private industry will be inducted to turnaround companies that have potential for revival. A Board for Reconstruction of Public Sector Enterprises (BRPSE) was set up in December, 2004 to examine inter alia the cases of sick/loss making CPSEs referred to it by the concerned administrative Ministries/Departments. While examining the cases of sick and loss making CPSEs the BRPSE takes into consideration various aspects including those relating to objectives, business policy, resources etc. The Board made recommendations in respect of 41 cases of CPSEs for revival and two for closure till 31.3.2007, the Minister added.

1018. (16-5-2007) NEW DELHI : Shri Kamal Nath, Union Minister of Commerce & Industry, has said that the US move on utilisation of the special H1B visa by Indian IT companies restricting movement of skilled professionals would have an adverse impact on the rapidly expanding services trade and has warned that it would be difficult for India to enhance its commitments in the services negotiations in the World Trade Organisation (WTO) unless there is forward movement by trading partners like US in such areas. Shri Kamal Nath has also said that he will raise this issue with Ms. Susan Schwab, the United States Trade Representative (USTR) and in the G-4 meetings scheduled to be held in Brussels on May 17-19, 2007. Following is the full text of the statement by Shri Kamal Nath on this subject: "A letter written by two members of the US Senate Judiciary Committee (Sub-Committee on Immigration, Border Security and Refugees) to some prominent Indian IT companies has been brought to my notice. The letter seeks details about the utilization of the special HIB visa programme by these companies. I am surprised both with the form and content of the letter. Issues such as work visas are inter-governmental in nature and should be dealt with accordingly. Temporary movement of skilled professionals is an essential component of the global services economy and bears no relation to immigration issues. Any move which creates uncertainty and unpredictability about such movements will naturally have an adverse impact on the rapidly expanding services trade. In recent years, India and the US have significantly expanded their bilateral engagement in services trade to mutual advantage. Indeed, the importance of knowledge-based services trade in the trade basket is a unique feature of India-US trade. For quite some time now, we have been discussing with the US regarding further liberalization of their regime for movement of skilled professionals to facilitate further expansion of this trade. At this juncture, we would be extremely concerned if there are efforts to circumscribe the existing levels of liberalization in this area in the United States. I will be raising this issue with Ambassador Susan Schwab, USTR and in the G-4 meetings being held in Brussels on May 17-18, 2007. In previous discussions, I have informed Ambassador Schwab that while India continues to liberalise its services economy, it expects at least equal movement from important trading partners like the US in areas of our interest like Mode-4. Unless we see forward movement in such areas, it will be difficult for India to enhance its commitments in the services negotiations. Services are an important component of the breakthrough in the current WTO negotiations and any move which vitiates the current progress will only frustrate the progress in bringing the round to a successful completion. I would like to assure Indian industry that India will not subscribe to any WTO conclusion without a satisfactory outcome in services".

1019. (16-5-2007) NEW DELHI : Gitdabling is a tiny hilly village situated on the foothills of north-eastern Himalayas about 48 kilometres from Kalimpong, a sub-divisional town famous for its home-made cakes and pastries in the Darjeeling district of West Bengal. Most of the people living in the nearby villages here are Lepchas who prefer to call themselves a primitive tribe. Gitdabling was best known for its rich ginger harvest. But a series of bad crops in 1990s ruined the villagers. Their effort to save the harvest siphoned-off their hard earned savings. They lost hope and gave up the traditional ginger cultivation. Regimith, a Lepcha tribal lady, 37 year old, and her husband Lok Bahadur Chhetri, aged 40, were no exception to this misery. To earn a living, Lok Bahadur started working in Doctor Graham Homes' Dairy at Kalimpong for some time. It was here that an idea to set up a mini dairy farm of his own at Gitdabling struck him. He approached the local Gramin Vikas Bank for help. Regimith, who had got a job in the village panchayat helped secured him a loan of Rs. 15,000 under the self-employment scheme. With this money and a saving of Rs. 5,000 the couple purchased six cows of local breed. They built a bamboo shed near their house and thus began the first cottage dairy of Gitdabling. His experience at Doctor Graham Homes' Dairy helped Lok Bahadur to look after his cows and milk business. Initially the Chhetri family had 30-35 litres milk daily which they supplied to Doctor Graham Homes' Dairy and Himul Cooperative Dairy. They motivated fellow villagers to follow them and soon increased their milk collection. The couple also started diversifying into production of curd, butter, paneer (cheese), ghee etc. Their hard work brought them good fortune and affluence. The resultant success gradually motivated the fellow villagers, into cattle-farming and Gitdabling into a 'dairy village'. Today, this chain of milk business has spread out to nearby villages of Upper Beyong, Lower Beyong, Changdung, Tugang, Payelong and Payechak. Every morning people from these villages bring their milk to the collection centre at Chhetris' house. For the last seven years, not only the Chhetri couple but the whole valley has never looked back. Impressed by Chhetris' determination and success the Cooperative Bank sanctioned a loan of Rs. 50,000 to them which they soon paid back. Now the local Gramin Bank has issued a five year term-loan to Regimith. Today about 137 families of the area are involved in a daily business with Chhetris' and their cottage dairy's daily collection of milk has exceeded 400 litres. Lok Bahadur got a special boost when Himalaya Dugdh Sahkari Sansthan recognized him as its regular member. The credit for the Chhetri's gradual but steady progress goes to the *Panchayati Raj* system and a chain of rural banks in the Darjeeling villages. The couple's untiring efforts are the key inspiration to the sea-change that has been seeping-in, in this hilly region.

1020. (16-5-2007) NEW DELHI : Export of gems and jewellery has bee identified as a thrust sector in the Foreign Trade Policy (2004-09). In the Foreign Trade Policy as updated on 19.4.2007, following facilities have been extended to the sector: Import of gold of 8 carat and above allowed under the replenishment scheme subject to the import being accompanied by an Assay Certificate specifying the purity, weight and alloy content. Duty Free import entitlement of consumables, tools, machinery and equipments for metals other than Gold and Platinum equal to 2% and for Gold and Platinum equal to 1% of FOB value of exports during the preceding financial year. In case of rhodium-finish silver jewellery, entitlement will be 3% of such jewellery. Duty free import entitlement of gems & jewellery samples in a financial year upto Rs. 300,000/- or 0.25% of the average of last three years export turnover of gems and jewellery items, whichever is lower. Duty free re-import entitlement for rejected jewellery upto 2% of the FOB value of exports in preceding year. Cutting and polishing of gems & jewellery, treated as manufacturing for the purposes of exemption under Section 10A of the Income Tax Act. Import of precious metal scrap/used jewellery allowed for melting, refining and re-export of jewellery. However, such import will not be allowed through hand baggage. Gems & Jewellery exporters allowed to export jewellery on consignment basis as per Rules. Gems & Jewellery exporters allowed to export cut and polished precious and semi-precious stones for treatment and re-import as per Rules. In the Union Budget 2007-08 following facilities have been provided to this sector:Import duty on cut and polished diamond abolished. Import duty on unworked corals reduced from 30% to 10%. Import duty on rough synthetic stones reduced from 12.5% to 5%. Introduction of Income Tax on turnover basis for assesses engaged in diamond manufacturing and trading who declare profits from such activities at 8% or more of turnover. Other facilities extended to this sector are promotion of gems and jewellery products through advertisements, publicity campaigns and participation in international fairs, organizing buyer-seller meets abroad, etc. The Government also encourages creation of training infrastructure in this sector.

1021. (16-5-2007) NEW DELHI : Only such applications which satisfy the requirements laid down in the Special Economic Zones Act, 2005 and the Special Economic Zones rules, 2006 and have been duly recommended by the State Governments concerned, are considered by the Special Economic Zones (SEZs) Board of Approval. It is not possible to estimate the number of SEZs that would be set up in the next three years. However, after the SEZ Act, 2005 and SEZ Rules, 2006 came into effect on 10th February, 2006, 237 formal approvals for setting up SEZs have been granted of which 103 SEZs have been notified while 3 have been withdrawn/cancelled. This was stated by the Minister of State for Commerce, Shri Jairam Ramesh in a written reply in the Rajya Sabha today.

1022. (16-5-2007) NEW DELHI : The Newspapers have carried reports today about some suggestions that I should stand as a candidate for the post of President of India. I want to state categorically that I have no desire to occupy that office. The NDA will announce its choice for the post of President of India shortly.

1023. (16-5-2007) NEW DELHI : Various issues concerning the Special Economic Zones (SEZs) policy including issues relating to land acquisition for SEZs have been considered by the Government and it has been decided that the State Governments would not undertake any compulsory acquisition of land for such SEZs approved after 5th April, 2007. It has also been decided to fix the upper limit of the area required for multi product SEZs at 5000 hectares with the provision that the State Governments may prescribe a lower limit. Further, the Ministry of Rural Development has been requested to reformulate a comprehensive Land Acquisition Act to address all relevant issues and also to work out a comprehensive Resettlement and Rehabilitation Policy ensuring livelihood from the project to at least one person from each displaced family. Extent of land involved in SEZs formally approved in the case of Brandix India Apparel City Private Ltd., Infosys Technologies, Jindal Stainless Ltd., Tata Consultancy Services Ltd., Mahindra Gesco Developers Ltd., M/s. Reliance, M/s. Ascendas and The Chatterjee Group.

1024. (16-5-2007) NEW DELHI : The export of Indian products including Agricultural products are governed by Foreign Trade Policy which is formulated keeping interest of all stakeholders including domestic consumers. Major export destination/major importing countries for Indian agricultural products are European Union, USA, Gulf countries, China and Japan. This was stated by the Minister of State for Commerce, Shri Jairam Ramesh, in a written reply in the Rajya Sabha today.

1025. (16-5-2007) NEW DELHI : No instance of flouting of SEZ guidelines by promoters has come to the notice of the Government so far, Minister of State for Commerce, Shri Jairam Ramesh stated in a written reply to a question in the Rajya Sabha today.. The empowered Group of Ministers (EGOM) at its meeting held on 5th April, 2007 had inter alia decided to fix the upper limit of the area required for multi product SEZs at 5000 hectares with a provision that the State Governments may prescribe a lower limit. In the 234 formal approvals granted so far, none of the SEZs has an area over 5000 hectares and therefore, the question of reviewing permission granted in these 234 formal approvals does not arise. In cases where in principle approvals have been granted, the developers are required to submit proposals for formal approvals. The decision of the EGOM would be applicable to all these cases as well as new proposals received.

1026. (16-5-2007) NEW DELHI : Total foreign exchange earned by the Export Oriented Units (EOUs) during the year 2004-05, 2005-06 and 2006-07 (April-December) were to the extent of approximately US $ 8700 million, US $ 11200 Million and US $ 8100 Million (provisional) respectively. The share of EOUs in the total exports of the country was about 10.45%, 10.84% and 9.07% during the year 2004-05, 2005-06 and 2006-07 (April-December) respectively. Units under export oriented scheme are eligible for fiscal concessions which include duty free import, domestic procurement and reimbursement of Central Sales Tax (CST) on capital goods, raw materials, consumables for their production activities and corporate tax exemption on export income for a period of 10 years. This was stated by the Minister of State for Commerce, Shri Jairam Ramesh, in a written reply in the Rajya Sabha today.

1027. (16-5-2007) NEW DELHI : The 'Ministry of Company Affairs' has been renamed as the 'Ministry of Corporate Affairs' vide Presidential Notification dated the 9th May 2007 amending the Government of India (Allocation of Business) Rules, 1961. "The new name not merely reflects a change in the form but also in the vision and approach that drives the initiatives of the Ministry", said the Minister, Shri Prem Chand Gupta while recounting the reasons for changing the name. The focus of the Ministry's working is no longer limited to the administration of companies but has increasingly acquired an all-inclusive role of addressing a wide sweep of functions-Corporate Governance reforms and the emerging legal framework. With the introduction of the 'Limited Liability Partnership Bill' proposing a new corporate structure, the amendments in the Acts governing the three professional institutions viz. the Institute of Chartered Accountants of India, the Institute of Costs & Works Accountants of India, and the Institute of Company Secretaries of India, notification of Accounting Standards, the initiatives being taken towards operationalisation of the 'Competition Commission of India', etc., the Ministry has, during the period of last two years, re-oriented itself to meet the expectations of a vibrant corporate sector in its march towards the global competitive environment. The implementation of MCA21 e-Governance Project, a mission mode project under the National e-Governance Plan, has brought about a complete turn around in the manner of delivery of services to the corporate sector. It is online, it is fast, it is transparent and it has largely eliminated the need for the stakeholders to physically visit the Registrars' offices and the drudgery of queuing-up with loads of paper. With more than 4.5 crore sheets of legacy records having been scanned and digitised, and the continuous enrichment of the electronic registry on an on-going basis the citizens can view public documents on-line any time anywhere from the comforts of their offices or homes. The Ministry is engaged in a complete revamp of the legal framework for the corporate sector. A new form of body corporate is proposed to be enabled through the proposed legislation on Limited Liability Partnerships for which the Bill has already been introduced in the Parliament. It is expected that this new framework will provide a significant boost to the growth of professional and knowledge domain in the country in an organised form. Similarly, amendments to the Competition Act, 2002 are at advanced stages of processing to enable operationalisation of a full-fledged Competition Commission of India. The Companies Act, 1956 is itself under a comprehensive revision. Having followed the process of wide consultation with the stakeholders and examination of the proposals by an Expert Group headed by Dr. JJ Irani, the draft for the new Company Law is at the vetting stage. "We can understand the anxiety of the corporate world who have been waiting for this new law but it has to be appreciated that the Companies Act, 1956 is the single largest piece of legislation and it takes time to re-write a piece of legislation which is envisaged to be not only simple and easy to understand but also forward-looking in keeping with the dynamic process of change in an international environment," explained the Minister. The notification of Accounting Standards is another milestone to bring the Indian corporate financial reporting systems in line with the international practices. The new Accounting Standards are not only expected to strengthen the system of disclosures for the stakeholders but also bring about parity with the international standards in a significant manner. This has become important in view of the Indian corporate stretching their operations beyond the national boundaries.

1028. (16-5-2007) NEW DELHI : Government has not of late reviewed or revised the iron ore exports policy, Minister of State for Commerce Shri Jairam Ramesh informed in a written reply to a question in the Rajya Sabha today. The existing iron ore exports policy regulates and promotes judicious use of iron ore for domestic purpose and export of surplus quantity. Production of iron ore is in excess of current domestic demand. Besides, the surplus iron ore fines, produced during mining as well as sizing and calibrating lumpy ore has to be evacuated through enabling exports as there is meager demand for it by domestic steel industry. Its accumulation would lead to curtailment of production resulting in unemployment predominantly in tribal areas, increased cost of production, reduction in economic activities and export earnings in addition to causing environmental hazards, he said.

1029. (16-5-2007) NEW DELHI : An Indian youth, Shri Sher Dhillon, accompanied by Mr. Jason Lewis, an Englishman, have travelled on board their boat without sails and without motor for 47 days and about 3000 kms. across the Indian Ocean from Mumbai to Djibouti during March 2007. Government has instituted the

"Tenzing Norgay National Adventure Awards" which cover such achievements on land, air and water. This achievement may be considered in making selection for the Awards this year, subject to the completion of the required formalities. This information was given by Shri Mani Shankar Aiyar, Minister of Panchayati Raj, Youth Affairs & Sports and DoNER in the Lok Sabha today in a written reply to a question by Shri M.K. Subba.

1030. (16-5-2007) NEW DELHI : Around 13000 sportspersons are being trained in different centres under various schemes being implemented by the Sports Authority of India (SAI). Further, around 3500 sportspersons (including some trainees in the SAI's centres) are being trained every year under National Coaching Camps in the context of international events. The 3rd Commonwealth Youth Games are being held at Pune in October, 2008 and the 19th Commonwealth Games are scheduled to be held in Delhi in October, 2010. International Championships/competitions in different disciplines are allotted by the World/International body concerned normally about a year in advance. As per information received from Federations concerned, the World Badminton Championship in 2009, the 10th Jr. and 4th Cadet World Archery Championships in 2008 and the 17th Commonwealth Table Tennis Championship in 2007 are proposed to be hosted by India. The Government is taking systematic steps for the creation/upgradation of the sports infrastructure required for the Commonwealth Games, and for up-gradation of the civic infrastructure and creation of other required facilities for the smooth and successful conduct of the Games. As far as the performance of Indian players is concerned, the Government is already providing assistance to National Sports Federations (NSFs) for holding national/international sports events in India and for participation of Indian sportspersons/teams in international tournaments abroad to enable them to get adequate competition exposure; for training and coaching in India (and abroad) through Indian and foreign coaches, with requisite scientific, technical and equipment support; and, for procurement of equipments etc., in terms of Long Term Development Plans (LTDPs) agreed between NSFs and Government. Detailed discussions are also being held with the NSFs and other stakeholders, including the Indian Olympic Association (IOA) and SAI, with a view to ensuring focused attention by all concerned on various measures for the improvement of performance at the international level. In addition, Government also provides financial assistance to identified meritorious sportspersons for the purchase of equipment, scientific support, and training and participation in events within the country and abroad under the schemes relating to 'Talent Search and Training' and the 'National Sports Development Fund'. A provision of Rs. 150 crores has been made during 2007-08 for preparations for the Commonwealth Games.

1031. (16-5-2007) NEW DELHI : The Minister of State for Coal Dr. Dasari Narayana Rao informed the Lok Sabha while replying to a question in the House today that 57 coal blocks have been allocated for power sector of which 9 coal blocks have been allocated for existing power plants and the remaining for expansion/new power plants to public and private sector companies.

1032. (16-5-2007) NEW DELHI : Bharat Heavy Electricals Ltd. (BHEL) has emerged as an active player in ensuring country's energy security related to electrical power by playing a larger role than just being a manufacturer and supplier of equipment. This was stated by Shri Sontosh Mohan Dev while addressing the Parliamentary Consultative Committee Meeting attached to his Ministry, here last night. Outlining the achievements of BHEL, the Minister said, BHEL recorded a turnover of Rs.18,702 crore (prov.) during 2006-07 – a growth of 29% over the previous year, after registering similar higher growth levels in the preceding two years. BHEL built thermal sets achieved the highest-ever Plant Load Factor (PLF) of 78.3%, higher than the national average by 1.5%. Further, BHEL make 200/210/250/500 MW thermal sets, which form the backbone of the country's thermal generating capacity, operated at a PLF of 83.5% & Operating Availability (OA) of 88.7%. Notably, 75 BHEL make sets achieved PLF of over 90% and 6 thermal sets of various ratings out of these operated at record PLF of 100%. BHEL has been consistently investing in R&D and had accelerated its R&D efforts recently. During the year 2006-07, the R&D spend has been Rs.238 crore, 58% higher than the previous year. The company has plans to increase it further by four times by 2011-12. BHEL is enhancing its manufacturing capacity to 10,000 MW p.a. by December 2007 at a cost of Rs.1600 crore and it plans to further hike this capacity to around 15,000 MW p.a. by December 2009 by investing around Rs.3200 crore. This enhancement of manufacturing capacity is possible only because of the availability of basic infrastructure and qualified and trained technical manpower in BHEL. The incremental investments, which are brown field expansion, is most economical to expand capacity, as against green field investment by any other company. During the year 2006-07, BHEL manufactured and supplied 7589 MW of power plant equipment and commissioned 7863 MW of power plants much beyond its capacity of 6000 MW p.a. catering to all sectors of domestic utilities, captive power plants for industry and overseas customers as part of its best efforts to meet the requirement of bunching of orders, Shri Dev added. Shri A.K.Puri, CMD, BHEL said that there were some reports suggesting that there was a proposal under consideration for setting up of a power equipment and engineering company on the lines of BHEL. This would be a sub-optimum solution to the problem of equipment manufacturing capacity constraints and the need for technology upgradation, he added. He said that from the details available so far, it was not clear as to why capacity additions in BHEL would not be sufficient to meet growing demand. A new company that operates in the same areas would be setting up similar capacities too. It is better to support an existing entity like BHEL where economies of scale for utilizing 15,000 MW p.a. capacity would outweigh setting up new manufacturing capacities where the gestation period could range from 3-4 years, not considering the skill requirements and capability building needed. Shri Puri said it remained a questionable idea even if the intention was to attract private capital by involving a domestic company or an MNC. Instead, BHEL itself can raise capital or access technology by taking on strategic partners.

1033. (16-5-2007) NEW DELHI : RBHs are not being incentivized by giving tax breaks or soft loans, but by converging extant schemes of State and Central Governments, as well as financing institutions/banks and promotional bodies, to promote integrated business relationships between decentralized rural production units and larger corporate entities through the intermediation of the Panchayats. The Electricity Act, 2003 enjoined the Central Government to formulate a National Policy for rural electrification and for the management of local distribution in rural areas through Panchayati Raj Institutions (PRIs) or franchisees. The Rural Electrification Policy, approved in 2006, stated that electricity has been recognized as a basic human need and further that a village would be classified as electrified based on a Certificate issued by the Gram Panchayat. The Gram Panchayat shall certify and confirm the electrified status of the village as on 31st March each year. Panchayati Raj Institutions would have both a supervisory as well as advisory role in rural electrification and electricity supply. The State Government could encourage Panchayati Raj Institutions to take on the responsibility of franchisees as and when they are deemed ready to undertake contractual obligations, raise resources and discharge associated legal responsibilities. Panchayati Raj Institutions will have an important role in overseeing the delivery of services by franchisees in accordance with their identified responsibility, in an advisory capacity. Under the Franchisee Guidelines of the Rajiv Gandhi Grameen Vidyutikaran Yojana 2006, Panchayati Raj Institutions are perceived as the primary interface for communication and advocacy of a participatory approach towards rural distribution management. With these provisions in view, a series of MoUs have already been entered into in the State of Karnataka between Panchayati Raj Institutions and electricity generation and distribution companies (both public and private sector), to promote Rural Business Hubs. This information was given by Shri Mani Shankar Aiyar, Minister of Panchayati Raj, Youth Affairs & Sports and DoNER in the Lok Sabha today in a written reply to a question by Shri Kailash Meghwal.

1034. (16-5-2007) NEW DELHI : Approximately seventy three per cent electors in the country have been issued Electors Photo Identity Cards (EPIC). In Kerala and Puducherry all electors have been issued photo identity cards. In West Bengal more than 95 per cent electors have been issued with EPIC followed by Punjab with 93 per cent and Haryana 87 per cent. The state-wise progress of issue of EPIC.

1035. (16-5-2007) NEW DELHI : The Department of Shipping has formulated the National Maritime Development Programme (NMDP). Under the Programme, a total of 387 projects involving an investment of Rs.1,00,339 crores have been identified to be taken up for implementation over a defined period. Out of this, 276 projects involving an investment of Rs.55,804 crores have been identified in the 12 Major Ports. The projects in the Major Ports relate to deepening of port channels, development of berths, modernization and upgradation of cargo handling equipment, enhancement of rail/road connectivity between the ports and the hinterland and other associated projects. Out of the investment for the Major Ports, Rs.34,505 crores are envisaged through private investment mainly in commercially viable activities like berths/terminals. The projects identified under the Programme are expected to be taken up for implementation over a period upto 2011-12. However, the year-wise financial outlays would depend on the timeframes involved in various processes like approval of the Competent Authority and the award of work for individual projects under the Programme as also the pace of execution and related factors including the demand projection and the funds availability. The objective is to upgrade and modernise the port infrastructure in India which will enable it to benchmark its performance against global standards. This information was given by the Minister of Shipping, Road Transport and Highways, Shri T.R. Baalu in a written reply in the Lok Sabha today.

1036. (16-5-2007) NEW DELHI : In order to strengthen coastal service, Government have given certain concessions, viz., (i) Coastal ships have been exempted from filing a bill of coastal goods at load ports and bill of entry at the discharge port; (ii) Coastal ships are exempted from light dues; (iii) Dedicated terminals have been provided for coastal shipping at various major ports in India; (iv) Vessel related charges for coastal vessels and cargo related charges for coastal cargoes have also been reduced and are now at 60% of the rate charged from other (foreign going) vessels; and (v) Tonnage tax is available to coastal ships registered under Merchant Shipping Act. Shipping service between India and Bangladesh is treated as international service. The 10th Plan did not make any specific reference to international service between India and Bangladesh. As such, there is no proposal to operate coastal service between India and Bangladesh. However, there is a feeder service operating on the 'Chennai-Kolkata-Chittagong,' route that caters to the east coast of India shipments to the Bangladesh Port. Also, another feeder service operating on the 'Colombo-Chittagong' route caters to shipments from west coast of Indian Ports to Bangladesh. No programme has been drawn to expand coastal service between India and Bangladesh in the Eleventh Plan. This information was given by the Minister of Shipping, Road Transport and Highways, Shri T.R. Baalu in a written reply in the Lok Sabha today.

1037. (16-5-2007) NEW DELHI : During the past 3-4 years, order book position of Indian shipyards has shown a phenomenal growth specially in export orders. The order book position has increased from Rs.150 crore in 2002 to about Rs.14,000 crore in 2006. India is expected to soon move up in the global ranking with the proposed capacity addition by various shipyards. Presently, there are no reservations for small scale industries in the shipbuilding sector. This information was given by the Minister of Shipping, Road Transport and Highways, Shri T.R. Baalu in a written reply in the Lok Sabha today.

1038. (16-5-2007) NEW DELHI : The National Highways Authority of India (NHAI) proposes to set up wayside amenities on the Golden Quadrilateral in line with international models. The wayside amenities would include the following facilities: Eating place, drinking water and toilets; Dormitory for rest; Facility of telephone; Fuelling facilities; Sufficient parking space for different categories of vehicles segregating the parking for buses and trucks from car and other light vehicles; Repair shops (mechanical and electrical) and shops for spare parts; A kiosk for sundry items; A space for spreading awareness about various government welfare programmes including first aid facility; and Landscaping. The wayside amenities at km 24 and km 78 on Ahmedabad-Vadodara Expressway are operational. In addition to above, wayside amenities at the following locations are under various stages of implementation: Km 20.057 to Km 20.357 Right Hand Side (RHS) on NH-8 (Jaipur Bypass) in the State of Rajasthan. Km 20.432 to Km 20.732 Left Hand Side (LHS) on NH-8 (Jaipur Bypass) in the State of Rajasthan. Km 46.700 to Km 46.900 (LHS) on NH-4 in the State of Karnataka. Km 61.130 to Km 61.330 (LHS) on NH-7 in State of Tamil Nadu. Km 528.200 on NH-2 in the State of West Bengal. Km. 617.530 on NH-2 in the State of West Bengal. Km 170.243 to Km 170.661 on NH-76 in the State of Rajasthan. Km 213.425 to Km 213.725 on NH-5 in the State of Andhra Pradesh. Km 285.396 to Km 285.656 on NH-5 in the State of Andhra Pradesh. Km 355.575 to Km 355.890 on NH-5 in the State of Andhra Pradesh. Km 81.0 on NH-5 in the State of Andhra Pradesh. Km 18.425 to Km 18.575 on NH-2 in the State of Uttar Pradesh. Km 235.473 to Km 253.673 on NH-5 in the State of Orissa. Km 305.225 to Km 305.375 on NH-5 in the State of Orissa. This information was given by the Minister of State for Shipping, Road Transport and Highways, Shri K.H. Muniyappa in a written reply in the Lok Sabha today.

1039. (16-5-2007) NEW DELHI : The Ministry of Shipping Road Transport & Highways provides funds to the State Governments under the schemes of the Central Road Fund (CRF) including the scheme of economic importance and interstate connectivity (EI&ISC) for development of State roads.

1040. (16-5-2007) NEW DELHI : The contractor engaged for the execution of the work has the responsibility to procure/provide crushed gravel/crushed shingle/ crushed stone aggregate, as specified in the Ministry of Shipping, Road Transport & Highways' "Specifications for Road and Bridge Works (Fourth Revision)", required for the work. No separate provision is made in the projects, sanctioned by the Ministry regarding setting up of stone-crushers. This Ministry has specified that the contractor has to take all precautions for safeguarding the environment during the course of construction and to abide by all the laws/rules related to pollution and environmental protection prevailing in the area of work. Moreover, the contractor shall take every precaution to reduce the levels of noise, vibration, dust and emissions from his plant and shall be fully responsible for any claims for damages caused to the owners of property, fields and residences in the vicinity. This information was given by the Minister of State for Shipping, Road Transport and Highways, Shri K.H. Muniyappa in a written reply in the Lok Sabha today.

1041. (16-5-2007) NEW DELHI : The National Highways Authority of India (NHAI) is implementing HIV/AIDS awareness campaign through Non-Governmental Organizations (NGOs) along NH-2 (Delhi-Kolkata), NH-28 (Lucknow –Muzaffarpur) NH-26 and NH-7 (Lalitpur to Anantpur-Andhra Pradesh/ Karnataka Border) and NH-76 and NH-25 (Chittorgarh-Jhansi). Presently, four NGOs have been awarded contracts for implementing HIV/AIDS awareness campaign along NH-28 (Lucknow-Muzaffarpur). Presently, the NHAI's HIV/ AIDS Prevention and Control Programme is being implemented as part of loan commitments to the World Bank and the Asian Development Bank (ADB) along the identified stretches as mentioned above. The estimated expenditure in this respect is around US $ 4.32 million (Rupees 19.44 crores approximately). This information was given by the Minister of State for Shipping, Road Transport and Highways, Shri K.H. Muniyappa in a written reply in the Lok Sabha today.

1042. (16-5-2007) NEW DELHI : The Union Government has approved the four laning of NH 22 from Ambala to Shimla, under NHDP –IIIA; The following stretches of NH-22 have been included in National Highways Development Project Phase-III A for four laning on Build, Operate and Transfer (BOT).

1043. (16-5-2007) NEW DELHI : During implementation of National Highways Development Project (NHDP) works, the contractors working in various States at times have informed about adverse law & order situation prevailing in the area hampering the progress of the projects. As per records, various companies/ contractors working on NHDP works have reported killing of five workers/staff during last three years. The matters with respect to adverse law & order situations are regularly taken up with concerned State Governments for providing adequate security to the personnel and equipments involved in the execution of the projects. In response, States have provided security at vulnerable locations at different points of time. This information was given by the Minister of State for Shipping, Road Transport and Highways, Shri K.H. Muniyappa in a written reply in the Lok Sabha today.

1044. (16-5-2007) NEW DELHI : Cluster Development approach is considered as an effective approach for inducing competitiveness in the industry by ensuring inter-firm cooperation based on networking and trust. Due to geographical proximity of units and homogeneity of products, development interventions can be made for a large number of units and simultaneously leading to higher gains at lower cost of implementation. This was stated by Shri Mahabir Prasad, Union Minister for Small Scale Industries & Agro and Rural Industries, while addressing the

Parliamentary Consultative Committee Meeting attached to his ministry, here today. He said that industrial cluster occupied the driver's seat for propelling economic activities in micro & small enterprises sector. Detailed study of the features of the clusters with due care and application were essential prerequisites for selection of a cluster of the right type, the Minister added. The criteria may vary to some extent depending on the type of clusters and the goals sought to be achieved through the cluster development initiatives. Shri Prasad also outlined the programmes and achievements under Prime Minister's Rozgar Yojana (PMRY). Some of the Members suggested that more and more clusters should be set up in various parts of the country, especially in the South. Assuring the Members, the Minister said that while selecting the clusters, an all India perspective would be kept in mind. Dr.Chandrapal, Secretary, SSI & ARI, Smt. Kumud Joshi, Chairperson, KVIC and Shri A.C. Jose, Chairman, Coir Board also spoke on this occasion.

1045. (16-5-2007) NEW DELHI : The Government proposes to set up a Centre for Communication Security Research and Monitoring. This was stated by Dr. Shakeel Ahmad, Minister of State for Communications and Information Technology in a written reply to question by Shri Bhartruhari Mahtab in Lok Sabha today. Dr. Ahmad said that the main objective for setting up the above Centre is to provide mandatory access to law enforcement agencies for intercepting, monitoring and analysis of the activities of the criminal elements and their social networking both proactively, online and through post-analysis of information. He further stated that Centre for Development of Telematics (C-DOT), an autonomous body of the Government of India has been appointed as the nodal agency for implementation of the project. A budget provision of Rs. 50 crores has been provided during 2007-2008 for setting up the above centre, he added.

1046. (16-5-2007) NEW DELHI : A modernization plan for the paramilitary forces which includes providing them superior arms and ammunition, strategic equipment, effective transport vehicles, state-of-the-art communication, surveillance and body guarding systems, is under implementation. The latest and modern technologies with respect to these items are being introduced for the modernization process. The expenditure on modernization is met out of the regular provisioning budget provided to the paramilitary forces. During the last 3 years, the total budget allocated for provisioning was Rs. 4654.72 crore and out of this an amount of Rs. 1292.34 crore was spent on modernization. This information was given by the Minister of State for Home, Shri Sriprakash Jaiswal in a written reply to a question in the Rajya Sabha today.

1047. (16-5-2007) NEW DELHI : Several measures have been taken to expedite customs, security and immigration clearances in order to reduce the hardships faced by foreign passport holders/tourists at the international airports. These measures inter alia, include (1). manning of all X-ray machines and security check points at the international airports for expeditious security clearance, (2). with regard to Customs clearance, 95% of the incoming passengers are cleared thorough the Green Channel, wherein the passengers simply walk through with their baggage and only passengers carrying dutiable goods report to the Red Channel. Facilitation desks are in place to assist the outgoing passengers and (3). computer systems have been upgraded, Immigration Control System Software, Passport Reading Machines (PRMs) and Questionable Document Examiner (QDX) machines have been installed at immigration counters at major international airports, to ensure expeditious immigration clearance. At present, there are separate immigration counters for Indians and Foreigners at Delhi, Chennai and Kolkata airports. This information was given by the Minister of State for Home, Shri Sriprakash Jaiswal in a written reply to a question in the Rajya Sabha today.

1048. (16-5-2007) NEW DELHI: Surprise name mentioned at a meeting of National Democratic Alliance leaders here on Tuesday in the context of the upcoming presidential race. It is learnt that Trinamool Congress leader Mamata Banerjee said Mr. Vajpayee should be the NDA's candidate for the post. This was acceptable to all allies. However, officially NDA convener George Fernandes told reporters that the NDA had "authorised Mr. Vajpayee" to consult allies and "monitor the situation related to the presidential election" and decide who the NDA candidate would be in the event of a contest. The NDA leaders would meet again on the issue of presidential election. It seems that with the Left parties having rejected a second term for A.P.J. Abdul Kalam—no President has been given a second term except the first President Rajendra Prasad—and with the Congress keen on its own candidate, the NDA would like to contest the election. Vice-President Bhairon Singh Shekhawat is not averse to being a candidate. BJP sources confirmed that a couple of days ago Mr. Vajpayee, and leaders of the Opposition in the two Houses L.K. Advani and Jaswant Singh called on Mr. Shekhawat. It is not known what transpired at the meeting, but there were indications that it was held to find out if he was willing to be the NDA candidate in the event of a contest.

1049. (16-5-2007) NEW DELHI : Research Department of All India Radio and Doordarshan have initiated a study of Emergency Warning Broadcast System (EWBS) suitable for Indian environment. Limited experimental transmissions have also been carried out on Medium Wave and FM transmitters in Delhi. Prasar Bharati has large transmitting infrastructure. This can be selectively used to convey emergency messages to public concerned about natural disasters after incorporation of the EWBS. However, manufacturers will have to provide EWBS ready TV and ready receivers. Prasar Bharati has informed that the EWBS has been in operation in Japan since 1985, in which emergency messages are transmitted on all transmitters (public/private, digital/analogue) during natural disasters for (i) relaying life-saving information on the preventive measures and (ii) the rescue measures undertake. EWBS ready radio and TV receivers can receive alarm signal and emergency broadcast signal even in sleep mode. This information was given by Minister of Information & Broadcasting and Parliamentary Affairs, Shri P. R. Dasmunsi in written reply to a question in Rajya Sabha today.

1050. (16-5-2007) NEW DELHI : For implementation of various Schemes under the North East Industrial and Investment Promotion Policy, 2007 a sum of Rs.89.99 crore has been earmarked during the current financial year. Since NEIIPP, 2007 has been announced only a month and a half ago, no funds have been sanctioned under it so far. The 'North East Industrial and Investment Promotion Policy (NEIIPP), 2007' for industrial development in the North Eastern Region including Sikkim has been announced on 1.4.2007. A copy of the Policy is placed below. North East Industrial and Investment Promotion Policy (NEIIPP), 2007 The Government has approved a package of fiscal incentives and other concessions for the North East Region namely the 'North East Industrial and Investment Promotion Policy (NEIIPP), 2007', effective from 1.4.2007.

1051. (16-5-2007) NEW DELHI : Separate data on the share of business sector in GDP is not available with Central Statistical Organization (CSO). However, data available on contribution of organized sector in the Net Domestic Product (NDP) indicates that the share of organized sector has increased from 39.6 percent in 2000-01 to 42.0 percent in 2004-05. The average annual growth rate of organized sector during 2000-01 to 2004-05 was 11.2 percent. The share of operating surplus (which consists of rent, interest and profits) in the NDP increased from 37.4 percent in 2000-01 to 46.2 percent in 2004-05. This was stated by the Minister of State for Industry, Shri Ashwani Kumar, in a written reply in the Rajya Sabha today.

1052. (16-5-2007) NEW DELHI : The Industrial Park Scheme, 2002 is an ongoing Scheme. As per the Scheme, Government do not set up Industrial Parks, instead approval is provided to the developer of Industrial Park to avail Income Tax benefits under section 80 IA of Income Tax Act, 1961. Applications are being continuously received and considered as per the Scheme. The Scheme provides for deductions, in calculating the tax payable, under the Income Tax Act 1961, on profits of industrial undertakings or enterprises, engaged in infrastructure development for a period of 10 consecutive years, in a block of fifteen assessment years after the commencement of business. As the Scheme envisages promoting quality industrial infrastructure, which is an essential component of industrialization, it is being found attractive by the developers.

1053. (16-5-2007) NEW DELHI : Bharat Heavy Electricals Ltd. (BHEL) has emerged as an active player in ensuring country's energy security related to electrical power by playing a larger role than just being a manufacturer and supplier of equipment. This was stated by Shri Sontosh Mohan Dev while addressing the Parliamentary Consultative Committee Meeting attached to his Ministry, here last night. Outlining the achievements of BHEL, the Minister said, BHEL recorded a turnover of Rs.18,702 crore (prov.) during 2006-07–a growth of 29% over the previous year, after registering similar higher growth levels in the preceding two years. BHEL built thermal sets achieved the highest-ever Plant Load Factor (PLF) of 78.3%, higher than the national average by 1.5%. Further, BHEL make 200/210/250/500 MW thermal sets, which form the backbone of the country's thermal generating capacity, operated at a PLF of 83.5% & Operating Availability (OA) of 88.7%. Notably, 75 BHEL make sets achieved PLF of over 90% and 6 thermal sets of various ratings out of these operated at record PLF of 100%. BHEL has been consistently investing in R&D and had accelerated its R&D efforts recently. During the year 2006-07, the R&D spend has been Rs.238 crore, 58% higher than the previous year. The company has plans to increase it further by four times by 2011-12. BHEL is enhancing its manufacturing capacity to 10,000 MW p.a. by December 2007 at a cost of Rs.1600 crore and it plans to further hike this capacity to around 15,000 MW p.a. by December 2009 by investing around Rs.3200 crore. This enhancement of manufacturing capacity is possible only because of the availability of basic infrastructure and qualified and trained technical manpower in BHEL. The incremental investments, which are brown field expansion, is most economical to expand capacity, as against green field investment by any other company. During the year 2006-07, BHEL manufactured and supplied 7589 MW of power plant equipment and commissioned 7863 MW of power plants much beyond its capacity of 6000 MW p.a. catering to all sectors of domestic utilities, captive power plants for industry and overseas customers as part of its best efforts to meet the requirement of bunching of orders, Shri Dev added. Shri A.K.Puri, CMD, BHEL said that there were some reports suggesting that there was a proposal under consideration for setting up of a power equipment and engineering company on the lines of BHEL. This would be a sub-optimum solution to the problem of equipment manufacturing capacity constraints and the need for technology upgradation, he added. He said that from the details available so far, it was not clear as to why capacity additions in BHEL would not be sufficient to meet growing demand. A new company that operates in the same areas would be setting up similar capacities too. It is better to support an existing entity like BHEL where economies of scale for utilizing 15,000 MW p.a. capacity would outweigh setting up new manufacturing capacities where the gestation period could range from 3-4 years, not considering the skill requirements and capability building needed. Shri Puri said it remained a questionable idea even if the intention was to attract private capital by involving a domestic company or an MNC. Instead, BHEL itself can raise capital or access technology by taking on strategic partners.

1054. (16-5-2007) NEW DELHI : A Government of India team jointly led by the Union Minister of Heavy Industries and Public Enterprises (HIPE), Shri Sontosh Mohan Dev and Minister of Petroleum and Natural Gas (PNG), Shri Murli Deora visited Bharat Pumps & Compressors Ltd. in Naini, Allahabad today. The team included Secretaries of the Ministries of HIPE & PNG. Other members included CMDs of ONGC, BHEL & EIL. Shri Sontosh Mohan Dev announced that a revival package for BPCL was approved by the Government to ensure its long-term sustainability including cash infusion of Rs.20 crore by BHEL and Rs. 150 crore by ONGC. The package also includes waiver of outstanding liabilities of Rs.150 crore and restructuring of the Board of Directors by including professionals from BHEL, ONGC & EIL. Shri Murli Deora, Minister for Petroleum and Natural Gas enquired about the problems, if any, being faced by BPCL in respect of Petroleum Sector. Shri Deora assured that ONGC would provide the required advance against supplies to be made by BPCL, including advance payment for next years projected supplies if needed. He also announced that he would ask the other public enterprises in the Petroleum Sector to give purchase preference, as admissible, to source their equipment from BPCL, in line with ONGC. However, BPCL should ensure no diversion of these funds. Shri Sontosh Mohan Dev handed over a cheque of Rs. 10 crore on behalf of BHEL to BPCL.

1055. (16-5-2007) NEW DELHI : Official visits between India and Israel take place to discuss issues of mutual interest including defence procurement issues. Defence Procurements are, however, done as per laid down procedures. M/s ELTA, Israel is the lowest bidder in response to a Request for Proposal (RFP) issued for procurement of some radars for the Indian Air Force. However, no contract has been signed with the firm. The defence purchases from Israel during the period 2002-07 have been over US $ 5 billion. Chief of the Army Staff visited Israel from 05th to 07th Mar 2007. This was a regular goodwill visit. This information was given by the Defence Minister Shri AK Antony in a written reply to Smt Shobhana Bhartia in Rajya Sabha today.

1056. (16-5-2007) NEW DELHI : While there are varying estimates about Pakistan's and China's defence expenditure, India's defence expenditure has been in the region of 2.3% in the 1st ten years. There is no decision of the Government so far to set up Aerospace Command. However, adequate measures are in place to address concerns of National security keeping in view the changing threat perception. This information was given by the Defence Minister Shri AK Antony in a written reply to Shri Ekkanath K Thakur in Rajya Sabha today.

1057. (16-5-2007) NEW DELHI : Armed Forces have a secular and apolitical character. Recruitment to the Forces is based on merit and is open to every citizen of the country without any discrimination on the basis of their case, creed, religion or region. All the personnel from all communities and regions work together without any distinction on the basis of caste, creed or religion. Therefore, it was not considered desirable to supply any data relating to particular religious community in respect of the Army as it would have affected the ethos and cohesiveness of the forces. This information was given by the Defence Minister Shri AK Antony in a written reply to Shri Syed Azeez Pasha in Rajya Sabha today.

1058. (16-5-2007) NEW DELHI : The Ministry of Rural Development has finalized targets for three schemes, the Swarnjayanti Gram Swarozgar Yojana (SGSY), the Sampoorna Grameen Rozgar Yojana (SGRY) and the Indira Awaas

Yojana (IAY) for 2007-08, under Prime Minister's 15-Point Programme. State-wise funds allocated under the SGRY and IAY and physical targets under SGSY are given in the Annexure. The funds are to be spent in accordance with the Guidelines of the Schemes. This was stated by the Minister of State in the Ministry of Rural Development, Smt. Suryakanta Patil in reply to a question in Rajya Sabha today.

1059. (16-5-2007) NEW DELHI : Out of 74,000 uncovered habitations which were reported uncovered as per Comprehensive Action Plan 99 (CAP 99) based on coverage in previous years, under Bharat Nirman programme for rural drinking water supply, it is proposed to cover uncovered habitations as well as to address issues of quality and slippages. During 2005-06, a total amount of Rs. 5946.25 crores have been utilized for covering 97215 habitations which included uncovered as also partially covered of CAP 99, slipped back and quality affected habitations. In the first three quarters of 2006-07, a total amount of Rs. 4207.05 crores have been utilized for covering 55452 habitations, which similarly included uncovered, partially covered of CAP 99, slipped back and quality affected habitations. The remaining uncovered habitations are proposed to be covered by 2008-09 under Bharat Nirman. This was stated by the Minister of State in the Ministry of Rural Development, Shri Chandra Sekhar Sahu in reply to a question in Rajya Sabha today.

1060. (16-5-2007) NEW DELHI : After the vacation of the stay order by the Hon'ble Supreme Court on 14.2.2006, the finalisation of BPL lists on the basis of BPL Census 2002 is being monitored regularly. The States of Arunachal Pradesh, Chhattisgarh, Jharkhand, Madhya Pradesh, Punjab, Uttar Pradesh, and Uttarakhand have already finalized the BPL lists. In the remaining States, the work is at various stages and the States have been advised to finalise the said lists by the end of June, 2007. The Ministry has already issued the guidelines to the States to ensure the transparency in preparation of BPL lists by getting it approved by the Gram Sabha and to minimize the subjectivity element. In order to remove the anomalies in the preparation of the BPL lists and to redress the public grievances, if any, a two-stage appeal mechanism has already been provided. The BPL Census is generally conducted after a period of 5 years. The objective of BPL Census is to identify the BPL households in the rural areas for targeting them under the programmes of the Ministry and not to determine the number of BPL households. The States have been advised to identify the number of rural BPL households as determined by the official estimates of Planning Commission. The methodology for BPL Census 2002 is score based ranking of the rural households for which 13 scorable socio-economic parameters have been prescribed. This methodology brings out the comparative level of deprivation of a rural household in an objective manner, therefore, the element of subjectivity has been minimized. No State has raised any major objection to the above methodology. The Ministry has not yet resorted to any penal action such as complete stoppage of Central funds for rural development works for non-finalisation of new BPL lists. This was stated by the Minister of State in the Ministry of Rural Development, Smt. Suryakanta Patil in reply to a question in Rajya Sabha today.

1061. (16-5-2007) NEW DELHI : As per 1991 census, the total percentage of household with latrine in rural area was about 22%, which has increased to about 45% by end of March 2007. The Millennium Development Goals (MDG) of the United Nations envisage halving by 2015, the number of people not having access to potable water or sanitation, taking 1990 as the base year. To accelerate the pace of rural sanitation coverage in India, a centrally sponsored programme, namely Central Rural Sanitation Programme (CRSP), was introduced in 1986. Central Rural Sanitation Programme was restructured in 1999 as Total Sanitation Campaign, with focus on demand generation through effective information, education and communication campaign. It is being implemented in rural areas taking district as a unit of implementation. Projects have been approved for 572 rural districts of the country. As a result, total percentage of household with latrine in rural area has increased to about 45% by end of March 2007. This was stated by the Minister of State in the Ministry of Rural Development, Shri Chandra Sekhar Sahu in reply to a question in Rajya Sabha today.

1062. (16-5-2007) NEW DELHI : The Ministry of Rural Development had provided Budgetary allocation of Rs. 3439.51 crores under three schemes namely, Sampoorna Grameen Rozgar Yojana (SGRY), Swarnjayanti Gram Swarozgar Yojana (SGSY) and Indira Awaas Yojana (IAY) for the year 2006-07 for the Scheduled Castes (SCs) and Scheduled Tribes (STs). State-wise and programme-wise funds utilized and quantitative benefits accrued to these sections are given in the Annexure. For 2007-08, Rs. 4339 crores have been allocated under these programmes for the benefit of SCs and STs. State-wise funds allocated under SGRY and IAY for 2007-08 are also given in the Annexure. Under SGSY, fifty percent of the total swarojgaris assisted shall belong to SCs/STs. This was stated by the Minister of State in the Ministry of Rural Development, Smt. Suryakanta Patil in reply to a question in Rajya Sabha today.

1063. (16-5-2007) NEW DELHI : The Finance Minister, in his Budget Speech of 28th February, 2005, identified Rural Roads as one of the six components of Bharat Nrman and has set a goal to provide connectivity to all villages with a population of 1000 (500 in the case of hilly or tribal areas) with an All-weather road by 2008-09. 66,802 habitations would be provided new connectivity under Bharat Nirman. This would involve construction of 1, 46,185 kms of new link roads. In addition, Bharat Nirman envisages upgradation/renewal of 1, 94,130 km of existing rural roads.

1064. (16-5-2007) NEW DELHI : As per Indira Awaas Yojana (IAY) guidelines, at least 60% of the total IAY allocation during a financial year should be utilized for construction/upgradation of dwelling units for SC/ST BPL households. A

Statement showing the number of houses constructed for SC/STs during the last three financial years, is at Annexure. At present financial assistance for an IAY house is provided at the rate of Rs. 25000/- for plain areas and Rs. 27500/- for hilly areas. These rates of assistance have been revised w.e.f. 1-4-2004. The financial assistance provided under IAY may not necessarily meet the total cost of an IAY house. Labour component is generally contributed by the beneficiary himself and sometimes beneficiary also mobilizes his/her own resources. The revision of norms of financial assistance under IAY is done from time to time keeping in view the factors such as rise in cost of material etc. The Working Group set up for preparation of 11th Plan proposals, have also recommended substantial increase in financial assistance for IAY houses in view of increase in cost of construction of houses. This was stated by the Minister of State in the Ministry of Rural Development, Smt. Suryakanta Patil in reply to a question in Rajya Sabha today.

1065. (16-5-2007) NEW DELHI : There is no direct co-relation between GDP and Budget Allocation. The Budget Allocation for different sectors mainly depends on the priorities determined by the Government and availability of Gross Budgetary Support. There has been a significant step up of allocation for Ministry of Rural Development over the years since 2002-03. The Budget Estimates for 2002-03 for Rural Development was Rs.13670.00 crores which has been increased to Rs.41060.00 crores (including Rs.4500.00 crores loan from NABARD) in the Budget for 2007-08 representing an increase of more than 200 per cent over 2002-03(BE). This was stated by the Minister of State in the Ministry of Rural Development, Smt. Suryakanta Patil in reply to a question in Rajya Sabha today.

1066. (16-5-2007) NEW DELHI : The Government proposes to conduct a survey over all the country to assess the number of child labour in the country. The Government is taking all measures to complete the survey as early as possible. Decennial Census conducted by the Registrar General of India and Census Commissioner is the most authentic source of information on the number of working children in the country. As per the 2001 Census, the number of working children in the country is 1.26 crore. The Central Advisory Board on child Labour is a tripartite committee in nature. The main function of the Board is to advise the Government on policy issues related to child labour. The Government is implementing the National Child Labour Projects (NCLP) Scheme in 250 districts of 20 States for the rehabilitation of children withdrawn from work. Under the Scheme, children withdrawn from work are provided with education, nutrition, stipend, vocational training and health care etc. and are finally mainstreamed to regular education system. So far, 3.92 lakh children have been mainstreamed into formal education system. This was stated by the Minister of State (Independent Charge), Labour & Employment, Shri Oscar Fernandes in a written reply in the Rajya Sabha today.

1067. (16-5-2007) NEW DELHI : The expenditure incurred by the State

Government on provision of medical care services is reimbursed to the State Governments by ESI Corporation on the basis of prescribed ceiling of Rs. 1000/- per Insured Person family unit per annum. ESI Corporation in its meeting held on December 23, 2006 approved the enhancement of ceiling on medical care from Rs. 900/- per Insured Person family unit per annum to Rs. 1000/- per Insured Person family unit per annum with effect from April 1, 2007. In addition to Rs. 1000/-, the ESI Corporation has also decided to give an incentive of Rs. 50/- per Insured Person family unit per annum to the State Governments on fulfilling the stipulated terms and conditions for improvement of medical scheme. There was no discussion in the meting of the ESI Corporation held on December 23, 2006 regarding reimbursement of expenses over the prescribed ceiling. The ESI Corporation has issued instructions conveying the enhancement of ceiling to State Governments on January 24, 2007. This was stated by the Minister of State (Independent Charge), Labour & Employment, Shri Oscar Fernandes in a written reply in the Rajya Sabha today.

1068. (16-5-2007) NEW DELHI : The government is implementing the scheme of National Child Labour Projects (NCLP) since 1988. Under the scheme, children withdrawn from work are put into special schools where they are provided with education, vocational training, nutrition, stipend and health care facilities etc. These children are kept in the special schools for a period of maximum three years to prepare them to join the regular education system. At present, approximately 3.30 lakh children withdrawn from work are enrolled in the special schools under the NCLP Scheme. So far, under the scheme, 3.92 lakh children have already been mainstreamed into formal education system. Out of this, 1.36 lakh children have been mainstreamed between the years 2003-04 to 2005-06. This was stated by the Minister of State (Independent Charge), Labour & Employment, Shri Oscar Fernandes in a written reply in the Rajya Sabha today. In another written reply Shri Fernandes said that Rs. 108 crore were spent under NCLP for rehabilitation of child labour during the last financial year.

1069. (16-5-2007) NEW DELHI : Shri Andimuthu Raja, has taken over as a new Minister of Communications & Information Technology here today. Earlier, Shri Raja was the Union Minister of Environment & Forests. He was received by the Secretaries of Department of Telecom, Posts, Information Technology, and several senior officials of BSNL and MTNL. While interacting with the media after taking over, Shri Raja said that his top priority area would be Rural telephony. He further said " during his tenure, his efforts and endeavour would be to provide the communication facilities to the people at the lowest ebb of the social order". Since the telecom sector is growing sector and all efforts required for maintaining its growth will continue, Shri Raja added. Elected as member to the 11th Lok Sabha for the first time in the year 1996, Shri A. Raja has also held earlier the positions in the central government as Minister of State of Rural Development and Minister of State of Health and Family Welfare.

1070. (16-5-2007) NEW DELHI : The Minister for Rural Development, Dr. Raghuvansh Prasad Singh while speaking in a one-day Workshop on Sustainability of Drinking Water Supply Schemes organized by the Deptt. of Drinking Water Supply, M/o Rural Development here today directed the State Governments to generate awareness about rain water harvesting for addressing the issues of availability, sustainability and quality in drinking water supply as there is no shortage of funds for the water sector. He further advised that his announcement on incentive for villages which have achieved 100% drinking water security has to be given a concrete shape after consultations with all stakeholders participating in the Workshop. Ms. Santha Sheela Nair, Secretary (Drinking Water Supply), in her opening remarks, stated that the objective of the Workshop is to address the problem of slipped back habitations in the Accelerated Rural Water Supply Programme (ARWSP) and to finalise the Technical Guidelines for building the component of sustainability in the rural drinking water supply schemes after consultations with experts in the sector, reputed NGOs, State Governments and other Central Government Departments dealing with Water Conservation and Management. In his keynote address, Shri B.M. Jha, Chairman, CGWB, highlighted that sustainability of drinking water sources is a challenging task. Shri K.D. Sharma, Director, National Institute of Hydrology-Roorkee stressed the need for demand management, integrated use of ground and surface water sources and recycling of waste water. Representatives from Planning commission, CGWB, Deptt. of Expenditure, Ministry of Water Resources, Deptt. of Land Resources., Deptt. of Rural Development, CAPART, National Institute of Hydrology, Central Pollution Control Board, National Institute of Communicable Diseases; international agencies like UNICEF, WSP-SA-World Bank and leading NGOs like Centre for Science and Environment, New Delhi; Tarun Bharat Sangh, Alwar; Dhan Foundation-Madurai, BAIF Research & Development Foundation-Pune, Kachchh Mahila Vikas Sangathan-Kachchh, Mr. Sahdevsingh Gohil – Sarpanch, Village Avaniya Taluka Ghogha, Distt. Bhavnagar & Smt. Shankuben Chaudhri, Sarpanch-Village Ekalva Ta Harij, Distt. Patan of Gujarat and representatives from State Governments participated in the Workshop. Participants from different Central Government Ministries and Departments underscored the importance of convergence of activities at the field level to optimize the outcome and the need for proper utilization of funds of the 12th Finance Commission. Though under the NREGS most of the works are water conservation related yet there is lack of commonality of vision amongst the stakeholders and this has to be debated and articulated properly for integration of the programme at the field level. Various reputed NGOs shared their experiences of mobilizing the communities and bringing about their effective participation for decentralized drinking water supply system.

1071. (17-5-2007) NEW DELHI : The Cabinet Committee on Economic Affairs today gave its approval for the following: (i) To grant financial assistance of Rs.352 crore to ITI for meeting the requirement of payment of statutory dues and grant towards VRS. (ii) Rs.25 crore will be provided as interest free loan simultaneously writing it off from the Government account.

1072. (17-5-2007) NEW DELHI : The Cabinet Committee on Economic Affairs today gave its approval for the Phase III of the National AIDS Control Programme with a financial out lay of the external aided component of Rs.3121.5 crore and domestic budgetary support of Rs.418.4 crore. The direct benefit of the programme is to reduce the transmission of HIV infection and halt and reverse the epidemic and to provide care and support to the people living with HIV / AIDS. The time frame for the Phase III of National AIDS Control Programme is 2007-2012.

1073. (17-5-2007) NEW DELHI : The Cabinet Committee on Economic Affairs today gave its approval for amendments in the guidelines of National Horticulture Mission (NHM) as follows: (i) to modify the pattern of the assistance involving credit linked back ended subsidy for activities relating to production of seeds and planting material, Integrated Nutrient Management (INM)/Integrated pest Management (IPM), Post Harvest Management (PHM) and Marketing infrastructure (ii) the projects relating to the activities indicated above will mostly be entrepreneur driven, through commercial ventures, for which the Central Government assistance for individual entrepreneurs/private sector will be credit linked back-ended subsidy @ 25% of the total project cost in general areas and @ 33.33% in case of Tribal/ Hilly areas. The State Government agencies, including institutions like cooperatives / registered societies/trusts and incorporated companies in the public/private sector will also be entitled for assistance in respect of such activities to the same extent. However, these institutions / agencies need not avail the credit from the bank / financial institutions and will ensure that their share of the project cost is met out of their own resources. The modification in pattern of assistance by de-linking the subsidy from bank credit for State Government agencies, including institutions like cooperatives / registered societies / trusts and incorporated companies in the public / private sector, would result in more efficient use of available funds and attract more players in the implementation of the programme.

1074. (17-5-2007) LUCKNOW: Uttar Pradesh Chief Minister Mayawati on Wednesday brought in Satish Chandra Mishra, the Brahmin face of the Bahujan Samaj Party, into her Cabinet in a special swearing in ceremony, even as a Minister resigned to contest for the Speaker's post. Mr. Mishra was administered the oath of office and secrecy at a brief ceremony at the Raj Bhavan by Governor T.V. Rajeswar. An eminent lawyer and Rajya Sabha member, he is credited with efforts to mobilise Brahmin support for the BSP chief. A close confidant of the Chief Minister, Mr. Mishra is likely to be given an "important portfolio." Mr. Mishra was the Advocate-General of Uttar Pradesh during an earlier tenure of Mr. Mayawati. Earlier, Sukhdev Rajbhar, who was sworn in Minister on Sunday, resigned after he was chosen the party candidate for the Speaker's post.

1075. (17-5-2007) NEW DELHI : The Cabinet Committee on Economic Affairs today gave its approval for the MSPs for 2007-08 kharif crops, as under: (i) Price per quintal Commodity Variety MSP for 2007-08 Increase in MSP over previous year's MSP Paddy Common 645 65 Grade A 675 65 Jowar Hybrid 600 60 Maldandi 620 65 Bajra- 600 60 Ragi- 600 60 Maize-620 80 Tur (Arhar)-1590 180 Moong-1740 220 Urad-1740 220 Groundnut-in-shell-1550 30 Soyabean Yellow 1050 30 Black 910 10 Sunflower Seed-1510 10 Sesamum-1580 20 Niger Seed-1240 20 Cotton Medium Staple Length 1800 30 Long Staple Length 2030 40 (ii) the prices for different varietal groups of rice be derived from the minimum support prices of paddy on the basis of hulling / milling ratios as well as the processing and incidental charges obtaining in different States; (iii) The MSP approved for Medium Staple Length relates to F-414/H-77/J-34 variety of kapas with technical parameters of Basic Staple Length (2.5% span) of 24.5 mm and Micronaire Value 3.8-4.8 (iv) The MSP approved for Long Staple Length relates to H-4/H-6 variety of kapas with technical parameters of Basic Staple Length (2.5% span) of 28.0 mm and Micronaire Value 3.6-4.5; (v) In the case of cereals, FCI and other designated States Agencies will continue to provide price support to the farmers, as in the past. NAFED would to continue to be the nodal agency for procurement of oilseeds and pulses and losses if any, will be fully reimbursed by the government of India. NAFED would also continue to undertake cotton procurement, in addition to Cotton Corporation of India.

1076. (17-5-2007) NEW DELHI : Congress Spokesperson Shri Abhishek Singhvi said that it is deeply regrettable and unfortunate that a constitutional functionary holding a high constitutional position of chief minister of Punjab should choose to make highly irresponsible statements. The Congress Party wishes to put on record that it has nothing whatsoever to do with the events in Punjab. The Chief Minister of Punjab should first set his own house, his own state, his own party in order before indulging in irresponsible finger-pointing. He must not forget that when he tries to point an accusing finger, three fingers, in fact, are pointing accusingly at him. It is very clear that the Chief Minister of Punjab is trying to sidetrack the issue, to transfer responsibility, to indulge in the politics of digression and diversion. The Congress Party which ruled Punjab for five years or so did not allow it to degenerate into irresponsible mudslinging or law and order problem which seem to occur even within the so-called honeymoon period of 90 days as far as the new government is concerned. Instead of enjoying this honeymoon period we have a govt., not tasting honey but stewing poison, giving excuses like the moon transferring responsibility. We also univocally condemn the violence in Punjab and the law and order situation there but most of all we think it is fully unbecoming and unethical for a constitutional functionary like the Chief Minister to try to transfer blame in this irresponsible manner and would like to end by making an appeal and a call for peace. To a question that BJP has said that Dr. Manmohan Singh is the weakest Prime Minister in the country, Shri Singhvi said that when Congress Party was existing and governing and winning elections, it is certainly not because of the certificates or lack of certificates to the BJP. I don't think Dr. Manmohan Singh requires any such certificate. To a question that Congress Party was being supported by the Dera Sucha Sauda, Shri Singhvi said that let us be clear that there is no question of Congress Party taking support, seeking support on the basis which has been suggested. In an election a group or institution or any such body decides to support the Congress or chooses to vote for the Congress Party, there is no question of the Congress Party going out of its way and taking out advertisements, accepting or denying such support. This is purely electoral process and there is no question of Congress Party going out and seeking the support of one particular Dera. To a question whether Left allies approves of the Congress Party candidate Pranab Mukherjee for the President, Shri Singhvi said that your question is highly premature one. As I told you the process of selection and election of the President is a process for the highest post in the country and that process will go on, certainly not before the Media glare. You have to wait and at an appropriate time when the decision is taken you shall come to know. To a question as to why Congress President is not taking responsibility for the drubbing in Uttar Pradesh elections, Shri Singhvi said that I am sorry that I don't agree with your perception at all. Family or party, that is not correct at all. A statement in the Congress Parliamentary Party meeting was made by the Congress President which is something on which there is already a process of deep introspection on, namely, how to strengthen the party. We do agree and do realise that the party needs strengthening in Uttar Pradesh. That is not the negative process, it is not a finger-pointing process, it is not a blame allocation process. It is a genuine constructive process to find a way of strengthening the party and the organization and we are in Uttar Pradesh for the long haul. We are in it to strengthen every unit, every block, every remote area of Uttar Pradesh as far as our party is concerned. To a question as to how the Congress Party is going on with its introspection on Uttar Pradesh results, Shri Singhvi said that the process is ongoing, continuous and the momentum will increase in the near future. And when we decide to choose to make an official statement on it ,in term of the results of that introspection, we will let you know.

1077. (17-5-2007) NEW DELHI : The Union Cabinet today gave its approval for introduction of a new legislation to provide for constitution of an Authority for Advance Rulings on Central Taxes as a substitute for the Authority for Advance Rulings constituted under section 245-O of the Income Tax Act, 1961, and the Authority for Advance Rulings (Central Excise, Customs and Service Tax) constituted under section 28-F of the Customs Act, 1962 and for matters connected therewith or incidental thereto and for making amendments to the Central Excise Act, 1944, the Central Sales Tax Act, 1956, the Income Tax Act, 1961, the Customs Act, 1962, and the Finance Act, 1994. The approval will facilitate the constitution of a common Authority for Advance Rulings. Ministry of Finance will undertake the Legislation on introduction of the Authority for Advance Rulings on Central Taxes Bill, 2007 in the ensuing session of Parliament.

1078. (17-5-2007) NEW DELHI : The Union Cabinet today gave its approval for National Policy on the Voluntary Sector. The Policy has six parts: (a) Preamble

(b) Scope of the Policy (c) Objectives of the Policy (d) Establishing an Enabling Environment (e) Partnership in Development (f) Strengthening the Voluntary Sector The main objectives of the policy include: (i) Creating an enabling environment for Voluntary Organisations (VOs) that not only stimulates their effectiveness but also protects their identity and safeguards their autonomy. (ii) Enabling VOs to legitimately mobilize the necessary financial resources from India and abroad. (iii) Identifying systems by which the Government may work together with the Voluntary Sector. (iv) Encouraging VOs to adopt transparent and accountable systems of governance and management. In the part 'Establishing Enabling Environment' it will examine the feasibility of enacting a simple and liberal central law to register societies, trusts and non-profit companies. Under 'Partnership in Development', three instruments of partnership between the Government and the voluntary sector have been recognized and elaborated upon. In the part 'Strengthening the Voluntary Sector', there is a commitment to encourage independent philanthropic institutions to provide financial assistance to deserving VOs. The National Policy on the voluntary sector aims to provide an enabling environment for the voluntary sector and also make it accountable, so that VOs can play their constructive role in development activities effectively.

1079. (17-5-2007) NEW DELHI : The Union Cabinet today gave its approval for concluding a Bilateral Investment Promotion and Protection Agreement (BIPA) with Government of the United Mexican States. The broad intent of the Agreement, between the two countries, is to promote and protect investments from either country. Under Article 1, "Investment" is defined as every kind of asset, including Intellectual Property Rights in accordance with laws and regulations of the country in which the investment is made. The core of the Agreement lies in Articles 3 and 4 with the positive assertion of the principles of Most Favoured Nation (MFN) Treatment and National Treatment. It would like to increase investments between India and United Mexican States. BIPA have been signed by the Government of India, till 30th April 2007, with 63 countries.

1080. (17-5-2007) NEW DELHI : The Union Cabinet today gave its approval for signing on behalf of the Customs administration of the government of India with the Customs administration of the republic of the Federal Republic of Brazil, an Agreement for cooperation and mutual assistance in Customs matters. The Agreement will help in the availability of reliable, quick and cost-effective information and intelligence for the prevention and investigation of Customs offences and apprehending of Customs offenders.

1081. (17-5-2007) NEW DELHI : Agreement between India and the Republic of South The Union Cabinet today gave its approval for signing on behalf of the Customs administration of the government of India with the Customs administration of the republic of South Africa, an Agreement for cooperation and mutual assistance in Customs matters. The Agreement will help in the availability of reliable, quick and cost-effective information and intelligence for the prevention and investigation of Customs offences and apprehending of Customs offenders.

1082. (17-5-2007) NEW DELHI : The Union Cabinet today gave its ex-post-facto approval for Signing, on behalf of the Customs administration of the Government of India with the Customs administration of the Russian Federation, a protocol for Exchange of Information on movement of goods and conveyances between the Republic of India and the Russian Federation. The protocol will help in accomplishing the objectives of trade facilitation and better enforcement, through electronic exchange of Customs data and to improve the efficiency and effectiveness of Customs administration by faster Customs clearance of goods and conveyances moved between the countries. The exchange of information shall enable identification of discrepancies in the data on goods and conveyances moved between the states of the Parties.

1083. (17-5-2007) NEW DELHI : The Prime Minister said that I am delighted to participate in the inauguration of the Conference on development of East and North-East India. I am happy that the Conference is bringing together intellectuals, industrialists, political leaders and societal transformers concerned with the development of East and North East India comprising of Bihar, Orissa, West Bengal, Jharkhand, Sikkim, Arunachal Pradesh, Manipur, Meghalaya, Nagaland, Assam, Mizoram and Tripura particularly to bring the benefits of national economic growth to the rural people in different parts of this region. This region accounts for over 260 million people. I have visited all the States of East and North-East a number of times. Every time I visit, I see the natural environment with multiple bio-diversity, beautiful rivers, forests, mountains, valleys, plains, and above all hard-working people. With these resources I am confident that this region with its multiple core competence and Investment Plan can get transformed into a developed region well before 2020.

1084. (17-5-2007) KOLKATA : The Prime Minister said that I am delighted to address and interact with the eminent thinkers of Calcutta Club Limited. My greetings to the President, CEO, Managing Committee Members and all the other professional members during the centenary celebrations of the Club. West Bengal is famous for innovative thinking and was responsible for many initiatives in literary and poetic excellence, social reforms, spiritual awakening, pioneering scientific innovation and generation of many Nobel laureates. As I am with this distinguished audience, I was thinking what thoughts I can share. How to achieve a peaceful, prosperous and happy India? This indeed is a challenging mission for us today. Keeping this in mind, I have selected? Dynamics of Peace and Prosperity? as the topic for initiating discussion today.

1085. (17-5-2007) NEW DELHI : Union Urban Development Minister Shri S. Jaipal Reddy says that most cities in the country have reached the saturation point and integrated development of towns beyond the cities has emerged as a viable alternative for new growth centres. He was delivering the inaugural address at the annual convention of Indian Buildings Congress in New Delhi today. He stated that towns need a long term-planning framework and prioritize infrastructure investment. Shri Reddy is of the view that integrated development should involve the stakeholders to foster ownership and to allow benefits to every section of the society. Speaking on the occasion, the secretary, Urban Development, Shri Ramachandran said that we need to be geared, as urbanization in the coming years will be much faster. He said that the urban-rural ratio would be 50-50 in 2007. Shri Ramachandran also stated that four factors are to be considered while focusing on development of small towns such as a vision for directing the development, sources of finance, capacity to formulate projects and plans, and finally the type, form and method of development of these towns. Earlier, Shri Jaipal Reddy presented awards and released a souvenir. The Director General Works, Central Public Works Department also spoke on the occasion.

1086. (17-5-2007) NEW DELHI : The Government on 29.3.2007 approved the continuance by Indian Oil Corporation Ltd.(IOCL) of the system of direct chartering of ships without going through TRANSCHART. Replying to a question in the Rajya Sabha today on giving freedom to oil PSUs to hire tankers on their own for importing crude oil, Shri Dinsha Patel, Minister of State for Petroleum & Natural Gas said that Bharat Petroleum Corporation Ltd. and Hindustan Petroleum Corporation Ltd. may charter ships for oil imports directly, instead of going through TRNASCHART. All the companies would follow all applicable regulations relating to hiring of ships including those relating to the Indian flag and shipping on FOB basis. Shri Patel further said that the system of direct chartering by IOCL has generally worked efficiently and satisfactorily during the last one year.

1087. (17-5-2007) NEW DELHI : As per current Preferential Traffic Schedule General Order No. 81, the priority for allotment of rakes for various commodities is determined broadly in the following order: Priority 'A' – Military Traffic. Priority 'B' – (i) Goods for emergency relief work for victims of national calamities like floods, drought, earthquake etc. (ii) Food grains and levy sugar for Public Distribution System or other welfare schemes sponsored by Food Corporation of India. Priority 'C' – All programmed traffic of coal, edible salt, raw-material for steel plants, fertilizer and Petroleum Oil & Lubricants (POL) when sponsored by government agencies and accepted by Railway authorities. Priority 'D' – All traffic not included in Priority 'A to 'C'. This information was given by Shri R. Velu, Minister of State for Railways in a written reply to a question in Lok Sabha today.

1088. (17-5-2007) NEW DELHI : Ministry of Railways have decided that existing safety surcharge now stands subsumed in passenger fares in form of a development charge for partial funding of Dedicated Freight Corridor project. It is expected that Rs. 845 Crore per annum would accrue in form of development charge. No additional levy has been imposed to fund Dedicated Freight Corridor project. Western Dedicated Freight Corridor will start from Jawaharlal Nehru Port and will be routed via Vadodra-Ahmedabad-Palanpour-Rewari to Tughlakabad/ Dadri. As per the present estimate, the project costing Rs. 16,592 Crore will be completed in about 5 years after the start of construction of the project. This information was given by Shri R. Velu, Minister of State for Railways in a written reply to a question in Lok Sabha today.

1089. (17-5-2007) NEW DELHI : All stations having reservation related workload qualify for provision of PRS facility. (ii) At least one PRS, railhead or non-railhead, in every district, in every district, irrespective whether the location is in District Head Quarter or otherwise, need to be provided. PRS at places, other than District Headquarters would be finalized on the recommendation of District Collector and concerned Zonal railway. District authorities will have to provide free-of–cost accommodation at non-railhead locations. Other cost towards air conditioning, channel, and equipment etc. is to be borne entirely by the Railways (iii) Important tourist or hill stations and pilgrimages centres etc. also qualify for PRS facilities. (iv) Such railway stations, where there is no PRS within a vicinity of 50 Kms, may be considered for combined PRS-cum-UTS offices based on adequate justification provided by the concerned railway. (v) Additional PRS may be opened for such satellite locations in such Metro cities, which are thickly populated, having population of 4 lakhs and more and where no PRS centre is available within a radius of 15 Kms. The railways may also recommend additional PRS centres in metro and other big cities, where urban population is increasing and leading to congestion in the existing PRS centres. (vi) No new conventional PRS centres be generally and exclusively provided at Universities, Institutions, Airports, Courts, etc. barring highly exceptional cases. They may be advised to tie up with IRCTC on the pattern of corporate houses on alternatively they may opt for internet kiosks to have Internet booking in their premises. In the Financial year 2006-07, approximately Rs. 6.89 crore has been sanctioned for opening of Computerized Reservation centres. Out of this approximately Rs. 3.16 crore have been utilized. For the Financial Year 2007-08, approximately Rs. 24 lakhs have been allocated uptill now. This information was given by Shri R. Velu, Minister of State for Railways in a written reply to a question in Lok Sabha today.

1090. (17-5-2007) NEW DELHI : Railways have recently approved the signing and ratification of the Inter-governmental agreement on Trans-Asian Railway. The Inter-government Agreement on Trans-Asian Railway was negotiated under the aegis of United National-Economic and Social Commission for Asia and the Pacific (UN-ESCAP) and was opened for signature during the Ministerial Conference on Transport at Busan in November 2006. The Agreement defines and lists the railway lines of international importance including the missing links and lays down the guiding principles relating to technical characteristics for providing seamless transport on the Trans Asian Railway network. The Agreement does not estimate the total investment required on the net work. However, the missing link in India is from Jiribam to Tamu in Myanmar. The construction of this missing link, as per the feasibility study conducted by Ministry of External Affaris through RITES Limited, is estimated to cost Rs. 2941 crores. On this portion, Ministry of Railways has sanctioned construction of the 97 kilometres new rail link between Jiribam and Tupul (Short of Imphal) costing Rs. 727.56 crores. This information was given by Shri R. Velu, Minister of State for Railways in a written reply to a question in Lok Sabha today.

1091. (17-5-2007) NEW DELHI : The Railways have a proposal to revamp the security arrangement at the railway stations in Northern Railway. Indian Institute of Technology (IIT), Delhi has been assigned the task of carrying out a security audit of Delhi Main Junction Railways Station with a view to prepare a composite security plan. The above mentioned project is a sort of pilot project. For the first time such a project has been assigned to IIT, Delhi by the Indian Railways. The terms and conditions specified by the Indian Institute of Technology for taking up this project have been accepted by the Railways and a Liaison Officer has been nominated from the Railways for day to day coordination. Further action will be taken by the Railways on receipt of the report. This information was given by Shri R. Velu, Minister of State for Railways in a written reply to a question in Lok Sabha today.

1092. (17-5-2007) NEW DELHI : The Railways are considering to reduce the weight of the coaches to improve their efficiency. A new design of light weight coaches was acquired under transfer of technology agreement with M/s Linke Hoffman Busch (LHB) and about 400 such coaches have already been manufactured indigenously at Rail Coach Factory, Kapurthala. These coaches are lighter than the existing Integral Coach Factory (ICF) design coaches.

1093. (17-5-2007) NEW DELHI : The delegations of Indian Railways and Pakistan Railways met in Islamabad from 7th to 9th April, 2007 and agreed to extend the existing Agreement relating to rail communication between India and Pakistan via Attari – Wagah for running of Samjhauta Express for a further period of three years with effect from 20.1.2007 to 19.1.2010. This information was given by Shri R. Velu, Minister of State for Railways in a written reply to a question in Lok Sabha today.

1094. (17-5-2007) NEW DELHI : Rajasthan Tourism Development Corporation (RTDC), which is the nodal agency for booking of tourists for the Palace on Wheels train have registered 7380 requests and out of these 4120 are confirmed bookings for the 'Palace on Wheels' upto 30th April, 2009. RTDC and the Ministry of Railways have decided to introduce second 'Palace on Wheels' train to run on the same sector as in the existing Palace on Wheels to cater to the demand of foreign and domestic tourists. No time frame has been set for the launching of the train. However, as and when the rake is ready to run, the train will be put on operation. This information was given by Shri R. Velu, Minister of State for Railways in a written reply to a question in Lok Sabha today.

1095. (17-5-2007) NEW DELHI : Proposal for construction of 8.82 Km long tunnel at Rohtang alongwith approach roads and alternative road to Leh via Darcha-Padam-Nimu has been approved at the cost of Rs.1355.82 Crore. Works are proposed to be completed by 2013-2014. With the completion of works, the distance between Manali and Leh will reduce by 47 Km and road will be available to users for longer time in the year. This will result in the saving in cost of vehicular operation for all users and cost of Air maintenance for the Army. This will also give boost to socio-economic development of the region by way of growth in industries related to tourism, agriculture and horticulture in part of Himachal Pradesh and Jammu & Kashmir. This information was given by the Defence Minister Shri AK Antony in a written reply to Shri S.K. Kharventhan in Lok Sabha today.

1096. (17-5-2007) NEW DELHI : Trishul missile system is not a failure. Technically it has met the performance objectives as per original Qualitative Requirements (QRs) though delayed. The main reason for this delay are technical problems in achieving perfect 3-beam guidance and obtaining millimetric wave components from abroad. Trishul missile project is required even after the successful test of firing of Agni-3 Missile. Trishul missile is a low-level, quick-reaction, short range, surface-to-air missile against air targets whereas, Agni-III is a long range surface-to-surface missile against fixed strategic targets. As the realization of Trishul missile system got delayed, Users (Army, Air Force, and Navy) resorted to acquisition from abroad as the QRs and operational requirements got modified over time. Dialogue is still on with Air Force to accept the system developed and produced for deploying in certain locations and for training/fire control/air defence practices. This information was given by the Defence Minister Shri AK Antony in a written reply to Shri Rakesh Singh in Lok Sabha today.

1097. (17-5-2007) NEW DELHI : Owing to an incident of forced landing of a Dhruv helicopter in November, 2005 due to failure of its tail rotor blade, Hindustan Aeronautics Limited (HAL) advised its customers to withhold flying of Dhruv helicopters till the cause of the incident is investigated by a Board of Inquiry (BoI). The tail rotor blades of all the Dhruv helicopters delivered to the Indian Armed forces till the date of incident have been replaced by HAL as per the recommendations of the BoI. The helicopters have started flying since February, 2006. This information was given by the Minister of State for Defence Production Rao Inderjit Singh in a written reply to Shri E G Sugavanam in Lok Sabha today.

1098. (17-5-2007) NEW DELHI : The aircraft carrier Gorshkov is scheduled to be delivered by the end of 2008. The Russian side has assured at the highest level that the ship will be delivered as per contract. The aircraft carrier is undergoing necessary repairs / modifications in Russia at present. The project is being closely monitored by the Empowered Apex Committee headed by the Defence Secretary and the Steering Committee headed by the Controller of Warship Production and Acquisition. This information was given by the Defence Minister Shri AK Antony in a written reply to Shri Ravi Prakash Verma and Shrimati Manorama Madhavaraj in Lok Sabha today.

1099. (17-5-2007) NEW DELHI : The Defence Forces propose to acquire night vision devices. The acquisitions are proposed to be made through floating of Global Request for Proposals/Foreign Military Sales route. The evaluations/trials are in progress in some of the cases. Divulging the details in this regard on the Floor of the House would not be in the interest of national security. The procurement of these devices would enhance the night-fighting capabilities of the Armed Forces. This information was given by the Defence Minister Shri AK Antony in a written reply to Shri Adhir Chowdhury and Shri Nikhil Kumar in Lok Sabha today.

1100. (17-5-2007) NEW DELHI : No defence personnel in the Officers' cadre has been reported missing. The details regarding number of Personnel Below Officer Ranks (PBORs) reported missing are as follows: When a defence personnel becomes absent without leave (AWL), efforts are made initially to trace the individual. Subsequently, a Court of Inquiry is ordered to look into the circumstances in which the defence personnel went missing. If the Court of Inquiry establishes that the defence personnel is not a deserter and is missing, the terminal benefits as applicable except death gratuity or ex-gratia are released to the Next of Kin (NOK) of such personnel after one year from the date the individual is reported as missing, in accordance with the laid down procedure. However, in case where the Court of Inquiry establishes that the missing defence personnel is a deserter, the terminal benefits are not released. Efforts are also made to apprehend the deserter with the help of civil authorities.

1101. (17-5-2007) NEW DELHI : A decision has been taken to procure 155 mm guns and the procurement process has been initiated strictly in accordance with the Defence Procurement Procedure. This information was given by the Defence Minister Shri AK Antony in a written reply to Shri Santosh Gangwar in Lok Sabha today.

1102. (17-5-2007) NEW DELHI : BJP Goa President Mr. Shripad Naik today said that the impending defeat of the Congress Party in the forthcoming assembly elections becoming increasingly clear with every passing day, has resulted in mass scale desertions and massive infighting within the Congress Party. As a result of the huge public build up against the anti-people and corrupt policies of the Congress Government in Goa, the party is today seriously plagued by the problem of open mass scale desertions by its former leaders and supporters. While addressing a press conference today, the BJP State President pointed out that everyday the total tally of seats that the Congress Party is contesting is rapidly shrinking.

Initially as part of the alliance with the NCP, the Congress Party was contesting 34 seats. But with the sudden last minute desertion of the Chief Minister's son and Congress leader Vishwajit Rane and Babush Monseratte and their filing nominations as independent candidates, the Congress Party's effective tally of seats that they are contesting has been reduced to only 32. The problem has been further compounded with the earlier defection of Mr. Churchill Allemao which further reduces the Congress Party's total effective tally to a mere 31 seats that they can hope to effectively contest. In this context, the Congress Party can now only dream of winning the elections, he said. Mr. Shripad Naik further pointed out that in addition to the problem of mass scale desertions and massive infighting among its leaders, the Congress Party is also seriously suffering from a leadership issue. In a house of 40 MLAs, there already are five clear Congress Chief Ministerial aspirants including the incumbent CM Mr. Pratap Singh Rane, Mr. Ravi Naik, Francisco Sardinho, Mr. Luizinho Falerio, Mr. Dayanand Narvekar and finally Mr. Wilfred D Souza of the NCP. In addition to this, two former Congress leaders Mr. Churchill Allemao and Babush Monseratte will be ever willing to join this club of Chief Ministerial aspirants, he added. The BJP State President highlighted the fact that clearly stability is now no longer a Congress plank before the voters. Infact the clear choice before the voters of Goa is between a stable, pro-people, responsive, sensitive, progressive and development oriented BJP government under the able leadership of Mr. Manohar Parrikar and an unstable, anti-people, anti-Goa, corrupt, inefficient Congress government under a one among numerous chief ministerial aspirants. Mr. Naik said that the people of Goa would definitely vote in favour of the BJP and pointed out that the Congress had already lost the war even before the start of the battle.

1103. (17-5-2007) NEW DELHI : At present there is no proposal to seek foreign technology assistance with regard to the production of Arjun Tank. Issues related to production of Arjun Tank are being resolved. Indian Army has placed an indent of manufacturing of 124 Tanks on Ordnance Factory Board (OFB) in March 2000. Five tanks have been handed over to Indian Army. Nine more tanks are under Joint Receipt Inspection. This information was given by the Defence Minister Shri AK Antony in a written reply to Shri Dalpat Singh Parste in Lok Sabha today.

1104. (17-5-2007) NEW DELHI : India has been an active participant in the United Nation's peacekeeping missions since 1950. The number of Armed Forces personnel deputed to various peacekeeping missions, in the last three years is as under: As on March 2007, a sum of USD 228.99 millions (approx) is due from the UN towards reimbursements in respect of deployment on various missions. The deployment of troops & equipment and reimbursement of charges therefore is a continuous process which is followed up through the Permanent Mission of India at New York or by sending special teams from time to time. This information was given by the Defence Minister Shri AK Antony in a written reply to Shri Ramdas Athawale in Lok Sabha today.

1105. (17-5-2007) NEW DELHI : Shri Arjun Singh, Human Resource Development Minister has said that Prof. M.M. Sharma Empowered Committee's recommendations regarding science education are being implemented sincerely. Shri Singh was addressing the Consultative Committee attached to HRD here yesterday. The Consultative Committee deliberated upon science and technology education. Ministry had appointed Prof. M.M. Sharma Committee whose recommendations have been accepted by UGC. The recommendations are under implementation. For this purpose, Prof. M.M. Sharma Committee has also been converted into an Empowered Committee. The Minister also informed the Consultative Committee that the third Indian Institute of Science, Education and Research (IISER), Mohali has been established and will admit students in this academic year and IISER at Bhopal and Thiruvanantapuram will be set up during the current year. He also informed that it is proposed to set up three new IITs in the country during the 11th Five Year Plan – one each in Bihar in the East, Rajasthan in the West and Andhra Pradesh in the South. 'The Planning Commission has also accorded 'in principle' approval for setting up of two new schools in Planning and Architecture. These will be set up in Bhopal and Vijaywada in the lines of School of Planning and Architecture, New Delhi', he said. He also said that 20 new Indian Institutes of Information Technologies will be started in 11th five year plan under PPP mode. Shri Singh also informed that Parliament has also approved the Bill seeking to cover all National Institutes of Technology (NITs). They would be accorded status of institutes of national importance. During discussion, Members of the Consultative Committee raised the issues of expansion of technical education, assuring quality of technical education, providing access and affordability for technical education, curriculum development for various courses of technical education, web based learning, nano technology, promoting PhDs and research in science and technology education. Replying the queries, officials from the Deptt. of Higher Education informed the Members that Central Government would intervene in a big way during the 11th Plan in the polytechnic education. Sixty-Five polytechnics will be established with one time grant of about Rs. 12 crores per polytechnic from the Central Government in such especially identified districts which do not have any polytechnic at present. Similarly, 177 existing polytechnics would be given assistance for upgradation of infrastructure. The All India Council for Technical Education has proposed to allow polytechnics to have double shifts subject to certain conditions. It was also informed that the requirement for land for establishing a new polytechnic is being proposed to be reduced by 50%. It was also informed to the Members that all IITs and IISc, Bangalore have jointly developed 225 video and web based courses under the National Programme on Technology Enhanced Learning (NPTEL) which will be available for use by engineering colleges of the country.

1106. (17-5-2007) NEW DELHI : The Secretary, Ministry of Civil Aviation, Shri Ashok Chawla today reviewed the contingency plan for the proposed strike by the Air Corporation Employees' Union of Indian Airlines on 18th May 2007, with the CMD, Indian Airlines, senior officials of the Ministry and Indian Airlines. It was decided at the meeting that the Indian Airlines and the Ministry will make all possible efforts so that the travelling public is not inconvenienced. The Airlines has a detailed contingency plan in this regard which includes issuing travel advisory asking the people to travel light as well as report early for checking-in, seeking support of the Airports Authority of India and the CISF, setting up facilitation counters at the Airport, reducing cargo bookings etc. The Government and the Indian Airlines is committed to a reasonable solution to the demand for wage arrears for which the Employees' Union proposes to go on a strike. However, it has been firmly decided not to consider any unrealistic demand. The Management will take a tough stands in case of disruption of traffic movement tomorrow. The Management has also decided to lodge FIR in case agitating workers resort to physical violence. The Airlines has already issued notifications that the agitational action by the employees is illegal particularly in view of the matter already being seized in conciliation of the Chief Labour Commissioner (Central), Government of India. In view of this, any employee participating in such action will not be entitled to salary/wages for the day besides withholding of payments under Productivity Linked Incentives Scheme for the entire month in addition to any other disciplinary action that the competent authority might deem fit to initiate. The Central Labour Commissioners has commenced conciliation proceedings and the first round was held today. He has impressed upon the representatives of the employees union to reconsider their plan to go on mass casual leave on Friday, the 18th May, 2007.

1107. (17-5-2007) NEW DELHI : The Union Minority Affairs Minister Shri A.R.Antulay has stated that the Jain community has represented to the National Commission for Minorities, its anguish over the decision of the Gujarat legislature to amend the Gujarat Freedom of Religion Act and to declare Buddhists and Jains as Hindus for the purposes of religious conversion. A press note was issued by the National Commission for Minorities expressing the view that the right to profess, practice and propagate religion, guaranteed by Article 25 of the Constitution, is an essential ingredient of the country's multi-religious edifice. The State Government has been urged to maintain the sanctity of this provision and to resolve any misgivings/ misunderstandings through dialogue. This information was given in reply to a written question in the Lok Sabha today.

1108. (17-5-2007) NEW DELHI : The Union Minority Affairs Minister Shri A.R.Antulay has stated that The National Commission for Minorities (NCM) has forwarded recommendations on the report of the Sachar Committee on the following five items: (i) Education (ii) Economy and Employment opportunities (iii) Access to bank credit (iv) Access to social and physical infrastructure and government programmes and (v) Public employment and recruitment procedures. In reply to a written question in Lok Sabha today the Minister also informed that the recommendations of the Sachar Committee are under consideration of Government.

1109. (17-5-2007) NEW DELHI : The Ministry of Rural Development has released second instalment of Central share of funds amounting to Rs. 35.57 lakh under the 'Swarnjayanti Gram Swarojgar Yojana' (SGSY) during the year 2006-07 to 2 DRDAs of Uttar Pradesh, namely Jalaun (Rs.15.78 lakh) and Gonda (Rs.19.79 lakh) towards Restoration of cut on account of late submission. The amount should be utilized on the Programme as per approved guidelines of SGSY. The funding pattern will be 75:25 by the Centre and the State. The State Government should release its share within one month of the date of release of the Central assistance. Under SGSY, assistance is given to the poor family living below the poverty line for taking up self-employment. It actively promotes group approach by organising the rural poor into Self-Help Groups.

1110. (17-5-2007) NEW DELHI : The Ministry of Rural Development has released part payment of first instalment of Central share of funds amounting to Rs. 7.90 crore under the 'Swarnjayanti Gram Swarojgar Yojana' (SGSY) during the year 2007-08 to 16 DRDAs of Chhattisgarh. Details of the allocation are as under: The amount should be utilized on the Programme as per approved guidelines of SGSY. The funding pattern will be 75:25 by the Centre and the State. The State Government should release its share within one month of the date of release of the Central assistance. Under SGSY, assistance is given to the poor family living below the poverty line for taking up self-employment. It actively promotes group approach by organising the rural poor into Self-Help Groups.

1111. (17-5-2007) NEW DELHI : Addressing the plenary meeting of the 60th World Health Assembly in Geneva on 16th May, 2007, the Minister for Health & Family Welfare, Dr. Anbumani Ramadoss said that the World Health Organisation (WHO) needs to develop the capacities of many countries to participate in the Intellectual Property Rights (IPR) regime and reap its benefits. He said there are valid reservations on whether or not the IPR regime will lead to innovations in so far as neglected and tropical diseases are concerned. Ms. Jane Halton, President, World Health Assembly and Dr. Margaret Chan, Director-General, WHO were also present on the occasion. The following is the text of the Minister's speech: It is indeed a pleasure for me to address the WHA once again. Last year I also had the privilege of chairing the proceedings of Committee-A. This provided me with a deep insight into the wide gamut of issues placed before the World Health Assembly. While it was no doubt enlightening for me to participate in these deliberations I cannot but help suggesting that WHO needs to progressively assume a more proactive role on global health issues rather than on advocating remedial measures after events have taken place. In particular WHO can be a bridge between developed and developing countries on issues relating to human resources, technology transfers, building consensus as well as capacities on emerging issues such as Intellectual Property Rights, Innovation and Public Health. There is also a case for a fresh look on the representation of developing countries like India and China on different WHO fora considering their population size and share of global disease burden. The theme adopted by the 60th WHA, "Health Security" is of great interest to all of us. The global threat of emergihg and re-emerging infectious diseases has been demonstrated by the emergence of Human Immunodeficiency Virus (HIV) in the 1980s, Avian Influenza H5N1 in Hong Kong originally seen in 1997 and continuing through today and a global epidemic of Severe Acute Respiratory Syndrome (SARS) in 2003. No country is immune to the occurrence of these diseases. It is therefore altogether appropriate for the WHA to focus on health security. Development issues including health, nutrition, drinking water, education are today at the forefront of world politics. Health, as we all know is fundamental to social and economic development. The Millennium Development Goals 2015 are less than a decade away and most countries are feeling the pressure from all stakeholders to design policies which accelerate the achievement of the goals as per schedule. In India, the state supported public health delivery system is being comprehensively rejuvenated under the National Rural Health Mission which is the biggest and most ambitious programme in the health sector ever in India. The National Rural Health Mission which is a convergence of health, nutrition, sanitation and drinking water, seeks to provide accessible, affordable and accountable quality health services specially to the poorest households in the remotest rural regions, focusing on reducing IMR and MMR. The thrust of NRHM is on establishing a fully functional, community owned, decentralized health delivery system with inter sectoral convergence at all levels. Quality care through adoption of the Indian Public Health Standards, focus on outcomes and adoption of evidence based strategies are some of the other salient features of NRHM. We realize the need to target programmes for our women and children. We are going for major capacity building initiatives both for human and physical resources to ensure nutritional adequacy, deliveries at institutions and by skilled birth attendants, referral transport and emergency obstetric care. The Janani Suraksha Yojana, a path breaking programme for cash support for institutional deliveries, has had an overwhelming response. Newborn and child health strategies range from the integrated management of neonatal and childhood illnesses, immunisation strategies, including this year, a US$300 million polio eradication programme and the recently launched Norway-India partnership initiative. We have more than 400,000 Accredited Social Health Activists (ASHAs) who are empowered village women forming a link between the government and our clients for better service delivery. The double burden of diseases experienced by a large number of low and middle income countries of the world has made it necessary for these countries to initiate mechanisms for effective prevention and control mechanisms.

1112. (17-5-2007) NEW DELHI : The Minister of Tourism and Culture Smt. Ambika Soni has said the total number of tourist visits, domestic and foreign taken together, to Srinagar during January-April 2007 has decreased by 39% as compared to the corresponding period of 2006. While the number of domestic tourist visits has decreased, that of foreign tourist visits has increased. The figures are given below:-In view of the 20% growth in foreign tourist visits to Srinagar during January-April 2007 in comparison to the figures for the corresponding period of the year 2006, possible loss of foreign exchange is not expected. In a written reply in the Lok Sabha today she said, attractive tourist packages are offered by the private sector and the Jammu & Kashmir Tourism Development Corporation (JKTDC). Lack of such packages is not perceived as the reason for decline in number of tourists.

1113. (17-5-2007) NEW DELHI : Participating in the inaugural ceremony of India Herbal Garden at WHO Headquarters in Geneva, the Minister for Health & Family Welfare, Dr. Anbumani Ramadoss said that the aim of the country is to move away from being an exporter of raw materials of medicinal plants to exporters of finished products of quality standards. The Minister is currently on an official visit to Geneva to attend the 60th World Health Assembly. The India Herbal Garden was inaugurated by Dr. Margaret Chan, Director General, WHO on 16th May, 2007. Dr. Samlee Plianbangchang, Regional Director of SEARO, WHO and the Indian Ambassador were also present on the occasion.

1114. (17-5-2007) NEW DELHI : Minister for Tourism and Culture Smt. Ambika Soni has said that there is no information that the minarets and towers of any of the protected monuments are tilting. Archaeological Survey of India has taken up a detailed study on the stability of the minarets of Taj Mahal by Geodetic and Research Branch on the Survey of India, Dehradun. The study has revealed that the minarets are stable and there was no tilting. In a written reply in the Lok Sabha today she said, seismic studies on the Qutb Minar are in progress.

1115. (17-5-2007) NEW DELHI : The Airports Authority of India (AAI) plans to construct a cargo terminal facility adjacent to the Terminal Building at the Trivandrum Airport. This information was given by Shri Praful Patel, Minister for Civil Aviation in the Parliament today. Presently, air cargo at the Trivandrum Airport is being managed by the Kerala State Industrial Enterprise (KSIE) at custodian appointed by the Customs Department. The AAI has, however, offered to develop and operate its proposed international cargo facility on the available piece of land near the new International Terminal Building in Joint Venture with KSIE. The AAI is currently constructing a new International Terminal Building at the Trivandrum Airport.

1116. (17-5-2007) NEW DELHI : Minister for Tourism and Culture Smt. Ambika Soni informed the Lok Sabha today that the paintings at Ajanta are safe and are in good state of preservation. Apart from undertaking regular conservation, preservation and maintenance, the Archaeological Survey of India has assigned Geological Survey of India (GSI) to conduct geo-technical studies of the Caves and recommend methods for conservation of the Caves and prevent them from natural disintegration. The GSI would also recommend methods for arresting seepage of water into the Caves. As already suggested by the Panel of Experts,

Archaeological Survey of India has taken up a programme for providing surface water drainage which is expected to minimize seepage into the Caves. It is proposed that the design of the surface drainage would be prepared by the Central Water Power Research Station (CWPRS), Pune. In a written reply Smt. Soni said sustained preservation measures are implemented as per annual programme. These include consolidation of painted plasters, monitoring of environmental parameters, dusting of painted surface, spraying of insecticides on the unpainted portions of the plaster; other preventive measures include regulating the movement of visitors inside the painted caves to control the relative humidity and Fibre optic light system is installed in five painted caves eliminating the harmful effects of heat and other ultraviolet and infrared radiations.

1117. (17-5-2007) NEW DELHI : Depending on the depths available in the entrance channels and berths, and the availability of equipment, vessels of various sizes are handled at Indian Ports. The ability of a port to attract large size vessels and to handle them depends on various factors which include the traffic volumes, proximity to international routes and markets, good road/rail connectivity, large backup area and supporting hinterland. It is the endeavour of the Government to develop the necessary port infrastructure for attracting and handling such vessels, keeping in view the demands of maritime trade, as part of the overall development of ports. Under the National Maritime Development Programme (NMDP) formulated by the Department of Shipping, 276 projects involving an investment of Rs.55,804 crores in the 12 Major Ports have been identified to be taken up for implementation over a period upto 2011-12. These include 25 projects for deepening of port channels, 76 projects for construction/reconstruction of berths/ jetties etc., 52 projects for procurement of equipment etc., 45 projects for improvement in rail/road connectivity to the Major Ports and 78 other associated projects. The objective is to upgrade and modernise the port infrastructure in India which will enable it to benchmark its performance against global standards. This information was given by the Minister of Shipping, Road Transport and Highways, Shri Thiru T.R. Baalu in a written reply in the Rajya Sabha today.

1118. (17-5-2007) NEW DELHI : Any accident including the death or injury to any seafarer of any nationality on board a ship registered in a foreign country while the said vessel is on or near the coast of India can be investigated by an officer appointed under section 359 of the Merchant Shipping Act, 1958. During the course of investigation, the vessel or its crew can be detained for the purpose of conducting the investigation. However, if the death is due to any criminal act such as murder, the relevant provisions of the Indian Penal Code/Criminal Penal Code would apply and the Merchant Shipping Act, 1958 does not have any provisions to address such issues. In cases where an Indian seafarer gets injured and dies on a foreign registered ship while the vessel is at high seas, it is the jurisdiction of the respective flag administration to conduct investigation into the cause of such accident or criminal incident. The Government of India, being a substantially interested state, however, has also now started participating as an observer in such investigation wherever possible. Further, whenever feasible, the Indian Embassy /High Commission officials are deputed to investigate the matter in the first port of call in the foreign countries. The Merchant Shipping Act addresses the subject of protecting the interests of Indian sailors through its various sections. However, to further strengthen the exiting provisions, the following additional measures have been initiated by the Directorate General of Shipping. (i) Recruitment and Placement Rules, 2005 have been notified to regulate various manning agents who employ Indian Seafarers. This notification requires mandatory registration of such manning agents operating out of offices registered in India. This has ensured that manning agents, who employ Indian seafarers on Indian as well as foreign registered vessels, are held accountable for the welfare of such Indian seafarers. (ii) A psychometric test has been introduced at the entry level of officers in maritime training courses, which will help in determining his/her attitude and aptitude for the sea. It assists the entrants in taking corrective measures to mentally prepare themselves for the rigours of a life at sea. (iii) The Directorate General of Shipping has also given wide publicity in leading newspapers with regard to the scheme of recruitment through the registered Recruitment and Placement Shipping Agents for employment in the marine sector. (iv) A new course module has been formulated to sensitize the trainees with regard to the rights of seafarers as laid down under the Merchant Shipping (Recruitment and Placement) Rules, 2005 in all the Pre-sea Training Institutes. (v) The matter has also been taken up with the International Maritime Organization (IMO) with regard to consolidating the international conventions with regard to shipping casualties and making the law stringent to bring around the non-responsible flag states to carry out their responsibility. (vi) MS Notice No. 5-A has been issued by the Director General of Shipping. This notice requires mandatory reporting and plan of action to deal with causalities involving Indian seafarers on foreign flag ships. This information was given by the Minister of Shipping, Road Transport and Highways, Shri Thiru T.R. Baalu in a written reply in the Rajya Sabha today.

1119. (17-5-2007) NEW DELHI : The Defence Minister Shri A K Antony will inaugurate a two-day conference of the General Managers of Ordnance Factories, in New Delhi on Friday, May, 18, 2007. A brief background note is accompanied below: Indian Ordnance Factories Organisation, a conglomerate of 39 Ordnance Factories, set up to produce land based military hardware exclusively for Defence use started its journey in 1802 when the British established the first factory on the bank of Hooghly near Kolkata to repair wooden gun carriages. The expansion of the organization thereafter was need based and concentrated in the years immediately after war for manufacture of products whose need was felt during the war. Since Indian Industry was at the infant stage when most of the Ordnance Factories came up, in-house manufacture of military products was planned from virgin metal. This fully integrative production approach was subsequently dispensed with when Indian Industry matured and today creation of capacity in Ordnance

Factories is restricted either in strategic area or for the inputs that Indian trade cannot meet qualitative and quantitative requirement. The share of Indian trade now has risen to 46% of turnover. Indigenous content in Ordnance factories products is about 98% for established items. Even when new items under productionisation are counted, import content varies at best between 5 to 6%. This high order of indigenisation helped Ordnance Factories to exploit surge capacity at a very short notice to meet increased requirement during war despite sanction imposed by overseas states. Today Ordnance Factories manufacture wide range of products starting from troop comfort items including small arms, ammunitions, weapons artillery guns transport and armoured vehicle, optical equipments required by Artillery Infantry Air Defence and Mechanised Forces. The organization is around the first 20 of Defence Industry contractors of the world with turnover of around 1.5 billion US $ per annum. Production capacity in Ordnance Factories was created to meet war time requirement. Exploitation of installed capacity in full always poses a challenge requirement, during peace time being less. Notwithstanding the limitation of product centric manufacturing capacity, constant endeavour made to assess and develop products for non Defence sector has led to develop market for almost 20% of turnover in other than Defence sector. Though Ordnance Factories supply to Defence Forces most of the products (except products manufactured in unorganized sector) at a price less than market price, Ordnance Factories do not have any scope to make profit from Defence sector as supply to Defence sector is on cost as per policy. However the price for products meant for non Defence sector is market driven. As such Ordnance Factories earn profit from supply to civil sector including export and pass on the benefit to Defence sector by calibrating price. Modernisation of infrastructure is another thrust area pursued continuously to upgrade technology to undertake manufacture of futuristic products in minimum response time. The organization has invested Rs. 2505 Cr. during IXth and Xth Plan for procurement of plant and machinery with upgraded technology. The modernization plan is regularly fine tuned matching with change in product mix brought about by Defence Forces at the time of induction of new products and funded through internal resources without taking any budgetary support from Govt. of India. Improved productivity, modernization and optimum capacity utilization has resulted in generation of surplus/profit.

1120. (17-5-2007) NEW DELHI : Most of the members of the Parliamentary Consultative Committee attached to the Ministry of Chemicals and Fertilisers and Steel have strongly supported a proposal to earmark 20 per cent of the MP Local Area Development Fund for assistance to critically ill patients suffering from selected diseases like cancer, heart and kidney problems, particularly form the weaker sections. The recommendation for this had come from the Pharmaceutical Advisory Forum in its latest meeting held in New Delhi recently. Giving details of the proposal, the Minister for Chemicals, Fertilisers and Steel Shri Ram Vilas Paswan said, the funds could be directly disbursed to the hospitals providing treatment thus ensuring transparency. He said, Parliament Members are often flooded with requests for such help and the present institutional mechanism is highly inadequate. Describing the move as historic some members said, they will support the move in the MP-LAD committee. Members also urged the government to ensure early approval of the National Pharmaceuticals Policy presently under consideration of the Group of Ministers. They said, this is required to ensure availability of medicines at affordable prices. They also demanded the introduction of the National Health Insurance Scheme. The Minister appraised the members that the scheme is part of the Draft NPP. Shri Paswan said, the proposed scheme can ensure timely treatment to all BPL families at an estimated expenditure of Rs.3000 Crore. The Minister also said that the Draft Pharma Policy also has a proposal to set up Drug Banks at District Hospitals in order to give benefit to the BPL families. The drug banks would be in operation on the lines of the Rajasthan Model. The Members welcomed this move announced by the Minister. The Minister said several steps have been taken to ensure price stability. Among them compulsory printing of the Maximum Retail Price inclusive of all taxes on all medicine packs, monitoring of prices of non scheduled formulations and the Pharma Industry's voluntary decision of bilingual labelling on medicine packs. Members of the Committee suggested that the Department should advertise throughout the country in regional newspapers the decision to print the MRP inclusive of all taxes to increase awareness among the people. The Minister also informed the Members of the decision of the Government that the annual limit of price hike of non-scheduled formulations, monitored by NPPA, has been reduced to 10 percent from the earlier 20 percent. Shri Paswan said, as per the commitment given by the present government, sick public sector units like the Hindustan Antibiotics and the Bengal Chemicals and Pharmaceuticals have been revived. The Union Cabinet will soon consider rehabilitation of the Indian Drugs and Pharmaceuticals Limited. Some members said there is shortage of anti rabies vaccine in the market. The Minister assured the members that the Bengal Chemicals and Pharmaceuticals will be asked to ensure adequate production and supply with the help of Pasteur Institute, Coonoor. The Members expressed their concern over the issue of spurious drugs. The Members also expressed concern about the issue of untrained people working as Pharmacists with the local chemists. The Members expressed the view that the Pharma Companies should take the responsibility of training pharmacists, through a specially designed short-term course.

1121. (17-5-2007) NEW DELHI : According to the data maintained by the Indian Seafarers Database (INDoS) there are 1,46,245 registered Indian seafarers. The exact number of seafarers employed on Indian ships and foreign owned ships are not known. However, the approximate number of Indian seafarers working at any point of time on Indian flag ships is between 30,000 – 32,000 and on foreign flag ships, it is between 52,000-54,000. The age profile of foreign ships, where Indian seafarers are working is also not known. Barring Single Hull Oil Tankers above 25 years of age, there is no restriction for any other types of ships to ferry cargo to Indian ports provided these ships are duly surveyed and certified for compliance with International Maritime Organization (IMO) Conventions, rules and regulations. Single Hull Oil Tankers above 25 years of age are not allowed to ferry oil cargo to Indian ports. Foreign ships visiting Indian ports are randomly inspected by the Mercantile Marine Department (MMD) Surveyors under the Port State Control regime. If foreign ships are found sub-standard or un-seaworthy during these inspections, ships are detained till such time all deficiencies are rectified. During the year 2006, MMD Surveyors inspected a total of 653 foreign flag ships at various ports and out of these, 99 ships were detained due to deficiencies. Almost 80% of 99 ships detained were above 25 years of age, and out of the total number of 653 inspections carried out about 30% were above 25 years of age. Reported deaths of Indian seafarers working on foreign flag ships of more than 15 years old since January 2005 are as follows: In the year 2005, five deaths in the five incidents, in 2006, three deaths in one incident and in the year 2007, two deaths in two incidents involving foreign ships which were more than 15 years old. This information was given by the Minister of Shipping, Road Transport and Highways, Shri Thiru T.R. Baalu in a written reply in the Rajya Sabha today.

1122. (17-5-2007) NEW DELHI : Prof. Saifuddin Soz, the Union Minister for Water Resources has said that the availability of water resources in our country is highly uneven in time and space. An accurate assessment of the available water resources, the surface and ground water is needed for optimum planning, design and operation of the water resources projects. In the area of water availability, National Institute of Hydrology (NIH) has studied many important issues for various states and central organizations. He was addressing at the Consultative Committee Meeting of Ministry of Water Resources to discuss "The Role and Functions of the National Institute of Hydrology" here today. The Minister said that the considerable expertise generated and technological advances made by NIH over the years in the area of Hydrology and water resources has been utilized by different Central and State Government Organizations of the country. The Institute has established regional centres in the country to develop understanding and tackle the hydrological problems of different regions. Prof. Soz has said that Terrorism and Climate Change are two biggest threats, the world is facing today. He called upon NIH to include Climate Change also in its studies. Referring to the Interlinking of the rivers in the country he said that the Government is fully committed to the interlinking of rivers and the work on five projects of interlinking of rivers is under progress. He also informed the Members that in the 11th Five Year Plan the Ministry of Water Resources is getting funds for Flood Management. The Members raised several issues regarding the hydro technology, digging bore-wells and quality of underground water in the Meeting. The Members of Parliament who participated included S/Sh.Parshuram Majhi, S.P.Y Reddy, Abu Ayes Mondal Dr. Rattan Singh Ajnala, Dr. Gyan Prakash Pilania, Hiten Barman, Kunnur Manjunath Channappa and Smt. N.P. Durga. Minister of State for Water Resources Shri Jai Prakash Nararan Yadav, Secretary Water Resources Smt. Gauri Chatterjee and senior officials of the Ministry of Water Resources and its subordinate offices attended the Meeting.

1123. (17-5-2007) NEW DELHI : National Highways Development Project (NHDP) is being implemented by National Highways Authority of India (NHAI). Wherever 4/6 laning works under NHDP are under implementation, to keep the existing roads in traffic worthy condition, the maintenance of existing roads are carried out by the Contractor/Concessionaire as part of their obligations under contract/concession agreement. In case of sections identified under NHDP where 4/6 laning has not yet started, the maintenance of existing roads are being carried out by NHAI, State Public Works Departments (PWDs)/Border Road Organisation (BRO) through funds provided by the Ministry of Shipping, Road Transport and Highways. This information was given by the Minister of State for Shipping, Road Transport and Highways, Shri K.H. Muniyappa in a written reply in the Rajya Sabha today.

1124. (17-5-2007) NEW DELHI : The Ministry of Shipping, Road Transport and Highways has approved 4229 Nos. projects for improvement of State roads from the Central Road Fund (CRF) for an aggregate amount of Rs.8142.99 crore as on January, 2007 since the year 2000-2001. 758 and 759 road projects were approved for CRF during 2003-04 and 2005-06 respectively and amounts of Rs.778.95 crore and Rs.1299.27 crore were released during the year 2003-04 and 2005-06 respectively. This information was given by the Minister of State for Shipping, Road Transport and Highways, Shri K.H. Muniyappa in a written reply in the Rajya Sabha today.

1125. (17-5-2007) NEW DELHI : The average cost per km for Phase-II of National Highways Development Project (NHDP) was approved at Rs. 4.75 crore for upgradation to 4-lane for flexible pavement and Rs. 6.45 crore per km for rigid pavement at 2002 prices. However the cost as considered in the Financing Plan for NHDP Phase-II, approved by Committee on Infrastructure, is now Rs. 6.52 crore per km at 2006 prices. The awarded contracts for NHDP Phase-II provide for price escalation and therefore, final cost of construction can be assessed only after completion of the project. This information was given by the Minister of State for Shipping, Road Transport and Highways, Shri K.H. Muniyappa in a written reply in the Rajya Sabha today.

1126. (17-5-2007) NEW DELHI : Minister for Tourism and Culture Smt. Ambika Soni informed the Lok Sabha today that her ministry is working on modalities for modernization of Nehru Memorial Museum and Library (NMML). In addition to the normal plan allocation of Rs. 350 lakhs for the year 2007-08, the Finance Minister in the Budget Speech for 2007-08 has announced a grant of Rs. 20 crores. The details and modalities are required to be worked out. As such, the exact time schedule by which the modernization of Nehru Memorial Museum & Library is likely to be completed cannot be specified. In a written reply she said, there is no Proposal/ Scheme for setting up of libraries in the country. However, Raja Rammohan Roy Library Foundation (RRRLF) has a Scheme for establishment of children's corner in the existing public Libraries. Under this Scheme an amount of upto Rs. 1.50 lakhs is granted to each library for setting up of RRRLF Children's Corner.

1127. (17-5-2007) NEW DELHI : Minister for Tourism and Culture Smt. Ambika Soni has said that there were apprehensions that vibration caused by the low flying aircrafts may adversely affect the historic temples of Khajuraho. This was taken up with the airlines and also the Airport Authority of India. In a written reply in the Lok Sabha today she said, the Airport Authority of India has initiated corrective measures like changes in landing and departure procedures and various amendments in the Air Traffic Control (ATC) procedures which would minimize the possibility of aircraft flying over these monuments.

1128. (17-5-2007) NEW DELHI : Gross telephone subscribers in the country reached 196.71 (million in January, 2007) as compared to 189.92 million in December, 2006. The overall tele-density reached 17.45 per cent in January, 2007 as compared to 16.83 per cent at the end of December, 2006. This was stated by Dr. Shakeel Ahmad, Minister of State for Communications and Information Technology in a written reply to question by Smt Supriya Sule in Rajya Sabha today. He further stated that there is no specific target set for tele-density for the year 2007-08. However, the target set was to achieve a tele-density of 7 per cent by the year 2005 and15 per cent by the year 2010, which had already been achieved. Also there is a target of 250 million telephones by the end of December, 2007 and 500 million telephones by the end of year 2010. Informing further, Dr. Ahmad said that out of total 607491 villages in the country, 552824 villages have been provided Village Public Telephone (VPT) facility as on 31-03-2007. Bharat Sanchar Nigam Ltd. (BSNL) has entered into an agreement with Universal Service Obligation Fund (USOF), DOT in November, 2004, for providing VPTs facility to 66822 accessible, undisputed and undisturbed uncovered villages having population more than 100 as per census 1991, which are planned to be provided with VPT facility progressively by November, 2007 in accordance with the terms and conditions of the said agreement. Out of the awarded village, BSNL has provided VPT facility to 46969 villages up to 31.03.2007. Also, a scheme is being launched by Government of India to provide support for the provision of mobile services, including WLL services, in specified rural and remote areas, where there is no existing fixed or mobile services and is likely to be made operational by June, 2008. About 2.12 lakh villages are likely to be covered under this scheme.

1129. (17-5-2007) NEW DELHI : The Department of Posts is expecting a revenue of Rs. 500 crores from the Speed Post Service in 2007-08. This was stated by Dr. Shakeel Ahmad, Minister of State for Communications and Information Technology in a written reply to question by Smt Supriya Sule in Rajya Sabha today. The National Speed Post network was extended to eighteen more cities on

January 1, 2007. It was further expanded to twenty five cities on March 1, 2007 and to another fifty five cities in on April 2, 2007. He further said that the Department of Posts earned Rs. 408 crores from Speed Post Service during 2005-06 and Rs. 449 crores during 2006-07. It is expected to earn revenue of Rs. 500 crores during 2007-08. The network of Speed Post service is extended as required taking into account the market requirements, customer needs, expected business, transport facilities available etc.

1130. (17-5-2007) NEW DELHI : The Minister of State for Coal Dr. Dasari Narayana Rao informed the Rajya Sabha in a written reply today that Government has allocated 60 coal blocks to the private sector companies so far. Of these, 7 private parties have started mining of coal. These 60 blocks have estimated coal reserves of over 7900 Million Metric Tonnes (MMT). The Minister further said that the Ministry of Coal has initiated various measures such as quarterly review at the Ministry level, bi-annual review by the Coal Controller, laying down of specific time bound milestones for development of coal blocks, introduction of bank guarantee deposit etc. in order to ensure timely development of coal blocks allotted to private companies. "Based on the periodic monitoring, the Ministry reviews the cases and wherever found necessary, the Ministry takes appropriate measures on merits, including deallocation of block where warranted" Dr. Rao told the House.

1131. (17-5-2007) NEW DELHI : The Minister of State for Coal Dr. Dasari Narayana Rao informed the Rajya Sabha in a written reply today that the assessed all India coal demand for Annual Plan 2007-08 is 494.50 Million Metric Tonne (MMT). This comprises of a demand of 38.04 MMT on the part of Singareni Collieries Company Limited operating in the State of Andhra Pradesh. He further informed that the estimated raw coal demand of 494.50 MMT in 2007-08 is planned to be met from domestic supply of 461.89 MMT, which includes domestic production of 460.50 MMT and a stock draw down of 1.39 MMT from Coal India Ltd.(CIL) sources. This leaves a gap of 30.61 MMT which will be entirely met by proposed import of 20 MMT of coking coal for steel sector and 10.61 MMT of non-coking coal for power, cement and other sectors. The Minister elaborated a number of steps taken by Government to increase domestic production to reduce the gap between demand and supply. As many as 130 coal blocks have been allotted to different consumers to be operated by private/public sector for captive end uses/commercial mining. CIL has identified to take up 119 coal projects for an ultimate capacity of 256 MMT with a contribution of 111.08 MMT in 2011-12, the terminal year of XI Plan. SCCL has identified to take up 25 projects for an ultimate capacity of 43.35 MMT with a contribution of 5.75 MMT in the terminal year 2011-12 of XI Plan. Further, CIL under "Emergency Coal Production Plan" has identified 16 opencast projects/mines where production from the existing mines/projects will be enhanced to a higher level yielding additional 71.3 MMT. Improvement in equipment utilization, mechanization/modernization of existing mines and increasing productivity in underground and opencast mines are some of the other significant steps taken in this direction.

1132. (17-5-2007) NEW DELHI : Expressing serious concern over the quality gap between public schools and private schools, the Prime Minister, Dr. Manmohan Singh has emphasized the need to bridge it if good education is not to become a preserve of the privileged classes only. Reiterating the Government's commitment to pursue effective Policies for the empowerment of Dalits, Tribals, Minorities, Other Backward Classes and women, the Prime Minister asserted that if there are ideas about the problems faced by poor children from other sections of the community, they should also be taken on board. He made these observations at the Conference on 'Empowerment of Scheduled Castes, Schedules Tribes and Minorities through Elementary Education' organized by the All India Forum of Legislators (SCs/ STs) & Others in association with the Ministry of Human Resource Development, here today. Stating that a high quality public schooling system is the only guarantor of equality of opportunity to all groups, irrespective of their social or economic conditions, the Prime Minister said that improving the public school system requires greater attention to teacher training and attending to the unique problems of first generation learners. "Greater attention needs to be paid to improving the teaching of science and mathematics in schools as numeracy skills and scientific knowledge are the key to success in the knowledge economy", he stressed. Former Prime Minister, Shri I.K. Gujral, Leader of Opposition, Shri L.K. Advani, Union Power Minister, Shri Sushil Kumar Shinde, Deputy Speaker, Lok Sabha, Shri Charanjit Singh Atwal, Chief Ministers of Nagaland, Meghalaya, Arunachal Pradesh, Union Ministers, MPs, MLAs and others participated in the Conference. Following is the text of the Prime Minister, Dr. Manmohan Singh's address on the occasion: "I join Advani ji in congratulating Sardar Charanjit Singh Atwal for having taken this initiative to convene this very very important Conference. Let me begin on a personal note. I would not have been what I am today and could not have done what I have been able to do in my life but for the light of education that my family lit for me. As a young adult, I had no other asset or advantage other than the benefit of a good education. That benefit I got both because of my family's commitment to my education and because of the various public scholarships that our State provided for students. I was able to earn as my education progressed. My own experience is a testimony to the role that education can play in our people's empowerment. Education enhances human capabilities. This, in turn, empowers us both socially and economically. That is why our Government has taken several initiatives to increase public investment in education, attract more private investment and to offer scholarships at all levels of education to the needy and the deserving. But I do recognize that what has been done is not enough. More needs to be done and new pathways have to be found to realise education as a fundamental human right of all our children. The world in which we now live and the new world that is now emerging, is a world in which knowledge will be the key to social and economic development, political power and strategic capability. The very fact that there is no developed, industrial economy with a literacy rate below 80%, testifies to the central role of education in processes of social and economic development. It is no longer access to land, or even capital, that differentiates the haves from the have-nots. The key differentiator today is access to modern education. Access to quality vocational education, access to modern science and technology and access to advanced skills and capabilities. These are crucial determinants of social mobility. I sincerely believe that the route to the social and economic empowerment of all disadvantaged groups-be they dalits or tribals; be they women or minorities – is through education. That is why our successive Governments have placed special emphasis on education. The Scheduled Castes constitute close to 16% of our population. While they suffer from many handicaps, the lack of access to education has been one of the foremost barriers to their sustained progress. The lower educational achievement among them is in turn, closely associated with the denial of a right to education in the past.

1133. (18-5-2007) NEW DELHI : The External Commercial Borrowing (ECB) policy is constantly reviewed by the Government in consultation with the Reserve Bank of India (RBI) to keep it in tune with the evolving macroeconomic situation, changing market conditions, sectoral requirements, the external sector and the lessons of experience. Based on such a review, it has been decided to modulate the capital inflows through ECB by modifying some aspects of the policy as indicated below: As per the extant ECB policy, utilization of ECB proceeds for real-estate is not permitted. However, the term 'real-estate' excludes development of integrated township as defined by Press Note 3 (2002 Series) dated January 04, 2002 issued by Ministry of Commerce & Industry. It has been decided to withdraw the exemption accorded to the 'development of integrated township' as a permissible end-use of ECB. In view of the upgradation of the country's sovereign credit ratings, existing all-in-cost ceilings are revised as follows:

1134. (18-5-2007) NEW DELHI : Government of India have announced the sale (re-issue) of "7.38 per cent Government Stock, 2015" for a notified amount of Rs. 5,000 crore (nominal) through a price based auction using multiple price method. Government of India have also announced the sale (re-issue) of "8.35 per cent Government Stock, 2022" for a notified amount of Rs. 3,000 crore (nominal) through a price based auction using multiple price method. The auctions will be conducted by the Reserve Bank of India, Mumbai Office, Fort, Mumbai on May 25, 2007 (Friday). Up to 5% of the notified amount of the sale of both the stocks will be allotted to eligible individuals and Institutions as per the Scheme for Non-Competitive Bidding Facility in the Auction of Government Securities. Bids in the prescribed form obtainable from the Regional Director, Reserve Bank of India, Mumbai Office (Public Debt Office), Fort, Mumbai-400 001 and RBI website www.rbi.org.in should be submitted to that Office on May 25, 2007. The NDS members should submit competitive as well as non-competitive bids in electronic format using Primary Market Operation (PMO) module of NDS. All bids should be submitted by 12.30 P.M.

1135. (18-5-2007) NEW DELHI : The Government has decided to accept nearly all the recommendations/suggestions of the Sachar Committee and taken the following major decisions for their implementation: Targeted intervention is proposed for improvement of basic amenities and employment opportunities in 90 identified minority concentration districts which are backward in terms of various developmental parameters. Appropriate measures will be taken to improve the deficiency in civic amenities and economic opportunities in 338 identified towns and cities with a substantial population of minorities, including Muslims. An inter-ministerial task force is already working on this to recommend appropriate strategies in this regard. An inter-ministerial group will plan and monitor the implementation of a comprehensive programme for skill and entrepreneurship development among the Muslim community and for ensuring easy and smooth access to credit to the minorities, and Muslims in particular. "Clusters", having a substantial presence of the Muslim community, especially of those engaged in artisanal activities, will be given focused attention. Public sector banks will open more branches in Muslim concentration areas, banks and financial institutions will promote micro-finance among the minorities, especially women, public sector banks will monitor the disposal of loan applications for minorities and maintain reasons for rejection, RBI will maintain district-wise and bank-wise data regarding disposal of applications on its web site and the flow of credit to the minorities, including Muslims would be monitored regularly. The data can be accessed under the Right to Information Act. A multi-pronged strategy will be adopted for addressing the problem of educational backwardness of the Muslim community. The outreach of upper primary schools will be expanded, particularly for Muslim girls, and where necessary, with "girls only" schools, more Kasturba Gandhi Balika Vidyalayas (KGBV) will be opened in areas with substantial Muslim population; priority would be given to the opening of secondary and senior secondary schools in areas of Muslim concentration, a special literacy drive will be taken up in districts with a substantial population of Muslims, Block Institutes of Teacher Education (BITEs) would be established to impart pre-service and in-service training to primary, upper primary and secondary level teachers in such areas, additional allocation will be made for opening women's hostels in schools and universities, the Madarasa Modernization Programme will be revised to enhance the components eligible for assistance, the mid-day meal scheme will be extended, especially in educationally backward Muslim concentration blocks and the question of equivalence of qualifications from madarsas for subsequent access to higher education will be addressed.

1136. (18-5-2007) NEW DELHI : The All-India Consumer Price Index for Agricultural and Rural Labourers (Base 1986-87 = 100) increased by two points each during April 2007 to stand at 394 points for Agricultural Labourers and 395 points for Rural Labourers. The rise and fall in index varied from state to state. In case of Agricultural Labourers 17 states reflected an increase in indices ranging between 1 to 9 points while in two states the indices went down by 3 to 4 points. It remained stationary in one state. In case of Rural Labourers, 18 states reflected an increase ranging between 1 to 9 points, in two states the indices fell by three points each. Manipur experienced the highest increase of 9 points each in respect of Agricultural Labourers and Rural Labourers. The rise has been mainly due to increase in the prices of Rice, Mixed Spices, Vegetables & Fruits and Pan Leaf. On the other hand, the indices in respect of Assam showed a maximum decrease of 4 points for Agricultural Labourers while in respect of Rural Labourers Assam and Bihar recorded the maximum decrease of 3 points each mainly due to decrease in the prices of Rice, Wheat Atta, Onions, Green Chillies, Vegetables & Fruits, and Sugar. Punjab and Rajasthan with 426 points each for Agricultural Labourers and Punjab with 427 points for Rural Labourers figured at the top of the index table. Manipur with 343 points each for Agricultural Labourers and 344 points for Rural Labourers remained at the bottom of the index.

1137. (18-5-2007) NEW DELHI : The Prime Minister, Dr. Manmohan Singh, has condemned the bomb blast in Hyderabad and has urged members of all communities to maintain peace and communal harmony. He expressed his condolences to the relatives of the victims.

1138. (18-5-2007) NEW DELHI : The Prime Minister, Dr. Manmohan Singh, has advised the state government of Punjab to maintain utmost vigil and ensure law and order and protection to life and property of all citizens. He has condemned the violence in the state and has urged the people to maintain peace and harmony.

1139. (18-5-2007) NEW DELHI : The centre is keeping a close watch on the situation arising out of the bomb blast in Hyderabad today. It is in constant touch with the Andhra Pradesh government. The Rapid Action Force contingent stationed in Hyderabad has been placed at the disposal of the State Government. A team of forensic experts has been rushed to Hyderabad to help investigate the nature of the blast. The Union Home Minister, Shri Shivraj Patil spoke to the Andhra Pradesh Chief Minister, Dr. Y.S. Rajasekhara Reddy and assured him of all possible assistance from the Centre. Strongly condemning the blast, the Union Home Minister conveyed his sympathies to the kins of those killed. He cautioned people about the evil designs of the forces which are trying to foment communal trouble. Shri Patil appealed to people to remain calm and cooperate with the government in maintaining peace and harmony. He also reiterated the Government's resolve to sternly deal with the perpetrators of such incidents.

1140. (18-5-2007) NEW DELHI : Dr. Dasari Narayana Rao, Minister of State for Coal announced at the meeting of Parliamentary Consultative Committee attached to his Ministry here last evening that in order to meet the coal demand, 81 additional coal blocks with geological reserves of about 20 billion tones have been identified by his Ministry for allocation to Government companies/private companies for permissible end use. Of these, 41 blocks with reserves of 15.7 billion tones are earmarked for power sector. These blocks for the power sector, have been further categorized in 3 separate lists on the basis of method of allocation which are, Government Company Dispensation Route (10 blocks with 6072.15 million metric tonne estimated reserves), Screening Committee Route (15 blocks with 3622.44 MMT reserves) and Tariff based Bidding as per Ministry of Power Guidelines (16 blocks with 6015.30 MMT reserves). The remaining 40 blocks with a total reserves of 4.3 billion tonne would be considered for allocation for the non-power sector under Government Company Dispensation Route (17 blocks with estimated 1847.75 MMT reserves) and Screening Committee route (23 blocks with 2464.23 MMT reserves). As many as 1422 applications have been received for 38 blocks advertised for allocation through Screening Committee. These have been forwarded to the State Governments and Administrative Ministries concerned for their views/recommendations. For allocation under Government Company Dispensation route about 200 applications have been received for allocation of 27 blocks. Comments on applications received for power sector have been obtained from the Ministry of Power and the matter is under consideration for approval of the Government. Further, the Ministry of Power has also been requested to take further action for the remaining 16 coal blocks earmarked for the power projects to be set up on the basis of tariff based competitive bidding system. Emphasising the importance of quick development, the Minister informed that specific time-bound milestones have been prescribed for development of coal blocks. An effective system of monitoring at the level of Ministry as well as the Coal Controller's Organisation has been put in place. A system of bank guarantee has been introduced, and it would get forfeited if the allocattee fails to achieve the guaranteed level of coal production. He further informed that of the 19 coal blocks allotted prior to 2002, 11 have commenced production so far. 6 more coal blocks are expected to come into production during the current financial year. Other coal blocks are at different stages of development. Elaborating the significance of coal to meet energy needs, Dr. Rao told the members that out of the four major Indian fuel sources-oil, natural gas, coal and uranium – coal has the largest domestic reserves base with nearly 55% of the total commercial energy needs met by coal. He stressed that even after 20 years, the scenario is going to be more or less the same.

1141. (18-5-2007) NEW DELHI : The Minister for Steel and Chemicals and Fertilisers Shri Ram Vilas Paswan has called for establishing socially just and casteless society through empowerment of the downtrodden through education. The Minister was speaking at the concluding session of a two-day conference on Empowerment of Scheduled Castes/Scheduled Tribes and Minorities through Elementary Education in New Delhi today. Advocating the cause of basic education he said, that villages with more than 40 percent population of SC/ST and minorities and backward communities should be adopted as Model Villages and should be provided with quality residential education institutions. He also advocated reservation of seats in private schools for the students from BPL families in order to provide them equal opportunities in quality education. Criticising those who get admission on the basis of capitation fees Shri Paswan asked is it not another kind of reservation where a less deserving candidate gets preference over a deserving candidate. Shri Paswan demanded separate allocation of funds in the budget for the SC/ST, minorities and backward communities. The Minister said it is essential to provide equal opportunities in elementary education for the sake of fair competition. Quoting the history Shri Paswan said that Muslim, Christians, Sikhs and Buddhists and other minorities are not foreigners. Dr. Ambedkar chose to convert to Buddhism not because the Buddha was a SC/ST or backward but because he preached and practiced equality. Those who converted to Buddhism with Dr. Ambedkar were mostly dalits. He said that depriving SC/ST and minorities of their constitutional rights is a serious and a long standing problem and needs to be addressed with all out efforts. Expressing concern over diminishing job opportunity in public sector undertakings in the wake of disinvestments, the Minister said reservation is justified in private sector also.

1142. (18-5-2007) NEW DELHI : Shri Jairam Ramesh, Minister of State for Commerce, co-chaired the Second Meeting of the Joint Trade Committee (JTC) between India and Tanzania along with the Tanzanian Minister of Industry, Trade and Marketing, Mr. Basil P Mramba, here this afternoon and underlined India's desire for further expansion and diversification of bilateral trade and investment with Tanzania. Shri Ramesh highlighted that mutually beneficial engagement between India and Tanzania was possible in several areas and valued Tanzania as an important destination for India's increasing requirements of gold and rough diamonds, cashew, leather etc. "Indian would like to forge a Long-Term relationship with Tanzania with regards to sourcing of raw materials while looking to cooperate with Tanzania to help it move towards value added production and manufacturing", he said. The Minister also offered India's help in the field of training, HRD and skill development. Mr. Basil P Mramba hoped that the Indian companies would invest more in Tanzania and highlighted areas such as power, leather, horticulture and infrastructure etc. where Indian investments could benefit Tanzania. Tanzanian side also requested India to assist in the preparation of a feasibility study for the establishment of a cyber city in Kilimanjaro International Airport (KIA) area (Arusha Cybercity) following which India has agreed to provide technical support for preparation of a feasibility report. Meanwhile, during the discussions, Shri Jairam Ramesh offered to lead a multi-sectoral delegation to Tanzania in August 2007 to look at the different opportunities between two countries and to take concrete and timely steps for entering into mutually beneficial economic projects. The Tanzanian Minister welcomed Shri Ramesh's suggestion and the two sides will workout the details of the visit in due course. Meanwhile, BHEL has offered to set up two 125 MW gas or coal/oil based power plants in Tanzania and an agreement to this effect may be signed during the proposed visit. NTPC also offered to provide technical assistance to upgrade the efficiency of power plants in Tanzania and to train the Tanzanian technical personnel.

1143. (18-5-2007) NEW DELHI : The Defence Minister Shri A K Antony has called upon Ordnance Factories to maintain quality and delivery schedule so as to keep its customer base intact. Stressing the need to give a fresh momentum to country's indigenization efforts so that the country can achieve self reliance in the field of defence production, the Minister said a major part of the responsibility to achieve this goal lies with the ordnance factories. Inaugurating the Conference of General Managers of Ordnance Factories in New Delhi today, Shri Antony expressed the hope that the conference will chart out a futuristic roadmap for ordnance factories. He said, 'there is an urgent need to thoroughly review the fixation of targets, placement of indents and authorization for expenditure'. The Defence Minister said that the procurement procedure of OFB too needs to be streamlined to avoid time and cost overruns. Referring to the complaints regarding quality of the products as well as feedback from the customers that the products are not delivered on time, Shri Antony said, customer satisfaction is and should be guiding force of any enterprise. He said OFB has so far been functioning only as a departmental production agency without any commercial orientation. He said 'in fact, the OFB should strive to become commercially proactive'. He also called upon the Defence Production agencies to shed old mindsets and excessive secrecy. The Defence Minister said ordnance factories must equip themselves to face competition and re-orient themselves as proactive and viable commercial organizations. He called upon the ordnance factories to work in close tandem with the end user, *i.e.* Armed Forces so that production and supplies are planned and executed in a scientific manner. 'Our objective should be long-term planning for target fixation and production' Shri Antony said. Underlining the need for a high-level consumer satisfaction, the Minister asked ordnance factories to seek feedback reports from the consumers on a regular basis and carry out time-bound re-appraisal based on the feedback and rectify the defects in the products. Referring to the defence procurement procedure, the Defence Minister asked ordnance factories to strive to maximize transparency in their financial dealing and management as procurement is done on a large-scale and from various sources. In his key note address the Secretary Defence Production Shri K P Singh complemented ordnance factories for having played a very crucial role in achieving self-reliance in defence production. However, he said, self-reliance in defence not only means self reliance in production but also self-reliance in developing new products so that our armed forces are fully equipped to meet all kinds of threat that the nation faces today. He regretted that the performance of the ordnance factories in this sphere was not encouraging. Shri Singh said, 'ordnance factories have not shown the ambition of developing major products and have been content with the role of a technology recipient'. In this connection, he asked ordnance factories to emulate the example of HAL which has developed world class products like ALH and IJT. Shri Singh said OFB is in the armament business where major customers are armed forces and the paramilitary forces. He said, 'OFB does not have the luxury to choose its customers and therefore has to earn the respect from the customers for product quality, timely deliveries and cheaper products to earn the good will. Unfortunately, Indian army does not perceive OFB as a manufacturer of defence equipment of global quality standards.' He further added that huge manufacturing infrastructure available with the factories will always play a crucial role in the national defence and the time has come for the efficient utilization of these productive resources. The General Managers of all the 39 ordnance factories, senior officials of the OFB, Ministry of Defence and the Services are attending the two-day conference.

1144. (18-5-2007) NEW DELHI : Representatives of the Congress Party in Assam, led by Shri Bhubaneshwar Kalita, President Assam Pradesh Congress Committee and Shri Himanta Biswa Sarma and Members of Parliament from Assam led by Shri Santosh Mohan Deb, Union Minister called on the Prime Minister Dr. Mammohan Singh here today to congratulate him on his election to the Rajya Sabha. The Prime Minister thanked the people of Assam for once again supporting him and renewing their trust in him. The Prime Minister said that it has been an honour to represent Assam in the Rajya Sabha since 1991. In the past three years representatives from various states had offered to elect the Prime Minister to Parliament, he however chose to remain faithful to his adopted state of Assam, the Prime Minister said. He asked the representatives calling on him to convey his best wishes to all MLAs and the people of Assam.

1145. (18-5-2007) NEW DELHI : The President of India, in his capacity as the Visitor of Aligarh Muslim University, has approved the appointment of Prof. (Dr.) P.K. Abdul Azis as the Vice Chancellor of the University for a period of five years with effect from the date he assumes charge of his office. The office of the Vice Chancellor of the University fell vacant from the afternoon of 7th April, 2007 following resignation of the previous Vice Chancellor, Shri Naseem Ahmad. Prof. Azis, holder of D.Sc in Ecology, has been serving as the Vice Chancellor of Cochin University of Science and Technology since 2004. The new initiatives undertaken by him at Cochin University include Modern Marine Engineering Campus, Department Aerospace Technology, M.Sc. in Nano Science, Rajiv Gandhi Chair in Contemporary Studies. He has 77 research papers to his credit published in various journals/books/proceedings.

1146. (18-5-2007) NEW DELHI : Shri Arjun Singh, Minister for Human Resource Development has said that Ministry is making all out efforts to ensure that SCs, STs, and Minorities have full access to education. It is a well established fact that education is a means for advancement of all individuals and to ensure political rights for them. But what exactly is holding back the matter is lack of sense of fair play, justice and commitment. Shri Arjun Singh said this while addressing in the concluding session of the International Conference on Empowerment of SCs,

STs and Minorities through Elementary Education here today. This Conference was organised by All India Forum of Legislators (SCs/STs) & others in association with Ministry of Human Resource Development. Shri Arjun Singh also said that we are still battling for the rights of the SCs/STs & Minorities. He said the reservation for backward classes is an attempt to make the entire higher education inclusive. He explained that when issue of reservation for backward classes in higher education came up, it was pointed out that it conflicts with the advantages for the unreserved candidates. He said if general category seats were to be curtailed and given to the backward classes in higher education institutions, then their grievance would have been genuine, but government adopted a unique level headed approach in which the general category seats were increased so that reservation to backward classes do not affect them. The Minister appealed to all sections of society to join to bring out an awakening for the rights of SCs, STS and Minorities. Dy. Speaker Lok Sabha Shri Charanjeet Singh Atwal gave a vote of thanks. In his address he summed up the proceedings of the two-day Conference and said that there was a popular demand to pool up population equivalent proportion of plan funds, now presumably being spent by various ministries for SC/ST welfare under SCP/TSP at the centre and state government level into one kitty before they are actually allocated to the ministries and to place it under SC,ST Development Authority at the centre, state and district levels. The concluding session was attended by Vice President, Shri Bhairon Singh Shekhawat; Dy. Speaker Lok Sabha, Shri Charanjeet Singh Atwal; UPA Chairperson, Smt. Sonia Gandhi; Dy. Chairman Rajya Sabha, Shri K. Rehman Khan; Chemicals & Fertilizer Minister Shri Ram Vilas Paswan; Small Scale Industry Minister Shri Mahavir Prasad, Social Justice & Empowerment Minister, Ms. Meira Kumar; and Labour Minister Shri Oscar Fernandes and others.

1147. (18-5-2007) NEW DELHI : The total approximate earnings of Indian Railways on originating basis during the period 1st May – 10th May 2007 were Rs. 1784.13 crore compared to Rs. 1633.81 crore during the same period last year, registering an increase of 9.20 per cent. The total goods earnings have gone up from Rs. 1075.95 crore during 1-10 May 2006 to Rs. 1160.91 crore during 1-10 May 2007, showing an increase of 7.90 per cent. The total passenger revenue earnings during the period 1–10 May 2007 were Rs. 559.39 crore compared to Rs. 504.04 crore during the same period last year, an increase of 10.98 per cent. The revenue earnings from other coaching amounted to Rs. 50.23 crore during this period compared to Rs. 43.49 crore during the same period last year, an increase of 15.50 per cent. The total sundry earnings have gone up from Rs. 10.33 crore during 1-10 May 2006 to Rs. 13.60 crore during 1-10 May 2007, showing an increase of 31.66 per cent. The total approximate number of passengers booked during the period 1–10 May 2007 were 187.57 million compared to 179.49 million during the same period last year, showing an increase of 4.50 per cent. In the suburban and non-suburban sectors, the number of passengers booked during 1-10 May 2007 were 100.58 million and 86.99 million compared to 98.75 million and 80.74 million during the same period last year, registering an increase of 1.85 per cent and 7.74 per cent respectively.

1148. (18-5-2007) NEW DELHI : The services in any Oil Field covered under item 17 of the First Schedule of the Industrial Disputes Act, 1947 will continue to be public utility for another six months with effect from May 19, 2007. The Labour Ministry in a notification issued here said that this has been done in public interest. The services in this industry were earlier declared public utility for six months from November 19, 2006. The employees in this industry, as a result, would among other things be required to give notice to their employer six weeks in advance of proceeding on strike so that conciliatory proceedings could be started. During the conciliatory proceedings and seven days after their completion, the employees cannot go on strike.

1149. (18-5-2007) NEW DELHI : The Union Minister of Shipping, Road Transport and Highways, Thiru T.R. Baalu has called for an early report on the state of equipment being used by the Centres of Indian Institute of Maritime Studies to ensure that the level of education is of world standards. He was addressing the fourth annual general meeting of the Indian Institute of Maritime Studies here today. Addressing the Meeting, the Minister also asked the authorities to immediately address the problem of shortage of seafarers and said that the Indian Maritime community should rise to the occasion and strive to make the country's maritime education and training amongst the best in the world. He hoped that with the setting up of Indian Maritime University, maritime education would get a boost and it would provide a platform for research, innovation and a place for higher education in specific fields of the Shipping industry. The Minister said that the University would cater to the large demand of the shipping industry in times to come. He said that we should aim at over all growth of the shipping industry while we also aim for aggressive marketing of Indian Seafarers on foreign flagships. Referring to the shortage of faculty in the four institutes of the maritime studies, Thiru Baalu said that immediate steps should be taken to remedy the situation to keep up the standards of the faculty and the infrastructure. He assured his Ministry's assistance in this regard. Commending the role of Indian seafarers, officers and seamen the Minister said that they have done yeomen service to the Indian shipping in particular and international shipping in general. He said Indian seafarers are employed in most of the shipping companies worldwide and informed that they stand 5th in the world on manning international shipping and close to the top in the world on manning shore establishments like management and ship owning companies. The Indian seafarers are preferred world over because of their strong academic background, excellent English language skills and highest entry level standards with well founded social values like harmonious living and traditional respect for environment, the Minister added.

1150. (18-5-2007) NEW DELHI : The twenty-seventh meeting of the Kendriya Sainik Board (KSB) will be inaugurated by the Prime Minister Dr. Manmohan

Singh in New Delhi tomorrow. The KSB functions under the chairmanship of the Defence Minister. The Chief Ministers/Lt. Governors of States/ UTs and Service Chiefs are its members. The board meets annually to review policy, achievements and deliberate on pending issues concerning Ex-Servicemen (ESM) welfare. There exists a vast reserve of skilled, disciplined and committed Human Resource available in the country in the form of ESM. The Government of India has declared the year 2007 as the year of the placement of ESM with a view to achieve the dual task of offering veterans a meaningful second career, while also harnessing this invaluable resource towards nation building. Approximately 60,000 Armed Forces personnel retire from their active service every year. These are retired only metaphorically, they are otherwise young, enthusiastic, disciplined and skilled, and who can be utilized for the benefit of the Nation on the one hand and a dignified life through meaningful second career options will also motivate the future generation, towards the Armed Forces on the other. The centre and state governments have accepted the joint responsibility for resettlement of Ex-servicemen and to provide them rehabilitation through provision of employment in the organized sector or through self employment. At the Centre, the Ex-Servicemen Welfare (ESW) department of the Ministry of Defence (MoD) is responsible for formulation of the policy guidelines and schemes for resettlement of the ESM. Working under the same banner, the Directorate General of Resettlement (DGR) and Kendriya Sainik Board (KSB) function conjointly towards the welfare and resetltment of ESM. In the states and Union Territories, The Rajya Sainik Boards, and at the District level the Zila Sainik Boards attend to the problems of ESM and assist in executing various schemes. The KSB which looks after the Armed Forces Flag Day Fund, functions under the DGR for implementing all schemes. This fund is utilized for various welfare measures for ESM, widows and their dependents besides giving grants to Paraplegic Rehabilitation Centre, located at Khadki and Mohali, St. Dunstan's Blind Institute at Dehradun, Cheshire Homes and Red Cross Old Age home at Bangalore. The DGR lays down the policies and schemes for resettlement of retiring and retired ESM fraternity, widows of martyrs and their dependents. The present ESM population in the country today is 24 Lakh in which widows population is over 4.2 Lakh. The bulk of Personnel below Officers Rank (PBOR) retire between the age group of 35-45 years and officers between 52-55 years depending on the rank held. Besides, a large number of short service commissioned officers are released from service after having served from 5 years to 14 years of contractual service. The early release / retirement of Armed Forces Personnel is resorted to in order to maintain youthful profile of the Armed Forces.

1151. (18-5-2007) NEW DELHI : In order to evolve the concept of 'Merchant Airports', Secretary, Ministry of Civil Aviation, Shri Ashok Chawla held a meeting with various stakeholders with a view to finalizing a policy initiative on the subject shortly. 'Merchant Airports' have been conceptualized as airport infrastructure entirely in private sector with private resources and with no Government funding. The entrepreneur is expected to set up and operate airport on the basis of commercial viability subject to the safety and security oversight of the Government. Such a proposal would dispense with the requirement for investment of Government resources and therefore, a more liberal and only a license based approval procedure could be considered. It is proposed to allow 100% FDI in such airports. At the meeting it was noted that though there are no set international practices in this regard, which could be used as benchmarks, in the context of rapid growth of civil aviation and the need for commensurate infrastructure being put in place, airports working purely on commercial viability basis in private sector was required. It was felt that such airports would be especially useful for creating cargo hubs, thereby providing a thrust to the cargo and freight handling. These airports are expected to come up in areas of high population density and more air traffic. However, large parcels of land are required to develop airports. Thus though 'Merchant Airports' would be totally built by private companies, land being a State subject, the assistance of State Government would be necessary. Similarly, facilitation by the Central Government in terms of clearances from Defence, Environment etc. would be essential besides the regulatory oversight. The need for 'Merchant Airports' has been felt because the Civil Aviation Sector in India is witnessing unprecedented growth. While international air traffic has been growing at a rate of about 15% p.a., the growth in domestic passenger traffic has at times surpassed even 40%. This growth has placed tremendous burden on the existing airport infrastructure. In order to create, develop and modernize airport infrastructure, the Government have taken several policy initiatives in recent past. The airport sector, which has traditionally been in public sector, has been opened up for private sector participation. The airports at Delhi and Mumbai have been restructured through JV route. Two new Greenfield airports are under construction at Bangalore and Hyderabad and are likely to become operational within one year. Proposals in respect of several other Greenfield airports are under consideration. Government has already permitted 100% FDI, through automatic route, in the Greenfield airports projects. The 'Policy on Airport Infrastructure' puts in place the policy and procedural requirements for development of new airports. The airport development being a long gestation period activity, Government has been considering various options to expedite development and modernization. Further, India expects to add aircraft worth about US$80 billion by 2020. This would necessitate an investment of about US$ 30 billion in airport infrastructure.

1152. (18-5-2007) NEW DELHI : Shri Jairam Ramesh, Minister of State for Commerce, co-chaired the Second Meeting of the Joint Trade Committee (JTC) between India and Tanzania along with the Tanzanian Minister of Industry, Trade and Marketing, Mr. Basil P Mramba, here this afternoon and underlined India's desire for further expansion and diversification of bilateral trade and investment with Tanzania. Two-way trade between India and Tanzania has more than doubled in the last five years – having gone up from US $ 166 million in 2001-02 to almost US $ 360 in 2005-06. The upward trend is continuing during the current year as well. India's exports to Tanzania were valued at around US $ 240 million and

India's imports from Tanzania were US $ 119 million in 2005-06. Economic reforms in both countries and the major role played by the Indian community in Tanzania's overseas trade had contributed to the rapid growth in the volume of trade from the 1990s onwards.

1153. (18-5-2007) NEW DELHI : The President of India, as advised by the Prime Minister, has been pleased to appoint Smt. V. Radhika Selvi as Minister of State in the Union Council of Ministers. The President administered the oath of office and secrecy to Smt. V. Radhika Selvi at a ceremony held in the Rashtrapati Bhavan, today. Further, as advised by the Prime Minister, the President of India has directed that Smt. V. Radhika Selvi be allocated the portfolio of Minister of State in the Ministry of Home Affairs.

1154. (18-5-2007) NEW DELHI : The Ministry of Rural Development has released part payment of first instalment of Central share of funds amounting to Rs. 3.31 crore under the 'Swarnjayanti Gram Swarojgar Yojana' (SGSY) during the year 2007-08 to 20 DRDAs of Haryana.

1155. (18-5-2007) NEW DELHI : BJP National Spokesperson and State Incharge of Goa Shri Rajiv Pratap Rudy today charged the Congress Party of trying to use the recently shelved Goa Regional Plan 2011 to pursue a divisive agenda of fomenting social tensions in the state. While on the surface the Goa Regional Plan 2011 apparently came across as a land and cash scam with the issue of environment being on the forefront, in reality the plan had a much deeper and nefarious long term divisive design that sought to lay the foundation of creating ethnic division for posterity in Goa. Mr. Rudy said that the Goa Regional Plan 2011, was not a development programme but a "Goa Disaster Plan 2011", the implementation of which could have had far reaching implications. The plan was created with a multi pronged strategy of filling the coffers of the Congress Party on the one hand, and on the other hand also fulfilling the long term strategy of the Congress Party of ensuring that greed and influx inundated Goa. Over time, this would result in serious demographic changes whereby the local population would eventually feel threatened and demographically challenged and disturb the current social equilibrium of the state. He added that the underlying nefarious design of the Congress Party in Goa was in tune with the divisive policies being followed by the central Congress Party since independence. Arguing further, Mr. Rudy said that there was distinct evidence of the involvement of the Congress leadership of prompting change in the demographic profile as witnessed in several states across the nation that had resulted in creating social and ethnic tensions. Mr. Rudy added that this was the well known and often used strategy of the Congress Party of creating a problem and social tensions between various ethnic groups first, and later politicizing it for electoral gains. This unfortunate strategy had been successfully encouraged and followed by the Congress Party in many states such as Bihar, West Bengal, Assam and other states in the north east region, he said. The massive demographic changes in Assam having been implemented and with similar danger lurking for other smaller states of the north east, there is a very real potent threat of the same strategy being systematically unveiled in Goa, he added. Mr. Rudy recalled the recent statement of the National Security Advisor to the Prime Minister Mr. Narayanan about investment in the real estate sector and flow of foreign funds parked in the real estate and hotel business as being a potent tool for unleashing terrorism. He said that a similar trend has been noticed in recent times whereby massive investments in the real estate sector may be a potential threat for targeting Goa as a safe haven for terrorist activities and spoiling the peace harmony of the tourist state for all times to come. Mr. Rudy said that the people of Goa deserved national recognition and have been applauded across the country for the timely detection and recognition of the inherent divisive dangers of the Goa Regional Plan 2011. The alert citizens of Goa have successfully forced the government to put on hold the implementation of this dangerous policy document. By halting the implementation of the Goa Regional Plan, the citizens of the state had successfully put on hold a divisive, destructive demographic time bomb which was capable of seriously impacting Goa's rich cultural heritage of the past, its present and the future of its children.

1156. (18-5-2007) NEW DELHI : The Ministry of Rural Development has released grants-in-aid amounting to Rs. 14.96 crore to 22 DRDAs of Andhra Pradesh towards part payment of first instalment during the year 2007-08 under the 'Swarnjayanti Gram Swarojgar Yojana' (SGSY).

1157. (19-5-2007) NEW DELHI : The Prime Minister Dr. Mammohan Singh has underlined the need for a mechanism at the district and state level to monitor the redressal of the grievances of the ex-servicemen. Inaugurating the 27th Meeting of the Kendriya Sainik Board in New Delhi today, the Prime Minister has also urged to accord high priority to the needs of war widows and the war disabled. He said their welfare should be given high priority. He said state governments should also consider introducing e-enabled services for dissemination of relevant information and guidance for the benefit of ex-servicemen through dedicated websites. The Defence Minister Shri A K Antony in his address called for optimal utilization of the services of the ex-servicemen by the State Governments. In this regard he suggested that every state and union territory should raise, at least, one battalion each of ex-servicemen for afforestation. Shri Antony called upon the states to fill up the posts lying vacant in various Rajya Sainik Boards and Zila Sainik Boards. Referring to the ex-servicemen contributory health scheme, the Defence Minister urged the State Governments to provide necessary assistance in land acquisition and construction of poly-clinics so that the scheme becomes fully operational. Referring to the increased understanding between the defence services and the corporate sector with regard to the employment opportunities for the ex-servicemen, the Minister thanked ASSOCHAM for making a commitment for absorbing about 10,000 ex-servicemen in the corporate sector. Shri Antony said Directorate General, Resettlement is exploring the possibility of providing

Ex-Servicemen suitable jobs in Delhi Transport Corporation and Delhi Metro. With the Commonwealth Games scheduled in the year 2010, there will not be any dearth of employment opportunities for Ex-Servicemen, he added. Earlier the Prime Minister gave away trophies to the States and Union Territories for their performance in the collection of Armed Forces Flag Day Fund during the year 2006. The trophy for highest collection in the state category was bagged by Maharashtra while in the Union Territory category it went to Chandigarh. The trophy for highest per capita collection in the State category went to Tamil Nadu while in the Union Territory category it was again the turn of Chandigarh. The meeting was attended by Minister of State for Defence Shri M M Pallam Raju, Minister of State for Defence Production Rao Inderjit Singh, Governor of Punjab, Chief Ministers of Haryana and Uttarakhand, the three Service Chiefs, Defence Secretary Shri Shekhar Dutt and various other high dignitaries from States, Union Territories. The Kendriya Sainik Board is an apex body of the Government of India which makes recommendation towards formulating policy for the welfare of ex-servicemen, war widows, disabled soldiers and their families. The Board is headed by Defence Minister. Chief Ministers / Ministers of various states and union territories and three Service Chiefs are among its members.

1158. (19-5-2007) NEW DELHI : Following is the full text of the speech delivered by Defence Minister Shri A K Antony at the 27th Meeting of the Kendriya Sainik Board held in New Delhi today: I welcome you all to the inauguration of XXVII Kendriya Sainik Board (KSB) meeting. It is indeed a privilege that the Hon'ble Prime Minister is here with us on this occasion. His presence and words of advice will surely motivate and encourage us in our endeavour. Our Armed Forces have been serving the nation with dedication and commitment, braving extreme weather conditions. They have to live away from their families, which makes their task even more difficult and challenging. During my visit to forward areas, I have had a first-hand experience of the difficult conditions. Thus, special attention by the Central and State Governments and support and care by the local administrations towards their families is really crucial. We want our troops to maintain a high morale and perform their duties without any worries. Nearly 60, 000 Armed Forces personnel either retire, or are released each year. They are between 35-45 years of age and are a rich repository of knowledge in different fields. We cannot and must not let this potential go unutilized. Moreover, keeping in mind their service to the nation, it is our moral responsibility to give them ample opportunities for reemployment and resettlement. Keeping this in view, the Government has declared 2007 as "The Year of the Placement of Ex-servicemen." Our Government has taken several measures for the welfare of ex-servicemen. The Prime Minister's Scholarship Scheme for wards of Ex-servicemen for their technical and professional education has been launched from the academic session this year. Many State Governments have taken steps to promote the welfare of Ex-servicemen by employing them in police force, to man forests, as well as toll plazas. I strongly urge all State Governments to optimally utilise the services of Ex-servicemen for mutual benefit. I also request all State Governments and Union Territories to raise at least one battalion each for afforestation.

1159. (19-5-2007) NEW DELHI : The Prime Minister, Dr. Manmohan Singh lauched the EDUSAT satellite based educational programmes in Haryana today. Following is the text of Prime Minister's address on the occasion: "I am happy to be here today to launch the EDUSAT Satellite based educational programmes in Haryana. I must begin by paying homage to the memory of two great Indians who are responsible for satellite based educational programmes in our country. First and foremost, I pay homage to our beloved leader and former Prime Minister, Smt. Indira Gandhi. Second, I pay homage to that great scientist, industrialist and visionary, Vikram Sarabhai. Indiraji grasped the vital role of satellite television in our vast sub-continental nation. Dr. Sarabhai emphasized its role in spreading literacy and awareness. The EDUSAT Programme is a realization of their dreams. I am seriously concerned at the slow progress of literacy in our country. We need a crash programme to increase literacy to over 80 per cent in all regions of the country. I am also concerned about the poor functioning of our government schools, especially in rural areas. The quality of education in the government school system is not satisfactory. There is a belief that the quality gap between public schools and private schools is increasing. I believe that greater effort is required to bridge this quality gap if good education is not to become a preserver of the privileged classes only. To have a high quality public schooling system, we need better teacher training and more importantly, better teaching of science and mathematics. Numeracy skills and scientific knowledge are the key to success in the knowledge economy and the EDUSAT programme can an important tool for improving science education in schools. I hope these objectives are addressed and served by the EDUSAT progrmme, I request those who are associated with the programme to ensure that the quality of programming is good. That it is both educational and entertaining. We have invested crores of rupees in good quality hardware. We must ensure that the software is equally good. Educational programmes should not be bored and dull. The television should not just become a podium from which lectures are giving. It is necessary to develop good visuals, graphics and other material that can be shown to the viewer. I hope students enjoy learning through EDUSAT. EDUSAT can also be used for a variety of purposes by district authorities, like teleconferencing, data transmission and so on. I hope the best use will be made of this technology in promoting rural development. I am happy to launch this prograqmme here. I wish you all the best. Haryana is making great strides in all walks of life and is a dynamic state of our union."

1160. (19-5-2007) NEW DELHI : The Prime Minister, Dr. Manmohan Singh, has said that the subject of welfare of ex-servicemen has been identified as the thrust area of the government's functioning and the Prime Minister's Office is monitoring it regularly and very closely. Speaking after inaugurating the XXVII meeting of Kendriya Sainik Board, here today, Dr. Singh said that ex-servicemen are national resources and "by drawing on this very valuable national resource we would not only be helping our ex-servicemen but also provide skilled human resources in many critical areas of our economy and indeed not to utilize this vast talent pool would be an act of not doing justice to the vast latent talent bank that exists amongst our ex-servicemen. " Union Defence Minister, Shri A.K. Antony, Ministers of State in Defence Ministry, Shri Pallam Raju and Shri Rao Indrajit Singh, were among those present on the occasion.

1161. (20-5-2007) NEW DELHI : The Pension Fund Regulatory and Development Authority (PFRDA) issued a Primary Information Memorandum and Expression of Interest (EOI) package for appointment of Pension Fund Managers for the New Pension System (NPS) on 11th May 2007. The last date for submission of EOI is 25th May 2007. The EOI document has been posted on the website of PFRDA (www.pfrda.org.in). Recently, reports have appeared in a section of the media that PFRDA proposes to allow foreign and private firms to manage pension funds. It is clarified that PFRDA has invited EOI only from public sector entities for sponsoring pension fund managers. As per the EOI, only Government entities, such as Central Government companies, public financial institutions etc. in which not less than 51% paid up share capital is held by Central Government or partly by Central Government and partly by one or more State Governments can apply. Further, to be eligible, the sponsors must have at least 5 years experience of fund management and average assets under management of the sponsors must not be less than Rs. 10,000 crores for the month of March 2007. Thus, even amongst public sector entities, only those with sufficient experience and financial strength can apply. The selected public sector entity would be required to incorporate the pension fund manager as a separate public sector company. Both the sponsor as well as the pension fund manager would, therefore, be in the public sector. Direct or indirect foreign investment in the pension fund manager, if any, shall not exceed 26% of its paid up share capital. This is in accordance with the report of the Standing Committee on Finance which examined the PFRDA Bill, 2005. Thus, it is clarified that in terms of PFRDA's invitation to submit EOI, no foreign or private firm would be eligible to apply for the pension fund business.

1162. (20-5-2007) NEW DELHI : The Military World Games Organising Committee (MWGOC), constituted under the Ministry of Defence, has given the prestigious broadcast/telecast rights of the Fourth Military World Games to be held in Hyderabad and Mumbai later this year, exclusively to Prasar Bharati. An MOU to this effect was signed between the MWGOC and Prasar Bharati here earlier this week. The Military World Games is the biggest sporting event, only next to the Olympic Games. Over100 countries are going to participate in this great event being conducted in Asia for the first time. It is expected that around 6000 uniformed sports persons will be participating in the15 disciplines. As per the

MOU, Prasar Bharati would telecast / broadcast the opening and closing ceremonies live on DD 1 and at least 8 hours of daily live telecast of the events in its sports channel, DD Sports. All other news channels would be given some daily feed by Prasar Bharati. The MOU also confers Prasar Bharati, full rights for multiple telecast / broadcast of matches / highlights of the matches on all or any of its channels in perpetuity. Prasar Bharati would also provide free publicity in the run up to the games on all its channels including DD-1, DD-News and DD-Sports. Prasar Bharati would also show at least half an hour of highlights of the sports events on DD-1, and all other channels of Prasar Bharati on all days during the conduct of the Games. Similar arrangements will be made by All India Radio for the broadcast of the Games across the country. Broadcast/Telecast of the Games on Prasar Bharati will be subject to programme exigencies of National significance. Prasar Bharati would pay 50 per cent of the net surplus earned by it through the exclusive telecast of the Games to MWGOC.

1163. (21-5-2007) NEW DELHI : Mr. Alderman John Stuttard MA, the Rt Hon Lord Mayor of the City of London called upon the Minister of Corporate Affairs, Shri Prem Chand Gupta here today. He was accompanied by a delegation of leading financial and legal experts from the U.K. The Lord Mayor is also the Ambassador of the Indo-UK industry with its headquarter in the city of London and includes the regional financial centres such as Edinburgh, Glasgow, Leeds, Manchester and Bristol as part of his ambassadorial role for financial services. He also receives visiting heads of states and governments on behalf of the British government. It is understood that Lord Mayor's business initiatives for his year in office will focus on the developing London as a city of Financial Learning. Mr. Stuttard has wide international experience including in China. In 1981 he was seconded for two years to the UK Cabinet Office, to advice on the nationalized industries and their privatization. During the meeting with Shri Prem Chand Gupta, the delegation discussed areas of mutual concern relating to the regulatory framework of preparation, presentation and audit of financial information of companies. The discussions also covered institutional mechanisms for Regulation of accountancy professionals and impact of financial reporting on corporate governance. Government of the two countries have already agreed to set up an Indo-UK Joint Working Group for mutual cooperation on all issues relating to corporate matters, including corporate laws and corporate governance. The Lord Mayor's special focus on learning was also discussed, and it was agreed that possibilities of collaboration between selected U.K institutes and the proposed "Indian Institutes of Corporate Affairs", being set up by the Ministry, would be explored.

1164. (21-5-2007) NEW DELHI : The Government has approved the nomination of two independent Members and three Members representing employers' organisations who will be common to both the Wage Boards for Working Journalists and Non-Working Journalists. This is besides the appointment of Dr. Justice K. Narayana Kurup as Chairman and of Shri K.M. Sahni, as full-time Member

Secretary of the two Wage Boards. Dr. Justice K. Narayana Kurup is a former Judge of Kerala High Court and has also served as the Acting Chief Justice of Madras High Court. Shri K.M.Sahni is former Labour Secretary, Government of India.

1165. (21-5-2007) NEW DELHI : According to the provisional findings of Shri R.K.Kardam, Commissioner of Railway Safety, North Eastern Circle. Lucknow who held a statutory inquiry into the collision of 5028 Dn. Gorakhpur-Hatia, Maurya Express train with a tractor trolley at unmanned level crossing between Bhatpar Rani and Bankata Railway Stations on Bhatni-Chhapra Kachery section of Varanasi Division of North Eastern Railway on 02-05-2007, the accident occurred due to "Failure of person other than Railway staff". The findings of the preliminary report are under the consideration of the Government. As a result of the accident 4 persons were killed, 9 sustained grievous injury and 2 sustained simple injury. The killed includes 3 road users.

1166. (21-5-2007) NEW DELHI : Productive absorption of under employed and surplus labour force in the rural sector has been a major focus of planning for rural development. In order to provide direct supplementary wage employment to the rural poor through public works, many programmes were initiated by the Government of India, namely, National Rural Employment Programme (NREP), Rural Landless Employment Guarantee Programme (RLEGP) and Jawahar Rozgar Yojana (JRY). NREGA Programme: The National Rural Employment Guarantee Act has been implemented all over the country with the objective to provide wage employment in rural areas, create durable rural infrastructure and to ensure food security. It provides an indispensable lifeline to the millions of poor in the rural areas of the country. This social security measure, makes the right to work a fundamental legal right-a new, radical deal for India's poor. Parliament has approved the National Rural Employment Bill, 2005 seeking to provide 100 days assured employment every year to every rural household. The legislation has received wide support among political parties, social movements and the public at large. Prime Minister Manmohan Singh described it as the "most important piece of legislation" in Independent India. It marked a new beginning in the efforts for social equity and justice. He hoped that in the next four or five years it would cover all rural districts. Dr. Singh said "this legislation will give bargaining power to the poorest of the poor and help those belonging to the Scheduled Casts, Scheduled Tribes, landless class and women. We are offering a modest, gainful employment that will fetch Rs. 500 per month for a family. This will bring landless families in the social safety net".

1167. (21-5-2007) NEW DELHI : Shri Ashwani Kumar, Minister of State for Industry, while delivering the Ministerial Statement at the Sixty-Third UN ESCAP (United Nations Economic and Social Commission for Asia and the Pacific) Session today at Almaty, Kazakhstan, called upon UN ESCAP to make use of

Gandhiji's talisman to focus its priorities towards the poor and the deprived of Asia and the Pacific region. "Development in its wider manifestation must positively impact on the lives of those who live on the margins", he said. The three-day Ministerial Segment of the Session was inaugurated by President Nursultan Nazarbayev of Kazakhstan. The Segment deliberated on how to help poor countries in Asia and the Pacific to achieve the Millennium Development Goals (MDGs) by 2015, and on promoting investment in health services in member countries and the region. While noting the robust economic growth of the region, Shri Kumar observed that economic growth must necessarily be inclusive and transform the lives of the poor and the marginalized. He complemented ESCAP for selecting "Development of Health Systems" as the theme for the 63rd Annual Session. The Minister highlighted India's initiatives to provide affordable and universal healthcare. The Minister congratulated ESCAP on its 60th Anniversary and said that both India and ESCAP started an exciting journey in 1947. He stated that the current century is destined to be an Asia-Pacific century and to turn this vision into a reality, we need to meet many challenges and focus on our strategies and priorities. He stressed the need for an urgent and purposive response for improving the living standards of the poor in accordance with the MDGs to which India remains irrevocably committed. The Minister called for strengthening the architecture of international institutions to meet the challenges of the new world order. The Asia-Pacific region continues to register a high rate of growth. Developing countries in ESCAP have recorded a GDP growth of 7.9% in real terms in 2006. In terms of purchasing power parity, these countries account for nearly 30% of the world's GDP and 33% of the world's GDP growth. The region has also accumulated sizeable foreign exchange reserves totalling nearly US $ 3 trillion. "This growth momentum is likely to be sustained during the coming decades and would be a critical driver of global growth. For economic growth to be sustainable, it needs to be inclusive and equitable. The challenge is indeed formidable when one looks at the other side of reality. In 2004, less than 80% of the population had sustainable access to an improved water source in East Asia, compared to 85% in South Asia. Of the 727 million people who lived on less than US$ 1 per day, two-thirds live in the five giant Asian economies. 81 million children are underweight in the Asia-Pacific region alone", Shri Kumar said.

1168. (21-5-2007) NEW DELHI : The Minister of State for Commerce, Shri Jairam Ramesh yesterday flagged off the first consignment of Banganpalli mangoes from Tirupati— in Andhra Pradesh's main mango-cultivating district of Chittoor— to Japan. The consignment was of 1 tonne (about 2500 mangos) and it is expected that by the end of this season (end-July) about 35-40 tonnes would be exported. This is the first full season that India is exporting mangoes to Japan after the 20-year ban was lifted for six varieties in June 2006. These varieties are Alphonso, Banganpalli, Chausa, Kesar, Langra and Mallika. In addition, market access for Malda and Dushehari varieties are also now under review. Each Banganpalli mango is expected to retail for Rs 200 in Japanese stores. Agricultural and

Processed Food Products Exports Developments Authority (APEDA) has already established a Vapur Heat Treatment (VHT) plant at Vashi near Mumbai and is setting up three more—at Tirupati and Nuzvid in Andhra Pradesh and at Saharanpur in Uttar Pradesh. The investment at each of the VHTs is around Rs 8 crore. Three VHTs have already come up in the private sector at Chittoor, Thane and Nashik. The VHT plants are essential for treating Indian mangos so that they meet Japanese health standards. Andhra Pradesh is India's leading producer of mangos, accounting for about 30% of the country's mango production. It also accounts for about 80% of the country's mango pulp production. Under the National Rural Employment Guarantee Scheme, about 6000 acres of assigned lands of scheduled caste families in Chittoor district has come under mango cultivation in 2006/07 and another 15,000 acres is being taken up in 2007/08. Banganpalli cultivation is being encouraged in these lands, in preference to Totapuri variety which goes entirely into pulp production. Exports of mangoes to USA have already started and the irradiation facility for processing mangos to meet US health standards is at present located at Lasal Gaon, Nashik. If needed, APEDA will collaborate with BARC to set up such facilities at other places as well.

1169. (21-5-2007) NEW DELHI : The Ministry of Rural Development has released part payment of first instalment of Central share of funds amounting to Rs. 11.30 crore under the 'Swarnjayanti Gram Swarojgar Yojana' (SGSY) during the year 2007-08 to 27 DRDAs of Karnataka.

1170. (21-5-2007) NEW DELHI : The Government has approved the appointment of Dr. Justice K. Narayana Kurup as Chairman of the Wage Board for Working Journalists and the Wage Board for Non-Working Journalists. A notification to this effect would be issued shortly. Dr. Justice K. Narayana Kurup is a former Judge of Kerala High Court and has also served as the Acting Chief Justice of Madras High Court. Shri K.M. Sahni, former Labour Secretary, has been appointed as Member Secretary to operationalise the Wage Boards. The two Boards will have ten members each. Besides the Chairman, the full-time Member Secretary, two independent Members and three Members representing employers' organisations will be common to both the Boards. The remaining three Members in each Board will be from employees' organisations representing working journalists and non-working journalists respectively. The Boards will start functioning with immediate effect for submission of Reports within the stipulated period of three years.

1171. (21-5-2007) NEW DELHI : The Ministry of Rural Development has released Grants-in-aid amounting to Rs. 15.13 crore as third/additional instalment of Central assistance to 18 districts of Haryana for the implementation of the Sampoorna Grameen Rozgar Yojana (SGRY) during the financial year (2006-07).

1172. (21-5-2007) NEW DELHI : The Ministry of Rural Development has released Grants-in-aid amounting to Rs. 31.38 crore as third/additional instalment of Central assistance to 26 districts of Rajashtan for the implementation of the Sampoorna Grameen Rozgar Yojana (SGRY) during the financial year (2006-07).

1173. (21-5-2007) NEW DELHI : The Ministry of Rural Development has sanctioned Rs. 1.89 crore of Grants-in-aid to 30 District Rural Development Agencies (DRDAs) of ORISSA towards part payment of first instalment of Central Share for the year 2007-08 under DRDA Administration.

1174. (21-5-2007) NEW DELHI : The Prime Minister, Dr. Manmohan Singh, is to inaugurate a two-day National Conference on Rural Roads on May 23, 2007 in New Delhi. He will also release the document "Rural Roads Plan : Vision-2025", prepared by the M/o rural Development for future development on rural roads in the country on the occasion. The conference organized by the Ministry of Rural Development will have a series of technical sessions in which the stakeholders would share their experience about development of rural roads. Around 1500 key experts from the Central and State Governments, Financial Institutions, R & D institutions, Field Engineers from States, Consultants, Machinery Manufacturers and Private Sector Construction Agencies are expected to participate in the conference. A technical exhibition to exhibit various materials and machinaries and to showcase the achievements in the flagship rural roads development programme has also been planned during the conference. Organising partners of the conference are National Rural Roads Development Agency(NRRDA), established under the Ministry of Rural Development in January, 2002 as a professional and multi-disciplinary body to extend management and technical support to the Ministry and the States for implementation of Pradhan Mantri Gram Sadak Yojana (PMGSY) and the road component of Bharat Nirman and Construction Industry Development Council (CIDC), an apex body set up in 1996 by the Planning Commission along with the construction industry to bring together all the stakeholders of the industry and provide a platform for formulating collaboration strategies.

1175. (21-5-2007) NEW DELHI : The Minority Affairs Minister, Shri A.R. Antulay will inaugurate a one-day annual conference of the Managing Directors of the State Channelising Agencies (SCAs) and Secretaries in charge of Minority Welfare of the State Governments here tomorrow. The Conference is being organized by the National Minorities Development & Finance Corporation (NMDFC), an apex Corporation under the Ministry of Minority Affairs, incorporated in September 1994 as a Section 25 company for providing consessional credit to the poorer section amongst the minorities for various income generation activities. Its schemes are implemented through the State Channelising Agencies (SCAs) nominated by the State Governments and Non Government Organisations (NGOs) through a network of Self Help Groups (SHGs). The Conference will decide on allocations for the current year and discuss about the progress made by the SCAs and sort out outstanding issues of various States to speed up the process of implementation.

1176. (21-5-2007) NEW DELHI : The President of India Dr. A.P.J. Abdul Kalam today presented the awards to young scholars of Sanskrit, Pali/Prakrit, Arabic and Persian. The Presidential Awards of Certificate of Honour and Maharshi Badrayan Vyas Samman Awards were presented to 30 recipients of the year 2006. Presidential Award of Certificate of. Honour is announced on the eve of Independence Day every year in recognition of the outstanding contribution of various scholars of eminence over 60 years of age in the field of Sanskrit, Arabic, Persian and Pali/Prakrit in recognition of their teaching experience, published work and their efforts in keeping the tradition of these languages alive. This scheme envisages a monetary grant of Rs. 50,000/- per annum for life, apart from a Sanad and a Shawl, which is presented to each of the awardees by the President of India. The award is conferred on a maximum number of 15 eminent scholars of Sanskrit, 1 scholar of Pali/Prakrit and 3 scholars each of Arabic and Persian every year. Young scholars of Sanskrit, Pali/Prakrit, Arabic and Persian in the age group of 30 to 40 years, who have made a breakthrough in the interdisciplinary studies involving contribution of these languages or the ancient Indian wisdom, to the process of synergy between modernity and tradition are granted Maharshi Badrayan Vyas Samman on this occasion every year. This carries a one-time cash award of Rs.1.00 lakh along with a sanad and a shawl, which is presented by the President. A Maximum number of 5 young scholars of Sanskrit and one each in Pali/Prakrit, Arabic and Persian is conferred every year.

1177. (21-5-2007) NEW DELHI : Shri Kamal Nath, Union Minister of Commerce & Industry, and Mr. Eduardo Sojo Garza-Aldape, Minister of Economy of Mexico, signed the Memorandum of Understanding (MOU) on the Establishment of a Bilateral High Level Group (HLG) on Trade, Investment and Economic Cooperation between India and Mexico, here today. The objective of MOU includes promotion of economic and trade relations between the two countries; facilitating better access to their respective markets and avoid imposition of new barriers to trade and investment; creation of bilateral consultative mechanism to include trade and economic cooperation. The functions of the HLG formed under the MOU includes – to devise specific measures for further promotion of bilateral cooperation in fields to be mutually identified; to maintain liaison between two countries in economic, commercial, technical and other related fields; to review progress of economic commercial and technical cooperation between the two countries and suggest measures for strengthening them and to formulate proposals and submit recommendations to the respective governments for coordinated efforts in furthering economic benefits for both countries. The HLG will be co-chaired from the Indian side by Minister of Commerce & Industry and the Secretary of Economy from Mexico or by their representative. The HLG will meet once a year alternatively in each country unless otherwise agreed and special meetings of Working Groups or ad hoc Expert Groups may be arranged when required by both countries. The Indian exports to Mexico during 2005-06 was US $ 432.85 million while imports from Mexico were US $ 96.18 million. Major item of exports from India include transport equipment, drugs & pharmaceuticals, readymade garments, inorganic/organic/agro chemicals etc., while major import items include electronic goods, Metalifers ores & metal scrap, iron & steel, plastic material etc.

1178. (21-5-2007) NEW DELHI : The Defence Minister Shri AK Antony has urged the Air Warriors to make all efforts for developing Indian Air Force (IAF) into a dominant Aerospace power. Inaugurating the three-day long Air Force Commanders' Conference here today, the Minister said that the IAF is in the process of transformation and modernization. Several important projects are in various stages of implementation. He said the Government is aware of the challenges, issues and requirements of the IAF. Adding further, that the IAF is a the technology intensive force, he said our attempts should be to enhance the strategic reach of IAF and integrate potent capabilities in air defence surveillance, space based assets and advance weapon systems to develop it into a dominant aerospace power. He said, "we must also develop asymmetric capabilities against superior forces". The Minister said that IAF has an ambitious action plan for acquisition of new systems and upgradation of existing ones over the next three years. Given the substantial amount of public money being used for these efforts, it is imperative that these financial resources are utilized honestly, efficiently and optimally. He said that we have been relying on outside suppliers to meet the requirement of our Defence Forces for quite some time. However, he remarked that a country like India cannot 'indefinitely' continue to rely on outside suppliers and self-reliance and indigenization must be our top priority. The Minister said, "self-reliance through indigenization should be the 'mantra' for companies in both the public as well as the private sector". Complimenting the IAF for its excellent flight safety record in the last financial year, the Minister said all possible efforts must be made by aviation related organizations to ensure that loss of human and financial resources through accidents remains minimal and if possible eliminated altogether. In this context, he stressed upon the need of training and strict adherence to Standard Operating Procedures relating to flight safety. Referring to the problem of serviceability, the Minister said, though long term business agreements have been signed a lot more remains to be done. Emphasizing the need of meticulous planning with regard to procurement of spares, he asked the Chief of Air Staff to chalk out a concrete action plan in this regard. Deliberating on India's friendly and cordial relations with all nations, especially country's in our immediate neighbourhood, the Minister said our relations with Pakistan show signs of improvement. However, Pakistan needs to match its words with actions on dismantling the terrorists and 'jehadi' infrastructure. He said, "though we deserve peace with Pakistan and want to continue talks with Pakistan on various issues, it is imperative for us to maintain eternal vigil all along our borders".

1179. (21-5-2007) NEW DELHI : India and Mexico signed the Agreement on Bilateral Protection and Promotion of Investments, here today. While Finance Minister, Shri P. Chidambaram signed the Agreement on behalf of India, Mexican

Minister of Economy, Dr. Eduardo Sojo signed on behalf of Mexico. The Agreement seeks to promote and protect investments from either country in the territory of the other country with the ultimate objective of increasing bilateral investment flow. It requires each country to encourage and create favourable conditions for investors of the other country to make investments in its territory and to admit investments in accordance with its laws. The Agreement would remain in force for a period of ten years and is expected to serve as a catalyst in boosting investment flows between the two countries. The term investment includes every kind of asset including intellectual property rights in accordance with laws and regulations of the country in which the investment is made. Principles of Most Favoured Nation Treatment and National Treatment (NT) have been asserted in the agreement. It also provides for free repatriation of funds of an investor of either country. Welcoming the Mexican delegate headed by Dr. Eduardo Sojo Garza-Aldape, Shri Chidambaram referred it as a historic day when the two countries added another golden page in the annals of longstanding bilateral relations between the two countries. He said that starting from the visit of India's first Prime Minister Shri Jawaharlal Nehru to Mexico in the year 1961, the two countries has had a series of visits of high level dignitaries from both sides. Very soon the new Mexican President Mr. Felipe Calderón is also scheduled to visit India. Shri Chidambaram mentioned that in the last decade the bilateral trade has grown almost 5 times and has reached the level of almost 2 billion US $. The investments in Mexico by the investors of Indian origin have also crossed US $ 1.5 billion. He also emphasized that given the fact that Mexico is a member of important free trade associations including the NAFTA, this Agreement will certainly be remembered as one of the most important Treaties, which India has signed in recent times. Shri Chidambaram said that today is the third anniversary of the UPA Government and hence it could not have been more appropriate than signing such an important Agreement on this day. Dr. Sojo mentioned that this is the first major Agreement which the present Government of Mexico has signed. He referred to the rapid growth of bilateral trade and Indian investments in Mexico and assured that the Indian investors would be provided with all possible incentives and comfort in establishing and reinforcing their investments in Mexico. India and Mexico have signed several important bilateral agreements including, Cultural Exchange Agreement, Agreement for Cooperation in Science and Technology, Agreement on Economic Cooperation, Agreement for Tourism Cooperation, Agreement exempting visa requirement for Official and Diplomatic Passport-holders and MoU on Cooperation in the field of SMEs. India and Mexico also have a number of other bilateral cooperation instruments in the fields of banking, telecommunications, culture and education, trade, industrial cooperation etc.

1180. (21-5-2007) NEW DELHI : To commemorate the 'Indian Coast Guard Aviation – Silver Jubilee' various events are being organized at Indian Coast Guard Air Station Daman on 21 and 22 May 07. Defence Minister Shri AK Antony would inspect the ceremonial parade, interact with the men and witness air display on

22 May 07. A series of events planned would showcase the multi faceted capabilities of the Coast Guard Aviation. The Best Aviation unit Trophy would also be awarded during the ceremonial parade. Indian Coast Guard (ICG) which was constituted as an Armed Force on 01 Feb. 1977 ushered in the aviation wing on 02 May 1982 with commissioning of the first Coast Guard Air unit at Goa. The growth of the fledgling air arm has been exponential. From just two helicopters in 1982, the ICG Aviation today boasts of 45 aircraft, two air stations, two air enclaves and number of air squadrons. The yeoman service being rendered by the Coast Guard Aviation is being recognized by the maritime community for their dedication and commitment in saving lives of seafarers, providing succour to marooned fishermen, combating marine pollution and effective monitoring of the vast Maritime Zones. 3896 lives have been saved at sea till to date. Indian Coast Guard on numerous occasions has demonstrated its operational versatility while handling relief and disaster operations such as Tsunami, BHN fire and pollution response at sea. The aviation wing in fulfilling the Indian Coast Guard's motto "WE PROTECT" has invoked a sense of safety and security amongst the maritime fraternity.

1181. (21-5-2007) NEW DELHI : The Pension Fund Regulatory and Development Authority (PFRDA) issued a Primary Information Memorandum and Expression of Interest (EOI) package for appointment of Pension Fund Managers for the New Pension System (NPS) on 11th May 2007. The last date for submission of EOI is 25th May 2007. The EOI document has been posted on the website of PFRDA (www.pfrda.org.in). Recently, reports have appeared in a section of the media that PFRDA proposes to allow foreign and private firms to manage pension funds. It is clarified that PFRDA has invited EOI only from public sector entities for sponsoring pension fund managers. As per the EOI, only Government entities, such as Central Government companies, public financial institutions etc. in which not less than 51% paid up share capital is held by Central Government or partly by Central Government and partly by one or more State Governments can apply. Further, to be eligible, the sponsors must have at least 5 years experience of fund management and average assets under management of the sponsors must not be less than Rs. 10,000 crores for the month of March 2007. Thus, even amongst public sector entities, only those with sufficient experience and financial strength can apply. The selected public sector entity would be required to incorporate the pension fund manager as a separate public sector company. Both the sponsor as well as the pension fund manager would, therefore, be in the public sector. Direct or indirect foreign investment in the pension fund manager, if any, shall not exceed 26% of its paid up share capital. This is in accordance with the report of the Standing Committee on Finance which examined the PFRDA Bill, 2005. Thus, it is clarified that in terms of PFRDA's invitation to submit EOI, no foreign or private firm would be eligible to apply for the pension fund business.

1182. (21-5-2007) NEW DELHI : The Prime Minister, Dr. Manmohan Singh, has approved the constitution of a Wage Board for Working Journalists. Formal orders regarding this will be issued shortly by the Union Labour Ministry. Working Journalists may be re-assured that the Prime Minister has fulfilled the assurance he had given them when they had called on him last year.

1183. (21-5-2007) PANAJI : BJP National Spokesperson and State Incharge of Goa Mr. Rajiv Pratap Rudy today appreciated the State Election Commission for taking cognizance of the electoral malpractices being undertaken by candidates of the Congress. While appreciating the active role being played by the Election Observers of the state in seizing cash from a Janata Dal candidate and distribution of various gifts to voters by Vishwajit Rane, son of the Chief Minister, Mr. Rudy emphasized that this was the outcome of the vigilant and alert approach of the Election Observers. Mr. Rudy pointed that as the date of elections draws closer, the Congress Party and other smaller regional parties on sensing the massive public mood build up in favour of the BJP, will in sheer desperation definitely seek to influence the voters through various unfair means and corrupt practices. These would include distribution of money, liquor and various gifts to influence the free and fair voting of the electorate. In this context, Mr. Rudy said the Election Observers need to remain even more vigilant and constantly monitor the field activities in every nook and corner of the state including sprucing up the intelligence network. The BJP Spokesperson said that people's expectations and confidence in the Election Commission has been enhanced every since they have witnessed free and fair elections being conducted earlier across the country and Bihar and Uttar Pradesh in particular. In this context, the Election Commission has to live upto these expectations and ensure that no malpractices occur in Goa. The BJP also demands that the Election Commission effectively deploys paramilitary forces across the state and assures all cooperation for the smooth conduct of elections. Mr. Rudy also highlighted that the BJP was formally launching its election campaign today with the rally at Azad Maidan in Panaji being addressed by the Leader of the Opposition Shri Lal Krishna Advani. To effectively expose the misdeeds of the Congress Government in the state before the people, Mr. Rudy said that the party had prepared a detailed campaign plan whereby a number of the central party's star campaigners would actively campaign in the state alongwith the local leadership including State President Mr. Shripad Naik, Mr. Manohar Parikkar and other state leaders. While addressing the press, Mr. Rudy said that the key BJP campaigners included Leader of the Opposition Mr. L K Advani who was formally launching the election campaign with the rally in Azad Maidan this evening followed by BJP General Secretary and MP Mr. Arun Jaitley who would release the party's Election Manifesto on the 22nd. Other senior leaders and star campaigners who would also hit the campaign trail over the next ten days included former BJP National President Mr. Venkaiah Naidu, senior party leader and MP Smt Sushma Swaraj, Vice President of the Party and MP Mr. Mukhtar Abbas Naqvi, BJP General Secretary Mr. Gopinath Munde, National Spokesperson Mr. Prakash Javadekar, BJP Maharashtra President Mr. Nitin Gadkari and popular television star Smruti Irani, among others. In addition to this, cricketing icon and MP

Mr. Navjot Singh Sidhu had agreed to hit the campaign for a second time later this month. Mr. Rudy highlighted that the Goa Election Campaign would touch its peak with the arrival of the BJP National President Mr. Rajnath Singh on the 29th and 30th of May who would address a series of rallies and meetings across various constituencies.

1184. (21-5-2007) NEW DELHI : Employees in Government offices, public sector undertakings and other public institutions throughout the country took pledge today in connection with the Anti-Terrorism Day. The Home Minister, Shri Shivraj Patil administered the oath to the officers and staff of the Ministry of Home Affairs in the North Block lawns here. Every year, 21st May is observed as Anti-Terrorism Day. The objective behind observance of Anti-Terrorism Day is to wean away the youth from terrorism and cult of violence by highlighting the sufferings of common people and showing how it is prejudicial to national interest. The objective is achieved through activities like pledge-taking, organisation of debates/ discussions in schools, colleges and universities, holding of symposia/seminars, lectures, etc. on the dangers of terrorism and violence.

1185. (21-5-2007) NEW DELHI : Results of All India JEE 2007 (Bsc. Hospitality and Hotel Administration Programme) have been declared. The Examination was held by National Council for Hotel Management and Catering Technology (NCHMCT), Pusa, New Delhi on 15th April, 2007. The results are available on NCHMCT's website www.nchmct.org

1186. (22-5-2007) NEW DELHI : The Prime Minister, Dr. Manmohan Singh, today released 'Report to the People 2006-07' on the occasion of completion of three years of the UPA Government. Following is the text of his address on the occasion: "We are gathered here, once again, to present our annual *Report to the People,* highlighting the important programmes and policies implemented by our Government. Friends, this annual exercise in accountability and transparency has set a new benchmark for governance in our country. It is my sincere hope that the contents of this report are widely disseminated and are discussed by our people at large. I would like to take this opportunity to place on record my sincere and heartfelt gratitude to the UPA chairperson, respected Soniaji, to all the leaders of all the parties constituting the UPA and our Left allies. It is their support that has given us the strength to try and redeem our pledge to our people to the best of our ability. I have been fortunate in having the unstinted support and cooperation of respected Soniaji. She is a source of immense inspiration for us all, particularly for all poor people across the length and breadth of our country. Under her leadership, the UPA has worked hard to implement the National Common Minimum Programme. It is my sincere hope and firm belief that by the end of our tenure in Government we would have delivered more than we had promised. The main objective of our Government in the past three years has been to ensure that, while sustaining higher rates of economic growth, the improved performance of the economy should contribute to employment generation, poverty reduction and human development. In this 60th year of our Independence, the country should have the satisfaction of recording for the fourth year in succession, a rate of economic growth of over 8.5%. The recent acceleration of growth to 9% per annum has been made possible by an unprecedented increase in the rate of investment which is at an all-time high of around 35% of our national income. Higher rates of investment and growth have helped generate employment and reduce poverty. However, we recognize that high national income growth alone does not address the challenge of employment promotion, poverty reduction and balanced regional development. Nor does growth by itself improve human development. The National Common Minimum Programme is based on the recognition that economic growth must be socially inclusive and regionally balanced. This has been the guiding principle of our Government's policies in the past three years.

1187. (22-5-2007) NEW DELHI : Government issued 10 notifications No.23/2007 to 32/2007-Service Tax, here today giving effect to some of the provisions of the Finance Act, 2007 relating to service tax. Seven services which are added in the category of taxable services shall come into force from 1st June, 2007. Renting of immovable properties for use in commerce or business shall be leviable to service tax with effect from 1st June, 2007. However, property tax paid on immovable property is specifically excluded from the levy of service tax by way of an exemption notification. Works Contract Service shall also be leviable to service tax with effect from 1st June, 2007. However, an optional Composition Scheme for payment of service tax on Works Contract Service has been notified. Under this Scheme, provider of Works Contract Service is given the option to pay service tax at a flat rate of 2% of the total value of the contract instead of paying service tax at the standard rate. Certain conditions are prescribed to avail the optional Composition Scheme. Section 65 defines taxable services and various terms used in relation to taxable services. Section 66 is the charging section and provides for levy of service tax on taxable services. These two sections have been amended in the Finance Act, 2007 to be effective from 1st June, 2007.

1188. (22-5-2007) NEW DELHI : The Secretary Minority Affairs, Shri M. N. Prasad while inaugurating the one day Annual Conference of the State Channelising Agencies of National Minorities Development & Finance Corporation (NMDFC) here in New Delhi has said that the Government is contemplating a significant role for NMDFC in the revamped "15 Point Programme of the Prime Minister". The Government is committed to provide higher allocations to NMDFC in order to substantially increase the coverage. Shri Prasad also informed that the participants representing the State government viz. Secretaries In-charge and Managing Directors of the State Channelising Agencies that the Central Government has taken cognizance of the deficiencies of the State Channelising Agencies. Accordingly a scheme has been launched for "Strengthening the State Channelising Agencies: in the plan for the current financial year. The scheme is being finalized and would be introduced very shortly. He also said that the Government has formed a "High Level Expert Committee" of the eminent bankers and financial sector experts to review the functioning of NMDFC. The committee has already submitted their report to the Ministry of Minority Affairs. The report is being processed and decision on recommendations is being finalized. The Conference was attended by Principal Secretaries of 9 States and the Managing Directors of the State Channelising Agencies of 32 States/UTs. The conference was convened for finalizing the Annual Allocations for the respective States/UTs for the current financial year *i.e.* 2007-08.

1189. (22-5-2007) NEW DELHI : The Government is working out a schedule for the replacement of the ageing platforms and systems of the Coast Guard in the forthcoming Annual Acquisition Plans. Speaking at the Silver Jubilee function of the Indian Coast Guard (ICG) Aviation at Daman this morning, the Defence Minister Shri AK Antony emphasized the need for faster modernization of the Coast Guard in view of emerging seaward threat. He, however, said that there would be no compromise on transparency while going through the process of modernization. The Defence Minister said that as India gains international stature and becomes an economic powerhouse, the Coast Guard's responsibilities are bound to increase. Shri Antony said that infiltration from land borders is becoming difficult for the terrorists due to constant vigil by security forces and changing environment in Jammu & Kashmir. However, there is no room for complacency He said, "as the pressure on terrorists on land increases, this threat is more likely than ever to come from the sea". In such a scenario, it is important for the Coast Guard to act in close cooperation with the other wings of our Armed Forces", the Defence Minister said adding that 73 coastal state police stations will soon be set up for better vigil along the country's vast coastline. The Defence Minister said that the government is aware of the need for acquiring new aircraft and surveillance equipment for the Coast Guard for it to perform its multifarious role effectively. "Enforcement of Maritime Laws is another domain that is becoming increasingly important due to rising threat of terrorism from the sea. To meet such varied challenges, upgradation and modernization of aviation assets is necessary", Shri Antony said. Praising the role played by the Coast Guard in pollution control, Shri Antony said that 3 Pollution Control Vessels would be procured during this year. The Defence Minister admitted that the delay in acquisition of various requirements of Armed Forces was a serious problem. He however emphasized that the government was committed to faster modernization of Armed Forces without compromising on transparency and the procedures were being constantly improved to facilitate this. The Defence Minister also said that indigenisation was an integral part of the modernization of Armed Forces. Earlier the Defence Minister reviewed a ceremonial parade at the Coast Guard Air Station, Daman. He also gave away the trophy for the Best Aviation Unit that was jointly awarded to the Kolkata-based No. 700 Squadron flying the Dornier aircraft and the Chetak Flight operating at Port Blair. An impressive flypast by Advanced Light Helicopters and Chetak preceded the peel-off sequence by five Dornier aircraft in a head-on approach. Also present on the occasion were Vice Admiral RF Contractor, Director General, Indian Coast Guard and Commanders of the Coast Guard regions of East, West and Andaman and Nicobar.

1190. (22-5-2007) NEW DELHI : Grants-in-aid amounting to Rs.57.49 lakh has been released by the Ministry of Rural Development to 5 DRDAs of Nagaland towards part payment of first instalment of Central share of funds under the 'Swarnjayanti Gram Swarojgar Yojana' (SGSY) during the year 2007-08.

1191. (22-5-2007) NEW DELHI : The United Progress Alliance (UPA) Government completes three years in office today. The Government and the Congress party will mark this event in predictably propagandistic manner. The propaganda, however, looks increasingly laboured, artificial and unenthusiastic. It can barely hide the growing discordant voices within the UPA. I have seen the performance of every government at the Centre since Independence. But I have not seen a government that is so utterly lacking in credibility, confidence and cohesion. For the first time in our Republican history, here is a government that is headed by a non-Prime Minister, run by a person who is not accountable to Parliament, and is surviving on life-support system provided by parties that behave more like the opposition. Last week, when the Finance Minister was replying to the debate on the Budget in the Lok Sabha, the MPs belonging to the Left parties joined the opposition NDA in staging a walk-out in protest. Now, a senior minister in the government, Shri Mani Shankar Aiyar, has himself publicly stated that the "UPA is no more *aam aadmi's* government." According to him, Dr. Manmohan Singh's is a government whose economic policy "may not get the *'aam aadmi's'* endorsement." I do not know why Shri Aiyar is being allowed to say such things by the Congress high command without being reprimanded. According to some analysts, this may be part of a deliberate attempt to distance the party's supreme leader from the failures of Dr. Manmohan Singh's government, so that at an opportune time in the near future the nominal and nominated Prime Minister can be dispensed with. I have no comments to offer on this analysis, except to say that the Congress party has surrendered itself to a slavish culture in which the reigning "Dynasty" never does wrong and is never responsible or accountable for any failure. I was rather amused to read in newspapers last week when both Shrimati Sonia Gandhi and her son blamed "the party" for its failure in the recently concluded UP assembly elections. One cannot expect any honest stocktaking of the three years of the UPA Government from this kind of imperious and dynastic leadership, which thinks that it is its birth-right to rule India. However, as the main opposition party, the BJP believes it to be its duty to present the true picture before the people.

1192. (22-5-2007) NEW DELHI : The Minister of Civil Aviation, Shri Praful Patel today officially announced that after the merger of Air India and Indian, the new entity will be known as 'Air India'. While the new company will have its registered office in New Delhi, its corporate office will be in Mumbai and its office for domestic operations as well as the Strategic Business Units will be mostly based in Delhi. The Mascot of the merged airline will be the Maharaja. The new livery and logo of the merged airline were also unveiled by the Minister today. As 'Air India' is a globally and nationally recognized brand name, as well as the designated airline in international bilaterals-the 'AI' code being available only to the existing name, it has been decided that the merged entity would continue with the same name. The design components of the new logo and livery have been drawn after merging some of the current features of both Air India and Indian Airlines. The logo of the new airline is a Flying Swan with the Konark Chakra placed inside it. The Flying Swan has been morphed from Air India's characteristic logo, 'The Centaur' whereas the 'Konark Chakra' is reminiscent of Indian's logo. The new logo will feature prominently on the tail of the aircrafts. Individually the Konark Chakra will also feature on all the engines of the aircrafts. The choice of colours namely red for "Flying Swan" and orange for "Konark Chakra" are meant to signify vigour and advancement. Further the colours also have a strong association with two carriers thereby retaining the earlier imagery of traditional hospitality and service. While the aircraft will be ivory in colour, the base will retain the red streak of Air India. Running parallel to each other will be the Orange and Red speed lines from front door to the rear door, subtly signifying the individual identities merged into one. The brand name 'Air India' will run across the tail of the aircraft.

1193. (22-5-2007) NEW DELHI : Kazakhstan has sought India's assistance in setting up of industrial clusters in textiles and cooperation in areas of hi-technology and financial services. This was stated by Mr. Marat Tazhin, Foreign Minister of Kazakhstan in a meeting with Shri Ashwani Kumar, Minister of State for Industry at Atmaty today. Shri Ashwani Kumar assured Mr. Tazhin of India's willingness to collaborate with Kazakhstan to share its experiences in building strong and vibrant industrial clusters. The Minister further highlighted India's need for energy security in view of India's dependence on oil and gas imports. "Participation of Indian oil and natural gas companies in Kazakhstan would be a win-win situation for both Kazakhstan and India", Shri Kumar said. He complemented the Government of Kazakhstan for strong economic growth in the recent years and hoped that Kazakhstan would play a significant role in bringing peace, stability and prosperity to Central Asia. Shri Kumar also met Ms. Zhanar Aitzhanova, Deputy Minister of Industry & Trade and Chief Negotiator on WTO Issues. Ms. Aitzhanova made a brief mention of the current status of negotiations with India for WTO accession. Recalling the support pledged by Mr. Kamal Nath, Commerce and Industry Minister, for Kazakhstan's WTO accession, she urged Shri Kumar to expedite India's signing of the Protocol in this regard. "India fully supports Kazakhstan's accession to the WTO. I hope that not only would outstanding issues be resolved but the bilateral relations also be further strengthened during the forthcoming bilateral meeting between India and Kazakhstan", Shri Kumar said.

1194. (22-5-2007) NEW DELHI : A Conference on Public Private Partnership in State Highways is being organized by the Central Government on May 25, 2007. The Conference will serve as a forum for sharing knowledge and experience aimed at attracting private investment on a much larger scale for the development of State highways through Public Private Partnership (PPPs). According to tentative estimates, the States should mobilize over Rs. 30,000 crores from PPPs during the Eleventh Five Year Plan. If successful, this initiative could rejuvenate over 30,000 km of state highways constituting one-fourth of this important segment of the road network. The Conference will be inaugurated by Shri Montek Singh Ahluwalia, Deputy Chairman, Planning Commission. The valedictory address will be delivered by Shri T.R. Balu, Minister of Shipping, Road Transport & Highways. Senior officials of the Central and State Government will participate in the Conference along with Stakeholders and experts from the private sector including senior bankers, lawyers and consultants as well as investors in PPP projects. They include Shri Vijay Singh, Secretary, Road Transport, Dr. D. Subba Rao, Secretary, Department of Economic affairs, Shri T. K. Viswanathan, Secretary, Department of Legal Affairs and Shri Pradeep Kumar, Chairman, NHAI. Speakers include Shri Gajendra Haldea of the Planning Commission, Shri Rajiv Lall of IDFC, Smt. Bharti Ramola Gupta of PWC and Shri D.P. Gupta, former DG, Road Development. It may be recalled that significant progress has been made in initiating an expanded National Highway Development Programme (NHDP) with an estimated outlay of Rs.2,20,000 crores. The bulk of the highway programme is proposed to be undertaken through Public Private Partnership (PPP) as a means of attracting private capital, improving efficiencies and reducing costs. This would include expressways, six-laning and four-laning projects, and also selected two-lane highways. The policy and regulatory framework, including a model concession agreement, is already in place and the roll out of projects has been accelerated. State Highways Development Programmes based on similar lines would be critical for growth of the States. Some of the States have already initiated ambitious programmes for PPP projects while others are in different stages of the process. There is a need for further streamlining and accelerating of the pace of project preparation and award, as these projects would benefit road users at least cost to the Government. Government of India supports the efforts of State Governments by providing financial assistance to PPP projects and by making available standard documents, based on best practices, for adoption by States. Many of the State Highways projects that have adopted standardized bid processes and transaction documents based on best practices have been approved for financial assistance of up to 20% of their respective capital costs under the Scheme for Financial Support to PPP projects. In addition, Government of India has set up the India Infrastructure Finance Company (IIFC) for providing financial assistance through long-term debt upto 20% of the capital costs of the project.

1195. (22-5-2007) NEW DELHI : India's share in world trade has gone up significantly since 2004. According to the latest information published in the

World Trade Statistics by the World Trade Organisation (WTO), India's share in total world trade (which includes trade in both merchandise and services sector) has gone up from 1.1% in 2004 — *i.e.*, the initial year of the Foreign Trade Policy (2004-09) – to 1.5% in 2006. "Based on the current rates of growth of merchandise and services trade, it is expected that India's share in world trade covering merchandise plus service sector trade may well double from the level of 2004 to cross 2% mark in 2009", Shri Kamal Nath, Minister of Commerce & Industry, has said. As far as merchandise trade alone is concerned, India's share in global merchandise trade may increase from 1.2% in 2006 to 1.5% in 2009. It may be recalled that India's share in merchandise trade has increased from 0.9% in 2004 to 1.2% in 2006, thereby crossing one per cent share of world trade. At the same time, India's services trade has recorded an even higher growth performance resulting in an increase in the share in world services trade from 2% in 2004 to 2.7% in 2006. In the Foreign Trade Policy announced by Shri Kamal Nath in August 2004, a medium term horizon for India's export growth was envisaged and as part of this, the share of India's merchandise trade in world trade was targeted to double in 2009. According to the World Trade Statistics of the WTO in 2006, India's total merchandise trade (export + import) was valued at US $ 294 billion in 2006 and India's services trade inclusive of export and import was US $ 143 billion. Thus, India's global economic engagement in 2006 covering both merchandise and services trade was of the order of US $ 437 billion, up by a record 72% from a level of US $ 253 billion in 2004.

1196. (22-5-2007) NEW DELHI : India is the largest producer of mangoes in the world (approximately 14 Million Tons) contributing more than 50% share of the world production. Many Indian Mango varieties have gained international acclaim due to their unique colour, flavour, aroma & taste. The Indian mango is a special product conforming to the highest standards of quality and is packed with nutrients. A single mango can provide up to 40% of the daily dietary fiber needs – a potent protector against heart disease, cancer and cholesterol build-up. In addition, this luscious fruit is a warehouse of potassium beta-carotene and antioxidants. Approved Indian varieties in Japan are Alphonso, Kesar, Benganpalli, Langra, Chausa and Mallika. In addition to the usual post-harvest procedures followed for other destinations, a special VHT (Vapour Heat Treatment) is also carried out for exports to Japan, strictly in accordance with the Japanese import regulation. As part of the India-Japan Friendship Year celebration the Agricultural and Processed Food Products Export Development Authority (APEDA) Ministry of Commerce & Industry, Government of India in coordination with Japan India-Business Cooperation Committee (JIBCC) is organizing the Mango Festival from 23rd-28th May 2007. The festival will be launched by Shri Kamal Nath, Commerce & Industry Minister. Ministers of the concerned Ministries of the Government of Japan, members of the JIBCC, prominent members of the Indian Community, members of the media, importers & exporters, members of the Japan & Tokyo Chambers of Commerce &Industry and Senior Indian officials would be attending the festival. A short film on Indian Mangoes will be screened at the launch party and there would be a display of the various varieties of Indian mangoes.

1197. (22-5-2007) NEW DELHI : Grants-in-aid amounting to Rs.57.49 crore has been released by the Ministry of Rural Development to 7 DRDAs of Arunachal Pradesh towards part payment of first instalment of Central share of funds under the 'Swarnjayanti Gram Swarojgar Yojana' (SGSY) during the year 2007-08.

1198. (22-5-2007) NEW DELHI : The Ministry of Rural Development has released part payment of first instalment of Central share of funds amounting to Rs. 17.11 crore under the 'Swarnjayanti Gram Swarojgar Yojana' (SGSY) during the year 2007-08 to 30 DRDAs of ORISSA.

1199. (22-5-2007) NEW DELHI : Five envoys presented their credentials to the President of India, Dr. A.P.J. Abdul Kalam at a ceremony at Rashtrapati Bhavan here today. The envoys who presented their credentials were:-His Excellency Mr. Paek Young-sun, the Ambassador of Republic of Korea, His Excellency Dr. Igor Polikha, the Ambassador of Ukraine, His Excellency Mr. Mohamed Ghassan Mohamed Adnan Shaikho, the Ambassador of Bahrain, Her Excellency Mrs. Teresita Vega Berner, the Ambassador of the Philippines and His Excellency Dr. Geza Palmai, the Ambassador of Hungary. The credential presentation ceremony was attended by the senior members of the missions, senior officials of the Ministry of External Affairs and Rashtrapati Bhavan.

1200. (23-5-2007) NEW DELHI : The Prime Minister, Dr. Manmohan Singh, released a book titled "1965 War – Inside Story" written by Shri R.D.Pradhan, here today. The Union Defence Minister, Shri A.K.Antony and Marshal of the IAF, Shri Arjan Singh, DFC were among the dignitaries present at the function. Following is the text of the Prime Minister's address on the occasion: "I am delighted to release my friend, Shri R.D. Pradhan's book. It is a labour of love and with good reasons. Shri Yashwantraoji Chavan, whose diary is the basis of this book, was one of our tallest national leaders in the post-Independence period. He was a great son of Maharashtra and a truly pan-Indian personality. Like Shri R.D. Pradhan, I had the privilege of working very closely with Shri Y.B. Chavan when he was our Finance Minister. I learnt a great deal from him in gaining awareness of various factors shaping our polity and economy. He was a great patriot and was deeply committed to both growth and social equity. I am happy that Shri Pradhan has published this book, making available to the public the thinking of Shri Chavan on a matter of great national importance. Yashwantraoji was a thinking politician and a thinking man's politician. Having made his mark on the important political stage of Maharashtra, Yashwantraoji arrived on the national scene at a momentous time. Panditji picked him to succeed the redoubtable V.K. Krishna Menon. Few in the country could have stepped into Krishna Menon's shoes with greater ease than Yashwantraoji did. He served both Panditji and Indiraji with great distinction. Yashwantraoji took little time in widening his horizons and growing in stature as a national leader. His grasp of administration, his understanding of national issues, his keen interest in matters relating to national security and economic policy stood him in good stead. Shri Pradhan has done great service both to the memory of Shri Chavan and to public policy in our country by publishing this book. The book helps us understand the mind of Shri Chavan and that of our national leaders during a critical phase in our recent history. I think civil servants have a responsibility to record for posterity the factors that shaped decision-making on important issues. There is a stronger tradition of such scholarship in the West, aided by access to government papers. I compliment Shri Pradhan for taking the trouble to put together this book. What comes through this book is the mature and balanced relationship that existed, and continues to exist, in our country between our political and military leadership. India stands as a shining example of a democracy with highly professional armed forces, working in a disciplined manner under civilian leadership. We have good reasons to be proud of this inheritance of our freedom movement and we must jealously guard it. All around us, and in much of the developing world, we see short-lived experiments in democracy snuffed out by soldiers in uniform. What Shri Pradhan's book shows is that it is not just in normal and peace-time that the civil-military relationship is normal and well-oiled, but even during times of national crisis and war. The 1962 war, the 1965 war and the 1971 war were important tests for a newly liberated, poor developing country like ours. Given the fact that we were still a young nation, barely integrated, such external threats could have been used to upset the balance in the civil-military relationship.

1201. (23-5-2007) NEW DELHI : The 'RURAL ROAD DEVELOPMENT PLAN: VISION 2025' was released here today by the Prime Minister, Dr. Manmohan Singh during the inaugural session of the two-day National Conference on Rural Roads organized by the organized by the National Rural Roads Development Agency (NRRDA), an autonomous agency under the Ministry of Rural Development and the Construction Industry Development Council (CIDC). Some of the salient features of the Plan are given below: In order to give a boost to rural connectivity, a Rural Roads Programme known as the Pradhan Mantri Gram Sadak Yojana (PMGSY) was launched in December 2000 as a 100 percent centrally funded scheme. It is estimated that about 1.79 lakh unconnected habitations need to be taken up under the PMGSY programme. This would involve new construction in a length of about 375,000 km at an estimated cost of Rs. 78,000 crore and improvements of 372,000 km at an estimated cost of Rs. 59,000 crore. Upto the end of December, 2006, a total of about 83,000 habitations have been covered and rural road works for an amount of Rs.38,387 crore have been sanctioned. Besides the balance work of PMGSY which in itself is an ambitions task, there is need to tackle the requirement of connectivity to habitations with lower population in the interest of social justice and removing sense of isolation of remote villages and bring them into main stream of national life. The objective has to be to provide full connectivity to all habitations including provision of bridges and culverts. Accordingly, the following vision for new connectivity has been recommended.

1202. (23-5-2007) NEW DELHI : I am delighted to participate in the presentation of Kabir Puraskar and the National Communal Harmony Awards for the year 2006. I would like to congratulate Shri Ram Babu Singh Chauhan of Uttar Pradesh, for receiving the Kabir Puraskar award for promoting peace and tranquility in his region. Also my congratulations to Shri Ravindranath Upadhyaya of Assam and the Institute for Socialist Education of Delhi for receiving National Communal Harmony Awards. By honouring such noble individuals and institutions, the significance of the awards has further increased. I would like to talk to you on the topic "Tolerant India, Tolerant World". The purpose of human life is beautifully described in "Bhagawat Gita". In the battle scene, where Arjuna was hesitating to fight against his own kith and kin in Kurushetra, Lord Krishna showed Arjuna a vision of Vrindavan where the whole garden was blossoming with beautiful flowers and fragrance and the flowers attracting honeybee. It was an enchanting scene. In another vision of the garden all the flowers which blossomed in the morning had now fallen on the ground. Lord Krishna says to Arjuna, "See the flower, how generously it offers beauty, fragrance and honey. It gives to all, gives freely its essence. When its work is done, it falls away quietly. Try to be like the flower, unassuming despite all its qualities". Lord Krishna conveys this message to the humanity. These characteristics must be imbibed in every youth by the parents and teachers at an early age so that they preserve the Dharma and contribute to the societal welfare.

1203. (23-5-2007) NEW DELHI : The annual Bhartendu Harishchandra awards for the years 2004 and 2005 were presented to writers for their original books in Hindi on journalism and mass communication, national integration, women's problems and children literature. The Secretary, Ministry of Information & Broadcasting Smt. Asha Swarup gave away the prizes at a function in New Delhi today. Smt. Swarup in her remarks said that the awards are an honour for those related to Hindi journalism. The awardees in their works have reflected different perspective of journalistic practices. She appreciated the topics reflecting the issues concerning children and women. Smt. Veena Jain, Director, DPD in her welcome address outlined the various activities undertaken by the Division. For the year 2005 in the journalism and mass communication category, the first prize was given to Dr. Gyanprakash Pandey for his book 'Jansanchar: Sidhant evam Shodh' and the second prize went to TV journalist Ms. Vartika Nanda for her book 'Television aur Apradh Patrakarita'. Social activities Shri Vijay Mohan Tiwari got the third prize for his celebrated book 'Harsood, 30 June'. Five authors received commendation prizes. For the year 2004, communicator Dr. Ashok Jerath received the first prize for his manuscript 'Yeh Akashwani Hai' and the second prize was jointly awarded to Shri K.S. Mehta and Sh. Chandrakant Sardana for their book 'Jansanchar – Kal, Aaj aur Kal'. Shri Ami Adhar 'Nidar' bagged the third prize for the book 'Samachar: Sankalpana evam Anuvad'. Three authors received commendation prizes in this category. In the women's problems category, the first prize was given to Ms. Ramanika Gupta for her book 'Stree Vimarsh: Kalam Aur Kudal ke Bahane' for 2004, and to Smt. Alka Pathak's manuscript 'Peer Pathara Gayee Hai' for 2005. S/Shri Suryakumar Pandey and Akhilesh Srivastava 'Chaman' were awarded the first prizes in children's literature category for 2004 and 2005 respectively. Shri Gulshan Rai Monga's book 'Poorvottar Bharat: Darshan aur Chintan' got the first prize in national integration category for the year 2004. In the journalism and mass communication category the first prize carries Rs. 35,000 cash while Rs. 25,000 and Rs. 20,000 are given for the second and third prizes respectively. For books on women's problems, national integration and children's literature Rs. 15,000 and Rs. 10,000 are given to the first and the second prize winners respectively. All the awardees also received a citation. Named after the father of Hindi journalism, Bhartendu Harishchandra Awards are given by the government since 1983 to encourage original book writing in Hindi on topics related to journalism and mass communication. Later, in 1992-93 three more categories, namely-national integration, women's problems and children's literatures, were also included for the awards.

1204. (23-5-2007) NEW DELHI : The Finance Minister, Shri P. Chidambaram, addressing the Convocation Ceremony of the first Batch of Tax Return Preparers (TRPs) held here today said that the TRP scheme was a unique initiative of the Government to encourage young men and women graduates to embark upon a successful career as TRPs and eventually as financial advisors to small and marginal taxpayers. Projecting direct taxes as a progressive tax and the taxes of the future, the Finance Minister emphasised that an unprecedented and highest ever tax collection of Rs.2,29,505 crore was achieved by the Income Tax department at the lowest cost of 0.59%. Allaying the common misconception that tax laws and procedures in India were among the most complicated in the world, the Finance Minister emphasised that the tax return forms, specially the return form ITR-I, were among the simplest in the world. The TRPs would help collect more taxes and inculcate the habit of voluntary tax compliance among small and marginal taxpayers. The Finance Minister personally distributed certificates to 23 TRPs, each of whom had scored 100% in the certification test. Shri Chidambaram said that more than 90,000 people applied for the training as TRPs, of which 47,227 candidates were short listed by the training partner NIIT for entrance examination. 4517 candidates joined the training, out of which 3737 candidates scored 60% marks or more in their 'end of course examination' to qualify for certification. He said that it is heartening to note that 966 candidates which is 27.46% of the candidates qualified as Tax Return Preparers are women. He said that Government intends to forge a long-term relationship with the TRPs. The Departmental Website, website of the Tax Return Preparer Scheme and a Toll free help line will provide the contact details of the TRPs to the taxpayers who propose to utilize their services. In her welcome address, Chairperson, CBDT, Smt. Indira Bhargava said that the Tax Return Preparer Scheme announced in the union budget 2006-07 is one of the boldest attempts by the Income-tax department to provide quality taxpayer service to the small and marginal taxpayers so that the citizens can fulfil their tax obligation with ease. She said, the scheme gives a unique opportunity for the Income Tax Department to provide self-employment opportunities to the bright youth of the country and give them a platform to extend a helping hand to the members of their community. The Department has already set up a Resource Centre that is headed by a Commissioner of Income-tax to monitor the implementation of the scheme. The Resource Centre will constantly monitor the work of the TRPs in the field and issue quality alerts to them, as and when needed. The TRPs will also be required to undertake periodic on line training and exam.

1205. (23-5-2007) NEW DELHI : India has one of the richest and most diverse cultural heritages associated with the use of medicinal plants. It represents a striking example of intimate link between biological diversity and cultural diversity. India is one of the 17-mega diversity countries and is home to 7% of the world biodiversity. There are 16 agro climatic zones, 45,000 different plants species of which about 7000 to 8000 species are used in various traditional and folk systems of medicine. The richness of Indian civilization with its glorious past has given the humanity vast knowledge about the usage of plants for food and health care. The strong tradition of health care practised and documented for more than 3000 years in the form of Ayurveda, Unani, Siddha and Yoga & Naturopathy systems of medicine have evolved through centuries of usage and have stood the test of times in providing holistic health care to the people and are based on a very intimate and well researched understanding that biotic and non-biotic components of the environment play in promoting holistic health care. There is growing interest in the world about the use of these systems and increasingly the developed world is prepared to adopt Indian systems. Today, Yoga has become popular the world over. It is now globally recognized that traditional, alternative complementary systems of medicine provide health care to almost 80% of the population in developing and less developed countries. Even in the developed world, there is a growing realization that the modern system of medicine alone is not able to address all the health problems particularly related to the life style diseases like diabetes, hypertension, AIDS, cancer, etc. It is in this context that scientific wisdom contained in the traditional health care system can be made use of to find solutions to the present day problems. India is fortunate to have inherited rich bio-diversity, both in plants and animals and the ethno botanical knowledge which need to be explored and researched to find solutions to the health problems of today as well as those that may emerge in times to come. Not only this, it needs to be understood that we have to move away from a single health care system to a pluralist health care system under which people are given options to choose the systems of medicine which they would like to access for health care. It is this philosophy that the Government of India is very actively promoting for development and promotion of the traditional systems of medicines like Ayurveda, Unani and Siddha. One of the important initiatives in this direction has been to mainstream AYUSH systems of medicine in the health care under the National Rural Health Mission (NRHM).

1206. (23-5-2007) NEW DELHI : Congress Spokesperson Smt. Jayanti Natrajan said that the Indian National Congress would like to extend its heartfelt congratulations to the Prime Minister Dr. Manmohan Singh and to the entire UPA alliance for successfully and productively completing three years in government yesterday. The Prime Minister has already released a report card on the work being done by his government and on behalf of the Indian National Congress we would like to place on record our felicitations. The main goal of the government has been development, socially inclusive growth, empowerment of the most disadvantaged sections of society, society free of communal tension and violence, National environment free from the worldwide challenge of terrorism, and above all the welfare of the Aam admi or the common man. This government has achieved all-round progress in all these areas and has brought-about a landmark legislation, such as the, Right to Information Bill, important schemes like Bharat Nirman, National Rural Employment Guarantee scheme and is restoring land to tribals in the forest area. These successes are also reflected in our external environment and all the successes achieved by the government on the External Affairs front. We would like to place on record our congratulations to the government to carry forward the good work already done in the years to come. To a question as to what is Congress Party's reaction to the comment made by Shri Mani Shanker Aiyer, Smt. Natarajan said that the view of the Congress Party is that government has done a spectacular job in taking the concern of the "Aam admi" as well as assuring the growth of 8 to 9 per cent. There has been a great increase in agriculture investment, there has been a particular focus on addressing the debt-trap the farmers have fallen into. It is completely incorrect for anybody to say that this government has not focused on the Aam admi. To a question that Shri Aiyer has clearly said that UPA government policies were only benefiting a few and not the Aam admi, Smt. Natrajan said that the Indian National Congress does not agree with his view. We believe that the Prime Minister has reflected his concern over inflation. The Party and the government are not blind to the various problems that have arisen. From time to time, from this forum, the party has requested the government to take steps to address pressing concern of inflation. We are all aware of those issues but at the same time there can be no doubt that the focus of the party and of this government is the common man. To a question that does it bother the Congress Party on their defeats in assembly elections in Punjab, Uttarakhand and Uttar Pradesh, Smt. Natarajan said that Congress Party takes winning and losing elections in a democratic spirit and accepts the verdict of the people. In that sense any defeat needs introspection. However, I do not believe that this is a reflection on the work done by this government at the Centre. To a question on controlling price rise, Smt. Natarajan said that the Prime Minister himself has said in his report card that price rise has been brought under control. We had from this forum requested the government to address this issue and the government has taken appropriate steps to control price rise.

1207. (23-5-2007) NEW DELHI : Concerted efforts were made to increase domestic production of fertilizers and improve timely availability of major fertilizers in adequate quantity during the three years of the UPA Government. The demand of ferilisers as assessed by the Department of Agriculture was fully met by the Department of Fertiisers during the last three years. Addressing a Press Conference here today the Minister for Chemicals & Fertilisers and Steel, Shri Ram Vilas Paswan said the backlog of fertiliser subsidy amounting to over Rs. 8000 crore will be cleared by this month end. Responding to questions the Minister said, the Government is trying to augment the supply of fertilizer in the long run through establishment of joint ventures abroad. Initial talks have been held for joint ventures for production of urea in Saudi Arabia, Kuwait, Nigeria, Egypt and Mozambique. The Government is considering joint venture projects in phosphorous rich countries like Tunisia, Algeria, Morocco and Jordan. Shri Paswan said the new pharmaceutical policy currently being considered by the Group of Ministers has several new features to ensure availability of medicines at affordable prices particularly to those Below the Poverty Line (BPL).

1208. (23-5-2007) NEW DELHI : A 30-member team of Civil Servants from Bangladesh, on a study tour of India, led by Mr. Iqbal Mahmood, Senior Joint Secretary, Government of Bangladesh called on the Union Minister for Railways, Shri Lalu Prasad here today. The study tour has been organized by the Indian Institute of Public Administration (IIPA) under a Memorandum of Understanding with Bangladesh Public Administration Centre. The Minister of State for Railways, Shri Naranbhai J. Rathwa, Chairman, Railway Board, Shri J.P. Batra, Member (Staff), Shri K.C. Jena were also present on the occasion. They were earlier given a presentation by Shri Sudhir Kumar, Officer on Special Duty, Ministry of Railways about the significant turn around by the Indian Railways. In his address, Shri Lalu Prasad informed the Civil Servants that when he took over as Minister for Railways, there was financial crisis in the Railways and there was talk of privatization and retrenchment of employees. Today the Railways have again become financially sound without any retrenchment and privatization etc. The year 2006-07 saw a record cash surplus before profit of Rs. 20,000 crore and the operating ratio is now 78 per cent. The Minster said that the aim was to modernize the entire Railway system at par with world standards. The length of popular trains is being increased to 24 coaches and simultaneously the length of platforms is also being increased. Fully airconditioned Garib Rath trains are also being run, where AC 3-tier charges are 40 per cent less than AC 3-tier charges in other trains. Work on Dedicated Freight Corridors (DFC) is likely to start from next month. The completion of

DFC will result in reduced congestion on the existing tracks. In his concluding remarks, the Minister said that the main objective of the Ministry was to work with honesty, commitment and vision so that Railways could become number one as in the world. Earlier the civil servants from Bangladesh thanked the Minister for the presentation on Indian Railways and for the warm hospitality given to them.

1209. (23-5-2007) NEW DELHI : The Delhi based NGO Hriday (Health Related Information Dissemination Amongst Youth)-Shan (Student Health Action Network) actively engaged in tobacco control awareness, advocacy and research along with students representing 17 Delhi schools met the Union Health Minister, Dr. Anbumani Ramadoss today expressing their support for Pictorial Health Warnings on Tobacco Products. The members of Hriday-Shan conveyed their support for notifying the mandatory placement of pictorial health warnings on tobacco products with the target date of implementation as June 01, 2007. However, the Government has constituted a Group of Ministers (GoM) to reconsider the issue and suggest further course of action. The GoM will meet in the evening today to discuss the issue.

1210. (23-5-2007) NEW DELHI : The President, Dr. A.P.J. Abdul Kalam, presented Kabir Puraskar and National Communal Harmony Awards to Shri Ram Babu Singh Chauhan, Shri Rabindra Nath Upadhyaya and Institute of Socialist Education, here today. The Vice President, Shri Bhairon Singh Shekhawat, the Prime Minister, Dr. Manmohan Singh, Union Home Minister, Shri Shivraj Patil, Leader of Opposition in Lok Sabha, Shri L.K.Advani, Minister of State in Home Ministry, Shri Sriprakash Jaiswal were present on the occasion. Following is the text of the Prime Minister, Dr. Manmohan Singh's remarks on the occasion: "I have great pleasure in congratulating the distinguished awardees of the Kabir Puraskar and National Communal Harmony Awards. Each one of them is a source of inspiration for us all. I wish them well in all their future endeavours. In honouring them, we reaffirm our nation's commitment to the value system enshrined in our constitution. The founding fathers of our republic were firm in their belief and convictions to promote communal harmony and amity and good will among all sections of the population. Shri Ram Babu Singh Chauhan has been deeply inspired by the life of Sant Kabir. Through his padayatra from Hathras to Agra to promote national integration, he has sought to further the ideals of the great Saint Kabir. Shri Ram Babu in his thoughts and deeds represents the universal values enshrined in all great religions of helping the underprivileged and those in need. Unmindful of his own safety, he acted boldly to protect a Muslim woman and secure justice for her when she became a victim of rape. He has also taken up various causes of farmers and other disadvantaged sections of society. Shri Rabindra Nath Upadhyaya is a freedom fighter from Assam. It gives me added pleasure, therefore, to compliment him. His rich experience in our struggle for independence, in the Bhudan and Gramdan movements has inspired him through life to serve society's under privileged sections I am truly Proud of the good work his organization, Tamulpur Anchalik Gramdan Sangha, has done to secure peace in the communally disturbed areas of Assam, Arunachal Pradesh, Manipur and Tripura.

1211. (23-5-2007) NEW DELHI : The President Dr. A.P.J. Abdul Kalam presented the National Communal Harmony Awards and Kabir Puraskar for 2006 at a ceremony here today. The National Communal Harmony Award was presented to venerable Gandhian, Shri Rabindra Nath Upadhyay, from Assam in the individual category and the Institute for Socialist Education, Delhi in the organisation category. The award carries a citation and a cash prize of Rs. 2 lakh in the individual category and a citation and cash prize of Rs. 5 lakh in the organisation category. The National Communal Harmony awards are given for promotion of communal harmony, fraternity and national integration. Kabir Puraskar Grade III was presented to Shri Ram Babu Singh Chauhan of Uttar Pradesh. The award in Grade III carries a certificate, a citation and a cash amount of Rs. 50,000. Kabir Puraskar is given to promote communal harmony by recognizing acts of physical and moral courage as also display of humane approach by an individual for saving the lives and properties of the members of another community during communal riots, caste conflicts and ethnic clashes. In their speeches on the occasion, the President Dr. A.P.J. Abdul Kalam, the Vice President, Shri Bhairon Singh Shekhawat, the Prime Minister, Dr. Manmohan Singh, the Home Minister, Shri Shivraj Patil and the Minister of State for Home Shri Sriprakash Jaiswal stressed the importance of promoting communal harmony and amity among all sections of the society. They expressed confidence that the awardees would inspire others also to work for communal harmony and amity. They also cautioned the gathering about the forces of communalism and religious extremism who pose great danger to the country's unity and integrity. From the year 2007, another award for the students' union category carrying a citation and cash amount of Rs. three lakh has been instituted.

1212. (23-5-2007) NEW DELHI : The Prime Minister, Dr. Manmohan Singh, while inaugurating the National Conference on Rural Roads, here today, organized by the National Rural Roads Development Agency (NRRDA), an autonomous agency under the Ministry of Rural Development and the Construction Industry Development Council (CIDC), has said that rural roads connectivity is a critical component of the overall strategy for rural development as it promotes access to economic and social services and facilitates the growth processes in the rural economy. He further said that expansion of rural network will have wider multiplier positive impact on development, well-being and welfare of the people. Dr. Singh stressed the need for quality benchmarks and quality assurance for rural roads like National Highways and evolving cost effective technologies that are low cost and use locally available materials for construction of rural roads. For this, there is a need for a policy and strong institutional framework for mainstreaming these alternatives to the maximum possible extent for expansion and development of rural roads, he opined. He also underscored the requirement of making road construction as labour intensive as possible with the help of labour based methods without compromising on the quality in order to increase employment potential in road construction by at least five times. This can create a synergy between the Bharat Nirman and the National Rural Employment Guarantee Programme

(NREGP), he remarked. He further outlined the importance of regular maintenance and upkeep of rural roads as a necessary pre-condition for sustaining the benefits of rural road connectivity and promoting decentralized systems for maintenance and management of rural road network. Dr. Montek Singh Ahluwalia, Dy. Chairman, Planning Commission, while speaking on the occasion, has said that rural roads are critical elements to build rural infrastructure and for inclusive growth in the country. Rural road connectivity is the single most determinant to remove poverty because of its direct effect on income generation. Eleventh Plan strategy focuses on rural roads and has set clear target for rural connectivity under PMGSY and Bharat Nirman and funds have been made available for both the programmes. He hoped that the Conference will be able to come out with specific policies on contract management and standardization of contract documents and deliberate on maintenance of rural roads, formulation of district plans and district road network and impact of rural road connectivity on economic activities. Dr. Raghuvansh Prasad Singh, Rural Development Minister, in his welcome and introductory speech has said that under PMGSY and Bharat Nirman, time-bound and targeted programmes are in progress to ensure rural road connectivity and that more than 1,22,000 Km. of roads have been completed under PMGSY so far and that work is in progress in respect of projects covering another one lakh Km. States are taking steps to overcome various constraints in the implementation of the programme like contractor shortage, material shortage, etc. He hoped that the Conference, which is first of its kind, will be able to set a new direction for the future development of rural roads in the country.

1213. (23-5-2007) NEW DELHI : The National Productivity Awards for the Agriculture Sector for the years 2005 and 2006 will be given away in the presence of Shri Sharad Pawar, Union Minister for Agriculture at a function organized by National Productivity Council here tomorrow. The awards shall be distributed by Dr. Akhilesh Prasad Singh, Minister of State for Agriculture, Consumer Affairs, Food & Public Distribution. These awards are presented every year in 14 sub sectors namely, Agricultural Extension Services, Animal Feed Processing Units, Bio-Fertilizer Producers, Command Area Development & Irrigation Projects, Dairy Development and Production in Cooperative and Public Sector, Dry Land Farming, Horticulture Development in Cooperative Sector, Inland & Marine Fish Production in Cooperative Sector, Poultry Production and Development, Seed Corporation in Public Sector, State Agro Industries Corporation, State Farm Corporation, State Marketing and Oilseed Federations in Cooperative Sector and Warehousing Sector. The Awards serve as a catalyst to promote the concept of productivity which has assumed further significance due to the ongoing process of economic reforms in the context of globalization and WTO regime. The Productivity Awards are decided after a consideration of both the quantitative and qualitative factors while undertaking assessment of the participants with regard to their commitment to productivity improvement on a continuous basis.

1214. (23-5-2007) NEW DELHI : Kazakhstan has sought India's assistance in setting up of industrial clusters in textiles and cooperation in areas of hi-technology and financial services. This was stated by Mr. Marat Tazhin, Foreign Minister of Kazakhstan in a meeting with Shri Ashwani Kumar, Minister of State for Industry at Atmaty yesterday. Shri Ashwani Kumar assured Mr. Tazhin of India's willingness to collaborate with Kazakhstan to share its experiences in building strong and vibrant industrial clusters. The Minister further highlighted India's need for energy security in view of India's dependence on oil and gas imports. "Participation of Indian oil and natural gas companies in Kazakhstan would be a win-win situation for both Kazakhstan and India", Shri Kumar said. He complemented the Government of Kazakhstan for strong economic growth in the recent years and hoped that Kazakhstan would play a significant role in bringing peace, stability and prosperity to Central Asia. Shri Kumar also met Ms. Zhanar Aitzhanova, Deputy Minister of Industry & Trade and Chief Negotiator on WTO Issues. Ms. Aitzhanova made a brief mention of the current status of negotiations with India for WTO accession. Recalling the support pledged by Mr. Kamal Nath, Commerce and Industry Minister, for Kazakhstan's WTO accession, she urged Shri Kumar to expedite India's signing of the Protocol in this regard. "India fully supports Kazakhstan's accession to the WTO. I hope that not only would outstanding issues be resolved but the bilateral relations also be further strengthened during the forthcoming bilateral meeting between India and Kazakhstan", Shri Kumar said.

1215. (23-5-2007) NEW DELHI : The number of consequential train accidents have come down from 473 in 2000-01 to 234 in 2005-06. During the preceding five years, the Commission of Railway Safety inquired into 28.5 train accidents per year on an average and there were 131 passenger fatalities per year in serious train accidents on an average. The passenger fatalities in the year 2005-06 were 177. Human failure continues to be the single largest cause for 88.3 per cent of all consequential train accidents which occurred on the Railways during the year 2005-06. The Commissioners of Railway Safety inspected 185.454 kilometres of new lines, 249.756 kilometres of doublings, 721.803 kilometres of gauge conversion works and 598.695 kilometres of Railway Electrification works for their suitability for public carriage of passengers and introduction of electric traction. These figures include the opening of the Delhi Metro Rail Corporation lines also. During the year under review, investigations into 23 train accidents were carried out by the Commissioners which required statutory inquiry and were considered serious enough by the Commissioners. The damage to railway property from all consequential train accidents was of the order of Rs. 41.75 crores. Failure of driving crew accounted for 44.45 per cent of the train collisions. There were 75 accidents at Level Crossings out of which 69 accidents occurred mainly on account of negligence of road users. Based on statutory inquiry conducted into serious train accidents, the Commission of Railway Safety has made 133 recommendations to the Ministry of Railways to improve safety and avoid recurrence of such accidents in future.

1216. (23-5-2007) NEW DELHI : Continued policy reforms and institutional development are a sine qua non for sustained economic growth in India. In his opening statement on behalf of India, at the World Trade Organisation (WTO)'s Trade Policy Review for India, to be held in Genera from 23-25 May, 2007, Shri G.K. Pillai, Commerce Secretary, said: "We are of the view that continued and sustained growth of the Indian economy is not only good for India but also for the rest of the world. We also believe that in a more integrated global economy, it is necessary that other less developed countries also grow significantly so that they are able to get the benefits of globalization. The Government of India is acutely aware that there is no inevitability of high growth and that sustained rapid growth cannot be taken for granted. For sustained economic growth, there is need for continual reform as well as a matrix of institutions and public policies tailored to the new needs of the economy. As brought out in the trade policy report, a slew of policy reforms have indeed been implemented over the last decade. There have been changes of Government over the last fifteen years, however, the momentum of economic reforms has not abated. In a vibrant and complex democracy such as India, the reform process can and will have some fits and starts but the overall direction of the Indian economic reforms has always been positive". Referring to non-tariff barriers to imports from developing countries, the statement said that non-tariff barriers in the form of restrictive regulations were impediments that significantly affected not only exports but also the capacity to trade and as a result, even after more than two decades of rapid trade growth, the pattern of trade remained highly skewed in favour of the developed world. "High-income countries representing 15% of the world's population still account for two-thirds of world exports. The share of world exports of Sub-Saharan Africa, with 689 million people, is less than one-half of that of Belgium, with 10 million people", the statement added. "We have a historic opportunity to partially correct this imbalance in the current Doha Development Round. India is extremely concerned at the slow pace of negotiations. While the suspended talks have resumed, the political will on the part of developed countries is still not evident. Unless the development dimension of the Doha Round is met and the developing countries prosper, global trade will always be at risk. The rapid economic growth of developing countries is a must for a truly global trade order to flourish. India stands committed to meet its obligations under the mandate of the July Framework and the Hong Kong Ministerial Declaration. Developed countries must recognize that our destinies are intertwined", the statement said.

1217. (23-5-2007) NEW DELHI : Expressing serious concern over corruption in road construction projects, the Prime Minister, Dr. Manmohan Singh has emphasized the need to implement both Pradhan Mantri Gram Sadak Yojana and Bharat Nirman without this affliction and in a transparent manner. Inaugurating the National Conference on Rural Roads, here today, Dr. Singh underscored the need for quality benchmarks and quality assurance for rural roads on the lines of national highways. "I am concerned about the fact that we invest crores of rupees every year on road construction and maintenance, and yet with every monsoon our roads get worn", he said. The Prime Minister also stressed the need to evolve cost-effective technologies for construction of rural roads as well as the need to make road construction as labour intensive as possible. He released a book on 'Rural Roads: Vision 2025' at the Conference which was attended by the Union Rural Development Minister, Dr. Raghuvansh Prasad Singh, Deputy Chairman, Planning Commission, Shri Montek Singh Ahluwalia, Ministers of State in the Ministry of Rural Development, Smt. Suryakanta Patil and Shri Chandrasekhar Sahu and other dignitaries. Following is the text of the Prime Minster's address on the occasion: "Let me, at the very outset, compliment my valued colleague, Shri Raghuvansh Prasad Singhji for organizing this important conference. He has been taking keen interest in all aspects of rural development and his vision, his dedication, his commitment to rural development is something truly remarkable and inspiration to all. I am happy to be associated with this conference today. Rural connectivity is a key component of rural development. Without connectivity, our rural economy will not be able to develop. Through bharat Nirman, our Government has made an important commitment to invest in rural connectivity – connectivity through power, connectivity through telephones and connectivity through roads. We have a vast road network of over 3 million kilometres spread across the length and breadth of our country. I believe there are three priority areas in road development. First, we need multi-laned highways connecting our vast country. This we are doing through a massive expansion of the National Highway Development Programme in which we are investing Rs.220,000 crores. Second we need a network of rural roads, linking our villages to towns, to market centres and to our highways. Third, we need good quality border roads and better road connectivity in the North-eastern region of our country. Rural road connectivity is a critical component of our overall strategy for rural development. It promotes access to economic and social services and facilitates the growth processes in our rural economy. Improved connectivity reduces the cost of transportation of inputs and outputs, promotes diversification of crops and creation of non-farm employment opportunities in our rural areas. According to some studies, a million rupees spent on roads has seven times the impact on poverty reduction as compared to similar spending on specific anti-poverty programmes.

1218. (24-5-2007) NEW DELHI : Dr. Akhilesh Prasad Singh,Minister of State for Agriculture has called for an all out effort to improve productivity in Agriculture to achieve the targeted 4% growth rate in the 11th plan. Giving away the National Productivity Awards for the Agricultural Sector here today, the Minister said, in view of the trade liberalization and globalisation, diversification in to higher value output is imperative to remain competitive. Women need to be given greater encouragement in agricultural avocations as the demographic pattern in rural areas is fast changing owing to urban migration etc., he added. 60 awards for the years 2005 and 2006 in 14 categories of Agriculture were distributed by the Minister to those organisations/units who have distinguished themselves in productivity enhancement in their respective fields. The awards serve as a catalyst to promote the concept of productivity, which has assumed further significance due to the ongoing process of economic reforms in the context of globalisation and WTO regime.

1219. (24-5-2007) NEW DELHI : The main objective of UPA Government in the past three years has been to ensure that, while sustaining higher rates of economic growth, the improved performance of the economy should contribute to employment generation, poverty reduction and human development. In this 60th year of our Independence, the country should have the satisfaction of recording for the fourth year in succession, a rate of economic growth of over 8.5%. The recent acceleration of growth to 9% per annum has been made possible by an unprecedented increase in the rate of investment which is at an all-time high of around 35% of our national income. Higher rates of investment and growth have helped generate employment and reduce poverty. However, it is recognized that high national income growth alone does not address the challenge of employment promotion, poverty reduction and balanced regional development. Nor does growth by itself improve human development. The National Common Minimum Programme is based on the recognition that economic growth must be socially inclusive and regionally balanced. This has been the guiding principle of the UPA Government's policies in the past three years. Taken together, all the major initiatives of the Government, in agriculture and rural development, in industry and urban development, in infrastructure and services, in education and health care and in every other facet of life, are aimed at promoting this "inclusive growth".

1220. (24-5-2007) NEW DELHI : In a first ever case in the Army, kidneys and liver of an accident victim were successfully retrieved here late last right. They were transplanted today to two army personnel in Army Hospital (R&R) in New Delhi and one lady in the Naval Hospital, Ashwani in Mumbai. Shri Ramesh Chand, 60 years old father of Havaldar Madan Mohan of the Indian Army and Corporal Kamlesh Kumar of the Indian Air Force was injured critically in a hit and run road accident at Faridabad on Monday last. He was operated upon at Army Hospital (R&R) here. He however breathed his last late last evening. Mrs. Hemlata, wife of the deceased desired to donate the organs. However being a road accident case, postmortem was a legal requirement. Through postmortems are generally not carried out in Army Hospitals, so as to facilitate the speedy retrieval of organs, Dr. Khakha Alexander of Safdarjung Hospital carried out postmortem in Army Hospital itself. In a nightlong procedure, one kidney and liver were retrieved and transplanted to two serving soldiers in Delhi. One kidney was airlifted late at night yesterday to Mumbai, where it was transplanted to the wife of a serving soldier. All the recipients are doing well. With a computerized data bank of patients in need of various organs, Army doctors are now in a position to send organs from are place to another with the required urgency. This move of a kidney from Delhi to Mumbai is also a first of its kind move of organs. The entire procedure was carried out under the supervision of Maj Gen OP Mathew, Brigadier RP Choubey and Col AK Seth of Army Hospital (R&R). In the last two months, this is the fourth case of organ transplant in Army Hospital (R&R).

1221. (24-5-2007) NEW DELHI : Shri Kamal Nath, Union Minister of Commerce and Industry and Mr. Akira Amari, Minister of Economy, Trade and Industry of Japan today signed the Memorandum of Understanding (MoU) between India and Japan for cooperation in the field of Intellectual Property Rights at Tokyo. Capacity building, human resource development and public awareness programmes are the three main areas of cooperation covered in the MoU. Information exchange and experience sharing are also envisaged in the agreement. Both countries will draw up Annual Action Plans to implement the MoU which will include the detailed planning for carrying out of the cooperation activities including the scope of the action. It is hoped that the MoU will go a long way in fostering the cooperation between India and Japan. The MoU follows the Joint Statement towards Japan-India Strategic and Global Partnership made by Prime Minister Dr. Manmohan Singh and Prime Minister Mr. Shinzo Abe on 15th December, 2006 which confirmed the willingness of the two Governments to continue to cooperate in capacity building activities in intellectual property, including in developing human resources.

1222. (24-5-2007) NEW DELHI : The unbeatable combination of an ancient civilization embracing economic globalisation in a context that is open and democratic makes India one of the bulwarks for the Future of Asia, Shri Kamal Nath, Union Minister of Commerce & Industry, said while addressing the Nikkei "Future of Asia Conference 2007" in Tokyo today, adding that, "in fact, at this conference discussing the Future of Asia, I can very confidently say that the future is Asia". Emphasising the importance of inclusive growth, Shri Kamal Nath said: "A few years ago we sensed the dangers that rapid growth without "inclusive" development can pose to the social polity. We found that our growth process was not creating as many jobs as we needed and the industrial and services sector growth was very urban centric. For the last three years we have, therefore, been moulding policies which, while ensuring that growth continues unhindered and faster, make the benefits more evenly spread, and reach the common man – what we in India call the 'aam aadmi'." He said the attraction of India lay in three distinct aspects: First, India's current and potential economic growth making it very attractive to the world at large. Second, India's politico-legal complexion based on sound and time-tested tenets fully acceptable to the civil society around the world. And third, the inherent stability of India's democratic institutions, its multi-culturalism and its hugely successful diaspora. Referring to the Doha round Shri Kamal Nath said: "The virtual suspension of the Doha Round negotiations last July has brought into focus not only the substantive issues which are the subject of discord, but also the institutionalised power asymmetries which continue to pervade the WTO. While its professed objective is greater openness in all aspects of trade, in practice this objective is observed in a highly selective manner that reflects the predilections and concerns of developed countries. Let me give just a few examples of this selective openness: National borders should matter less and less for merchandise trade and capital flows. But we are told – don't talk about technology flows and labour flows. Subsidies are bad for industrial sectors, but on agricultural subsidies, the only thing we hear is that we'll get back to you. Tariffs should be transparent and ad valorem in the industrial sector. In agriculture, now, that's something else! The private interests of IPR holders are sacred; issues of public interest regarding intellectual property are of a second order. Talk of a Development Round remains largely rhetorical. Issues of serious concern like cotton, ushering in fair and undistorted agricultural world trade, Duty Free Quota Free Treatment for LDC's, Implementation Issues, etc. remain unresolved. The fundamental principle of special & differential treatment for developing countries to address their concerns of policy space in the major areas of negotiations remains deadlocked. There is as yet, no recognition by some developed countries that the basic premise of a Development Round is primacy for the development needs of developing countries, and not market access for developed countries. The unity amongst the developing countries has been our strength; it has withstood all pressures to undermine the development promise of the Doha Round. In our work ahead, I intend to continue working with my colleagues in order to create that balance of give-and-take across the Doha Work programme as a whole that will make winners of each of us".

1223. (24-5-2007) NEW DELHI : The Vice President, Shri Bhairon Singh Shekhawat, while delivering the valedictory address at the National Conference on Rural Roads, organized by the National Rural Roads Development Agency (NRRDA), an autonomous agency under the Ministry of Rural Development and the Construction Industry Development Council (CIDC), has said here today that rural prosperity ought to be the ultimate focus of our public programmes for development and the major challenge that the nation faces today is that of balancing the growth process and bridging the various "divides" and the "divide" between the urban and rural areas has been among the most significant ones. He expressed concern that incomes of many in the rural areas have dwindled and farm households have become more prone to stress and insecurity. The greatest developmental challenge is to secure all inclusive development which is socially equitable and regionally balanced, he stressed. Shri Shekhawat further said that in the strategy and planning for rural development, rural connectivity has tremendous importance as a necessary pre-condition for sustainable reduction of rural poverty. Roads become a lifeline to new markets, new businesses, new incomes and above all to new opportunities. The Pradhan Mantri Gram Sadak Yojana (PMGSY) has given a new thrust to development of rural roads and its success in achieving the targets will certainly go a long way in improving the much-needed rural infrastructure. He expressed satisfaction that the construction of rural roads is now aimed to be taken up on the basis of systematic network planning and that there is distinctive focus on quality assurance. The Vice President made the observation that the issue of adequate maintenance and upkeep of the entire network of rural roads in a holistic manner is of critical importance and it needs to be tackled collectively by all stakeholders. Further, complete information on construction of rural roads including allocation of funds, progress of expenditure should be widely disseminated to ensure efficient and corruption-free utilization of public funds under the watchful eyes of the public. He expressed satisfaction that the Conference provided opportunity to all the participants for sharing of experiences and evolving strategies for integrated development of rural roads. He hoped that the conclusions & recommendations of the Conference would make significant impact on the development of rural areas. The Vice President released the "Quality Assurance Handbook for Rural Roads" on the occasion. Speaking on the occasion, the Minister for Rural Development, Dr. Raghuvansh Prasad Singh, informed that to check quality of rural road construction, the system of technical audit has been introduced, a 3-tier system of quality monitoring has already been put in place and to ensure transparency in programme implementation, all the details have been made available in the Citizens' domain. Dr. Singh assured that the recommendations and suggestions of various technical and experience-sharing sessions will be positively considered and put into practice. He hoped that the States would also come out with State road development plans on the lines of 'Rural Roads Plan : Vision 2025'. Shri M.V. Rajasekharan, Union Minister of State for Planning in his speech said that without rural roads there can be no mainstreaming of the people with society and the economy and rural connectivity is critical for servicing the transportation needs of farmers to provide the much-needed impetus to the agricultural and rural manufacturing industries and thereby creating new areas of employment and reducing poverty. He further said that PMGSY within a short span has already set precedence in effective project management. Earlier, the Minister of State for Rural Development, Shri Chandra Sekhar Sahu, welcomed the gathering. Dr. Subas Pani, Secretary (Rural Development) proposed a vote of thanks.

1224. (24-5-2007) NEW DELHI : The Minister for Civil Aviation, Shri Praful Patel has asked British investors to participate in a big way in India's development. He was addressing "Indian Infrastructure – way forward" a Conference organized by the Indian Business Forum at the London Business School, yesterday evening. Speaking on the occasion, the Minister said that the Indian Government was committed to reforms but it had to be inclusive. He said that India had a great potential and immense growth prospect because of its sheer size and population and the British investors should avail the opportunity to participate in India's rapid development process. The Indian Government, he said, was taking a number of steps to improve the infrastructure of the country including power, roads, aviation, shipping and transport. It was for the first time in India's history that a Committee on Infrastructure development, headed by the Prime Minister of the country had been formed. The implementation of the projects in the seven key infrastructural areas were being monitored by the Prime Minister's Office. According to the estimates of the Committee on Infrastructure, India's infrastructure sector alone can absorb more than 150 billion dollars of Foreign Direct Investments (FDI) over the next five years. He said that India's total FDI inflow in 2006 was close to 11 billion dollars and bringing in 30 billion dollars a year in infrastructure alone would give a huge boost to the economic reform process that was going on in the country. Speaking about the Civil Aviation sector in India he said that the sector had undergone a sea change in the past few years. Just two years ago there were only 135 passenger aircraft catering to a one billion population, while today India has placed the largest order of aircraft ever. The public carriers themselves have placed an order of 111 aircraft. The civil aviation infrastructure was also expanding significantly. Speaking about the Mumbai and Delhi airports, the Minister said that the bidding process for these airports had been done in a most transparent manner and they were now being built in Public-Private-Partnership with international consortiums. The Minister also said that there has been a change in the mindset as to how the world looks at India. The world's focus towards India cannot be ignored.

1225. (24-5-2007) NEW DELHI : The Vice President of India Shri Bhairon Singh Shekhawat has said that it is important that rural prosperity ought to be the ultimate focus of our public programmes for development. Delivering Valedictory address at the "National Conference and Exposition of Rural Roads" here today, he said that we need to address the concerns, the needs and aspirations, the apprehensions and the anxieties of our rural people in all developmental plans and projects. Shri Shekhawat expressed his concern that a major challenge we face today is that of balancing the growth process and bridging the various 'divides'. The 'divide' between the urban and rural areas has been among the most significant ones. It is rather unfortunate that in the rural areas, incomes of many have dwindled and farm households have become more prone to stress and insecurity. The problem of farmers' suicides is a matter of grave anxiety that highlights the urgency to take up programmes for integrated rural development. Shri Shekhawat opined that the complete information on construction of rural roads including allocation of funds, progress of expenditure should be widely disseminated; for this information and knowledge being in public domain will be the most effective way to ensure efficient and corruption-free utilization of public funds under the watchful eyes of the public. Shri Shekhawat said that not only the 'Pradhan Mantri Gram Sadak Yojana' is being given a new thrust but development of rural roads constitutes one of the six components of "Bharat Nirman Initiative". Success in achieving the targets under these programmes would certainly go a long way in improving the much needed rural infrastructure. The development of rural roads is now aimed to be taken up on the basis of systematic network planning and that there is distinctive focus on quality assurance. Shri Shekhawat released "Quality Assurance Handbook for Rural Roads" on the occasion. He congratulated the Ministry of Rural Development for taking the initiative to develop Vision Document for Rural Roads Planning for the next 20 years and hoped that the conclusions and recommendations of this Conference would result in significant impact on the development of our rural areas. Following is the text of the Vice President's address on the occasion: "I am happy to be amidst you in this Conference which represents the national commitment to build dependable rural infrastructure for all-round rural development. I thank Shri Raghuvansh Prasad Singh, Hon'ble Union Minister of Rural Development for having given me this welcome opportunity. I offer my greetings to all participants of the Conference. At the inauguration of the Conference yesterday, the key to open the door for discussion was handed over to you. Now I am here to take the key back and close the workshop. This implies that discussions being over, it is time to digest the conclusions and get set for the hard work ahead in implementation so as to successfully achieve the objectives of Vision Document for Rural Roads : 2025.

1226. (24-5-2007) NEW DELHI : The telecom sector further expanded by adding 4.9 million in the number of telecom subscribers during the month of April 2007 thereby taking the total number of telephones in the country to more than 211.7 million, as compared to 146.20 during April 2006, *i.e.*, a growth of 44.8% during May 2006- April 2007. The GSM segment has also shown an increase of 4.13 million during the month of April 2007. While the CDMA segment registered an increase of 1.01 million the fixed segment has declined by 0.23 million. All these made the teledensity to improve further to 18.7%. In the GSM segment, Tamil Nadu telecom circle added more than 4.4 lakh subscribers during April 2007. In the CDMA segment, Uttar Pradesh (W) added 1.96 lakh subscribers during the period. The growth of broadband connections improved further and at the end of March 2007, about 2.29 million broadband connections were provided and coverage of broadband connectivity by public sector service providers has reached 962 cities. Further, the total number of existing ISP licencees is 382. Under Bharat Nirman Programme, out of the 66,822 villages, so far 47747 villages have been provided with Village Public Telephones (VPTs). The remaining 19075 villages are to be covered by November, this year.

1227. (24-5-2007) NEW DELHI : The Ministry of Rural Development has released Grants-in-aid amounting to Rs.2.44 crore as part of first instalment to the 6 districts of JAMMU & KASHMIR as central assistance for the implementation of the Sampoorna Grameen Rozgar Yojana (SGRY) during the financial year (2007-08).

1228. (24-5-2007) NEW DELHI : The Ministry of Rural Development has sanctioned Rs. 2.76 crore of Grants-in-aid to 48 District Rural Development Agencies (DRDAs) of Madhya Pradesh towards part payment of first instalment of Central Share for the year 2007-08 under DRDA Administration as per Annexure. The funding pattern under the scheme is 75:25 between Centre and the State. The utilization of funds is to be in accordance with the DRDA administration guidelines and the release of the second instalment during 2007-08 is subject to the fulfillment of all the conditions as per the DRDA Administration guidelines.

1229. (24-5-2007) NEW DELHI : The Union Minister of External Affairs, Shri Pranab Mukherjee today left on an official visit to four countries, namely Cyprus, Libya, Germany and Belgium. His first stop would be in Cyprus where apart from a one-to-one and a delegation-level meeting with H.E. Mr. Yiorgos Lillikas, the Foreign Minister of Cyprus, Shri Mukherjee will call on the President of Cyprus, H.E. Mr. Tassos Papadopoulos. Talks are expected to cover bilateral relations, and regional and multilateral issues of mutual interest. The visit to Cyprus follows the decision arrived at during the visit to India of the President of Cyprus in April 2006 to constitute a high level Ministerial dialogue between the two countries to take the traditionally close and warm relationship between the two countries forward in the light of the changing global and regional situation and to better utilize each other's complementarities in trade and economic matters. This will be the first visit by an Indian External Affairs Minister in over two decades. Prime Minister Shri Vajpayee had visited Cyprus in October 2002 and Minister of State for External Affairs Shri Omar Abdullah had visited Cyprus in April 2002. India and Cyprus have traditionally supported each other on issues of importance to each other. Cyprus' membership of the EU has given rise to greater scope for closer collaboration between our two countries. India has consistently supported the sovereignty and territorial integrity of Cyprus. India supports a peaceful resolution of the Cyprus problem in accordance with relevant Resolutions of the UNSC. Both countries share similar views on the need to combat and eradicate the scourge of terrorism. Within the UN, both countries share the need for early conclusion of the Comprehensive Convention on International Terrorism.

1230. (24-5-2007) NEW DELHI : Implementation of Centrally sponsored scheme "skill development initiative" The Cabinet Committee on Economic Affairs today gave its approval for implementing the scheme "Skill Development Initiative" at a total cost of Rs.550 crore. The Scheme is a Centrally Sponsored Scheme with 100% Central Assistance. The objective of the Scheme will be: (i) to provide training to school leavers, existing workers, ITI graduates, etc. to improve their employability by optimally utilizing the infrastructure available in government and private institutions and industry. Existing skills of the persons can also be tested and certified under this scheme; (ii) to build capacity in the area of development of competency standards curricula, learning material and assessment standards in the country. The training under SDI scheme will be provided by various Vocational Training Providers (VTPs) under Central Government, State Government, Public and Private Sector and Industrial establishments. To begin with, 1896 Govt. ITIs and 3218 private ITCs affiliated to the national council for Vocational Training (NCVT) will be eligible to participate in the scheme as VTPs. Once the scheme takes off, the mechanism will be evolved for empanelment of other private VTPs by the Apex Committee. One million persons would be trained or their existing skills tested and certified over a period of five years. About 200 modules for employable skills as per industry and labour market demands would be identified and course curriculum developed. On an average, expenditure of Rs.5000/- per persons is expected to be incurred on imparting training and certification of work force. Therefore, direct expenses for a million persons is 10,00,000 x Rs.5000 = Rs.500 crore. In addition, expenditure on training support services, studies administrative cost would be Rs.50 crore. The minimum age limit for persons to take part in the scheme is 15 years but there is no upper age limit. Directorate General of Employment & Training will appoint assessing bodies to assess the competency of the workforce. The assessing body will be an independent agency, which will not be involved in conducting the training programmes. This, in turn, will ensure quality of training and credibility of the scheme to a greater extent.

1231. (24-5-2007) NEW DELHI : The Union Cabinet today gave its approval for the following: (i) Jammu & Kashmir Reconstruction Plan for earthquake affected areas at a cost of Rs.635.88 crore to be implemented over a period of two years *i.e.* 2006-07 and 2007-08. (ii) Additional Central Assistance to the State of Jammu & Kashmir for implementing the Reconstruction Plan in the form of grant component of Rs.572.29 crore and loan component of Rs.63.59 crore. (iii) Release of a grant of Rs.150.00 crore during 2006-07 and Rs.146.58 crore during 2007-08, to the State of Jammu & Kashmir, totalling a net grant of Rs.296.58 crore. This will enable the State of Jammu & Kashmir to undertake long-term reconstruction of the damaged infrastructure including housing.

1232. (24-5-2007) NEW DELHI : The Union Cabinet today gave its approval for exemption of all textiles and all textile machinery manufactured in India from textiles Committee Cess under section 5E of the textiles Committee Act, 1963. The exemption of textiles Committee cess under section 5E of the Textiles Committee Act, 1963 will rationalise the tax and cess burden on the textile sector in the changed scenario of global competitiveness and thus improve competitiveness of Indian textile sector in global markets.

1233. (24-5-2007) NEW DELHI : The first stage written examination to be conducted by the Railway Recruitment Board, Bhopal for Employment Notice No. 02/2005 for category No. 01 to 04 for Jr. Clerk, Jr. Accounts Clerk, Commercial Clerk, Trains Clerk fixed on 27.5.2007 and 03/06/2007 at Bhopal, Jabalpur, Kota, Bilaspur, Raipur, Nagpur, Bhilai-Durg and Indore is postponed till further orders. New dates for the above examination will be advertised later.

1234. (24-5-2007) NEW DELHI : The Railways have generated Rs.3619.92 crore of revenue earnings from freight traffic during the month of April 2007 as compared to Rs. 3327.77 crore during the corresponding period last year, registering an increase of 8.78 per cent. Railways carried 60.68 million tonnes of freight traffic during April 2007 as compared to 58.09 million tonnes carried during the corresponding period last year, an increase of 4.46 per cent. The Net Tonne Kilo Metres (NTKM) went up from 39420 million during the month of April 2006 to 39552 million during April 2007, an increase of 0.33 per cent. Of the total earnings during the month of April 2007, Rs. 1376.95 crore came from transportation of

26.45 million tonnes of coal, followed by Rs. 298.55 crore from 3.08 million tonnes of foodgrains, Rs. 327.84 crore from 6.29 million tonnes of cement, Rs. 240.56 crore from 2.84 million tonnes of petroleum oil and lubricant (POL), Rs. 257.07 crore from 3.62 million tonnes iron ore for exports, Rs. 156.33 crore from 2.14 million tonnes of fertilizers, Rs. 170.11 crore from 1.55 million tonnes of iron & steel for steel plants, Rs. 169.76 crore from 4.49 million tonnes of raw material for steel plants and Rs. 622.75 crore from 10.22 million tonnes of other goods.

1235. (24-5-2007) NEW DELHI : Urging the Indian industry to make our growth processes both efficient and inclusive, the Prime Minister, Dr. Manmohan Singh outlined a Ten Point Social Charter for this purpose. Inaugurating the National Conference and Annual Session 2007 of the Confederation of Indian Industry (CII), here today, Dr. Singh invited corporate India to be a partner in making ours a more humane and just society. The Ten Point Social Charter spelt out by the Prime Minister includes healthy respect for workers and investment in their welfare, corporate social responsibility, employment to the less privileged, resist excessive remuneration and discourage conspicuous consumption, and investment in people and in their skills. Elaborating further, the Prime Minister asked the industry to desist from non-competitive behaviour, invest in environment-friendly technologies, promote enterprise and innovation, fight corruption at all levels and promote socially responsible media and finance socially responsible advertising. Reminding the captains of industry that we are what we are because of what our Motherland has given us, Dr. Singh said, "the time has come for us to ask ourselves what can we give her back. India has made us. We must make Bharat." Shri R. Seshasayee, Shri Sunil Bharti Mittal, Shri S.S. Mehta, diplomats, representatives of business and industry were among those present.

1236. (24-5-2007) NEW DELHI : The Union Cabinet today gave its approval for exemption of all textiles and all textile machinery manufactured in India from textiles committee Cess under section 5E of the textiles Committee Act, 1963. The exemption of textile committee cess under section 5E of the Textiles Committee Act, 1963 will rationalize the tax and cess burden on the textile sector in the changed scenario of global competitiveness and thus improve competitiveness of Indian textile sector in global markets.

1237. (25-5-2007) NEW DELHI : Following are the excerpts from the Report to the people 2004-07 specifically on the programmes run by the Ministry of Rural Development.. The Report was released by the Prime Minister Dr.Manmohan Singh on 22nd May, 2007. Bharat Nirman is a four-year programme (2005-09) for achieving identified goals in six selected areas of rural infrastructure of which drinking water, housing and roads is managed by the Ministry of Rural Development. In these areas the aim is to have universal coverage, where every village will have access to safe drinking water and – for a population of at least one thousand, or

500 in hilly / tribal areas – access to all weather road. In addition, we intend to build 60 lakh houses and add one crore hectares of irrigation capacity. The estimated investment is over Rs. 1,74,000 crore. Internal and extra-budgetary resources also contribute to investment under the programme. The goal for drinking water is to ensure that estimated 55,000 habitations without safe source of drinking water, estimated 2.8 lakh habitations that have slipped back from full coverage, and estimated 2.17 lakh habitations that have problems of water quality are provided access to safe drinking water. 66,802 habitations will be connected to a road aimed over the period 2005-09 through construction of 1.46 lakh km of roads and upgrading of 1.94 lakh km of existing roads at an investment of approximately Rs. 48,000 crore. Most of the yearly targets have been met for projects undertaken through Bharat Nirman, except in a few States. Programmes for rural roads, rural housing and rural drinking water supply are on track. 9,481 habitations had been connected by January 2007, with over 30,000 km length of new roads and nearly 29,000 km length of upgraded roads. Over 23 lakh houses had been constructed. 1.5 lakh habitations had been provided save drinking water as per norms. The National Rural Employment Guarantee Act has been passed. For the first time, it recognises the right to work as a fundamental legal right and entitles the rural poor to guaranteed employment for hundred days. Over 1.4 crore households have benefited under the Rural Employment Guarantee Scheme under the Act made operational in 200 districts initially with expansion to another 130 districts during 2007. Over 500,000 works are under operation under the Act in different parts of the country, of which over half are in the area of water conservation and drought-proofing, contributing to rebuilding of the natural resource base. A social safety net of this dimension has not been undertaken ever before anywhere in the world. The law commits the Government to expand the Rural Employment Guarantee Scheme throughout the country within five years.

1238. (25-5-2007) THIRUVANANTHAPURAM: Kerala Chief Minister V.S. Achuthanandan said here on Thursday that the disciplinary action taken by the Communist Party of India (Marxist) against party leaders had raised concern among the cadre. The party Polit Bureau will discuss the issue at its meeting in New Delhi on May 25 and 26. Replying to questions at a press conference, the Chief Minister said the Polit Bureau had received complaints from party leaders on the action taken against leaders in Thrissur and other places recently. As a Polit Bureau member, he had also received copies of the complaints.

1239. (25-5-2007) NEW DELHI : Following are the excerpts from the Report to the people 2004-07 on the Ministry of Minority Affairs. The Report was released by the Prime Minister Dr.Manmohan Singh on 22nd May, 2007. Minority affairs have been given focus through creation of the Ministry of Minority Affairs. A bill for providing Constitutional status to the Minorities Commission has been introduced in Parliament. A Commission has been set up to identify how best the welfare of socially and economically backward sections among minorities, including through reservation in education and government employment, may be ensured. A High Level Committee chaired by Justice Rajindar Sachar has submitted its report on the social, economic and educational status of the Muslim community in India and the report has been tabled in Parliament. The UPA Government is following up on the recommendations, with a view to acting swiftly on the recommendations so that effective measures are taken soon for amelioration of the condition of minorities. The overall communal situation remained under control and there has been a sharp fall in the number of communal incidents. Timely and effective action was taken in some of the recent communal incidents. The National Integration Council has been reconstituted and has met after a gap of 12 years. The Communal Violence (Prevention, Control and Rehabilitation of Victims) Bill has been introduced in Parliament for prevention and control of communal violence, protection of witnesses, expeditious disposal of cases, immediate and effective steps for relief, rehabilitation and compensation to the victims of communal violence, and expeditious investigation and trial. The trend of communalisation of education has been reversed. The National Curriculum Framework for School Education has been revised. All autonomous bodies under the Ministry of HRD were requested to review those activities that have possibly given rise to the perception of communalisation of education and to take suitable corrective measures. The Prime Minister's 15-Point Programme for Welfare of the Minorities has been recast as follows to make it monitorable, to focus action sharply on issues intimately linked with the social, educational and economic uplift of minorities, to provide for earmarking of outlays in certain schemes and through location of developmental facilities in minority concentration areas, and to prevent communal disharmony and violence.

1240. (25-5-2007) NEW DELHI : The Union Minister of Shipping, Road transport & Highways, Thiru T.R. Baalu has asked the States to formulate the plans for developing and strengthening the State Highways on the lines of National Highways Development Programme (NHDP) which is under implementation for the National Highways. Thiru Baalu was delivering the Valedictory address at the Conference on 'Public-Private Partnership (PPP) in State Highways' here today. Thiru Baalu said that the Planning Commission has already written to the Chief Ministers suggesting the formation of a State Highway Development Programme (SHDP). Thiru Baalu informed that some of the States have initiated ambitious programmes for such PPP projects while others are in different stages of the process. In this context, he said that States like Andhra Pradesh, Chhattisgarh, Gujarat, Kerala, Madhya Pradesh, Maharashtra, Punjab, Rajasthan, and Tamil Nadu have adopted PPP approach for development of roads in their states. Thiru Baalu said that just as the development of the National Highways is considered essential for the socio-economic development of the country, the State Highways are an equally important component in the infrastructure development roadmap of the country. The accelerated development of State Highways, in a phased and time-bound manner, would not only provide an improved hinterland connectivity but would also kick-start the accelerated socio-economic development in the hitherto lesser developed regions of the nation and the State Highways need to be strengthened and developed on the lines of the development strategy envisaged for the National Highways of the country, he said. Thiru Baalu said that to effectively take up the state highway development programmes, similar organisations like the NHAI need to be created in the States for implementing the SHDP. The State Governments may evolve a suitable mechanism for harnessing the benefits of the PPP regime for all round development of the State Highways. In this context, he also informed that the National Highways Authority of India has been vested with sufficient powers to sanction projects on a fast-track basis. The NHAI is also being strengthened further to enable it to take up larger programmes at an accelerated pace. The Minister said that the Centre has laid down comprehensive policy guidelines for private sector participation in highways sector and have also announced several incentives such as tax exemptions and duty-free import of road building equipment and machinery. He informed that Model Concession Agreements have also been finalised for major road projects. He pointed out that the huge upfront capital investment and high risk of revenue collection have been recognised as potential deterrents to private sector participation and to address this, in addition to giving several incentives, the Government has also decided to offer some projects on annuity basis and a number of projects have been taken up on annuity payment system. Thiru Baalu said that the development of road infrastructure on PPP mode has not only come to stay in India but has made its inroads in the developing world as well. In India, under the NHDP, the NHAI has awarded 78 contracts aggregating to a length of around 4,550 kms at a cost of Rs.300.50 billion. So far 15 projects aggregating to a length of 896 kms at a cost of Rs.46 billion have been completed. During the financial year 2007-08, a length of 2,995 kms at an estimated cost of Rs.196.50 billion are to awarded on PPP basis under NHDP Phase-V for six laning of identified National Highways. Similarly, 3,278 kms of National Highways have been identified for development to 4/6-lanes at an estimated cost of Rs.213 billion on the PPP mode under the NHDP Phase-III. Giving details of the new five phases of NHDP, Thiru Baalu said that it includes four-laning of 12,109 kms of National Highways under the NHDP Phase-III, two-laning with paved shoulders of 20,000 kms of National Highways under the NHDP Phase-IV, six laning of 6,500 kms of stretches of Golden Quadrilateral and other high density stretches under the NHDP Phase-V, construction of 1,000 kms of Expressways under the NHDP Phase-VI and construction of flyovers, ring roads, interchanges and bypasses under the NHDP Phase-VII. He said that these phases are slated for completion by 2015 at an estimated cost of Rs.2,35,430 crores.

1241. (25-5-2007) NEW DELHI : The UPA Government has just completed three years in office. On this occasion, it released a "Report to The People", setting out in great detail the policies and programmes it has been pursuing to make India's economic growth processes socially and regionally more inclusive. The guiding principle of the Government has been to ensure that, while sustaining higher rates of economic growth, the improved performance of the economy must contribute to employment generation, poverty reduction and human development. The aim of each of its flagship programmes is to ensure that growth is more equitable and that it empowers the most deprived of citizens. However, the government recognizes that it has a long way to go in addressing the needs and concerns of all sections of society, especially the poorest. The UPA Government came to power to address their felt needs and aspirations. It remains committed to that goal and that vision.

1242. (25-5-2007) NEW DELHI : The Central Government has revoked the prohibition imposed on transmission/re-transmission of FTV.com India Channel on all platforms with effect from today. Otherwise, the 60-day ban was to continue till May 30, 2007. The revocation is subject to the condition that the suspended period of prohibition of six days shall be added to the penalty in case of any future violation of the Cable Act/Rules. FTV.com India Channel have regretted their error and assured that such error will not be repeated in future. They have assured that they have put in place a strict vigilance committee to oversee the programme content telecast on FTV.com India Channel so that there is no violation of Programme Code contained in Cable Television Networks (Regulation) Act, 1995 and also assured that any programming considered inappropriate by the Ministry will be immediately removed. The Central Government had imposed a prohibition of two months on transmission of FTV.com India Channel for telecasting programmes such as 'Midnight Hot' that were against good taste and decency and were likely to adversely affect public morality with effect from 01.04.2007.

1243. (25-5-2007) NEW DELHI : Following are the excerpts from the 'Report to the People 2004-2007' on Ministry of Corporate Affairs. The report was released by the Prime Minister Dr. Manmohan Singh on 22nd May, 2007. "Drafting and introduction in Parliament of a new bill to comprehensively revise the Companies Act is targeted during 2007-08 for providing a legal frame that is easy to understand and implement and responsive to dynamic changes in the international business scenario. In order to ensure a suitable regulatory regime for competition, the Ministry has introduced a bill in the Parliament to amend the Competition Commission Act so that issues that had prevented the Competition Commission of India from becoming fully operational on a sustainable basis get resolved. The Commission will function not only as a market regulator for preventing anti-competitive practices, but will also serve as an expert body having advisory and advocacy functions. During the year 2007, the Government aims to complete the process of enactment of amendments to the Competition Act, 2002, select the chairperson and members of the Competition Commission of India and the Competition Appellate Tribunal, appoint the staff of the Commission and Tribunal, and provide for infrastructure and amenities for the Tribunal. The interface of industry with regulatory bodies like taxation authorities and registration authorities is being made transparent, simple and hassle-free through initiatives like the MCA-21 and income tax computerisation e-governance projects under the National e-Governance Plan. The offices of Registrars of Companies (RoCs) have been restructured. Under MCA21, all registration related functions of the Registrar of Companies have been transformed successfully into e-governance mode, with 80% documents now being filed by companies and professionals from their offices or homes. In order to provide greater freedom with accountability in the professions of chartered accountants, company secretaries and costs and works accountants, the related statutes have been amended. New Indian Accounting Standards, incorporating international best practices, have been developed and notified. A bill to provide for limited liability partnerships (LLPs) has been introduced in Parliament to provide for a new form of business organisation that combines the limited liability aspect of companies with the high degree of flexibility in internal management available in partnerships. This structure is expected to significantly benefit small enterprises and professionals engaged in providing various services, and also encourage venture capital investments. The National Foundation for Corporate Governance has been set up in association with industry and professional associations to serve as a platform for deliberations on issues related to corporate governance, with the focus being on adoption and implementation of a country strategy on corporate governance with active involvement and participation of all stakeholders, dissemination of good corporate governance practices to small and medium enterprises and creating an interface on corporate social responsibility. The Government proposes to establish an Indian Institute of Corporate Affairs to provide policy research and knowledge support."

1244. (25-5-2007) NEW DELHI : The 16th Session of the Indian-Iraqi Joint Commission Meeting for Economic and Technical Cooperation took place in New Delhi on May 22-25, 2007. The Iraqi delegation was led by Dr. Hussain Al-Shahristani, Minister of Oil of the Republic of Iraq and Shri Murli Deora, Minister of Petroleum and Natural Gas of the Republic of India led the Indian delegation. The talks were held in an extremely cordial and friendly atmosphere reflecting complete understanding and common bonds of strong ties of brotherhood of the people of the two countries. The Joint Commission reviewed with great interest bilateral commercial, economic, industrial, scientific and technical cooperation as well as the achievement in this regard since the last session. Deliberations in the Joint Commission included discussions for enhancing cooperation in the areas of trade, finance, investment, private sector cooperation, oil & gas, industry, electricity, transportation including railways, telecommunication and agriculture. Technical, educational, scientific & cultural cooperation including cooperation in higher education, offer of ICCR and other scholarships, cooperation in culture & tourism and science & technology, cooperation in human resources development and health and mutual legal assistance were also discussed. India and Iraq agreed to convene the 17th Session of the Joint Commission in Baghdad on a date to be mutually agreed upon.

1245. (25-5-2007) NEW DELHI : The Health Minister said that I am delighted to participate in the Convocation of Pt. B.D. Sharma Post Graduate Institute of Medical Sciences (BDSPGIMS), Rohtak. I congratulate all the graduate and post-graduate students for their academic performance and the faculty members for shaping the young minds. My greetings to the Director, faculty members, scientists, technologists, government functionaries, students and distinguished guests. During the last forty seven years, the Institute has generated more than six thousand medical professionals who are playing a key role in providing quality Medicare to the needy patients in different parts of Haryana and other parts of the country and abroad. Of course PGI Rohtak every year removes the pain of the people using the best of technology and care of over 1.6 lakh outpatients and over 73,000 inpatients. I would like to present the "Profile of Medicare". Dear Graduating students, when I see you all, in front of me, a scene of our country appears which links the new doctors and their role in the national mission. What is that scene? In our country, 700 million people live in 600,000 villages equivalent to 200,000 panchayats. We have 2020 Vision Document prepared by TIFAC, which indiates about the typical disease pattern which will be faced by the country during the period now to the year 2020. It is expected that HIV/TB combination, water borne diseases, cardiac diseases will be the predominant diseases and we have to find solutions for diagnosing and treatment. Also there are challenges for researchers for discovering molecule leading to drugs for various diseases such as diabetics, cancer, allergic diseases, inflammatory diseases, and certain type of new pattern of diseases in the tribal sector such as sickle cell disease. Many of you may take up healthcare practice in various fields and some of you may opt for research and development. The opportunities for you in the country, will be challenging equally both in the urban and rural areas. With the development of electronic connectivity and knowledge connectivity, and the spreading of health care centres and quality education we should be able to provide quality health care to our rural citizens. I am sure many of you will find working in rural areas to be really challenging. First and foremost, it is necessary to activate all the 411 Primary Health Centres and 85 Community Health Centres. Tele-medicine, in combination with PHCs and CHCs will bring the best possibilities in diagnostic and treatment from urban to rural areas. Another area which is knocking at our doors is preventive healthcare. Some of you may participate in the research, development and use of vaccines against HIV, malaria and even against the cardiac diseases. There are several other avenues such as application of stem cell therapy for many ailments like treatment of heart failure and diabetics. Students should be aware of such developments taking place in the country and elsewhere. I have selected the topic for discussion "Removing the pain is God's Mission."

1246. (25-5-2007) NEW DELHI : Inaugurating the second review meeting of health sector programmes in North Eastern States, the Union Minister for Health & Family Welfare, Dr. Anbumani Ramadoss said that I am very happy that the eight NE states had responded enthusiastically to the institutional restructuring and embraced the National Rural Health Mission (NRHM) strategies with zeal. I know there are many difficult and tenacious problems relating to restructuring of systems, convergence within the Health Department and its management structures, convergence with other Departments, shortages of manpower, etc. which need to be still resolved and require vigorous and sustained efforts from your side. The Mission provides you with the opportunity to take proactive action and I am sure that the opportunity provided will not be squandered. Besides Health Ministers from the eight North Eastern States, Union and State Health Secretaries, Secretary, AYUSH, Mission Directors and senior officials from the Centre as well as North Eastern States were present at the meeting. Appreciating the efforts made by the States to improving health care of the people under the NRHM, the Minister said the second year of NRHM has also seen increased focus on improvement in institutional deliveries and immunisation, further strengthening the institutional framework right down to the Block levels, focused stress, greater convergence within the health sector programmes, etc. in keeping with the Mission's aim of providing universal access to health care in accordance with the needs of the people, bringing about reduction in child and maternal mortality, population stabilisation, communicable disease control, etc.

1247. (25-5-2007) NEW DELHI : In the 15 months since the Special Economic Zones (SEZ) Act and Rules were notified on 10th February 2006, investments of the order of $ 8 billion have already been made and another $25 billion investment is underway. This was indicated in the reply on behalf of India by Shri G.K. Pillai, Commerce Secretary, at the World Trade Organisation (WTO) Trade Policy Review Meeting for India in Geneva today. "As far as SEZs are concerned, I think the WTO Secretariat was a little premature in expressing doubt about their effectiveness in boosting both investment and employment… So far, over 31000 people have got direct employment and this is expected to rise to 100,000 by the end of this calendar year and to 4 million by the end of 2010. The large number of textile, gems and leather SEZs being established would provide employment for a less skilled labour force", he said, allaying WTO doubts expressed in the WTO Secretariat report on this score. Underlining macro-economic sustainability, the reply states that the recent rise in inflation is due to (i) the global acceleration in inflation and the rise in world commodity prices, including food and energy; (ii) the slower rise in Indian interest rates that lagged the rise in world rates. The fiscal situation, which earlier used to raise some disquiet among the international financial community, is now firmly under control. Since the passing of the Fiscal Reform and Budget Management Act, in July 2004, the fiscal deficit has declined steadily to reach 6.3% of GDP in 2006-07(BE). Thus, one of the major factors that could lead to higher long-term inflation is now in abatement as a result of extensive fiscal reforms. "India's trade basket is diversifying rapidly. Moreover, the direction of India's trade, both exports and imports is increasing with developing countries in Asia, East Asia, Africa and Latin America. India also proposes to introduce, in a phased manner, the Duty Free Quota Free Scheme for LDCs this year", he said. Referring to concern expressed by several delegations that in addition to tariffs, India imposes several other taxes on imports, Shri Pillai clarified the position as follows: "In the first place, India levies basic customs duties on imports. In addition, imported articles are liable to an additional duty which is equal to the excise duty leviable on a like article produced or manufactured in India. This provides a level playing field to domestic production vis-a-vis imports. That apart, a special additional duty of customs @ 4% has been imposed on imported articles to counterbalance the sales tax, State value added tax, local tax or any other charges leviable on a like article on its sale, purchase or transportations in India. Once again, only to provide a level playing field".

1248. (25-5-2007) NEW DELHI : Following are the excerpts from the 'Report to the people 2004-07' on tourism & culture. The report was released by the Prime Minister Dr. Manmohan Singh on 22nd May, 2007. '11.5 Tourism: There has been impressive growth in foreign tourist arrivals, foreign exchange earnings and employment generation. The UPA Government has encouraged public-private partnerships in tourism. A new scheme of Creation of Land Bank for Hotels has been introduced to help meet the shortage of hotel accommodation all over the country, especially in view of the Commonwealth Games 2010. Policy and guidelines on eco-tourism have been formulated for involving local community and minimizing the likelihood of conflicts between use of resources for tourism and livelihood of local inhabitant. Long-term multi-entry tourist visas of five-year duration have been introduced for nationals of 18 countries'. '11.7 Classical languages: A new category of classical languages has been created and Sanskrit and Tamil have been notified as classical languages. A scheme has been launched for providing scholarships for Tamil scholar'.

1249. (25-5-2007) NEW DELHI : It has been the clear and consistent policy of the Election Commission that the bye elections shall be held at the earliest possible opportunity in order to ensure that no segment of the Indian people remain unrepresented for long time. There is 1 (one) clear vacancy in Legislative Assembly of Tamil Nadu from 142-Madurai West Assembly Constituency due to death of sitting member Shri S.V.Shanmugam on 5.2.2007.

1250. (25-5-2007) NEW DELHI : Shri Ashwani Kumar, Minister of State for Industry in a meeting with Mr. Salaheddine Mezouar, Minister of Industry, Trade and Economy Upgrading of Morocco at Rabat yesterday, emphasised the fields of aeronautics, information technology, automobiles, pharmaceuticals, textiles, tourism and infrastructure as the most prospective areas of joint cooperation and partnership between India and Morocco. "In the present day world of globalisation, strategic geographical location of Morocco and its extant FTA agreements with several countries, offer substantial opportunities for enhancement of trade exchanges as well as joint ventures which can eventually be utilised for export to American, European, Arab and African markets.", Shri Kumar said. The Moroccan Minister expressed his appreciation of the growing presence of Indian companies in Morocco and highlighted the recent agreement signed by Morocco with Tata Consultancy Services to establish an off-shoring delivery centre and a project to impart national training and e-governance. He also stressed that both countries should intensify their exchanges and work together for mutual benefit of both the nations. Shri Ashwani Kumar is on a visit to Morocco to participate in the Symposium on 'South-South Cooperation in the fields of energy and industry – challenges and opportunities' being held today.

1251. (25-5-2007) NEW DELHI : The Ministry of Rural Development has sanctioned Grant-in-aid of Rs.4.72 Lakh to the Gangtok DRDA of Sikkim towards part payment of first instalment of Central share for the year 2007-2008 under DRDA Administration. The funding pattern under the scheme is 75:25 between Centre and the State. The utilization of funds is to be in accordance with the DRDA administration guidelines and the release of the second instalment during 2007-08 is subject to the fulfillment of all the conditions as per the DRDA Administration guidelines.

1252. (25-5-2007) NEW DELHI : Civil Works for various Renewable Energy Systems and Landscape Development has been started at Renewable Energy Park at Bhanjakhri Water Falls, Gangtok. This State level Park is getting Rs. One Crore as grant from Union Ministry of New and Renewable Energy (MNRE). Public awareness activities such as Rajiv Gandhi Akshay Urja Diwas, District Advisory Committee functions, New Renewable Source Energy (NRSE) exhibitions and Solar Energy and Small hydro power programmes are organized under this project. Dr. N.P. Singh, Advisor, MNRE discussed this project with Shri K.S. Tobegy, Director of Sikkim Renewable Energy Development Agency (SREDA) at Gangtok today along with proposals for 2007-08. The Ministry of New Renewable Energy has been implementing comprehensive programmes for the development and utilization of various renewable energy sources in the country. As a result of a number of technologies and devices have been developed and have become commercially available. These include bio-gas plants, improved wood stoves, solar water heaters, solar cooker, solar lanterns, street lights, ponds, wind electric generators etc. Energy technologies such as hydrogen, fuel cells and bio-fuels are being actively developed.

1253. (25-5-2007) NEW DELHI : Government has notified International Centre for Automotive Technology (iCAT) as an accredited "Type Approval and homologation" agency of India under Central Motor Vehicle Rules. iCAT is a state-of-the-art centre coming up at Manesar, about 60 km from Delhi, under the ambitious National Automotive Testing and R&D Infrastructure Project (NATRiP) for providing wide range of testing, research and development services to the automotive industry within and outside the country. NATRiP is a Rs.1718 crore mission of the Department of Heavy Industry to set up world class automotive testing, homologation and R&D infrastructure in India. Currently, iCAT has an investment of Rs.62 crore and the facilities are spread over more than 8 acres of land. The Centre has already started rendering valuable support services to the automotive industry in the country. An investment of Rs.400 crore under NATRiP for setting up added facilities by way of tracks and testing infrastructure is currently underway on additional 42 acres of land being allotted by the Government of Haryana. Once completed by 2010, iCAT would be one of the most modern automotive technical centres in this part of the world and would meet the country's full range of testing, R&D and homologation requirements. iCAT will be equipped with the state-of-the-art facilities to test and validate all categories of vehicles including two/three wheelers, cars, MUV/SUVs, light, medium and heavy commercial vehicles, gensets and entire range of off-road vehicles. The facilities at iCAT would be versatile and capable of testing and developing vehicles propelled by alternative fuels and alternate propulsion systems. The infrastructure coming up at iCAT includes two state-of-the-art Centres of Excellence in the areas of Noise, Vibration & Harshness (NVH) and component designing and development, both being focus areas for advanced automotive research in India. This would enormously help the automotive industry, especially the component industry of this region, which accounts for nearly one third of the national auto sector turnover. iCAT would also provide global trade related testing and certification services to OEMs within India and outside in active collaboration with the Vehicle Certification Agency (VCA), of the UK Government with which NATRiP has signed an MoU. iCAT's birth as an independent type approval agency reflects reaching of a major milestone by NATRiP.

1254. (25-5-2007) NEW DELHI : The Prime Minister Dr. Manmohan Singh will inaugurate and address the Conference of Chief Ministers of States/UTs on power related issues, scheduled to be held here on Monday, the 28th of this month. The conference, Chaired by the Prime Minister, will have the following issues as its agenda: (i) programme for rapid expansion of generation in the next five years (ii) reduction of losses (T&D/ATC) through a crash programme (iii) Improving functioning of electricity markets by ensuring greater competitiveness, including through open access (iv) Rural electrification; and (v) Energy conservation and demand side management The scheduled conference is a follow up of the recently concluded States Chief Secretaries/Power Secretaries last month. In that conference, there was a general consensus on the issues relating to reduction of losses, control of power theft, accelerated expansion of generation capacity in the next five years, need for facilitation and encouragement by States in 'open access' in transmission and distribution. It may be recalled that in the Chief Secretaries' Conference the progress of rural electrification under the *Rajiv Gandhi Grameen Vidyutikaran Yojana* was also reviewed and the States were asked to formulate their plans for rural electrification and share them with the Ministry of Power at the Centre.

1255. (25-5-2007) NEW DELHI : Deputy Chairman, Planning Commission, Dr. Montek Singh Ahluwalia today called upon the Private Sector to prepare for a bigger role in the development of infrastructure. Inaugurating the Conference on Public Private Partnership in State Highways, here, he said latest estimates of the Planning Commission indicate that economy was likely to grow at an average of 9 per cent plus during the Eleventh Plan period. This would need a major increase in the investment requirement for infrastructure. He said the scale of investment in infrastructure sector would require an increase of about 3.5 per cent over the current level of 4.5 per cent of GDP by the terminal year of the Plan. With commitments to fund huge investments in social sectors including education, agriculture, health and rural infrastructure, it would be difficult for government to meet investment requirements for infrastructure sector, particularly the large capital intensive projects. The private sector will have to play a crucial role in participating in building national and State highways through public private partnership. The requirements would have to be scaled down if the entire programme is to be carried out by public sector alone, he cautioned. He said the tolling alone cannot ensure the money required for funding road programmes and the government would have to make capital subsidy available. For this purpose, we have in place the viability gap scheme where a number of projects from different States have already been sanctioned. He said the Model Concession Agreement clearly lays out the framework for ensuring the interests of both the contractual parties like risk allocation. For this purpose viability gap funding scheme has been introduced and a number of projects from different States have already been sanctioned. Member Secretary Planning Commission R.R Shah said a whopping Rs.1, 30,000 crores would be needed for upgrading the state highways. H said money was being routed for building roads through the Viability Gap Funding while money was also being provided by the India Infrastructure Finance Company Limited. Pointing out that Rs.43,000 crores were required to give facelift to the rural roads, he said the government has provided Rs.8,000 crores for upgrading roads in the Northeastern region. The Conference has been organized by Central Government to serve as a forum for sharing knowledge and experience aimed at attracting private investment on a much larger scale for the development of State highways through Public Private Partnership (PPPs). It may be recalled that significant progress has been made in initiating an expanded National Highway Development Programme (NHDP) with an estimated outlay of Rs.2,20,000 crores. The bulk of the highway programme is proposed to be undertaken through Public Private Partnership (PPP) as a means of attracting private capital, improving efficiencies and reducing costs. This would include expressways, six-laning and four-laning projects, and also selected two-lane highways.

1256. (25-5-2007) NEW DELHI : As per available information 1,21,410 employees of media organizations are covered under the Employees' Provident Fund Scheme. Out of these contribution in respect of 1,06,611 employees is being received regularly.

1257. (25-5-2007) NEW DELHI : Retail prices of most of the essential commodities at four main metropolitan centres have remained stable over the week ending 22nd May except some marginal variations in the prices of some commodities. At Delhi, prices of mustard oil and potato declined; price of loose tea increased; and prices of wheat, atta, rice, sugar, gram, onion, vanaspati, tur dal, packed salt and groundnut oil remained steady. As part of measures taken by the Government to check rise in prices of essential commodities, zero duty on import of pulses has been further extended upto 31st March 2009.

1258. (25-5-2007) NEW DELHI : Shri Kamal Nath, Union Minister of Commerce and Industry and Mr. Akira Amari, Minister of Economy, Trade and Industry of Japan signed the Memorandum of Understanding (MoU) between India and Japan for cooperation in the field of Intellectual Property Rights, at Tokyo yesterday. Capacity building, human resource development and public awareness programmes are the three main areas of cooperation covered in the MoU. Information exchange and experience sharing are also envisaged in the agreement. Both countries will draw up Annual Action Plans to implement the MoU which will include the detailed planning for carrying out of the cooperation activities including the scope of the action. It is hoped that the MoU will go a long way in fostering the cooperation between India and Japan. The MoU follows the Joint Statement towards Japan-India Strategic and Global Partnership made by Prime Minister Dr. Manmohan Singh and Prime Minister Mr. Shinzo Abe on 15th December, 2006 which confirmed the willingness of the two Governments to continue to cooperate in capacity building activities in intellectual property, including in developing human resources.

1259. (25-5-2007) NEW DELHI : Pawan Hans has been given NOC to operate as 'Scheduled Operator' in India. The Company will now join the club of scheduled airlines such as Indian Airlines, Air India etc. The Company is also exploring possibilities of venturing into fixed wing operations. Pawan Hans, an ISO 9001:2000 certified, is one of India's leading helicopter company. The Company was incorporated in 1985 with the objective of providing helicopter services to the petroleum sector, linking inaccessible areas of the country and operating charters for promotion of tourism. Since inception the company has operated a number of helicopters and offered a wide range of services through its fleet of 34 helicopters consisting of Bell 206L4, Bell 407, Dauphin SA 365N, Dauphin AS 365N3 and Mi-172. In addition, Pawan Hans is also acquiring two new Dauphin N3 helicopters and delivery of these helicopters would be in Sept/Oct., 2007. Pawan Hans is a leader in providing offshore helicopter support in India. Its helicopters operate for ONGC at Bombay High and Hardy Exploration at Chennai. PSUs such as GAIL use them for pipeline surveillance. The company also has a strong presence in the North East. Its helicopters are deployed in the States of Arunachal Pradesh, Meghalaya, Sikkim and Tripura. Regular passenger services are being run under the aegis of these State Governments. The company also provides helicopters to Andaman & Nicobar & Lakshadweep islands for inter-island helicopter services.

1260. (25-5-2007) NEW DELHI : The Industry Minister said that I am indeed delighted to visit the Maruti Udyog plant in Gurgaon and address the members of this unique institution. I greet Shri Jagdish Khattar, Managing Director, Management team, scientists, engineers and managers of Maruti Udyog Limited. I congratulate the Maruti team for pioneering action in introducing the people's car which has become affordable for the large sections of Indian population today, in spite of stiff competition faced by the entry of many international companies. From the study of Maruti profile, Maruti is now generating a profit of around Rs. 1560 Cr. in the financial year 2006-07. Maruti is presently producing over 6.7 lakh vehicles per annum using a plant which designed to produce 3.5 lakh vehicles annually. I understand, this has been achieved through continuous application of productivity enhancement strategy, particularly relating to dynamic inventory management, continuous implementation of cost reduction system. It is heartening to find that the price of Maruti models have virtually remained unchanged during the period 2001-02 to 2006-07, whereas in some case, the price has actually come down. These are notable development achievement and the nation is thankful to all the members of Maruti team for this singular contribution. With this background, I would like to discuss with you on the topic "Dynamics of Automobile Industry".

1261. (26-5-2007) NEW DELHI : The first set of national identity cards under the Pilot Project on Multipurpose National Identity Card (MNIC) was handed over to the citizens of Pooth Khurd at Narela by Shri D.K. Sikri, Registrar General, India & Registrar General of Citizens Registration, here today. A Pilot Project to understand and develop the processes for collection and management database of citizens as well as for smart card technology has been under implementation in Andhra Pradesh, Assam, Delhi, Goa, Gujarat, Jammu & Kashmir, Rajasthan, Tripura, Uttar Pradesh, Uttarakhand, Tamil Nadu, West Bengal and in the union territory of Pondicherry. The Pilot Project on MNIC has followed the census approach for collection of particulars of each individual in the pilot areas. Alongwith the particulars of individuals, photographs and finger biometrics have also been collected of all those who are 18 years of age and above. For management of citizens database, 20 centres have been set up, one at each Tehsil/Block headquarters equipped with computer terminals and on-line connectivity. The back-end management of these centres has been out-sourced to Bharat Electronics Limited (BEL). The personalization of cards has been entrusted to the Consortium of Central Public Sector Undertakings (CPSUs) comprising Bharat Electronics Limited (BEL), Electronics Corporations of India Limited (ECIL) and Indian Telephone Industries (ITI). The design of the card has been prepared with the help of National Institute of Design and carries a unique National Identity Number (NIN) for each of the citizens. The identity card being given to each individual citizen, has a micro processor chip with a memory of 16 KB which is a secure card. Besides having several physical features into the design of the card, it is the cyber security using 'asymmetric key cryptography' and 'symmetric key cryptography' that has made the card secure against the risk of tempering and cloning. The National Informatics Centre has made a major contribution towards developing the processes for database management and smart card technology. The rest of the citizens in the pilot areas shall be delivered cards by post for which special arrangements have been made with the Department of Posts for delivery. The cards will be sent to them in a packet which is tear-proof, temper-proof and waterproof. This has been specially designed for this project.

1262. (26-5-2007) NEW DELHI : The Union Home Minister, Shri Shivraj Patil has strongly condemned today's blast in Guwahati. He expressed condolences to the kins of those killed and wished speedy recovery to those injured in the incident. The Home Minister said that such incidents would not succeed in weakening the resolve of the Government of India to deal strongly with divisive forces in Assam and other north eastern states. Following the blast, the Home Ministry is in constant touch with the State Government and monitoring the situation regularly. The Union Home Minister has spoken to the Assam Chief Minister, Shri Tarun Gogoi. The State Government has been advised to remain vigilant and ensure that peace is maintained. The State Government has been assured of necessary help.

1263. (26-5-2007) NEW DELHI : The Union Minister of External Affairs, Shri Pranab Mukherjee began his tour of Cyprus by paying homage at the bust of Mahatma Gandhi located next to the Cyprus Parliament on Jawaharlal Nehru Avenue in Nicosia (the only such bust of a foreign leader in the area), yesterday. He then offered flowers at the statue of late President Archbishop Makarios III. Shri Pranab Mukherjee had arrived in Cyprus on May 24 night on his tour of Cyprus, Libya, Hamburg (ASEM Meeting), Brussels and Berlin (Indo-EU Troika). Shri Mukherjee called on President Tassos Papadopoulos. The discussions recalled the traditional long-standing and deep rooted friendship between Cyprus and India, India's consistent support for the territorial integrity of Cyprus as well as the UN Security Council Resolutions relating to the Cyprus problem. Bilateral relations particularly the possibilities of closer cooperation in trade and investment, knowledge-based industries, pharmaceuticals and energy were discussed. President Papadopoulos assured EAM of strong support from Cyprus as a member of the EU on matters of interest to India. Shri Mukherjee had one-to-one meeting with Cyprus Foreign Minister Yiorgos Lillikas followed by delegation level talks which carried on over lunch. Bilateral relations were discussed in detail in the context of traditional friendship between the two countries and the history of close cooperation and support in the international forum. Possibilities of Cyprus playing a useful and cooperative role for promoting India-EU relations in political and economic terms were discussed. Cooperation in trade and investment, energy, tourism, pharmaceuticals, IT were discussed including through setting up of joint ventures. Closer and regular consultations between the two Foreign Ministries were also agreed upon. Cyprus reiterated their strong support for India's candidature as a Permanent Member for UN Security Council. Other issues discussed included India's civil nuclear programme, terrorism, climate change and developments in SAARC. Three agreements were signed between India and Cyprus– Agreement on Abolition of Visa Requirement for Diplomatic and Official Passport Holders,

Agreement on Combating International Terrorism, Organised Crime and Illicit Drug Trafficking, and Executive Programme on Cultural, Educational and Scientific Cooperation. Later, Shri Mukherjee met the President of Foreign Affairs Committee in the House of Representatives, Mr. Averof Neophytou. The following is the text of Shri Pranab Mukherjee's opening remarks at the joint press interaction: "I am delighted to be here in Cyprus, a country with which we have traditionally had very warm and close ties. I am here in pursuance of a decision taken when the President of Cyprus visited India in April 2006 to launch a high level ministerial dialogue between our two countries to prepare our relationship for the 21st century. It would interest you to know that this is my first visit to Europe since I assumed charge as the External Affairs Minister of India late last year. We are very happy that Cyprus is now a member of the EU. We have a strategic partnership with the EU and a comprehensive joint action plan to implement that partnership. Cyprus in the EU means that we have one more close friend in the Union. I have had a very productive and useful exchange of views with my counterpart and before that I was received by the President of the Republic. We have had substantive discussions on how best to take forward our bilateral relationship and have signed three important agreements. We also discussed regional and international issues of interest to both our sides. India has always supported Cyprus in its quest for unity and territorial integrity. Cyprus, in turn, has always been supportive of India's interests including in such important areas as our quest for permanent membership of the UN Security Council, our desire to expand our civil nuclear energy programme and our fight against terrorism. I am confident that my visit will help further strengthen the ties of friendship and cooperation that bind India and Cyprus."

1264. (26-5-2007) NEW DELHI : The Prime Minister, Dr. Manmohan Singh has condemned the violent bomb blast, which led to the killing of innocent citizens and injuries to many others in Assam. "Violent acts of this nature serve no purpose other than harm the life of ordinary people", he said. The Prime Minister has expressed his grief at the loss of lives and has sent his condolences to the families of the bereaved.

1265. (27-5-2007) NEW DELHI : The Committee of Experts set up by the Ministry of Tribal Affairs to look into the polices and action for the Primitive Tribal Groups (PTGs) of Andaman and Nicobar Islands has stressed the need of separate policies for each of PTGs namely Shompen, Great Andamanese, Onges and Sentinelese at the earliest. It has expressed concern over alarming increase in the population of the Islands and recommended immediate steps to restrict the population influx into the islands. The Expert committee which had its first meeting here today under the Chairmanship of Secretary, Ministry of Tribal Affairs was of the view that the vehicular traffic on the Andaman Trunk road passing through Jarawa Reserve should be substituted with the sea going vehicles and construction work on the road which runs through middle of Great Nicobar should be stop immediately. The details of the conclusions arrived at the expert committee meeting are as follows:-Within the distinctly different nature of the five PTGs of the Andaman and Nicobar Islands, it is important to have separate policies for each of the PTGs. A policy already exists for the Jarawa tribe, but there is no policy for the remaining four PTGs namely Shompen, Great Andamanese, Onges and Sentinelese. A policy for each of these PTGs needs to be put in place at the earliest. To enable these policies to be framed fixed studies of approximately three months duration need to be taken up. Though a policy exists for Jarawa tribe, it is not being implemented properly or monitored adequately. The Expert Committee will look closely into the implementation of Jarawa policy. While separate policies may be made for each of the PTGs, certain efforts which affect all the PTGs on the islands as a whole are necessary to be taken if these tribes and the environment ecology of the islands are to survive. An alarming increase in the population of the islands needs to be addressed forthwith. While a carrying capacity study has been commissioned to arrive at the optimum level of population the islands can sustain, it is not advisable to delay taking action until the results of the study are available. Acute shortage of drinking water, large scale construction resulting in the destruction of the environment is already apparent. Therefore, immediate steps need to be taken to restrict the population influx into the islands. There is a lack of sensitivity amongst the general population in the islands be in officials, settlers, school children or others regarding the situation of the PTGs. They are being seen as a curiosity item and that due to the adverse impact of the various activities on these heritage groups, they are on the brink of extinction, is little appreciated.-In the case of two PTGs namely Great Andamanese and Onges who are in full contact with the general population, the education that is being imparted needs to be carefully looked at and quickly reviewed. Though some efforts have been made to prepare material in their mother tongue namely Great Andamanese and Onge for teaching their children, no worthwhile efforts have been made to implement teaching in mother tongue. The quality of teaching material in Great Andamanese and Onge also needs a lot to be desired from the pedagogical point of view. It is also necessary to immediately look at this material and introduce it in a proper form in the schools and provide teachers knowing their language.-A portion of Andaman Trunk Road (ATR) passes through Jarawa reserve. The Supreme Court has ordered that vehicular traffic on this stretch of road be stopped. However, a stay has been obtained and the vehicles continue to ply and in fact their number has increased in the recent years. If the Jarawas are to be protected, from unwarranted and undesirable interaction with other people, it is important to impose significant restrictions on the volume of traffic on the ATR and to have a plan to discontinue all the traffic within the Jarawa reserve within a certain time frame.

1266. (27-5-2007) NEW DELHI : The Government has introduced Energy Conservation Codes for commercial buildings. Initially, implementation of the codes will be voluntary but will be made mandatory soon under the Energy Conservation Act 2001 for the buildings having connected load of 500 kw or more. The implementation of the codes will reduce energy consumption from 25% to

40% and will yield annual saving of about 1.7 billion units. The codes sets a minimum efficiency standards for external wall, roof, glass structure, lighting, heating, ventilation and air conditioning of the commercial buildings in all the five climatic zones in the country. The State Government will have the flexibility to amend these codes to suit local or regional needs and notify them accordingly. Launching the codes here today, Minister for Power, Shri Sushil Kumar Shinde said that the codes aimed at bringing down the energy consumption of the commercial buildings through the efficient design and use of resources. Highlighting the Government's efforts to increase power production in the country, Shri Shinde said that the plans had been made for capacity addition of about 70 thousand MW during the 11th Plan and by 2012 the country would be self sufficient to the great extent in the power sector. He said that efficient use of energy and check the leakages in energy consumption is must as by conserving only 20% of energy the country would save about Rs. 20,000 crore. The Minister said that very soon the Government would put in place appropriate institutional structure to oversee implementation of the codes throughout the country with involvement of states and other stakeholders. Effective awareness and outreach programme would be launched to overcome strong first cost bias that usually needs owners to under-invest in energy efficiency during building design and construction. The State Governments would be requested to integrate the energy codes in city bylaws through municipalitie, he added.

1267. (27-5-2007) NEW DELHI : The Third Meeting of the India-GCC Industrial Forum is scheduled to be held in Mumbai on 29 and 30 May, 2007. Shri Kamal Nath, Union Minister of Commerce & Industry, will lead the Indian delegation to this important meeting, which is expected to be attended by Commerce & Industry Ministers of the six Gulf Cooperation Council (GCC) States – namely, Bahrain, Kuwait, Oman, Qatar, Saudi Arabia and the United Arab Emirates (UAE), besides the Secretary General of GCC. The delegation from GCC will be around 300 strong. The event will focus on 'India-GCC Investment Opportunities' and would comprise of plenary sessions on Investing in India, Investing in GCC and on four sectors namely, Real Estate, Energy (Oil, Gas and Power), Petrochemicals and Infrastructure. At the Plenary Session on Opportunities for Investment on 29th May, 2007, there will be presentations on 'Investment Scenario in India' by Dr. Ajay Dua, Secretary, Department of Industrial Policy & Promotion and on 'Special Economic Zones – Opportunities for Investment in India' by Shri G.K. Pillai, Commerce Secretary. The Session on "Opportunities in Infrastructure" on 30th May will be chaired by Shri T.K.A. Nair, Principal Secretary to the Prime Minister. The Protocol of the Third meeting will be signed on 30th May at the valedictory session which will be addressed by Shri Kamal Nath and the GCC Ministers.

1268. (27-5-2007) THIRUVANANTHAPURAM: The Polit Bureau of the Communist Party of India (Marxist) has sent a strong and unequivocal message to the party's leaders, cadres and the people of Kerala with its unprecedented decision to suspend simultaneously, and in a seemingly even-handed manner, V.S. Achuthanandan and Pinarayi Vijayan from the Polit Bureau. The Polit Bureau decision, subject to review by the Central Committee, will not immediately affect the positions they hold, Chief Minister and State secretary respectively, but it is a major turn in the history of the CPI(M) in Kerala. What the CPI(M) Polit Bureau has tried to communicate to all concerned is that it would not allow the party to be caught in a complex web of factional pulls and pressures or let any differences between State party leaders to result in the frittering away of the massive mandate that the people of Kerala gave the CPI(M) and the Left Democratic Front (LDF) in 2006. It also speaks volumes for the difference between the CPI(M) and many other parties, national and regional, which have seldom been able to act decisively to end factionalism. The immediate cause for the Polit Bureau decision are certain remarks made by Mr. Achuthanandan and Mr. Vijayan against each other. Mr. Achuthanandan is reported to have implied, while replying to a question at a press briefing following a Cabinet meeting last week, that Mr. Vijayan was also responsible for leaking party-related information to the media.

1269. (28-5-2007) NEW DELHI : News item has appeared in print and electronic media that individual taxpayers have to submit Form 16 – a certificate of tax deducted at source – along with income tax returns to obtain refunds. It is hereby clarified that the Government has amended Rule 12 of the Income Tax Rules so as to notify the new income tax return forms for assessment Year 2007-08 with effect from 14th May 2007. These new return forms (other then new Form ITR-7 for charitable/religious trusts and institutions) are annexure-less. A taxpayer is not required to file any document relating to computation of income or challans or TDS certificates (Form 16 or form 16A) or TCS certificates alongwith these annexure-less returns, irrespective of whether a refund is claimed or not. In view of the above position, the contents of the news item regarding the need to file Form 16 for claiming refund is baseless. The taxpayers are advised to strictly follow the instruction annexed with the new return forms and Rule 12 of the Income Tax Rules. The new return forms along with the instruction and Rule 12 are available on the website http://incometaxindiaefiling.gov.in.

1270. (28-5-2007) NEW DELHI : Following are the concluding remarks of the Prime Minister, Dr. Manmohan Singh at the Chief Ministers Conference on Power Sector, here today. " We have had a very fruitful exchange of opinions on a wide range of issues concerning the Power Sector. As I had said earlier in my opening remarks, electricity is vital for sustained economic growth and the purpose of this conference was to focus on finding practical, pragmatic solutions to the problems of this sector. From the tenor of our discussions, I believe that there is broad agreement among us on the measures to be taken to improve the availability of power while at the same time improving the financial health of utilities. We have covered in detail all the five themes listed in the agenda. A number of valuable suggestions were made by Chief Ministers which may require a review of some of our policies, programmes and approaches. I am sure that the Power Ministry will take due note of each and every suggestion made by the Chief Ministers. Some Chief Ministers have also drawn attention to a few other issues having a bearing on the Power Sector –such as availability and pricing of gas, royalties for coal, incentivising capacity additions in coal-rich states, securing environmental clearances in a timely manner, timely and adequate coal linkages, benefit sharing in hydro-projects and many other suggestions were also made. The resolutions that we are adopting today broadly lay down the parameters on which we agree to move forward to improve the performance of the Power Sector. I would like to dwell on a few of these and also on some other issues. I am happy that there is general agreement on the need to rapidly reduce T&D losses. Building on our resolve today, I request all Chief Ministers to launch a campaign against theft in their states. The Electricity Act provides for constitution of special courts for speedy disposal of such cases. These courts should be set up and operationalised soon. At the same time, the Centre will provide financial assistance for upgrading transmission and distribution systems. As losses come down to agreed levels, we will reward performing states appropriately. For this purpose, the ARDRP scheme is being revised and the contours of this revised scheme will be announced within two months. The Planning Commission, the Finance Ministry and the Power Ministry should finalise this scheme within this time-frame. It is satisfying that the States are rolling out ambitious capacity addition plans so that we can eliminate power shortages by the year 2012. Put together, the capacity addition plans of the Centre and States, in the 11th Plan are over three times the achievement in the 10th Plan. While these ambitions are laudable, we need to have effective project implementation and monitoring structure in place. We will set up a dedicated, professionally managed National Power Project Management Board attached to the Ministry of Power. This Board will keep track of all projects which are to be completed in the 11th Plan and will assist state and central utilities in ensuring that project implementation milestones are met for every single power project. This is the only way we can achieve the ambitious targets we have set for ourselves.

1271. (28-5-2007) NEW DELHI : A seven-member delegation from the United Arab Emirates (UAE), led by their Under Secretary, Ministry of Interior, Lt. General Saif Abdulla Al-Shaafar held discussions with an Indian delegation, led by the Union Home Secretary, Shri Madhukar Gupta here today. Issues of security-related cooperation between India and UAE were discussed during the meeting which lasted over an hour. Both sides agreed to move forward meaningfully in this direction. The delegation will now be having further detailed discussions with the concerned officers and agencies in the Government of India to work out details of agreements and institutional arrangements to carry forward this cooperation. The UAE delegation also called on the Union Home Minister, Shri Shivraj Patil.

1272. (28-5-2007) NEW DELHI : Dr. Pradipto Ghosh, Secretary, Ministry of Environment and Forests, said the new methodology used for tiger census is different from the previous one. Interacting with Media in New Delhi today, he said earlier only pugmarks were obtained to identify individual tigers. Continuous monitoring of individual tigers in a particular area was done over a time period to arrive at this figure. The new methodology uses camera trap, sighting, pugmarks and genetical tests amongst others. This has been approved by veteran Scientist Dr. Madhav Gadgil and endorsed by the Ministry. Dr. Ghosh added it is not possible to count juvenals in the new methodology. He said we would accept the findings by the Wildlife Institute of India which will be ready by the end of this year. Regarding the trade of tiger organs he stressed that this is illegal. China has a large number of conservation in citu and they use various organs for pharmaceutically and other products. We have requested China to identify usage of tiger organs on the packaging of their products. China has about 5000 tigers in their farms. Regarding rehabilitation of Asiatic lions, Dr. Ghosh reiterated that lion is the pride of India not just of Gujarat. Government of Gujarat is at the forefront of conservation, but they are not joining this project. Palampur Sanctuary in Mahdya Pradesh is ready for this purpose and lots of communities have been rehabilitated to prepare the sanctuary, which is a second home to lions. On the decline number of vultures it is difficult to say without scientific survey. It is wrong to jump on any conclusions, he added. Refuting SEZ in the forest area, he said the Ministry does not have any plan of this kind. He clarified that there is multi structural partnership for afforestation in waste lands of forests, where sharing of benefits are negotiated between local community, land owning agency and other stake holders. A legal basic contract for these parties is under preparation.

1273. (28-5-2007) NEW DELHI : The Minister for Overseas Indian Affairs, Shri Vayalar Ravi launched the Overseas Indian Facilitation Centre (OIFC) here today. Addressing the gathering, he said that OIFC would function as a non-profit body with the objective of Promoting Overseas Indian Investment in India and facilitating Business-to-Business partnership between Indian Business and Overseas Indians and extend a host of advisory services to PIO's and NRI's. He further said that this will be "one stop shop" for the Overseas Indians where at one platform they can get information, assistance and handholding services. This will be function in a Public-Private Partnership mode. While the Ministry will provide the policy support, the centre will be managed by the Confederation of Indian Industry (CII), he added. Elaborating the objects of the OIFC, Shri. Ravi said that it would promote the overseas Indian investment into India and facilitate business partnerships, by giving authentic and real time information and also by provide paid for handholding services to the potential Overseas Indian Investors. It will establish and maintain a Diaspora Knowledge Network, by creating a database of Overseas Indians to leverage the knowledge resources through an electronic platform and function as a clearinghouse for all investment related information. It will also assist States in India to project investment opportunities to overseas Indians in the infrastructure and social sectors. The objectives of the OIFC will be to bring the Indian States, Indian Business and potential Overseas Investors on the same platform and to facilitate the investors to identify the investment opportunities. The OIFC would provide a host of advisory services to PIO and NRIs. These would include matters such as consular issues, stay in India, investment and financial issues etc. As regards Overseas Indian Workers; our aim is to help transform them from mere savers to investors. 23 billion dollars which comes as remittance mostly goes into bank deposits and consumption expenditure. The challenge before us is to convert these savings into investments, he added. The Minister further said that India is emerging as a much sought after destination for investment in the world. Overseas Indians estimated at over twenty five million spread across 130 countries are an important economic constituency with the ability and willingness to invest in the emerging opportunities in their home country. We would like the vast and diverse Overseas Indian community to benefit from investment opportunities in India. The establishment of OIFC would serve all these purposes.

1274. (28-5-2007) NEW DELHI : Army Chief General JJ Singh, who is also Chairman Chief of Staffs Committee (COSC) returned today after leading a week long Tri-Service Military Delegation to China. This was the third visit of an Indian Army Chief and the first by any Chairman of the COSC to China. General JJ Singh's visit to China was the follow up of the MoU signed by the two countries for defence cooperation, during the visit of Mr. Pranab Mukherjee, the then Defence Minister to China last year. The visit marked a decision in the engagement and mutual confidence building mechanism by seeking to hold periodic joint military training exercises between the two Armies. General JJ Singh arrived in Beijing on 21 May to a ceremonial welcome by his Chinese counterpart General Liang Guanglie at the headquarters of the Central Military Commission (CMC), the top military organ of China. During the weeklong visit, the General held wide ranging talks with his counterpart as well as General Guo Boxiong, Vice Chairman of the CMC and other senior defence officials. His schedule included a call on the Chinese Vice President Zeng Quinghong and the newly appointed Foreign Minister, Yang Jiechie as well as visits to operational formations and higher military training institutions like Academy of Military Sciences (AMS), Beijing. The Indian delegation visited various PLA formations and institutions including the 15 Airborne Corps at Wuhan, 28 Air Division at Hangzhou and a naval base at Shanghai. The two Armed Forces have upgraded military to military cooperation in a graduated manner which began from setting up of "peace and tranquility" mechanism along the LAC and has over the past few years graduated to holding of cultural and sports events amongst forces deployed in the border areas; allowing each other's military "observers" at military exercises and maneuvers; extending facility of attending courses of instructions at each other's military training facilities and finally leading to inviting high level visits by respective military delegations to each other's military establishments.

1275. (28-5-2007) NEW DELHI : Following the text of Dr. Montek Singh Ahluwalia Speech at the Conference of Chief Ministers and Power Ministers of

States. I consider it a privilege to have the opportunity to address this meeting of Chief Ministers on the Power situation facing the country. The National Development council has mandated that the Eleventh Five Year Plan should aim at the twin objective of achieving faster and more inclusive growth. Both these objectives require a massive improvement in the situation facing the Power Sector. The 9 percent growth target we have set certainty requires a much faster increase in supply of electricity than we have had thus far, and with much less dependence on high cost captive power. Expansion in electricity supply is also needed if we want growth to be more inclusive. Improvement in the quality of life in rural areas is a key objective of the Eleventh Plan and yet, large numbers of our population in rural areas remain without access to electricity. The percentage of unelectrified rural households varies from a low of 10% of rural households in Punjab to 80% in Uttar Pradesh Orissa and West Bengal and as high as 95% in Bihar. Lack of reliable uninterrupted supply of electricity from the utilities is also a major constraint on the ability of our small and medium industries to improve their competitive strength and to grow in a competitive world. And yet it is precisely these industries that are crucial for inclusiveness since they are most likely to generate the increase in employment and the regional spread of industrialization that we need in the Eleventh Plan. I believe we are today at a critical point for policy credibility in this sector. We have been talking of power sector reform for over a decade. And yet, actual performance in this sector falls well below expectations, and indeed below the level of other infrastructure sectors. Consider for example the performance of telecommunications where we began the process of reforms some years after the power sector but where the sector has shown a dramatic improvement for some years. This is also beginning to be evident in roads, ports, airports and more recently the railways. The Eleventh Plan should be the occasion to achieve a decisive turnaround in the power sector also. Since time is limited, I will touch only very briefly on some important issues. Capacity creation is one of the themes of the conference and it is obviously critical. A rapidly growing economy, and especially one which wants to meet the large unfilled need for rural electrification, must plan for a bold expansion in generating capacity. The base documents distributed for the conference lay down a target of around 78,000 MW of additional capacity in the Eleventh Plan. This is indeed an appropriate target on the basis of need, which includes elimination of peaking shortages. However it is a formidable target in comparison with what we have achieved thus far. In the Tenth Plan period, against a target of adding 41000 MW, our actual achievement was only a little over 21000 MW.

1276. (28-5-2007) NEW DELHI : The three Delhi based AF Schools *i.e.* Air Force Golden Jubilee Institute (AFGJI), The Air Force School (TAFS) Subroto Park and Air Force Bal Bharati School (AFBBS) Lodhi Road have achieved more than 96% pass percentage in the recently declared all India Senior Secondary School Examination (Class – XII) conducted by CBSE. In all a total 611 children appeared in Class XII CBSE Examination and out of which 269 children scored more than 75% marks while 23 children scored 90%. Miss Snigdha Sahi of Air Force Golden Jubilee Institute (AFGJI), Subroto Park scored 95.2% marks in science stream (PCM with computer science) Sarakshi Chadha and Sangeetha Esther of AFBBS scored 100 marks in Mathematics and Informatics Practices respectively. Five children have scored 99 marks in various subjects. Over the years these schools have been achieving excellent results in the Board Examination.

1277. (28-5-2007) NEW DELHI : Some of the parameters for improvement in the quality of education as normally understood starting from enrolment to reduction in the dropout rates, from the pass percentage to the attendance of the teachers in the primary schools marked a quantum rise in Nagaland between 2002 to 2004. So also the case in the efficiency of the village health service delivery system measured in terms of number of child and adult patients visiting health centres in rural Nagaland. It also indicates improvement in the staff attendance, visit of the medical officers and even in the staff attitude. All this is reflected in a report by the UNICEF on the impact assessment of cummunitisation of public institutions and services in Nagaland. The unique scheme for involving the community was conceived under the stewardship of the then Chief Secretary of the state Shri R. S.Pandey and was launched after the passage of an act in 2002. Initially. The scheme focused on three very important areas : Elementary eduction, Grass root health services and Electricity management. The experiment evolved from the need to revitalize the massive welfare infrastructure and vast network of delivery services set up by the government which had become ineffective and dysfunctional. It is based on the philosophy of communitisation as an alternative to privatization as well as management by government. This philosophy attempts to combine the best of both approaches by substituting the private profit motive with enlightened collective self interest. It holds among other tenets, that when the empowered are not adequately motivated to perform, it makes sense to empower the motivated.

1278. (28-5-2007) NEW DELHI : India is conducting the 4th CISM Military World Games in Hyderabad and Mumbai in October this year. Nearly 127 countries are expected to participate in this mega event. Going by the size, this event is considered as the biggest sporting event, next only to the Olympics. In Olympics almost 25% of the medal winners are from the armed forces from world over. These Champions will comprise the 6000 strong participants world wide. India is conducting this mega event for the first time. The Military World Games are held under the aegis of CISM – Counseil International du Sport Militaire or the International Military Sports Council, better known by its acronym CISM, pronounced "*sizum*". Founded in February 1948 with five member nations, it is today the second largest multi disciplinary sports organisation in the world, and *the* largest authority for military sports. CISM with a membership of 127 nations, 38 from Europe, 45 from Africa, 26 from Asia and 18 from the Americas is recognised by the IOC and the UN, and is a key player on the international sport scene. The Military World Games is its biggest event, held once in four years, in the year preceding the Olympics. The participants are service personnel from the militaries of member nations, the finest and fittest fraternity of young men and women in the world! Though the five founding nations– Belgium, Denmark, France, Luxembourg and Netherlands – were from Europe, CISM had a global vision from its inception; its primary purpose was the promotion of worldwide good will through competitions in sport. CISM, open to the armed forces of all nations, aims to develop friendly relations between them and contribute to the international effort for universal peace. It promotes sport, physical education and harmonious development of military personnel, while encouraging solidarity and mutual support. Physical fitness is mandatory in the military sport as part of training ensures the military is 'fighting fit'! The concept of a healthy body hosting a healthy mind is not just a cliché in the forces. CISM while focusing on physical fitness and excellence in sport aims to use this as a building block in promoting selflessness, sportsmanship and brotherhood of mankind. The ideals and principles of CISM are enumerated in the Mission Statement adopted on its 50th anniversary, during the General Assembly held in Baden, Austria in 1998. CISM is an apolitical organisation, which fosters through sport, friendship between military athletes to promote international harmony. It adheres to the universal principle that "all human beings are born free and equal, in dignity and in rights", as stated in the Universal Declaration of Human Rights. CISM condemns all forms of discrimination towards a nation or a person on the basis of race, religion or political belief. It upholds democratic principles in its functioning, one nation represents one voice, majority rules and the General Assembly of member nations is its supreme authority. CISM by encouraging member nations to organize sports competitions in a spirit of equal opportunity, friendship, solidarity and fair play has succeeded in giving soldiers the opportunity to participate in some of the best international amateur competitions available. The council cooperates with all international institutions and organizations that share its objectives and encourages the assembly of citizens of the world.

1279. (28-5-2007) NEW DELHI : The following are the excerpts from the "Report to the People 2004-2007" on Heavy Industries & Public Enterprises. The report was released by the Prime Minister Dr. Manmohan Singh on 22nd May, 2007. The UPA Government has taken a number of measures through the Budget mechanism as well as through Plan programmes to improve the competitiveness of Indian industry. This has resulted in robust growth in the last three years, particularly in the manufacturing sector, which is the main driver of growth in the economy. The growth rate of the manufacturing sector has risen steadily from 8.7% in 2004-05 to 9.2% in 2005-06 to 11.3% in 2006-07. More importantly, this growth has been widespread, covering almost all segments of the manufacturing sector. Capital formation in the manufacturing sector is estimated to have grown by over 30% per annum during this period. 762 guidelines relating to Central Public Sector Enterprises have been withdrawn, and a number of other guidelines have been modified or merged to simplify their administration. Government has given greater managerial and commercial autonomy to successful Central Public Sector Enterprises. The powers of Navratna and Miniratna PSEs in regard to investment in subsidiaries and joint ventures, and for delegation of powers relating to human resource management, have been enhanced. The Government has delegated to Navratna and Miniratna PSEs powers for mergers and acquisitions and has relaxed the conditions relating to Government guarantee for retaining Navratna and Miniratna status. Powers to incur capital expenditure have been enhanced for Miniratna and other profit-making PSEs. A mechanism has been created for expeditiously including/deleting Central PSEs from Navratna category. The Government is considering guidelines on corporate governance for Central PSEs.

1280. (28-5-2007) NEW DELHI : The following are the excerpts from the "Report to the People 2004-2007" on Small Scale Industries & Agro and Rural Industries. The report was released by the Prime Minister Dr. Manmohan Singh on 22nd May, 2007. The Micro, Small and Medium Enterprises Development Act, 2006 provides the first-ever legal frame for covering services along with manufacturing under the concept of enterprises, progressive classification of enterprises, statutory consultative mechanism, establishment of a fund for promotion and development of such enterprises, preference in government procurement of products and services of such enterprises, effective mechanism for mitigating problems of delayed payments, etc. A major promotional package has been announced and this includes measures to address most of the concerns in areas of credit, cluster-based development, technology upgrade, marketing, infrastructure upgrade, etc. The corpus of the Credit Guarantee Fund is being revised from Rs. 1,132 crore in March 2006 to Rs. 2,500 crore over a period of five years. Following the credit policy for small and medium enterprises announced in 2005, outstanding credit to the sector increased from Rs. 135,200 crore in 2005 end to Rs. 173,460 crore in 2006 end. A major step has been taken towards provision of social security to labour in the unorganised sector in rural areas through enactment of the National Rural Employment Guarantee Act. The National Commission on Enterprises in the Unorganised Sector has been set up to act as an advisory body and a watchdog and to submit periodic reports to the Government. Its terms of reference cover broadly the entire gamut of issues relating to unorganised sector and it has done significant work on relevant legislation through wide-ranging consultations with stakeholders, particularly state governments with the objective of providing a social security net, including health insurance and other schemes for these workers. The Commission has also undertaken a review of labour laws in India for improving productivity and ensuring greater competitiveness and employment generation in various sectors, like textiles, IT and SEZs, consistent with labour rights. Cluster based growth poles, skill formation through public-private partnership, provision of micro-finance have been identified as priority areas. Measures are also being identified for protecting and promoting livelihoods for self-employed workers, through provision of credit, right to common property and natural resources, and use of public space to engage in economic activity. The report of the National Commission for Enterprises in the Unorganised Sector is near finalisation.

1281. (28-5-2007) NEW DELHI : The National Consumer Helpline, NCH has reported that it has been receiving the largest number of complaints from telecom companies. In April, it received 621 calls against main telecom service providers. The complaints related to delay in activation, unsolicited calls, excess billing, poor network coverage, wrong promises etc. Among the telecom service providers, MTNL, Idea and Tata Teleservices have been providing regular feedback to the consumer helpline on the complaints sent to them.Talks are being held with VSNL and Reliance also to have voluntary mechanism of forwarding complaints by NCH and receiving feedback from the companies. The NCH is available at toll-free-no 1800-11-4000. Through this helpline, consumers are guided in finding solutions to problems related to products and services. The helpline also facilitates filing of complaints by consumers against defaulting service providers.

1282. (28-5-2007) NEW DELHI : The Prime Minister, Dr. Manmohan Singh has stressed the need for a wide range of power sector reforms including open access and competition. Emphasizing the role of States and Centre in this reform process, the Prime Minister suggested that interstate transmission needs to be truly opened up to competition and a separate and independent government entity be set up to control the National Load Despatch Centre. In addition, he underscored the importance of reducing transmission and distribution losses, launching a crash programme for capacity addition and taking steps to attract private investment. Dr. Manmohan Singh said this while inaugurating the Conference of Chief Ministers on the Power Sector, here today, which was attended by Shri P. Chidambaram, Union Minister of Finance, Dr. Montek Singh Ahluwalia, Deputy Chairman, Planning Commission, Shri Sontosh Mohan Dev, Minister of Heavy Industries and Public Enterprises, several Union Ministers, Chief Ministers of States and Power Ministers of States. Speaking on the occasion the Prime Minister called for a National Mission on Conservation of Energy. Urging all Chief Ministers to reduce T&D losses to acceptable levels, Dr. Singh said, "The Centre will support the initiative through a revised Accelerated Power Development and Reforms Programme (APDRP) scheme through which we will reward performing states by converting loans to grants in an appropriate manner on achieving certain benchmark results." Stressing the need for a crash programme for capacity addition aimed at eliminating shortages latest by the year 2012, the Prime Minister said, "The targets are no doubt ambitious and a 'business as usual' approach will not suffice. We need specialized project management and monitoring capabilities to ensure timely commissioning of projects."

1283. (28-5-2007) NEW DELHI : The Steel Authority of India Limited (SAIL) will increase its installed capacity to 24.98 million tones by 2010 form the current level of 13 million tones. Initially the expansion plan of the company was to raise its capacity to 22.5 million tones by 2010 with an investment of Rs.37,000 crore. The revised estimate for the higher installed capacity along with the ongoing programme has been pegged at Rs.43,000 crore. Reviewing the progress of the expansion programme of SAIL here today, the Minister for Steel, Chemicals and Fertilisers Shri Ram Vilas Paswan urged the top management of the company to implement the programme on time. He also asked the chairman of SAIL to come up with a revised schedule for implementing the expansion plan with-in two days. The Minister said responsibility should be fixed for any kind of delay at different stages and action may be taken. Shri Paswan has also asked the Secretary, Ministry of Steel to review the progress in the first week of each month. There will be further reviews following the deadlines for important milestones with a six monthly appraisal. Officials not meeting the deadlines will be held responsible and action will be taken. Shri Paswan asked SAIL to avoid delay in the execution of the programme which costs the exchequer substantially. The Minister said, economic progress has thrown up a great opportunity to create a solid base for the steel sector and we will loose the opportunity unless we take timely action. He said, the Board of Directors of the Navaratna PSUs like SAIL have been given autonomy to take decisions and if there are any procedural snags it may be taken up with the CVC. The Chairman of the Steel Authority Shri S.K.Roongta made a presentation on the progress of the expansion programme and explained the difficulties faced. Secretary Ministry of Steel, Shri R.S. Pandey, Special Secretary Shri A.K.Rath and other senior officials were present during the review.

1284. (28-5-2007) NEW DELHI : The Prime Minister, Dr. Manmohan Singh has stressed the need for a wide range of power sector reforms including open access and competition. Emphasizing the role of States and Centre in this reform process, the Prime Minister suggested that interstate transmission needs to be truly opened up to competition and a separate and independent government entity be set up to control the National Load Despatch Centre. In addition, he underscored the importance of reducing transmission and distribution losses, launching a crash programme for capacity addition and taking steps to attract private investment. Dr. Manmohan Singh said this while inaugurating the Conference of Chief Ministers on the Power Sector, here today, which was attended by Shri P. Chidambaram, Union Minister of Finance, Dr. Montek Singh Ahluwalia, Deputy Chairman, Planning Commission, Shri Sontosh Mohan Dev, Minister of Heavy Industries and Public Enterprises, several Union Ministers, Chief Ministers of States and Power Ministers of States. Speaking on the occasion the Prime Minister called for a National Mission on Conservation of Energy. Urging all Chief Ministers to reduce T&D losses to acceptable levels, Dr. Singh said, "The Centre will support the initiative through a revised Accelerated Power Development and Reforms Programme (APDRP) scheme through which we will reward performing states by converting loans to grants in an appropriate manner on achieving certain benchmark results." Stressing the need for a crash programme for capacity addition aimed at eliminating shortages latest by the year 2012, the Prime Minister said,

"The targets are no doubt ambitious and a 'business as usual' approach will not suffice. We need specialized project management and monitoring capabilities to ensure timely commissioning of projects." Urging the States to continue the initiative on rural electrification on a war footing and reach electricity to all un-electrified villages by the year 2009, Dr. Singh said, "We, however, need to focus on development of appropriate revenue models for rural areas, protection of rural electrification assets and most importantly, deliver electricity through the wires!" Earlier, welcoming the Chief Ministers and delegates to the Conference and speaking on the occasion Shri Sushilkumar Shinde, Union Minister of Power, has said that today's conference was to address various issues which were critical for achieving the objectives of "power for all" and providing adequate electricity for various economic activities. The Minister hoped that the conference would help in renewing the common resolve to move forward collectively. In this the biggest challenge, he said, was to ensure rapid capacity addition in order to overcome the present shortages and also to meet the expected grown in demand for electricity in the country The state sector bears a heavy responsibility while its share in the installed capacity has been declining continuously in the last three decades which was 82.5 per cent at the end of the Fifth Five Year Plan in 1979 came down to 54 per cent at the end of the Tenth Five Year Plan. He said the role of Central Government is expanding though it was a supplementary, he said. Shri Shinde further said that the tremendous response from project developers to the ultra mega power projects has demonstrated that large investments could be mobilized through a transparent and competitive template providing a level playing field and in this process also deliver a very attractive and economic tariff for electricity. The Centre will pursue this scheme for at least in nine locations of the country. Shri Shinde informed the Conference that the Union Ministry of Power would launch within a month a new scheme called "Bachat CFL" at low cost, affordable even by the BPL families with a buy back provision for fused lamps so as to minimize environmental hazard through negligent disposal.

1285. (28-5-2007) NEW DELHI : Recent terror related incidences in various parts of the Country confirm our apprehensions that there exists a *Trance National Terror Network* operated and facilitated by ISI of Pakistan. The rise in ULFA terror activities, double push in infiltration across the borders of Pakistan, Bangladesh and Nepal, massive explosion in Hyderabad, arrest of a Imam with Arms and Ammunition in Ahmedabad, and arrest of terrorists with fake Indian currency in Delhi are all pointers to this *Trance National Terror Network.* The ULFA has triggered seven blasts in Assam in May alone killing 9 persons and injuring 100 others including attacks on migrant labour is a cause of concern. The central and the state government have completely failed in intelligence and tackling the situation. A bomb planted near Marwari Maternity Hospital, adjacent Fancy Bazar, successive blasts in Athgaon area, a blast in FCI godown, an explosion in Sibsagar town in upper Assam and an explosion in Bongaigaon district in lower Assam is a well thought out plan of ULFA to distabilise the state and drive out Hindi speaking people. Pakistan backed militants are desperately trying to infiltrate into Jammu and Kashmir and the infiltration attempts have nearly doubled in the past two months. What is worry some feature of these attempts, is that infiltrators are using Nepal and Bangladesh borders through launch pads setup by the ISI. It seems that militants across the border have regrouped and consolidated their position and are pushing through Poonch, Rajouri and Kupwara sectors. The connection of Huji-a militant outfit operative in Bangladesh, in bomb blast in Mecca Masjid in Hyderabad has added a new dimension to militancy in India confirming the existence of *Trance National Terror Network.* The arrest of Imam in Ahmedabad is also directly linked to this blast. All these developments have to be viewed on the backdrop of continuous demand by PDP for troop pull out and government's soft attitude exhibited in Round Table Conference. The UPA government has faltered in taking a tough stand against terrorism due to political expediency and vote bank politics. Bharatiya Janata Party demands immediate establishment of *Anti Terror Operative Unit* combining manpower and intelligence of various security and other agencies to deal with *Trance National Terror Network.*

1286. (28-5-2007) NEW DELHI : The Steel Authority of India Limited (SAIL) will increase its installed capacity to 24.98 million tones by 2010 form the current level of 13 million tones. Initially the expansion plan of the company was to raise its capacity to 22.5 million tones by 2010 with an investment of Rs.37,000 crore. The revised estimate for the higher installed capacity along with the ongoing programme has been pegged at Rs.43,000 crore. Reviewing the progress of the expansion programme of SAIL here today, the Minister for Steel, Chemicals and Fertilisers Shri Ram Vilas Paswan urged the top management of the company to implement the programme on time. He also asked the chairman of SAIL to come up with a revised schedule for implementing the expansion plan with-in two days. The Minister said responsibility should be fixed for any kind of delay at different stages and action may be taken. Shri Paswan has also asked the Secretary, Ministry of Steel to review the progress in the first week of each month. There will be further reviews following the deadlines for important milestones with a six monthly appraisal. Officials not meeting the deadlines will be held responsible and action will be taken. Shri Paswan asked SAIL to avoid delay in the execution of the programme which costs the exchequer substantially. The Minister said, economic progress has thrown up a great opportunity to create a solid base for the steel sector and we will loose the opportunity unless we take timely action. He said, the Board of Directors of the Navaratna PSUs like SAIL have been given autonomy to take decisions and if there are any procedural snags it may be taken up with the CVC. The Chairman of the Steel Authority Shri S.K.Roongta made a presentation on the progress of the expansion programme and explained the difficulties faced. Secretary Ministry of Steel, Shri R.S. Pandey, Special Secretary Shri A.K.Rath and other senior officials were present during the review.

1287. (28-5-2007) NEW DELHI : The Prime Minister, Dr. Manmohan Singh has stressed the need for a wide range of power sector reforms including open access and competition. Emphasizing the role of States and Centre in this reform process, the Prime Minister suggested that interstate transmission needs to be truly opened up to competition and a separate and independent government entity be set up to control the National Load Despatch Centre. In addition, he underscored the importance of reducing transmission and distribution losses, launching a crash programme for capacity addition and taking steps to attract private investment. Dr. Manmohan Singh said this while inaugurating the Conference of Chief Ministers on the Power Sector, here today, which was attended by Shri P. Chidambaram, Union Minister of Finance, Dr. Montek Singh Ahluwalia, Deputy Chairman, Planning Commission, Shri Sontosh Mohan Dev, Minister of Heavy Industries and Public Enterprises, several Union Ministers, Chief Ministers of States and Power Ministers of States. Speaking on the occasion the Prime Minister called for a National Mission on Conservation of Energy. Urging all Chief Ministers to reduce T&D losses to acceptable levels, Dr. Singh said, "The Centre will support the initiative through a revised Accelerated Power Development and Reforms Programme (APDRP) scheme through which we will reward performing states by converting loans to grants in an appropriate manner on achieving certain benchmark results." Stressing the need for a crash programme for capacity addition aimed at eliminating shortages latest by the year 2012, the Prime Minister said, "The targets are no doubt ambitious and a 'business as usual' approach will not suffice. We need specialized project management and monitoring capabilities to ensure timely commissioning of projects." Urging the States to continue the initiative on rural electrification on a war footing and reach electricity to all un-electrified villages by the year 2009, Dr. Singh said, "We, however, need to focus on development of appropriate revenue models for rural areas, protection of rural electrification assets and most importantly, deliver electricity through the wires!"

1288. (28-5-2007) NEW DELHI : The first meeting of India-UAE Trade Policy Forum was held here today, preceded by a one-to-one meeting between Shri Kamal Nath, Union Minister of Commerce & Industry and Shaikha Lubna Al Qasimi, Minister of Economy of the United Arab Emirates (UAE). Both the Ministers underlined the strong partnership that India and UAE enjoy in the field of trade and commerce, while noting that the partnership was still way below the potential. Both the Ministers expressed the hope that the Ministerial level Gulf Cooperation Council (GCC)-India Industrial Conference beginning in Mumbai tomorrow would promote a greater thrust to India's economic cooperation with the Gulf region as a whole. The two Ministers discussed a range of issues with a view to increasing the level of trade between the two countries. Shri Kamal Nath took up with the UAE Minister issues relating to opening of branches of Indian banks in UAE, including the State Bank of India (SBI), lifting of the ban on import of poultry products and removal of trade barriers such as registration guidelines, restrictive work permits, visa regime etc. relating to import of pharmaceutical and chemicals and allied products. The UAE in turn referred to anti-dumping measures on UAE products and companies and matters relating to the successful establishment and implementation of Orissa Alumina Joint Project. Trade between India and UAE stood at US $ 12.9 billion in 2005-06. Of this, India's exports to the UAE were valued at US $ 8.59 billion and imports from the UAE at US $ 4.31 billion. UAE is India's top trading partner in the entire WANA region, as the UAE alone represents 75% of India's export to GCC countries. Indian exports to the UAE account for 6% of India's global exports. Dubai is a major trade centre of re-exports and a gateway for the whole of Arab world. Revival of oil prices since late 1999 has strengthened the trading position of GCC countries in general and UAE in particular.

1289. (28-5-2007) NEW DELHI : The Finance Minister said that I am delighted to participate in the inauguration of India Development Marketplace-2007 (IDM-2007) organized by the World Bank. My interest to participate in this meet arises from the focus of the programme towards sustainable rural development in India. My greetings to all the participants who have submitted the proposals, award winners, experts, juries and distinguished guests. I had participated in the inauguration of India Development Marketplace-2004 (IDM-2004) where 20 innovations were selected. Out of these, two innovations have found place in today's exhibition based on its sustainable operation in the rural sector. One pertains to dew harvesting for drinking water in coastal Gujarat. I understand dew condensers have been successfully installed in a school, a warehouse and a few private homes in the area. The second one is on Assam's River Network Harnessing System being used as a medical delivery system to isolated regions. The originally conceived boat as a "ship of hope" is now being used to ferry medical teams to deliver healthcare throughout the year to the people in Assam region.

1290. (28-5-2007) NEW DELHI : A concept report titled 'Master Plan for Artificial Recharge to Ground Water' prepared by Central Ground Water Board (CGWB), aims at providing area specific artificial recharge technique to augment the ground water reservoir based on the twin important requirements of source water availability and capability of ground water reservoir to accommodate it. The report has been circulated to all the States/UTs.

1291. (28-5-2007) NEW DELHI : The Ministry of Rural Development has released Grants-in-aid to Assam amounting to Rs. 63.51 crore as third/additional instalment of Central assistance to 16 districts as central assistance for the implementation of the Sampoorna Grameen Rozgar Yojana (SGRY) during the financial year (2006-07) as per details below:

1292. (28-5-2007) NEW DELHI : The Ministry of Rural Development has sanctioned Rs. 4.54 crore of Grants-in-aid to 70 District Rural Development Agencies (DRDAs) of UTTAR PRADESH towards part payment of first instalment of Central Share for the year 2007-08 under DRDA Administration as per details below: The funding pattern under the scheme is 75:25 between Centre and the State. The utilization of funds is to be in accordance with the DRDA administration guidelines and the release of the second instalment during 2007-08 is subject to the fulfillment of all the conditions as per the DRDA Administration guidelines.

1293. (28-5-2007) NEW DELHI : The Ministry of Rural Development has released Rs. 200.00 crore as part payment of second instalment of Phase-IV for the projects under Pradhan Mantri Gram Sadak Yojana (PMGSY) to the Uttar Pradesh Gramin Sadak Vikas Abhikaran, which is the autonomous agency for receiving funds under the programme in the State. The grant is towards the Plan expenditure and will be subject to the conditions laid down from time to time in the guidelines of the Pradhan Mantri Gram Sadak Yojana and supplementary directions. PMGSY was launched in December 2000 as a 100 per cent Centrally Sponsored Scheme with a target of connecting every habitation that has a population of more than 1000 within the next three years and every habitation with a population of more than 500 by the year 2007 *i.e.* by the end of the 10th Five Year Plan through good all-weather road. A sum of Rs.20,400.70 crore has been released to the States/UTs towards the programme and up to December 2006, 35,868 roadworks covering a length of 1,07,569.08 Kms. have been completed.

1294. (28-5-2007) NEW DELHI : The Central Board of Trustees (CBT) of the Employees Provident Fund Organisation deferred its decision about the rate of the interest to be paid to EPF subscribers for 2006-07 and 2007-08 in view of the modal code of conduct for the Goa Assembly Elections. This was stated by the Minister of State (Independent Charge) for Labour and Employment, Shri Oscar Fernandes whiled talking to media persons after the meeting here yesterday evening. He said the next meeting of the CBT is likely to be held on July 2, 2007. This was the fifth meeting in a row of the CBT to decide the issue of interest rate to be credited to the accounts of over 4 crore subscribers of the Employees Provident Fund for the previous financial year. Earlier presiding over the meeting, Shri Fernandes, who is also chairman of the Central Board of Trustees, said, "the most telling effect of non-declaration of rate of interest will be felt in updation of annual accounts and furnishing of information of balances to members. The delay also leads to accumulation of Interest Suspense Account which draws adverse attention. It will also have implications in further roll out of the Re-inventing EPF India Project in other offices." He said that the para 60 of the EPF Scheme has been recently amended to allow crediting of interest at the previous rate for outgoing members to mitigate their hardships.

1295. (28-5-2007) NEW DELHI : According to media reports the Indo-US nuclear deal is almost ready for the approval of the governments of the two countries. A senior U.S. official has claimed that the deal is ninety ready. Constitutionally the Government of India is not required to seek parliamentary approval before signing an International agreement. Yet in this case the Prime Minister had given certain specific assurances to the Parliament of India last year.

Therefore, it is incumbent upon the Prime Minister to satisfy both Houses of Parliament before confirming India's commitment to the deal that the assurances he had given have been fulfilled. This is all the more necessary given the controversy generated by some provisions of the legislation passed by the U.S. Congress.

1296. (28-5-2007) NEW DELHI : The Prime Minister, Dr. Manmohan Singh has stressed the need for a wide range of power sector reforms including open access and competition. Emphasizing the role of States and Centre in this reform process, the Prime Minister suggested that interstate transmission needs to be truly opened up to competition and a separate and independent government entity be set up to control the National Load Despatch Centre. In addition, he underscored the importance of reducing transmission and distribution losses, launching a crash programme for capacity addition and taking steps to attract private investment. Inaugurating the Conference of Chief Ministers on the Power Sector, here today, Dr. Singh called for a National Mission on Conservation of Energy. Urging all Chief Ministers to reduce T&D losses to acceptable levels, Dr. Singh said, "The Centre will support the initiative through a revised Accelerated Power Development and Reforms Programme (APDRP) scheme through which we will reward performing states by converting loans to grants in an appropriate manner on achieving certain benchmark results." Stressing the need for a crash programme for capacity addition aimed at eliminating shortages latest by the year 2012, the Prime Minister said, "The targets are no doubt ambitious and a 'business as usual' approach will not suffice. We need specialized project management and monitoring capabilities to ensure timely commissioning of projects." Urging States to continue the initiative on rural electrification on a war footing and reach electricity to all un-electrified villages by the year 2009, Dr. Singh said, "We, however, need to focus on development of appropriate revenue models for rural areas, protection of rural electrification assets and most importantly, deliver electricity through the wires!" The Union Finance Minister, Shri P. Chidambaram, Power Minister, Shri Sushil Kumar Shinde, Deputy Chairman, Planning Commission, Shri Montek Singh Ahluwalia, other Union Ministers, Chief Ministers and Power Ministers from various States were among dignitaries present on the occasion.

1297. (28-5-2007) NEW DELHI : Following are the excerpts from the "Report to the People 2004-2007" on Railways. The report was released by the Prime Minister Dr. Manmohan Singh on 22nd May, 2007. The UPA Government has succeeded in ensuring a turnaround of the Indian Railways. Over the past two and a half years, railway freight volumes have grown by 8-10 per cent and growth in passenger volumes has doubled. As a result of improved supply and demand management, rational utilasation of capacity and a market-driven pricing policy, the Indian Railways are once again on track. Infrastructure development through public-private partnerships is being promoted. There has been on encouraging response to the offer to allow private container trains. Preliminary work on the proposed Dedicated Rail Freight Corridors has begun. Container business has been opened to the private sector. Increase in axle load, coupled with reduction in turnaround time of wagons from seven to five days, has contributed to incremental loading capacity of 120 million tonnes, resulting in incremental revenues of Rs. 7,000/ crore. Tariff has been rationalised by reducing the number of classes from over 4,000 to 18. Pricing policy has become market-driven and dynamic, with attractive discounts during the lean season and surcharge on busy routes during the busy season. The old strategy of resource allocation has given way to resource leveraging. Improvement in customer services and reduction in passenger fare, particularly for poorer sections, have been effected. Reforms have been introduced a human face, without losing sight of social obligations. In order to meet the transport demand of the economy and industry on the Delhi-Mumbai and Delhi-Kolkata trunk routes, building of two connected dedicated multi-modal freight corridors has been taken up on fast-track basis through a special purpose vehicle called the Dedicated Freight Corridor Corporation of India Ltd. at an estimated cost of Rs. 30,000 crore, with completion targeted during the Eleventh Plan period. The project will provide necessary infrastructure support for container, coal and other mineral traffic and will also improve passenger traffic on these routes. The UPA Government also proposes to undertake pre-feasibility studies and preliminary engineering-cum-traffic surveys for taking up freight corridors along the Golden Quadrilateral.

1298. (28-5-2007) NEW DELHI : The Union External Affairs Minister, Shri Pranab Mukherjee was received for an hour-long discussion by Libyan leader H.E. Col. Muammer Al Gaddafi at his desert camp near the coastal town of Sirte, yesterday. After a two-day visit to Cyprus, Libya is the second stop for Mr. Mukherjee, who is on a four-nation tour. The wide-ranging discussions were held in a very warm and cordial atmosphere. Traditional friendship between the two countries, India's support for Libya's position and principled opposition to sanctions were recalled. Bilateral cooperation, particularly cooperation in the oil and petroleum sectors, as well as human resource development were discussed. Col. Gaddafi said that the sky is the limit for cooperation between the two countries. While discussing regional issues, Shri Mukherjee briefed the Libyan leader on developments in SAARC, India-Pakistan composite dialogue, India-China relations as well as Trilateral India-Russia-China dialogue. India's relations with Africa and greater cooperation in this regard were also discussed. Col. Gaddafi said that he would himself work towards further strengthening India-Africa partnership. On international issues, discussions focused on the need for reform in the UN, including the UN Security Council structure. Col. Gaddafi reiterated that India has a right to have a permanent seat on the UN Security Council. Shri Mukherjee handed over a letter from Prime Minister Dr. Manmohan Singh inviting Col. Gaddafi to visit India. The Libyan leader said that he looked forward to visiting India.

1299. (29-5-2007) NEW DELHI : Following are the Prime Minister, Dr. Manmohan Singh's closing remarks at the 53rd meeting of the National Development Council's

Special Session on Food and Agriculture, here today: "We have reached the end of a long and fruitful discussion on the problems of our agriculture sector and possible strategies for revitalizing it in the next few years. The discussion was appropriate in many ways. It has focused our collective attention on agriculture and firmly placed it at the top of our priorities –both at the Centre and in the States. This is as it should be, given that over 60% of our people still depend on it for sustenance and livelihood. I also note that there is a broad agreement on the approach to be taken for improving the conditions of our farmers and the performance of our agriculture. We have covered a large number of issues impacting on all aspects on agriculture. At the end of the day's discussion, I am hopeful that our collective will and resolve can make a positive difference to future of our agriculture. In this room, we have a collection of the most important levels of national leadership in the nation and a wealth of wisdom. I am confident that if we commit ourselves individually and collectively to the task of revitalizing our agriculture, we can certainly transform our agriculture. I am also confident that the goal of 4% annual growth in agriculture and allied activities in 11th Five Year Plan is certainly feasible and achievable if only we are willing to take tough decisions and back it up with concerted action. During the course of our discussions, a number of very valuable suggestions were made by the Chief Ministers. The Planning Commission has taken note of each of these suggestions and will reflect on them in the coming months. What is striking from your comments is the diversity in views and opinions and the wide variation in priorities between states. This is but natural. We are all simultaneously all united to do everything in our power to get our agriculture once again on the road of prosperity. There are differences in the requirements of highly irrigated states and those of relatively dry states with very low rainfall. There are states, which have exhausted their groundwater potential whereas there are others, which still have a lot of groundwater to tap. There are states, which are concerned about low institutional credit coverage while there are others worried about high farmer indebtedness. Some states are concerned about diversifying into more remunerative crops while others are bothered about low productivity. This only confirms the prognosis of the NDC Sub-Committee that the problems of agriculture need localized solutions taking into account local resources endowments, capabilities as well as constraints. This, I am even more convinced, is the only way forward. This is reflected in the resolution we have adopted today.

1300. (29-5-2007) NEW DELHI : Following is the text of Dr. Montek Singh Ahluwalia Speech at the 53rd meeting of the National Development Council held on 29th May, 2007 at Vigyan Bhavan, New Delhi: The major issues facing this meeting have been outlined by the Prime Minister in his opening address and have been further elaborated by the Hon'ble Minister for Agriculture. The Planning Commission has been working on these issues to evolve a strategy for the 11th Plan. In this process, we have reviewed the work of several expert groups and the report of the NDC Committee. Our present perception is summarised in the paper on "Agricultural Strategy for the Eleventh Plan : Some Critical Issues" which has been distributed to all participants as an input into the deliberations of this meeting. I will, therefore, limit my remarks to only a few issues. The Prime Minister has already referred to the emergence of a technology fatigue in Indian agriculture. This is reflected in the fact that the yield of new varieties released in recent years has plateaued. However, there is still considerable scope for increasing productivity in the field because the yields actually being achieved on the field for many crops in many States are much below the realiasable potential even of existing varieties if best cultivation practices are used.

1301. (29-5-2007) NEW DELHI : 123 Army Schools spread through out the country have excelled in CBSE class X & XII exams, results of which were announced recently. While 97 percent of students of Class X have passed the exam, 94 percent have passed Class XII. As compared to overall national pass percentage, this is higher by above 14 percent for Class XII. 83 percent of the students of Class X & XII have obtained first division. These results assume greater significance, as most children in Army Schools are wards of Personnel Below Officer Ranks who belong largely to rural background.

1302. (29-5-2007) NEW DELHI : India and Uganda today agreed to strengthen cooperation in the field of agriculture, especially technical exchanges in this area. An agreement on farm trade is to be signed between the two countries at Kampala tomorrow. In the meeting held between the visiting Indian Minister of State for Agriculture Shri Kanti Lal Bhuria and the Fisheries Minister of Uganda, Mr. Fred Mukisa the two sides stressed on greater cooperation between their agricultural research institutions. Earlier, Shri Bhuria had discussion with Internal Affairs Minister of Uganda, Mr. Ruhakana Rugunda.

1303. (29-5-2007) NEW DELHI : A review of India's Foreign Direct Investment (FDI) policy is currently under way and the results of this review will be announced by June-July 2007. This was stated by Dr. Ajay Dua, Secretary, Department of Industrial Policy and Promotion (DIPP), Ministry of Commerce and Industry, in a presentation on "Investment Scenario in India" at the Plenary Session on "GCC-India Investment Opportunities" at the 3rd meeting of the India-GCC Industrial Forum in Mumbai today. The results of the review would be in the direction of liberalization, as was the case with similar policy reviews in the past, he indicated. In a detailed presentation, Dr. Dua outlined the growing attraction of India as an investment destination and identified the following as the six sectors with potential – automobiles and auto ancillaries; information technology (IT) and IT – enabled services; pharmaceuticals; biotechnology; food processing; and telecommunications. He mentioned in this context that FDI had started coming into the telecon sector in India in a big way now. In all these sectors, the basis for optimism about future growth stemmed from India's cost competitiveness, supplied side strengths including a large intellectual capital base and the expanding domestic market, he said. He emphasized that India had deliberately followed a process of calibrated liberalization of its FDI regime – from the pre-1991 policy when FDI was allowed selectively upto 40% and thereafter, in 1991 upto 51% under the automatic route for 35 priority sectors to the year 1997 when it was decided first to allow upto 74/51/50% in 111 sectors under the automatic route and 100% in some sectors. In 2000, upto 100% was allowed under the automatic route in all sectors except a negative list, while more sectors have been opened, equity caps raised and conditions relaxed in the post-2000 phase, he said, underlining that there were no restrictions on FDI in the manufacturing sector where upto 100% FDI had been allowed. According to RBI data, FDI equity inflows into India upto January 2007 amounted to US$ 16.4 billion. With the addition of reinvested earnings, the total FDI inflows were US$ 19 billion in 2006-07.

1304. (29-5-2007) NEW DELHI : India is in the process of negotiating a Free Trade Agreement (FTA) with the Gulf countries and the talks in this regard are likely to be concluded very soon. This was indicated by Shri Kamal Nath, Minister of Commerce and Industry, in his keynote address at the Inaugural Session of the 3rd meeting of the India-GCC Industrial Forum, in Mumbai today. Stating that India is privileged to host this year's Forum, the Minister expressed the hope that the deliberations would further enhance the expanding economic relations between India and the Gulf Cooperation Council (GCC) countries. "In the last five years, India's total trade with the GCC countries has risen more than four-fold – from US$ 5.55 billion in 2000-01 to US$ 23.42 billion in 2005-06. The period witnessed buoyancy in both exports and imports. Signing of the Framework Agreement on Economic Cooperation between India and GCC countries in 2004, was another milestone in the Indo-GCC economic relations", he added. Dr. Al Yamani, Minister of Commerce and Industry, Saudi Arabia and Mr. Maqbool bin Ali bin Sultan, Minister of Commerce and Industry, Oman, were present on the occasion along with members of the GCC delegations, including the GCC Chambers and leading representatives of Indian Industry headed by the Confederation of Indian Industry (CII) and the Federation of Indian Chambers of Commerce and Industry (FICCI). Underlining the importance of the Gulf countries to India, Shri Kamal Nath observed that the Gulf region was on par in terms of demand creation when compare to even the US. "It is already a target market for more than three-quarters of India's main export products including fresh fruits and vegetables", he said. The Minister outlined a whole of range of opportunities in India for investors from the Gulf, specially the huge opportunities in infrastructure. "There are obvious synergies between India and the Gulf. The GCC countries continue to be a major supplier of oil to India, meeting almost two-thirds of our oil requirements. India is looking at providing refining services to the Gulf. I invite oil companies from the Gulf to set up their facilities in India as it will not only add a new dimension to our India-GCC trade but also help in enhancing capacities. At the same time, we should also look at partnering in areas that go beyond just oil. Infrastructure is one area where India offers immense opportunities for investment. We have estimated the requirement of infrastructure sector to be about US$ 320 billion in the next five years. India plans to add 100,000 MWs of power in the next ten years. There is potential for investment in LNG terminals as India is a gas deficient country. Air passenger traffic has grown in excess of 30 per cent in the last three years. I expect investors from this region to actively participate in the ongoing airport modernization programmes across the country", he said Exciting opportunities also exist in India on farm and food processing sector, as value addition in this area is only 16%, despite the fact that India is among the world's largest producer of milk, vegetables and fruits, he said adding that India's investment requirement in this would be around 15 billion. Gems and jewellery, healthcare and biotechnology were the other areas flagged by Mr. Kamal Nath for Gulf investors. "I invite investors from the GCC countries to make the most of the opportunities that India provides by entering into joint ventures, collaborations and partnerships in different sectors. There is political will on both sides to take the India-GCC trade to the next higher level of engagement and now the onus is on the trade and investment community to translate this will into a reality that augurs well for both sides", he stressed.

1305. (29-5-2007) NEW DELHI : The total import of sensitive items for the period April 06-March 07 has been Rs.18555 crores as compared to Rs.16789 crores during the corresponding period last year thereby showing an increase of 10.5%. The gross import of all commodity during same period of current year was Rs.820568 crores as compared to Rs.635013 crores during the same period of last year. Thus import of sensitive items constitute 2.6% and 2.3% of the gross imports during last year and current year respectively. Imports of cotton & silk, spices and tea & coffee have shown a decline at broad group level during the period. Imports of items viz. edible oil, fruits & vegetables (including nuts), food grains, products of SSI, rubber, automobiles, marble & Granite, Alcoholic beverages and milk & milk products have shown increase during the period under reference. In the edible oil segment, the import has increased from Rs.8954 crores last year to Rs.9351 crores for the corresponding period of this year. A significant feature of edible oil import is that import of crude oil has gone up by 9.7% and that of refined oil have gone down by 34.7%. The growth in edible oil import is mainly due to significant increase in import of Crude Palm Oil and its fractions which has gone up by 39%. Imports of sensitive items from Indonesia, China P RP, United States of America, Malaysia, Russia, Cote D' Ivory, Australia, Thailand, Germany, Sri Lanka DSR, Japan, Ukraine, Benin etc. have gone up while those from Brazil, Guinea Bissau, Tanzania REP, Egypt A RP, Argentina etc. have shown a decrease.

1306. (29-5-2007) NEW DELHI : The Government has issued notifications constituting the Wage Boards for Working Journalists and Non-working Journalists of newspapers and news agencies w.e.f.24th May, 2007. These Wage Boards have been constituted for the purpose of fixing or revising rates of wages of working journalists and newspaper employees and non-journalists newspapers employees in accordance with the provisions of the Working Journalists and Other Newspaper Employees (Conditions of service) and Miscellaneous Provisions Act, 1955. The headquarter of the Wage Board will be New Delhi. The Boards have been asked to submit their reports within the stipulated period of 3 years. Both the Wage Boards will have 10 members each headed by Dr. Justice K. Narayana Kurup. Dr., Justice K. Narayana Kurup is a formal Judge of Kerala High Court and has also served as Acting Chief Justice of Madras High Court. As per the notification, Shri K.M. Sahni, former Labour and Employment Secretary would be the Member Secretary for both the Boards. The other independent members common to both the Boards are Shri B.P. Singh and Shri P.N. Prasanna Kumar. Shri Naresh Mohan (Indian Newspaper Society), Shri Gurinder Singh (All India Small and Medium Newspapers Federation), Shri Prataprai Tarachand Shah (Indian Language Newspaper Association) will be representing employers on both the Wage Boards. Shri K. Vikram Rao (Indian Federation of Working Journalists), Shri Nand Kishore Trikha (National Union of Journalists (India) and Shri Suresh Akhouri (Indian Journalists Union) will represent the Working Journalists on the Wage Board for Working Journalists. Shri Madan Phadnis (All India Newspaper Employees Federation), Shri Uma Shankar Mishra (National Federation of Newspaper Employees) and Shri M.S. Yadav (Press Trust of India) will represent non-journalists on the Wage Boards for Non-Working Journalists.

1307. (29-5-2007) NEW DELHI : The UPSC has declared the results of written exams for Central Police Forces (Asstt. Commandant) Examination 2006. These candidates have qualified for Physical and Medical Standard Tests and Physical Efficiency Tests on the basis of the result of written part of the exam held by the Union Public Service Commission in October 2006. The Border Security Force, (Nodal Authority nominated by Ministry of Home Affairs) will intimate to the candidates about the date, time and venue of the Physical and Medical Standards Tests and Physical Efficiency Tests (PET), to be conducted by them. In case, any candidate does not receive the call letter for Physical and Medical Standards Tests and Physical Efficiency Tests by the 2nd Week of June, 2007, they may contact the Border Security Force on Telephone No.011-24368233, 24364850/Ext.342 or on Fax No.011-24361794. The marks of candidates who have not qualified in both papers of CPF (ACs) Examination, 2006 shall be available on the Commission's website within 30 days from the publication of this Press Note and would be available on the website for a period of 60 days.

1308. (29-5-2007) NEW DELHI : Following is the text of the intervention of Finance Minister, Shri P. Chidambaram at the 53rd meeting of National Development Council on issues relating to Agriculture, here today: "I am happy that this meeting of the National Development Council brings agriculture to where it belongs – at the top of the agenda of policy makers. In my Budget Speech for 2007-08, I had quoted Jawaharlal Nehru, who said "Everything else can wait, but not agriculture."

Self-sufficiency or mere self-sufficiency in essential food items is not, in the Indian context, an academic or ideological issue. It is a matter of dire necessity. No country as large as India can hope to meet the requirements of its people for cereals, pulses, oil seeds, sugar, milk, etc. through imports on a large scale. While supply-demand gaps are not unusual in any economy, especially a growing economy, any supply-demand gap in essential food articles has the effect of exacerbating the problems relating to maintenance of price stability. While imports are a short-term answer to the supply-demand gap, practical experience shows that India does not have too much room to manoeuvre. It is a matter of satisfaction that we have put behind us the years of high inflation. I may recall that in 1979-80 the average inflation measured by WPI was 17.1 per cent. In the years immediately after the reform process started, between 1990 and 1995 average inflation was 11.0 per cent. As recently as the period between 2000 and 2004 it was 4.9 per cent. But the tolerance level for inflation has come down sharply. Therefore, we aim to control inflation at between 4.0 and 4.5 per cent. The recent spell of inflation was largely due to the spurt in prices of primary articles – and that includes, apart from metals, food articles. The contribution of primary articles to WPI inflation was as much as 43.8 per cent on May 12, 2007. Needless to say, inflation has other consequences and obliges Government and the RBI to take strong measures. Therefore, even from the point of view of sound macro-economic management, it is necessary that we maintain adequate supplies of food articles and the resulting price stability.

1309. (29-5-2007) NEW DELHI : On arrival in Hamburg, Germany yesterday for the Asia-Europe Meeting (ASEM), External Affairs Minister, Shri Pranab Mukherjee started a round of bilateral discussions on the sidelines of the Meeting. He had a 40-minute meeting with China's Foreign Minister Yang Jiechi. This was the first meeting between Shri Mukherjee and the new Chinese Foreign Minister. The two Ministers reviewed bilateral relationship in the light of the ten-pronged strategy to strengthen bilateral relations that was spelt out during President Hu Jintao's visit in November 2006. They said that high-level contacts should continue (meeting on G-8 sideline, Foreign Minister level discussions, Foreign Office Consultations etc.) They reviewed the trade and economic relationship and noted that bilateral trade has crossed US $ 25 billion and at this rate we should be able to meet the target of US $ 40 billion by 2010. Chinese Foreign Minister said that in first four months this year bilateral trade has reached US $ 11.4 billion (56 % rise). The two Ministers also reviewed progress under MOU for defence cooperation (2006) and said that dates would be fixed for the annual meeting of the Defence Dialogue Mechanism. The discussion also touched upon the boundary question and it was agreed that Special Representatives will continue with their work with the encouragement and guidance of the political leadership. Other issues discussed included cooperation for the success of the India-China Tourism Year and Youth exchanges. Multilateral issues, particularly UN reforms, including Security Council reforms were also discussed. Shri Mukherjee also had a half an hour meeting with Polish Foreign Minister Ms. Anna Fotyga. Discussions covered bilateral relations particularly trade and investment, cooperation in multilateral fora and the situation in Afghanistan.

1310. (29-5-2007) NEW DELHI : Central Ground Water Authority constituted under section 3(3) of Environment (Protection) Act of 1986 to regulate the development and management of ground water resources in the country has undertaken the following measures to check over-exploitation of ground water: Central Ground Water Authority is regulating withdrawal of ground water by new industries/projects in Over-exploited. Critical and Semi-critical areas by according clearance only in areas where there would be no adverse effect on ground water regime. CGWA has notified 43 Over-exploited areas in the country for regulation of ground water development and management. In these notified areas, installation of new ground water abstraction structures is not permitted without prior specific approval of the Authority. For enforcement of the regulatory directions issued under Section 5 of EPA, 1986, concerned Deputy Commissioners/District Magistrates have been authorized to take necessary action in case of violation of directives of CGWA in the notified areas. For more effective regulation of ground water development and management, Advisory Committees under the Chairmanship of District Collector/Deputy Commissioners with members drawn from various organizations have been constituted. Such committees will render advise to the District Collectors/Deputy Commissioners in matters pertaining to regulation of ground water development and management. Advisory Committees for notified areas of Diu, Ghaziabad, Gurgaon, Jothwara, Jhunjhunu, Mundwa, Chirawa, Buhana and Pushkar Valley have already been constituted. Constitution of Advisory Committees for the remaining areas is under consideration of Authority on the basis of proposals from the states. CGWA have also notified 65 OE areas in various States, for registration of ground water abstraction structures, which showed a very steep decline in ground water levels and required action for regulation. CGWA has issued directions to all the Chief Secretaries of States having Over-exploited blocks to take all necessary measures to promote/adopt artificial recharge to ground water/grain water harvesting. Directions have been issued to Group Housing Societies, Institutes, Hotels, Industries, Farm Houses, etc. in the notified areas of Delhi, Faridabad, Gurgaon and Ghaziabad and other areas of NCT Delhi where ground water is 8 metre from ground surface to adopt roof top rain water harvesting system. The last date for adoption of rain water harvesting has been extended upto 30th June, 2007.

1311. (29-5-2007) NEW DELHI : The total approximate earnings of Indian Railways on originating basis during the period 11th May – 20th May 2007 were Rs. 1806.72 crore compared to Rs. 1618.05 crore during the same period last year, registering an increase of 11.66 per cent. The total goods earnings have gone up from Rs. 1080.14 crore during 11-20 May 2006 to Rs. 1200.67 crore during 11-20 May 2007, showing an increase of 11.16 per cent. The total passenger revenue earnings during the period 11–20 May 2007 were Rs. 542.35 crore compared to Rs. 484.49 crore during the same period last year, an increase of 11.94 per cent. The revenue earnings from other coaching amounted to Rs. 50.23 crore during this period compared to Rs. 42.61 crore during the same period last year, an increase of 17.88 per cent. The total sundry earnings have gone up from Rs. 10.81 crore during 11-20 May 2006 to Rs. 13.47 crore during 11-20 May 2007, showing an increase of 24.61 per cent. The total approximate number of passengers booked during the period 11–20 May 2007 were 179.16 million compared to 169.28 million during the same period last year, showing an increase of 5.84 per cent. In the suburban and non-suburban sectors, the number of passengers booked during 11-20 May 2007 were 95.88 million and 83.28 million compared to 88.80 million and 80.48 million during the same period last year, registering an increase of 7.97 per cent and 3.48 per cent respectively.

1312. (29-5-2007) NEW DELHI : The performance of Indian Railways in respect of loading has gone up from 58.09 Million Tonnes during April 2006 to 60.68 Million Tonnes during April 2007, an increase of 4.46 per cent. Freight earnings have also gone up from Rs. 3221.51 crore during April 2006 to Rs.3561.99 crore during April 2007, registering an increase of 10.57 per cent. Passenger earnings have gone up from Rs. 1383.89 crore during April 2006 to Rs.1557.17 crore during April 2007, an increase of 12.52 per cent. The Integral Coach Factory (ICF) produced 56 coaches during April 2007 exceeding the target by 4 coaches. Chitranjan Locomotive Works (CLW), Diesel Locomotive Works (DLW) and Rail Coach Factory (RCF) produced 7 electric locomotives, 17 locomotives and 85 coaches respectively equaling the targets set by them while Rail Wheel Factory (RWF) produced 6928 wheels and 4285 axles against the target of 10873 wheels and 4719 axles during the same period. The punctuality percentage of mail/express trains was 91.7 per cent in Broad Gauge and 99.5 per cent in Metre Gauge during April 2007 compared to 91.7 per cent and 97.3 per cent respectively during the same period last year.

1313. (29-5-2007) NEW DELHI : Union Agriculture Minister, Shri Sharad Pawar today called upon States to prepare State-specific plans on agriculture, keeping in view the agro-climatic conditions, natural resource and available technology. These Plans should integrate various schemes in the agriculture sector with rural development programmes, irrigation projects and other related programmes. Shri Pawar was addressing the 53rd Meeting of the National Development Council called here specially to discuss the food and agriculture sector. The State Plans, the Minister said, would need to be backed up with an effective extension system which should provide assistance to farmers not only on crop related activities but also on animal resource development. The Minister observed that the deceleration in agricultural growth in the recent years has coincided with the falling share of agriculture, irrigation and rural development in the State Plan outlays. Enhancing investment and plan outlays has to be complemented with effective implementation of the programmes and schemes, he said. Shri Pawar further emphasized the need for higher investments in these sectors. 'The twin objectives of ensuring food security and improving the lot of our farmers can be achieved through higher investments in the agriculture and allied sectors, including irrigation. However, the allocation to this crucial sector, in relation to other sectors, has been going down over the years. This needs to be reversed', he stated.

1314. (29-5-2007) NEW DELHI : The Government has approved the appointment of Shri V. Thulasidas as Chairman and Managing Director and Shri Vishwapati Trivedi as Joint Managing Director of the merged entity 'Air India' from the time the merged entity comes into being. According to the decision of the Government, Shri V. Thulasidas and Shri Vishwapati Trivedi will continue as Chairman and Managing Director of Air India Ltd., and Indian Airlines Ltd. respectively, till such time as the merged entity comes into being. From the date on which the merged entity comes into being, Shri V. Thulasidas will be the Chairman and the Managing Director of the merged entity till the date of his retirement *i.e.* 31st March 2008 or until further orders of the Government, whichever is earlier. From the date on which the merged entity comes into being, Shri Vishwapati Trivedi will be the Joint Managing Director of the new entity till 31st March 2008 or until further orders, whichever is earlier. The Government has also approved that the pay and perquisites of Shri V, Thulasidas as CMD, Air India Ltd., and Shri Vishwapati Trivedi as CMD, Indian Airlines Ltd., shall remain protected. Shri V. Thulasidas is an IAS officer of 1972 batch, Manipur-Tripura Cadre; and Shri Vishwapati Trivedi is an IAS officer of 1977 batch, Madhya Pradesh Cadre.

1315. (29-5-2007) NEW DELHI : The Prime Minister, Dr. Manmohan Singh addressed the 53rd meeting of the National Development Council's Special Session on Food and Agriculture, here today. Following is the text of the Prime Minister's address on the occasion: "I am extremely happy to welcome you all to this 53rd meeting of the National Development Council. We last met in December 2006 to discuss the Approach Paper to the 11th Five Year Plan. While endorsing the overall approach to the Plan and expressing cautious optimism about achieving a growth target reaching 10% in the last year of the 11th Plan, there was a sense of urgency about the need to redress the emerging weaknesses in our agricultural sector. At less than 2% per annum growth, the growth of the agriculture sector since the mid-1990s has been a cause for concern. In view of the seriousness of the situation, I had then proposed to call a meeting of the National Development Council to discuss exclusively and deal with issues related to the management of our food and agricultural economy. We are here today to reflect on this very important matter and identify steps that we can collectively and individually take to improve the lot of our farmers and agriculture sector as a whole. Earlier, in the 51st meeting of the NDC held in June 2005, we had agreed to constitute an NDC Sub-Committee on "Agriculture and Related Issues" under the Chairmanship of my distinguished colleague Shri Sharad Pawar, the Union Agriculture Minister.

The purpose of the sub-committee was to examine in-depth the problems facing Indian agriculture and to suggest implementable action programmes. The NDC Committee has worked diligently on this important subject, setting up several sub-Committees chaired by some distinguished Chief Ministers. The report of the NDC Committee, which has been circulated for this meeting, draws on a number of other reports of expert groups and presents a broad agenda of the policy changes we urgently need in managing our agricultural economy. I would like to congratulate my distinguished colleague, Shri Sharad Pawar Ji for his leadership in getting the NDC Committee to complete its work in a relatively short period of time. In order to build on the Committee's recommendations and develop an agricultural strategy for the 11th Plan, I had directed the Planning Commission to work with the Ministry of Agriculture and come up with specific proposals to promote State specific agricultural strategies. The Planning Commission has been interacting with the Ministry of Agriculture to come up with the main components of this strategy. Later on, I would like the Agriculture Minister and the Deputy Chairman, Planning Commission to highlight the key features of this strategy that is suggested for revitalizing our agricultural sector. Before we go on to hear the detailed presentation by the Deputy Chairman and the interventions of my cabinet colleagues, the Agriculture Minister and the Finance Minister, I would like to share some of my thoughts with you.

1316. (29-5-2007) NEW DELHI : The Ministry of Tribal Affairs released Rs. 104 crore to the States during 2006-07 for taking up minor irrigation schemes for land owned by STs. The objective of the scheme is to ensure over all development of tribals by providing 100% financial assistance to those STs who are engaged in farming and usually reside in remote, far-flung and often inaccessible areas with undulating terrain. Their land holdings are fragmented and small with poor irrigation facilities. The assistance is provided for taking up irrigation projects aimed at enhancing productivity of land belonging to tribal communities through water harvesting and soil conservation so as to improve socio-economic conditions, conserve and improve biodiversity and provide employment leading to poverty alleviation. The assistance is released to the States on the basis of projects submitted by them.

1317. (29-5-2007) NEW DELHI : The Ministry of Rural Development has released Grants-in-aid amounting to Rs. 6.57 crore as third/additional instalment of Central assistance to 11 districts of Jammu & Kashmir for the implementation of the Sampoorna Grameen Rozgar Yojana (SGRY) during the financial year (2006-07).

1318. (29-5-2007) NEW DELHI : The Ministry of Rural Development has released Grants-in-aid amounting to Rs. 24.67 crore as third/additional instalment of Central assistance to 14 districts of Bihar for the implementation of the Sampoorna Grameen Rozgar Yojana (SGRY) during the financial year (2006-07). Grants amounting to Rs.52.15 crore as second instalment has also been released to 12 districts of the State under the scheme for the year 2006-07.

1319. (29-5-2007) NEW DELHI : The Ministry of Rural Development has released Grants-in-aid amounting to Rs. 23.33 crore as third/additional instalment of Central assistance to 6 districts of West Bengal for the implementation of the Sampoorna Grameen Rozgar Yojana (SGRY) during the current financial year (2006-07).

1320. (29-5-2007) NEW DELHI : he following is the text of the External Affairs Minister, Shri Pranab Mukherjee's interventions on Afghanistan and Iran at the ASEM meeting in Hamburg: "I use the opportunity you have provided me today to share some thoughts on Afghanistan. In 2002, there was a strong international consensus and commitment that the rebuilding and reconstruction of Afghanistan must continue apace with a stabilization of the security situation. The Bonn, Tokyo and Berlin conferences, the Regional Economic Cooperation Conference (RECC) on Afghanistan in New Delhi, the successful completion of Presidential and Parliamentary elections-all these are prominent landmarks of the gains so far. But the challenges remain, indeed they have grown and the resurgence of the Taliban has set the entire process on precarious ground. The increase in suicide attacks, kidnappings and most of all the growing strength of the Taliban through Afghanistan's south make us now confront a problem which has acquired threatening proportions and which calls for a well thought our counter strategy. An oft repeated truism stares us in the face; if we forget history, we will be condemned to repeat it. The international community must do all that it can to prevent the reenactment of the ghastly dance of death of the past. The area of instability now covers both sides of the Durand Line. It radiates and projects its influence in all areas west of the Indus. Early warning signs of this happening were perhaps ignored. We now face a situation where in a large swathe of Southern Afghanistan, international development activity has slowed down to the point of being non-existent.

1321. (30-5-2007) NEW DELHI : Shri Kanti Lal Bhuria, Minister of State for Agriculture signed an agreement at Kambala today with Mr. Hilary Obek, Minister of Agriculture, Animal Industry and Fisheries of the Republic of Uganda for strengthening bilateral cooperation in Agriculture. The agreement envisages exchanges in the areas of cooperation, animal husbandry, agri-sciences and technology. It will also open the door for joint ventures in various fields of agri-business. Other features include Research and Training related exchanges of people and materials, extension management, agri-trade, plant protection and horticulture. A joint group will also be set up to oversee implementation of the agreement. After signing the agreement, Shri Bhuria expressed the hope that the agreement will further strengthen the friendly ties between the two countries. Shri Bhuria is leaving for Rwanda later tonight.

1322. (30-5-2007) NEW DELHI : The newly constituted National Commission for Scheduled Castes held its first meeting under the chairmanship of Dr. Buta

Singh, the newly appointed Chairman of the Commission, here today. The other Members of the Commission, viz., Prof. N.M. Kamble, Vice Chairman, Shrin Mrutyunjay Nayak, Shri Mahendra Boudh and Smt. Satya Bahin, Members were also present. The Commission under the leadership of Dr. Buta Singh first participated in the Centenary Celebrations of Babu Jagjivan Ram being held at Parliament Annexe, New Delhi and paid glowing tributes for his sterling services to the nation and the down trodden. Thereafter, the Commission in its meeting placed on record the contribution made by Late Dr. Suraj Bhan, Chairman of the first N.C.S.C for the upliftment of SCs over the decades. They paid tribute to him by observing one minute silence in his memory. The Commission decided to take up the monitoring of various organizations connected with the welfare and development of SCs population in the country on regular basis. Henceforth the Commission will hold two meetings in a month. It decided to monitor the resolution of local problems in remote parts of the country by the concerned State Government and Departments/authorities through spot visits. The Commission also resolved to visit all States at least once a year for interaction with the State Governments and various organisations, associations and bodies of the Scheduled Castes for speedy resolution of issues connected with their welfare.

1323. (30-5-2007) NEW DELHI : Dr.Kassu Ilalla, Ethiopian Minster of Urban Development and Small Scale Industries called on Shri Mahabir Prasad, Union Minister of Small Scale Industries & Agro and Rural Industries here today. Both the leaders discussed various issues pertaining to the micro, medium and small industries in India as also in Ethiopia. Dr. Ilalla evinced keen interest in the micro industries in India. Welcoming the visiting dignitaries, Shri Mahabir Prasad said the MSME Sector in India attracted attention in recent years because of its massive potential. Shri Prasad urged the visiting Minister to take note of the various steps taken by the present UPA Government to boost this sector. Elaborating on the subject, he said recently the Government announced a package for the benefit of Small Scale Sector. He also remarked that adding the nomenclature of 'micro' to the existing concept of small industries would go a long way in ensuring the steady growth of this sector. Shri Mahabir Prasad explained the progress and benefit of 'cluster development schemes' that have been taken up in various States to the visiting delegation. He expressed the hope that the good age-old relationship between the two countries would continue to grow and India would help Ethiopia in every possible way towards the growth of MSME sector. India's excellent institutional mechanism for the growth of SSI sector could be explored by Ethiopia, the Minister added. Dr. Ilalla thanked the minister for the hospitality and assured all cooperation from his country. He said Ethiopia has a free market economy and the small scale sector is a major employer to the teeming millions like India.

1324. (30-5-2007) NEW DELHI : In the 18th USIC International Tennis Championship at Prerov, Czech Republic, Indian Railways beat Russia by 3 –1 in the finals and won USIC tennis Championship 2007. In the last USIC Tennis

Championship held in 1999, Indian Railways won the Bronze Medal. Of the 31 member countries of USIC, 18 countries have participated in the said Championship. The Indian Railways team was headed by Rakesh Yadav, Secretary, Railway Sports Promotion Board and Shri B.N. Mohapatra, Treasurer, Railway Sports Promotion Board. The team included 4 players viz. Aditya Medkekar (Western Railway), Vishnu Vardhan and PC Vignesh (South Central Railway) and Manoj Kumar (Eastern Railway). The Indian Railways beat Finland in Quarter Finals and Switzerland in Semi-finals.

1325. (30-5-2007) NEW DELHI : Industrial development is important for economic growth, employment generation and improvement in the quality of life. However, industrial activities without proper precautionary measures for environmental protection are known to cause pollution and associated problems. If ecological and environmental criteria are forsaken, "industrialise and perish" will be the nature's retort. Now, there is a global consensus about the threat posed by the climate change. The disagreement is only, on how to go about altering human activities that unleash greenhouse gases, fuelling global warming. The recent report of the Intergovernmental Panel on Climate Change (IPCC) is the latest scientific assessment of the impact of global warming on human, animal and plant life. The culprit is greenhouse gases, notably carbon dioxide, methane and nitrous oxide. These are accumulating to unprecedented levels in the atmosphere as a result of profligate burning of fossil fuels, industrial processes, farming activities and changing land use. The greenhouse gases act like a blanket around the earth, trapping too much of the heat that would otherwise have escaped into space. The IPCC is a body of 2500 scientists that brings out reports, considered the last word on the Science of Climate Change. "Warming of the Climate System is unequivocal", says the IPCC in its latest report, pointing to the increased global, air and ocean temperatures, widespread melting of snow, and ice and rising sea levels. If the introduction of these greenhouse gases continued to soar, global temperature could rise up by 2.40C to 6.40 C by the end of the century, with far-reaching consequences for the climate, warned the IPCC. The report has given fresh impetus to finding solutions to the global warming problem. The summit meeting of the Group of Eight Industrialised countries (G8) to be held in June in Germany is expected to launch new initiatives for collective action by both rich nations and fast growing developing countries to combat climate change. The report provides hope that concerted action can make a real difference in the next quarter century. The panel is convinced that greenhouse gases in the atmosphere can be pegged at relatively safe levels, with measures that will not affect GDP growth. It is little surprise that the panel found that owing to human activity, gas emissions, primarily CO2, rose by 70 percent between 1970 and 2004.

1326. (30-5-2007) NEW DELHI : Government has decided that private parties purchasing wheat in excess of 50,000 MT (total purchases made throughout the country) under the Wheat (Stock Declaration by Companies or Firms or Individuals)

Order, 2007 will continue to submit weekly returns upto June, 2006 to the Department of Food & Public Distribution. From July, 2007 the companies are required to file monthly returns upto December, 2007. In the notification issued on 1.3.2007 weekly returns were stipulated upto May, 2007.

1327. (30-5-2007) NEW DELHI : Ten new FM radio channels have been commissioned during April 2007 taking the total of private FM radio channels in the country to 68. These include, four FM channels by Adlabs Films Ltd., namely, BIG FM for Bareily, Bhubaneshwar, Guwahati and Jalandhar, two of Entertainment Network (India) Ltd. (ENIL) named Radio Mirchi for Patna and Jalandhar, three of Puran Multimedia, namely, Mantra FM for Bareily, Karnal and Jalandhar and MY FM Channel at Jalandhar, belonging to Synergy Media. The Government received a sum of Rs. 7.28 crores as annual fee from the private FM radio broadcasters during the period. During the month, permissions were also granted to three companies to uplink their TV channels from India. These are TG Angel Media Pvt. Ltd., Triveni Media Ltd. and Creative Channel Advertising and Marketing Pvt. Ltd.

1328. (30-5-2007) NEW DELHI : The census of tiger is being done following new methodology which is being applied since last two years. This new methodology has new components and aspects of today's advanced science. Referring to reports in some newspapers, Dr.Pradipto Ghosh, Secretary, Ministry of Environment and Forests, made it clear that the previous methodology was not wrong at all. That was relevant at the time of implementation as whatever science could contribute for the census at that time. Dr. Ghosh further stated that while the Government is not aware of the results to be presented by the Wildlife Institute of India, since it had commissioned the study and approved the methodology, the Ministry would accept the findings. He also said that both the methodology can not be compared.

1329. (30-5-2007) NEW DELHI : The Defence Minister of Republic of Korea Mr. Kim Jang Soo called on Defence Minister Shri AK Antony in Defence Headquarters here today. The two leaders discussed matters of mutual interest. Various steps to strengthen the existing Defence Cooperation between both the countries were also discussed, which includes training of Armed Forces personnel, exchange of visits and strengthening the mutual cooperation between the Coast Guard of two countries and widening the scope of sea-lane communications. It may be recalled that India and Republic of Korea signed a Memorandum of Understanding on Defence Logistics and Supplies in the year 2005. This was the first ever visit by any Korean Defence Minister to India. The visit by the Korean Defence Minister is expected to give a boost to the existing Defence Cooperation between India and Republic of Korea. Mr. Soo who is on a four-day State visit to India, arrived on May 28, 2007 and visited Taj Mahal at Agra. The Korean Defence Minister will visit Western Naval Command Headquarters at Mumbai later today. Republic of Korea is a pioneer in shipbuilding and has a thriving Private Sector Defence Industry.

1330. (30-5-2007) NEW DELHI : The Ministry of Housing and Urban Poverty Alleviation is organizing a two day National Conference on "Affordable Housing for All" jointly with Confederation of Indian Industry and Government of Maharashtra in Mumbai from 1st June, 2007. The Minister of State (Independent Charge), for Housing And Urban Poverty Alleviation Kumari Selja will address the inaugural session, the Chief Minister of Maharashtra, Shri Vilasrao Deshmukh will be the Chief Guest and the Minister of State for Finance, Shri Pawan Kumar Bansal will be the Guest of Honour also. There will be a Plenary Session on Legislation and Policy Reforms, which will be chaired by Kumari Selja. There will be four parallel Sessions also on Land Availability and Use, Finance, Innovative Technologies and Social Housing. The Valedictory Session will be addressed by Kumari Selja and Shri Vilasrao Deshmukh. The Conference provide platform for the financing institutions, to come together and share their knowledge, experience and views and reviews the status of housing finance extended by the banks and the housing finance institutions in the country. It will also provide an opportunity to the delegations to suggests measures and recommend suitable financing interventions consistent with the above objective of "Affordable Housing for All". The Conference will be attended by over 800 delegates from Real Estate Developers, Builders, NGOs, Civil Society, Financial Institutions, Government Representatives both from Centre and States.

1331. (30-5-2007) NEW DELHI : The following are the excerpts from the "Report to the People 2004-2007" on Ministry of Water Resources. The report was released by the Prime Minister Dr. Manmohan Singh on 22nd May, 2007. Water Conservation: A substantial proportion of funds under the schemes mandated by the National Rural Employment Guarantee Act is earmarked for Water Conservation works. A National Project for Repair, Renovation and Restoration of Water Bodies used by farmers has been launched on pilot basis. The DPAP and IWDP, the two programmes for watershed development, have been brought under a common guideline. States have been asked to direct municipal bodies to make rainwater-harvesting part of design approvals by local bodies. A number of states have done work on rainwater harvesting and taken steps to amend municipal or building laws. Initiatives in dry-land farming: A National Rain-fed Area Authority is being established to look into all dimensions of managing water resources in rain-fed areas. Interlinking of rivers: Agreement for the first inter-linking of rivers project for Ken and Betwa rivers has been signed between Madhya Pradesh and Uttar Pradesh and completion of the detailed project report is targeted by mid 2008. On the Parvati-Kalisindh-Chambal link, consensus has been arrived at between Madhya Pradesh and Rajasthan and both the states are working out the details of draft MoU. Flood Management: In the purview of states. Nevertheless, the Centre is assisting them. The recommendations of a Task Force on short and long term measures for addressing problems associated within floods have been circulated to state governments concerned. The jurisdiction of Farakka Barrage has been extended for speedy implementation of anti-erosion works and other measures are at various stages of approval and implementation.. Critical flood control and anti-erosion schemes in the Ganga basin states have been approved with a total cost of Rs. 305 crore. The Government has approved schemes amounting to Rs. 225 crore for taking up critical flood control and anti-erosion projects in the Brahmaputra and Barak valleys during 2006-07. A State Sector scheme of the Ministry of Water Resources amounting to Rs. 166.68 crore benefiting all northeastern states as well as West Bengal has also been approved.

1332. (30-5-2007) NEW DELHI : India's relations with the Gulf countries received a big boost with the 3rd India-GCC Business Conference (Industrial Forum) adopting the Mumbai Declaration to enhance economic engagement between the two sides in number of new areas and with both sides agreeing to expedite conclusion of the proposed Free Trade Agreement (FTA) between India and the Gulf Cooperation Council (GCC) countries. A major outcome has been the decision to facilitate and expedite projects in the field of agriculture and food processing which has been identified as a new sector with significant opportunities for trade and investment. GCC States would receive and facilitate the visits of Indian agro processing companies particularly of the Agricultural and Processed Food Products Export Development Authority (APEDA) of India and India will reciprocate. It has also been decided that in order to promote joint venture projects of Small and Medium Enterprises (SMEs) in both India and GCC countries, a holding company would be set up with private and public sector participation in India and GCC States.

1333. (30-5-2007) NEW DELHI : Congress Spokesperson Smt. Jayanti Natrajan said that the Indian National Congress strongly condemns the brutal police firing resulting in the death of 14 people in Rajasthan. The state government of Rajasthan has miserably failed to maintain law and order and this has resulted in the tragic loss of lives. This is a situation that should have been prevented by the state government. It should have been anticipated and effective steps should have been taken to prevent the loss of lives and injury to citizens. The elected representatives of the state were too busy depicting the chief minister as the goddess to divert their attention from pressing problems in the state. The chief minister while remaining a mute accomplice to her own deification failed to fulfil her constitutional obligations to maintain law and order. The entire responsibility for this loss of life and injury lies on the shoulder of the chief minister and the Rajasthan government. The Law and order should be immediately restored and all steps to be taken to ensure that security, peace and harmony returns to Rajasthan. To a question that does the Congress Party support the demand of the Gujjars, Smt. Natarajan said that this is a serious and complicated issue. There can be no piecemeal solution to this issue. This is something on which a decision can be taken only after wide-ranging discussions at the national level. To a question on the issue of an audio CD made public by suspended Congress Party MLA from Hiamchal Pradesh, Sh. Vijay Singh Mankotia, Smt. Natarajan said that the party leadership is seized of the entire issue. We are in the process of ascertaining all the facts and necessary steps will be taken, if required. To a question on Prakash Karat's statement that has the Congress Party joined hand with communal party in West Bengal, Smt. Natarajan said that I am not aware what Mr. Karat is actually referring to and whatever he has said, I am sure the Congress leadership will come to know about it. The Congress Party does not join hands with any communal party in any state of India or outside India.

1334. (30-5-2007) NEW DELHI : The Parliamentary Committee for examining 'The Gram Nyayalayas Bill, 2007, has invited views from the public/organisations interested in the subject. The Bill seeks to provide for establishment of the Gram Nyayalayas for the purposes of providing access to justice, both civil and criminal, to the citizens at the grassroots level and to ensure that opportunities for securing justice are not denied to any citizen by the reasons of social, economic or other limitations. The Gram Nyayalayas Bill, 2007, introduced in the Rajya Sabha on the 15th May, 2007 and pending therein, has been referred to the Department Related Parliamentary Standing Committee on Personnel, Public Grievances, Law and Justice, headed by Dr. E. M. Sudarsana Natchiappan, M.P., for examination and report. Those desirous of submitting memoranda to the Committee may send two copies (either in English or Hindi) thereof to Smt. Sasilekha Nair, Under Secretary, Rajya Sabha Secretariat, Room No. 528-A, Fifth Floor, parliament House Annexe, New Delhi-110001 (Tel: 23035308 and Fax 23794328, 23016784, E-mail: lekha.n@sansad.nic.in). The memorandum which might be submitted to the Committee, would form part of the records of the committee and would be treated as confidential and would not be circulated to anyone, as any act contrary thereto would constitute a breach of privilege of the Committee. The Bill was published in the Gazette of India, Extraordinary, Part II, Section 2, dated the 15th May, 2007. Its copies can be had on written request to the above-mentioned Officer or can be down loaded from the official web-site of the Rajya Sabha (http://rajyasabha.nic.in), under the caption "Bills with the Committee".

1335. (30-5-2007) NEW DELHI : Following are some of the important highlights of the activities of the organizations under the Ministry of Civil Aviation in the month of April 2007. On 24th April 2007, Air India took delivery of the first of the two A310 aircraft, which were being converted into freighter for starting dedicated cargo services, at the EADS (European Aeronautic. Defence & Space Company) facility in Germany. As per MoU signed between IAF and Air India, the IAF has relased its first list of 14 pilots to be sent to Air India, which consists of 6 Air Vice marshals, 7 Air Commodores and 1 Group Captain. Air India has concluded negotiations with Malaysian Airlines for six additional landing slots at London's Heathrow airport. Air India will not be paying, any money to Malaysian Airlines for the slots. Successful conclusion of the agreement would allow Air India to operate 6 more flights to UK Air India, along with India and SATS, have been chosen as one of the two Ground Handling Service Providers for the upcoming new Greenfield Airport at Shamsabad, Hyderabad, which is likely to be operational on 1st March, 2008. A total of 107 tourist charter flights were permitted during the month. 975 flights clearances were issued which includes overflying/landing/ technical landing and departure to foreign destinations by Indian Registered Aircraft. Under the Satellite Based Augmentation System (SBAS) Project the connectivity test of the Indian Reference Station (INRES) at Port Blair with Indian Master Control Centre (INMCC) at Bangalore is in progress. The Geo integration of iterative testing and tuning is in progress. Request for Proposal (RFP) draft for implementation of Operational GAGAN system has been prepared and discussed at ISRO Bangalore on 9th April, 2007. TDS-Extended of GAGAN Final System Acceptance Test (FAST) is planned in the month of May 2007.

1336. (30-5-2007) NEW DELHI : The Union External Affairs Minister, Mr. Pranab Mukherjee had two bilateral meetings on the sidelines of ASEM Meeting at Hamburg (Germany) yesterday. The first meeting was with the Foreign Minister and the Deputy Foreign Minister of Vietnam. The two Ministers reviewed bilateral relations and looked at concrete steps that needed to be taken to expand these relations. In particular, they hoped that India and Vietnam could reach the bilateral trade target of US $ 2 billion by 2010. Mr. Mukherjee reiterated India's desire to cooperate with Vietnam in the hydro-carbon sector and the power sector. This cooperation could be facilitated by offering soft loans to Vietnam as well as credit loan. Foreign Minister of Vietnam discussed the forthcoming visit of Prime Minister of Vietnam to India. He also took the opportunity to reiterate Vietnam's support for India's candidature to the permanent membership of the UN Security Council. The second meeting was with Mr. Javier Solana, Secretary General of the European Council and High Representative for the Common Foreign and Security Policy. Mr. Mukherjee and Mr. Solana reviewed India-EU relations and expressed their keenness to intensify political contacts. More frequent and informal contacts were agreed upon. They had an exchange of views on the Iran nuclear issue. Mr. Mukherjee also briefed Mr. Solana on the 14th SAARC Summit and positive developments like the setting up of the SAARC Development Fund, South Asian University and SAARC Food Bank. He also briefed Mr. Solana on the India-Pakistan composite dialogue and the CBMs that have already been put in place between the two countries.

1337. (30-5-2007) NEW DELHI : Shri Kamal Nath, Union Minister of Commerce and Industry, will present awards to exporters of engineering goods for their outstanding performance at the All India Awards Function of the Engineering Export Promotion Council (EEPC) here on 1st June, 2007. On this occasion, the Minister is also scheduled to release the Report on Engineering Process Outsourcing (EPO), prepared by the EEPC in association with M/s. Fergusson & Company. Engineering exports from India are estimated to have touched US $ 26 billion mark in 2006-07 making the engineering sector one of the major contributors to India's rapidly growing exports.

1338. (30-5-2007) NEW DELHI : The Ministry of Rural Development has released Grants-in-aid to Himachal Pradesh amounting to Rs. 4.25 crore as third/ additional instalment of Central assistance to 8 districts during the financial year (2006-07) for the implementation of the Sampoorna Grameen Rozgar Yojana (SGRY). Grants amounting to Rs.1.72 crore as part of first instalment to the 5 districts of the State as central assistance for the implementation of the scheme during the current financial year (2007-08) were also granted.

1339. (30-5-2007) NEW DELHI : The Ministry of Rural Development has released Grants-in-aid amounting to Rs. 91.89 crore as of part of first instalment Central assistance to 47 districts of Uttar Pradesh for the implementation of the Sampoorna Grameen Rozgar Yojana (SGRY) during the financial year (2007-08). The details of the allocation are at Annexure. The release is towards plan expenditure and will be utilized for approved items of works subject to the conditions laid down in the SGRY Guidelines. No deviations from the guidelines is permissible.

1340. (31-5-2007) NEW DELHI : The Union Cabinet today gave its approval for introduction of a new Central Sector Scholarship Scheme of Top Quality Higher Education to Students belonging to Scheduled Tribes, to be implemented from 2007-08. The Scheme will cover students beyond 12th class, whose total family income from all sources does not exceed Rs.2.00 lakh per annum. The ST students will be awarded a scholarship to meet the requirements for – (i) full tuition fee and other non-refundable dues in respect of Government/Government funded institutions. However, there will be a ceiling of Rs.2.00 lakhs p.a. per student for private sector institutions and Rs.3.72 lakhs per student for the private sector flying clubs for Commercial Pilot Training; (ii) Living expenses will be provided as per actuals subject to maximum ceiling of Rs.3000/- per month per student; (iii) Books and stationery @ Rs.3000/- per annum per student; (iv) Full cost of a latest computer along with its accessories limited to Rs.45,000/- as one time assistance during the course. The Scheme will be funded by the Ministry of Tribal Affairs on 100% basis. In the first year of implementation of the Scheme, a sum of Rs.20.46 crore will be required, which will go up to Rs.60.42 crore in the fifth year. The Scheme is likely to benefit 635 students in first year and 7910 students during the five year period of its operation.

1341. (31-5-2007) NEW DELHI : The Union Cabinet today gave its 'In principle' approval for construction of a new airport of international standards through PPP at Navi Mumbai, Maharashtra. The new international airport at Navi Mumbai will meet requirement of increasing air traffic in the Mumbai metropolis.

1342. (31-5-2007) NEW DELHI : The Union Cabinet today gave its approval for the: (i) Constitution of a "Tiger and Other Endangered Species Crime Control Bureau" (Wildlife Crime Control Bureau) with headquarters at New Delhi, having four existing Regional Offices and three Sub Regional Offices, one new Regional Office and strengthening five existing sensitive border customs posts for overseeing works relating to trafficking of wildlife, their body parts and derivatives, with additional posts; (ii) Creation of a new post of Additional Director in the rank of Inspector General of Police; (iii) In principle endorsement of the additional staff needed for the proper functioning of the Bureau. The constitution of a multidisciplinary Bureau will conserve the natural heritage of the country by establishing a credible data base on wildlife items and trade, and helping to convict criminals and their accomplices at National and International levels. It will facilitate training to the field staff in intelligence gathering, crime detection and prosecution. It will also strengthen the ongoing efforts for control of poaching and illegal trade. The Bureau will address the growing concern among public and media on wildlife crime and launch a meaningful initiative to combat illegal wildlife trade.

1343. (31-5-2007) NEW DELHI : The Union Cabinet today gave its approval for the following: (i) Making both men and women eligible for short Service Commission (SSC) in the Flying branch of Indian Air Force; (ii) Revision of the SSC ceiling in Flying branch to 20% (iii) Revision of the term of engagement of SSC officers in Flying branch to 14 years, with no extension. It would help in overcoming the shortages in Flying branch and to enhance the SSC strength in flying branch.

1344. (31-5-2007) NEW DELHI : The Union Cabinet today gave its approval for withdrawal of the Private Universities (Establishment and Regulations) Bill, 1995 from the Rajya Sabha. The Bill which is pending since 1995, will be removed from the list of pending bills, since the UGC Regulations, 2003 which were upheld by the Supreme Court adequately address the concern regarding mushrooming of private universities and also take care of the Centre's obligation in regard to the coordination and maintenance of standards of higher education.

1345. (31-5-2007) NEW DELHI : The Government today gave its approval for the construction of an International Airport at Navi Mumbai. The Airport will be developed as a Greenfield Airport through Public Private Partnership (PPP) along the lines of the Greenfield Airports at Hyderabad and Bangalore. The Ministry of Civil Aviation had sought an 'in principle' approval of the Government for the construction of a second international airport in Mumbai as the updated air traffic forecasts had revealed that if there were no constraints, the number of passengers at Mumbai would reach 27.5 million per annum (mpa) around 2010, close to 40 mpa in 2015 and more than 80 mpa in 2026. Inspite of the restructuring and modernization of the Chhatrapati Shivaji International Airport by the JVC Mumbai International Airport Pvt. Ltd., and significant improvements of existing airport infrastructure, the current airport would be fully saturated by 2013. It was therefore, felt imperative that the proposed second airport at Mumbai should be operational before 2013 to meet the increasing air traffic demand as well as uninterrupted economic growth of the region. The State Government of Maharashtra, had, proposed a site in Navi Mumbai for the second airport because of the availability of developed infrastructure, power, water supply, roads and communication, minimal environmental disturbance and limited rehabilitation issues. A techno-economic feasibility study was conducted by the City and Industrial Development Corporation of Maharashtra Ltd., (CIDCO). A detailed simulation study was also carried out by the International Civil Aviation Organisation (ICAO) to ensure conflict free operation at both the airports, *i.e.* the existing and the one proposed at Navi Mumbai. The simulation study has revealed that with the appropriate procedures in place, simultaneous operation of both Mumbai and Navi Mumbai International airports is feasible. The Government of Maharashtra has intimated that the proposed international airport at Navi Mumbai had been considered on several parameters. Prominent amongst these is the fact that Navi Mumbai is expected to absorb the future growth in population, business and commercial activities of the Mumbai region. The proposed airport is located on NH4B at a distance of 35 km. from Santacruz Airport near Panvel town in the geographical centre of Navi Mumbai. An area of approx. 1140 Hectares (Ha) has been earmarked for the development of the second airport. Out of this about 620 Ha of land is in possession of CIDCO. Another 225 Ha of government land is being transferred to CIDCO and remaining 295 Ha is private land, which is under acquisition.

1346. (31-5-2007) NEW DELHI : Disinvestment Secretary, Shri P.V. Bhide takes over as Secretary, Deptt. of Revenue, Ministry of Finance tomorrow. Shri Bhide is a member of the Indian Administrative Service of 1973 Batch-Andhra Pradesh Cadre. He has also served as Additional/Special Secretary, Ministry of Home Affairs, Govt. of India. Shri Bhide had earlier worked as Director in the Department of Economic Affairs and was deputed to the World Bank during 1988-92 as Technical Advisor. In the State Government, he has served in various capacities including Finance Secretary & Energy Secretary. He was also CMD in APCO and Godavari Fertilizers & Chemicals Ltd. Both the Boards – Central Board of Direct Taxes and Central Board of Excise & Customs under Deptt. of Revenue will have new Chairmen from tomorrow. Shri B.M. Singh, IRS 1970 Batch, will take over as Chairman, Central Board of Direct Taxes. He succeeds Ms. Indira Bhargava who retires this afternoon. Shri S.K. Shingal, IRS (C&CE) also of 1970 batch, will take over as Chiarman, Central Board of Excise & Customs succeeding Shri V.P. Singh who relinquishes the charge of the post on his superannuation.

1347. (31-5-2007) NEW DELHI : The National Commission for Enterprises in the Unorganised Sector (NCEUS) today met the Central Trade Unions and National level organizations representing unorganised sector workers to ascertain their views on two draft Bills proposed by it relating to Conditions of Work and Promotion of Livelihoods for Agricultural and Non-agricultural Workers respectively. These discussions were held in New Delhi as part of the regional and national consultations organized by the Commission on its various proposals in a run up to finalising its report for submission to the Government. It may be recalled that the Commission had earlier submitted a detailed report and Draft

Bill on social security to the government a year ago on which the Cabinet took a decision in its meeting of May 24, 2007. Today's meeting of the Commission with the National workers' organizations was presided over by Dr. Arjun Sengupta, Chairman of the Commission and a brief presentation on the main contents of the proposals was made by Dr. Ravi Srivastava, Member of the Commission. Representatives of eight Central Trade Unions, namely W. R. Varadarajan (CITU), Abani Roy (UTUC), R. A. Mital (HMS), S. N. Thakur (AITUC), Naresh (INTUC), S. P. Singh (BMS), C. Chattopdhyay (NIFTU), K. Chakraborty (UTUC-LS), Jaya Arunachalam (Working Women's Forum), Shalini Trivedi (SEWA), Subhash Bhatnagar and R. Geetha (National Campaign Committee for Unorganized Sector Workers), N. P. Samy (National Centre for Labour, were among those who attended. In the deliberations on the issue of working conditions and protection and promotion of livelihood of unorganised workers the union representatives appreciated the detailed report of the Commission. They agreed with the thrust of the measures proposed by the NCEUS for improving the lot of the unorganized workers.

1348. (31-5-2007) NEW DELHI : Union Minister of Petroleum & Natural Gas Shri Murli Deora has called on the international community to lay higher emphasis on scientific and technological innovations and conservation to meet global need for energy security. Speaking at the Ministerial Conference on Energy in a Changing World at UNESCO headquarters in Paris today he said the oil recovery rate improvement by 5% could tentamount to adding oil reserves of 50 billion barrels which means that reserve to production ratio would go up by 2 years. On significance of conservation through energy efficiency, he said 2% cut in the oil consumption would mean saving of almost 2 million barrels each day. He said this cut in consumption would meet the current shortfall in the sector. Shri Deora also referred to various initiatives underway in India to enhance more efficient and environment friendly availability of fuels. He said that India's energy programmes and policies are devised to focus on improving energy efficiency, providing hydro and renewable energy, carrying out structural reforms by setting up regulatory authorities, innovative use of science & technology and R&D along with environment management. Shri Deora further recalled that the late Indian Prime Minister Mrs. Indira Gandhi had rightly pointed out at the Stockholm Conference that poverty is the biggest pollutant. He added that India is fully committed to bring about all round prosperity and happiness for a billion Indians through multi pronged strategies outlined in the Common Minimum Programme of UPA Government. With a significant decline in poverty from over 51 per cent in 1977-78 to about 26 per cent in 1999-2000, the Government is working towards reduction of poverty levels by 15 percentage points by 2012.

1349. (31-5-2007) NEW DELHI : Central Board of Excise and Customs (CBEC), Department of Revenue has issued Notification no. 55/2007-Cus (N.T) dated 31st May, 2007 notifying tariff values of edible oils and brass scrap (all grades) as shown in the Table below. The tariff values of six palm group oils and crude soyabean oil remain unchanged. However, tariff value of brass scrap (all grades) has been reduced.

1350. (31-5-2007) NEW DELHI : Finance Minister Shri P. Chidambaram expressed his happiness over the results of the GDP growth rate of 9.4% released by Central Statistical Organisation, here today saying that the report confirm our belief that the Indian economy has shifted to a higher growth trajectory. Briefing the media persons, he said that because we have high growth, we can make bold to claim that we would do everything possible to make the growth inclusive.

1351. (31-5-2007) NEW DELHI : The All India Consumer Price Index for Industrial Workers (CPI-IW) for April 2007 based on new series (2001=100) increased by one point to stand at 128 points. The Index in 78 centres during March 2007 and April 2007.

1352. (31-5-2007) NEW DELHI : The All India Consumer Price Index Number for Industrial Workers (CPI-IW) (base 2001-100) during April 2007 increased by one point to stand at 128 (one hundred and twenty eight) points. The index recorded an increase of 7 points in Sholapur Centre and 5 points in Rangapara-Tezpur centre. The index also witnessed an increase by 4 points each in 4 centres and by 3 points in 8 centres, 2 points in 9 centres and one point in 27 centres.. The Rise/Fall in index varied from centre to centre. The index during April 2007 decreased by 2 points each in Quilon and Nasik centres. It decreased by one point in 6 centres.. While in the remaining 20 centres the index remained stationary. The increase of 7 points in Sholapur centre was the outcome of increase in the prices of Rice, Wheat, Jowar, Arhar Dal, Masur Dal, Groundnut Oil, Milk, Garlic, Vegetable & Fruit Items, Country Liquor, Stationery items etc. The decrease of 2 points in Quilon centre was mainly on account of the fall in the prices of Rice, Fish Fresh, Coconut etc. while in Nasik centre the decrease was mainly due to decrease in the prices of Wheat, Coconut, Onions, Vegetable & Fruit items, Electricity Charges etc. The point to point rate of inflation, based on the CPI-IW on base 2001=100 has decreased from 6.72% in March, 2007 to 6.67% in April, 2007.

1353. (31-5-2007) NEW DELHI : Smt. Santosh Chowdhary, Chairperson of the National Commission for Safai Karamcharis visited All India Institute of Medical Science (AIIMS) today to know the socio-economic, living, working, service and educational conditions of safai Karamcharis and their dependents. She held a meeting with the concerned officials and representatives of Safai Karamcharis of AIIMS to discuss the various problems faced by them. She said Commission wants that all the temporary Safai Karamcharis should be made permanent and posts lying vacant should be filled soon. She advocated minimum wages for temporary Safai Karamcharis. She also asked the AIIMS authorities to clear all the pending pension and GPF cases of retired Safai Karamcharis. Smt. Chowdhary said free medical check up of Safai Karamcharis and welfare campaign about policies for them should be take up on priority basis.

1354. (31-5-2007) NEW DELHI : It has been decided to extend the period of procurement of wheat by Government agencies in Punjab and Haryana upto June 15, 2007. The incentive bonus of Rs. 100/- per quintal for procurement of wheat over and above the MSP of Rs. 750/- per quintal payable by the FCI and State agencies will continue to be applicable in this period, subject to the condition that the concerned State Government fully exempts this bonus amount from all State taxes and levies.

1355. (31-5-2007) NEW DELHI : A seven member delegation of the United Arab Emirates, led by their Under Secretary (Interior), Major General Saif Abdulla Al-Sha'afar met the Indian delegation, headed by the Union Home Secretary, Shri Madhukar Gupta here on 28th and 29th of this month. The talks were held in a friendly and cordial atmosphere. Both sides noted with satisfaction the strong traditional and friendly ties between the two countries and underlined the need to enhance bilateral security cooperation. It was noted that discussions are underway on the agreements on transfer of sentenced persons, and on combating international terrorism, organized crime and illicit drug trafficking. It was decided that these agreements would be finalized, as far as possible, within three months. Both sides underscored the need to firmly and effectively combat terrorism and other related crimes. In this connection, they noted the importance of exchange of operational information and intelligence in the areas of terrorism, organized crime, financing of terrorism, smuggling of small arms and explosives, and agreed to set up an institutional mechanism to coordinate and facilitate such exchange on a continuing basis. This mechanism will also discuss ways to facilitate greater cooperation and speedy action in criminal investigations including Red Corner Notices and extradition cases. Both sides also discussed passport, visa and immigration related issues and agreed to find ways and means to reduce vulnerability of passports, prevent issuance of forged travel documents, take steps to control the activities of unscrupulous middlemen and also address the problems faced by Indian expatriate workers in the UAE. It was decided that the institutional mechanism would address these issues also. It was also agreed that both sides would avail of facilities in either country for enhancing capacity and skills of their respective police personnel. Both sides agreed that to ensure early operationalisation of the institutional mechanism, both sides will convey to each other within two weeks the names of respective competent authorities / nodal points.

1356. (31-5-2007) NEW DELHI : India Post has brought out a set of commemorative postage stamps on five National Parks of India. Dr. Shakeel Ahmad, Minister of State for Communications and IT released the stamps in the presence of Shri Namo Narain Meena, Minister of State for Environment and Forests at a function here today. Each stamp is in the denomination of rupees five and is on Mudumalai, Bandipur, Bandhavgarh, Periyar and Kaziranga National

Parks of India. Speaking on the occasion, Dr. Ahmad said that these stamps will spread the message of conservation and will educate the public about the efforts made in this direction. The stamps are released at a time when India Post is already running an exhibition of stamps on "Nature and Wildlife", he added. India Post has issued about 117 stamps on Nature, Wildlife and Environment including those on Jim Corbett, Ghana Bird Sanctuary, Kanha National Park and Project Tiger. The Department also issued a set of four stamps on Endangered Birds of India last year.

1357. (31-5-2007) NEW DELHI : The Board of Approval (BOA) of the Special Economic Zones (SEZs) met here today to consider proposals for setting up of Special Economic Zones and also approve other miscellaneous requests pertaining to notified SEZs. In this meeting, 40 new applications were considered. Out of this, 22 Formal approvals and 6 In principle approvals were granted. One proposal for conversion of In principle approval to formal approval was also granted. Prominent among the Formal approvals are: IT/ITES SEZ by ETA Technopark Pvt. Ltd. in Tamil Nadu, IT/ITES SEZ by GENPACT INDIA in Andhra Pradesh; Multiproduct SEZ by Gopalpur SEZ Limited in Orissa; IT/ITES SEZ by Shivajimarg Properties Limited in Delhi; Biotech SEZ by Gujarat Industrial Development Corporation, Vadodara, Gujarat; Gems and Jewellery SEZ by Shirpur Gold Refinery Limited at Dhulia, Maharashtra and Three SEZs for Textiles, Leather and Engineering Goods by Uttar Pradesh State Industrial Development Corporation (UPSIDC), at Kanpur, Uttar Pradesh. Prominent In principle approvals granted are : Multi product SEZ by SRM Infrastructure Private Limited in Alwar, Rajasthan; Multi services SEZ by Society for Innovative Education and Development at Alwar, Rajasthan and a Carpet and Handicraft SEZ by UPSIDC in Bhadohi, Uttar Pradesh.

1358. (31-5-2007) NEW DELHI : The Appointments Committee of the Cabinet has approved the following appointments: Shri Arun Ramanathan, IAS (TN, 1973) presently in the cadre as Secretary, Department of Chemicals and Petrochemicals (Ministry of Chemicals and Fertilizers. Ms. Meena Gupta, IAS (OR, 1971) presently Secretary, Ministry of Tribal Affairs, as Secretary, Ministry of Environment and Forests. Shri R.C Joshi, IAS (MH, 1973) presently Special Secretary, Department of Atomic Energy as Member (Finance), Atomic Energy Commission and Member (Finance), Space Commission. Shri Gautam Buddha Mukherji, IAS (OR, 1973) presently in the cadre as Secretary, Ministry of Tribal Affairs. Shri P.V. Bhide, IAS (AP, 1973) presently Secretary, Department of Disinvestment, Ministry of Finance, as Secretary, Department of Revenue, Ministry of Finance.

1359. (31-5-2007) NEW DELHI : Science and technology should be at the heart of economic development if the country is to achieve the growth rate between 8 to 9 per cent. This was stated by the Union Minister for Science & Technology and Earth Sciences, Shri Kapil Sibal while briefing the media person on the three years achievements of his Ministry here today. He said that this requires well planned and focused strategy to make available to the people of India, especially the disadvantaged, all the benefits that science and technology can confer. Speaking on the occasion, the Shri Sibal said that the three major legislations will change the way the things are being done. These are Survey of India Bill for restructuring of the Department, Public Funded R&D Bill for Protection, Utilization & Regulation of Intellectual Property and Medical Devices Regulation Bill. He said the foundation stone for a modern India is being laid where S&T will touch the lives of common man. Listing out the achievements of two Ministries namely Ministry of Science & Technology (MoST) and Ministry of Earth Sciences (MoES) Shri Sibal said that focused programmes and initiatives are mounted.

1360. (31-5-2007) NEW DELHI : Union Minister for Science & Technology and Earth Sciences, Shri Kapil Sibal launched "STANFORD-INDIA BIODESIGN PROGRAMME" a collaborative venture of the Department of Biotechnology, Ministry of Science and Technology with Standford University, USA, here today. The objective of the programme is to create medical technology innovation in India in partnership with Stanford University, USA by developing leaders in biomedical technology. The programme seeks to provide training to young engineers from IITs, leading engineering institutions with partner medical institution to identify major health needs in India and develop solutions that are cost-effective and widely deployable across a broad socio-economic spectrum. The goals of the programme are: (i) to introduce the Stanford model of biodesign into educational system of these institutions (ii) to establish Centre of Excellence at each IIT in partnership with a medical institution (iii) identify opportunities through observation of patients by a multidisciplinary team comprised of biologist, engineer, chemistry and medical persons, then to select at least one new technology for group to be designed and develop it into a prototype. The focus of the programme will be on the development of implants, medical devices and bioinstrumentation. The initial development phase will include an intensive design and planning process based on the national needs. The faculty and fellows would be trained in the design innovation process by providing hands-on training at Stanford University, USA. Once the training will be over, the team will come back to India and start designing process and identifying clinical needs/challenges in India based on their experience at Stanford University, USA.

1361. (31-5-2007) NEW DELHI : The following are the excerpts from the "Report to the People 2004-07" on Women and Child Development. The report was released by the Prime Minister, Dr. Manmohan Singh on 22nd May, 2007. In order to give greater focus to issue relating to women, an independent Ministry of Women and child Development has been created first time. Forty-two laws which are either specifically related to women or contain provisions affecting them, administered by various Ministries/Departments, have been under the scrutiny of the Government. The Government has set up an Inter-Ministerial Committee to monitor the status of amendments to such laws with a view to making them more women-friendly. So far, the Government has amended six laws, enacted two new laws and issued executive orders in respect of five statues. Through coming into force of the Protection of Women from Domestic Violence Act, 2005, more effective protection has been provided to women who are victims of violence of any kind occurring within a family. The Act enables women to negotiate non-abusive and nonviolent available in the criminal law regime. The Hindu Succession Act, 1955 has been amended to make Hindu women's inheritance rights in coparcenary property equal to men's across states, overriding any inconsistent state laws. A bill for compulsory registration of marriages is under active consideration. Amendments to the Commission of Sati (Prevention) Act, 1987 are being introduced to make the provisions of the Act more stringent, deterrent and effective and help re-orient the existing perception of the woman attempting to commit sati as an offender and, instead, treat her as a victim of prolonged social conditioning. Amendments have been passed by Parliament prohibiting arrest of women after sunset and before sunrise; medical examination of persons accused of committing or attempting to commit rape; and mandatory judicial inquiry in case of rape while in police custody. The Sexual Harassment of Women at Work Place (Prevention, Prohibition and Redressal) Bill is being finanalised. Steps are being initiated to eliminate female foeticide. In order to provide flexibility in the matter of employment of women during night while requiring the employer to ensure measures for safety and protection, the Government has introduced a bill in Parliament to amend the Factories Act, 1948. The Government has introduced a bill in Parliament for amending the Immoral Traffic (Prevention) Act, 1956 in order to make the provisions of law more stringent, deterrent and effective against traffickers, pimps and brothel-owners, omit such provisions of the Act as are discriminatory towards women who are victims of commercial sexual exploitation, provide for in camera proceedings to protect the privacy and dignity of victims, and provide for setting up a Central authority as well as state authorities for effectively preventing and combating trafficking in persons. Amendments are also being considered to the Indecent Representation of Women (Prohibition) Act, 1986, the Dowry Prohibition Act, 1961, the Medical Termination of Pregnancy Act, 1971, the Guardians and Wards Act, 1890, the Hindu Adoptions and Maintenance Act, 1956, the Foreign Marriage Act, 1969, the Hindu Minority and Guardianship Act, 1956.

1362. (31-5-2007) NEW DELHI : The Annual Plan of Punjab for the year 2007-08 has been approved in a meeting between the Deputy Chairman, Planning Commission, Shri Montek Singh Ahluwalia and the Chief Minister of Punjab Sardar Prakash Singh Badal, here today. The Annual Plan size was agreed at Rs.5111 crores. This includes additional Central assistance of Rs.150 crores for projects linked to skill development programme and Rs.125 crores under the new ACA scheme for agriculture. In his opening remarks Deputy Chairman, Planning Commission, Dr. Montek Singh Ahluwalia said the economy of Punjab has traditionally revolved around success in the agriculture sector but the present agriculture system was increasingly becoming ecologically and economically untenable. Renovations of existing agriculture system, diversification of agriculture production patterns and agri-processing should acquire prominence in the government's planning process. He said against a growth target of 6.4 per cent for the Tenth Plan, the State was likely to achieve an average growth rate of only 5.03 per cent. Per capita income of the State at constant prices has increased from Rs.15071 in the year 2000-01 to Rs.17864 in year 2006-07 from number one among the major States it has slipped down to number four. Shri Ahluwalia said that the State should work towards higher growth targets for the Eleventh Plan and identify means to fund higher plan. Complimenting the State for achievements in the human resource development, Mr. Ahluwalia said the State has done well in mid-day meal, Serva Shiksha Abhiyan and encouraging NGOs participation in development process. The State Government was advised to focus on development of infrastructure vital for creating investor friendly environment. The State was advised to go for capacity addition in power sector. Skill up-gradation should also get focused.

1363. (31-5-2007) NEW DELHI : Union Finance Minister, Shri P. Chidambaram has approved 23 Foreign Direct Investment proposals recommended by Foreign Investment Promotion Board (FIPB) in its meeting held on 18th May, 2007. The approval amounts to Rs. 418.3333 crore. The proposals relate to Ministries/ Departments, namely, Agriculture & Cooperation, Commerce, Food & Public Distribution, Heavy Industry, Information & Broadcasting, Industrial Policy & Promotion, Power, Telecommunications and Economic Affairs. The major investment proposals pertain to the Ministry/Departments of Commerce, Telecommunications and Economic Affairs.

1364. (31-5-2007) NEW DELHI : The Defence Minister Shri AK Antony leaves New Delhi tonight for Singapore to attend the Sixth Asia Security Conference (The Shangri-La Dialogue-2007). Shri Antony will address the second plenary session on China and India : Building International Stability. The Shangri-La Dialogue has been recognized as a key event for defence and security diplomacy for the region. Since its inaugural meeting in 2002, the Dialogue has become a recognised part of the architecture of Asian defence diplomacy and is seen as the region's premier and most inclusive security institution. The Shangri-La Dialogue continues to serve as the best available vehicle in the Asia-Pacific region for developing and channelling astute and effective public policy on defence and security. The dialogue is organized by the International Institute for Strategic Studies, London. During his three-day stay in the island country, the Minister will also hold bilateral meetings with his Singaporean counterpart besides the Sri Lankan Foreign Minister Mr. Rohitha Bogollagama, the US Secretary of Defence Dr. Robert M Gates, the Deputy Prime Minister and Minister of National Defence of Cambodia General Tea Banh, the Japanese Minister of Defence Mr. Fumio Kyuma, the Minister of State for the Armed Forces of the United Kingdom Mr. Adam Ingram, The

Secretary General of National Defence of France Mr. Francis Delon, the Secretary of National Defence of Philippines Mr. Hermogenes E Ebdane Jr, the Minister of Defence of Australia Dr. Brendan Nelson and the Chief of Army Staff of Bangladesh General Moeen U Ahmed. Shri Antony will also call on the Singaporean Senior Minister Mr. Goh Chok Tong, the Singaporean Minister Mentor Mr. Lee Kuan Yew and the Singaporean Prime Minister Mr. Lee Hsien Loong. Shri Antony will return home on June 03, 2007.

1365. (31-5-2007) NEW DELHI : The Union Minister of Shipping, Road Transport and Highways Thiru T.R. Baalu today handed over the 30,000 DWT bulk carrier 'M.V. Good Providence' to M/s Goodearth Maritime Limited at Vishakhapatnam today. Built at a cost of US $ 17.51 million, this is the first vessel of a series of four numbers 30,000 DWT vessels to be built by the public sector Hindustan Shipyard Ltd. for M/s Goodearth Maritime Ltd. Thiru Baalu commended the employees of the Shipyard for completing the vessel in about one and a half years' time in tough working environment when the company was facing even working capital problems. The Hindustan Shipyard Ltd. has got an order book of 20 vessels which accounts for Rs. 2,000 crore in terms of value. With the proposed restructuring which is under consideration of the Government of India, the HSL will achieve long term profitability and with modernization schemes coming through, it is poised to become one of the best shipyards in the country. The Union Government has already taken several measures including release of additional funds for replacement and renewal of plant, machinery and equipment to help the Shipyard during the last three years. Thiru Baalu earlier reviewed the functioning of Vishakhapatnam Port Trust and directed the Port authorities to work expeditiously on the plans and programmes to be implemented during the next five year plan.

1366. (31-5-2007) NEW DELHI : An analysis of employment among rural households from 1974-75 to 1999-2000 (25 years) has revealed an upward trend. According to a Report by the Labour Bureau entitled "Rural Labour Enquiry on Employment and Unemployment of Rural Labour Households – 1999-2000", men worked for 298 in 1999-2000 as against 250 days in 1974-75. Similarly the increase for women has been 200 days from 185 days during the same period. Consequently, the actual unemployment, *i.e.*, the number of days not worked for want of work has also shown a downward trend. For the men workers it declined from 99 days in 1974-75 to 67 days in 1999-2000. In respect of women workers, it declined from 160 days to 109 days. However, when compared to last such survey held in 1993-94 there has been a decrease in number of working days during 1999-2000. Their number went down in case of men from 305 days in 1993-94 to 298 days in 1999-2000 for all classes, 300 days to 294 for SCs and 314 days to 308 days for STs. Similarly in respect of women it went down 265 days in 1993-94 to 256 days in 1999-2000 for 'all classes', 254 days to 249 days for SCs and 282 days to 267 days for STs.

1367. (31-5-2007) NEW DELHI : The following is the text of External Affairs Minister Shri Pranab Mukherjee's Intervention on Counter Terrorism at the ASEM Meeting in Hamburg, Germany yesterday: "Mr. Chairman, colleagues and friends, I am grateful for the opportunity to share India's perspectives on combating terrorism, an issue that has serious implications for global peace and security. Terrorist acts anywhere, whether in Mumbai and Hyderabad or in Bali and London, endanger the peace and security of all States. The possibility that terrorists may acquire and use weapons of mass destruction has added an alarming new dimension to this threat. The international community has long recognized that terrorism requires a comprehensive and multi-pronged global response. At the outset, all of us must continue to strongly condemn terrorism in all its forms and manifestations, committed by whomever, wherever and for whatever purposes. We must make it absolutely clear that no cause or grievance can ever justify acts of terrorism. All states must also abide by their commitment enshrined in the UN Global Counter-Terrorism Strategy adopted by the UN General Assembly in September 2006, to refrain from organizing, instigating, facilitating, participating in, financing, encouraging or tolerating terrorist activities and to take appropriate measures to ensure that their territories are not used for terrorist installations or training camps or for the perpetration or organization of terrorist acts intended to be committed against other States or their citizens. Apart from security and low-enforcement measures to prevent terrorist acts, we must also take steps to deny funds to terrorists and dismantle their financing channels. India regards combating the financing of terrorism a crucial element of its counter-terrorism strategy. We are an observer at the Financial Action Task Force and are working towards joining it as a member. The Financial Intelligence Unit of India is an observer at the EGMONT Group and is working towards joining it as a member. We are also a member of the Asia-Pacific Group on Money Laundering.

1368. (31-5-2007) NEW DELHI : The Union External Affairs Minister Shri Pranab Mukherjee chaired a day long Conference of India's Heads of Missions in EU States, in Brussels yesterday. Twenty-one Heads of Missions attended the Conference. Addressing the Heads of Missions, Shri Mukherjee underlined the importance of the Strategic Partnership between India and the EU, which is now India's largest trade partner. EU is also the source of one-fifth of India's FDI as well as an important destination for Indian investment. The Strategic Partnership is underpinned by an extensive Joint Action Programme adopted in 2005. Summits have been held annually since 2000 and the next Summit is expected to be held in New Delhi late in 2007. India's effort is to increasingly move the relationship beyond trade and economic relationship into areas such as Science & Technology, cooperation in Counter Terrorism, access to new energy and renewable energy technologies, space, environment etc. Negotiations are also expected to begin on a wide-ranging Free Trade Agreement between India and EU soon. The Heads of Missions briefed the Minister on aspects of the Indo-EU Strategic Partnership, principal issues of bilateral relations between India and countries of their accreditation as well as important developments in Europe/EU and NATO.

1369. (31-5-2007) NEW DELHI : The Ministry of Rural Development has released Rs.37.51 lakhs as part payment of first instalment of the Central share under the 'Swarnjayanti Gram Swarojgar Yojana' (SGSY) during the year 2007-08 to 8 DRDAs of Mizoram.

1370. (31-5-2007) NEW DELHI : The Ministry of Rural Development has released Rs.81.24 lakhs as part payment of first instalment of the Central share under the 'Swarnjayanti Gram Swarojgar Yojana' (SGSY) during the year 2007-08 to 3 DRDAs of Meghalaya.

1371. (31-5-2007) NEW DELHI : The Ministry of Rural Development has released Grants-in-aid amounting to Rs. 60.54 lakh as part of first instalment, out of the allocation of Rs.363.23 lakhs as Central assistance to the Uttarkashi District of Uttarakhand for the implementation of the Sampoorna Grameen Rozgar Yojana (SGRY) during the current financial year (2007-08). The release is towards plan expenditure and will be utilized for approved items of works subject to the conditions laid down in the SGRY Guidelines. No deviations from the guidelines is permissible. The expenditure on implementation of the programme with regard to cash component is to be shared on 75:25 basis between the Central and the State Government, respectively. The Sampoorna Grameen Rozgar Yojana (SGRY) is a Centrally Sponsored Scheme (CSS) to provide additional wage employment to the rural areas as also food security, alongside the creation of durable community assets, socio-economic infrastructure in the rural areas. Under the Scheme, foodgrains are provided every year, free of cost to the State Governments and Union Territory Administration.

1372. (31-5-2007) NEW DELHI : The Ministry of Rural Development has released Grants-in-aid amounting to Rs. 1.61 crore as part of first instalment to two districts of Punjab,viz. Sangrur (Rs. 74.68 lakhs) and Patiala (Rs. 86.66 lakhs) as Central assistance for the implementation of the Sampoorna Grameen Rozgar Yojana (SGRY) during the current financial year (2007-08). The release is towards plan expenditure and will be utilized for approved items of works subject to the conditions laid down in the SGRY Guidelines. No deviations from the guidelines is permissible. The expenditure on implementation of the programme with regard to cash component is to be shared on 75:25 basis between the Central and the State Government, respectively. The Sampoorna Grameen Rozgar Yojana (SGRY) is a Centrally Sponsored Scheme (CSS) to provide additional wage employment to the rural areas as also food security, alongside the creation of durable community assets, socio-economic infrastructure in the rural areas. Under the Scheme, foodgrains are provided every year, free of cost to the State Governments and Union Territory Administration.

1373. (1-6-2007) NEW DELHI : Government of India have announced the sale (re-issue) of "7.49 per cent Government Stock, 2017" for a notified amount of Rs. 6,000 crore (nominal) through a price based auction using multiple price method. Government of India have also announced the sale (re-issue) of "8.33 per cent Government Stock, 2036" for a notified amount of Rs. 3,000 crore (nominal) through a price based auction using multiple price method. The auctions will be conducted by the Reserve Bank of India, Mumbai Office, Fort, Mumbai on June 5, 2007 (Tuesday). Up to 5% of the notified amount of the sale of both the stocks will be allotted to eligible individuals and Institutions as per the Scheme for Non-Competitive Bidding Facility in the Auction of Government Securities. Bids in the prescribed form obtainable from the Regional Director, Reserve Bank of India, Mumbai Office (Public Debt Office), Fort, Mumbai-400 001 and RBI website www.rbi.org.in should be submitted to that Office on June 5, 2007. The NDS members should submit competitive as well as non-competitive bids in electronic format using Primary Market Operation (PMO) module of NDS. All bids should be submitted by 12.30 P.M. The result of the auctions will be announced on June 5, 2007 and payment by successful bidders will be during banking hours on June 6, 2007 (Wednesday). Both the Stocks will be eligible for "When Issued" trading in accordance with the guidelines on 'When issued transactions in Central Government Securities' issued by the Reserve Bank of India vide circular No.RBI/ 2006-07/178 dated November 16, 2006.

1374. (1-6-2007) NEW DELHI : The Prime Minister, Dr. Manmohan Singh chaired a meeting to review the state of higher education in India and address the challenge of increasing enrolment while improving access to and quality of higher education in India. The Prime Minister directed the University Grants Commission and the Planning Commission to jointly prepare a strategy for this. The Prime Minister also declared that the Government of India will setup at least one Central University in every State and assist State Government to ensure that there is at least one degree college in every district. There are presently 20 Central Universities in the country, while 16 States do not have a Central University. The Prime Minister said that each Central University should become a symbol of excellence, a model of efficiency and an example in terms of academic standards and university governance for other State Universities to emulate. 350 districts where enrolment is below national average will be brought upto national average. The Prime Minister also reiterated his commitment to offer more scholarships to increase the gross enrolment rate at the college level.

1375. (1-6-2007) NEW DELHI : The President Dr.A.P.J.Abdul Kalam today presented Bal Shree Honour 2006 to 22 children at a function in Rashtrapati Bhavan. "National Bal Shree Scheme" is a unique endeavour of National Bal Bhavan to honour the most creative children of India. The Bal Shree Honour is an effort to provide proper conditions for overall development of children's personality by nurturing their creativity in four streams *i.e.* Creative Performance,

Creative Arts, Creative Scientific Innovation and Creative Writing. Creative children of India within the age group of 9 to 16 years are thus identified in the above fields through this scheme.

1376. (1-6-2007) NEW DELHI : Congress Spokesperson Smt. Jayanti Natrajan said that the situation in Rajasthan has completely spiralled out of control and right now there is a very serious situation and grave security threat to the lives of citizens in Rajasthan. The Indian National Congress has already made an appeal for peace and harmony and security to be restored, but unfortunately the situation has deteriorated considerably leading to serious concern. The chief minister of Rajasthan should accept the entire moral responsibility for this dangerous turn of events while everybody was aware that there was sufficient warnings that such clashes were likely to occur. The chief minister of Rajasthan chooses to remain abroad for over 20 days and failed to take a single step to prevent these incidents from happening. It is for this reason that she should accept moral responsibility for this culpable inaction and failure on her part. The national level BJP, as well, has failed to take a single step to direct the chief minister or request her to restore normalcy. The Indian National Congress would like to once again make an appeal to all the people of Rajasthan to maintain peace and harmony. It is the responsibility of the chief minister to restore peace and security of lives at the earliest possible. To a question that Congress Party is talking about peace but Congress MPs and MLAs are sitting on dharna, Smt. Natrajan said that Congress MPs and MLAs would not add to any confusion as the direct representatives of the people. They have a right to bring out the serious situation that exists in Rajasthan to the notice of authorities in Delhi as well as attend to the grievances of their constituents. To a question as to what is Congress Party's reaction on the situation, Smt. Natrajan said that our appeal to the Rajasthan government is to restore peace and harmony without further delay. Our charge against the Rajasthan government and the chief minister specifically is that notwithstanding all the earlier information that was available, she failed to take steps to contain the situation. To a question as to what is the Congress Party's stand in giving ST status to the Gujjar community, Smt. Natrajan said that this is a serious and complicated issue and this requires the widest possible consultation at the national level with all the stockholders. We would definitely urge the government that talks are held at the national level and a consensus is arrived at the earliest possible date. However, the chief minister has failed to fulfil her constitutional responsibility of providing the data or forwarding whatever data that was available to the Central Government. To a question as to what the Central government is doing to contain the situation, Smt. Natrajan said that I speak for the Indian National Congress and I am very confident that the Central Government will take whatever steps necessary and required on their part to contain the situation. Even now, whatever has been salvaged is only because of the presence of Central and paramilitary forces. There is absolutely nothing done by the state government. To a question on the sting operation against Shri R.K. Anand in the BMW case, Smt. Natrajan said that the court is now seized of the matter as to whatever that has appeared on TV. The party will wait for the outcome of the stand taken by the court before arriving at any calculation. To a question that UPA government has achieved 9.4% GDP growth, Smt. Natrajan said that certainly, the robust growth of our economy is some thing that we are very proud of what the government has achieved, but at the same time we strongly believe what the Hon'ble Prime Minister has said that growth should be inclusive growth and this will be the continued effort of the Indian National Congress to ensure that growth is not jobless but inclusive growth.

1377. (1-6-2007) NEW DELHI : The quarterly quota of non-levy sugar for April, 2007 to June, 2007 has been increased to 41 lakh tonnes from 38 lakh tonnes announced earlier. This has been done in view the summer demand for sugar. Accordingly, the non-levy sugar quota for the month of June, 2007 has been increased to 16 lakh tonnes from 13 lakh tonnes. The sugar released for the month of June, 2007 is required to be sold within the month. The higher non-levy quota is expected to maintain the retail prices of sugar in the open market at reasonable level.

1378. (1-6-2007) NEW DELHI : Dr. Justice K. Narayana Kurup has assumed the office of the Chairman of the Wage Boards for working journalists and non-working journalists of newspapers and news agencies here on Thursday. Dr. Justice Kurup heads the two Wage Boards having 10 members each. The Wage Boards have been constituted for the purpose of fixing or revising wages of working journalists and newspaper employees and non working journalists newspaper employees in accordance with the provisions of the Working Journalists and other Newspaper Employees (Conditions of Service) and Miscellaneous Provisions Act, 1955. The Board is to submit its report within 3 years. Dr. Justice Kurup is a former judge of Kerala High Court and has also served as an Acting Chief Justice of Madras High Court.

1379. (1-6-2007) NEW DELHI : Visiting Union Minister of Petroleum and Natural Gas Shri Murli Deora held bilateral talks with his Russian and Sudanese counterparts on the sidelines of the UNESCO's Ministerial Conference at Paris late yesterday evening. During his discussions with Mr. Victor Khristenko, Minister of Industry and Energy, Russia, Shri Deora invited Russian oil & gas sector to invest in India. He said Indian Oil PSUs are simultaneously keen to invest in Russia particularly in the exploration and production activities. Both the Ministers said that there is tremendous potential to further enhance mutual cooperation in the sector. Mr. Khristenko pointed out that the Russian companies could utilize the investment opportunities in India in the oil & gas sector in general and in the downstream activities in particular. The meeting took place in the back-drop of the discussions held during Russian President Mr. Vladimir Putin's visit to India about accelerating cooperation in the oil sector. During the talks between Indian Minister and his Sudanese counterpart, Mr. Awad Ahmad Alijaz, Minister of

Energy, Sudanese Minister invited Indian oil & gas companies to aggressively participate in the coming round of bidding for exploration blocks in Sudan. The two Ministers reviewed the existing cooperation and projects in oil & gas sector. They expressed satisfaction regarding the progress of the projects under implementation/production. The Sudanese Minister also expressed his great appreciation of the role played by ONGC Videsh Ltd. in development of Sudanese upstream sector (exploration and production) and the community welfare projects implemented in Sudan. Mr. Awad praised the Indian company for completing the pipeline project in Sudan before schedule.

1380. (1-6-2007) NEW DELHI : Meena Gupta has taken charge as Secretary in the Ministry of Environment and Forests (MoEF). A 1971 batch IAS officer of the Orissa cadre, she worked in the same Ministry as Chief of this Regulatory Agency in 2003. Prior to that, she was the health secretary of the Orissa government. She had been assigned the GEAC role briefly, earlier in 2003. Bureaucratic circles were very impressed with her handling of the health issues in the aftermath of the super cyclone that hit the Orissa coast in 2001. Terming the job of GEAC challenging work, she did commendable job for recombinant streptokinase drug's clearance. Before joining Ministry of Environment and Forests, she worked as Secretary, Tribal Affairs.

1381. (1-6-2007) NEW DELHI : The following are the excerpts from the "Report to the People 2004-07" on Tribal Affairs. The report was released by the Prime Minister, Dr. Manmohan Singh on 22nd May, 2007. National Tribal Policy: the Government has formulated a draft National Tribal Policy covering all important issues that concern tribal people, such as alienation of tribal land, tribal-forest interface, resettlement and rehabilitation, primitive tribal groups, empowerment, enlisting support of NGOs, tribal culture, traditional knowledge, development and administration of tribal areas, scheduling and de-scheduling of tribes, etc. A plan of Action for three years is being incorporated in the draft policy itself. The resettlement and rehabilitation policy regarding displacement of tribal people is being reworked to provide for suitable legal provisions. Rights of forest dwelling STs in forest: the Scheduled Tribes and other Traditional Forest Dwellers (Recognition of Forests Rights) Act, 2006 will improve the lives of members belonging to the scheduled tribes and other traditional forest dwellers living in forest since generations by vesting various forest rights, such as rights over forest land occupied by them agriculture and ownership of minor forest produce, including the right to collect, use and dispose of such produce, and certain other traditional and customary rights. It will remove the threat of eviction from forestland under their occupation. This will also make them entitled to the benefits of various schemes of the Government. In undisputed cases, the distribution of pattas and Green cards is targeted on 14.11.07. for disputed cases, distribution is targeted by 26.1.08. Institutional focus: the Cabinet Committee on Tribal Affairs has been set up to address issues concerning tribal development on a continuing basis. The

Committee of Ministers on Dalit Affairs has been set up to bring greater focus on dalit affairs. Separate national Commission have been set up for scheduled castes and scheduled tribes. A commission has also been set up on denotified tribes. Developing lands of SCs and STs: the National Rural Employment Guarantee Scheme provides for improvement of fields of farmers belonging to the Scheduled Castes and the Scheduled Tribes. A National project for the Repair, Renovation and Restoration of Water Bodies used by farmers especially in dry land, remote and tribal areas, has been launched on irrigation potential. This gives priority to SC/ST farmlands. The Accelerated Irrigation Benefits Programme guidelines have been revised to also include surface minor irrigation in non-special category states for tribal and drought-prone areas and this is expected to predominantly benefit Scheduled Castes and Scheduled Tribes. A programme has been initiated to provide assistance for minor irrigation schemes for land belonging to the Scheduled Tribes. Creation of irrigation potential of 10 lakh hectares by 2009 under Bharat Nirman through groundwater will primarily benefit small and marginal farmers among the Scheduled Castes and the Scheduled Tribes. Outlays for the Scheduled Castes and Tribes: the allocation for Scheduled Castes and the Scheduled Tribes has been substantially enhanced each year. The allocation for schemes benefiting them has increased to Rs. 17,691 crore in 2007-08 from Rs. 12,592 crore in 2006-07.

1382. (1-6-2007) NEW DELHI : The Chief Minister of Mizoram, Shri Zoramthanga met the Union Home Minister, Shri Shivraj Patil here yesterday to discuss the issue of repatriation of Bru (Reang) migrants from Tripura to Mizoram. They agreed that this is a humanitarian problem and needs to be resolved at the earliest. The Home Minister offered to provide all possible help from the Centre to the State Government for rehabilitation of Bru migrants. The Mizoram Government will expedite identification of migrants to satisfy itself that they belonged to Mizoram before they migrated to Tripura. The Ministry of Home Affairs has been making persistent efforts for repatriation of Bru migrants who have gone to Tripura since 1997.

1383. (1-6-2007) NEW DELHI : India's merchandise exports during April 2007 are valued at US $ 10575.11 million ($ 10.57 billion) which is 23.06 % higher than the level of US $ 8593.51 million ($ 8.59 billion) during April, 2006. In rupee terms, the exports were Rs.44572.18 crores, which is 15.39% higher than the value of exports during April 2006. India's merchandise imports during April 2007 are valued at US $ 17635.33 million representing an increase of 40.69 % over the level of imports valued at US $ 12534.53 million in April, 2006. In Rupee terms, the imports increased by 31.93%. Oil imports during April, 2007 are valued at US $ 4424.91 million which is 11.4 % higher than oil imports valued at US $ 3972.19 million in the corresponding period last year. Non-oil imports during April 2007 are estimated at US $ 13210.42 million which is 54.29 % higher than the level of such imports valued at US $ 8562.34 million in April, 2006. The trade deficit for April 2007 is estimated at US $ 7060.22 million which is higher than the deficit at US $ 3941.02 million during April, 2006.

1384. (1-6-2007) NEW DELHI : Vice Admiral RF Contractor, Director General Coast Guard visited Japan from 26-31 May 07. He was there on an official visit to conduct High Level talks with the Japan Coast Guard authorities in addition to oversee the Japan Coast Guard Sea Review at Tokyo and the VIIIth Indo Japan Coast Guard Joint Exercise at Nagoya. The DG was accorded a very warm welcome by Commandant Hiroki Ishikawa, Chief of Japanese Coast Guard. During his official meetings with his Japanese counterpart and other agencies, various issues such as cooperation in the field of search and rescue, anti-piracy, drugs and arms trafficking, illegal immigration, environmental protection, disaster management and response, boarding Operations and training were discussed. The DG Coast Guard also took the Salute of Indian Coast Guard Ship-Sagar during the steam past by the ship. Indian and Japanese Coast Guards have been conducting joint exercises every year since the year 2000 alternately in India and Japan. Last year on November 24th, a memorandum of Cooperation was signed between the two Coast Guards at Mumbai. The visit of this High Level delegation led by the Indian Director General thus assumes great significance in the context of Indo-Japan strategic and Global Partnership dialogue initiated during Prime Minister Dr. Manmohan Singh's visit to Japan in December last year.

1385. (1-6-2007) NEW DELHI : Hydrogen holds the promise to provide clean, reliable and sustainable energy supply for meeting the growing energy needs for transportation and power generation in the coming years. Hydrogen can be used directly as a fuel for producing mechanical / electrical energy through internal combustion engines. It can also be used in fuel cells to generate electricity for stationary, portable and transport applications. Hydrogen is environmentally benign and has the potential to replace liquid fossil fuels in the future and thereby provide energy security to India. Recognizing the importance of hydrogen as an energy carrier for the future, the Ministry of New and Renewable Energy, as the nodal Ministry for this sector, has been implementing a broad based Research, Development and Demonstration Programme on Hydrogen Energy and Fuel Cell Technologies for more than two decades. In recent years, significant progress has been reported by several countries including India in the development of hydrogen as an alternative fuel both for automotive and stationary applications. A National Hydrogen Energy Road Map (NHERM) was prepared by a Steering Group set up by the National Hydrogen Energy Board (NHEB which was set up earlier in October 2003), under the Chairmanship of Shri Ratan Tata. The National Hydrogen Energy Road Map was approved by the National Hydrogen Energy Board in January, 2006. The NHERM has identified research, development and demonstration efforts to be undertaken in the country for bridging the technological gaps in different areas of hydrogen energy, including its production, storage, transportation and delivery, applications, safety, codes and standards and capacity building for the period up to 2020. The Road Map has emphasised on development of the total hydrogen energy system, which includes all the above components of hydrogen energy sector. Keeping in view the present status of development of hydrogen energy, the NHERM has recommended two major initiatives for promoting the use of hydrogen as a fuel for Green Transportation (Green Initiative for Future Transportation-GIFT) and Green Power Generation (Green Initiative for Power Generation-GIP). The National Hydrogen Energy Road Map has visualized that by 2020, one million hydrogen fuelled vehicles, mostly two and three wheelers, and 1,000 MW aggregate hydrogen based power generation capacity would be established in the country. A total investment requirement of Rs.25,000 crores has been projected in the Road Map for creating the required hydrogen supply infrastructure to realize the goals of one million vehicles and 1,000 MW power generation capacity by 2020, including Rs.1,000 crores for research, development and demonstration activities. The Road Map is a public-private partnership driven process.

1386. (1-6-2007) NEW DELHI: The Union Home Ministry on Thursday carried out a detailed review of the situation in Rajasthan in the wake of continued Gujjar violence in different parts of the State. After a detailed discussion with senior officials of the Ministry, Union Home Secretary Madhukar Gupta held a video-conference with the State Chief Secretary and the Director-General of Police. At the high-level meeting, where the Directors-General of the Border Security Force (BSF), the Central Reserve Police Force (CRPF) and the Railway Protection Force (RPF) were present, Mr. Gupta also reviewed the availability of paramilitary forces in the State. Special Secretary (Internal Security) Mahendra Kumawat was present.

1387. (1-6-2007) NEW DELHI : Suspension of operations agreement with the National Democratic Front of Bodoland (NDFB), a militant outfit operating in Assam, has been extended for a period of 6 months upto 30.11.2007. The agreement has been in operation since 01.06.2005.

1388. (1-6-2007) NEW DELHI : Prof. Saifuddin Soz, the Union Minister for Water Resources participated in the Asian Regional Dialogue on Water and Sanitation at Shanghai on May 31, 2007, organized by the UN Secretary General's Advisory Board on Water and Sanitation (UNSGAB) along with the Asian Development Bank (ADB) and the Government of China. This was the second ever such regional dialogue to build on the Hashimoto Action Plan adopted in Mexico in March, 2006 to improve water and sanitation access on a global scale. The Dialogue was chaired by HRH Prince Willem-Alexander of the Netherlands. In his address at the forum, Prof. Soz noted that the National Water Policy of India accorded primacy to drinking water needs of the population. Government of India was implementing a dedicated Accelerated Rural Water Supply Programme to extend supply to all rural inhabitants in the country. He also stressed the fact that Government of India attaches great importance to extension of irrigation and sanitation facilities on a wider scale. Prof Soz. underlined the need for sustaining the created facilities which can be done effectively by fully involving the stake holders at grass-root level, in the process of its planning, implementation and operation. He noted that over 60,000 Water User Associations had already been established in the country, which were energetically performing the intended role. Prof. Soz had a bilateral meeting with his Chinese counterpart H.E. Chen Lei on June 1, 2007. The Ambassador of India in China, Ms. Nirupama Rao, was present at the meeting. He congratulated Minister Chen on his assumption of office recently, and commended China's timely initiative to convene the Dialogue. He stressed the need for sustained bilateral cooperation in water resources, which directly affects the well-being of people of both countries and hoped that the canvas of cooperation would broaden further, in line with the understanding reached during His Excellency President Hu Jintao's visit to India in November 2006. He expressed the hope that the bilateral expert level mechanism to discuss cooperation in this field would be convened at an early date. He also invited Minister Chen to visit India. Minister Chen welcomed Prof. Soz's visit to China which had provided a useful opportunity for an exchange of views between the two sides. Recalling the visit of his predecessor to India in 2004, he observed that India-China cooperation in the water sector, which was important for both countries, was steadily expanding. He said that China was working towards the early convening of the expert level meeting and that preparations were on in this regard. Minister Chen added that he looked forward to visiting India and also invited Minister Soz to return to China on a bilateral visit."

1389. (1-6-2007) NEW DELHI : Central Water Commission (CWC) under Ministry of Water Resources is monitoring storage position of 76 important reservoirs spread all over the country, of which as many as 31 reservoirs have significant hydro-power benefits with installed capacity of more than 60 MW each. The combined live storage in these 76 reservoirs at the beginning of monsoon *i.e.* 1st June, 2006 was 22 per cent of their designed capacity and stood at 51 per cent of the designed capacity as on 24th May 2007. The present storage is 112 per cent of the last year's storage and 153 per cent of last 10 years average storage during the same period. Out of these 76 reservoirs there are presently 8 reservoirs where this year's storage is 80 per cent or less than the average of previous 10 years and in the remaining 58 reservoirs the storage is more than 80 per cent of the average of previous 10 years. In order to derive the best possible benefits from the available water, Central Water Commission is keeping in touch with the Department of Agriculture and Cooperation and providing information of the weekly storage position to the Crop Weather Watch Group for evolving suitable crop strategies and also apprising the situation to various Departments and Ministries involved in Water Resources Planning.

1390. (1-6-2007) NEW DELHI : A special free roaming plan is being introduced by Bharat Sanchar Nigam Limited (BSNL) and Mahanagar Telephone Nigam

Limited (MTNL) on 3rd June, 2007 for their customers. Announcing the new plans of their respective organizations at joint press conference here today, Shri AK Sinha, CMD, BSNL and Shri RSP Sinha, CMD, MTNL stated that this unique plan will provide freedom to the customers from incoming roaming charges up to 300 minutes / 5 hours of free talk time per month. Shri AK Sinha further informed that this plan provides free incoming roaming of 300 minutes at a very special post-paid plan of Rs. 550/-per month on a network which has its reach from Kashmir to Kanyakumari and from Dibrugarh to Dwarka. The scheme will be open to all BSNL's Cellone customers who can avail this facility without any additional charges.

1391. (1-6-2007) NEW DELHI : 1. The Chief of Air Staff, Air Chief Marshal Fali Major 'flagged off' a 'Round the World' Microlight expedition today from Air Force Station Hindon. The Microlight expedition has been undertaken by two IAF pilots Wg Cdr R Monga and Wg Cdr Anil Kumar. This expedition is a part of ongoing IAF platinum jubilee celebration, with a purpose of living the spirit of adventure and international goodwill. 2. The expedition has been undertaken in a German manufactured Microlight aircraft called the 'CSTW Advance'. The Microlight aircraft would be attempting to cover more than 39,000 kms in about 45 days. In addition, rest and maintenance activities have been planned on 19 days. This would also be an attempt to set a new world record for fastest time in circumnavigating the world in 300-500 kg weight category. The route has been approved by the Aero Club of India, which represents Federation Aeronautique International (FAI), the governing body for aerosports. 3. In an address prior to the flagging off, Air Chief Marshal Major said " I wish I could take the place of the expedition's crew for what they are setting out to accomplish has all the ingredients of a great adventure-challenge, excitement hint off danger, unpredictability of elements of nature, foreign lands & unfamiliar route". Giving example of various aviation adventurist from Wright brothers to Mr. Vijaypat Singhania he said "Aviation & flight are very embodiment of human striving and sprit of adventure". He also said "as the prime custodian of the legacy of aviation in India, the IAF has responsibility not only to push the envelop itself but also to promote aero-sport activity in the country. This would also help inculcate an air-mindedness in our people". The chief wished the crew 'bon-voyage' on behalf of the IAF. 4. Wg Cdr Monga, on being asked how he feels to be going around the world for the expedition, said "We are keen on getting on with the expedition. I am proud to represent the country and the Indian Air Force in such an event. Me and my entire team have put in a lot of effort 'planning' the expedition, it's time to live it. With God's grace and well wishes of the entire country we will be successful". 5. The Empty weight of Microlight is 300 kgs and it has a range of 1400 km. The Microlight has ceiling of 14,000 feet. It has a glass cockpit, and electronic flight instrumentation system (EFIS), internal GPS, a satellite tracker and a VOR coupled R/T set. It is also fitted with an emergency parachute recovery system. 6. The IAF is attempting an expedition requiring great fortitude. The expedition will be a true test of both men and machine. There will be challenges of extremes of weather, change of time zones, flying through different countries and interacting with various agencies all across the world. The crew would be totally independent; even for undertaking scheduled servicing. In addition to highlighting the capability of IAF in undertaking such an expedition, it also embodies the true sprit of adventurous aviation. The route of Microlight would be from Delhi (India)-Myanmar-Thailand-China-Russia-Canada-Alaska-Greenland-EU Countires-Turkey-UAE-Oman and back to India.

1392. (1-6-2007) NEW DELHI : Shri Subodh Kant Sahai, Minister of State (Independent Charge), Food Processing Industries Ministry is on a twelve-day official tour to the United States of America. During his visit the Minister will meet the US Agriculture Secretary, Mr. Mike Johannes in Washington. Shri Sahai will have a meeting with the representatives of the US Industry in New York and visit the Chicago Board of Trade in Chicago and the Culinary Institute of America located at St. Helena. He will also meet with the Captains of the Food Processing Companies in Los Angles and visit Melissa's World Variety Produce at Vernon. The issues that would come under discussion during his visit include integrated cold chain facilities, packaging issues, irradiation facilities and food parks.

1393. (1-6-2007) NEW DELHI : The Ministry of Rural Development has released the payment of Grants-in-aid amounting to Rs. 97.25 lakh as part of first instalment to Dehradun district of Uttarakhand State as Central assistance for the implementation of the SGRY during the current financial year (2007-08). The grant is towards plan expenditure and will be utilized for approved items of works subject to the conditions laid down in the SGRY Guidelines. No deviations from the guidelines is permissible. The expenditure on implementation of the programme with regard to cash component is to be shared on 75:25 basis between the Central and the State Government respectively.

1394. (1-6-2007) NEW DELHI : The Minister for Social Justice and Empowerment, Smt. Meira Kumar said that the Human Rights violation of children and youth, particularly, the girl children is a cause of prime concern and the Government is committed to ensure the human rights of the girl child. She was speaking at the 15th Rotary India Award function here today. She advocated for an urgent need to repeal existing laws and regulations and remove customs and practices, which discriminate against and cause harm to the girl child so that effective protection and promotion of human rights of girl child may be ensured. In order to safeguard the future sustainability of the actions initiated towards the protection of the girl child, she said that there is an urgent need to further strengthen the national and international mechanisms and programmes for the defence and protection of under-privileged and disadvantaged children in particular the girl child. Smt. Meira Kumar informed that the Ministry of Social Justice and Empowerment is dedicated towards educational empowerment of girl child. The Ministry provides Pre and Post Matric Scholarship to disadvantaged girls, particularly, those belongs to the SC and other backward classes. The Ministry has increased the central funding from 50% to 100% for the Construction of Girls Hostel by revising the scheme for construction of hostels for SC boys and girls so that they can pursue their education in a protected and enabling environment. She further said that gender disparity in education still remains a matter of serious concern in our society. This is evident from the drop out rates among girls, which are still on the higher, particularly in the rural areas. It is estimated that for every ten girl children who enroll in Class 1, only three reach Class X. The Government under "Sarva Shiksha Abhiyan" has started offering compulsory elementary education to all children in the age Group of 6 to 14 so that social, regional and gender gaps may be eliminated. The Minister also urged the voluntary organizations, corporate institutions and social activists to make sustained efforts in promoting equality of opportunity for the girl child so that their personal, economic and social aspirations and potentials may be fulfilled so that they get protection from all forms of exploitation. Vatsalalya, an NGO in Lucknow was selected for the Award for year 2006 for protection and care of the girl child. Former Prime Minister, Shri. I.K. Gujral was also present in the function.

1395. (2-6-2007) NEW DELHI : Following violence in parts of Rajasthan, the Prime Minister, Dr. Manmohan Singh has issued the following appeal, here today. "The events of the past few days in parts of Rajasthan have caused a great deal of pain and distress to large numbers of people. Sadly, many lives have been lost, plunging their families into grief. My heart grieves for all those who have lost their family members and those who have suffered injuries. I appeal to all the people of Rajasthan and also those in neighbouring States to maintain peace and calm. I appeal to all sections of society to desist from actions which may lead to further violence and distress and which will disrupt the lives of ordinary citizens."

1396. (1-6-2007) NEW DELHI : Following is the text of the speech delivered by the Defence Minister Shri A K Antony at the Second Plenary Session on 'China and India: Building International Stability' of the 6th Asia Security Conference, also known as the Shangri-La Dialogue-2007. "Most of us gathered here today are professionally focussed on security issues. We deal with different dimensions of security-from internal and regional, to the continental and global. We also envisage the definition of security in varied ways-from the traditional hard security viewpoint to its larger and softer concepts. We have been made aware too that the nature of threats that societies face are constantly changing. Obviously, our responses which are so critical to ensuring international stability must keep pace with those changes. Today, I share India's thinking on these subjects, less as a projection of static interests vis-a-vis an external world, and more as a viewpoint of a country integrating with a larger global canvas. I hope thus to bring out how India's security policies contribute to building international stability. For some international stability is the absence of conflict among the major powers. As was notably the case during the Cold War, international stability in this perspective is also related to a balance of power between major contenders for influence. The Cold War is gone but the concepts of deterrence, balance, arms races and arms control are still seen as important factors in international stability. This point of view may still be valid to a degree but just as our view of security has evolved so too must our view of international stability. Given today's unprecedented globalisation in trade, technology, media, and a host of other areas, our lives are linked together in myriad ways. This interdependence is in itself a major dampener of conflict, reducing the incentive for major players to seek a resolution of differences by a show of strength. However, globalisation has highlighted new threats to international stability such as meltdown of currencies and financial markets-a new domino theory if you will-cascading protectionism, pandemics, uncontrolled migration flows and inability of states to handle change and conflict within thereby generating instability and conflict. Globalisation and interdependence have also changed radically the nature of old threats and enhanced the threat potential of non-state actors. For example, India had to cope with terrorism in the 80s. It was seen by many as India's problem. Today, post 9/11, international terrorism is seen from a very different perspective. The old concepts of balance of power and accommodation of rising powers through slow adjustment of existing frameworks need to be updated and supplemented if we are to successfully handle these challenges to international stability. In this background and as Minister of Defence, how do I see India's security priorities? India is the world's most populous democracy. The well-being of its billion plus citizens has to be any Indian Government's first task. This well-being is not only economic. Our Constitution embodies a host of rights and guarantees and directs us to remove social and economic disparities. When security is accompanied by such a broad sense of well being, we can be more certainly assured of stability. Meeting aspirations in the midst of substantial change is, however, a very complex challenge. Yet, it has to be seriously undertaken because mitigating grievances and addressing expectations are central to the management of such change. Values, beliefs and ideologies can make their contribution, both positively and negatively. The point I wish to emphasise is that an effective management of India's internal security at a time of rapid modernisation is itself a key contribution to international stability. When one sixth of the world demonstrates an ability to meet its wants, manage its expectations and govern itself effectively, the significance of that achievement cannot be overvalued.

1397. (3-6-2007) NEW DELHI : The Union Minister of External Affairs, Shri Pranab Mukherjee today said that to reclaim its heritage and realise the full potential of South Asia, it is essential that existing barriers that restrict the movement of people, goods and investments within and across the region be dismantled. It is with this perspective that India has extended its hand of friendship and cooperation to all her neighbours and proactively addresses whatever differences there may be, he said while addressing the concluding session of the conference of parliamentarians from the SAARC region organized by South Asian Free Media Association (SAFMA) on 'South Asian Parliament: Evolving South Asian Fraternity', in Shimla today.

1398. (3-6-2007) NEW DELHI : General of the Army Alexei Fedorovich Maslov, Commander-in-Chief, Russian Land Forces would be on a five day visit to India from Monday. The visit by a Commander-in Chief, Russian Land Forces is being undertaken after a gap of almost eight years since the last visit. The visit assumes special significance in the light of enhanced defence cooperation between the two countries. Indo-Russian bilateral relations are historical, multifaceted and based on mutual trust and confidence. Russia has been the major defence equipment supplier to Indian Armed Forces. Presently the ongoing defence cooperation encompasses equipment procurement, exchange of delegations, conduct of joint exercises, and joint designing, development and marketing of military equipment. The first ever joint Airborne exercise between the two Armies was conducted in 2005 in India and next joint exercise is planned to be conducted in Russia this year. During the visit, the Land Forces Commander will meet the Chief of the Army Staff, Chief of Naval Staff, Chief of Air Staff, Defence Secretary and other dignitaries. He will also visit important institutions of the Indian Armed Forces. The visit of the Commander-in-Chief, Russian Land Forces would give an impetus to the existing defence cooperation and also aim to further diversify Army to Army cooperation in the field of training and exchange of experts in the field of mutual interests.

1399. (4-6-2007) NEW DELHI : The President of India, Dr. A.P.J. Abdul Kalam conferred the Jawaharlal Nehru Award for International Understanding on President Luiz Inacio Lula da Silva of Brazil at a function here today. Following is the text of the President's address on the occasion: "I am indeed delighted to confer the Jawaharlal Nehru Award for International Understanding on President Luiz Inacio Lula da Silva of Brazil who is one of the foremost leaders of Latin America and also one of the leading personalities on the world stage. I am going to discuss with you a few thoughts on "Reaching the Unreached", that is indeed the mission of President Luiz Inacio Lula da Silva. As we honour President Lula with the Jawaharlal Nehru Award, we realize the Award has been enriched. At this point of time, let me recall Pandit Jawaharlal Nehru's sterling contribution to India's development through major national programmes of industrialization, establishment of great science institutions, promoting of science and scientific temper, agrarian and land reforms, infrastructure and energy development. Nehru was also an exponent of people's prosperity, a means to address long-standing national challenges.

1400. (4-6-2007) NEW DELHI : In order to encourage work of excellence in taxonomy-the science of identification, classification and naming of organisms-the Ministry of Environment & Forests has instituted a National Award named after the late Prof. E.K. Janaki Ammal-an eminent Indian scientist & botanist of international repute. The Janaki Ammal National Award on Plant Taxonomy for the year 2006 goes to Dr. N.P. Balakrishnan and the Janaki Ammal National Award on Animal Taxonomy for the year 2006 goes to Prof. (Mrs.) Veena Tandon. Dr. N.P. Balakrishnan has contributed substantially to the understanding of family Euphorbiaceae in the Indian sub-continent. He edited three volumes of 'Flora of India', was responsible for establishment of Andaman & Nicobar Circle of Botanical Survey of India and had done considerable work on plant resources of Andaman & Nicobar Islands. Dr. Balakrishnan has published 185 scientific articles, authored 10 books and has to his credit 19 taxonomic revisions and five monographic works. Prof. (Mrs.) Veena Tandon has worked extensively on Taxonomy of helminth parasites in the North Eastern region of India. She has 33 years of Post-Graduate teaching experience, has guided 12 Ph.D. students, authored 122 research papers & two books and is continuing teaching & research in the North Eastern Hill University, Shillong.

1401. (4-6-2007) NEW DELHI : The Minister for Overseas Indian Affairs, Shri Vayalar Ravi called upon the Indian Community in Suriname to explore areas for grater trade and investment in various sectors, such as energy, mining, agriculture, IT, etc. He was speaking at the Lalla Rookh Foundation in Paramaribo, Suriname. During his meeting with a selected group of businessmen of Indian origin, he discussed issues pertaining to economic, business and trade. He assured India's full support for closer trade and economic relations. During his visit to Suriname, the Mr. Ravi attended the India Arrival Day celebration, organized by Global Organization of Persons of Indian Origin (GOPIO). In his speech, he commended the heroic struggle of the Indians through generations in preserving their culture and tradition alive. He expressed his deep appreciation of role which the present day Persons of Indian Origin (PIOs) of Suriname have been playing in contributing to the unity and prosperity of the country while keeping alive their ancestral link of culture and language. On the occasion, Vice President of Suriname, Ramdien Sadjoe praised the role of the PIOs of Suriname in the economic development and unity of the country. Shri. Ravi also visited St. Vincent and the Grenadines (SVG) and Trinidad and Tobago before arriving Suriname. During his visit to SVG, he attended the India Arrival Day as Chief Guest. In his remark, he praised the Indian Community and IHF for their commendable efforts for celebrating the Indian Arrival Day. He said India like the Caribbean, was also symphony of various cultures. Prime Minister of SVG, Dr. Ralph Gonsalves lauded the contribution of PIOs to economic development of the island. Shri. Ravi also discussed the mutual interest with Prime Minister of SVG. Dr. Ralph sought India's help in area like agro-processing, education, IT, etc. During his visit to Trinidad and Tobago, Shri Ravi attends the 162nd anniversary of the Indian Arrival Day celebrations in Port of Spain. Speaking to gathering consisting of Minister of Culture Joan Yuille-Williams and Christine Sahadeo, Minister of Finance and many other dignitaries, the Minister said he came from India, the land of Mahatma Gandhi and those great ancestors of the PIOs of Trinidad and Tobago. He spoke about the tribulations faced by those who came to this country as indentured labourers, which, he said was another form of slavery, and despite all the hardships managed to preserve their culture and traditions. This culture now formed the heritage of Trinidad and Tobago. He said India was an example of unity in diversity like Trinidad. Shri Ravi held a meeting with President of Trinidad and Tobago, Prof. George Maxwell Richards, Prime Minister Patrick Manning and several other Ministers and exchanged views on matters of bilateral interest. Minister also had a meeting with Leader of the Opposition Kamla Persad-Bissessar. The President raised the issue of greater cooperation in education and academic fields and need for efforts to bridge the trade deficit. Prime Minister Patrick Manning said that the economy of Trinidad was fast expanding and diversifying and also noted the contribution of Indian investment in the economic development of Trinidad and Tobago.

1402. (4-6-2007) NEW DELHI : Government of India have announced the sale (re-issue) of "6.65 percent Government Stock, 2009" under Market Stabilization Scheme for a notified amount of Rs. 5,000 crore (nominal). The Government Stock will be sold through price based auction using multiple price method. The auction will be conducted by the Reserve Bank of India, Mumbai Office, Fort, Mumbai on June 6, 2007 (Wednesday). Up to 5% of the amount notified for the sale of stock is reserved for allotment to eligible individuals and Institutions on non-competitive basis as per the Scheme for Non-Competitive Bidding Facility in the Auction of Government Securities. Bids in the prescribed form obtainable from the Regional Director, Reserve Bank of India, Mumbai Office (Public Debt Office), Fort, Mumbai-400 001 and RBI website www.rbi.org.in should be submitted to that Office on June 6, 2007. The NDS members should submit competitive as well as non-competitive bids in electronic format using Primary Market Operation (PMO) module of NDS. All bids should be submitted by 12.30 P.M. The result of the auction will be announced on June 6, 2007 and payment by successful bidders will be during banking hours on June 7, 2007 (Thursday).

1403. (4-6-2007) NEW DELHI : Shri Murli Deora, Minister (Petroleum & Natural Gas) called on the President, Brazil H.E. Mr. Luiz Nacio Lula Da Silva here today and discussed the potential for collaboration and cooperation between India and Brazil as both are growing economies and the international economic interests of the two nations are similar. Shri Deora thanked H.E. President of Brazil for facilitating the signing of the Heads of the Agreement among ONGC, OVL and Petrobras which was signed earlier today in the presence of Hon'ble President of Brazil and Hon'ble Prime Minister of India. This will lead to enhanced cooperation between the two nations, Mr. Deora said.. The Union Minister also congratulated the President Brazil on being conferred the Jawahar Lal Nehru Award for International Understanding for the year 2006. He lauded the immense contribution made by H.E. towards the strengthening of bilateral relations between India and

Brazil and the award is a recognition of the achievements of the President as an individual and the nation of Brazil. He also requested for expediting action on the issues of joint collaboration for which an MOU was signed between OVL and Petrobras on 12th September, 2006. This will lead to joint participation by ONGC/ OVL and Petrobras for acquiring Exploration and Production (E&P) assets in Brazil, India and third countries. Minister, Petroleum & Natural Gas expressed satisfaction on the present level of collaboration in E&P by ONGC/OVL and Petrobras. Minister, Petroleum & Natural Gas indicated that Indian Navratna National Oil Companies like ONGC, IOC, BPCL and GAIL are further interested in E&P in Brazil. Shri Deora informed the President that on the Brazilian example, India has also started mixing of Ethanol with Petrol. Presently 5% ethanol blended petrol (EBP) programme has been launched in major parts of India. Minister, Petroleum & Natural Gas requested that India would like to collaborate with Brazil on EBP for better technology to gain from the experience and expertise of Brazil. The President of Brazil reciprocated the sentiments and views expressed by Minister (P&NG) and hoped for closer cooperation between the two countries. He was accompanied by Shri M.S. Srinivasan, Secretary Petroleum & Natural Gas, Shri Sundareshan, Additional Secretary, Ministry of Petroleum & Natural Gas, Shri R.S. Sharma, CMD, Oil & Natural Gas Corporation Limited (ONGC) and Shri R.S. Butola, Managing Director, ONGC Videsh Limited (OVL).

1404. (4-6-2007) SHIMLA: External Affairs Minister Pranab Mukherjee on Sunday dismissed Pakistan's charge that India had heavily militarised Jammu and Kashmir. Security forces in the State were trying to restore normality, he said. Addressing a two-day conference titled 'Towards South Asian unity,' organised by the South Asian Free Media Association (SAFMA), he said: "I don't agree with suggestions that there is militarisation in Kashmir. Security forces and law-enforcing agencies are maintaining law and order in the State." Mr. Mukherjee said the committee set up by the Centre in April to consider the demand for reduction of troops in the State was doing its job. Pakistan had been claiming that India had posted some 7 lakh troops in Jammu and Kashmir and insisting that their strength be reduced. Asked if India and Pakistan were close to finding a solution to the Kashmir issue, he said they were discussing outstanding issues within the framework of the composite dialogue process. Three rounds of talks had already been concluded and the fourth was now in progress. "I do hope that we will be able to resolve" the issue, he said.

1405. (4-6-2007) NEW DELHI : Gen of Russian Army Alexie Feodorovich Maslov, Commander in Chief, Russian Land Forces arrived here in the early hours today. He is accompanied by his wife Mrs. Natalia and a delegation comprising of two other officers. After laying a wreath at Amar Jawan Jyoti, he was accorded a guard of honour at South Block Lawns. The Russian Army Chief had wide ranging talks with his Indian counterpart, Gen JJ Singh. Gen Maslov was born in 1953 in Kursk region of Russia. After graduation from the Military Academy of the Armoured Forces, he has held various appointments to include Divisional Commanding Officer in the Volga-Urals Military District. After graduation from the General Staff Military Academy, he served as Commander of the Baikal Military District in charge of combat training, and as Army Corps Commander in the Siberian Military District. In March 2003 he was as appointed Chief of Staff and First Deputy Commander of the North Caucasus Military District. He is holding the present appointment since Nov. 2004. Gen Maslov was briefed on India's Security perspective at the Army Headquarters. He later visited the BrahMos organization. His schedule includes meetings with the Air Force and Naval Chiefs and Defence Secretary, Shri Shekhar Dutt.

1406. (4-6-2007) NEW DELHI : BJP President Shri Rajnath Singh said that he was satisfied with the final outcome of the talks between the Rajasthan Government and leaders of the Gujjar and other communities. Speaking to the media the BJP President said that over the last few days the agitation over the issue of reservation by the Gujjar community in Rajasthan and some other neighbouring states had finally reached a satisfactory and harmonious conclusion this evening. Shri Rajnath Singh in particular thanked the leaders of the Gujjar and Meena Communities for playing a constructive role in the talks with the Rajasthan Government. Shri Singh added that he was confident that in addition to the Gujjar and Meena communities, all other communities would also play a positive and constructive role in maintaining social harmony and cohesion. The BJP President at the same time conveyed his heartfelt condolences and sympathies to the families of those people who lost their lives during the agitation. BJP Vice President Shri Yashwant Sinha and party spokesperson Shri Ravi Shankar Prasad were also present during the briefing.

1407. (4-6-2007) NEW DELHI : The recession of Glaciers is a worldwide phenomenon including the icy continent of Antarctica. The glaciers show recession both in area and volume. Recession of Himalayan glacier is a natural cyclic process sensitive to climate fluctuation wherein the rise in global average temperature results in melting of the glaciers. The studies carried out by Geological Survey of India have revealed that the majority of glaciers of Himalayan Region are passing through a phase of recession for over a century now. The recession may result due to sub-normal snowfall, higher temperature during summer, less severe winter or a combination of all of them. Thus, the recession of the glaciers does not necessarily mean rapid melting. Due to enhanced melting of ice, consequent upon faster recession the run off the Himalayan rivers may increase initially but it may ultimately lead to some reduction of water availability in future, as the size and number of glaciers may reduce. However, the Himalayan Rivers will continue to flow as the major parts of the water in these rivers come from seasonal snowfall, groundwater, precipitation, etc. Hence, the presumption of recession of glaciers will lead to reduction in water availability is not well founded. As the recession of the glaciers is a natural process, it cannot be checked in absolute terms.

However, the Government of India has identified the possible measures for reducing the recession of glacier which include conservation activities such as afforestation, removal of garbage, restriction on human interference on glaciers and promotion of sustainable ecotourism. ISRO and Ministry of Environment & Forests are carrying out a comprehensive programme on inventory of glaciers, their retreat and mass balance studies. This programme will help in monitoring the glaciers in the Himalayas.

1408. (4-6-2007) NEW DELHI : A survey conducted by the National Sample Survey Organization (NSSO), shows that the total employment in both the organized and the unorganised sectors in the country is 39.7 crore, of which 2.8 crore are in the organized sector and 36.9 crore (about 93%) are in the unorganised sector. Of this, 23.7 crore workers are in the agricultural sector and 1.7 crore are engaged in construction sector. Remaining workers are engaged in mining, manufacturing and services sector. On account of their unorganised nature, these workers do not get adequate social security and welfare. Some welfare schemes are being implemented by the Central Government for specific occupational groups of unorganised sector workers such as beedi workers, non-coal mine workers, cine workers, handloom weavers, fishermen, etc. These are apart from the National old Age Pension Scheme and National Rural Health Mission. Some of the State Governments have also been implementing welfare programmes for certain categories of the unorganised sector workers. Some NGOs are also providing social security to certain categories of workers. Despite all these efforts, there is a deficit in the coverage of the unorganised sector workers in the matter of labour protection and social security measures.

1409. (4-6-2007) NEW DELHI : Climate change due to rising levels of Carbon dioxide in the atmosphere is one of the most serious environmental concerns of our time. General expansion of economic activity, increased population and use of fossil fuels are responsible for man made emission of Green house Gases (GHG). To address the problem posed by Climate Change the international community set up the United Nations Framework Convention on Climate Change (UNFCCC) in 1992, based on the principle of "common but differentiated responsibilities and respective capabilities of countries". The objective of UNFCCC is to stabilize GHGs concentration in the atmosphere to prevent dangerous anthropogenic interference with the climate system. Later in the year 1997, Parties adopted the Kyoto Protocol which sets legally binding targets for GHG reductions by industrialized countries during "first commitment period", 2008-2012, totalling 5.2% below their aggregate 1990 emissions. The projected climatic change indicates adverse impacts on developing countries in many ways resulting in changes in frequency, duration and intensity of extreme events such as heat waves and heavy precipitation events. Climate change would also increase the threats to human health due to increase in vector borne diseases. The impacts of climate change would fall disproportionately upon developing countries and would further exacerbate inequities in health status, access to food, clean water and other resources. India in particular is seriously concerned about the climate change because of its dependency on climate sensitive sectors like agriculture and forestry for livelihoods. The Clean Development Mechanism (CDM) is one of the flexible arrangements under the Kyoto protocol to the United Nations Framework Convention on Climate Change (UNFCCC) supporting the implementation of sustainable and environmentally friendly technologies in developing countries and thereby, facilitating industrialized countries in meeting their emission reduction obligations in a cost-effective manner. India's CDM potential represents a significant component of the global CDM market. As on 23rd May 2007, 235 out of total 674 projects registered by the CDM Executive Board are from India, which so far is the highest by any country in the world. Also as on date the National CDM Authority has accorded Host Country Approval to 615 projects facilitating an investment of Rs. 54,536 crores. These projects are in the sectors of energy efficiency, fuel switching, industrial processes, municipal solid waste and renewable energy.

1410. (4-6-2007) NEW DELHI : The Ministry of Rural Development has approved the release of 3392 MT of Common Rice during the year 2007-08 to Durg District of Chhattisgarh State through Food Corporation of India depots in the State under the Sampoorna Grameen Rozgar Yojana (SGRY) scheme. The grant is towards plan expenditure and will be utilized for approved items of works subject to the conditions laid down in the SGRY Guidelines.

1411. (4-6-2007) CHENNAI: Dravida Munnetra Kazhagam (DMK) president and Chief Minister M. Karunanidhi on Sunday said his party would strive further for ensuring that only secular Governments come to power in the country both at the Centre and the States. Addressing a public meeting held here to mark his 84th birthday, he said that it was the DMK, which laid the foundation at a critical time for bringing back a secular Government at the Centre. Now it had to be ensured that only secular Governments were installed in every State. The DMK should go down in history as stabilising this process, he said.

1412. (4-6-2007) NEW DELHI : The Ministry of Rural Development has sanctioned Rs. 20.04 crore to the State Government of Haryana towards balance of first instalment of funds against the provisional allocation of Rs.60.13 crore made for the Government of Haryana under Accelerated Rural Water Supply Programme (Normal) of Rajiv Gandhi National Drinking Water Mission, during the year 2007-08. Up to 15 per cent of funds released under this sanction may be utilized for Operation & Maintenance and up to 5 per cent of funds may be spent for taking sustainability measures. States have been requested to delegate powers for management of Rural Water Supply Schemes through the Panchayati Raj Institutions (PRIs) as per the Constitution of India. As such Operation and Maintenance of the completed RWS Scheme should be transferred to the PRIs. No expenditure shall be incurred on taking water quality problems form the present release, as there is a separate allocation for the purpose. This release is being made for execution/completion of schemes to provide safe drinking water facilities to rural habitations and schools under the Centrally Sponsored ARWSP. Priorities set in ARWSP guidelines and through other instructions issued from time to time shall be followed for coverage of rural habitations and rural schools.

1413. (4-6-2007) NEW DELHI : The Ministry of Rural Development has released Rs. 180.36 crore as balance payment of first instalment of Phase-IV under ADB assisted RRSIP and Rs.258.05 crore as Grants-in-aid for Phase-VI as balance payment of first instalment to the MADHYA PRADESH RURAL ROADS DEVELOPMENT AUTHORITY (MPRRDA), which is the Autonomous Agency for receiving the funds for the programme under Pradhan Mantri Gram Sadak Yojana (PMGSY). The grant is towards the Plan expenditure and will be subject to the conditions laid down from time to time in the guidelines of the PMGSY and supplementary directions. PMGSY was launched in December 2000 as a 100 per cent Centrally Sponsored Scheme with a target of connecting every habitation that has a population of more than 1000 within the next three years and every habitation with a population of more than 500 by the year 2007 *i.e.* by the end of the 10th Five Year Plan through good all-weather road. A sum of Rs.20,400.70 crore has been released to the States/UTs towards the programme and up to December 2006, 35,868 roadworks covering a length of 1,07,569.08 Kms. have been completed.

1414. (4-6-2007) NEW DELHI : The National Hydrogen Energy road Map lays down the pathway for the development of Hydrogen energy infrastructure in the country including introduction of Hydrogen Fueled Vehicles by 2020. Giving a Presidential address in the conclave on National Hydrogen Energy Road Map : Opportunities for Public Private Partnership (PPP), the Minister of State for the Ministry of New and Renewable Energy, Shri Vilas Muttemwar sad that the Ministry is confident of achieving over ten per cent of the total installed power generating capacity in the country by 2012 from Renewable Power. The Minister further said about 10 lakh solar photovoltaic systems are being used for domestic lighting purposes. Today India has largest programmes on renewable energy technologies in the world. The total power generating capacity in the country as of March 2007 was about 1,33,000 MW. Renewable power generating capacity is about 10,252 MW, which contributes 7.75 per cent of the installed power generating capacity. Among renewable power technologies the major contributions are from Wind Power (7092 MW) Small Hydro Power (1976 MW), Bio Energy (1187 MW) and 155 MW of grid distributed renewable power. Our Ministry has been appointed as the nodal Ministry for the overall coordination of the National Bio Fuel Programme. Bio Fuels provides short term answer to alleviate the problem of climate change, the long term answer has been recognized the world over to come from hydrogen which is being called the free fuel for future. India is actively involved in hydrogen and fuel cell research and development for more than two decades in academic institutions universities, research and development institutions and industry. The Minister added recognizing the importance of hydrogen as a green future fuel, the Ministry set up a National Hydrogen Energy Board in 2003. The Board has set up a Steering Group under the Chairmanship of Shri Ratan Tata to prepare a National Hydrogen Road Map. Under this initiatives about 1 million Hydrogen Fuel vehicles, of which about 75 per cent vehicles are expected to be two and three wheelers, would be plying on the Indian Roads. Aggregate hydrogen based power generating capacity of 1000 MW would be set up by that time. Dr. R.Chidambaram, Principal Scientific Advisor, Government of India, in his special address said that hydrogen is a source of clean energy. He said per capita electricity consumption and female literacy are main factors for development of any country. Apart from water, distillery waste bagasse etc. can be used to produce hydrogen fuel. Shri Ratan Tata, Chairman Tata Group and Chairman Steering Group, NHEB, Tata said hydrogen fuel will be alternative to fossil fuel on which national economy can be build. He said hydrogen may remain illusive for long term because there are challenges to generated, to store and to deliver it. India has enormous strength of scientists and manpower and I am confident that if not us, our future generation will definitely have clear fuel. Dr. Montek Singh Ahluwalia, Dy Chairman, Planning Commission, giving inaugural address, said to reduce emission clean fuel like hydrogen will help. The Ministry is looking for new energy which has high potential. We should develop more technologies and put efforts in more research.

1415. (4-6-2007) NEW DELHI : The Repair, Renovation and Restoration work in 619 Water Bodies has been completed till March, 2007. Ministry of Water Resources has approved 1098 Water Bodies for 26 district projects in 15 States, namely, Andhra Pradesh, Bihar, Chattisgarh, Jharkhand, Karnataka, Madhya Pradesh, Orissa, Rajasthan, Tamil Nadu, West Bengal, Himachal Pradesh, J&K, Gujarat, Kerala and Maharashtra at an estimated cost of Rs. 299.92 crores. The World Bank Loan Agreement signed with Tamil Nadu for Rs.2182 crores to restore 5763 water bodies having a CCA of 4 lakh hectares. The negotiations for the project "Andhra Pradesh Community-Based Tank Management Project" at the cost of about Rs.1000 crores have been completed in March 2007 for restoration of 3000 water bodies with a CCA of 2.5 lakh hectares. The Projects of Karnataka, Orissa and West Bengal are at the different stages of appraisal by the World Bank. Under the scheme of "National Project for Repair, Renovation and Restoration of Water Bodies, it is proposed to restore water bodies throughout India to their original glory which is likely to upgrade the storage capacity significantly. Pilot projects were to be taken up for the purpose in at least five districts. For this purpose, a pilot scheme has been approved by Government of India in January, 05 at an estimated cost of Rs. 300 crores to be implemented during the remaining period of the Xth Five Year Plan. This scheme is a state-sector scheme and the proposed funding pattern is Centre: State-75: 25. Under the scheme, projects are to be taken up in one or two districts each in the states. The states are to take up restoration of water bodies having original irrigation culturable command area of 40 ha upto 2000 ha to revive, augment and utilize their storage and irrigation potential. The projects are to be completed within a period of two years. Detailed Project Reports (DPR's) are to be prepared by the states as per the guidelines and submitted for approval of Ministry of Water Resources and consideration for funding. Detailed Project Reports (DPRs) duly approved by the States Technical Advisory Committee (TAC) are to be submitted to Central Water Commission (CWC). CWC, after examination, will forward the DPRs with their considered views and recommendations to Ministry of Water Resources for approval and funding under the scheme. A high level Selection Committee of the Ministry of Water Resources will select the projects for approval of the Ministry. Central share of funds will be released to states for implementation of the district projects and states will provide 25% share.

1416. (4-6-2007) NEW DELHI : Brazil has emerged as India's largest trading partner in Latin America with bilateral trade crossing the record $ 2 billion mark in 2006, Shri Kamal Nath, Union Minister of Commerce and Industry, indicated in his keynote address at the inaugural session of the Business Seminar on India and Brazil here today. He further indicated that both the governments have set a bilateral trade target of US $ 10 billion by 2010. Two-way trade between India and Brazil has registered a quantum increase-from a meagre US $ 488 million in 2000 to US $ 2.4 billion in 2006. The inaugural session of the Seminar organised by the Confederation of Indian Industry (CII) was also addressed by Mr. Miguel Joao Jorge Filho, Brazilian Minister for Development Industry and Foreign Trade. Referring to the partnership between India and MERCOSUR, of which Brazil is a part, Shri Kamal Nath informed that following the conclusion of a Preferential Trade Agreement (PTA) in March 2005, "India and MERCOSUR have agreed to give tariff concessions, ranging from 10% to 100% to the other side on 450 and 452 tariff lines respectively. The PTA will come into force as soon as ratified by the legislatures of Brazil and Argentina. Meanwhile the process of expansion of the coverage of the PTA has also been initiated in persuasion of the IBSA Declaration made by the Heads of India, Brazil and South Africa on September 13th 2006. I hope, the operationalisation of PTA will help achieving the target of 10 billion two-way trade in years to come". A trilateral arrangement between India, MERCOSUR and SACU (South Africa Customs Union) is also on the way to widen the scope of South-South Cooperation, he added. "Indian investments in Brazil have also increased in recent years, particularly in the field of information technology, biotechnology and pharmaceuticals. Indian companies such as Tata Consultancy Services, Ranbaxy and Dr. Reddy's Laboratories, Strides among others have made a mark in the Brazilian market. Many others including other TATA group companies are exploring the opportunities for investment in Brazil", he said. Shri Kamal Nath had a separate bilateral meeting with Mr. Miguel Joao Jorge Filho, later in the evening when both the Ministers underlined the immense scope for increasing bilateral trade and investment given the huge opportunities that the two countries offer to each other. He also had a separate interaction with the Brazilian business delegation led by Mr. Armando Monteiro Neto, President of the National Confederation of Industry and Member of the Chamber of Deputies, the lower house of the Brazilian Parliament.

1417. (5-6-2007) NEW DELHI : Shri Mohammed Amin, a newly elected Member of Rajya Sabha, representing the State of West Bengal, has made and subscribed affirmation today in the Chamber of Chairman, Rajya Sabha.

1418. (5-6-2007) NEW DELHI : The President, Dr. A.P.J. Abdul Kalam has called on the World Space Community to evolve a Space Vision that will enable mankind to meet the challenges of the 21st Century. The President was speaking today from Rashtrapati Bhavan through video conferencing to the "International Conference on Space-A Conceptual Challenge to Defence", organised by the Centre of Aerospace Strategic Studies and the National Centre for Space Studies of France in Paris. Dr. Kalam said the "World Space Vision 2050" has three components: 1. Space exploration and current application missions 2. Comprehensive space security; and 3. Large scale societal missions and low cost access to space. This would enhance the quality of human life, inspire the spirit of space exploration, expand the horizons of knowledge and ensure space security for all nations. Dr. Kalam suggested that the conference could consider evolving a World Space Council to formulate and implement this vision. Such a unified approach, the President felt, will enable the world to see a quantum jump in the progress of space, Science and Technology. The President also said that the greatest asset of space research is that in many cases, the technology used in space has gone on to have applications in everyday life, thus enhancing the quality of life of the common person around the globe. Space technology has also helped the development process of nations, the President felt. Dr. Kalam has also briefly touched on the history of the Indian Space programme from the vision of Professor Vikram Sarabhai in the 1970s to its present capabilities. The President said India is now working on its 2nd space vision. He said he forsees that India will make an important contribution to low cost access to space and missions to the Moon and Mars. Dr. Kalam also answered questions from the audience after his address.

1419. (5-6-2007) NEW DELHI : A Hundred Member Indian Youth Delegation will be visiting China from 7th June to 16th June, 2007. Shri Mani Shankar Aiyar, Minister of Panchayati Raj, Youth Affairs & Sports and DoNER will be leading this delegation. Prior to the visit a two-day Workshop was held in New Delhi from 4th to 5th June for the youth selected for this delegation. Speaking in the valedictory session of the Workshop Shri Aiyar said that the hundred young boys and girls selected for this delegation are among the best and brightest of the generation. The Minister said that the selection process for this was very vigorous and various categories of delegates have been selected. These categories include: Scholars of China from India, scholars of other disciplines who have distinguished themselves in their field, young entrepreneurs doing different types of businesses, those who have distinguished themselves in social work, group of bravery award winners, sportspersons distinguished in Table Tennis & Badminton, cultural artists, dancers, musicians, singers, a large number of those who hold elected position in local Government. Two physically challenged youth are also members of the delegation. Shri Aiyar expressed confidence that this visit will further cement ties between India and China. The Chinese Government and the All China Youth Federation has drawn up a very interesting calendar of places of visit during the youth delegation' stay in China. Starting from Beijing, they not only meet the First Secretary of the Communist Youth League of China and Honorary President of the All China Youth Federation, visits are also arranged to see the Tsinghua University as well as the "Bird's Nest"-the main Olympic stadium. Besides the must see Forbidden City and the Great Wall, they also meet up with the Vice Chairman of the Standing Committee of National People's Congress, closing the evening with a reception hosted by India's Ambassador to China. The Youth Delegation then stops over at Kunming, the Capital of Yunnan Province. They get an opportunity to interact with the students of Yunnan University as well as a visit to Pharmaceutical companies as well as the World Horticulture Expo. There is a very interesting planned visit to the Nationalities' Village.

1420. (5-6-2007) NEW DELHI : The Prime Minister, Dr. Manmohan Singh has granted assistance to physically challenged Rani Verma of Varanasi. Miss Rani Verma of Dallipur Village, Badagaav, Varanasi lost both her hands in an accident when she was studying in the fifth standard. Despite the severe handicap Rani Verma continued her education and the 14 year old has appeared in the matriculation exam using her feet to write the exams. The Prime Minister, moved by her courage and determination to beat all odds and continue with her studies, has sanctioned one lakh rupees from the Prime Minister's Discretionary Fund as financial assistance to Ms. Rani Verma. The amount of rupees one lakh is to be deposited as a fixed deposit in the name of the father Shri Ramesh Chandra Verma and the monthly interest may be withdrawn by the father for the educational expenses of Rani Verma. The principal amount of rupees one lakh will be given to Rani Verma on her attaining 18 years of age.

1421. (5-6-2007) NEW DELHI : The Prime Minister, Dr. Manmohan Singh, chaired a meeting here today to take stock of the implementation of the National Rural Health Mission (NRHM). The Union Minister for Health and Family Welfare presented a detailed outline on action taken till now and identified three categories of States in terms of the implementation of the NRHM. The best performing States so far have been identified as Andhra Pradesh, Assam, Haryana, Gujarat, Madhya Pradesh, Orissa, Rajasthan, Sikkim, Tamil Nadu and Tripura. The average performing States have been identified as Arunachal Pradesh, Bihar, Chhattisgarh, Himachal Pradesh, Meghalaya, Mizoram, Punjab and Uttarkhand. The States which have so far not performed well in the implementation of NRHM programmes are Jammu & Kashmir, Jharkhand, Karnataka, Kerala, Maharashtra, Manipur, Nagaland and Uttar Pradesh. The Prime Minister urged all State Governments to pay adequate attention to health care issues and ensure efficient functioning of public health services. He also emphasized the need for greater investment in medical education, including nursing, especially in States where there is an acute shortage of seats in nursing and medicine. The Prime Minister will convene a special meeting of the National Development Council to discuss issues relating to health care, disease control and public health.

1422. (5-6-2007) NEW DELHI : The Prime Minister, Dr. Manmohan Singh, has set up a High Level advisory group on climate change issues. The Prime Minister's Council on Climate Change will include the following: (a) Government Representatives:-Minister of External Affairs; Finance Minister; Minister of Environment & Forests; Minister of Agriculture; Minister of Water Resources; Minister of Science & Technology; Deputy Chairman, Planning Commission; Dr. R. Chidambaram, Principal Scientific Advisor to PM; Shri V. Krishnamurthy, Chairman, NMCC; Dr. C. Rangarajan, Chairman, EAC; Shri Ajay Mathur, Chairman, Bureau of Energy Efficiency; Foreign Secretary; Secretary, Environment & Forests and Principal Secretary to PM (Convenor) (b) Non-Government Members:-Dr. R.K. Pachauri, Chairperson, TERI; Dr. Prodipto Ghosh; Dr. Nitin Desai; Dr. Sunita Narain; Shri Chandrashekhar Dasgupta (Retd. Diplomat); Shri Ratan Tata, Chairman, Investment Commission; Shri Raj Chengappa, Executive Editor, India Today; Dr. R.Ramachandran, Science Editor, The Hindu. The Council will coordinate national action plans for assessment, adaptation and mitigation of climate change. It will advise government on pro-active measures that can be taken by India to deal with the challenge of climate change. It will also facilitate inter-ministerial coordination and guide policy in relevant areas.

1423. (5-6-2007) NEW DELHI : The Prime Minister, Dr. Manmohan Singh has issued the following message on the occasion of the World Environment Day: "On the occasion of World Environment Day, I urge every one of our citizens to recall the wise words of the Father of our Nation, Mahatma Gandhi, that our planet has enough to meet everyone's need but not everyone's greed. It is incumbent upon all of us to think of future generations and the very future of our planet each time we undertake an act of consumption. The threat of climate change is real and unless we alter our lifestyles and pursue a sustainable model of development, our future will be at peril. India is committed to pursuing environmentally sustainable development strategies. While we have a long way to go in meeting the aspirations of our people and while we must rid our county of the scourge of poverty, ignorance and disease, we should do so in a manner that is environmentally sustainable. The challenge before us is, therefore, to protect our environment and ensure the well-being of future generations, even as we seek to accelerate the pace of economic growth, pursue industrialization and the modernization of agriculture and improve the quality of life of all our people.

1424. (5-6-2007) NEW DELHI : The theme for this year's World Environment Day-Melting Ice-Hot Topic focuses on the challenges facing the people and ecosystem that we live in, as a result of rapid environmental and climatic changes. It also links to the wider world where glaciers are sinking and an increasing number of extreme weather events are triggering more frequent droughts, and floods which we are also facing in India. Addressing a function organized by the Ministry of Environment and Forests, to celebrate World Environment Day today Shri Paranab Mukherjee, Minister of External Affairs further said that in India we have taken major initiatives including adopting a National Environment Policy (NEP) 2006. Our NEP is a response to our national commitment to clean environment. It synergies environmental and economic policies and appropriate institutional mechanisms to support the integration of three pillars of sustainable development; economic development, social development and environmental protection. Shri Mukherjee said as a signatory to the United Nations framework convention on climate change we are committed to climate friendly sustainable development. The Energy Conservation Act 2001 has set energy consumption norms for each industry. Regarding National Museum of Natural History, he said it has maintained the spirit to provide an out of school facility for education of children and to promote environmental awareness among the masses. The Minister added it should be remembered that conservation and management of the environment is not the sole responsibility of the Government alone. Individuals, their families, communities and institutions have to come forward for preservation of environment. Shri Namo Narayan Meena, Miinister of State for Environment and Forests said climate change due to rising levels of carbondioxide in the atmosphere is one of the most serious environmental concerns of our times. General expansion of economic activity, increased population pressure and use of fossil fuels are responsible for emission of Green House Gases, which lead to global warming. He suggested to learn from sound knowledge of the historical adaptive processes that are still functional. He referred to rain water harvesting systems in India including the Havelis of Jodhpur, Bandh and Bandhuna of Satna, Virda of Gujarat, Khadins of Rajasthan, ahar-pynes of Bihar, eri of Tamil Nadu, dhora of Aravalis and other earthworks. Thiru S.Raghupati, Minister of State for Environment and Forests, said that climate is the most important determinant of vegetation patterns globally and has significant influence on the distribution, structure and ecology of forests. Climate change is likely to force some plants and animals to migrate if they are unable to adapt to their changing environments. This causes a future problem for conservation and biodiversity. We therefore, need to protect and augment our forests resources at all costs. Secretary, Ms. Meena Gupta, appealed to reduce pollution in each form. Use of mass transportation, saving power, conservation of water and involvement in afforestation activities, will save our planate, she said. The Environment Day was also a festive occasion for winners for environmental and forest preservation activities.

1425. (5-6-2007) NEW DELHI : The Parliamentary Standing Committee on Personal, Public Grievances, Law and Justice has invited views/suggestions on the Gram Nyayalayas Bill, 2007 from individuals and organisations interested in the subject matter of the Bill. The memoranda containing views/suggestions either in Hindi or English may be sent in duplicate to Smt. Sasilekha Nair, Under Secretary, Rajya Sabha Secretariat, Room No. 528-A, Fifth Floor, Parliament House Annexe, New Delhi, 110001 within thirty days of the publication of this advertisement. The memoranda addressed to the Committee would form part of the records of the Committee and would be treated as confidential and would not be circulated to anyone. The Gram Nyayalayas Bill, 2007 was introduced in the Rajya Sabha on 15th May, 2007 and subsequently referred to Department related Parliamentary Standing Committee on Personal, Public Grievances, Law and Justice headed by Dr. E.M. Sudarsana Natchiappan, M.P., for examination and report. The Bill was published in the Gazette of India Extraordinary on the same day. It seeks to provide for establishment of Gram Nyayalayas for providing justice, both civil and criminal, to the citizens at grassroots level and to ensure that opportunities for securing justice are not denied to any citizen by the reasons of social, economic or other limitations. MLD/L&J-44 (Parl St Comm. On Gram Nyayalays Bill)

1426. (5-6-2007) NEW DELHI : The Ministry of Rural Development has approved the release of 868 MT of Common Rice during the year 2007-08 to West Khasi Hills District of Meghalaya State through Food Corporation of India depots in the State under the Sampoorna Grameen Rozgar Yojana (SGRY) scheme. The grant is towards plan expenditure and will be utilized for approved items of works subject to the conditions laid down in the SGRY Guidelines.

1427. (5-6-2007) NEW DELHI : The Ministry of Rural Development has released Rs. 56.03 crore to M/s. National Hydroelectric Power Corporation Ltd. for implementation of 52 road work packages in Bihar under Pradhan Mantri Gram Sadak Yojana (PMGSY) for the year 2007-08. The grant is towards the Plan expenditure and will be subject to the conditions laid down from time to time in the guidelines of the PMGSY and supplementary directions. PMGSY was launched in December 2000 as a 100 per cent Centrally Sponsored Scheme with a target of connecting every habitation that has a population of more than 1000 within the next three years and every habitation with a population of more than 500 by the year 2007 *i.e.* by the end of the 10th Five Year Plan through good all-weather road. A sum of Rs.20,400.70 crore has been released to the States/UTs towards the programme and up to December 2006, 35,868 roadworks covering a length of 1,07,569.08 Kms. have been completed.

1428. (5-6-2007) NEW DELHI : The Ministry of Rural Development has sanctioned Rs. 13.14 crore to the State Government of Tripura towards balance of first instalment of funds against the provisional allocation of Rs.39.43 crore made for the Government of Tripura under Accelerated Rural Water Supply Programme (Normal) of Rajiv Gandhi National Drinking Water Mission, during the year 2007-08. Up to 15 per cent of funds released under this sanction may be utilized for Operation & Maintenance and up to 5 per cent of funds may be spent for taking sustainability measures. States have been requested to delegate powers for management of Rural Water Supply Schemes through the Panchayati Raj Institutions (PRIs) as per the Constitution of India. As such Operation and Maintenance of the completed RWS Scheme should be transferred to the PRIs. No expenditure shall be incurred on taking water quality problems form the present release, as there is a separate allocation for the purpose. This release is being made for execution/completion of schemes to provide safe drinking water facilities to rural habitations and schools under the Centrally Sponsored ARWSP. Priorities set in ARWSP guidelines and through other instructions issued from time to time shall be followed for coverage of rural habitations and rural schools.

1429. (5-6-2007) NEW DELHI : The Ministry of Rural Development has sanctioned Rs. 134.80 crore to the Maharashtra Jeevan Pradhikaran, Mumbai towards balance of first instalment of funds against the provisional allocation of Rs.404.40 crore made for the Government of Maharashtra under the centrally sponsored Accelerated Rural Water Supply Programme (Normal) of Rajiv Gandhi National Drinking Water Mission, during the year 2007-08. Up to 15 per cent of funds released under this sanction may be utilized for Operation & Maintenance and up to 5 per cent of funds may be spent for taking sustainability measures. States have been requested to delegate powers for management of Rural Water Supply Schemes through the Panchayati Raj Institutions (PRIs) as per the Constitution of India. As such Operation and Maintenance of the completed RWS Scheme should be transferred to the PRIs. No expenditure shall be incurred on taking water quality problems form the present release, as there is a separate allocation for the purpose. This release is being made for execution/completion of schemes to provide safe drinking water facilities to rural habitations and schools under the Centrally Sponsored ARWSP. Priorities set in ARWSP guidelines and through other instructions issued from time to time shall be followed for coverage of rural habitations and rural schools.

1430. (5-6-2007) NEW DELHI : Eravikulam National Park has the largest surviving population of Nilgiri Tahr. This endangered animal is endemic to the southern Western Ghats in Kerala and Tamil Nadu area. As per the provisional analysis, there are about 42 newborn Nilgiri Tahrs in Eravikulam National Park area this time. A good news for nature lovers as it will help protecting this endangered species. The monsoon season is also the mating season for the Nilgiri tahr. And its birth season ranges from January to February. Eravikulam National park remains closed for visitors during the breeding season. This time the re-opening of the Park for visitors was extended upto March as the birth season for some Tahrs were delayed. The conservation of tahr is crucial in preserving the eco system of the region. The shola-grassland ecosystem is a strange admixture of temperature and tropical qualities. It is exceptionally rich in orchids and balsams. As per the schedule I of the Indian Wildlife (Protection) Act, 1972, the Nilgiri tahr is listed as an endangered and categorized as vulnerable by the IUCN.

Another noteworthy thing is that it is endemic to the hill ranges of Western Ghats of South India, where a suitable mosaic of montane grass lands and rugged terrain exists. It inhabits at elevations from 1200 to 2600 meters. The tahrs generally inhabit the fringes of the grassy plateau and move on to the steep slabs and cliffs bordering it, occasionally visiting the shrub lands along the base of the cliffs. Tahrs avoid sholas, but sometime forage along their periphery. Dense forests at the lower end surround these grassland habitats. The Nilgiri tahrs were formerly found over these grasslands in large numbers. But indiscriminative trespassing into the forest areas in 19th century adversely affected the population of tahrs. And it came down to a dangerous level of about 100 in the beginning of 20th century. But the efforts to preserve this endangered species have achieved remarkable success. Now in the Eravikulam area alone, there are about 700-800 Nilgiri tahrs. And with nearly 40 new born, this number will increase significantly in the coming years. Apart from the Eravikulam National park the Nilgiri Hills are reported to have more concentration of Nilgiri tahrs. Smaller population is found in Periyar National Park, Palani Hills, Annamalai Hills and some other pockets in the Western Ghats south of Eravikulam. Nilgiri tahr is co-generic with the Himalayan tahr (H. jemlahicus) which occurs along the southern flanks of the Himalayas and the Arabian tahr (H.jayakari) which inhibits the arid mountains of Oman. Peculiarities of the Nilgiri Tahr are:-the coat of the Nilgiri tahr is shorter than that of Himalayan tahr. This may be because of the adaptation to the wet climate this species inhabits. Among the Nilgiri tahr itself there are differences between mature males and females. The fully-grown male, known as 'saddle back', is much bigger and darker than the female and has a silvery saddle like patch on its back. Females and immature males are an overall yellowish-brown to grey. When the male ones grow, their pelage darkens to a deep chocolate or even blackish-brown-a process which begins at two years of age and takes over four years to complete. The shoulders, neck, and legs turn nearly black, with white knee-spots marking the interior surface of the front legs. A distinctive silvery saddle-patch marks the back of mature male Nilgiri tahr, starting out as an indistinct light tan area at five years of age and becoming lighter and more defined until around eight years.

1431. (5-6-2007) NEW DELHI : No child labour has been found employed in three plantation industries, viz., Tea, Coffee and Rubber plantations. This has been stated by the Labour Bureau in its Report on Occupational Wage Surveys in three plantation industries. According to the Report, 9.78 lakh workers are employed in these plantation industries. Of them 53.54 percent are female workers, 45.25 percent male workers and 1.21 percent adolescent workers. Majority of the workers constituting 89.48 percent are employed as 'Plantation Labour" followed by "Rubber Tapper' who account for 3.80 percent of workers. 80.79 percent of workers are employed on piece-rate system of wages, whereas the remaining 19.21 percent workers are employed on time rate basis. Rubber Plantations workers are the highest paid with an average daily wage rate of Rs.89.77 followed by Rs.71.66 in Coffee Plantations and Rs.54.27 in Tea Plantations. However, the overall daily wage rate for all workers in three plantations stood at Rs.58.37. Although the women workers outnumbered the male workers in employment, their average daily wage was found to be less than their male counterparts in all three plantations with the exception of one occupation each in Coffee and Tea Plantations and three occupations in Rubber Plantation. The Report is part of the 6th Round of Occupational Wage Survey (OWS) being conducted by the Labour Bureau with effect from 2002. In all, 56 industries are to be covered under this round of OWS. The Bureau has already released its report on four Service Sector industries.

1432. (5-6-2007) NEW DELHI : The Board of Approval for the Special Economic Zones (SEZs) met here today to consider proposals for setting up of Special Economic Zones and also approve other miscellaneous requests pertaining to notified SEZs. In the meeting, 42 new applications were considered. Out of this, 24 Formal approvals and 9 In-principle approvals were granted. Two in principle approvals of: M/s SRI City SEZ for a multi product SEZ in Andhra Pradesh and M/s Reliance Haryana SEZ Limited for a multi services SEZ in Gurgaon, Haryana, were also approved for grant of Formal Approval. Prominent among the Formal approvals are: Agro processing SEZ by MIDC in Maharashtra; IT/ITES SEZ by MIDC in Thane, Maharashtra; Gems and Jewellery SEZ by Royal Palms India in Maharashtra; IT/ITES SEZ by WIPRO Limited in Andhra Pradesh; Multi product SEZ by Indiabulls Industrial Infrastructure Limited in Maharashtra; Two IT/ITES SEZs by TIDCO in Tamil Nadu; IT/ITES SEZ by APIIC in Andhra Pradesh; Airport based multi product SEZ by GMR Hyderabad International Airport Limited in Andhra Pradesh; Handicrafts and Artisan SEZ by Gujarat Growth Centres Development Corporation Limited in Gujarat; Electronic Hardware SEZ by SIPCOT in Tamil Nadu; Handicrafts SEZ by Mansarover Industrial Development Corporation in Rajasthan. Prominent In principle approvals granted are: Gems and Jewellery SEZ by Gitanjali Gems Limited in Maharashtra; Leather industry SEZ by MIDC in Maharashtra; Steel SEZ by Jaibalaji Sponge Limited in West Bengal; Multi Services SEZ by Gitanjali Gems Limited in Maharashtra; Multi product SEZ by Indiabulls Builders Limited in Maharasthra; Textile SEZ by DLF Limited in West Bengal; Multi product SEZ by Rewas Ports Limited in Maharashtra.

1433. (5-6-2007) NEW DELHI : Sarva Shiksha Abhiyan (SSA) has made remarkable progress in increasing access and narrowing gender and social gaps. The projected infrastructure gaps in schools has reduced at primary level with the opening of more than 2.40 lakh new schools till December, 2006 and Construction of 1.57 lakhs school buildings, 6.50 lakh additional classrooms, 1.57 lakh drinking water facilities and 2.03 lakh toilets. The country has universaliszed access at primary level. A large number of children studying in Education Guarantee Scheme (EGS) and Alternative & Innovative Education (AIE) schools have been mainstreamed giving an opportunity to many children to study in a regular school. The country is approaching near universalization of enrolment at the primary stage. The overall enrolment currently stands at 94% in the age group of 6-14 years {Selected Educational Statistics (SES) 2004-05}. The Gross Enrolment Ratio (primary 2004-05) 108.56%-boys 111.41%; girls 105.48%. The Drop out rate has declined by 10.54 percentage points at primary; 15.08 percentage points decline for girls (2001-02 to 2004-05). Share of SC students 18.64% at elementary level {District Information System for Education (DISE) 2005-06}. Share of ST students 9.02% at elementary level (DISE 2005-06). Transition Rate from primary to upper primary is 83.36% (DISE 2005-06). The gender gap overall has closed and is reflected in the steady increase in the Gender Parity Index (GPI). At the primary level, several states have reached a GPI above 90 and at the upper primary level the GPI has increased to 0.88 The number of out-of-school children has reduced from 3.20 crore in 2001-02 to 70 lakh (as on April 2006). The challenge however, remains, in certain groups like SC, ST and minority children, where the number of out-of school children needs further attention. The programme is focusing on bringing the 'hardest to reach' children into the schooling system. SSA is now providing greater attention to completing access and retention rates at upper primary level and providing greater emphasis on improving quality of learning. 8.22 lakh teachers have been appointed and 6.12 eligible children given free textbooks till December 2006. Intensive teacher training to all in-service teachers; remedial teaching to over 43 lakh children; computer aided learning at upper primary level and independent testing of children have been put in place for improving quality of education. The Sarva Shiksha Abhiyan or "Education for All Programme" is the national flagship programme to provide quality elementary education to all children in the 6-14 years age group through a time bound approach, in partnership with States.

1434. (6-6-2007) NEW DELHI : Shri Kamal Nath, Union Minister of Commerce & Industry, in a meeting with Sheikh Abdullah Bin Zayed Al-Nahyan, Minister of Foreign Affairs, United Arab Emirates (UAE), here today, sought greater trade between India and UAE in agro products. "Greater trade in agro products with UAE and the entire Gulf region is important to India. Our top priority for exports to UAE is vegetables, fruits, processed foods, poultry etc.", the Minister said. The UAE Minister concurred with Shri Kamal Nath's suggestion that a delegation from Agriculture and Processed Food Export Development Authority (APEDA) can visit UAE to discuss the possibilities in food and agriculture sector with the importers in UAE. The possibility of setting up laboratories in India for testing the quality of food exports to meet the standards set by UAE authorities was also discussed. The UAE Minister informed that less than 1% of all UAE investments were in India and UAE was keen to focus on investing in India's economy including the agriculture sector. The trade between India and UAE was US $ 12.9 billion in 2005-06. Exports from India were US $ 8.59 billion while imports were US $ 4.31 billion. Main items for import from UAE includes pearls, precious and semi-precious stones, gold, electronic goods etc. and the main export items from India includes gems & jewellery, non-ferrous metals, plastics, manmade yarn etc.

1435. (6-6-2007) NEW DELHI : A high level selection committee to identify "Raksha Udyog Ratnas" submitted its report to the Defence Minister Shri AK Antony in New Delhi today. The Committee, headed by Shri Prabir Sengupta former Secretary Defence Production and former Director, Indian Institute of Foreign Trade, examined the possibility of engaging particular industries in the country in Defence Production. The Committee was asked to identify various industries which could be involved in the production of large weapon systems and other requirements of the Defence Forces. The other members of the committee were Shri N R Mohanty, former Chairman, HAL, Shri S H Khan, ex-Chairman-cum-Managing Director, IDBI and Shri Bakul Dholakia, Director IIM Ahmedabad. Experts from the three armed forces, Integrated Defence Staff (IDS), Defence Research and Development Organisation, Finance officials from Defence Ministry and Engineers India Limited assisted the committee. M/s Engineers India Limited provided technical assistance to the Committee. The committee was set up on May 09 last year in pursuance of the Government's policy to identify Tier-I industries in the country and to systematically encourage their involvement in Defence Production so as to assume the role of system integrators of large weapon systems and producers of platforms required by the Defence Forces. The companies recommended by the committee will be notified only after the proposals are approved by the Defence Acquisition Council.

1436. (6-6-2007) NEW DELHI : Defence Minister Shri AK Antony gave away RM's Trophy for the Best Run Command Hospital under Armed Forces for the year 2006 to Command Hospital (Northern Command), Udhampur in New Delhi, today. Maj Gen Naresh Kumar, Commandant of the hospital received the trophy and a cash award of Rs 2 lakhs. Speaking on the occasion, the Defence Minister praised the yeoman service rendered by the Armed Forces Medical Services (AFMS) over the years both during war and peace. He said AFMS has also brought laurels to the nation whenever deployed in UN or humanitarian missions in various countries. Shri Antony said the swiftness with which medical relief was despatched for earthquake victims of Indonesia has been appreciated all over the world. I have no doubt that the health of our troops, the ex-servicemen and their families is in safe hands, the Minister added. The Director General Armed Forces Medical Services Surgeon Admiral Yogendra Singh highlighted the modernisation programme of the Medical Services and reassured that they were fully prepared to meet any challenge. The Minister of State for Defence Shri MM Pallam Raju, the three Service Chiefs, Defence Secretary Shri Shekhar Dutt, Secretary Defence Production Shri KP Singh and various other senior civil and military officials were present on the occasion. The Raksha Mantri's Trophy was instituted in 1989 to create a healthy competition among the Command Hospitals of the Army and its equivalent Hospitals in the Navy and Air Force. The best hospital is adjudged on the basis of a number of objective criteria by a Committee headed by Director General Hospital Services (Armed Forces). The Joint Secretary (Estt), Ministry of Defence is also a member of the Committee.

1437. (6-6-2007) NEW DELHI : The Minister for Overseas Indian Affairs, Shri Vayalar Ravi called on the President of Suriname, Shri Runaldo Ronald Venetiaan in Paramaribo, Suriname. Both the leaders discussed economic, trade and bilateral issues. President Venetiaan recalled the sacrifices of the ancestors of Surinamese Indians, who have laid the foundation for a multi-ethnic and multi-religious society. Shri. Ravi also met with the Vice President, Ramdien Sardjoe and Chairman of the National Assembly of Suriname, Paul Somohardjo and exchanged matters of bilateral importance. Vice President Sardjoe, who is himself a Person of Indian Origin (PIO) lauded the significant contribution made by the Indian community for the prosperity and unity of the country. The Speaker also congratulated PIOs of Suriname for having contributed to the well being and prosperity of the country and for having integrated so well into the multi-ethnic fabric of the society. Shri Ravi also met with Minister of Social Justice and Police, Shri Chandrikaprasad Santokhi, Ministers for Home Affairs, Defence, Attorney General, and former Vice President Ajodhia, Members of the Council of States and Assembly and several representatives of the Surinamese Government as well as Indian community during a lunch function, hosted by Surinamese government. On the occasion, Minister Santokhi recalled the cordial bilateral relations between India and Suriname and said that there were immense possibilities for further intensification of cooperation. Several Ministers of the Government drew the attention of Shri Ravi to areas of cooperation where India has been generously supporting technical, educational and cultural cooperation. Shri Ravi in his remarks thanked the Government of Suriname for having hosted his visit, which has been memorable. He spoke about India's ever growing relations with the Caribbean countries and India's engagement with CARICOM. He said that India had been actively supporting the cause of the developing countries. Commenting that Suriname was rich in land and water resources, he called upon the Government to devise a long term strategy to use its extensive mineral, physical and human resources to play a significant role in the Caribbean region and beyond.

1438. (6-6-2007) NEW DELHI : Speaking at the meeting of Health Ministers of polio affected States organized today to review the status of polio eradication efforts, the Minister for Health & Family Welfare, Dr. Anbumani Ramadoss said that it is critical to sustain the high level of immunity in all polio-affected States by vaccinating all children under the age of five both through routine immunization and Supplementary Immunization Activities (SIAs), so that the polio virus does not get a chance to re-establish its circulation. Besides the Minister of State for Health & Family Welfare, Smt. Panabaka Lakshmi, Health Ministers from Uttar Pradesh, Bihar, Uttranchal, Maharashtra, Delhi, Haryana and Gujarat and senior officials representing the States of Andhra Pradesh, Madhya Pradesh and Rajasthan were present at the meeting. In addition, senior officials from the Ministry of Health & Family Welfare, representatives from WHO, ICMR, UNICEF and Rotary International also participated in the discussions. Appreciating the efforts made by the State Governments, the Minister said the number of polio cases have been lower-both during the peak and the trough of the last outbreak-as compared to 2002-2003. The core districts of western UP, responsible for the outbreak, have not had a single case of type 1 poliovirus for the last six months, the longest period so far. Though the type 3 poliovirus cases are up slightly, they remain geographically restricted to western UP. The poliovirus transmission has also been low in Bihar. Since early this year, extraordinary efforts have been made in Uttar Pradesh and Bihar with frequent immunization rounds every four-week using a monovalent polio vaccine with the focus on reaching the youngest children specially the newborns, in the highest risk areas. Some areas in Bihar have already had six immunization rounds. The programme has been integrated into the National Rural Health Mission and the community link workers (ASHA) are effectively involved for polio eradication. Social mobilisation initiatives have been expanded and intensified to reach out to all sections of the society, specially the marginalized. These measures together have improved the quality of immunization rounds. In order to boost the immunity in children before the onset of high transmission season the May immunization round was extended to vulnerable states where the immunity level is comparatively low, like Andhra Pradesh, Chhattisgarh, Orissa, Assam, Rajasthan, Gujarat, Punjab and Haryana. The Minister asked the States to be cautiously optimistic as the risks and challenges remain-of type 1 poliovirus spreading to other states. To further improve the quality of SIAs, the Minister asked the States to improve health infrastructure, fill the vacancies of Medical officers, Auxiliary Nurse Midwives (ANMs) and ASHAs. The Minister asked the Health Ministers of UP and Bihar to strengthen political oversight and engagement to further improve and sustain the quality of the immunization rounds. He said regular interactions with district magistrates and health staff would be very productive to ensure the best quality programme. As per the recommendation of the Indian Expert Advisory Group (IEAG) immunization rounds would be held in the high-risk areas in June, August and September followed by two rounds later in the year with monovalent vaccines. "Our job now is to contain the disease from spreading further and to safeguard the significant progress made over the last few months" said Dr. Ramadoss. "We can do that with the strategy we have in place. The Ministers today gave their pledge to ensure that no children are left unimmunized in the crucial next few polio campaigns" and ensure achieving zero polio transmission by 2008.

1439. (6-6-2007) NEW DELHI : The Union Minister of Shipping, Road Transport & Highways Thiru T.R.Baalu, has said that his Ministry is working in right earnest on the 250 Kms Bangalore Ring Road project. During a meeting with the Chief Minister of Karnataka, Shri H.D. Kumaraswamy in Bangalore today, Thiru Baalu informed him that the consultants have already been appointed for preparing the Detailed Project Report (DPR) for the 250 Km Ring road project. Thiru Baalu said that after finalization of the DPR, this project would be included in the appropriate phase of the National Highway Development Programme (NHDP). The Minister for State for Road Transport & Highways Shri K.H. Muniyappa was also present during the meeting. Thiru Baalu also reviewed the ongoing central road sector projects in the state of Karnataka during this meeting which was also attended by the Members of Parliament from the State. Apart from the ongoing projects, the terminated projects of Golden Quadrilateral *i.e.* from Belgaum-Maharashtra border to Nelamangala were also reviewed. The Minister directed the National Highway Authority of India (NHAI) to ensure that rebidding for the two terminated packages *i.e.* Chitradurga Harihar & Harihar-Haveri is completed on priority. On the issue of the need to repair that Shiradi Ghat road stretch, Thiru Baalu advised the State PWD to formulate the fresh proposals keeping in view the revised schedule and changes in the cost of construction material etc. The North-South Corridor project from Andhra / Karnataka Border to Bangalore was also reviewed and it was pointed out that progress on some of the stretches have been affected due to delay in acquisition of land and shifting of utilities. Thiru Baalu asked the State Government to address these issues expeditiously to ensure that the project is completed in a time-bound manner. Earlier Thiru Baalu inspected the works on the Elevated Highway Project from Silk Board Junction to Electronic City Junction on Bangalore-Hosur section of NH7 along with Shri K.H. Muniyappa. During the inspection he directed the officials to improve safety arrangements to ensure safety of the road users. He expressed satisfaction on the progress of work and traffic management plan being implemented at the site during construction activities. The Minister also directed that appropriate measures should be taken to ensure that the project is completed by July next year. It may be recalled that in Karnataka, 670 Km length of National Highways are being taken up by NHAI for 4/6-laning of NHDP Phase-III. The work of widening to 4/6-lanes in 180 Kms at a cost of Rs.1450 crore in three packages of Bangalore-Nelamangala section of NH4, Bangalore-Kolar-Mulabagal section of NH4 and Nelamangala-Devihalli section of NH48 have been awarded in the last four months and the work on these stretches is expected to start shortly. In addition to the ongoing projects of NHDP Phase-I, II and III, NHAI has also taken up the feasibility study / DPR for construction of Ring Road to Bangalore city. Besides this, the feasibility study of 4/6-laning of Kundapur-Karnataka / Goa border of NH17 (192 Km), Hassan-Mangalaore section of NH48 (137 Km) and Hospet-Bellary section of NH63 (70 Km) is also being taken up.

1440. (6-6-2007) NEW DELHI : The 51st meeting of the Central Wakf Council under the Chairmanship of Mr. A.R. Antulay, Minister for Minority Affairs held here recently has reviewed its Educational and Development programmes and functioning of its Planning and Advisory, Education and Women Welfare, Wakf Development and Monitoring Committees. Accordingly, it has been decided that the educational and development programmes of Council may continue with the riders that (i) no grant be given by the Central Wakf Council to those organizations which have received grant from Maulana Azad Education Foundation for vocational training/ITI; and (ii) once the grant is released by the Central Wakf Council to an organization, no request for further grant be considered within five years. On the issue of Maulana Azad Education Foundation's refusal to consider the applications of educational institutions run by various Wakf Boards, it was decided that the M/o Minority Affairs wll take appropriate action to make such Wakfs become eligible for grants from the Foundation. It was also decided that the monitoring of the projects under the Scheme for the Development of Urban Wakf Properties and Educational Programmes will be improved through regular inspections. For this, a local expert and a member of the Central Wakf Council, residing in that area may be engaged. In case there is no member of the Council in that area then a member residing nearer to the area may be requested to make the inspection with the help of an expert locally available. The Meeting also approved Revised Estimates for the Council for the year 2006-07 and Budget Estimates for the year 2007-08. The Annual Report and Audit Report of the Council for the year 2005-06, adopted by the Planning & Advisory Committee was also ratified.

1441. (6-6-2007) NEW DELHI : The Minister of Tourism and Culture Smt. Ambika Soni took part in 'India on Canvas' paintings series by making a painting with noted painter Ms. Madhavi Parekh here today. The painting depicts Shakti (Durga) and Lion. The spontaneous work was completed in about an hour. The Minister said she was comfortable with the theme of the painting and enjoyed working with Ms. Madhavi Parekh. The painting will be auctioned in October this year in Mumbai for charity purposes.

1442. (6-6-2007) NEW DELHI : The Ministry of Rural Development has sanctioned Rs. 63.79 crore to the State Government of West Bengal towards balance of first instalment of funds against the provisional allocation of Rs.191.37 crore made for the Government of West Bengal under the centrally sponsored Accelerated Rural Water Supply Programme (Normal) of Rajiv Gandhi National Drinking Water Mission, during the year 2007-08. Up to 15 per cent of funds released under this sanction may be utilized for Operation & Maintenance and up to 5 per cent of funds may be spent for taking sustainability measures. States have been requested to delegate powers for management of Rural Water Supply Schemes through the Panchayati Raj Institutions (PRIs) as per the Constitution of India. As such Operation and Maintenance of the completed RWS Scheme should be transferred to the PRIs. No expenditure shall be incurred on taking water quality problems form the present release, as there is a separate allocation for the purpose. This release is being made for execution/completion of schemes to provide safe drinking water facilities to rural habitations and schools under the Centrally Sponsored ARWSP. Priorities set in ARWSP guidelines and through other instructions issued from time to time shall be followed for coverage of rural habitations and rural schools.

1443. (6-6-2007) NEW DELHI : The Ministry of Rural Development has sanctioned Rs. 17.63 crore to the State Government of Punjab towards balance of first instalment of funds against the provisional allocation of Rs. 52.91 crore made for the Government of Punjab under Accelerated Rural Water Supply Programme (Normal) of Rajiv Gandhi National Drinking Water Mission, during the year 2007-08. Up to 15 per cent of funds released under this sanction may be utilized for Operation & Maintenance and up to 5 per cent of funds may be spent for taking sustainability measures. States have been requested to delegate powers for management of Rural Water Supply Schemes through the Panchayati Raj Institutions (PRIs) as per the Constitution of India. As such Operation and Maintenance of the completed RWS Scheme should be transferred to the PRIs. No expenditure shall be incurred on taking water quality problems form the present release, as there is a separate allocation for the purpose. This release is being made for execution/completion of schemes to provide safe drinking water facilities to rural habitations and schools under the Centrally Sponsored ARWSP. Priorities set in ARWSP guidelines and through other instructions issued from time to time shall be followed for coverage of rural habitations and rural schools.

1444. (6-6-2007) NEW DELHI : The Ministry of Rural Development has sanctioned Rs. 4.50 crore to the State Government of Andhra Pradesh towards balance of first instalment of ARWSP-DDP funds against provisional allocation of Rs.13.52 crore for the year 2007-08 under Accelerated Rural Water Supply Programme (ARWSP)-DDP Areas of Rajiv Gandhi National Drinking Water Mission (RGNDWM). The release is being made for execution/completion of schemes to provide safe drinking water facilities to rural habitations and schools under the ARWSP-DDP Areas as per the priorities indicated in the Guidelines for implementation of Rural Water Supply Programme. The terms and conditions for the release of ARWSP-DDP funds are included in the Guidelines for implementation of Rural Water Supply Programme.

1445. (6-6-2007) NEW DELHI : Shri Ashwani Kumar, Minister of State for Industry, met leading international bankers and private equity fund managers at an interactive breakfast meeting in New York yesterday and briefed them on the state of Indian Economy and on the potential India provides for leading investors. In his presentation, Shri Kumar highlighted the phenomenal growth witnessed in the country cutting across various sectors. While outlining major policy initiatives such as the recently announced policy on Petroleum, Chemicals and Petrochemicals Investment Regions (PCPIRs), he emphasized the Government's commitment to continuing the process of economic reform. "The resilience of India's democratic institutions has contributed to the economic growth of the country consistent with equality and freedom of its people", he said. Highlighting some of the success stories in India in fields such as real estate and manufacturing, the Minister stressed that the qualitative distinction of India's success story was defined by the state's commitment to proactively intervene with a view to impacting positively on the living standards of the poor. The Presentation was followed by a discussion with the bankers, fund managers and CEOs on the future growth potential of the Indian economy and the vast opportunities available to foreign investors. "Nearly 98 percent of the Indian economy is now open to foreign direct investment through the automatic route", Shri Kumar informed. He encouraged US companies to invest in major growth sectors such as infrastructure, both physical and social infrastructure, which hold significant promise. "At least one-third of the estimated US$ 550 billion required to be invested in the infrastructure sector alone could come by way of Foreign Direct Investment & Foreign Institutional Investment", the Minister said. Speaking about the Indo-US Agreement on Civil Nuclear Cooperation, Shri Kumar said that the Agreement was dictated by the need to access clean sources of energy for India's industrialization and economic growth. Earlier, the Minister also released the India Factor Report prepared by Societe Generale Bank.

1446. (6-6-2007) NEW DELHI : Congress Spokesperson Smt. Jayanti Natrajan said that on behalf of the Congress President, the Indian National Congress would like to thank the people of Goa for the confidence that they have reposed in the Indian National Congress and for having voted the Congress-led government back to power. This is a vindication of the excellent work that has been carried out by the Congress government in Goa and by the party organisation in Goa and guided by the Party leadership in Delhi. There has been a tremendous vote of confidence in the Indian National Congress and its policies and the new Congress-led government in Goa will ensure that the people of Goa gets a good responsive, transparent government which will ensure the future development of Goa and continue the good work that has already been done. To a question that Congress only won 16 seats in an assembly of 40 seats, Smt. Natrajan said that the fact of the matter is that Congress government formation is off course with its allies. The Congress government will come back to power and those Congress candidates who have been defeated will learn their lessons and go back to the people with greater vigour. To a question as to what is Congress Party's reaction to the Third Front meeting in Hyderabad, Smt. Natrajan said that the Congress Party is not at all perturbed about the formation of the Third front. This again is a natural process in a democracy and if a healthy Opposition exists that carries out its duty to the people, we would be willing to face that opposition with all the vigour at our command and we will emerge more successful than ever before. The Congress Party would like to totally deny any charges that the policies of this government are wrong. This government has acted in good faith and with great success to fulfil all the promises made in the Common Minimum Programme and has brought about path-breaking legislation on many important fronts and is totally committed to inclusive growth and all-round development. Therefore criticism from the opposition is something that is in the normal course and this criticism by them is completely unjustified and we are very sure that we will face them on an electoral field or on any policy discussion and shall emerge successful and correct as against their policies. To a question on the Presidential election, Smt. Natrajan said that we are absolutely confident that a strong and secular person, supported by the UPA and its allies, will emerge as the next President of India. To a question that BJP alleges that the Congress and BSP have arrived to some understanding as the UP Governor did not allow CBI to prosecute Mayawati in the Taj Corridor case, Smt. Natrajan said that it is very wrong and condemnable on the part of the BJP to caste aspersions on the high constitutional office of the Governor. The Indian National Congress has nothing to do with this issue. It is a matter on which a Governor has exercised his authority as a Constitutional functionary. It is the old habit of the BJP to indulge in irresponsible attacks on high Constitutional offices like the Chief Election Commissioner, Governors and even the President of India and this is not a healthy trend in a democracy.

1447. (6-6-2007) NEW DELHI : Representatives of mega cities' corporations, senior officials from banks and financial institutions, apex industries' organizations, state government representatives met in a daylong conference in New Delhi yesterday (5th June 2007). The objective of the meeting was to take stock of the implementation vision of the Jawaharlal Nehru National Urban Renewal Mission, JNNURM projects in the mega cities of Delhi, Mumbai, Ahmedabad, Bangalore, Chennai, Kolkata, and Hyderabad. Shri M. Ramachandran, Secretary, and Urban Development Ministry chaired the conference. The meeting felt that the projects, which are amenable to Public Private Partnership, PPP, should be listed by the cities. Assistance of financial institutions should be enlisted and more attention should be paid to simultaneously moving further on the PPP route. The conference felt that success shown like the Latur (Maharashtra) Water supply project where private participation has been successful should be widely circulated. Considering that about Rs. 26,500 crore worth of projects are now being taken up in the mega cities of India, the conference also delineated on the magnitude of contracting ability required in execution of these projects. Cities have been reporting constraints in the execution capacity and there is a need to attract large engineering firms to ensure timely execution of projects. The engineering firm representatives felt that tender systems have to be standardized to eliminate uncertainties. The conference agreed that the commercial banks have an increasing role in financing urban infrastructure projects and the banks have committed to have a second look at the terms and conditions. The conference has prepared a subsidized interest rate regime for financing viable urban infrastructure projects by banks and financial institutions. The proposed Urban Infrastructure Fund, which the Ministry of Urban Development is proposing, could be an effective vehicle for the multinational financial institutions, national financial institutions and the banks to earmark more resources for urban infrastructure projects. The Secretary, Ministry of Urban Development has constituted groups to coordinate with the banks, look at the possibility of standardizing tender related issues and improving the pace of implementation. The Secretary has asked the Secretary, Urban Development, Tamil Nadu to suggest the possibility of having a single focal point in the mega cities which could be an immediate and effective contact point for all those interested in taking up projects in the cities, PPP initiatives and implementing best practices. JNNURM, which is the country's flagship programme for urban local bodies, focuses on urban infrastructure improvement and provision of basic services for the poor with a focus on 63 mission cities (with population of 120.6 million). A related programme is covering the remaining 5098 cities and towns of India.

1448. (6-6-2007) NEW DELHI : The Prime Minister said "I am visiting Germany to attend the Summit Meeting of G8 and Outreach Countries (Brazil, China, India, Mexico and South Africa) being organised at Heiligendamm by the German G8 Presidency on June 8. At the summit, I will have the opportunity to present India's viewpoint on the global issues that have been identified by the G8 for special focus including climate protection, energy efficiency, and the conclusion of the Doha round of talks. Our viewpoint, and the viewpoint of much of the developing world on these issues, is that while addressing them due care must be taken not to allow growth and development prospects in the developing world to be undermined or constrained. At the summit, I will speak on issues related to climate change. I will emphasize the need not to lose sight of the fundamental and universally accepted principle of common but differentiated responsibility and respective capabilities between the developed and developing worlds. It is also a fact that more and not less development is the best way for developing countries to address themselves to the issue of preserving the environment and protecting the climate. Prior to the meeting with leaders of the G8, the President of Mexico will host a meeting of leaders of the Outreach countries in Berlin on June 7, where we will discuss our positions on global issues that are of special relevance to the developing world. On the sidelines of both these Summit Meetings, I will also have the opportunity to hold bilateral meetings with some of the leaders present, including Chancellor Merkel of Germany who is our host, other leaders of the G-8, and the leaders of China, Mexico, Nigeria as also the Secretary General of the United Nations.

1449. (7-6-2007) NEW DELHI : Strict dope testing measures will be followed during the conduct of the forthcoming Military World Games to be held in Hyderabad and Mumbai from October 14 to 21, 2007. Samples of all record breaking winners, in addition to random samples, will be sent to special laboratories in Bangkok on a daily basis to ensure highest international standards in this biggest ever sporting event to be held in India so far. This was disclosed at the high level meeting taken by the Defence Minister Shri AK Antony here today. The meeting was attended among others by the Minister of State for Defence Shri. MM Pallam Raju, the Defence Secretary Shri Shekhar Dutt, the Vice Chief of Army Staff Lt. General Deepak Kapur and senior functionaries of the Games Organising Committee. So far, nearly 4700 participants from 72 countries have already confirmed their participation in the 15 events to be conducted at the Fourth Edition of the Games which is going to be held for the first time in Asia. The largest contingents will be from the host country besides China and Germany which will be fielding over 200 each sportspersons from their Armed Forces. Continent-wise, Europe will be sending the maximum number of countries. 34 out of the total of 38 member nations of Europe will converge for the Games which is seen as a precursor to the Olympic Games. The Organising Committee in association with the Andhra Pradesh Government is making all efforts to make the conduct of the Games a success. Massive infrastructures are coming up in Hyderabad and the existing facilities at Mumbai are being upgraded to international standards to meet the requirements of the Games. Addressing the members, Shri Antony said that the event must be conducted in the best possible manner and should provide a benchmark for all future Games in India. He assured that the Ministry will provide all support in this regard. The Military World Games (MWG) are conducted under the aegis of International Military Sports Council (CISM) Brussels (Belgium) at an interval of every four years. CISM is an International Sports Association, which is open to the armed forces of all nations. India joined CISM in 1999 and thereafter has been an actively involved in all the activities of the organisation. 15 sports disciplines would be contested for during the Games. All the events will be conducted at Hyderabad except the Sailing and Triathlon which would be conducted at Mumbai. Both men & women will participate in all events expect boxing, wrestling and handball. The list of competitive disciplines are Military Pentathlon, Shooting, Parachuting, Football, Handball, Volleyball, Triathlon, Sailing, Swimming, Track & Field, Judo, Boxing and Wrestling. Hockey and Kabaddi will be the demonstration sports.

1450. (7-6-2007) NEW DELHI : It has been reported in some of the newspapers that Ministry of Railways has approved of a scheme for privately owned and operated local trains in Mumbai. It is clarified that there is no plan to privatize the operation of commuter passenger trains.

1451. (7-6-2007) NEW DELHI : The total approximate earnings of Indian Railways on originating basis during 1st April-31st May 2007 were Rs. 11001.05 crore compared to Rs. 9913.49 crore during the same period last year, registering an increase of 10.97 per cent. The total goods earnings have gone up from Rs. 6642.37 during 1st April-31st May 2006 to Rs. 7309.66 crore during 1st April-31st May 2007, an increase of 10.05 per cent. The total passenger revenue earnings during first two months of the financial year 2007-08 were Rs. 3283.59 crore compared to Rs. 2929.17 crore during the same period last year, registering an increase of 12.10 per cent. The revenue earnings from other coaching amounted to Rs. 312.10 crore during April-May 2007 compared to Rs. 262.35 crore during the same period last year, an increase of 18.96 per cent. The total sundry earnings have gone up from Rs. 79.60 crore during April-May 2006 to Rs. 95.70 crore during April-May 2007, an increase of 20.23 percent. The total approximate number of passengers booked during April-May 2007 were 1059.99 million compared to 1004.92 million during the same period last year, showing an increase of 5.48 per cent. In the suburban and non-suburban sectors, the number of passengers booked during April-May 2007 were 549.80 million and 510.19 million compared to 525.49 million and 479.38 million during the same period last year, an increase of 4.62 per cent and 6.43 per cent respectively.

1452. (7-6-2007) NEW DELHI : Agricultural & Processed Food Products Export Development Authority (APEDA) and Spices Board under the Ministry of Commerce and Industry, is initiating several projects in Chhindwara, including setting up of Pack Houses, Collection Centres and Spices Park. Two Pack Houses one each at Umranala and Saunsar will handle oranges and other fruits & vegetables to provide value-addition of fresh produce through cold chain, washing, packaging etc. APEDA will provide Rs.8.9 crore for setting up of the Pack Houses and the project will be implemented by NAFED. The Umranala project is already under implementation and will be completed by the year-end while the Saunsar project will be completed in a year's time. APEDA is also funding Rs.5.5 crore to set up Seven Collection Centres (Chhindwara, Mohkhed, Saunsar, Bichua, Parasia, Singodi and Chauria), which will provide the primary sorting and grading services before the fresh agriculture produce is taken to the Pack Houses. The Collection Centres are expected to be operational in 3-4 months timeframe. "These projects will benefit the farmers and allow them to get a better price for their produce, apart from generating employment in this sector", Shri Kamal Nath, Minister for Commerce & Industry, said. The Spices Board will set up a Spices Park in an area of 9 acres at Umranala of which, 6 acres has already been acquired. The Park will provide facilities for dehydration of garlic products and coriander leaf, green chilli extracts and medicinal herbs and turmeric. Funding of Rs.9.95 crore for the Spices Park has been sought under the ASIDE Scheme (Assistance to States for Infrastructure Development of Exports). The project will include setting up of a world-class testing laboratory to be set up jointly by STC and Spices Board. Further, NAFED is also setting up a Seed Processing Unit at Kusmali at a total cost of Rs.1.25 crore. Meanwhile, keeping in view the serious problem of Gummosis (phytothora) disease in oranges grown in Chhindwara District, the National Horticulture Mission had recently approved the proposal for rejuvenation of 10348 hectares of orange cultivation with a total outlay of Rs. 5.91 crore. In addition, NAFED is conducting two training programme in pre and post-harvest management for farmers of oranges and vegetables in Chhindwara, while, three more training programmes will be taken up in the next 2-3 months

1453. (7-6-2007) NEW DELHI : The following are the excerpts from the 'Report to the People 2004-07' on Overseas Indian Affairs. The report was released by the Prime Minister, Dr. Manmohan Singh on 22nd May, 2007. The report in full and its highlights are available on PIB website: www.pib.nic.in Overseas Citizenship: The scheme for Overseas Citizenship of India has been extended to cover all overseas Indians who emigrated after January 26, 1950. Overseas Citizens have been granted parity with NRIs in respect of facilities in economic, financial and educational fields, with some exceptions, besides lifelong multipurpose multi-entry visa and exemption from registration with local authorities. Till 2006, over 78,000 online applications had been filed and over 36,000 overseas citizenship registration certificates had been granted. Voting by NRIs: A bill has been introduced in Parliament to permit Indian citizens outside India who are absent in their ordinary place of residence to get themselves registered in the electoral rolls of the constituency of their ordinary place of residence. Social Security: A Social Security Agreement has been entered into with Belgium, exempting overseas Indians on short-term contracts of up to five years from payment of social security contributions and providing for export of social security benefits for those on long-term contract, after they relocate to India on retirement. The Government has initiated the process for entering into similar agreements with other countries like The Netherlands, Sweden and France. The Government has entered into a bilateral MoU on manpower with the United Arab Emirates on a wide range of issues concerning the protection and welfare of overseas Indian workers, including non-payment or delay in payment of wages, harsh working and living conditions, substitution of contracts, retention of passports, cheating by intermediaries, physical abuse, etc. Conclusion of a similar MoU with Kuwait has been approved, which would facilitate recruitment of manpower, prohibit changes in terms and conditions of employment contracts to the detriment of workers, lay down the procedure for authentication for employment contract place responsibility on employers to arrange the work permits, and protect workers who are otherwise not covered under local labour laws. More such MoU are expected with other Gulf countries, including Bahrain, Saudi Arabia and Oman, as well as with Malaysia. NRI / PIO University: The UPA Government has approved a policy frame for setting up a university for children of NRIs and PIOs.

1454. (7-6-2007) NEW DELHI : The following are the excerpts from the "Report to the People 2004-07" on Textile Ministry. The report was released by the Prime Minister, Dr. Manmohan Singh on 22nd May, 2007. The report in full and its highlights are available on PIB website. Textile industry has been able to generate considerable employment and promote exports and improve its performance in the post-Multi Fibre Agreement regime. A major package, including tax relief, was provided. Basic customs duty on various textile machinery and spare parts has been reduced, additional capital subsidy has been provided for processing, duties on specified textile machinery items, raw materials and spare parts has been brought down, and excise duty on polyester filament yarn has been reduced. The scope and outlays of schemes like the Technology Upgradation Fund Scheme and the Technology Mission on Cotton has been augmented to modernize the industry and to ensure availability of quality raw material at competitive prices. The Scheme for Integrated Textiles Parks has been launched to strengthen infrastructure. Under the scheme, it is proposed to set up 30 Integrated Textiles Parks by 2008, with an investment of over Rs. 13,000 crore. These parks will generate annual production of over Rs. 20,000 crore, and create over half a million new jobs. Due to focused support to cotton-growers cotton production and productivity have touched record heights. The textiles sector has grown phenomenally since the phasing out of the Multi-Fibre Arrangement (MFA) after 2004. it is expected that by 2011-2012, the textiles sector will more than double to US$ 115 billion. The estimated investment during this period will be approximately Rs. 1,50,000 crore, which will generate employment for approximately 17 million workers. Investments in Textiles to create 17 million jobs by 2012. a focused approach to helping weavers is in place with an increase in the number of cluster development centres, more yarn depots, support to technology upgrade, health and life insurance cover for weavers, and a new 'Handloom Mark' for branding handloom products. 200 handloom clusters of over 5,000 handlooms each are targeted for taking up under the Integrated Handloom Devlopment Scheme during 2007-08. A comprehensive National Jute Policy has been announced for the first time to boost demand for jute and protect the interests of jute growers. Restructuring of the Jute Corporation of India has been undertaken. Steps are being taken to implement a Jute Technology Mission for holistic development of the jute sector at an estimated cost of Rs. 355 crore. The National Jute Board Bill, 2006 has been introduced in Parliament to provide for establishment of the National Jute Board to effect synergy in the activities of various organizations in jute sector. To ensure adequate demand, the level of compulsory packaging has been increased for sugar and food grains. The level of compulsory packing in jute bags for food grains and sugar has been continued at 100% for the jute year 2006-07.

1455. (7-6-2007) NEW DELHI : The Ministry of Rural Development has sanctioned Rs. 56.28 crore to the State Government of Orissa towards balance of first instalment of funds against the provisional allocation of Rs. 168.85 crore made for the Government of Orissa under Accelerated Rural Water Supply Programme (Normal) of Rajiv Gandhi National Drinking Water Mission, during the year 2007-08. Up to 15 per cent of funds released under this sanction may be utilized for Operation & Maintenance and up to 5 per cent of funds may be spent for taking sustainability measures. States have been requested to delegate powers for management of Rural Water Supply Schemes through the Panchayati Raj Institutions (PRIs) as per the Constitution of India. As such Operation and Maintenance of the completed RWS Scheme should be transferred to the PRIs. No expenditure shall be incurred on taking water quality problems form the present release, as there is a separate allocation for the purpose. This release is being made for execution/completion of schemes to provide safe drinking water facilities to rural habitations and schools under the Centrally Sponsored ARWSP. Priorities set in ARWSP guidelines and through other instructions issued from time to time shall be followed for coverage of rural habitations and rural schools.

1456. (7-6-2007) NEW DELHI : The Ministry of Rural Development has sanctioned Rs. 11.09 crore to the State Government of Haryana towards balance of first instalment of ARWSP-DDP funds against provisional allocation of Rs.33.28 crore for the year 2007-08 under Accelerated Rural Water Supply Programme (ARWSP)-DDP Areas of Rajiv Gandhi National Drinking Water Mission (RGNDWM). The release is being made for execution/completion of schemes to provide safe drinking water facilities to rural habitations and schools under the ARWSP-DDP Areas as per the priorities indicated in the Guidelines for implementation of Rural Water Supply Programme. The terms and conditions for the release of ARWSP-DDP funds are included in the Guidelines for implementation of Rural Water Supply Programme.

1457. (7-6-2007) NEW DELHI : The Ministry of Rural Development has approved the release of 2484 MTs of Common Rice during the year 2007-08 to Siliguri District of West Bengal State through Food Corporation of India depots in the State under the Sampoorna Grameen Rozgar Yojana (SGRY) scheme. The grant is towards plan expenditure and will be utilized for approved items of works subject to the conditions laid down in the SGRY Guidelines.

1458. (7-6-2007) NEW DELHI : The Leeds Metropolitan University of United Kingdom today conferred an honorary doctorate degree on the Minister for Civil Aviation, Shri Praful Patel. The University has stated that the conferment of the honorary doctorate degree on Shri Praful Patel is in recognition of his "outstanding contribution to the modernization of India's civil aviation industry". Accepting the degree the Minister said that it was "a recognition of the progress of civil aviation in India". According to the Minister, the past three years or so have seen the redefining of civil aviation in India. Air travel in India was originally for an elite few. Things have changed dramatically and now it is a mode of mass travel. There has been an unprecedented growth of over 50% in domestic passenger traffic in the year 2006. Further domestic air services are now available to/from more than 75 airports across the country as against 50 in the year 2000. Aviation is integral to the economy of the country. It has a big role in generating tourism, travel, industrial development, job creation and integration of the country. The sector has finally got momentum and is now poised for major growth. This growth is expected from the Level-II and Level-III cities across the country. The Indian economy has been growing at a healthy rate and should continue to do so for the years to come. The aviation sector, which has evolved over the past few years, should be able to take advantage of this growth. The change in mindset in both the public and private sector has led to more competition, competitive and affordable fares and more passengers. The Government's policies too are now clear and strong. It aims at providing healthy competition and level playing fields to both the public and private players. The Government shall continue in its role as a facilitator of the sector. One of the biggest challenges in aviation lies in the cargo sector. Today 40% of the world's cargo business, in terms of value, moves by air. India too is at the threshold of developing its air cargo business and moving high value goods and services across the country in cargo planes. This is going to happen mostly in the smaller cities giving a fillip to their economy. The next big challenge that the sector faces is that of infrastructure. "We have to catch up with the lost time and we are indeed doing so." In the next five years approximately Rs. 40,000-50,000 crores will be invested in developing the airports. Mumbai, Delhi, Kolkata and Chennai Airports are being upgraded and modernized. The Greenfield airports in Bangalore and Hyderabad will become operational in 2008.

More Greenfield airports will be coming up across the country. Work is in progress to develop 35 non-metro airports in the country. India needs and can easily have 400 airports across the length and breadth of the country.

1459. (8-6-2007) NEW DELHI : The Leeds Metropolitan University of United Kingdom today conferred an honorary doctorate degree on the Minister for Civil Aviation, Shri Praful Patel. The University has stated that the conferment of the honorary doctorate degree on Shri Praful Patel is in recognition of his "outstanding contribution to the modernization of India's civil aviation industry". Accepting the degree the Minister said that it was "a recognition of the progress of civil aviation in India". Each year the Leeds Metropolitan University confers honorary degrees on a small number of distinguished recipients. This year being the centenary year of the Leeds Met, it is being celebrated at the University's Headingley campus. The University has marked these celebrations with a special Honorary Awards ceremony. The decision of the University to confer the degree on Shri Praful Patel was conveyed to the Minister personally by Prof. Simon Lee, Vice Chancellor of the Leeds Metropolitan University.

1460. (8-6-2007) NEW DELHI : The Minister for Overseas Indian Affairs, Shri Vayalar Ravi assured India's full cooperation and support to Jamaica in the fields of IT, manpower training and educational and cultural exchanges, under the framework of cultural agreement signed by the two countries. He was discussing the bilateral relations with Jamaican Foreign Minister, Mr. Antony Hylton during his visit to Jamaica. He also called on the Jamaican Prime Minister, Ms. Portia Simpson-Miller and discussed the matters of mutual interest. Ms. Miller expressed her desire to visit India. Later addressing the members of the Indian Cultural Community, a nodal body promoting the diversity of Indian culture in Jamaica, Shri Ravi said that the Ministry of Overseas Indian Affairs was alive to cultural need of the overseas Indian Communities and assured the organization that their hands would be further strengthened. He also attended a reception hosted by the High Commissioner, where, he interacted with cross section of the Indian Community. The Minister called upon them to integrate further while maintaining their cultural and ancestral link with India. Before arriving Jamaica, Shri. Ravi also visited Curacao, the capital of Netherlands Antilles. In Curacao, he called on the Prime Minister of Netherlands Antilles, Emily de Jongh-Elhage. During the meeting, the Prime Minister deeply appreciated the contribution made by the Indian community for the economic development of the island and called upon the Minister to facilitate greater business and trade interaction with India. Shri Ravi in his reply said that India was an emerging global economic and knowledge power country. He also drew the Prime Minister's attention to the recent fires, which had taken place in the FTZ affecting interest of the Indian businessmen and he requested expeditious handling of the matter. He also took up the issue of general delay in visas and complicated procedure for obtaining visas for visiting Aruba and St. Martin, all three being part of the Netherlands Antilles. The Overseas

Indian Affairs Minister's visit to the Caribbean region included three larger countries Trinidad and Tobago, Suriname and Jamaica and two smaller nations St. Vincent and Grenadines (SVG) and Curacao (Netherlands Antilles) gave a significant exposure to the Ministry of Overseas Indian Affairs in understanding the needs and concerns of this important concentration of the diaspora.

1461. (8-6-2007) NEW DELHI : The Heads of State and/ or Government of Brazil, China, India, Mexico and South Africa held a meeting on June 7th afternoon in Berlin, Germany, at the invitation of Mexican President Felipe Calderon. The purpose of the meeting was to share perspectives and find convergences about the topics that they will discuss on June 8th in Heiligendamm during the outreach sessions of the G8 summit, as well as to exchange views on various significant international issues. The five countries also participated in the G8 Summits in Gleneagles (2005) and St Petersburg (2006). President Luiz Inácio Lula da Silva of Brazil, President Hu Jintao of China, Prime Minister Dr. Manmohan Singh of India, President Felipe Calderón Hinojosa of Mexico, and President Thabo Mbeki of South Africa reaffirmed their shared conviction that developing countries must participate more actively in the consolidation of strategies and initiatives that effectively address the challenges of a globalising and increasingly interdependent world. They agreed that their five countries, based on their undeniable political and economic strength, can make a decisive contribution to increase the participation of developing countries in this process. Regarding the matters that will be discussed in Heiligendamm with the G8 countries, the leaders will be pleased to note opportunities for joint collaboration in the fields of cross border investment, research and innovation, climate change, energy and development. The consensus view was that all of these challenges must be addressed from a multilateral, regional and bilateral perspective, taking into consideration the interests and capacities of the different States. During their talks, the leaders also stated their ideas about certain topics of particular relevance to developing countries, such as global governance, international trade, bio-fuels, migration and South-South cooperation. At the Berlin meeting, the Leaders shared views about the future of their participation in the Outreach Dialogue, and about the convenience of ensuring coordination and follow-up to the discussions among their five countries. They agree on having consultations on a regular basis on issues of common interest and to coordinate their positions. To this end they instructed their Foreign Ministers to meet on the margins of the next UN General Assembly. The Heads of State and/ or Government expressed their thanks to Chancellor Merkel for the invitation to participate at the G8 Heiligendamm Summit. The leaders of the five countries have met before on the margins of the Glenagles Summit at the invitation of President Mbeki of South Africa and the St Petersburg Summit at the invitation of President Lula of Brazil.

1462. (8-6-2007) NEW DELHI : The Union Public Service Commission has declared the final result of the Engineering Services Examination held in June

2006 and the interviews for Personality Test held in May 2007. The successful candidates have been recommended for appointment to Civil Engineering Group, Mechanical Engineering Group, Electrical Engineering Group and Electronics and Tele-Communication Engineering Group. The total number of candidates in the four lists is 308 including 56 candidates belonging to Scheduled Castes, 20 belonging to Scheduled Tribes and 94 belonging to the Other Backward Classes and 05 candidates belonging to Physically Handicapped. U.P.S.C. has a "Facilitation Counter" near Examination Hall Building in its Campus. Candidates may obtain any information/clarification regarding their recruitments on working days between 10.00 A.M. to 5.00 P.M. in person or over telephone Nos. 23385271 and 23381125 from this Counter. The results will be able to on UPSC website *i.e.* www.upsc.gov.in.

1463. (8-6-2007) NEW DELHI : There has been a news report in the Indian Express, dated 6th June, in which a person, Mr.B.K.Verma, has claimed to be working as a Law Officer in the Prime Minister's Office [PMO]. This is to clarify that there is no such Law Officer working in the PMO.

1464. (8-6-2007) NEW DELHI : The Department of Fertilisers has implemented Web based Fertilizer Monitoring System (FMS) which is able to track the dispatch, receipt and sale of fertilisers in each district in the country against the approved plans. Reviewing the position regarding availability of fertilizers in the country and the implementation of recent initiatives for its movement and distribution, here today, the Minister for Chemicals and Fertilisers and Steel, Shri Ram Vilas Paswan observed that availability of Urea, DAP and MOP is being planned and monitored on the basis of detailed districtwise, monthwise and companywise Supply Plans. This will ensure adequate availability of fertilizers against the assessed requirement upto the district level. The Supply Plans prepared by the State Governments concerned in consultation with the lead fertiliser company and other major fertiliser suppliers to the State require each fertiliser company to identify upto 3 Primary Stock Points (PSP's) in each district to which it is marketing fertilisers. The details of such identified PSP's have already been entered into the FMS. Receipt and sales of fertilizers in each district will be monitored through these PSP's. It has been decided that subsidy will be paid to the fertiliser manufacturers/suppliers with effect from 1.4.2007 only on the basis of actual receipt of fertilisers in the State. The details can be seen at www.urvarak.co.in. In respect of urea, fertilizer companies will be provided actual cost of transportation of fertilizers by way of primary freight upto the primary stock point and by way of secondary freight for movement beyond the primary stock point. In so far as budgetary provision for subsidy on fertilizers is concerned, the requirement of funds for 2007-08 including the carryover liability of Rs. 8082 crores as estimated by the Department is Rs. 50284.08 crores as against which, the B.E. allocation is Rs.22451 crores. The shortfall in the budgetary provision has been apprised to the Ministry of Finance. The DoF has also authorized creation of buffer stocks of urea in each of the major agricultural States to be operated by the lead fertilizer company. The buffer stock in respect of urea has been authorized to the extent of 5% of the seasonal demand. For the current season, the authorized buffer to be operated is 6.5 LMT of urea. The DoF also proposes to maintain a buffer in respect of DAP (2 LMT) and MOP (1 LMT) to meet any exigent situations. The pre-positioning of stocks is being undertaken to obviate any shortages at the local level during the season. It is proposed to pre-position stocks at the level of 75% of the monthly requirement by the Ist of the month and 100% of the requirement by 15th of each month. The requirement of fertilizers during the current Kharif season as assessed by the DAC is 131.65 LMT of Urea, 40.08 LMT of DAP and 16.52 LMT of MOP as against the assessed requirement during the last Kharif season of 122.37 LMT of Urea, 33.10 LMT of DAP and 14.66 LMT of MOP. This year's demand represents an increase of 7.5% in respect of Urea, 21% in respect of DAP and 13% in respect of MOP over the corresponding period last year. The availability of fertilizers during the first two months of the season has been satisfactory.

1465. (8-6-2007) NEW DELHI : As part of its continuous efforts to know its epidemic better, the National AIDS Control Organization (NACO) leads an annual process, together with national and international expert groups, including UNAIDS and WHO to estimate the number of adults living with HIV/AIDS in India (HIV prevalence). From 4-6 June, 2007, NACO convened a meeting of the Core Technical Working Group on Estimates and Projections, which provides guidance on the methods and assumptions used to develop national HIV prevalence estimates. This year the estimates would provide a more accurate picture of the epidemic because of availability of more information based on population based surveys and improved data from high risk groups. The Working Group is still in the process of analyzing the data to develop an updated estimate of national HIV prevalence and these figures will be available by the first week of July. Some trends can already be identified from the analysis of existing sentinel data. Although prevalence in antenatal clinics has shown a decline in some southern states, high levels of infection among the groups at higher risk, such as Men who have Sex with Men (MSM), and Injecting Drug Users (IDU) are of concern. Similarly, while data does suggest that the HIV prevalence levels are declining among sex workers in areas where targeted interventions have been implemented, particularly in the southern states, yet overall prevalence levels among this group continue to be high necessitating focused prevention interventions. Experience shows that where these groups are themselves engaged in prevention efforts they become strong leaders in prevention. Finally, the 2007 sentinel data clearly validates the prevention strategy being implemented by NACO.

1466. (8-6-2007) NEW DELHI : Smt. Renuka Chowdhury, Minister for Women and Child Development Women and President of the Commonwealth Women Parliamentarians Group has called upon women's to strive to ensure active participation in power structure and decision making so as to acquire their share in the leadership. 'Unless women's representation in all spheres of governance reaches their equitable share, women's impact on shaping the future of society will remain marginal'. The Minister was addressing the meeting of Parliamentary Forum on 'Women and Leadership in a Democracy' being hosted jointly by the Commonwealth Parliamentary Association Secretariat and Parliament of Uganda at Kampala today after inaugurating it. She asserted that that to make a qualitative and quantitative improvement in our democracies we need to ensure a 'critical mass' of 30% of women in politics. Mrs. Chowdhury said that women's political rights and their participation in decision-making are fundamental to the success of democracy. 'But women's exclusion from the leadership and decision-making raises many concerns regarding their empowerment and the achievements of democratic transformation. Highlighting the role of women in decision making the Minister said with women constituting a significant proportion of human population, it was illogical to conceptualize the development issues and to develop public policies without their equal participation in any decision-making process. Democracy cannot afford to be gender-blind and, therefore, equal engagement of men and women in the decision-making process is a sine qua non of any democratic framework, she added. Cautioning the political leadership about excluding women from positions of power and from elected bodies, Mrs. Chowdhury said that it inhibits the development of a just society. Without full participation of women in leadership and decision-making, the political process will be far less effective than what it can and should be. 'We must realize and recognize the role of women as a dynamic force and as a valuable asset for the overall development of our societies. Any development strategy that neglects the need for enhancing the role of women cannot lead to comprehensive socio-economic development'. She added that the need of the hour is to create an atmosphere which is conducive to the involvement of a larger percentage of women in the decision-making processes. Briefing about India's efforts in the area of empowerment of women, the Minister said that India had been successful in ensuring one-third representation for women at the local level bodies by effecting amending in constitution and it had resulted in over one million women being elected to rural and urban local bodies. With these arrangements, the socio economic condition of women folk in the country has shown considerable improvement.

1467. (8-6-2007) NEW DELHI : The Union Minister for Micro, Small and Medium Enterprises, Shri Mahabir Prasad has said that Khadi will have to match the standards of the new products that are available in the market. He said that competition in the market increased tremendously as a result of marketing and technological developments due to globalisation. He said that special attention should be given to specific technological requirements so that the standards of the KVI products were improved to make them face the competition in the market. Shri Prasad was inaugurating the first meeting of the National Khadi and Village Industries Board (NKVIB) here today. Elaborating on the performance of Khadi and Village Industries Commission (KVIC) Shri Prasad said, during the Tenth Plan, 1,21,961 units were established under Rural Employment Generation

Programme to which margin money assistance of Rs.1452 crore was released by the Government through KVIC to the beneficiaries. An estimated 25.25 lakh additional employment opportunities have been generated during the Tenth Plan. He said, there was an urgent need for substantially enhancing the wages of Spinners and Weavers from the present level. Earlier the Chairperson of KVIC, Smt. Kumud Joshi said, through KVI activities, 20 lakh additional employment could be created within 4 to 5 years at low capital investment. She said a proposal had already been submitted to the Government for additional fund requirement. She said an amount of Rs.3,475 crore was required for generating the additional employment and strengthening existing infrastructure. The day long meeting of NKVIB deliberated on various subjects like new schemes approved by the Government, ensuring remunerating wages, convergence with like minded originations, rebate system, opening of SC/STs new institution and clusters and export of Khadi through various exhibitions and outlets abroad etc. Members from all over the country attended the meeting.

1468. (8-6-2007) NEW DELHI : The Ministry of Petroleum & Natural Gas has accepted the Report of the Committee constituted to formulate transparent guidelines for approving natural gas price formula/basis for giving Government approval under the Production Sharing Contracts. The Committee, which was constituted by the Ministry in August 2006, was headed by Joint Secretary & Financial Advisor, Ministry of Petroleum & Natural Gas and had DG, DGH and concerned Joint Secretaries as other members. The Committee has recommended that in all situations, where a price discovery through competitive bidding is possible, there should be no need to apply any other principle for valuation of gas. Once a market-determined price has been discovered between the suppliers and customers through a transparent competitive bidding process, there should be no need for the Government to interfere with the same. Further, the committee has said that in the absence of a market determined price, discovered through a transparent bidding process, where valuation of gas has to be necessarily done by Government, it may be done based on the price in the most recent competitively determined contract in the region duly indexed to the present. Indexation is to be done as per provisions of the market determined reference contract, as each market determined contract sets out various terms and conditions of supply, including the price review mechanism. The Committee has noted that each contract, normally, has a price review clause every 5 years. If the price stands reviewed as per the reference contract, that may become the new reference price. For interim periods, the Committee has recommended that indexation may be linked to percentage increase in price of cheapest liquid fuel, *i.e.* Furnace Oil (FO) which is not only the cheapest liquid fuel but has also shown least price volatility in recent years. The committee was of the view that the above valuation may be applied only when actual supply has commenced and the price has not been discovered through the market mechanism. However, if the actual price at which any producer supplies to any consumer is higher than the one arrived at by above methodology, then the higher price is to be reckoned for Government take. It would be ideal if the Committee's approach had never to be applied but if the eventuality does arise, DG DGH and Director, PPAC will do the calculations based on Committee's recommendations. It would be DGH's responsibility to ensure that the Producer remits the Government's take accordingly. The Committee had put up its draft recommendations in the public domain through the website of the Ministry of Petroleum & Natural Gas in December, 2006 itself. The Committee had held extensive consultations with various stakeholders, including the producers as well as the consumers besides other expert organizations, before finalizing its report.

1469. (8-6-2007) NEW DELHI : The following are the excerpts from the 'Report to the People 2004-07' on Social Justice and Empowerment. The report was released by the Prime Minister, Dr. Manmohan Singh on 22nd May, 2007. The report in full and its highlights are available on PIB website. Reservations in jobs: A bill seeking to elevate reservations to a statutory right has been introduced in Parliament. A special recruitment drive to fill up the backlog of vacancies for reserved posts was launched and has been carried out with unprecedented success, with filling up of around 50,000 vacancies through direct recruitment or promotion over the past two years. A Group of Ministers has been set up to cover all dimensions regarding the question of reservation for the OBCs in backlog vacancies. A Group of Ministers, constituted to examine the issue of affirmative action in the private sector, initiated a dialogue with Industry to see how best the private sector could fulfil the aspirations of youth belonging to the SCs and the STs and submitted its report. A Coordination Committee, serviced by the Department of Industrial Policy and Promotion, has initiated the process of obtaining comments from the industry with a view to coming out with a concrete scheme of affirmative action. Education: Constitution has been amended to facilitate greater access to education for students belonging to the scheduled castes and tribes and the socially and educationally backward classes. The UPA Government has expanded scholarships to students belonging to these categories and has initiated the legislation enacted for widened access to higher education for the OBCs. To prepare candidates from among the SCs and the STs for selection to academic positions and for doctoral studies, the Rajiv Gandhi National Fellowship Scheme has been launched for funding 2,000 fellowships annually. 2,180 new residential Kasturba Gandhi Balika Vidyalaya schools have been sanctioned over the last three years for providing free residential education up to class VIII to girls belonging predominantly to the weaker sections of society or the minority communities. Rehabilitation of manual scavengers: To rehabilitate scavengers-empower the most deprived among the scheduled castes-in alternative occupations, the UPA Government has launched a new Self Employment Scheme for Rehabilitation of Manual Scavengers that provides assistance to them and their dependants in the form of credit-linked subsidy and loans at concessionary rates of interest for undertaking self-employment ventures as well as training up to one year for skill development. The aim is to eradicate the practice of manual scavenging within two years. Outlays for the scheduled castes and tribes: The allocation for scheduled castes and the scheduled tribes has been substantially enhanced each year. The allocation for schemes benefiting them has increased to Rs. 17,691 crore in 2007-08 from Rs. 12,592 crore in 2006-07.

1470. (8-6-2007) NEW DELHI : The Indian Railways, the lifeline and mainstay of the country's transport infrastructure, continue to achieve excellent performance in terms of revenue generation especially during the year 2006-07. This has come about through the turnaround strategy adopted by Indian Railways based on a perfect blend of commercial wisdom and empathy for the people. Indian Railways created a history by generating a Cash Surplus before Dividend of Rs. 20153.49 crore for the year 2006-07 as against Rs. 14,709.79 crore in the previous year. According to the latest financial statistics of Ministry of Railways, the gross earnings of Railways were Rs. 62367.55 crore during the year 2006-07 compared to Rs. 54404.56 crore during the year 2005-06. The fund balance as on 31st March 2007 was Rs. 16528.65 Crore. To add more in its pride, the operating ratio of Indian Railways has come down to 78.68 per cent during the year 2006-07 from 83.72 per cent during the year 2005-06. Railways have turned in a record breaking performance in goods earnings as well as passenger earnings during the year 2006-07. The total goods earnings have gone up from Rs. 36286.97 crore during 2005-06 to Rs. 41716.50 crore during the year 2006-07. The total passenger earnings were Rs. 17224.56 crore during 2006-07 compared to Rs. 15126.00 crore during 2005-06. The Net Payable Dividend of Indian Railways was Rs. 4247.52 crore during the year 2006-07 compared to Rs. 3667.92 crore during the year 2005-06 and this has been met fully.

1471. (8-6-2007) NEW DELHI : The Ministry of Rural Development has approved the release of 2008 MTs of Common Rice during the year 2007-08 to North Tripura District of Tripura State through Food Corporation of India depots in the State under the Sampoorna Grameen Rozgar Yojana (SGRY) scheme. The grant is towards plan expenditure and will be utilized for approved items of works subject to the conditions laid down in the SGRY Guidelines.

1472. (8-6-2007) NEW DELHI : The Ministry of Rural Development has released the payment of Grants-in-aid amounting to Rs. 27.42 lakh out of the Central allocation of Rs.164.53 lakh, as part of first instalment to Hamirpur district of Himachal Pradesh State as Central assistance for the implementation of the SGRY during the current financial year (2007-08). The grant is towards plan expenditure and will be utilized for approved items of works subject to the conditions laid down in the SGRY Guidelines. No deviations from the guidelines is permissible. The expenditure on implementation of the programme with regard to cash component is to be shared on 75:25 basis between the Central and the State Government respectively.

1473. (8-6-2007) NEW DELHI : The Ministry of Rural Development has sanctioned Rs. 93.92 crore to the State Government of Andhra Pradesh towards balance of first instalment of funds against the provisional allocation of Rs.281.78 crore made for the Government of Andhra Pradesh under the centrally sponsored Accelerated Rural Water Supply Programme (Normal) of Rajiv Gandhi National Drinking Water Mission, during the year 2007-08. Up to 15 per cent of funds released under this sanction may be utilized for Operation & Maintenance and up to 5 per cent of funds may be spent for taking sustainability measures. States have been requested to delegate powers for management of Rural Water Supply Schemes through the Panchayati Raj Institutions (PRIs) as per the Constitution of India. As such Operation and Maintenance of the completed RWS Scheme should be transferred to the PRIs. No expenditure shall be incurred on taking water quality problems form the present release, as there is a separate allocation for the purpose. This release is being made for execution/completion of schemes to provide safe drinking water facilities to rural habitations and schools under the Centrally Sponsored ARWSP. Priorities set in ARWSP guidelines and through other instructions issued from time to time shall be followed for coverage of rural habitations and rural schools.

1474. (8-6-2007) NEW DELHI : The UPSC has declared the results of Combined Defence Services Examination-II, 2005. The selected candidates have qualified on the basis of the results of the written examination and interview for admission to the 123rd Course of Indian Military Academy, Dehradun, Naval Academy, Goa and 182nd (Pre-Flying) Training Course of Air Force Station, Begumpet, Hyderabad. The number of vacancies for Indian Military Academy is 250, for Naval Academy is 30 and for Air Force Academy, the vacancies are 32. The result of Medical examination has not been taken into account in preparing these lists.

1475. (9-6-2007) NEW DELHI : The Award Jury of the World Environment Foundation, under the Chairmanship of Justice PN Bhagwati, former Chief Justice of India has selected the Corps of Engineers of the Indian Army as the winner of the Golden Peacock Eco-Innovation Award for the year 2007. The award is for the yeomen work done by the Corps of Engineers in arresting environmental degradation and instituting energy conservation measures in all Cantonments and Military Stations across the country. The path breaking efforts instituted include, planned afforestation, water conservation projects, drip irrigation projects, recycling of swimming pool water, soil conservation, rain water harvesting and projects relating to renewable energy sources. The Armed Forces are thus well on course towards being an energy conscious, environment friendly and a non-polluting force. The presentation of award was made at Palampur (HP) today, where the World Environment Forum is conducting a day-long convention on "Climate Change".

1476. (9-6-2007) NEW DELHI : Govt. of Maharashtra and Ministry of Railways must fulfil all their relief and rehabilitation commitments to the surviving victims of 7/11 within the next one month The serial bomb blasts in Mumbai's local trains on July 11 last year were one of the most warlike acts of Pakistan-sponsored terrorism that India has witnessed. As many as 187 innocent people lost their lives in blasts inside running trains at seven different locations and all within a span of about 10 minutes. It was the second instance of a terrorist attack on Mumbai in the form of serial bomb explosions, the first having taken place on 12 March 1993. I had come to Mumbai on July 12 last year, visited some of the sites of the bomb blasts and met the injured people in some of the city hospitals. In my interaction with the media, I had stated that this attack was carried out, with military precision, by enemies of the nation outside India with the collusion of anti-national elements within India. It is a matter of considerable concern that the UPA Government at the Centre, and the Congress-NCP Government in Maharashtra, have shown extreme lethargy and casualness, bordering on callousness, in investigating into this crime against the nation. The people of Mumbai – indeed, the entire country – have a right to know who were the culprits behind 7/11, and expect deterrent punishment to them. I therefore demand expeditious conclusion of the investigation and speedy justice to the guilty. There should not be a repeat of the experience of the March 1993 serial blasts; punishments for the guilty in the first serial bomb blasts are currently still being pronounced, after a gap of 14 long years. Today I visited two victims of 7/11 who are still in coma. They are – Shri Parag Sawant, who is at Hinduja Hospital and Shri Amit Singh at Jaslok Hospital. I pray for their speedy recovery. My party, the BJP, had demanded expeditious relief and rehabilitation to all the victims of the terrorist attack on 7/11. I myself wrote a letter to the Prime Minister in this regard on 30 August 2006, when it was brought to my attention that the various governmental agencies were slow and bureaucratic in fulfilling their promises to the surviving victims of 7/11. He had given detailed and specific assurances for prompt action in this regard.

1477. (10-6-2007) NEW DELHI : Shri Kamal Nath, Union Minister of Commerce & Industry, while addressing the Plenary Session on "The Emerging Power of Emerging Markets" at the 11th International Economic Forum at St. Petersburg today highlighted the change in the global trade that has come about as a result of the rise of the emerging markets and pointed out India as an example of the growing clout of these countries in global economy. "What better example to cite the growing clout of emerging economies than India, which has recorded the fastest GDP growth in 18 years, with the economy growing 9.4 per cent in 2006-07. While India continues to alter the coordinates of global trade, the country itself has seen robust growth in manufacturing with the sector growing 12.3 per cent in 2006-07 as compared to 9.1 per cent in the previous year... Very few countries in the world match these growth rates", he said. The Minister recorded the strides India has made in attracting foreign direct investment (FDI) and said that an estimated growth rate of 9% over the next five years starting 2007-08 would need an investment rate of 35.1% of GDP. He also informed about the huge investment potential in the upcoming knowledge process outsourcing (KPO) sector. "We are likely to capture around 15% of the over US $ 54 billion KPO industry worldwide by 2010", he said. Shri Nath also emphasised the opportunities presented by India's farm and food processing sector which has been identified as a priority area and also spoke of India's strength in the gems & jewellery and automobile and auto-components sector. Further, quoting a McKinsey study, he informed that the Indian pharmaceutical industry is projected to grow to US $ 25 billion by 2010. On the issue of the retail revolution, the Minister informed that organised retailing in India is expected to grow at the rate of 37% in 2007 and 42% in 2008. This is also offering opportunities in real estate sector, he stated. Shri Kamal Nath emphasised the need for "inclusive development" and said the biggest challenge before the emerging economies is to ensure that growth and development are more evenly spread.

1478. (11-6-2007) NEW DELHI : The Union Minister for Rural Development Dr. Raghuvansh Prasad Singh has emphasized the need for creating widespread awareness for the successful implementation of National Rural Employment Guarantee Act (NREGA). Speaking at a Review Meeting of State Rural Development Secretaries held here today, the Minister said that State Governments cannot have a different set of wages for NREGA and other developmental programmes. The minimum wages should be similar to the wages paid to agricultural labours for unskilled workers and must be at par with payment made for other developmental works carried out by other government agencies, he added. He said there should be no discrimination on gender basis over the payment of amount and the amount to be paid is on the basis of work actually done. The Minister stressed upon the judicious use of Central Grants and said that payment under NREGA is made only for 100 days of work. The Minister further clarified that the wages being paid under NREGA must be in conformity with minimum wages fixed under Minimum Wages Act and there can't be different wage structure for NREGA works alone. He said a 4-point strategy inclusive of strict vigilant monitoring, people's participation, transparency and accountability in implementing the NREGA in different States be opted and involvement of Local representatives including Member of Parliament of the area concerned should be ensured while making the Social Audit of the schemes. Dr. Singh asked for the timely revision of wages and verification of muster rolls on regular basis. Earlier the Rural Development Secretary, Sh. Subas Pani apprised the participants of the agenda of meeting and asked for adopting transparent approach while implementing NREGA in their respective States. The Meeting discussed various topics like deployment and training of personnel, muster roll verification campaign, social audit and the status of setting up of State Employment Guarantee Council etc.

1479. (11-6-2007) NEW DELHI : Shri Ram Awdhesh Singh has been nominated as the Member of National Commission of Backward Classes for a term of three years w.e.f 8th June 2007. He has been former Member of Bihar Legislative

Assembly, Lok Sabha and Rajya Sabha. He has been actively involved in the activities for the welfare and upliftment of backward classes.

1480. (11-6-2007) NEW DELHI : The Government proposes to expand the National Child Labour Project (NCLP) Scheme to all child labour endemic districts in the country during the 11th Plan. The Scheme is at present operational in 250 districts in 20 States wherein 7,328 special schools are functioning for the children withdrawn from work. Over 4.20 lakh children withdrawn from work are at present covered under the Scheme. The NCLP Scheme has been in operation since 1988. During the 10th Plan, the NCLP projects were enhanced from 150 to 250 districts. Under the Scheme children withdrawn from work are sent to special schools where they are provided with education, vocational training, nutrition, stipend, health care facilities etc. The children withdrawn from work are kept in special schools for a maximum period of three years to prepare them to join the regular education system. At present, approximately 3.30 lakh children withdrawn from work are enrolled in the special schools under the NCLP Scheme. So far, 3.92 lakh children have already been mainstreamed into formal education system. Out of this 1.36 lakh children have been mainstreamed between 2003-04 to 2005-06. The budget allocation for the Scheme was more than doubled during the 10th Plan. The allocation was increased from 249.60 crore in the 9th Plan to Rs. 602 crore during the 10th Plan. The implementation of the Scheme is being monitored through periodical reports submitted by the district authorities to the Labour and Employment Ministry. At the national level, the Central Monitoring Committee under the chairmanship of the Secretary, Labour and Employment monitors the functioning of the child labour projects at their level. In addition to NCLP Scheme, the Government is implementing the scheme of Grants-in-aid to voluntary organisations for the benefit of children withdrawn from work in the districts which are not covered by NCLP Scheme. 109 NGOs and 99 NGOs were given grants-in-aid during 2005-06 and 2006-07 respectively. Apart of these two Schemes, Government is implementing three other projects in collaboration with ILO *i.e.* INDUS, an Indo-US project being implemented in 21 districts of five states and Andhra Pradesh State Based Project being implemented in 3 districts in Andhra Pradesh. The third project is being implemented in Karnataka for the welfare of working children in two districts of the State. Census conducted by the Registrar General of India is the only authentic data in respect of number of child labour in the country. As per Census 2001, the number of child labourers in the country is 1.26 crore.

1481. (11-6-2007) NEW DELHI : State Government of Nagaland has been granted Rs. 10.90 crore towards balance of first instalment of funds by the Ministry of Rural Development against the provisional allocation of Rs.32.72 crore made for the Government of Nagaland under Accelerated Rural Water Supply Programme (Normal) of Rajiv Gandhi National Drinking Water Mission, during the year 2007-08. Up to 15 per cent of funds released under this sanction may be utilized for

Operation & Maintenance and up to 5 per cent of funds may be spent for taking sustainability measures. States have been requested to delegate powers for management of Rural Water Supply Schemes through the Panchayati Raj Institutions (PRIs) as per the Constitution of India. As such Operation and Maintenance of the completed RWS Scheme should be transferred to the PRIs. No expenditure shall be incurred on taking water quality problems form the present release, as there is a separate allocation for the purpose. This release is being made for execution/completion of schemes to provide safe drinking water facilities to rural habitations and schools under the Centrally Sponsored ARWSP. Priorities set in ARWSP guidelines and through other instructions issued from time to time shall be followed for coverage of rural habitations and rural schools.

1482. (11-6-2007) NEW DELHI : Under Accelerated Rural Water Supply Programme (Normal) of Rajiv Gandhi National Drinking Water Mission, Rs. 83.87 crore has been sanctioned to the State Government of Madhya Pradesh towards balance of first instalment of funds against the provisional allocation of Rs.251.62 crore by the Ministry of Rural Development during the year 2007-08. Up to 15 per cent of funds released under this sanction may be utilized for Operation & Maintenance and up to 5 per cent of funds may be spent for taking sustainability measures. States have been requested to delegate powers for management of Rural Water Supply Schemes through the Panchayati Raj Institutions (PRIs) as per the Constitution of India. As such Operation and Maintenance of the completed RWS Scheme should be transferred to the PRIs. No expenditure shall be incurred on taking water quality problems form the present release, as there is a separate allocation for the purpose. This release is being made for execution/completion of schemes to provide safe drinking water facilities to rural habitations and schools under the Centrally Sponsored ARWSP. Priorities set in ARWSP guidelines and through other instructions issued from time to time shall be followed for coverage of rural habitations and rural schools.

1483. (11-6-2007) NEW DELHI : Rs. 60.48 crore has been sanctioned to Gujarat Water Supply & Sewerage Board, Gandhinagar towards balance of first instalment of funds against the provisional allocation of Rs.181.44 crore made for the Government of Gujarat under the centrally sponsored Accelerated Rural Water Supply Programme (Normal) of Rajiv Gandhi National Drinking Water Mission, during the year 2007-08 by the Ministry of Rural Development. Up to 15 per cent of funds released under this sanction may be utilized for Operation & Maintenance and up to 5 per cent of funds may be spent for taking sustainability measures. States have been requested to delegate powers for management of Rural Water Supply Schemes through the Panchayati Raj Institutions (PRIs) as per the Constitution of India. As such Operation and Maintenance of the completed RWS Scheme should be transferred to the PRIs. No expenditure shall be incurred on taking water quality problems form the present release, as there is a separate allocation for the purpose. This release is being made for execution/completion of schemes to provide safe drinking water facilities to rural habitations and schools under the Centrally Sponsored ARWSP. Priorities set in ARWSP guidelines and through other instructions issued from time to time shall be followed for coverage of rural habitations and rural schools.

1484. (11-6-2007) NEW DELHI : Farm commodity prices monitored by the Department of Consumer Affairs have generally remained steady or have shown mixed trend in different centres across the country in the week ending 05.06.2007. Wheat prices remained steady at majority of reporting centres and declined at Patna and Bangalore. Wheat prices have shown increase only at Ahmedabad. Sugar prices remained steady across majority of the centres and declined at Guwahati and Chennai. There was marginal increase at Ahmedabad and Shillong. Gram prices remained steady over the week across most of the centres and declined at Ahmedabad, Bhuvaneshwar, Patna and Bangalore. Tur dal prices were also steady across most of the centres. As on 6th June, public sector agencies have contracted import of 6.375 lakh tonne pulses of which 1.72 lakh tonne has already reached Indian ports. At Delhi, no increase in prices has been reported over the week ending 5th June. Prices of wheat, atta, gram dal, tur dal, sugar, groundnut oil and packaged salt remained steady over one week and prices of rice, milk, potato and vanaspati remained steady over one month. Prices of tea loose and mustard oil declined.

1485. (11-6-2007) NEW DELHI : India and Russia have signed a Statement of Understanding to set up a Joint Task Force (JTF) to monitor the implementation of the Programme recommended by Joint Study Group (JSG) intending to reach a bilateral trade of US $ 10 billion by 2010 and to explore the feasibility of concluding Comprehensive Economic Cooperation Agreement (CECA) between the two countries. The Statement was signed by Shri Kamal Nath, Minister of Commerce and Industry of India and Mr. Gref, Minister of Economic Development and Trade of the Russian Federation, in St. Petersburg (Russia) on June 9, 2007. The Joint Task Force will further the objectives laid down by the JSG which was set up between India and Russia in February 2006, to formulate a programme for increasing the India-Russia bilateral trade through significant increase of mutual bilateral trade turnover between the two countries in a wide range of areas particularly with regard to trade in goods and services, investment and economic cooperation. Three meetings of JSG have been held so far and the fourth meeting is scheduled to be held in July 2007. The Joint Study Group is in the process of finalising a report that would analyse the current situation of bilateral trade and the prospects for expansion of trade and economic cooperation between Russia and India and contain a list of recommendations for the Russian and Indian Governments and business communities directed towards boosting bilateral trade and investment flows and developing the potential of Russian and Indian relations in the economic sphere.

1486. (12-6-2007) NEW DELHI : India will seek the support & cooperation of International community for the conservation of wildlife, and especially in India's endeavours for addressing concerns of tiger conservation. Minister for Environment & Forests, Shri Namo Narain Meena, who left early in the morning today to attend the Ministerial Round table Conference on Convention on International Trade in Endangered Species of Wild Fauna and Flora tomorrow at Hague, Netherlands will particularly talk about ban on illegal trade in tiger products.. The CITES convenes Conference of the Parties regularly. This is the 14th Convention of Parties which is convened at The Hague, Netherlands, from the 3rd June to 15th June 2007. During the present CoP, several issues relating to conservation of endangered species including Tiger, Elephant, Star tortoise, Sharks etc. would be discussed.

1487. (12-6-2007) NEW DELHI : As per the Quick Estimates of Industrial Production released by the Central Statistical Organization (CSO), industrial production in India registered a healthy growth of 13.6% in April 2007 as compared to 9.9% in April 2006. Industrial growth during 2006-07 went up by 11.5% as compared to 8.2% registered in the previous year. This is the highest growth of the industrial sector since 1995-96. The Manufacturing sector, which has about 80% weightage in the Index of Industrial Production, has registered a record growth of 15.1% in April 2007 as compared to 11.0% in April 2006. Earlier, a record growth of 12.5% was achieved during 2006-07 in the Manufacturing Sector, which augurs well for the 11th Plan, wherein a growth of 12% for the Manufacturing Sector has been envisaged. The Mining and Quarrying sector has shown a growth of 3.4%, whereas the Electricity sector has registered a growth of 8.7% during April 2007. The industries that have performed well in April 2007 include Wood and Wood Products; Furniture & Fixtures registering growth rates of 92.2%, 'Food Products' (55.0%), Machinery and Equipment (19.2%) 'Basic Metal and Alloy Industries' (18.0%), Jute and Other Vegetable Fibre Textiles (17.7%), Leather and Leather & Fur Products (14.7%) and Rubber, Plastic, Petroleum and Coal Products (14.1%). Among the use-base economic sub-groups, both Consumer Goods and Capital Goods have posted impressive rates of 17.7% during April 2007. Basic Goods, Intermediate Goods have recorded growth of 8.9% and 12.6% during April 2007.

1488. (12-6-2007) NEW DELHI : The Minister of Tourism and Culture Smt. Ambika Soni inaugurated " Dreams in Italy-an exhibition of paintings by Elizabeth Sass Brunner and Elizabeth Brunner" here today. The exhibition aims at showing a comprehensive picture of the art of the Brunner's in Italy covering their stay there both geographically and artistically. Elizabeth Sass Brunner (1889-1950) and her daughter Elizabeth Brunner (1910-2001) were artists of extraordinary talent and unique spiritual vision. From the total IGNCA collection of 852 paintings, a collection of 72 paintings done in Italy by the mother-daughter duo while on their way to India has been selected for focus in the exhibition. The paintings done by the two artists in Italy are completed with some of their important works painted in Hungary just before they left for the journey, and also some beautiful pieces done shortly after their arrival to India. These specifically trace their route from Hungary to Italy (Fiume, Bologna, Rome Naples, Sorrento, Capri and Sicily), to Libya (Tripoli) and finally India. Their attitude towards Italy was unusual, as their entire art was unique. The favourite tourist sites did not attract them. They were seeking for something more. The beautiful landscapes, the ancient monument conveyed them a spiritual message. They captured the message of the mighty Roman ruins, the catacombs of the first Christian communities, and the mighty forces of nature present in the rocks, the volcanoes and the mighty waves of the sea. Thus, the visitor of the exhibition will receive a full picture of their art in that period, and has the possibility to witness their artistic development from Hungary, through Italy to India. Italy, seen through the vivid imagination of the mother and the daughter coupled with their memory of glorious classical past, seems like a blossoming garden. There is a constant representation of the transformations that take place, the colours of sea and the Vesuvius and every city that they moved to is depicted in a unique predominant colour-Bologna, warm and yellow flower, changing like its flowers; Rome, glowing like the torches of the Coliseum and saints; Naples multicolored and crowded; Sorrento and Capri, changing blue and green of the Mediterranean. The horror of the First World War and the complete disintegration of the country did not dampen the artistic pursuits of the Brunner family. They depicted the landscape around the Balaton lake, the many forms of water sky and the garden, and indulged in self-reflection through self-portrait.

1489. (12-6-2007) NEW DELHI : A delegation representing the China National Biotec Group (CNBG) led by Madam Wang Lifeng, President and CEO of the organization along with four officials met the Union Minister for Health & Family Welfare, Dr. Anbumani Ramadoss today in New Delhi. The CNBG is Government owned, the largest vaccine manufacturer and supplier in China. Among other things, the delegation discussed the supply live of JE vaccine in order to protect Indian children from Japanese Encephalitis. Japanese Encephalitis is a life threatening disease to children in endemic countries in Asia, including China, India, Nepal, Korea, etc. Chengdu Institute of Biological Products (CNBG Chengdu Institute), one of subsidiaries of CNBG, developed a live attenuated Japanese Encephalitis vaccine SA14-14-2 (hereinafter referred as JE vaccine) and has supplied it in China since 1990. This vaccine has also been exported to Korea, Nepal and other Asian countries in recent years and protected millions of children against the life threatening Japanese Encephalitis in those countries. In February 2006, JE vaccine was licensed in India and 13.5 million doses of JE vaccine were supplied by CNBG Chengdu Institute to India in the first half of 2006. About 10 million Indian children between 1 to 15 years were vaccinated with JE vaccine in order to be protected from Japanese Encephalitis. The mass JE vaccination campaign were organized and monitored by Ministry of Health & Family Welfare,

Government of India, in a very efficient and effective manner. In 2007, the vaccination campaign for JE vaccine will be expanded to 22 districts in India and CNBG Chengdu Institute will supply more than 20 million doses of JE vaccine to Ministry of Health and Family Welfare, Government of India. Since last two years (05-06 and 06-07), the Ministry is procuring JE vaccine SA14-14-2 for JE vaccination campaign from Chengdu Institute of Biological Products on single source procurement basis.

1490. (12-6-2007) NEW DELHI : The Ministry of Rural Development has sanctioned Rs. 63.63 crore to the State Government of Tamil Nadu towards balance of first instalment of funds against the provisional allocation of Rs.190.90 crore made for the Government of Tamil Nadu under the Centrally sponsored Accelerated Rural Water Supply Programme (Normal) of Rajiv Gandhi National Drinking Water Mission, during the year 2007-08. Up to 15 per cent of funds released under this sanction may be utilized for Operation & Maintenance and up to 5 per cent of funds may be spent for taking sustainability measures. States have been requested to delegate powers for management of Rural Water Supply Schemes through the Panchayati Raj Institutions (PRIs) as per the Constitution of India. As such Operation and Maintenance of the completed RWS Scheme should be transferred to the PRIs. No expenditure shall be incurred on taking water quality problems form the present release, as there is a separate allocation for the purpose. This release is being made for execution/completion of schemes to provide safe drinking water facilities to rural habitations and schools under the Centrally Sponsored ARWSP. Priorities set in ARWSP guidelines and through other instructions issued from time to time shall be followed for coverage of rural habitations and rural schools.

1491. (12-6-2007) NEW DELHI : The Ministry of Rural Development has sanctioned Rs. 63.63 crore to the State Government of Tamil Nadu towards balance of first instalment of funds against the provisional allocation of Rs.190.90 crore made for the Government of Tamil Nadu under the Centrally sponsored Accelerated Rural Water Supply Programme (Normal) of Rajiv Gandhi National Drinking Water Mission, during the year 2007-08. Up to 15 per cent of funds released under this sanction may be utilized for Operation & Maintenance and up to 5 per cent of funds may be spent for taking sustainability measures. States have been requested to delegate powers for management of Rural Water Supply Schemes through the Panchayati Raj Institutions (PRIs) as per the Constitution of India. As such Operation and Maintenance of the completed RWS Scheme should be transferred to the PRIs. No expenditure shall be incurred on taking water quality problems form the present release, as there is a separate allocation for the purpose. This release is being made for execution/completion of schemes to provide safe drinking water facilities to rural habitations and schools under the Centrally Sponsored ARWSP. Priorities set in ARWSP guidelines and through other instructions issued from time to time shall be followed for coverage of rural habitations and rural schools.

1492. (12-6-2007) NEW DELHI : The Ministry of Rural Development has sanctioned Rs. 14.81 crore to the State Government of Meghalaya towards balance of first instalment of funds against the provisional allocation of Rs. 44.46 crore made for the Government of Meghalaya under Accelerated Rural Water Supply Programme (Normal) of Rajiv Gandhi National Drinking Water Mission, during the year 2007-08. Up to 15 per cent of funds released under this sanction may be utilized for Operation & Maintenance and up to 5 per cent of funds may be spent for taking sustainability measures. States have been requested to delegate powers for management of Rural Water Supply Schemes through the Panchayati Raj Institutions (PRIs) as per the Constitution of India. As such Operation and Maintenance of the completed RWS Scheme should be transferred to the PRIs. No expenditure shall be incurred on taking water quality problems form the present release, as there is a separate allocation for the purpose. This release is being made for execution/completion of schemes to provide safe drinking water facilities to rural habitations and schools under the Centrally Sponsored ARWSP. Priorities set in ARWSP guidelines and through other instructions issued from time to time shall be followed for coverage of rural habitations and rural schools.

1493. (12-6-2007) NEW DELHI : Rs. 138.83 crore has been sanctioned by the Ministry of Rural Development to the Uttar Pradesh Jal Nigam, Lucknow towards balance of first instalment of funds against the provisional allocation of Rs.401.51 crore made for the Government of Uttar Pradesh under the Centrally sponsored Accelerated Rural Water Supply Programme (Normal) of Rajiv Gandhi National Drinking Water Mission, during the year 2007-08. Up to 15 per cent of funds released under this sanction may be utilized for Operation & Maintenance and up to 5 per cent of funds may be spent for taking sustainability measures. States have been requested to delegate powers for management of Rural Water Supply Schemes through the Panchayati Raj Institutions (PRIs) as per the Constitution of India. As such Operation and Maintenance of the completed RWS Scheme should be transferred to the PRIs. No expenditure shall be incurred on taking water quality problems form the present release, as there is a separate allocation for the purpose. This release is being made for execution/completion of schemes to provide safe drinking water facilities to rural habitations and schools under the Centrally Sponsored ARWSP. Priorities set in ARWSP guidelines and through other instructions issued from time to time shall be followed for coverage of rural habitations and rural schools.

1494. (12-6-2007) NEW DELHI : Agriculture Minister Shri Sharad Pawar today said that it is necessary that farmers are given relevant information and guidance in simple language so that they assimilate it to generate better returns from farming activities. The Minister said that if farmers are guided about scientific use of inputs-especially balanced use of fertilizers, efficient use of water, marketing, animal husbandry, credit availability and other areas of farmers' interest, the adoption of new technologies and scientific agronomic practices will improve.

This in turn will improve the overall farm productivity, he argued. At the national level, the Minister said, the demand for foodgrains is increasing because of rising population and improving standards of living. In such a scenario, the only way to have sustained food security is to raise farm productivity. Extension and media can play a major role in doing so by providing proper guidance and information to the farmer, the Minister added. Shri Pawar felicitated Doordarshan and All India Radio on producing programmes on agriculture which, according to feedback reports, have generally been appreciated by farmers. However, there is need to improve the content to make the programmes more locally relevant and easy to assimilate. Besides guiding the farmer on farming matters, the programmes should also inform him about government's schemes and guide him to use them, he said. The Minister was speaking at the first meeting of the Apex Committee on Mass Media Support to Agriculture Extension. Besides concerned Departments, Doordarshan and All India Radio, States and farmers are represented in the Committee. Shri Pawar also launched a 'Content Scheduling and Monitoring Portal'. This portal gives details of agricultural programmes broadcast / telecast by all Stations of All India Radio and Kendras of Doordarshan. The portal is available at: dacnet.nic.in/csms

1495. (12-6-2007) NEW DELHI : The services in the Industry involved in Processing or Production of Fuel Gasses (Coal Gas, Natural Gas and the like)will continue as a public utility service under the Industrial Dispute Act, 1947 for another six months with effect from June 15, 2007. In a notification issued here, the Labour Ministry said that this is being done in the public interest. Earlier, the services in the industry were declared a public utility for six months from December 15, 2006. The employees in the said industry would, among other things, be required to give notice to their employers six weeks in advance of proceeding on strike so that conciliatory proceedings could be started. During the conciliatory proceedings and seven days after their completion, the employees cannot go on strike.

1496. (12-6-2007) NEW DELHI : Can an injury caused due to a syringe used on an AIDS patient infect the injured with HIV? No, it won't. Because HIV must enter your body in sufficient quantity for you to get infected. That's another reason why it is almost impossible to get infected with HIV from a barber's razor. Is it true most of the women infected with HIV are prostitutes? Myth again! Most women infected with HIV are housewives and a majority of them, over 70 percent in fact, get it through their husbands. Revealing facts like the ones above are samples from a set of 40 Q&As included in a three booklet set and a CD released by Surgeon Vice-Admiral Yogendra Singh, Director General, Armed Forces Medical Services (AFMS) in New Delhi today. The booklets and the CD were distributed to more than 100 participants at a workshop for Armed Forces Wives Welfare Associations. The participants, wives of serving soldiers, drawn from the three services, will form Peer Group Leaders, who will disseminate awareness on HIV/

AIDS among peer groups of about 20 wives of soldiers in the field units. The rapid spread of HIV/AIDS in the armed forces has alarmed authorities. Since the first detection of HIV in a soldier returning from a UN mission in 1992, the virus has affected 0.028 percent of the forces' strength, a statement laid before parliament last year said. 104 HIV-infected soldiers were discharged from service in 2004 alone. The workshop and the focus on Peer Group among wives of soldiers is part of a thrust programme in the armed forces to combat HIV/AIDS, the enemy within the ranks. Underlining the role women could play in checking HIV spread, Admiral Singh motivated soldiers' wives to create awareness and combat the menace. "The youthful, exuberant and aggressive attitude of our troops combined with the long separation from families and high mobility has compounded the risks faced by them," Admiral Singh said in his inaugural address to the two-day workshop. Mrs. Anupama Singh, Mrs. Maria Teresa Mehta and Mrs. Zareen Major, Presidents of Wives Welfare Associations of Army, Navy and Air Force respectively are attending the workshop. It has been organized by AFMS and the US Pacifc Command, in association with two NGOs-SOMA India and Partners in Development Initiatives (PDI).

1497. (12-6-2007) NEW DELHI : Based on the recommendations of Foreign Investment Promotion Board (FIPB) in its meeting held on 8th June, 2007, Finance Minister, Shri P. Chidambaram has approved 17 proposals of Foreign Direct Investment amounting approximately to Rs. 122.308 crore. The proposals relate to Ministries/Departments, namely, Biotechnology, Commerce, Defence Production, Heavy Industry, Information & Broadcasting, Information Technology, Posts, Tourism, Urban Development, Telecommunications and Economic Affairs. The major investment proposals pertain to the Ministries/Departments of Commerce, Urban Development and Telecommunications.

1498. (12-6-2007) NEW DELHI : Shri Kamal Nath, Union Minister of Commerce & Industry, has emphasized the importance of Special Products (SPs) and Special Safeguard Mechanism (SSM) for protecting the food security and livelihood security needs of India and strongly reiterated that "the issue would not be allowed to be diluted in any way by the developed countries to satisfy their demand for additional market access in the developing country markets." He was speaking at the meeting of the G-33-a grouping of countries with defensive interests in WTO agriculture negotiations. There was a general consensus among the 46 Member countries of the G33 to engage constructively with the developed countries on Indicators, which would yield the number of Special Products required by a developing country. Apart from the G-33 meeting, the Strategic meetings of the G-20 and the NAMA 11 Groups of developing countries were also held in Geneva yesterday. The G-20 and G-33 meetings were attended by Shri Kamal Nath and the Trade Ministers of many developing countries, including Brazil, Argentina, Indonesia, South Africa, Tanzania, Bolivia and senior officials. The G-20 meeting took stock of the latest offers on Agriculture subsidies and market access tabled by the US and the EC and concluded that there was hardly any movement in their positions from July 2006, when the Doha Round talks has to be suspended because of an impasse on these issues. The Members reiterated their commitment to the G-20 proposal of seeking effective and substantial cuts in the agriculture subsidies of the developed countries. They also emphasized that the developing countries, by agreeing to the principle of two-thirds overall proportionality in tariff cuts, were making an ambitious offer. However, this ambitious offer had to be met with an equally ambitious one from the developed countries-an expectation which was still to be fulfilled. The Members also noted that while the developed countries were very ambitious in seeking a drastic reduction in tariffs on industrial products (NAMA) in the developing countries, they were reluctant to follow the same principle for agricultural products in their own countries. This was leading to a palpable imbalance between agriculture and NAMA, which was contrary to the Doha Round mandate. The NAMA 11 meeting was chaired by the Commerce Minister of South Africa and attended by the Commerce or Trade Ministers of Argentina, Brazil, India, Indonesia and the senior officials of Venezuela, Namibia, Egypt, Tunisia and the Philippines. The Trade Ministers of China and Pakistan also attended the meeting. All the participants stressed on the need for a balanced and fair outcome in NAMA negotiations, rejecting the developed country proposal of a Swiss coefficient of 15 for the developing countries. They said it was inappropriate for the developed countries to place such extreme demands on the developing countries, in effect asking them to pay for the entire Round. They sought greater flexibilities for the developing countries to accommodate their development needs. Calling for a correction of the past imbalances in the multilateral trading system, they said that a successful outcome of the negotiations is only possible if the Round delivers on its development objectives. On Sectoral initiatives, a key demand of the US in this Round, it was pointed out that these initiatives were a voluntary modality to meet supplementary ambitions of the participants, that is cuts in addition to that achieved through the application of the formula.

1499. (12-6-2007) NEW DELHI : Indian Railways have carried 124.68 million tonnes of revenue earning freight traffic during April-May 2007. The freight carried shows an increase of 7.01 million tonnes over the freight traffic of 117.67 million tonnes actually carried during the corresponding period last year, an increase of 5.96 per cent. During the month of May 2007, the revenue earning freight traffic carried by Indian Railways was 63.77 million tonnes. There is an increase of 4.19 million tonnes over the actual freight traffic of 59.58 million tonnes actually carried by the Indian Railways during the same period last year, an increase of 7.03 per cent.

1500. (12-6-2007) NEW DELHI : A significant progress in the implementation of ICDS Scheme during the last 3 years has been registered, both in terms of increase in number of operational projects and Anganwadi Centres (AWCs) and coverage of beneficiaries. During a period of two and half years *i.e.* from 31.3.2004 to 30.9.2006, the number of beneficiaries for Supplementary Nutrition have increased from 415.09 lakh to 654.18 lakh. Similarly, the number of children (3-6 years) attending Anganwadi Centres for pre-school education has increased from 204.38 lakh to 271.28 lakh during the period. The ICDS Scheme has already been expanded twice in 2005-06 and 2006-07. During the 1st phase of expansion the Scheme was expanded to cover 466 additional Projects and 1.88 lakh Anganwadi Centres across the country, during 2005-06. The Government approved in December, 2006, 2nd phase of expansion of the Scheme for 173 additional Projects, 107274 Anganwadi Centres (AWCs) and 25961 mini Anganwadi Centre. Administrative sanctions for 166 additional Projects, 106726 Anganwadi Centres and 25943 mini anganwadi centres have since been issued to all States /UTs Administrations to cover the uncovered population/areas. Alongside gradual expansion of the Scheme, there has also been a significant increase in the budgetary allocation for ICDS (General), during the last three years. The allocation has increased from Rs. 1675.97 crore in 2003-04 to Rs. 1837.44 crore followed by Rs. 3610.30 crore, Rs. 4454.52 crore and Rs. 5204.00 crore for the years 2004-05, 2005-06, 2006-07 and 2007-08 respectively. Financial norms for supplementary nutritional under the ICDS Scheme, fixed in 1991, were revised in October, 2004. Existing financial norms have been doubled. Till 2004-05, States were responsible for providing supplementary nutrition as per nutritional and financial norms of the Scheme out of States own resources. It was also decided that from the year 2005-06 the Government of India would provide central assistance to States/UTs for supplementary nutrition also to the extent of 50% of the actual expenditure incurred or 50% of the cost norms, whichever is less. Grant-in-aid for supplementary nutrition, accordingly, is being released since the financial year 2005-06. Hitherto doubts persisted that supplementary nutrition under the Scheme is confined to beneficiaries hailing from low income (BPL) family. In super session of all previous instructions in this regard it has been clarified that supplementary nutrition is not be confined to beneficiaries of BPL families. In recognition of the significant services being provided by the Anganwadi Workers and Helpers (AWWs/AWHs), who are the critical grassroots-level functionaries in the ICDS set up, the honoraria being paid to them has been almost doubled with effect from 1st April, 2002. Anganwadi Workers and Helpers have also been allowed paid absence on maternity for a period of 135 days. In line with the aim of the Government to provide risk coverage for workers in the unorganized sector, a benefit has been extended to Anganwadi Workers and helpers through an insurance scheme under the Life Insurance Corporation's Social Security Group Scheme called the Anganwadi Karyakartri Bima Yojana.

1501. (13-6-2007) NEW DELHI : The Chief Labour Commissioner today declared the strike by the Indian Airlines employees union ACEU, illegal and liable for prosecution under the provisions of the Industrial Disputes Act 1947. This strike had been called for by the Air Corporation Employees Union (ACEU) which represents ground operations and clerical staff. The strike appears to be an attempt to create confusion by a few Union leaders for unknown reasons as all reasonable demands have been agreed to. The ACEU had threatened to go on strike with effect from 18th May 2007 regarding payment of wage arrears for the past 10 years. The management and the Union, in consultation with the Government, arrived at a reasonable settlement to the tune of Rs.267 crores and wage levels at par with their counterparts in Air India. Though the Company had financial problems in dealing with such a large amount of arrears, when PLI for the last 10 years in lieu of wage arrears had been regularly paid, the management and the Government, in the larger interest of harmonious industrial relations, had agreed to the same. On the late evening of 12th June, in the proceeding before the Chief Labour Commissioner, Union raised further unreasonable demands and suddenly went on a flash strike which is totally illegal and unwarranted. Indian Airlines has appealed to its employees, including the members of the ACEU, to refrain from such illegal industrial action considering that it is a peak summer holiday season and would cause distress to a large number of passengers, apart from being detrimental to the financial condition and image of the Company. In view of the strike, Indian Airlines has also decided to take stringent action against striking employees. Indian Airlines has also through a public message, requested all its passengers to bear with the inconvenience. While all efforts are being made to maintain the schedule to the extent possible, they have been requested to travel as light as possible and reconfirm their flights by calling a toll free No.1400/1401.

1502. (13-6-2007) NEW DELHI : A delegation led by Ms. Anna Kalata, Minister for Labour and Social Policy of Poland and the Indian delegation led by Shri Vayalar Ravi, Minister for Overseas Indian Affairs held a bilateral talks here today. Both sides discussed the perspectives of development of bilateral cooperation in the field of movement of workers especially in the context of employment of Indian citizens in Poland in the construction, agricultural and road-building sectors. The meeting focused on the possibilities of deepening cooperation in the field of labour and social policy with particular regard to exchange of experiences in the field of organization and management of migrant workers. Shri Ravi welcomed the step taken by the Polish Government to initiate a dialogue with India for developing a framework for bilateral cooperation to facilitate managed migration of Indian workers. He informed the Polish Minister that a robust statutory framework exists in India for facilitating managed migration and discouraging irregular migration and the same is now being fortified by implementing e-Governance. A skill upgradation programme has been launched recently to bring skills of potential migrants at par with the market demand. He emphasized that India has the capacity to supply high quality workers for construction, agricultural and road building sectors as well as for sectors like IT and Telecom. The Polish Minister for Labour and Social Policy has taken the initiative to promote recruitment of Indian workers in the construction, agriculture and road-building sectors. In response the Ministry of Overseas Indian Affairs had suggested a Memorandum of Understanding to the Polish side leading to the visit of the Polish Minister for Labour and Social Policy to India. The Polish side appreciated the statutory framework and the initiatives for migration management in India and agreed that the needs of the two friendly countries are complementary and call for an appropriate framework for bilateral cooperation. It was agreed that managed migration under the framework of bilateral cooperation will benefit both countries as well as the workers and their families. Both sides agreed to constitute a Joint Working Group to discuss and identify areas of cooperation and finalize the framework/Memorandum of Understanding.

1503. (13-6-2007) NEW DELHI : Shri K.M. Chandrasekhar assumed charge as the Union Cabinet Secretary here today. He belongs to the 1970 batch of the Indian Administrative Service (Kerala Cadre). Prior to this, he held a number of important positions in the Government of Kerala as well as in the Government of India with the latest one being the Revenue Secretary in the Ministry of Finance. He also held the posts of Ambassador & Permanent Representative of India to the World Trade Organisation, Geneva; Deputy Chief of Mission, Embassy of India, Brussels; Joint Secretary (Trade Policy Division) in the Ministry of Commerce and Chairman, Spices Board of India. As Revenue Secretary, he was instrumental in ensuring consistent high performance in revenue collection and ushering in systemic changes in revenue administration, procedures and policy. Shri Chandrasekhar was Chairman/ Chief Executive/Director of more than 40 public and private sector companies in India at various times. He has many achievements and major milestones to his credit in his distinguished career both in the Government of Kerala and in the Centre and also possesses vast international experience. Shri Chandrasekhar holds a B.A. (Hons.) Degree in Economics, M.A. (History) from the University of Delhi and M.A. (Management Studies) from the University of Leeds, U.K.

1504. (13-6-2007) NEW DELHI : There are some misconceptions regarding telephone interception by the Investigation Wing of the Income Tax Department. Phone interception is done only in very exceptional and the rarest of cases after obtaining due authorisation from the appropriate authority. Reports suggesting that the interception facility is used for routinely tapping corporate conversations or keeping a tab on top bracket taxpayers are totally baseless.

1505. (13-6-2007) NEW DELHI : Sections 11 and 12 of the Income Tax Act, 1961 provide for exemption of income of charitable and religious entities. In order to avail of such exemption, the entity is required to make an application for registration under section 12A in form No. 10 A to the Commissioner of Income Tax. Prior to 1st day of June. 2007, the application had to be made by the entity within one year from the date of its creation/establishment and the Commissioner had discretion to condone the delay if the application was filed belatedly. However, the Finance Act, 2007 has removed the requirement of filing the application for registration by the entity within one year and has also removed the power vested with the Commissioner for condonation of delay in respect of any application made on or after 1st day of June, 2007. A new clause (aa) to sub-section (1) of section 12A of the Income Tax Act has been inserted in this regard. Consequent to this, in order to harmonise the existing Rule 17 A and the Form No.10A Appendix II to the said Rule with the new provision, notification has been issued on 30th May, 2007 amending this Rule and Form to enable filing of application for registration by charitable and religious entities on or after the 1st day of June, 2007. Further, income received on behalf of certain charitable and religious entities is entitled for exemption from tax in terms of sub-clauses (iv),(v),(vi) and (via) to clause (23C) of Section 10. Till now, in order to be eligible for such exemption, the entities had to be notified by Central Government (sub-clause) (iv) or (v)) or had to be approved by the prescribed authorities (sub-clauses) (vi) and(via)). Vide Finance Act, 2007, the approvals in respect of sub-clauses (iv) and (v) have also to be granted by the prescribed authorities with effect from 1st June, 2007. Notifications have been issued on 30th May, 2007 to amend the relevant rules viz,.Rule 2C and Rule 2CA of the Income Tax Rules, 1962 to specify the Chief Commissioners of Income Tax/Directors General of Income Tax who will be the prescribed authorities for receipt of applications and grant of approvals in terms of sub-clauses(iv),(v),(vi) and(via) to clause (23C) of Section 10. From Nos. 56 and 56D in the Appendix II to the Income Tax Rules have also been modified consequent upon these amendments. The above notifications have been made effective from the 1st day of June, 2007.

1506. (13-6-2007) NEW DELHI : The Minister for Civil Aviation, Shri Praful Patel, today reviewed the flash strike called by Unions of Indian Airlines Ltd., from 9 p.m. yesterday. The Minister has called the strike illegal and unwarranted as negotiations and talks between the Management, the Union representatives and the Chief Labour Commissioner were at an advanced stage. Despite the fact that arrears are not payable in loss making Public Sector Undertakings the Ministry as well as the Management of Indian Airlines had agreed to pay a package of Rs. 267 crore as wage arrears and an agreement on this issue with the Union and with the employees had been finalized. Also career progression to bring the employees broadly at par to what they had demanded had been agreed on. However just before the final agreement could be reached the employees have gone on a strike without giving any notice to the Management. The Government and the Management of Indian Airlines have taken a very serious view of the situation. All steps including legal action are being considered. The Minister has warned that if the strike is not called off by this evening strict steps would be taken by the Ministry and the Management. The financial package that has been offered to the employees too might be withdrawn, the Minister said. The Minister has however, assured the travelling public that their convenience would be given the highest priority. All steps were being taken to bring back normalcy as soon as possible. The Minister pointed out that this being the holiday season a great number of people would be travelling and it was the obligation of the employees of Indian Airlines to ensure that they were not unnecessarily inconvenienced.

1507. (13-6-2007) NEW DELHI : Congress Spokesperson Smt. Jayanti Natrajan said that with great fanfare the BJP along with all its important national leaders trooped down to Gujarat to congratulate Narendra Modi on becoming the longest ever serving Chief Minister of Gujarat on his completion of 2063 days as Chief Minister. However the nation realizes that this is not an occasion for celebration, but one of sober introspection on the vagaries of democracy that the man who masterminded state sponsored genocide in the aftermath of Godhra, the man who in the words of the Supreme Court of India watched like Nero while Gujarat burned who unleashed a programme against minorities in the land of Mahatma Gandhi, can possibly be congratulated or felicitated in any way. Minorities, Dalits, women, labour and children are not safe in Gujarat today, Under Modi's Chief Ministership, normalization and strength are equated with a vindictive administration and political repression, where brute compromise is thrust, when acknowledgment of the horrors of mass crime are denied when villages, cities, mohallas are divided by borders when the victim, survivors and human right defenders who stand up for justice are threatened arrested and tortured and civil liberties brutally trampled upon. Five years after the genocide of the aftermath of Godhra, the most bleak period of India's post independence history, where the Chief Minister of Gujarat has been acknowledged by high constitutional authorities such as the Supreme Court, and the NHRC as the Chief author and architect of all that happened in Gujarat after the arson of Feb 27, 2002, it is important for all citizens to remember the true face of Narendra Modi. It is not as if the fascist repression of large sections of the people of Gujarat have stopped after Modi has been repeatedly pulled up by various authorities. Farmers were brutally repressed when the kisans agitated for their rights. Artists have been time and again made the target of Modi's repression and brute force. The film industry had borne the brunt of Narendra Modi's anger, and we witnessed the bizarre spectacle of film distributors being threatened not to exhibit the film Parzania. Recently in Vadodara brutal repressive tactics were employed against university students. Two girls have been cruelly raped and murdered in Junagadh and until today, the guilty have not been brought to book. And then there are the infamous and shameful encounter killings. When in a complete breakdown of law and order, a man is pulled out of a bus and shot. And his wife raped and murdered. All in the name of security, when policemen who are themselves meant to protect the citizens turn into aggressors and murderers who are protected by the Government, then no vestige of security is left for the average citizen to lead a safe life. Let me quote a BJP MLA Dhiru Gajera. "There is only one person safe in Gujarat and that is Narendra Modi. The rest of the state is at God's mercy!!...loot, robbery, murder and rape are common," The accused are not caught for days and months, while on the other hand false cases are thrust on political adversaries who are arrested and killed in fake encounters on the ground that they had plotted to kill Modi.

1508. (13-6-2007) NEW DELHI: Bahujan Samaj Party president and Uttar Pradesh Chief Minister Mayawati on Tuesday announced her party's unequivocal support to the United Progressive Alliance candidate for the Presidential election. At a press conference here, Ms. Mayawati said she gave the commitment to Congress president and UPA chairperson Sonia Gandhi at a dinner meeting on Monday. She, however, declined to reveal the name on which there was consensus. Ms. Gandhi would "soon" announce the candidate, she said adding that some names were discussed. Ms. Mayawati, said she wanted to make it "clear" that her party always struggled "against communal forces" and that was why there was no question of supporting a National Democratic Alliance (NDA) candidate. Coalitions with the BJP were formed in Uttar Pradesh under special circumstances, she said. "There was no clear mandate. We wanted re-election but people did not want another election to be foisted on them. But the BSP did not allow communal forces to rise and abandon its ideology and principles. If that were not the case, I would not have resigned before the terms were over. Even Mulayam Singh got a chance to cobble up a government because I resigned." Asked if the Congress president invited her to join the UPA Government now, she said: "In the government formation stage itself, the UPA chairperson invited us. But we decided against joining the UPA or the government. We were for outside support to prevent the NDA and communal parties from coming to power." Asked if the bonhomie would continue till the 2009 Lok Sabha elections, she said: "We were never enemies. We keep meeting." Asked whether her party would support Bhairon Singh Shekhawat in the Presidential poll, she said there was no question of considering a "second or third person." Ms. Mayawati denied that she imposed any conditions or made any claims for the Vice-President's post, which is also falling vacant, in lieu of her support to the UPA candidate.

1509. (13-6-2007) NEW DELHI : Defence Research and Development Organisation (DRDO) of the Ministry of Defence has signed a Memorandum of Understanding (MoU) with National Association of Software and Service Companies (NASSCOM), the premier chamber of commerce for software and services in India to strengthen cooperation and increase collaboration between the Indian IT industry and DRDO. This MoU is an initiative to further innovation and the development of Intellectual Property in the domestic market in India. The MoU will help establish a successful working relationship between DRDO and the Indian IT industry and will advance issues of mutual interest. This initiative will also strengthen cooperation for enabling a long-term involvement of IT software companies in DRDO's development projects. Speaking on the occasion Shri M Natrajan, Director General Defence R&D said DRDO has taken a lot of initiatives for promoting increased partnership of private sector industry in the development of major systems. He said 'as the modern military systems are becoming increasingly software intensive, we are keen to workout a long-term strategic arrangement with NASSCOM to enable Indian IT industry to partner DRDO labs in various software development activities mainly related to systems like Radars, Electronic Warfare Systems, Sonars, Flight Control, Avionics, Missile Systems, Command and Control Systems, Communication System etc.'. Shri Natrajan said the MoU seeks to facilitate defining long term strategic partnership with IT industry and to take further actions for finalizing methodologies for its effective implementation. Shri Kiran Karnik, President NASSCOM said creating upstream linkages with the Indian R&D institutions is a key part of NASSCOM's focus on developing India's innovation ecosystem. He said DRDO has been responsible for developing a number of leading technologies in multi-focus areas spanning across aero-space, control systems, communication etc. which makes it the obvious choice for such a partnership. Shri Karnik said through this MoU the DRDO-IT industry partnership could liverage the experience and best practices gained through these engagements.

1510. (13-6-2007) NEW DELHI : Shri Subodh Kant Sahai, Hon'ble Minister of State for Food Processing Industries (Independent Charge) visited the USA during 31st May to 11th June, 2007. The Minister was accompanied by a delegation of ten members of Indo-American Chamber of Commerce, representing various sectors like food processing, packaging, organic foods, etc. The delegation members had business-to-business meetings at all the cities with potential US investors. Food Processing Sector has been identified as the priority sector in India. The Vision Document adopted by the Government provides for an investment of about rupees one lakh crore, of which rupees ten thousand crore only is to come from the Government. There is, therefore, a need for larger private investment to establish adequate infrastructural facilities and supply chain for the food processing sector. The farmers are required to be linked to the market and they should start producing raw material for the use by the industry so that they are benefited with long term economic sustainability. Keeping the above mission in view, the Minister had visited Washington, New York, Chicago, San Francisco and Los Angeles and interacted with the potential US investors for their investment in technology transfer, capacity building and creating infrastructural facilities / supply chain and quality control laboratories. Shri Sahai met with the US Secretary for Agriculture Mr. Mike Johanns at Washington DC. Both the leaders discussed about the post-harvest and food processing initiatives in India and the India-US Agricultural Knowledge Initiative. Shri Sahai said that India is the largest producer of milk and second largest producer of fruits and vegetables. However, the food processing industry in India is at a nascent stage. Perishable food items in India have short shelf life and poor marketing facilities. The Honorable Minister said that the focus needed to be on areas of reducing post-harvest losses, building supply chain, cold chain, and developing linkages of farming to the processing industry. India-US Knowledge Initiative in Agriculture could play an important role in all these areas. Shri Sahai suggested setting up a Joint Laboratory for SPS standards in India to facilitate trade in agricultural items as well as processed food. The Minister said that India would be interested in expanding trade and investment in those areas and would welcome technology transfer from US to India in the Food Processing sector. Shri Sahai further mentioned that Ministry of Food Processing Industry was in talks with Cornell University for providing technical support for setting up a National Institute of Food Technology, Entrepreneurship and Management (NIFTEM) in India. As a goodwill gesture, the Minister presented a fresh consignment of Indian mangoes to the US secretary for Agriculture Mr. Mike Johanns. A meeting was also held with senior officials of World Bank in Washington. The World Bank officials considered the food processing sector as one of their priority areas and expressed their willingness to extend their support for building up supply chain and other infrastructure projects in India. Mr. Cal Dooley, President of the Association of Food Processing Companies has also met the Minister and discussed about investment of US companies in India. He is willing to visit India with a delegation consisting of representatives of US companies. Another large company in USA (M/s Tyson Company) dealing with poultry and meat processing has expressed keen interest to have joint venture with India for setting up / upgradation of abattoirs and poultry processing. The Honorable Minister visited Chicago Board of Trade and addressed a series of Road Shows in New York, Chicago, San Francisco, and Los Angeles on the opportunities in the Food Processing Industry in India. The Road Shows were attended by US companies looking to invest in the sector in India. Representatives from companies like Pepsi, Hershey, Cargill, JP Morgan, P&G, Sara Lee etc. and many others participated in these meetings. In dairy sector, US investor has requested for specific requirement of supply of about one to two million litres of flavoured milk in tetra packs per month, for which availability of suitable Indian partners are being explored.

1511. (13-6-2007) NEW DELHI : The Taj Mahal is the best known monument of India and undoubtedly the most magnificent monument in a series of mausoleums built by the Mughal Emperors. Shahjahan raised this grand mausoleum on the banks of river Yamuna in memory of his second wife Mumtaz Mahal. The construction of Taj Mahal started in 1631 and was completed in about 22 years. More than 20000 people were deployed to work on it and materials were brought out from all over India and Central Asia. The Taj rises on a high red sand base topped by a white marble terrace on which rests the famous dome flanked by tapering minarets. Within the dome lies the jewel inlaid cenotaph of the Queen. The Taj Mahal was declared as a protected monument in 1920 under the Ancient Monuments Preservation Act of 1904.

1512. (13-6-2007) NEW DELHI : There are reports in the print and electronic media raising concerns on grant of patent on Yoga postures by the United States Patent and Trademark Office (USPTO). The matter was checked up with First Secretary for Intellectual Property, US Embassy, New Delhi, who has reported that USPTO was not able to identify a single patent directed on yoga poses. The Controller General of Patents, Designs and Trademarks (CMPDTM) has also informed that preliminary search of USPTO database indicates that there is no patent on yoga postures per se. Patents granted by USPTO mostly include devices and accessories in Yoga. It is estimated that 131 patents have been granted in USPTO on yoga subject and there are 3700 trademarks which have been listed in the database of registered and pending trade marks by USPTO. Department of AYUSH, Ministry of Health & Family Welfare, who is the nodal Department for Yoga, have already written to Indian Ambassador in Washington to take all necessary steps to address the issue of misappropriation of Indian Yoga system through USPTO.

1513. (13-6-2007) NEW DELHI : Shri Kamal Nath, Minister of Commerce & Industry, today announced a package of wide ranging measures to counter the negative impact of rupee appreciation on India's exports. Following extensive interaction with a high-level delegation of the Federation of Indian Export Organisations (FIEO) and all Export Promotion Councils (EPCs) led by the FIEO President, Shri G.K. Gupta, the Minister announced the following measures: Ministry of Commerce would recommend to the Ministry of Finance the following: Duty Entitlement Pass Book (DEPB) and Duty Drawback rates may be enhanced by 5%. Rate of interest on pre-shipment and post-shipment credit be reduced for exporters to 6%. (At present, the rate of interest charged is in the range of 9 to 11%). Exchange Earners' Foreign Currency (EEFC) Accounts may be made interest bearing. (As on date, EEFC Account deposited is stated as current account and interest on it discontinued since 2000). Scheduled Commercial Banks may be mandated to meet 15% export credit disbursement target. Notify the Service Tax Exemption / Refunds for exports announced in the Foreign Trade Policy 2007 without further delay. All arrears of TED (Terminal Excise Duty) & CST (Central Sales Tax) reimbursement would be cleared by 30th June, 2007 and the Ministry of Finance will be requested to provide additional funds, if necessary. Export Credit & Guarantee Corporation (ECGC) will reduce its premia rates by upto 10% to make exports more competitive.

1514. (13-6-2007) NEW DELHI : For the implementation of the Sampoorna Grameen Rozgar Yojana (SGRY), Grants-in-aid amounting to Rs. 144.24 lakh as part of first instalment, out of the Central allocation of Rs.865.41 lakh, has been released to Jabalpur district of Madhya Pradesh State by the Ministry of Rural Development, as Central assistance during the current financial year (2007-08). The grant is towards plan expenditure and will be utilized for approved items of works subject to the conditions laid down in the SGRY Guidelines. No deviations from the guidelines is permissible. The expenditure on implementation of the programme with regard to cash component is to be shared on 75:25 basis between the Central and the State Government respectively.

1515. (13-6-2007) NEW DELHI : Rs. 4.47 crore has been sanctioned to the State Government of Sikkim by the Ministry of Rural Development towards balance of first instalment of funds against the provisional allocation of Rs.13.42 crore made for the Government of Sikkim under Accelerated Rural Water Supply

Programme (Normal) of Rajiv Gandhi National Drinking Water Mission, during the year 2007-08. Up to 15 per cent of funds released under this sanction may be utilized for Operation & Maintenance and up to 5 per cent of funds may be spent for taking sustainability measures. States have been requested to delegate powers for management of Rural Water Supply Schemes through the Panchayati Raj Institutions (PRIs) as per the Constitution of India. As such Operation and Maintenance of the completed RWS Scheme should be transferred to the PRIs. No expenditure shall be incurred on taking water quality problems form the present release, as there is a separate allocation for the purpose. This release is being made for execution/completion of schemes to provide safe drinking water facilities to rural habitations and schools under the Centrally Sponsored ARWSP. Priorities set in ARWSP guidelines and through other instructions issued from time to time shall be followed for coverage of rural habitations and rural schools.

1516. (13-6-2007) NEW DELHI : State Government of Mizoram has been sanctioned Rs. 10.62 crore towards balance of first instalment of funds against the provisional allocation of Rs.31.88 crore made for the Government of Mizoram under Accelerated Rural Water Supply Programme (Normal) of Rajiv Gandhi National Drinking Water Mission, during the year 2007-08 by the Ministry of Rural Development. Up to 15 per cent of funds released under this sanction may be utilized for Operation & Maintenance and up to 5 per cent of funds may be spent for taking sustainability measures. States have been requested to delegate powers for management of Rural Water Supply Schemes through the Panchayati Raj Institutions (PRIs) as per the Constitution of India. As such Operation and Maintenance of the completed RWS Scheme should be transferred to the PRIs. No expenditure shall be incurred on taking water quality problems form the present release, as there is a separate allocation for the purpose. This release is being made for execution/completion of schemes to provide safe drinking water facilities to rural habitations and schools under the Centrally Sponsored ARWSP. Priorities set in ARWSP guidelines and through other instructions issued from time to time shall be followed for coverage of rural habitations and rural schools.

1517. (14-6-2007) NEW DELHI : The President, Dr. A.P.J.Abdul Kalam has condoled the passing away of Mahatma Gandhi's grandson, Prof. Ramachandra Gandhi. In a condolence message to the late Professor's brothers, Shri Gopalkrishna Gandhi the Governor of West Bengal and Shri Rajmohan Gandhi, the President has said that Prof. Ramachandra Gandhi was a well-known personality, philosopher, visionary, writer and an outstanding scholar.

1518. (14-6-2007) NEW DELHI : Top Class Education for providing professional courses in medicine, engineering, law, fashion technology etc. through 127 institutes of eminence will soon be introduced by the Ministry of Social justice and Empowerment for the higher educational attainment of SC students. This was announced by Minister for Social Justice & Empowerment, Smt. Meira Kumar at the Conference of State Social Welfare Secretaries of States/UTs here today.

She said as far as the targeted educational development programmes for the students belonging to the Scheduled Castes, progress has been made in their educational advancement through scholarships/fellowships schemes. The National Overseas Scholarship Scheme and Scheme for Free Coaching for SC and OBC students has also been revised. Addressing the Social Welfare Secretaries, the Minister said that the Ministry has constituted a Committee to oversee the implementation status of the PCR and POA Acts so that focused attention to the problem of atrocities against the Scheduled Castes and Scheduled Tribes may be ensured. She further said that I had requested the Chief Ministers of States during February, 2006 to consider increase in the incentive amount for inter caste marriages to at least Rs. 50000/-of which 50% would be borne by central assistance. Further, in order to promote and increase awareness among the masses, the Ministry has taken an important and significant initiative by announcing a National Award during November, 2006 in the field of eradicating untouchability and combating offences against Scheduled Castes. She said that scavenging has also been one of our priority concerns. She asked the Secretaries to apprise about the follow up actions taken by States on the issues and progress made by the States in the rehabilitation of the manual scavengers. Speaking on the girls' education, She said Recognizing that the investment in girls education is key to empowerment of women, we have increased the Central funding from 50 to 100% for the Construction of SC Girls Hostel by revising the scheme so that the girl students can pursue their education in a protected and enabling environment. She said the Ministry has streamlined the procedure for sanction of grant in aid to the NGOs from the current financial year. Under the new procedure, we have introduced the concept of State-wise notional allocation so that the existing asymmetry in the fund flow may be corrected. Smt Meira Kumar also informed that the Ministry has enhanced the budgetary allocation under the Post Matric Scholarship Scheme from Rs. 35 crore in the year 2006-07 to Rs. 100 crore in the current financial year. Also under the scheme of financial assistance to voluntary organisations, we have identified training institutes of repute like Rural Development and Self Employment Training Institutes (RUDSET), Karanata and Apparal Training & Design Centre (ATDC), Gurgaon for providing specialized skill development programmes to the OBC beneficiaries, 'she added.

1519. (14-6-2007) NEW DELHI : A Memorandum of Agreement was signed today between the National Institute of Health & Family Welfare (NIHFW) and National Research Development Corporation (NRDC) for transfer of technology developed by the NIHFW in the fields of Thermo Stable Elisa Kits and Laboratory Kits for Testing Sperm Functions. The up scaling of technologies developed by the Institute will be taken up by NRDC for commercialization. Prof. Deoki Nandan, Director, NIHFW and Mr. Somenath Ghosh, Chairman & Managing Director, NRDC signed the Memorandum of Agreement. This is the first time that the technology developed by NIHFW is being taken up for commercialization. Thermo Stable Elisa Kits technology allows enzyme conjugate and antibody to retain their enzymatic and immunological activity respectively at 37 oC for three months or more than two years at 2 to 8 °C. The thermo stability technology for enzyme conjugate can have applicative value in those Elisa kits that are based on the use of enzyme horseradish peroxidase as label. The imported kits wherein horseradish peroxidase enzyme used are not thermo stable (can not with stand higher temperature of 37 °C for more than twenty four hours). They require cold chain for their transport and storage. The new technologies are useful in production of Thermo-Stable Elisa Kits. Three technological kits have been developed for testing Sperm functions. These will help to test many of the specialized functions of the sperms which otherwise are not routinely examined. It will strengthen the existing diagnostic tools in the male infertility diagnosis and management. It has the great potential to be routinely used in human sperm banks and can be extended in the same area for veterinary applications. At present no such laboratory kit for sperm function is available in the market. The kits do not require any imported material and have been developed indigenously. In addition, the institute has also developed a vaginal contraceptives technology, which is water based, very much effective, less expansive and expected to provide wide acceptability.

1520. (14-6-2007) NEW DELHI : The Central Board of Direct Taxes (CBDT) has decided that the first instalment of Fringe Benefit Tax, which is payable by tomorrow in respect of transfer or allotment of specified security or sweat equity shares to its employees, may now be paid by 15th of September, 2007 (the date of second instalment). CBDT is currently in the process of notifying the method for determination of the fair market value. In the meantime, the first instalment of advance tax in respect of fringe benefit tax falls due on 15th of June. In the absence of a method for determination of the fair market value, it will not be possible for an employer to determine the value of the first instalment of advance tax related to fringe benefit tax in respect of allotment or transfer of specified security or sweat equity shares to its employees. By virtue of the provision of clause (d) of sub-section (1) section 115 WB, introduced by Finance Act, 2007, an employer is liable to pay Fringe Benefit Tax on any consideration for employment provided by way of any specified security or sweat equity shares allotted or transferred, directly or indirectly, by such employer free of cost or at concessional rate to his employees. The value of the fringe benefit is determined as the fair market value of the specified security or sweat equity share on the date on which the option vests with the employee as reduced by the amount actually paid, by or recovered from the employee in respect of such security or shares. The fair market value for this purpose is to be determined in accordance with the method prescribed by the Board.

1521. (14-6-2007) NEW DELHI : The Indian Airlines Employees Union, ACEU, has called off its strike today. This was done after talks between the Ministry of Civil Aviation, the Indian Airlines Management and the Union leaders. The Secretary, Ministry of Civil Aviation, Shri Ashok Chawla along with senior officials of the

Ministry, the CMD and Director (Personnel) of Indian Airlines met with some of the representatives of the ACEU today morning. At the meeting an agreement has been reached between the employees and the Management of Indian Airlines. The wage arrears of Rs. 267 crores to be paid to the employees have been agreed upon. It will be paid in 18 months. Minor issue regarding career progression has also been amicably settled. The flight situation of Indian Airlines is expected to be normal very soon. Indian Airlines is informing all the passengers accordingly.

1522. (14-6-2007) NEW DELHI : The Ministry of Rural Development has approved the release of 314 MT of Wheat and 180 MT of Common Rice (Total 494 MT) during the year 2007-08 to Hamirpur District of Himachal Pradesh State through Food Corporation of India depots in the State under the Sampoorna Grameen Rozgar Yojana (SGRY) scheme. The grant is towards plan expenditure and will be utilized for approved items of works subject to the conditions laid down in the SGRY Guidelines.

1523. (14-6-2007) NEW DELHI : State Government of Karnataka has been sanctioned Rs. 10.93 crore by the Ministry of Rural Development towards balance of first instalment of ARWSP-DDP funds against provisional allocation of Rs.32.79 crore for the year 2007-08 under Accelerated Rural Water Supply Programme (ARWSP)-DDP Areas of Rajiv Gandhi National Drinking Water Mission (RGNDWM). The release is being made for execution/completion of schemes to provide safe drinking water facilities to rural habitations and schools under the ARWSP-DDP Areas as per the priorities indicated in the Guidelines for implementation of Rural Water Supply Programme. The terms and conditions for the release of ARWSP-DDP funds are included in the Guidelines for implementation of Rural Water Supply Programme.

1524. (14-6-2007) NEW DELHI : An amount of Rs. 81.90 crore has been sanctioned to the State Government of Karnataka towards balance of first instalment of funds against the provisional allocation of Rs. 245.72 crore by the Rural Development Ministry under the Centrally Sponsored Accelerated Rural Water Supply Programme (Normal) of Rajiv Gandhi National Drinking Water Mission, during the year 2007-08. Up to 15 per cent of funds released under this sanction may be utilized for Operation & Maintenance and up to 5 per cent of funds may be spent for taking sustainability measures. States have been requested to delegate powers for management of Rural Water Supply Schemes through the Panchayati Raj Institutions (PRIs) as per the Constitution of India. As such Operation and Maintenance of the completed RWS Scheme should be transferred to the PRIs. No expenditure shall be incurred on taking water quality problems form the present release, as there is a separate allocation for the purpose. This release is being made for execution/completion of schemes to provide safe drinking water facilities to rural habitations and schools under the Centrally Sponsored ARWSP. Priorities set in ARWSP guidelines and through other instructions issued from time to time shall be followed for coverage of rural habitations and rural schools.

1525. (14-6-2007) NEW DELHI : The Consultative Committee members attached to the Urban Development Ministry today met in the capital under the Chairmanship of Shri S.Jaipal Reddy, Urban Development Minister and discussed preparations for Commonwealth Games 2010. Shri Ajay Maken, Minister of State for Ubran Development Ministry was also present. The Parliament Members who attended the meeting include Shri V. Radhakrishnan, Shri Pannian Ravindran, Shri A.H. Khan Chowdhury, Shri Ravi Prakash Verma, Shri Sajjan Kumar, Shri Swadesh Chakrabortty, Shri Jagdish Tytler, Shri Prasanta Chatterjee, Ms. Krishna Tirath, Shri Anirudh Prasad Yadav, Ms. Prema Kariappa, Shri V. Narayanswamy, Shri Karnendu Bhattacharjee, and Shri Ram Narayan Sahu. DDA Vice Chairman, Shri Dinesh Rai and Director General, CPWD, Shri A.K. Chakrabarti gave presentations on the role of DDA and CPWD respectively on Development of Venues and Games Village for Commonwealth Games. In his introductory remarks the Chairman Shri Jaipal Reddy stated that the Delhi Development Authority, Government of Delhi and the Sports Authority of India are involved in the preparation for the Commonwealth Games. Shri Reddy said that the DDA is executing agency for the Commonwealth Games Village and the preparations are in advanced stage. The Urban Development Minister said that the Central Public Works Department is the executing agency for the Sports Authority of India. Shri Reddy asked the DDA Vice Chairman to make the presentation on the Commonwealth Games village for the benefit of the members. After the presentation, Shri Reddy invited the members for their suggestions. Shri Jagdish Tytler stated that the approach roads to various stadia are in bad shape and may be built in tune with the modernization and renovation of these stadia. He also suggested that building and maintenance of greenery and trees around these stadia. Shri Tytler stated that a four to five year old trees might be replanted around the stadia and adjoining areas to provide a green and beautiful outlook to the region. Shri Sajjan Kumar asked for relocation of a club near the Talkatora Stadium, as it is not in tune with the stadium atmosphere there. It may be shifted to another place and the club space may be left vacant to give good look to the region. He also suggested that the service providers might be given appropriate accommodation near the Commonwealth Games village preferably with in one or one and a half kilometres distance from the games village. Replying to a question, Shri Dinesh rai told the members that a lakh people would be visiting from local and abroad, for the opening ceremony of the Commonwealth Games. He said that the water harvesting techniques would be employed in the Commonwealth Games village. Shri Rai said that 1/3rd of the flats to be built would be returned to the DDA and the rest would be with the developers after the games are over. He said that 8,000 athletes would be accommodated in the Games Village and 2 athletes share a room and the residential accommodation in the village would be fully air-conditioned. Thanking the members the Urban Development Minister, Shri Jaipal Reddy, said that the Ministry will organize a visit for the Consultative Committee members to some of the Commonwealth Games sites for first hand knowledge. He said that this visit would help the Ministry to get more suggestions from the members for better execution of works. Earlier, Shri Jaipal Reddy informed the members about the major developments that took place since the last Consultative Committee meeting. These included the adoption of Delhi Master Plan 2021 and its notification, sending of papers relating to MPD 2021 including files to the Supreme Court, the proposal sending to the Cabinet for regularization of about 1500 un authorized colonies in Delhi, the empowered Group of Ministers approving the high speed express metro link from New Delhi Station to Indira Gandhi International Airport as per the revised alignments, introduction of Central Secretariat to Badarpur metro line in the Phase II and signing of a Memorandum of Understanding between India and Japan on Urban Development.

1526. (14-6-2007) NEW DELHI : The Prime Minister, Dr. Manmohan Singh, has condoled the demise of Professor Ramachandra Gandhi. In his message, he said: "I was deeply sad to learn of the passing away of Professor Ramachandra Gandhi. He was a distinguished academic and a learned scholar. He was also a truly devoted teacher who was held in high regard and with great affection by his students. As a symbol of simple living and high thinking, he came to epitomize the message of his grandfather, the Father of our Nation. I convey my sincere condolences to his family, his wide circle of friends and admirers and his many students."

1527. (14-6-2007) NEW DELHI : The Government has merged the erstwhile Ministry of Small Scale Industries and Ministry of Agro and Rural Industries and formed a new Ministry, namely, Ministry of Micro, Small and Medium Enterprises. A Notification of the Cabinet Secretariat has been issued to this effect. In keeping with the new name of the Ministry, the name of the Office of Development Commissioner (Small Scale Industries) has also been changed to Office of the Development Commissioner (Micro, Small and Medium Enterprises).

1528. (14-6-2007) NEW DELHI : The menace of wildlife crime and illegal trade in wildlife products continues to be a cause of concern. Addressing the 14th Convention on Parties of Convention on International Trade in Endangered Species (CITES) at Hague, Netherlands yesterday, the Union Minister of State for Environment and Forests, Shri Namo Narayan Meena further said that the enormity of the situation, and the whole gamut of factors involved calls for more conscious and concerted actions at regional, national and trans-national level. Shri Meena said that the International community has shown great commitment to regulate the trade in wildlife and crack down wildlife crimes. India has been a victim of growing illegal trade and its consequential impact on depletion of critically endangered flora and fauna. Referring to tiger he said that it is our national animal and our national heritage. We support the largest wide population of tiger in well established network of protected areas and tiger reserves. Despite of our efforts to conserve this magnificent animal, the illegal trade in tiger and its body parts across the international borders is the biggest problem. Coaching and illegal trade threatens its survival. The Minister reiterated to seek international support and cooperation to address concerns of tiger conservation, particularly, illegal trade in tiger products. Shri Meena informed that the Wildlife Protection Act of India strengthens enforcement mechanisms and to enhance the punishment for the wildlife criminals The National Wildlife Action Plan has identified this issue and its products as a priority area for action. He said India has also set up a multi disciplinary wildlife crime control bureau for dedicated and focused action on tackling wildlife crime. The Minister expressed the need to give more focus to the protection of our marine resources and timber resources. India is a signatory to many international treaties and conventions like CITES, Convention on Migratory Species, International Whaling Commission etc.

1529. (14-6-2007) NEW DELHI : It has been the constant endeavor of the Ministry of Tribal Affairs, Government of India to accelerate the pace of development in tribal areas to bridge the existing gaps in infrastructure and in turn to improve the human development index of the tribal community. To achieve the same, a number of initiatives have been taken by the Ministry. There are 2,474 forest villages/ habitations spread in 12 States. These settlements were established by the Forest Departments prior to independence for easy availability of manpower to carry out various forestry operations, mainly timber harvesting. They provided great service for forest and wildlife conservation. Most of the inhabitants of these villages/ habitations are tribals. The people living in these villages have skilled in various forestry operations however, after emphasis on conservation and ban on green felling, employment opportunities started shrinking and their conditions deteriorated. After the enactment of Forest (Conservation) Act, 1980, State Governments faced problems in taking up non-forestry developmental activities relating to infrastructure for improving socio-economic conditions of people living in the villages located in the forest areas.

1530. (15-6-2007) NEW DELHI : Dr. Manmohan Singh and Shri Kumar Deepak Das, the newly elected/ re-elected Members of the Rajya Sabha, today took oath of office. Both the members represent the State of Assam in the Upper House of Parliament. Dr. Manmohan Singh has been re-elected, where as Shri Kumar Deepak Das is the newly elected member.

1531. (15-6-2007) NEW DELHI : In a move to make Indian Railways world's number one Railway network, the Committee on Infrastructure approved the proposal for completing the first phase of modernization of the New Delhi railway station into a world-class station through Public Private Partnership before the Commonwealth Games, 2010 here today. For ensuring better inter-ministerial coordination, an Empowered Committee under the Chairmanship of the Cabinet Secretary has been constituted in which Chairman, Railway Board, Secretary (Planning Commission), Home Secretary, Secretary (Economic Affairs), Secretary

(Urban Development), Secretary (Environment and Forests), Chief Secretary (Government of Delhi), Vice Chairman (DDA) and Chairpersons of MCD and NDMC would be ex-officio members. Further, it has also been decided to constitute an Inter-Ministerial Group (IMG) under the Chairmanship of Chairman, Railway Board for finalizing Model Concession Agreement in which Secretaries of the Planning Commission, Department of Economic Affairs, Department of Urban Development and Department of Legal Affairs would be members. This Group has been directed to submit the Model Concession Agreement by October 31, 2007. In addition to New Delhi, following railway stations would also be developed as world class stations:-Agra, Ahmedabad, Amritsar, Anand Vihar, Bangalore, Bhopal, Bhubaneshwar, Bijwasan, Chandigarh, Chennai, Mumbai CST, Howrah, Jaipur, Lucknow, Mathura, Patna, Pune, Secunderabad, Thiruvananthapuram and Varanasi.

1532. (15-6-2007) NEW DELHI : The Prime Minister's Committee on Infrastructure which met here today has decided that Chennai Airport will be upgraded and modernized by the Airports Authority of India (AAI). The Committee has also asked for a pre-feasibility report for a greenfield airport near Chennai. The present airport in Chennai handle about 25 aircraft movement per hour and in the year 2006-07 it handled 97680 aircraft movement. The capacity of Airport to handle aircraft movement is expected to be saturated by the year 2014-15. The Airport handled 2.8 million passengers in its international terminal in 2006-07. The capacity of this terminal is 3 million annually and it is expected to be saturated by 2007-08. Similarly the domestic terminal which handled 5.9 million passengers in 2006-07 has a capacity to handle 6 million passengers annually and will be saturated by 2007-08. The Airport Cargo handling capacity is also expected to be saturated around the same time. The modernization and restructuring is expected to cost around approximately Rs.2350 crore of which cost of construction of runway, taxiway and apron would be around Rs. 1100 crore and cost of construction of terminal building, cargo building, car park and face Uplift would be Rs.1250 crore.

1533. (15-6-2007) NEW DELHI : The Two-day conference of Social Welfare Secretaries of States/UT concluded here today. In her remark on the occasion, Minister for Social Justice & Empowerment, Smt. Meira Kumar urged the Social Welfare Secretaries from States/UTs to ensure that the benefits of the Ministry's schemes should reach at grass root level in time. She said the funds provided by central government for the welfare schemes should be fully utilized in proper manner. She also urged the secretaries to conduct follow up actions after implementing the schemes. Expressing her concern over increasing drug abuses, she said there is a need to encourage NGOs to work against the drug abuses. To empower the SC students, she said Top Class Education for providing professional courses in medicine, engineering, law, fashion technology etc. through 127 institutes of eminence will soon be introduced by the Ministry of Social justice. On occasion addressing the Conference, the Minister of State for Social Justice and Empowerment Smt. Subbulakshmi Jagadeesan said the Ministry of Social Justice and Empowerment is implementing various educational schemes for improving their educational standard so that they can be brought into the national mainstream. She urged the states to send the complete proposals for grant of scholarships and for construction of hostels latest by the end of June, 2007 so that the financial assistance can be released immediately. She informed that the National Backward Classes Finance & Development Corporation provides financial assistance at concessional rates to the OBCs through State Channelising Agencies (SCAs) for supporting income generating activities. She urged to take up the matter with State Government and ensure that the Block Government Guarantees are released at an early date. We have brought under our schemes for Assistance to Voluntary Organizations working for the welfare of Other Backward Classes through skill upgradation, she added. Smt.Jagadeesan also informed that the Working Group for empowerment of Backward Classes during Eleventh Five Year Plan have recommended enhanced allocation of outlay for the above Schemes during XIth Plan. The recommendation of the working group has been submitted to Planning Commission for consideration. The approved 10th plan outlay for the above schemes was Rs.450 crores whereas the Ministry has sought an allocation of Rs.2250.00 crores from Planning Commission during the XIth Plan. The Planning Commission has already allocated Rs.100 crores for Post-matric Scholarship for the year 2007-08 against the allocation of Rs.35 crores during 2006-07. About 8 lakhs OBC students are likely to be benefited during the current year under the Post-matric Scholarship Scheme only. She also said that the Ministry assists in providing rehabilitation services to persons with disabilities through Composite Rehabilitation Centres, District Disability Rehabilitation Centres and NGOs. These Centres required constant supervision and support from the State Govt. so that they are able to provide the services to persons with disabilities. In accessible areas like North-Eastern States and Jammu & Kashmir also are not covered by the scheme. Therefore, this year we have made notional allocation of funds to every district in the country based on the proportion of disabled population. It is expected that NGOs and other implementing agencies of this scheme would organize disability camps according to the notional allocation and would ensure that the benefits reach in all the uncovered areas particularly in remote areas of North-Eastern region and the State of Jammu & Kashmir. She urged the Welfare Secretaries to take immediate action to implement the Act as soon as it comes into existence. She said that recognizing the lack of proper utilization of funds due to problem of non-receipt/delay in receipt of recommendations from the State Governments, we have streamlined the procedure of sanction of grant in aid to NGOs from the current financial year.

1534. (15-6-2007) NEW DELHI : The Central Board of Direct Taxes through Instruction No.1827 dated August 31, 1989 had brought to the notice of the assessing officers that there is a distinction between shares held as investment (capital asset) and shares held as stock-in-trade (trading asset). In the light of a number of judicial decisions pronounced after the issue of the said instructions, CBDT has issued circular no. 4/2007 dated 15th June, 2007 to update the above instructions for the information of assesses as well as for guidance of the assessing officers. The new circular is available on the websites www.finmin.nic.in and www.incometaxindia.gov.in.

1535. (15-6-2007) NEW DELHI : Kharif sowing is progressing in various states with the advent of South-West mansoon. Transplanting of rice has started in the states of Andhra Pradesh, Assam, Haryana, J&K, Karnataka, Kerala, Orissa, Punjab, Tamil Nadu, Uttarkhand and West Bengal covering an area of 11.61 lakh hectare against 10.65 lakh hectare last year. Jower covers an area of 1.406 lakh hectare while Bajra at 0.470 lakh hectare and Maize at 3.989 lakh hectare. The area covered under Cotton so far is 15.230 lakh hectare against 14.650 lakh hectare last year. Out of this, 8.68 lakh hectare is under Bt. Cotton. Sugarcane covers 44.020 lakh hectare and coverage under Jute has so far been reported at 7.819 lakh hectare, the weekly Crop Weather Watch Group meeting of the Ministry of Agriculture was informed here today.

1536. (15-6-2007) NEW DELHI : The Railways have generated Rs.7356.72 crore of revenue earnings from freight traffic during the months of April-May 2007 as compared to Rs. 6692.58 crore during the corresponding period last year, registering an increase of 9.92 per cent. Railways carried 124.76 million tonnes of freight traffic during April-May 2007 as compared to 117.67 million tonnes carried during the corresponding period last year, an increase of 6.03 per cent. The Net Tonne Kilo Metres (NTKM) went up from 79135 million during the months of April-May 2006 to 81126 million during April-May 2007, an increase of 2.52 per cent. The earnings from freight traffic during the month of May 2007 was Rs. 3752.91 crore, compared to Rs. 3364.69 crore during the corresponding period last year showing an increase of 11.54 per cent. Railways carried 63.85 million tonnes (MTs) of freight traffic during the month as compared to 59.58 million tonnes of freight traffic during the corresponding period last year, registering an increase of 7.17 per cent. The Net Tonne Kilo Metres (NTKM) went up from 39715 million during the month of May 2006 to 41188 million during May 2007, an increase of 3.71 per cent. Of the total earnings during the month of May 2007, Rs. 1484.17 crore came from transportation of 28.25 million tonnes of coal, followed by Rs. 323.88 crore from 6.32 million tonnes of cement, Rs. 275.77 crore from 2.98 million tonnes of foodgrains, Rs. 272.08 crore from 4.03 million tonnes iron ore for exports, Rs. 258.72 crore from 3.11 million tonnes of petroleum oil and lubricant (POL), Rs. 176.59 crore from 1.62 million tonnes of iron & steel for steel plants, Rs. 158.16 crore from 4.33 million tonnes of raw material for steel plants, Rs. 156.88 crore from 2.50 million tonnes of fertilizers and Rs. 646.66 crore from 10.71 million tonnes of other goods.

1537. (15-6-2007) NEW DELHI : Delhi will get 90 per cent of the power generated from the 980 MW second phase of National Thermal Power Corporation

(NTPC) Project, Dadri, in view of the forthcoming Commonwealth Games while the Uttar Pradesh will share 10 per cent of the power generated. This was stated by the Union Minister of Power, Shri Sushilkumar Shinde while laying the foundation stone of the State II-2X490 MW units of NTPC Dadri in Gautam Budh Nagar today. Congratulating the NTPC staff for continuous meritorious performance, the Minister said that NTPC will meet the expectations of the nation by completing this project in time for the Commonwealth Games. He said with this the total power generating capacity of the Dadri Project will rise to 2,650 MW from 1,670 MW. He further said that the project has played a significant role in power supply to the Northern Region and in overall development of the area. Listing the initiatives taken to develop the power sector, Shri Shinde said that a roadmap has been drafted to achieve the target of more than 78,000 MW capacity during the 11th Plan and all out efforts are being made in this direction. The Minister further said that sufficient power availability is also needed as India is set to achieve 9 to 10 per cent economic growth for the next few years. Power Ministry is giving priority to capacity addition, distribution reforms and rural electrification to achieve the target of "electricity for all by 2012".

1538. (15-6-2007) NEW DELHI : The monthly average circulation of various journals brought out by the Publications Division of the Ministry of Information & Broadcasting has touched 1.61 lakhs in 2006-07. The monthly magazine 'Yojana', published in 13 languages, had a combined circulation of 1.03 lakhs whereas 'Kurukshetra', the dedicated journal on rural development had a circulation of 38,500. Popular children's monthly in Hindi 'Bal Bharati' and the literary magazine 'Aajkal' had a monthly circulation of around 10,000 each. In its series Shodh Yatra, Yojana began highlighting the technologies development by rural population for their welfare. A news series called 'Do You Know' was launched in which basic facts on economic issues are analysed in layman's languages. The Division published 129 titles in English, Hindi and different regional languages during 2006-07, against the target of 120 titles for the year. Some of the important titles released during this period were: Great Masters of Indian Cinema-Dadasaheb Phalke Award Winners, 5000 years of Indian Architecture, The Story of India's Struggle for Freedom, A Career for You, Upbhokta Samrakshan Adhiniyam Aur Updhokta Adhikar, Krantikari Mahilayein, Sangeet Bachchon Ke Liye, Jallianwala Bagh etc. The Division earned a total revenue of Rs. 4.12 crores during this period.

1539. (15-6-2007) NEW DELHI : The Defence Minister Shri A K Antony will inaugurate the Unified Commanders'-in-Chief (UCC) Conference in New Delhi on Monday. Heads of Joint Services Headquarters, Commanders-in-Chief of Andaman & Nicobar Command and Strategic Forces Command and the Commandants of Tri-Services Institutions will attend the two-day conference being held at the headquarters of the Integrated Defence Staff. The conference will discuss strategy to bring about coordination between the Army, Navy and Air Force. Top strategists will also review the progress achieved so far in this transformation and try to work out a conceptual way forward.

1540. (15-6-2007) NEW DELHI : Delegations representing the Government of India and the Russian Federation met in Moscow on 14th June 2007, to discuss issues related to the cooperation between the two countries in the field of civil aviation. A mutually beneficial agreement was reached, under which the designated airlines of the two countries will continue to be permitted to over fly the territory of the other country without restrictions. Further, traffic rights were enhanced and capacity entitlements were increased from 46 to 52 weekly frequencies for both sides. The increase in flights will be to the cities of Ahmedabad and Amritsar each of which will get three additional flights from Russia. The Indian delegation was led by Mr. RK Singh, Joint Secretary, Ministry of Civil Aviation. The Russian delegation was led by Mr. G Loschenov, Chief Negotiator, Department of State Policy in Civil Aviation. The leaders of both delegations expressed satisfaction with the outcome of the discussions and re-affirmed the need to hold frequent consultations for further strengthening the civil aviation relationship between India and Russia.

1541. (15-6-2007) NEW DELHI : The Union Cabinet today accorded its approval for promulgation of an Ordinance, namely, the National Capital Territory of Delhi Laws (Special Provisions) Ordinance, 2007 to grant temporary relief from forcible action against unauthorized development in the form of encroachment by slum and jhuggi-jhompri dwellers, hawkers and urban street vendors and unauthorized development in the existing farm houses involving construction beyond permissible building limits and schools, dispensaries, religious institutions and cultural institutions in rural areas built on agricultural land for a period of one year in Delhi. The Ordinance would provide temporary relief against forcible action to people of the above categories as to avoid undue hardship and irreparable loss and also allow for a balanced and well-considered view to be taken on policies involving such unauthorized development thereby to formulate schemes to address these issues. A Bill will be moved in the coming session of Parliament to replace the Ordinance.

1542. (15-6-2007) NEW DELHI : The Union Cabinet today gave its approval for establishment of Indira Gandhi National Tribal University in Amarkantak, Madhya Pradesh with Central Government funding. It also approved introduction of the Indira Gandhi National Tribal University Bill, 2007 in the Parliament. This would ensure establishment of a teaching and affiliating University for facilitating and promoting avenues of higher education and research facilities for the tribal population of the country. The objects of the University include inter-alia, promoting studies and research in tribal art, culture, tradition, language, custom, medicinal systems, forest based economic activities, including special studies in the flora and fauna, and advancements in technologies relating to natural resources of the tribal areas. Apart from affiliating the colleges, the University has the power to establish such number of its own regional centres in tribal areas as the University may deem fit. There will be at least one school in every regional Centre, to serve as a model school for the schools of the region, wherefrom the tribal students would be expected to join the local colleges, the off-campuses or the University.

1543. (15-6-2007) NEW DELHI : The Union Cabinet today approved the ratification of the Amendment to the Convention on the Physical Protection of Nuclear Material, 1980 and also to amend the Extradition Act 1962. Becoming a Party to the Convention would strengthen the international legal framework to combat terrorism and also enhance international cooperation in investigation, prosecution and extradition of those who commit terrorist acts and acts of sabotage involving radioactive material or nuclear devices and facilities. The Amendment to the Convention : The States Parties, at a Diplomatic Conference held at IAEA Headquarters in July 2005, adopted an Amendment to the Convention with a view to strengthening the provisions of the Convention, in particular, for including terrorist acts and acts of sabotage against nuclear materials / nuclear facilities among the offences that States Parties are required to make punishable, under their domestic laws. The amended CPPNM will make it legally binding for States Parties to protect nuclear facilities and material in peaceful domestic use, storage as well as transport. It will also provide for expanded cooperation between and among States regarding rapid measures to locate and recover stolen or smuggled nuclear material, mitigate any radiological consequences of sabotage and prevent and combat related offences.

1544. (15-6-2007) NEW DELHI : The Union Cabinet today gave its approval for signing and ratification of a Bilateral Investment Promotion and Protection Agreement with the Republic of Mozambique. This Agreement is likely to increase investments between India and Mozambique.

1545. (15-6-2007) NEW DELHI : The Indian National Congress places on record its deep appreciation of the fact that in the 60th year of India's Independence, the UPA has chosen a woman as its candidate for the high office of President of India. In the words of the Congress President Smt. Sonia Gandhi, this is a historic moment for our democracy. In the years since our Independence, we have seen many eminent men occupy the position of President of our republic, and the greatness of our democracy lies in the fact that on several occasions men from remote villages, born into highly disadvantaged environment have risen through their hard work to adorn this position. Our country has thrown up the opportunities and possibilities for these persons to rise to the highest office in the land. They too, have served in that post with courage, grace and distinction. We are proud of the fact that we have had a Dalit president, Presidents from the minority community, and Presidents from all walks of life, but at the same time, it is an irony that women who represent over 50% of the population of our country, who fought shoulder to shoulder with men, during our Freedom Movement, who still toil in all walks of life in India, striving selflessly for the progress of the country and their families, be it in agriculture, in industry, in universities, or in every home, often with little reward, or even a word of gratitude, have never reached the high office of President. It is a matter of enormous pride for all Indians, particularly women, that today the UPA candidate for President is a distinguished woman, an she will be the next President of India....our country's first woman president. We would like to thank the UPA Chairperson Smt. Sonia Gandhi, the Prime Minister Dr. Manmohan Singh, and all our allies in the UPA for having come forward with this tremendous initiative, to put forward Smt. Pratibha Patil as the presidential candidate. This will send a highly encouraging signal, not only to all the women in our country, but also to the international community, that India is a country where women are valued, and taken seriously. This is not mere symbolism but rather, an important indicator that the UPA and its allies are totally committed to the cause of women, and their progress. Smt. Pratibha Patil is a woman of great distinction, and her accomplishments and service are second to none. She has served society, and our Party for several decades, as a legislator, as a Minister, as Dy. Chairman of Rajya Sabha, and as president of the MPCC. She has also worked tirelessly for the upliftment of women, the poor and the physically disadvantaged. She has rendered yeoman service to the cause of education. Thus her achievements, as a citizen, are as important a factor for her elevation as the presidential candidate, as the fact that when elected, she will be India's first woman President. It is very unfortunate, that at this crucial moment in India's history, the opposition BJP, does not have the political grace, the social commitment or the moral fibre to support the candidature of Smt. Pratibha Patil. Her eminent and impeccable track record, and the fact that India will have its first woman president, should have encouraged them to support her candidature. Its unfortunate that the BJP lacks the grace shown by the Congress Party when we sat in the opposition, and came forward to agree on Dr. Abdul Kalam as a consensus candidate, but also that they are so blatantly against the cause of women. Any political party, which has even a minimum commitment to the cause of women would have come forward to support the UPA in this historic initiative. It is obvious that the BJP is so bereft of ideology or commitment that it cannot bring itself to overcome its internal contradictions and hostility to support an eminent woman candidate. The people of India, particularly women will now understand the true colours of the BJP, and relegate them to the political oblivion which they richly deserve. We appeal to all right thinking parties and citizens to support the candidature of the UPA candidate Smt. Pratibha Patil, and are confident that, come July she will go to Rashtrapathi Bhavan as India's first woman President. We are very proud that our President, the UPA Chairperson Smt. Sonia Gandhi has taken this pathbreaking initiative, and even more proud to be a part of this historic moment in our democracy.

1546. (15-6-2007) NEW DELHI : The Union Cabinet today accorded its approval for concluding a Bilateral Investment Promotion and Protection Agreement with the Federal Democratic Republic of Ethiopia. This decision is likely to increase investment between India and Ethiopia. Bilateral Investment Promotion and Protection Agreements (BIPA) have been signed by the Government of India with 65 countries.

1547. (15-6-2007) NEW DELHI : The Union Cabinet today accorded its approval for concluding a Bilateral Investment Promotion and Protection Agreement with the Federal Democratic Republic of Ethiopia. This decision is likely to increase investment between India and Ethiopia. Bilateral Investment Promotion and Protection Agreements (BIPA) have been signed by the Government of India with 65 countries.

1548. (15-6-2007) NEW DELHI : Under the Sampoorna Grameen Rozgar Yojana (SGRY) scheme West District of Sikkim State has been released 419 MT of Common Rice through Food Corporation of India depots in the State during the year 2007-08 by the Ministry of Rural Development. The grant is towards plan expenditure and will be utilized for approved items of works subject to the conditions laid down in the SGRY Guidelines.

1549. (15-6-2007) NEW DELHI : Under Sampoorna Grameen Rozgar Yojana (SGRY), the Ministry of Rural Development has released Grants-in-aid amounting to Rs. 4.90 crore as balance of first instalment of Central assistance out of the Central allocation of Rs. 11.30 crore to the Durg District of Chhattisgarh for the implementation of the scheme during the current financial year (2007-08). Rs. 1.88 crore has already been released as part of first instalment under the scheme. The release is towards plan expenditure and will be utilized for approved items of works subject to the conditions laid down in the SGRY Guidelines. No deviations from the guidelines is permissible.

1550. (15-6-2007) NEW DELHI : Recently, it was reported in a section of the Press that Denmark has suspended all adoptions from India after the claim by a parent that his children were taken away without his consent. On the basis of these reports, Shri J.K. Mittal, Chairman, Central Adoption Resource Agency (CARA), a nodal body in the country under the Ministry of Women and Child Development in the matters of adoption, had ordered an inquiry into the matter. A preliminary inquiry has since been undertaken and it has come to light from available documents that the biological father himself approached the concerned adoption agency in Pune through a social worker to make his four children available for adoption/ rehabilitation (not two as reported in the Press). On a stamped paper, the biological father gave his consent on 9.4.2002 to the concerned agency to place his four children in adoption. This consent forms part of the relinquishment deed, which was signed, by his sister and brother-in-law as witnesses and the same was countersigned by the Chairman, Juvenile Welfare Board. The deed was written in Marathi, the Mother Tongue of the biological father who is stated to be a matriculate. Hence the deed could easily be understood by him. These facts lead CARA to believe that the adoption process of four children in this case was initiated with the consent of the biological father. However, detailed investigations are still in progress.

1551. (15-6-2007) NEW DELHI : Union Minister for Health & Family Welfare, Dr. Anbumani Ramadoss inaugurated today a videoconference system for counselling of seat allotment for medical and dental courses. This is the first time that the counselling is being done through videoconference connecting Delhi, Puducherry and Kolkata. DGHS is entrusted with the responsibility of allotting 15% All India Quota of MBBS/BDS courses and 50% All India quota of PG courses (MD/MS, PG Diploma & MDS) by the Hon'ble Supreme Court of India. In this allotment system, all MCI recognized Medical & Dental colleges (except in the states of Andhra Pradesh and Jammu &Kashmir) participate. First round of seat allotment for the MBBS/BDS courses start on 15th June 2007 and will end on 26th June, 07.

1552. (15-6-2007) NEW DELHI : On 18th June 2007 the Crescent Moon and Venus will make a breathtaking pair in the western skies immediately after sunset. They will be very close to each other. The Moon will seem to approach Venus and as the evening progresses will move in front of Venus at 9.30 p.m. (in Delhi) If the sky is clear the view of a bright Venus sleeping behind the dark Crescent Moon is like a shy maiden. This celestial love affair would be a beautiful sight. The best thing about this is that one does not need a telescope to view this phenomenon. Venus can be identified by its nearness to the Moon. Last time the event took place in November 2004 in the early hours of the day. It is this nearness which gives rise to the eerie feeling one gets, while viewing an event of this kind. It does not normally happen that two bright objects in the sky appear close to each other and this is going to be the coming together of the second and third brightest celestial objects in the sky. The time when Venus reappears from behind the bright crescent portion of the Moon, it will be too low in the sky to be visible. A lunar occultation happens when a celestial body appears to have moved behind the moon. Such events happen very frequently, but in most cases the star being occulted may be very faint. However, when bright stars or planets such as Venus are occulted by the moon, the event can be seen with the naked eyes. Lunar Occultation of Venus is a routine, but breathtakingly beautiful event. Normally, this would not even require a telescope or other equipment to view, as Venus is usually bright enough, not to be washed out by the glare of the Moon. Occultation of Venus by the Moon also happens when the Moon is in a crescent phase, thereby reducing the glare of the Moon. Nehru Planetarium and Vigyan Prasar, in collaboration with Science Popularisation Association of Communicators and Educators (S.P.A.C.E., an NGO) and the Amateur Astronomers Association of Delhi, will be conducting a public sky-watch at the Jantar Mantar on the evening of the 18th. The sky-watch will start at 5:00 PM at the Jantar Mantar, with Sun observations using the Ram Yantra. There will be demonstrations and live interactions related to observing the Sun, Moon and the planets. Telescopes will be set up within the Jantar Mantar complex to view the approach of Moon and Venus and also to view Saturn and Jupiter. The changing angle between Moon and Venus can be measured using the Ram Yantra and the Jai Prakas. Visitors will be given help to make these measurements on their own and compare their results with theoretical values. Visitors will thereby be able to appreciate the possible accuracies that the giant masonry instruments of the Jantar Mantar can achieve, as well as appreciate movements of the Moon and Planets in the sky against the relatively unchanging background of stars. The finale will be the actual occultation that is to take place at 9:30 PM, as seen from Delhi. If the horizon is clear, it will be captured by the 11" computerized GOTO telescope of Vigyan Prasar and visitors to the Jantar Mantar can view the event through live multimedia projection attached to this telescope. The event is visible from most parts of India, other than some locations in the east and south-east. Even from these locations, Moon and Venus would appear quite close to each other before they set. This is a view that does not require any precautions, unlike viewing the Sun. Anyone with a digital camera that is equipped with a good optical zoom, would be able to obtain good images of the Moon-Venus pair just before the occultation. Standing to the east of a historical monument, one would obtain wonderful images of the event against the architectural heritage of our country.

1553. (15-6-2007) NEW DELHI : Farm commodity prices monitored by the Department of Consumer Affairs have generally remained steady or have shown mixed trend in different centres across the country in the week ending 11.06.2007. Wheat prices remained steady at majority of reporting centres and declined at Ahmedabad. Sugar prices remained steady across majority of the centres and declined at Ahmedabad. Gram prices remained steady over the week across most of the centres; declined at Agartala and Bangalore; and increased at Delhi, Ahmedabad, Mumbai and Kolkata. Tur dal prices were also steady across most of the centres; declined at Lucknow, Ahmedabad and Bhubaneshwar; and increased at Jaipur. At Delhi, prices of wheat, atta, tur dal, sugar and groundnut oil remained steady over one week; those of rice, milk and potato remained steady over one month; and prices of vanspati remained steady for six months. Prices of the following commodities have increased at Delhi in the week ending 11th June: tea (loose), mustard oil, gram, onion and packaged salt. As on 11th June, public sector agencies have contracted import of 6.395 lakh tonne pulses of which 1.766 lakh tonnes has already reached Indian ports. The imported pulses include urad, moong, dunpeas, masoor, chana, yellow peas and tur.

1554. (16-6-2007) NEW DELHI : Following is the text of the speech delivered by the Defence Minister Shri A K Antony at the inauguration of New Facilities for R&D at Ghaziabad unit of Bharat Electronics Limited (BEL): "...It is a well-known fact that the establishment of defence industry base in India dates back to the 19th century. The expansion of defence industries has really taken place after independence. Today, we have eight Defence Public Sector Undertakings, apart from a chain of 39 Ordnance Factories. Research & Development is one of the most crucial components of our defence industry. The Armed Forces, the industry, and various Research & Development establishments must join hands and work in close coordination to enable our nation to become strong and self-reliant. The involvement of private industry in this sector has been growing over the years. The private industry continues to be the main source of supply of raw materials and components to the DPSUs and OFs. In May 2001, subject to licensing,-the Government had allowed the private sector to participate in defence production. We have issued guidelines for grant of licenses also. I understand that about 30 licenses have been issued so far. The Government is indeed committed to ensure that resources do not become a constraint in providing the best equipment to our Armed Forces. However, we want to meet our defence requirements from indigenous sources, as far as possible. Companies like BEL & HAL have done good work and I hope that they will continue to do better. However, companies like BEL need to step out of the protected environment and carve out a niche for themselves in the competitive market. Even for defence supplies, there will be many competitors within India coming up with production of sophisticated items, largely in collaboration with foreign partners. I have been told that recently, in a few cases, BEL has been able to win contracts in MoD in a multi-vendor situation. This is creditable, but I believe that the price quoted was much lower than the estimate made by Ministry of Defence. This clearly indicates that the process of nomination does not necessarily lead to a correct price discovery. BEL has been gaining contracts on a nomination basis and in such cases, it is necessary that the price is reasonable. Therefore, BEL should quote the best price it can offer to the Government. The recent cases of competitive bidding do indicate that BEL can certainly cut edges and reduce prices significantly. I hope that rigorous costing exercises are taken up, so that in case there is a nomination, the price quoted by BEL can be appropriately assessed. BEL has been investing significantly in R&D, which has enriched its overall technological base. It has been successful in developing new products on its own-as well as in collaboration with DRDO. In this age, when Research and Development is a key engine for economic growth and development, the impact of globalization demands increased responsiveness to meet threats to national security. R&D increases technological competitiveness and enhances capabilities for economic growth. Hence, it is imperative that our defence production industries modernize rapidly to match the changing needs.

1555. (16-6-2007) NEW DELHI : In a significant move at facilitating power generation in the country, Indian Railways have signed a Coal Transportation Agreement with M/s Nagarajuna Power Corporation Limited (NPCL) which is setting up a 1015 MW thermal power plant near Padubidri near Udipi in Karnataka on Konkan Railway. The Agreement was signed here yesterday among Southern Railway, Konkan Railway Corporation Limited and NPCL. Under the agreement, the coal required for the plant will be transported by rail from new Mangalore Port to the plant covering a distance of about 36 Kms. Coal required for the power plant will be imported at the port. While loading of coal and a small lead of 5 kms is in Southern Railway, unloading siding will be in Konkan Railway jurisdiction. Transportation of 2.8 MTPA of coal will be required for the power house. The present agreement is on the lines of the agreement earlier signed with M/s Rosa Power Company Limited.

1556. (16-6-2007) NEW DELHI : The Prime Minister, Dr. Manmohan Singh has welcomed the decision of the United Nations to observe October 2nd as International Day of Non-Violence. In a Statement, he said, "I am extremely happy that the United Nations will henceforth observe Gandhi Jayanti, October 2 as International Day of Non-Violence each year, following a unanimous decision of the General Assembly of United Nations yesterday. This decision originates in a declaration of the International Conference on Peace, Non-violence and Empowerment: Gandhian Philosophy in the 21st Century, convened in New Delhi in January this year commemorating the centenary of the Satyagraha Movement launched by Mahatma Gandhi. This is a tribute by the world community to the Father of our Nation. The universal relevance of Gandhiji's message of non-violence is more important today than ever before since nations across the world continue to grapple with the threat of conflict, violence and terrorism. This is also an occasion for all of us, the people of India, to re-dedicate ourselves to the ideals and values of Mahatma Gandhi, which shall continue to be our guiding light."

1557. (16-6-2007) NEW DELHI : Shri Ashwani Kumar, Minister of State for Industries has reiterated India's position on climate change issues in his meeting with former Vice President of the United States of America Mr. Al Gore on the margins of the UBS CEO's Summit (June 14-18) in Florence, Italy yesterday. The Minister stated that while there can be no difference of opinion as to the urgency of addressing critical issues related to climate change, the global debate should harmonise equitably the imperatives of development in the emerging economies and sustainable development. "The terms of the debate and the idioms of the dialogue should not be such as to unjustifiably transfer the major burden of sustainable development on developing countries", he said. Mr. Al Gore agreed with the Minister and also expressed a willingness to visit India to engage with all stakeholders on the various issues and challenges related to climate change and sustainable development, particularly taking into consideration the situation in India. Shri Kumar also met Zhang Zhiang, Former Vice Minister of Commerce of China, Sergio Marchionne, CEO of FIAT and Mr. Peter A. Wuffli, Group CEO of UBS AG. Shri Ashwani Kumar will today address the Session titled "Rapid Emergence of China and India as Global Economic Powers and their impact on the Developed World". Other key participants in the Session will include Shri Mukesh Ambani, CMD, Reliance Industries, Shri Sanjay Chandra, MD, Unitech Limited, Dr. Fu Yuning, Director & President, China Merchants Group, Eddie Wang, President, China Minsheng Banking Corporation.

1558. (16-6-2007) NEW DELHI : The Prime Minister, Dr. Manmohan Singh chaired the 11th Meeting of the Island Development Authority here today. In his remarks the Prime Minister said that the balanced development of Lakshadweep and Andaman & Nicobar Islands will be a focus area for the 11th Five Year Plan. The Union Cabinet Secretary has been asked to monitor all Inter-Ministerial issues on a quarterly basis to ensure that the Government of India is pro active in dealing with problems of infrastructure development, human development and disaster management in the islands. The Prime Minister expressed his concern at the slow progress of rehabilitation work, especially housing construction for the Tsunami affected households. He directed the Cabinet Secretary to pay urgent attention and ensure no further delay in Tsunami rehabilitation. The meeting took note of several issues of concern to the islands that were articulated by Shri Manoranjan Bhakta and Dr. P.P. Koya, Members of Parliament. He assured them that the Island Development Authority will meet on a regular basis to review infrastructure development in Lakshadweep Islands and Andaman and Nicobar Islands. The Prime Minister requested the Union Minister for Shipping Mr. T.R. Baalu to visit Port Blair and ensure early delivery of the required maritime infrastructure including ships. The Prime Minister assured the people of the Islands that the Central Government will focus on their developmental needs mindful of their aspirations, and the concerns of ecological and environmental sustainability and protection as well as national security considerations.

1559. (16-6-2007) NEW DELHI : The Prime Minister, Dr. Manmohan Singh reviewed the progress of the Jawaharlal Nehru National Urban Renewal Mission (JNNURM) and reiterated the need for State Governments to pay greater attention to the reform of urban governance and the modernization of urban infrastructure, with special focus on the lives of the poor in urban areas. The Minister for Urban Development, Shri Jaipal Reddy informed the Prime Minister that some States had taken the initiative to implement programmes under JNNURM. As a result, of the sixty three cities that have prepared city development plans, six cities covered by the programme will now have 100% water supply. These are Ahmedabad, Rajkot, Surat, Vadodara, Vijayawada and Vishakapatnam. Four cities will be fully covered by modern sewerage systems. These are Ahmedabad, Rajkot, Surat and Vijayawada. Four cities will have systems for collection, transportation, treatment and disposal of wastes. These are Agra, Kanpur, Lucknow and Rajkot. Six cities will have improved Bus Rapid Transit Systems. These are Ahmedabad, Bhopal, Indore, Pune, Thane and Vijayawada. Four cities in the North East, namely, Aizwal, Gangtok, Itanagar and Shillong will have municipal bodies. Thirty Three cities have implemented e-governance reforms. Forty cities have earmarked funds for services to urban poor. Eleven cities have achieved 85% coverage efficiency in property tax collection, while eight cities have achieved 90%. The meeting noted that there was very positive response from urban bodies to the JNNURM and urged State Governments to speed up the implementation of urban infrastructure development and municipal reform. The Prime Minister assured the meeting that adequate financial resources will be made available provided the commitments undertaken are fulfilled.

1560. (18-6-2007) NEW DELHI : A bilateral trade target of US $ 10 billion annually in goods and US $ 10 billion in services, set by the India-Canada CEOs Roundtable at its first meeting in New Delhi last March, was reaffirmed by participants at the second meeting of the Roundtable which was held in Montreal today. Shri Kamal Nath, Minister of Commerce & Industry, who participated in the Roundtable along with the Prime Minister of Quebec Mr. Jean Charest, told the CEOs that India and Canada must seize this opportunity to significantly increase two way trade and investment flows and suggested that alongside the target of US $ 10 billion each annually in bilateral goods and services trade to be achieved in 5 years, India and Canada should work to achieve US $ 5 billion a year in bilateral investment flows by 2012. He also expressed the hope that the completion of the Doha Round of WTO negotiations would go a long way in liberalising and enhancing trade and investment flows between the two countries. "It is heartening that in the last few months, Indian investment in Canada has picked up substantially. Last February, the Aditya Birla Group company Hindalco acquired Novelis for around US $ 6 billion. In April, the Essar Group acquired Algoma Steel for US $ 1.7 billion. Last year, the Tata Group had acquired Teleglobe, a telecommunications company, and the Birlas Minacs Worldwide, a BPO firm. This trend is likely to continue. I also hope that more Canadian companies will invest in India, to exploit the synergies that exist between the two sides", the Minister said. Referring to the economic scenario in India, Shri Kamal Nath informed the Canadian CEOs that the Indian economy had grown by 9% and the aim was to take this growth to 10% in the next couple of years. "Growth of this magnitude would unleash demand of various kinds. We are now faced with the need for better infrastructure, particularly power, roads, energy, environmental technology and raw materials. This would also open-up new opportunities for Indian and Canadian companies to work together in these critical areas. In this context, the recent visits to India by the Minister for International Trade, Mr. David Emerson, and the Canadian Infrastructure delegation, were very useful. We need more such visits from both sides", he said. Earlier, Shri Kamal Nath, who is on an official visit to Canada from 16-18 June, had bilateral meetings with Mr. David Emerson, Minister of International Trade, Canada; and Mr. Dalton McGuinty, Premier of Ontario, besides bilateral interaction with the Premier of Quebec. India and Canada have also concluded negotiations for a Bilateral Investment Protection Agreement to provide an impetus to the two-way investments, Shri Kamal Nath said.

1561. (18-6-2007) NEW DELHI : The Minister for Social Justice and Empowerment, Smt. Meira Kumar said that her Ministry is committed to the Official Language Policy and make out all possible efforts for maximum use of Hindi language in day-to-day official works of the Ministry of Social Justice and

Empowerment. She said this at the meeting of "Hindi Salahkaar Samiti" of the Ministry here today. During the meeting, the Minister informed the Samiti about the cent percent use of Hindi language in the Ministry, especially, while, issuing of official documents/ correspondence. Priority is given to ensure that all relevant information are made available in Hindi on Ministry's official website. The Minister reiterated that all Commissions, Departments under her Ministry would strictly follow the maximum use of Hindi Language in official works. She also informed that the Ministry of Social Justice and Empowerment was awarded with "Rajbhasha Navratna Shield" last year for excellent work in Hindi language.

1562. (18-6-2007) NEW DELHI : As part of the initiative taken by the Minister of Petroleum & Natural Gas Shri Murli Deora, a regional meeting of the three Northern Hill states of Himachal Pradesh, Jammu & Kashmir and Uttarakhand was held today (18.6.2007) at Srinagar to review the marketing and distribution of petroleum products in these States. Speaking at the meeting Shri Deora assured the three State Governments that the needs and requirements of these Hill States with respect to the energy sector shall be given due priority to ensure that the development of these States is not imparred. This meeting is part of a series of meetings held by the Minister of Petroleum & Natural Gas to be more responsive to the needs & the requirements of the State and to have a first hand knowledge of State specific issues. Earlier, such meetings have been held in Andhra Pradesh, Maharashtra, West Bengal, Tamil Nadu and Uttarakhand. Today's meeting was attended by the Union Minister (P&NG), Chief Ministers of Himachal Pradesh and Jammu and Kashmir, Union Minister of State (P&NG) and senior officers of Ministry of Petroleum and Natural Gas and the three State Governments. The States of Jammu & Kashmir, Himachal Pradesh and Uttarakhand are hilly regions where the logistics of reaching essential petroleum products continues to be a major challenge. Despite this, the public sector Oil Marketing Companies viz. IOC, BPC and HPC-under the Ministry of Petroleum and Natural Gas have set up an extensive infrastructure in these States for the marketing and distribution of petroleum products. There are 266 retail outlets (ROs) in Himachal Pradesh, 333 in J&K and 352 in Uttarakhand. Similarly, there are 120 LPG distributorships in Himachal Pradesh, 154 in J&K and 169 in Uttarakhand. Oil marketing Companies have plans to set up 25 more ROs and 3 more LPG distributorships in Himachal Pradesh, 49 ROs and 24 distributorships in J&K and 22 ROs and 3 distributorships in Uttarakhand. A major challenge for the people living in hilly regions, is to preserve the delicate ecological balance and protect the environment and rich forests in the area. The Ministry of Petroleum & Natural Gas had introduced 5kg. LPG cylinders several years ago keeping the hilly regions in mind.